ARTHUR J. GOLDBERG

ARTHUR J. GOLDBERG
New Deal Liberal

DAVID L. STEBENNE

New York   Oxford
OXFORD UNIVERSITY PRESS
1996

Oxford University Press

Oxford   New York   Toronto
Delhi   Bombay   Calcutta   Madras   Karachi
Kuala Lumpur   Singapore   Hong Kong   Tokyo
Nairobi   Dar es Salaam   Cape Town
Melbourne   Auckland

and associated companies in
Berlin   Ibadan

Copyright © 1996 by David L. Stebenne

Published by Oxford University Press, Inc.,
198 Madison Avenue, New York, New York 10016

Oxford is a registered trademark of Oxford University Press

Library of Congress Cataloging-in-Publication Data
Stebenne, David
Arthur J. Goldberg : New Deal liberal / David L. Stebenne.
p. cm.
Includes bibliographical references and index.
ISBN 0–19–507105–0
1. Goldberg, Arthur J. 2. Cabinet officers—United States—Biography.
3. Ambassadors—United States—Biography. 4. Judges—United States—Biography.
5. Liberalism—United States—History—20th century. I. Title.
E840.8G57S74   1996
973.92′092—dc20
[B]   95—48250

2 4 6 8 9 7 5 3 1

Printed in the United States of America
on acid-free paper

To my parents, William and Regina Stebenne

Preface

In view of the varying expectations about content that readers of biography have today, a brief explanation and caveat seem in order. This book has been conceived as both more and less than a conventional biography. It is more in the sense that it tells the story of the rise and decline of a certain social bargain, one that for all its problems remains central to the political economy of this society and all the other highly industrialized market systems. This book is also less than a conventional biography in that its primary focus is on Arthur Goldberg's connections to that larger theme rather than his life story as such. And although this biography does tell his story from beginning to end, the emphasis throughout is on what he did in his public life, rather than who he was in his private one. All biographers are, of course, confronted with issues of selection, of deciding what should be put in and what can be left out. My objective here has been to capture those aspects of Goldberg's life and career of greatest historical significance.

Most people today who produce this sort of book accumulate lots of debts to others along the way, and that has certainly been true for me. I owe the most to those who taught me history in college and graduate school. I first became interested in Arthur Goldberg when I was an undergraduate, in a seminar taught by John Blum on modern American political history. Like many students before and after, I have benefited from his exemplary teaching and especially from his gift for stimulating serious inquiry into the history of modern America. Also helpful was an early conversation with David Montgomery, which he has no doubt forgotten, but which I never did. My teachers in the graduate and law schools at Columbia University helped even more, especially Eric McKitrick, who kept a watchful and encouraging eye on me throughout my time there, and Eric Foner, who directed the dissertation on which this book is based. I owe a special debt to Alan Brinkley, who rashly agreed to read and edit what turned out to be a very long manuscript, and also helped in other ways too numerous to mention here.

    Then there are the debts owed to colleagues and friends. Thanks go to Karla Goldman, for initial inspiration and important assists along the way; to my graduate school colleagues Tyler Anbinder and Patrick Williams, who listened patiently and provided much useful advice; to Ellen Hamilton, with whom the issues discussed in Chapters 1 through 5 were debated at length; to Diana Shenk of Pennsylvania State University, for her invaluable assistance in using the papers of the Steelworkers Union; to Dan Schiller, who read an early draft and made many insightful comments; to Nick Spiliotes and Steve Fabry, for providing lots of encouragement and a careful reading of the final draft; to the members of the Manhattan Dinner Seminar, whose debates about political economy clarified my thinking in some important respects; to my literary agent Gerry McCauley, and Sheldon Meyer, Andrew Albanese, Carole Schwager, and others at Oxford University Press, all of whom made possible the transition from manuscript to book; to Dave Mason and Aaron Retish, who helped with the index and proofreading, respectively; to Frances Simonson Guilbert, who believed in this project and its author from the very beginning; and to the Listers: Chuck, Jennifer, Penny, and especially Sara, for their own very special and much appreciated form of encouragement. There are, of course, others who helped, too many, in fact, to list here. I am sure they know who they are, and can imagine how grateful I am for their contributions, big and small.
    Projects like this also depend on financial support, and I have been fortunate in that regard as well. Graduate school fellowships provided through Columbia University's history department and suport from the Whiting Foundation together made this book possible. I am also indebted to the following organizations for financing parts of my research: the American Historical Association, the Henry J. Kaiser Family Foundation, the John F. Kennedy Library Foundation, the Lyndon Baines Johnson Foundation, and the Harry S. Truman Library Institute. Last but not least, I am grateful for professional leave during the fall of 1993 from my teaching duties at Ohio State University, a respite that enabled me to finish the last major part of the writing.

Columbus, Ohio   D. L. S.
December 1995

Contents

ARTHUR J. GOLDBERG

*The twilight zone that lies between
living memory and written history
is one of the favorite breeding places
of mythology.*

C. VANN WOODWARD

1

Beginnings

Hᴉs ʀᴏᴏᴛs ʟᴀʏ in a neighborhood that has now all but disappeared, both literally and figuratively. Arthur Goldberg was born on August 8, 1908, in a working-class area on the West Side of Chicago known as Maxwell Street. A shopping district, its byways teemed with recent immigrants to America, many of whom were trying to scratch out a living as itinerant peddlers. Others operated small stores, stables, or hat and cap makers' shops, or worked in the meatpacking, shipping, and manufacturing industries on which Chicago's prosperity had been built. The neighborhood abounded, too, in the sort of cheap mass entertainments then becoming a fixture of working-class life. Among the most popular were three movie houses, which by the time Arthur reached an age appropriate for attendance, showed pictures about the First World War with such lurid titles as *Under the Heel of the Hun*. And wherever he went, there was the smell of food wafting from delicatessens, butter and egg stores, herring shops, pickle makers, and dry goods emporiums with their sacks of beans, spices, cornmeal, and cereals. So popular and even exotic was the shopping area that it drew tourists from all over the city, who came not only to buy but also for the fun of haggling with the local merchants.[1]

The neighborhood had, like other urban slums, more than a little social unrest, some of which found expression in radical politics. "There were a lot of socialists around the neighborhood," Goldberg later remembered, frequent strikes by workers, and a thriving left-wing press.[2] The same basic conditions also bred a good deal of crime, much of it mob related and violent, as well as political corruption. Tensions between people of Irish ancestry and the more recently arrived immigrants from southern and eastern Europe contributed still more to the area's volatility. In all, life in that world was much more raw, colorful, disorderly, and uncertain than it is for most Americans today. It was only just beginning to assume a shape that would be familiar to the grandchildren of those who grew up there.[3]

Maxwell Street reflected—as well as any Chicago neighborhood did in

3

those days—the energy, industry, and diversity for which the city justly became famous. Some indication of the extent to which the area possessed those qualities can be seen by considering some of its best-known progeny. In addition to Goldberg, Maxwell Street gave the world the musician Benny Goodman, the boxer King Levinsky, and the politician Jacob Arvey.[4]

That all of them were Jews was no coincidence, for many of the area's residents then were Jewish refugees from Russian pogroms. Such was the case for Goldberg's parents, who made their way to America from a Ukrainian village northeast of Kiev, known as Zhinkov. His father, Joseph Goldberg, the town clerk, came first by taking the less conventional eastward route, which led through Vladivostock, Alaska, California, and then Texas, where he landed in 1890. From there he crossed the Great Plains, pioneer fashion, by driving a horse and wagon all the way to Chicago. Upon arriving, he sent as soon as possible for his wife Rebecca and their daughter Mary.[5]

In order to provide for their transit and his own survival, Joseph Goldberg quickly obtained work as a peddler. For an educated man, it was a less than ideal way to make a living, but the only paying job he could find. Joseph Goldberg specialized in delivering produce from the South Water Street market to West Side shops and hotels. In that way he managed to support a family that grew substantially. In addition to Mary, who came with her mother from the Ukraine, the Goldbergs had six more children, the youngest of whom was a boy they named Arthur Joseph.[6]

Among his earliest memories were those of annual moves to new apartments, which allowed the Goldbergs to take advantage of the one month's free rent customarily given to new tenants. Other early impressions had to do with working for his father in the morning before school started. They used a wagon drawn by a horse with only one good eye, because they could not afford a horse with two of them. During that time, Arthur Goldberg also quickly came to understand that his father wanted his children to retain their Jewish heritage in the New World. While delivering food one day, Arthur encountered a kindly cook who offered him a ham sandwich. The boy politely accepted, only to have his father dash it from his hands when he returned to the wagon. The memory lingered, painful because it was only the first in a series of adjustments Arthur Goldberg would have to make between the values of his parents and those of the society's dominant culture.[7]

Another source of pain, both mental and physical, were Arthur's encounters with some of the Polish American and Irish American youths who harassed Goldberg on his way home from school with anti-Semitic epithets and who sometimes pelted him with stones. They were experiences he never forgot. He suffered, too, when the difficult immigrant life finally proved too much for his father. In 1916 Joseph Goldberg died at the age of fifty-one, leaving his wife and seven children to fend for themselves.[8]

In some respects, Arthur was the luckiest of the children, because as the youngest he was not obliged to quit school right away to help support the family. Some of his siblings did that, thereby giving him the chance to continue his education. Goldberg's performance at Theodore Herzl Elementary

School soon alerted his family that he had an unusual gift for learning. Wanting him to have the opportunity to develop it, his siblings—none of whom ever went beyond grade school—helped pay for brother Arthur's continuing education. He did his part, too, by doing such things as wrapping fish, selling shoes, and working as a page in a library. One of his favorite jobs was as a vendor at Wrigley Field. During the Prohibition years of the 1920s, he carried a large coffee urn strapped to his back and sold cups of it, rather than the traditional beer, to fans. In so doing, he developed a lifelong enthusiasm for baseball and Chicago's then-mighty Cubs. Arthur also learned to play the game, which to many children of immigrants was a badge of their new nationality.[9]

At school he worked even harder and, with the aid of his exceptional intelligence, excelled. In 1924, at the age of sixteen, he graduated from Benjamin Harrison Public High School, a milestone that none of his brothers or sisters ever reached. His class annual revealed that he had already set his sights on further schooling and a career in law. "Apparently I decided that as a kid," he remembered later, "and I don't know why. I grew up in a kind of typical immigrant family, none of my relatives were lawyers and . . . I guess it may have been a response to that."[10] The sensational Leopold and Loeb murder trial that Goldberg attended in 1923 "may have had an impact."[11] He may have been encouraged, too, by the mark that American Jews such as Louis Brandeis and Benjamin Cardozo had already made in the law. A scholarship from Crane Junior College, at which Goldberg soon enrolled, furthered his goal of legal education. His "academic moonlighting," as he later described it, also included taking a few courses at DePaul University.[12]

At Crane he met Lillian Herstein, a young woman who was teaching freshman English and, in her spare time, lecturing on labor topics in classes conducted by the Chicago branch of the American Federation of Labor (AFL). Herstein, the daughter of Lithuanian Jews who had left for the United States in the 1870s, was a highly effective speaker who impressed union leaders with both her enthusiasm for the labor movement and her articulate delivery. In those days unions were trying to organize immigrant garment workers, many of whom were women, and Herstein seemed the ideal person for the job. She soon won election to the executive board of the Chicago AFL, on which for many years she served as the only woman member. Herstein came out of the pre–World War I era of single-taxers, Debsian socialists, and farmer-laborites. Her presidential candidates were men such as Eugene Debs, Robert La Follette, and Norman Thomas. Upon encountering Goldberg at Crane, she spotted his potential and set to work educating him about issues of power and class. Goldberg later recalled that it was Herstein who first opened his eyes to the complexities of politics and awakened his interest in labor issues, through their talks and the books she suggested he read.[13]

It was the beginning of a lifelong friendship and interest in those subjects, but Goldberg's poverty precluded spending much time studying them in any formal way. Instead, he advanced through school at the considerable speed his intelligence allowed and by 1926 had moved on to Northwestern University, where he finished college one year later. Aided by a scholarship from North-western's law school and income from construction jobs, he realized his dream of becoming a lawyer. The regimen, however, proved taxing. Goldberg was a hod carrier and union man by day and a law student afternoons and evenings, a combination that wore so heavily that he often fell asleep in his classes. A somewhat disturbed dean called Arthur in to discuss the matter but could find little to fault in his academic performance: Goldberg received only one grade below an A in two and a half years as a law student. It was the best academic record in the history of Northwestern Law School, and it led to Goldberg's election as editor in chief of the *Illinois Law Review*. So impressed was the law school dean, John Henry Wigmore, that he selected Goldberg to assist with preparing the third edition of Wigmore's treatise on evidence, then as now, the leading text in that field.[14]

For Goldberg it was a time of real development, intellectual and otherwise. All this work made him strong if not very big. At his full height, which he reached around this time, Goldberg stood at five feet nine and weighed approximately 150 pounds. He had brown eyes, dark, wavy hair, and an attractive, serious face. His obvious intelligence and good looks attracted the attention of a young art student named Dorothy Kurgans. Like Goldberg, she had humble origins, high intelligence, and a warm, unpretentious manner. Although his heavy workload left little time for socializing, they soon began a steady courtship.[15]

Goldberg crossed the final academic hurdles with distinction at around the same time he reached adulthood. In 1928 he earned his bachelor of science in law (BSL) degree magna cum laude, followed one year later by a doctor of science in law (JSD) degree. His graduation at age twenty-one presented a problem, however, because Illinois Bar Association rules forbade admitting one so young. He sued. After Goldberg had argued his own case before an Illinois court, the judge waived the age restriction for him. The arduous period of schooling finally at an end, Goldberg promptly commenced the practice of law with the Chicago firm of Pritzger and Pritzger.[16]

His choice revealed much about the profession in those days. As a Jew, Goldberg was automatically barred from Chicago's oldest and largest firms, dominated by the older-stock elite who made their homes in fashionable communities north of Chicago along the shore of Lake Michigan. Only three years before Goldberg took up law practice, one such product of the Illinois gentry, named Adlai Stevenson, had, upon graduating from Northwestern Law School, secured a job as an associate with the long-established Chicago firm of Cutting, Moore and Sidley. He received the job, a Stevenson biographer later wrote, through a "combination of family and Princeton ties, personal friendship, acceptable education and social position. . . . It was a combination he used—later adding political ties—all his life."[17] Advancement through those means was closed to Arthur Goldberg, however. Barriers based on class and bigotry compelled him to choose in 1929 among less discriminatory and less socially prestigious firms composed largely of Catholics and Jews. He picked the Pritzger firm, founded by a family of German

Jews, among the wealthiest in Chicago and later one of the richest in Amer-ica.[18]

When not working at the firm, Goldberg spent his free time with Dorothy Kurgans, whom he married in 1931. Although these were very difficult years for the country as a whole, the Goldbergs' lives went very well. Theirs was a marriage, all observers agreed, in which the whole was truly greater than the sum of the parts. In time Dorothy gave birth to two children, a daughter, Barbara, in 1936, and a son, Robert, who arrived five years later, both of whom added to their parents' happiness.[19]

At his law firm Goldberg entered a world of prosperous and more assimi-lated German Jews, quite different from the one in which he had grown up. From them he learned to wear conservatively tailored suits and to adopt a more secular lifestyle. He eventually began eating ham and broke out of his parents' more confining immigrant Jewish milieu. While all this helped him to fit in to his new surroundings, Goldberg's work quickly demonstrated that he could also excel there. Soon he was mainly handling appeals to the state supreme court. Although very successful in his work, he never really felt comfortable at the Pritzger firm. The principal source of his unhappiness was the kind of assignments he was obliged to handle. During these years, the worst of the Great Depression, too many of his cases consisted of defending bondholder committees and bankruptcy proceedings, which were as unap-pealing to him as they were lucrative for the firm.[20] "It was during the Depression," Dorothy Goldberg later remembered, "and it was a wonderful job, Arthur was doing so well. . . . But Arthur decided he didn't want to spend his time foreclosing mortgages."[21] Accordingly, in 1933 he left the firm and opened his own law office.[22]

The decision revealed much about Goldberg's sense of himself and the world. In moving from a large firm controlled by others to his own shop, he was seeking a measure of independence. In that he reflected the worldview of the small, independent producer, who sought to compete with others on a more or less equal footing in what another Illinois lawyer named Abraham Lincoln once called "the race of life."[23] Most of the clients Goldberg found fit that description, as he himself did. His practice soon consisted mostly of representing small businessmen and other lawyers in modest-sized firms who retained him to handle appeals in the state court system.[24]

There are, of course, many kinds of small producer outlooks, but Gold-berg's seems to have been derived from that prevailing in the immigrant milieu out of which he had come, with its aversion to big business and focus on becoming a neighborhood merchant, combined with elements of the na-tion's dominant economic and political tradition that he had acquired at school. From Maxwell Street he drew a certain degree of alienation from large corporations, long-established elites and their culture, as well as the more recent arrivals who had wholeheartedly embraced it. And from Northwestern he acquired much of the prevailing American worldview of the late nineteenth and early twentieth centuries. Law schools during the 1920s were leading repositories of that heritage, and in that respect Northwestern was no excep-

tion. Among the most important elements of the older belief system that
Goldberg absorbed there were its emphasis on the role of law in providing
civil and political equality for all citizens, in limiting the arbitrary exercise of
state power, and in eliminating privately organized violence. Fused with those
beliefs was a strong hostility to the concentrated economic power Goldberg
had witnessed while growing up in the urban industrial America of the early
twentieth century. That hostility moved him, along with some others of his
background and perspective, increasingly toward advocating a larger role for
the state and labor unions as counterweights to corporate power.[25]

He rejected more radical solutions as unrealistic and, in any event, as
requiring too high a price in social strife. The poverty and sometimes naked
class conflict of the 1930s would sorely test his beliefs and move him to seek a
middle way. Not surprisingly, the first major party politician to interest Goldberg deeply was Franklin Roosevelt. As he later recalled, "In my youth there
were plenty of radicals around, but I was never even a Socialist, nor was
anyone in my family. . . . Roosevelt was the first man who had any strong
political appeal for me."[26] Before the advent of the New Deal, the two major
parties had not interested Goldberg very much. The sterile debate their
candidates conducted with one another during the 1920s offered little that
was new or inspiring. As the New Deal began to take shape in the spring of
1933, however, Goldberg became an ardent convert.[27]

His worldview also could be seen and was shaped by the organizations in
which he enrolled during the 1930s. Like most young lawyers starting out in
private practice, Goldberg was an avid joiner, although he shunned the business and professional organizations popular with conservative attorneys. Instead he became active in the Chicago-based Civil Liberties Committee,
which later became the Illinois Division of the American Civil Liberties
Union (ACLU).

One issue of particular importance to its members was censorship. In those
days the city of Chicago routinely banned films and theatrical productions
that the mayor's office considered obscene or politically subversive. Proscribed works deemed threatening to the public welfare included Henrik
Ibsen's *Ghosts* and George Bernard Shaw's *Man and Superman*. While in law
school Goldberg had developed a deep intellectual commitment to preserving
civil liberties. Even though he joined in efforts during the 1930s to use the
courts to resist such censorship, after several years they had made only modest
headway. As late as 1945 he blasted Chicago in a letter to *The Nation* for
"censorship of movies and plays which is the most flagrant and bigoted of any
American city, including Boston."[28]

In this activity, the influence of the nineteenth-century political tradition
was fairly clear. The Civil Liberties Committee's work was liberal in the
original sense, for it was aimed at limiting the power of the state, in this
instance over culture. Although controversial with some in Chicago—notably
the city's Roman Catholic hierarchy—the committee's activities did not imperil the rest of Goldberg's law practice. On the contrary, many of his clients
strongly supported his civil libertarianism. They were, Goldberg later re-

called, "the most enthusiastic supporters of my doing it. They were mostly Jews . . . inclined to be liberal, and they took pride that I would do this."[29]

The Civil Liberties Committee proved a formative experience for Goldberg, because at its meetings he first encountered many people who would become lifelong colleagues and, in some cases, close friends. Its members included such men as University of Chicago economist Paul Douglas and philosophy professor T. V. Smith, both of whom would later serve in Congress; Northwestern University anthropology professor Melville J. Herskovits; University of Chicago English professor and later governor-general of the Virgin Islands Robert Morss Lovett; as well as the somewhat less prominent civic activists Edgar Bernhard, Robert T. Drake, and Charles Liebman. Another was Sam Levin, Chicago leader of the Amalgamated Clothing Workers Union (ACW), with whom Goldberg soon developed a close friendship. Sensing both Goldberg's sympathy to organized labor and his legal talents, Levin invited Goldberg to serve as a public director of Chicago's Amalgamated Labor Bank. He accepted and thereby became exposed to one of the most influential sets of union leaders in America.[30]

The bank, founded in 1922, reflected ACW president Sidney Hillman's expansive view of organized labor's proper role in promoting workers' welfare. The bank's directors, however, were cautious administrators. "It was the most conservative bank in Chicago," Goldberg later recalled. He added, only half-jokingly, that "it would never make me a loan . . . if I needed one to pay my taxes."[31] The bank's prudent lending practices indicated how cautious the union had become by the 1920s in promoting its social agenda.[32]

At bank board meetings, Goldberg had the chance to meet Hillman and the other leaders of the Amalgamated and to discuss with them their ideas about the role of organized labor in society. Like Goldberg, Hillman was the child of Russian Jewish parents, although it was he and not they who had emigrated to the United States in the year before Goldberg was born. Even more important, Hillman lacked labor leaders' usual distrust of intellectuals, attorneys, and experts. Similar perspectives contributed to a meeting of the minds about ways to reform society, and especially labor's role in that process. From Hillman and his associates Goldberg began to see more clearly how labor unions could be used to make a market system more stable and egalitarian and less wasteful, rather than simply to drive up the pay of their members or form the nucleus of organizations aimed at overthrowing the existing order.[33]

Hillman's own views had emerged from the experience of clothing workers in places such as Chicago, Rochester, and Baltimore. In those cities, the clothing industry was characterized by large units of production and workforces in the hundreds or thousands, which produced, with the aid of sophisticated equipment, standardized apparel for the high end of the market. Such large producers felt threatened by the much more turbulent state of the rest of industry, which resulted from what labor historian Steve Fraser has called "the anarchic behavior of the mass of petty producers and worker-entrepreneurs."[34] The industry leaders operated enterprises sufficiently large that they required stable cost estimates and output levels to survive, and some executives began to see in unions a mechanism for ensuring such stability. Union supervision of the workforce and wages set by collective bargaining offered that promise and persuaded the heads of the industry's leading firm, the Chicago-based Hart, Schaffner and Marx Company, to be receptive when union leaders such as Hillman came along.

Hillman and his brethren, for their part, perceived such an arrangement as bringing benefits to both sides. By standardizing wage rates and work schedules and acquiring more say in governing the workplace, the workers, Hillman hoped, could improve their wages and working conditions while at the same time boosting output and profits. Those ideas first found support in the clothing industry during the years before the Depression, but would enjoy their greatest influence on the industrial economy after the onset of the New Deal.[35]

For Goldberg, the idea that an accord of some kind could be reached between workers and employers that benefited both was enormously appealing. First and foremost, that was because it promised to improve workers' quality of life. Such an approach's commitment to more planning and efficiency in the production process also struck him as one solution to the country's overall economic problems. The idea of a workable social contract for the industrial age fitted, too, with the immigrant Jewish milieu and the climate of Progressive-era reformism in which he had grown up. And at the same time, such a plan rationalized his support for labor's aspirations with his desire to move up in the established social order. His beliefs thus allowed room for both his conscience and his ambition.[36]

Many of the employers in the clothing industry were Jewish and shared a similar sensibility with Goldberg. They tended to support an arrangement with labor not only on the grounds of protecting profits but also because they sought a more humane and stable social order. They were willing to concede more to the industrial working class, partly because their historical tradition argued against exploitation and partly because they feared its potential consequences more than the older elite groups did. As Jews, they felt, especially during the 1930s, more vulnerable than did the Protestant gentry living on the North Shore. Such a program also promised to win for such employers a measure of respect from the established middle class for acting as "responsible" businessmen. For all these mutually reinforcing reasons, clothing industry leaders had contributed to the emergence of a more harmonious approach to what they were beginning to call "industrial relations."[37]

While the Civil Liberties Committee had enabled Goldberg to meet people who would prove of enduring usefulness and the Labor Bank to learn equally important ideas, his one other major extracurricular activity in those days—membership in the National Lawyers Guild (NLG)—was significant, too, although only in a negative sense. The Chicago chapter of the NLG in the 1930s contained both liberals and radicals working together in an uneasy and, as eventually became clear, unsustainable alliance. Goldberg joined the guild at the time of its formation to help create a counterweight to the more conservative American Bar Association (ABA).

By the middle 1930s the ABA had taken a strong stand against most New Deal legislation, a move that prompted liberal and more radical attorneys to develop an opposing institutional voice. It emerged as the NLG, which offered support within the legal community for such measures as the Social Security law and the National Labor Relations Act at a time when their constitutionality was under challenge in the courts. The two factions in the guild had managed to work with each other until 1938, by which time the growing number of Roosevelt appointees to the federal bench ensured that it would no longer oppose key New Deal enactments.[38]

At that point, conflicts began to emerge over the organization's future direction, with the more radical elements, whose ranks included some genuine communists, gaining the upper hand. Just as alienating, if not more so, were the means by which they had managed to do so. The radicals' tendency to try to make up with zeal for what they lacked in numbers infuriated Goldberg, as it did so many other liberals of that era. Consequently, by early 1939, he and other New Deal liberals had begun to leave the guild's Chicago chapter en masse. For them, the decision to depart was both difficult, because it left them without any organization of their own, and defining, because it confirmed to themselves and to others that their support for social change had its limits, which put such liberals at odds not only with conservatives but also with those leftists who were trying to bring about a revolutionary transformation of American society.[39]

Thus by the middle of Roosevelt's second term, Goldberg, by virtue of his outside activities, had taken clear public stands in favor of protecting civil liberties and promoting unions and against the program of the American Communist Party (CP). It was that combination, together with his growing reputation as a skilled courtroom lawyer, that brought him to the attention of Congress of Industrial Organizations (CIO) leaders in Chicago. In 1938 they asked him to use his skills on behalf of a group of newspaper employees who found themselves in serious trouble.[40]

II

Journalists in those days, like so many other American workers, were locked in a bitter contest with their employers over the issue of forming unions. Newswriters and editors, led by the well-known syndicated columnist Heywood Broun, had launched the American Newspaper Guild (ANG) in 1933 to gain better pay and more secure working conditions. Journalists' need for organization appeared compelling. Never a profession characterized by great job security, newswriting by 1933 enjoyed no immunity from Depression-era economic conditions. From 1929 to 1933, overall employment had fallen off sharply and so too had wages, down an average of 12 percent by the spring of 1934. In laying off employees and reducing their salaries, newspaper managers attempted to ease the hardship by explaining to writers that unless costs were cut, the payroll for mechanical employees could not be met. In that event, publishers explained, strikes by mechanical workers, all of whom were members of the old and powerful International Typographical Union (ITU), would shut down the paper and cost everyone his or her job.

Many newswriters got the message, but not in the way publishers had intended. During the years preceding the Depression, many such editorial employees had watched enviously as ITU locals negotiated better pay and benefits for their members than the writers themselves had obtained. As the differential grew in the wake of economic collapse, newswriters resolved to adopt the mechanical workers' already successful tactics.[41]

Roosevelt's National Industrial Recovery Act (NIRA), with its Section 7(a) acknowledging the right of workers to bargain collectively, seem to provide the needed opening. Publishers at first responded cautiously, urging that editorial employees, as professionals, should pattern their group along the lines of the American Bar Association. Broun and other writers, sensitive to the reluctance of some newswriters to join a body that exactly duplicated a trade union, adopted the less provocative name *guild*. The group's goals, however, soon marked it as a union in all but name. Publishers were outraged, claiming that the American Newspaper Guild (ANG) threatened freedom of the press. Roosevelt, for his part, proved unwilling to antagonize the already hostile news media, especially the Hearst chain, which had supported his candidacy in 1932. For that reason, he kept his distance from the guild, although Eleanor Roosevelt joined in January 1937 on the basis of her syndicated column.[42]

Bitterly contested strikes broke out in late 1934, with the Associated Press and Hearst as leaders of the antiguild publishers. They soon enlisted the American Federation of Labor and its affiliated Teamsters Union as allies. The AFL came to oppose the guild because the latter had in 1937 switched its affiliation to the CIO over the issue of jurisdiction. Like the other CIO-affiliated unions, the ANG's leaders were trying to organize newspaper employees on a shopwide basis rather than via the traditional AFL approach of forming unions by craft. The specific issue that divided the guild and the Teamsters had to do with the ANG's efforts to organize news deliverymen along with editorial employees. The Teamsters claimed jurisdiction over the carriers, and after the ANG's members left the AFL in 1937 the dispute became an ugly one, as teamsters sided with employers to break ANG picket lines.[43]

Chicagoans one year later witnessed the start of the longest, most famous, and probably most violent guild strike. It began as a dispute over the firing of several employees at the two Hearst newspapers in the city, the morning *Herald-Examiner* and the *Evening American*. All the dismissed workers were active in the guild, which claimed that Hearst was attempting to disrupt legitimate efforts to organize for collective bargaining. One guild veteran described a pattern of incidents that he said had begun as far back as 1936. "Strange things occurred," he wrote later.

[A] CNG (Chicago Newspaper Guild) officer's car was shoved into the Chicago river, the Guild office was burglarized and its membership files, scarcely of any value to any conventional burglar, were stolen. It clearly suggested that Chicago publishers didn't associate the Guild with the "gentlemen of the press" image held by many newsmen.[44]

Management replied that those fired had lost their jobs because of malfeasance or because financial problems dictated layoffs, not for their guild activities. At least one scholar has concluded, however, that William Randolph Hearst declared war on the guild everywhere because he saw it as a potential threat to his control over editorial expression and therefore that financial motives were of only secondary concern. Thus this struggle between workers and owners was, as in so many other instances during the 1930s and 1940s, only partly about pay and benefits. It also turned on issues involving control of the workplace and the production process. Hearst, like so many industrialists of that day, was accustomed to absolute control over his white-collar workers and was unwilling to grant them even a modest measure of job security, let alone authority in the workplace, a policy the *Herald-Examiner* management explained to its new employees with the warning, "When you work here, you work with your hat on."[45]

By December 15, 1938, the remaining workers balked at enduring any more such treatment. On that day they struck both papers, starting a fifteen-month walkout that would gain national attention and cost the union $125,000 for court costs and strike relief payments. Management deployed teamsters armed with crank handles and clubs to drive away picketers and thus break the strike. Hearst spokesmen claimed that exchanges ensued when the strikers tried to obstruct the movement of newspapers to delivery trucks. The guildsmen, on the other hand, contended that, as one of them later recounted,

at publisher Merrill C. Meigs' direction . . . circulation trucks backed up along the curb where the picket line had formed and deliberately raced their engines, choking the protesters with carbon monoxide fumes. When they remonstrated with the circulation men, the drivers responded by charging the picket lines with clubs and rubber hoses. All of those arrested were Guildsmen.[46]

The exchange earned the Hearst publisher the new nickname "Monoxide Meigs" among the strikers. Pictures of the violence, spread all over the pages of Chicago's other newspapers, appalled much of the city's middle class, already disturbed by the sharp increase in class antagonism nationwide that had accompanied both the adoption of the sit-down strike tactic by the CIO and the 1937/38 recession.[47]

The adverse publicity, however, failed to persuade Hearst executives to cease and desist. They soon chose instead to supplement their strong-arm tactics with legal maneuvers, hoping that the combination of the two would eventually break the strike. And so, soon after the walkout began, it evolved into two separate but related contests, one taking place in the streets of Chicago and the other in the city's courtrooms. Shortly after the first clash, Hearst's attorneys entered a state court seeking an order that would prohibit any further guild picketing on the grounds that strikers had used violence and illegal coercion. The newspaper's publishers also brought a libel suit against the leaders of the guild's Chicago chapter. The guild, Hearst claimed, had damaged the *Herald-Examiner*'s reputation, thereby costing it thousands of dollars in lost advertising revenues. The state court, one of many filled with appointees of dubious quality and suspect neutrality, soon granted Hearst a sweeping injunction. As a further blow, Judge Sullivan of the renter's court began sending out eviction notices to strikers in late January 1939. One account quoted the judge as having told the strikers to pay or get out because "you can work if you want to."[48]

The guild pickets chose to ignore the court orders, and the brawling continued, with an extremely ugly exchange on February 18. The Hearst management and its Chicago Teamster allies proved an intimidating combination, but the guild refused to give up, and so early in March, Hearst's attorneys went back to court. This time they asked to have the picketers arrested for defying the earlier injunction. The court obliged by swearing out warrants for many of them, an act that threatened to bring the strike to an end. After bailing out its members, the guild on April 4 brought a countersuit against the *Herald-Examiner* for the violent acts of its strikebreakers.[49]

Pending the outcome of the suit, clashes between the two sides continued. Strikers were assaulted and their sound truck dumped into Lake Michigan. One guild leader was attacked while entering his home, and his call to the police yielded no response until several hours after the incident. Chicago Mayor Edward J. Kelly's reluctance to intervene and thus prevent further disturbances angered many in the city's middle class, who formed a committee to aid the guild. Representatives from the National Lawyers Guild, the Civil Liberties Committee, and assorted church groups participated. In April, several denominations jointly published a report documenting Hearst's use of illegal terror tactics to break the strike.[50]

Hearst's methods also alienated many in Chicago's AFL unions, despite the publisher's claim that the strike was really a jurisdictional dispute between the CIO Guild and the AFL Teamsters. The AFL's leaders, including its president, William Green, were more worried, however, by the CIO than by Hearst and so followed his lead. Eventually they pushed through a resolution at the AFL's 1940 national convention denouncing the guild for "exploiting editorial workers, for promoting an alien doctrine, for being un-American, anti-American, and a menace to freedom of speech, freedom of the press, and freedom of assembly, as a peril to the advancement of journalism, and as having failed and betrayed the trust of American newspaper men and women."[51]

The guild in Chicago waged its own propaganda effort to persuade unionists, AFL and CIO alike, and sympathetic members of the middle class that the strike was being fought over unfair working conditions. The guild sponsored parades along the Loop and held a mass meeting that featured CIO president John L. Lewis, and guild national president Heywood Broun, as speakers. Airplanes flew over the city carrying proguild streamers, and guild sympathizers distributed handbills urging Chicagoans not to buy goods from merchants who still advertised in the *Herald-Examiner*. One account records that when detectives hired by Marshall Field & Company, the city's great shopping emporium, began ejecting guildsmen who were handing out fliers from the store, the strikers dispatched a "great hairy ape, with snarling jaws and emitting terrifying shrieks . . . [which] dashed through the startled throngs of shoppers one Saturday morning pointing to a sign on his chest which read, 'I DON'T BUY MY COCONUTS AT FIELD'S. THEY AD-VERTISE IN THE UNFAIR EXAMINER AND AMERICAN.'"[52] Through such strenuous and sometimes unorthodox efforts the guild managed to win considerable community support.[53]

Despite the headway workers were making in the streets and neighborhoods, Hearst's courtroom campaign progressed, thereby threatening to undermine what the union hoped to accomplish by direct action. On September 15, 1939, a judge fined the guild $500 for contempt. A new feature of the court's ruling was to forbid the guild from "linking together in one sentence any statement regarding the Swarts Company [an advertiser] and the strike being carried on by the Guild."[54] Hearst sought further court rulings to block the passing of handbills by anyone, including private citizens. The court also neared a decision on whether to imprison guildsmen who had defied the earlier order not to strike.[55]

For Goldberg and other civil libertarians, bans on handbills and strikes would have imperiled the First Amendment far more than the guild did. Thus when Chicago labor leader Van Bittner, the CIO's western region representative and coordinator of the strike, asked him to defend the picketers in court, Goldberg was receptive. He took the job, he said, "as a public service," because he was a civil libertarian and the court's action posed a threat to civil liberties.[56] That rationale was revealing, because it indicates that one key motivating force in persuading Goldberg to work on labor's behalf was his desire to protect it from government repression. Thus his entry into the labor field was based in part on traditionally liberal grounds, namely, that the state's power was being used arbitrarily and illegally, in this instance against workers.

There were, of course, other reasons. Goldberg's civil libertarian rationale was mixed with compassion for the workers and repugnance for the violence that had erupted in the city's streets. What seems to have been the most compelling motive of the three was his sympathy for a labor movement that was trying to make life better for the kinds of people with whom he had grown up, most of whom were unable to duplicate his success. As Goldberg later explained, "I got attached to the CIO in Chicago because they were the down-and-outers at that time."[57] A fourth catalyst emerged after some of his friends advised him against taking the guild as a client on the grounds that fighting a newspaper could harm the rest of his practice and any hopes he might have for appointment to the bench. The advice only encouraged him to take the case. "I don't like to be told," he said later, "that if I do this it will alienate so-and-so. Everything you do in life is like that."[58]

Also influencing him to take the case was the timing of Bittner's request, for in the previous six years the laws governing workers had undergone a profound transformation, one that offered Goldberg a real chance for an eventual triumph in the courtroom. The growth of workers' power on the shop floor that had begun in the early years of the New Deal was gradually bringing changes, albeit indirectly, in the nation's legal system.[59]

For lawyers, the decisive year was not 1934 when workers began joining unions in droves or 1935 when Congress passed the National Labor Relations Act (NLRA) but, rather, 1937 when the Supreme Court upheld it. Until then, Senator Wagner's new law appeared unlikely to survive a test of its constitutionality. Even many members of Congress who had voted for it thought the Court's conservative majority would eventually strike down the NLRA. Around that same time, the Court also held in the Associated Press cases that the First Amendment did not preclude editorial employee unions.[60]

Those decisions were followed only a year later by a Court ruling that the Norris–La Guardia Act was constitutional as well. The act, passed by Congress in 1932, was the result of organized labor's fifty-year struggle to curb the federal courts' discretionary use of sweeping antistrike injunctions. The labor injunction had first appeared in the 1880s, and courts had used it with increasing frequency thereafter. By the late 1920s, as labor historian Irving Bernstein has pointed out, it had become "the leading issue of labor policy."[61]

Union leaders protested that often when a strike broke out, the employer requested an injunction barring all picketing and typically gave as his or her reason for the request the belief that the union intended to damage the employer's property irreparably. Judges, not required to consult with the other side, routinely expressed their hostility to organized labor by granting broad court orders. Civil liberties expert Morris Ernst testified before a Senate committee in 1928 that "he had uncovered injunctions that forbade persons to pray on the roadside or sing in groups, that required pickets to be American citizens or to speak the English language, and that denied the rights of free assembly and communication."[62]

Such orders outraged unionists, who saw many strikes broken with them, and civil libertarians, who deplored them as assaults on the First Amendment. The first serious academic study of the issue had taken place in American law schools during the 1920s. Among the students learning about the subject then was Goldberg, who had taken a labor law course while at Northwestern. He had supported the Norris–La Guardia bill to curb the use of injunctions and observed with approval the Supreme Court's 1938 decision in *Lauf* v. *Shimer & Co.* to uphold the new law.[63]

Thus by the time Bittner approached Goldberg in late 1939 on behalf of the guild, the Supreme Court had just completed the transformation of labor law that had begun in the early 1930s. A lawyer by 1939 could defend the CIO's challenge to management's monopoly on power in the workplace and do so in the knowledge that such CIO efforts were protected by the law of the land. It was a combination that Goldberg, like many other lawyers during the late 1930s, found quite attractive.[64]

Bittner's motives in seeking out Goldberg's help were as complicated as the latter's in accepting it. Bittner, a seasoned veteran of countless strikes during his years as an organizer for the United Mine Workers, shared Goldberg's enthusiasm for unions as organizations that could democratize, humanize, and stabilize a market system. He respected, too, Goldberg's proven record as a skilled courtroom advocate and was also attracted by Goldberg's publicly expressed hostility to the program of the American Communist Party.[65]

That last point was a crucial one in Bittner's decision to ask for Goldberg's help. As Goldberg later recalled, "The reason they [Bittner and his associates] came to me . . . was that the Guild strike was bleeding the organization dry. . . . Furthermore, they didn't trust the representation they were getting from the Guild."[66] Local guild attorneys had achieved little success, and although the ANG's national office offered to send substitutes, Bittner refused them. His reason was simple. Internecine warfare between liberal and radical factions divided the organization in much the same way as it did the National Lawyers Guild. In 1939 Communists held the upper hand in the ANG's national headquarters in New York. Bittner, having spent years battling CP members in the UMW, distrusted them.[67]

Goldberg's legal aid, however, lived up to Bittner's expectations. At the time he took the guild as a client, Goldberg remembered, "three hundred reporters were held in contempt and might go to jail."[68] That month, September 1939, he began, as lead counsel, his efforts to breathe new life into the guild's legal counterattack. It was, he recalled, "a horrendous experience. I was in court every day for nine months. . . . It was a tough strike. . . . There were all kinds of things that happened, violations of the injunction, [strikers] getting into fights with the Teamsters, a variety of things for which they were hauled into court."[69]

His at that time still novel approach to winning the legal struggle was not to question the validity of the laws that workers were accused of having broken or to deny their actions but, instead, to attack Hearst for having acted unlawfully as well. As an initial move, he requested the court to enjoin the publisher from using violent tactics. "Is there any question in your honor's mind," he asked the judge, "[that] if the plaintiff [Hearst] had come into court with these specific allegations of violence[,] would the court hesitate from issuing the order?"[70] Above all, Goldberg's pleading emphasized the need for fairness, in the sense of treating both sides equally.[71]

To the delight of Bittner and the striking newspaper employees, Goldberg's tactics worked beautifully. He obtained the court order restraining Hearst, which an observer noted was "the first time in newspaper-labor history . . . an injunction was secured enjoining a publisher from employing violence as a weapon against the strike."[72]

When Hearst ignored the order, Goldberg brought contempt charges against the publisher and also appealed the $500 award against the guild. On December 15, 1939, the first anniversary of the strike, he delivered what was probably his first public address to a labor group, which had gathered at strike headquarters. In the speech he reviewed the legal situation and explained what he thought would come next.[73]

Goldberg's actions in and out of the courtroom attracted growing attention from trade union circles and more requests for assistance. CIO leaders in Chicago asked for his help in drafting a proposed Illinois statute that would explicitly bar state courts from issuing strike injunctions of the type obtained by Hearst. The state's own "little" Norris–La Guardia act had allowed such orders if acts of violence were imminent, but the law had been drafted so poorly that hostile state courts could construe the term *violence* to include the threat of it and thus bar most picketing on those grounds. Goldberg spoke to a CIO group to urge their support for such an amendment and, at the polls, to elect a more sympathetic judiciary. Recent Illinois history had revealed that both were important, for although the state had passed an anti-injunction law in 1935, Cook County judges in 1938 had issued fifty labor injunctions, underscoring the dual aspect of the unions' problem.[74]

Vigorous efforts by Goldberg and his co-counsel and friend, George Quilici, blocked Hearst's legal effort to break the strike. They argued that the Supreme Court in 1937 and afterward had ruled peaceful picketing legal. The guild's favorable odds of reversing lower court fines against it on those grounds helped persuade Hearst to give up. In May 1940, after nearly seventeen months, the strike ended with a settlement. Although the Hearst papers in Chicago soon closed, the guild worked out an agreement with the publisher for preferential hiring at other Hearst newspapers. That result was, however, "a Pyrrhic victory at best," as one participant concluded, for the guild sustained a defeat in its attempt to organize the new Hearst *Herald-American*.[75] Soon the Chicago guild members started quarreling over how to allocate the lump-sum award to cover back pay, which only further weakened their cause.[76]

If the Chicago chapter fared badly, the guild in a larger sense benefited from the strike, because it convinced the Hearst chain to give up its efforts to break the union nationwide. Only a year after the strike ended, Hearst signed an agreement with the guild permitting it to organize all of his newspapers. Large losses in advertising revenue as a result of strikes had taught the publisher an expensive lesson.[77]

For Goldberg, too, the whole episode had been an education, in more ways than one. He had learned much about labor law, in which he had not been very well versed, and about the union movement itself. "I had no labor practice," he explained. "Here I was representing lawyers and a few small corporations and . . . I was being called on to represent the labor movement."[78] Unions in those days could not really afford to pay lawyers much, and so Goldberg had never tried to add them to his firm as clients. He later observed that "in the nine months I represented the Newspaper Guild, if I got expenses out of it that was a great thing. Most of the time I didn't. . . . I had to support myself out of the other practice I had."[79]

Despite organized labor's somewhat precarious existence in the late 1930s, by the spring of 1940 the economy had begun to improve, and so, too, had the fortunes of most labor unions. By that time, a lawyer with real vision could expect that labor law might in time prove rewarding in a monetary sense as well as in other ways, and so in May when Bittner asked Goldberg to take the Steel Workers Organizing Committee (SWOC)'s western region as a client, he said yes. As important if not more so than pecuniary gain in persuading Goldberg to accept was his liking for both the clients and the work. He believed in the union cause, albeit within the limits outlined by Hillman and his associates at the labor bank.[80]

For Bittner's part, Goldberg seemed likely to become an effective aide in dealing with management and a loyal ally in what Bittner expected would be an eventual showdown for control of the CIO between its by-then dominant New Deal liberal faction and the more radical elements, which included, among others, communists and party sympathizers. That mattered even more to Bittner's deputy in the Chicago-based district of the SWOC, the outspoken, tough, and militantly anticommunist Joe Germano. "They wanted," Goldberg remembered, "a lawyer of stature and standing in the community . . . and . . . one who stood with them in the developing ideological battle within the trade union movement."[81]

In the 1930s, those divisions had not produced civil war within the CIO because both sides were content at first to work together in building strong workers' organizations. CIO president John L. Lewis, although himself a bitter foe of radicalism whose own United Mine Workers Union had enacted a constitutional ban on communists as members, nonetheless tolerated their presence in the new labor federation because they supplied him with a corps of talented, experienced organizers that he needed to build unions in several industries. He did not expect that they would ever pose a real threat to his control. "Who gets the bird," he asked in an oft-quoted remark, "the hunter or the dog?"[82]

For their part, the communists in the CIO saw in Lewis a well-financed supporter whose resources could be used to radicalize the working class and make it into the agent for a larger transformation of the whole society. The two sides worked together uneasily during the late 1930s but maintained what harmony there was only by putting off debates over the CIO's long-term program. A reorganization of the CIO's administrative structure in 1938 strengthened the Lewis faction's hold on the reins, but Bittner and his allies worried about what would follow Lewis's eventual retirement and the development of a more pluralistic CIO governing structure.[83]

Goldberg's decision to accept the job Bittner offered him thus did more than bring him some new clients for his law firm. It linked him, albeit indirectly, to the labor movement at a critical period in its evolution. At the time he took the job, it was still hard to see how things would eventually turn out. But at thirty-two years of age, Goldberg had found a route that would eventually lead him to the center of the forces that governed American society. The guild strike had marked a turning point not only in the lives of those on the picket lines but in his own as well.

2

The Crucible of Wartime

$\mathbf{A}$T THE SAME time the guild strike was in progress, events in the wider world began to intrude on Goldberg's life, as they did for so many others. In the same month that he had gone to the guild strikers' defense, Germany declared war on England and France. Eight months later, just as the strike was ending, German troops invaded France and in a mere six weeks defeated the French armies. The Third Republic's rapid collapse sent shock waves throughout the United States, shattering Americans' complacent belief that France and Britain would check any further Nazi advance. For liberals and especially Jews who viewed Hitler as a menace to humanity in general and European Jewry in particular, the need for U.S. government aid to Britain seemed compelling. And so when longtime Republican Progressive William Allen White, a staunch supporter of such aid as a way of avoiding American military intervention, established the Committee to Defend America by Aiding the Allies that spring, Goldberg quickly signed on as a member.[1]

The Chicago chapter of the White committee recruited most of its members from the internationalist Chicago Council on Foreign Relations, a circumstance that enabled Goldberg to make one of the most important political connections of his life. The council's members championed a more active role abroad for the United States government, one they believed was appropriate given the ever increasing expansion of American economic activity outside the Western Hemisphere. For years, however, they had been merely a band of lonely dissenters in the deeply isolationist Midwest. Among them was a former council president, Chicago attorney Adlai Stevenson, whom Goldberg had first met casually at a council meeting during the 1930s. Apart from that encounter, the two had had little contact with each other until the White committee assembled in May 1940. The reason for that was simple: They came from entirely different worlds. Stevenson was a wealthy patrician, the grandson of a Democratic vice-president of the same name, and by then a partner in one of Chicago's leading law firms; Goldberg was the striving son of immigrant Jews, with a reputation as a civil libertarian, and the head of his own small firm.[2]

When the Chicago chapter of the White committee elected Stevenson its president, however, the two began to get to know each other and eventually became quite friendly. "Both of us recognized," Goldberg explained, "the danger of Hitler dominating Europe and then beyond."[3] Their political philosophies were more or less congruent, although Stevenson's liberalism was much more nebulous and tentative, more an intellectual tendency than a collection of coherent and firmly held convictions, which contrasted sharply with Goldberg's more considered and passionate support for the New Deal. Stevenson's lineage, wealth, vaguely reformist impulses, and talent as a public speaker suggested his potential for public service to many, including his new colleague Arthur Goldberg. He was attracted to Stevenson by his obvious intelligence, wit, and willingness to speak out against an isolationist stance strongly supported by most of his well-to-do North Shore friends.[4]

Stevenson responded to Goldberg's good wishes, despite the obvious differences in their respective backgrounds. Although he had grown up in a world largely closed to Jews, Stevenson possessed enough openness of mind to probe beyond his peers' anti-Semitic cant. He did not, however, at that point at least, entirely reject it. Rather, Stevenson liked and respected Goldberg for reasons perhaps similar to those he gave for admiring another intellectually gifted Jewish lawyer, Harvard law professor Jerome Frank. Stevenson had served a brief stint at the U.S. Agriculture Department during the early 1930s while Frank was general counsel and described him in a letter

> as smart and able as can be. There is a little feeling that the Jews are getting too prominent [at the department] — as you know many of them are autocratic and the effect on the public . . . is bad. . . . I've noticed it from the start. . . . Frank has none of the racial characteristics and has done a dreadfully difficult job as well as could be hoped for — he's indefatigable & literally works most all night every night but he's brought several other Jews down who, tho individually smart and able, are more racial.[5]

Traces of social snobbery lingered but did not blind Stevenson to individual distinctions. He had graduated from Northwestern Law School three years before Goldberg and probably knew of his unsurpassed academic record there. In both Frank and Goldberg he could discern piercing legal intelligence, great industry, and humane principles. Stevenson, moreover, was capable of intellectual growth, open to new ideas and to people who had grown up in different circumstances. As one biographer noted, for example, under Stevenson's leadership the Council on Foreign Relations had "changed from a small elitist group of like-minded people to a larger, more public and more diverse group."[6]

Many of those members joined with Stevenson and Goldberg to debate Chicago's then-formidable isolationist establishment. Its most notable voice was the *Chicago Tribune*, the city's only morning newspaper, which daily blared forth publisher Robert R. McCormick's view that America should studiously avoid any involvement in the conflict. Chicago was then the only major U.S. city with a single morning paper, thanks largely to the guild strike, and thus the *Tribune*'s monopoly and tone contributed to the city's reputation as the capital of isolationist America.

There the America First Committee established its national headquarters. This leading isolationist group featured an executive board made up of such diverse public figures as Charles Lindbergh, Norman Thomas, Chester Bowles, Father Coughlin, and Alice Roosevelt Longworth, to name only a few. From the spring of 1940 through the late fall, it and the White committee sparred with each other in an increasingly bitter debate.

Stevenson's group organized a mass meeting in May at the University of Chicago, where he spoke to a crowd of several thousand. As Goldberg recalled later, "We all pitched in, we didn't have a big budget. It was a name committee."[7] They took out ads in Chicago's evening papers, raised money— most of it from Jewish businessmen—and engaged in a public debate that divided families, friends, and neighbors.[8]

The issue of American aid to Great Britain soon became linked to the 1940 presidential election. The Republicans, surprising even themselves, nominated former Democrat and political neophyte Wendell Willkie in late June. He campaigned at first as an internationalist who pledged to aid Britain but soon adopted a more neutralist stance. The Democrats provided a surprise of their own by drafting an eager Roosevelt to run for an unprecedented third term. They convened in Chicago during July and among those present was ardent FDR supporter Arthur Goldberg. He was not a delegate but attended as Illinois's secretary of the Norris–La Guardia Committee for the Re-election of Roosevelt, a group of liberal Republicans and independents united by that common goal.[9]

Goldberg was working for the independent group and not for Roosevelt's own party, because for many years he had viewed the city's Democratic machine with disgust. The cleavage between New Deal liberals and the machine had a long history in Chicago. It was rooted in the tendency of the mayor's office to back FDR on the national ticket but apply few, if any, New Deal ideas to governing the city itself. The mayor in those days, Edward J. Kelly, did little to disturb the patterns of dishonesty and graft that had made Chicago in the 1920s a synonym for corrupt municipal administration. For Goldberg and his colleagues on the Civil Liberties Committee, the only choice was that of a principled independence. The problem did not change much, though, despite their efforts at reform.

As late as 1945 Goldberg would write that Chicago was "a boss-ridden, politically dominated city, with an administration far more corrupt and inefficient than the old Tammany administration in New York."[10] He had no illusions about Mayor Kelly either, whom he saw as "the one man political czar of Chicago" and one whose ideals were "those dictated by political expediency."[11] For that reason, Kelly supported Roosevelt's quest for a third term, working in uneasy alliance with members of the reform faction such as Goldberg, who continued to distrust him.[12]

As the general election contest heated up, so too did the debate over intervention in Europe. The White committee favored all aid to Britain short of war, including the destroyers-for-bases deal FDR negotiated in August. They stepped up their efforts with a large mass meeting held at the Chicago Coliseum on September 18 that attracted more than 13,000 people. America First, however, had sponsored a rally only a few weeks earlier that had drawn more than twice that number.

Goldberg's dual role as worker for both the White committee and Roosevelt's reelection reflected the gradual merging of the two issues. Columnist Arthur Krock noted this development in a piece published in the *New York Times* just a week before the election. Writing from Chicago, he observed,

> An argument over foreign policy is running parallel to the Presidential campaign in this section, as in other parts of the country. In Chicago it is best exemplified by the rival views being stated by representatives of the William Allen White committee and an organization called the America First Committee. But despite the fact that both groups are making every effort to be nonpartisan, the debate parallel is being drawn closer to that of the campaign itself, which is turning out to be a very bad thing.[13]

The *Tribune*'s editor, Robert McCormick, did all he could to advance the related causes of America First and Wendell Willkie. The paper poured forth a steady stream of attacks on Roosevelt's foreign policy while the Republican candidate dominated the *Tribune*'s campaign coverage. Often McCormick's tactics were grossly unfair. Stevenson remembered later that "the *Tribune* used to send photographers to photograph all the empty seats, if any, in halls where we presented programs."[14]

Roosevelt's fairly narrow but still decisive victory seemed to turn the tide against the midwestern isolationists. To McCormick's apparent shock, he carried Illinois by 51.2 percent on the strength of a huge Chicago majority. Paul Douglas confirmed in his memoirs the vote's impact in the city on the related issue of aid to Britain. "Until Roosevelt swept the city, the state and the country in the 1940 election," he wrote, "the weight of articulate opinion seemed to be on the other side."[15]

The Roosevelt and White committee campaigns, along with the British people's gritty defense of their home island, shifted midwestern public opinion toward support for FDR's Lend–Lease program, which he soon proposed after winning a third term. The White committee members in Chicago gradually wound down their activities during the first three months of 1941 and viewed the debate as largely won when Congress passed Lend–Lease that March.[16]

The experience marked the emergence in public life of Stevenson and the core of what eventually became his most loyal political supporters. For the first time he had assumed a prominent role regarding a divisive political issue when most of his friends stood on the other side. He had attracted Roosevelt's attention and endeared himself to New Deal liberals in Chicago, including Arthur Goldberg. In December 1940 Goldberg, Douglas, and others on the Civil Liberties Committee asked their friend Adlai to serve on its executive board. Although he declined, giving other obligations as the reason, the offer testified to his growing popularity with them.[17]

Stevenson had also bolstered his standing with Chicago's Jewish community. In the wake of Roosevelt's victory, the *Tribune* published an article attributing to Jews the source of the funds for the White committee's Chicago chapter. Although most of the large contributions did come from them, the story was couched in such inflammatory language that it deeply offended both the city's Jewish community and White committee members. Stevenson asked the Anti-Defamation League of B'Nai Brith to draft a letter of protest, which he then edited and issued over his own signature. He had been at some pains to keep the Jewish backers of the White committee out of the limelight, both to prevent anti-Semitism from undermining the interventionist cause and to avoid giving the impression that it was supported only by those with a special interest in the conflict.

Stevenson wrote, for example, to M. J. Spiegel, who contributed the largest amount:

> I hope you will agree that it is probably best, at least at this stage, to keep the large Jewish support feature in the background. I am very apprehensive that, as time goes on, the "enemy within" may try to couple up anti-Semitism with appeasement with a consequent increase in confused thinking.[18]

This incident pointed up the dilemma faced by American Jews such as Goldberg: The more strident they became on the issues of aid to the Allies and the admission of Jewish refugees to the United States, the more likely their isolationist foes could — by accusing such Jews of pushing the United States into war for selfish reasons — use anti-Semitic feeling to bolster their own cause. Some American Jews feared their activities might backfire, and others worried about a loss of standing in American society as another possible consequence. Many, Goldberg included, were therefore grateful to Stevenson for working on their behalf.[19]

Such sentiments encouraged Stevenson to express openly to his colleagues and friends the political ambitions he had harbored for a long time. Early in 1941 he began looking for a job at the State Department and asked former *Chicago Daily News* publisher and current secretary of the navy, Frank Knox, to help him. Although Stevenson used all of the connections at his disposal, the hoped-for opening failed to appear. Finally Knox himself hired Stevenson in June as principal attorney to the Secretary. Both Theodore and Franklin Roosevelt had found the Navy Department a springboard to high office, and Stevenson seems to have had similar thoughts. When he confessed his desire to Goldberg, the latter used his new ties to the CIO to arrange Stevenson's first meeting with labor people in July 1941.

For Stevenson, the event constituted another milestone in his quest for public office. Goldberg had responded to Stevenson's expression of interest in running for office, by asking

> him a question. He lived in Libertyville. No one who put on a hard hat at that time lived in Libertyville . . . and so I said, "Have you ever met a labor person? [If] you want to go into politics, you're going to have to meet people." "No," [Stevenson had replied]. . . . It so happened there was a meeting at the Amalgamated Bank of the state CIO, which I then represented. . . . I took Adlai along with me and introduced him to his first sons of toil.[20]

Goldberg tried to advance Stevenson's political career by suggesting that he run for the U.S. Senate seat held by Republican C. Wayland Brooks, up for reelection in 1942. In July of the preceding year, Stevenson had written Goldberg urging him "not to forget that you have promised to let me know when you are in Washington. I am still enjoying glimpses from the dizzying mountain top to which you led me the other day."[21]

The dizzying mountaintop—Goldberg's proposal that he run for the Senate—Stevenson declined to attempt, possibly because he was preoccupied with marital problems and also unsure of his chances, especially after the Chicago Democratic bosses endorsed another candidate. Paul Douglas ran instead, losing to the machine's choice in the primary, whom Brooks in turn easily defeated.[22]

II

If Stevenson's fortunes suffered a reverse in the early 1940s, those of Goldberg's new CIO clients experienced just the opposite. When Goldberg agreed in the spring of 1940 to represent the steelworkers, their union faced a highly uncertain future. The Steel Workers Organizing Committee (SWOC), which had been created five years earlier by John L. Lewis and his lieutenants in the United Mine Workers Union (UMW), still had only a precarious existence. Although supported by some very active locals and hundreds of organizers, the organization lacked the broader and more energetic rank-and-file backing enjoyed by the other big CIO unions such as the UMW and the United Automobile Workers (UAW). SWOC had been greatly strengthened by U.S. Steel management's decision to recognize it in March 1937, but the recession that began the following summer threatened for the next two years to undo all that SWOC had accomplished.

The key problem was not relations with U.S. Steel, which had signed a contract with SWOC that would run until 1940, but, rather, the smaller companies in the industry, which had never been organized successfully. These firms, usually grouped under the somewhat misleading rubric of "Little Steel," included Bethlehem, Inland, Youngstown Sheet & Tube, Republic, National, and Armco. Executives at all of them had refused to follow the lead of their counterparts at U.S. Steel in recognizing SWOC and had broken the

SWOC-led strikes against them in the spring and summer of 1937. During the deep recession that had followed, they had led the way in imposing wage reductions and layoffs.

Large orders for steel to rearm America and meet the demands of European nations at war with Germany, however, shifted the balance of power once again in SWOC's favor. By February 1940 the American steel industry was operating at virtually full capacity, and that same month, SWOC won its first organizing victory in over two and a half years.

SWOC's leaders saw their opportunity and seized it by inaugurating a new campaign to organize the industry holdouts. So, like his decision to represent the guild, Goldberg's acceptance of SWOC as a client in May 1940 had come at an opportune moment.[23]

The drive formally began in October 1940 and was directed by the man who had hired him, Van Bittner. That big, strong-willed, and acid-tongued labor leader was a superb organizer, whose western region included many of the smaller steel companies' major plants. He and Goldberg soon became close friends, though their backgrounds differed in many ways. Bittner, like John L. Lewis and SWOC chief Philip Murray, had begun working in a coal mine when still a boy and knew at first hand the despair produced by steadily falling wages in times of depression, the bitterness that grew in the wake of countless failed strikes, and the grinding misery of coal-mining towns for which Harlan County, Kentucky, became a national symbol during the 1930s. And as was true for his better-known CIO colleagues, Lewis and Murray, Bittner had obtained little education beyond grade school. As a rule he and they distrusted professionals, but CIO leaders' growing need for skilled attorneys to represent SWOC before the National Labor Relations Board (NLRB) and the courts led them to hire many and to give them an increasing amount of responsibility.[24]

Goldberg soon received a lot from Bittner. The SWOC's western region encompassed no fewer than twelve districts. In order of decreasing size they were Chicago–Calumet, Cleveland, Milwaukee, Indianapolis, St. Louis, Peoria, California, Duluth, Detroit, Texas, Washington, and Utah.

As the SWOC organizing drive led by Bittner and the accompanying legal struggle directed by CIO and SWOC general counsel Lee Pressman proceeded during 1940 and 1941, they gradually wore down most of the remaining Little Steel companies. As in the mid-1930s, efforts to reshape power relations in the workplace eventually worked changes in the Nation Labor Relations Board's (NLRB) rulings and judicial opinions.

Pressman, a brilliant legal strategist, managed to secure a Supreme Court ruling in November 1940 that upheld an NLRB decision barring several specific employer practices that these firms had used to obstruct CIO organizing efforts. The following April, the NLRB ordered Youngstown Sheet & Tube to dissolve its company unions and permit an election regarding the issue of SWOC affiliation. One month later, a federal circuit court sustained an NLRB ruling favoring SWOC representation at Bethlehem Steel. Republic's senior executives, at last acknowledging that further resistance to SWOC would be futile, also agreed to recognize the organization once a majority of their workers signed union cards. By the fall of 1941, recognition had been won at all of the Little Steel companies except National and Armco.[25]

The largely successful effort by workers and full-time organizers to win union recognition generated a great deal of legal work for those at the secondary level, such as Goldberg. Many of the Little Steel plants were in the western region, and the organizing drives created enormous numbers of disputes over unfair labor practices, the reinstatement of discharged workers, grievance proceedings that were initiated to resolve a whole host of work rules issues, and modifications in the contracts negotiated by Pressman to meet special circumstances in individual plants. Goldberg proved very adept at those sorts of matters, and especially at contract negotiation.

His manner, then as throughout his association with the labor movement, was warm, down-to-earth, direct, and very firm when needed. He had an unusual gift for expressing complicated provisions in simple formulas. As one observer of his technique noted, Goldberg was a "meticulous man . . . [who] hates clutter and thinks systematically. He has the ability to reduce complex legal situations to understandable, almost simplistic language. This ability to strip matters down to bare essentials runs through his entire personality."[26] Dorothy Goldberg, an artist, described the same quality in terms of her own vocation. "If Arthur painted," she said, "he would be like Mondrian."[27]

Another clue to Goldberg's talent for contract negotiation lay in his tendency to leave some areas of disagreement to be solved later, once sufficient common ground had been reached. Dorothy Goldberg saw the technique as one that allowed "for a certain amount of gray area to exist, a certain ambiguity that permits the hurdling of obstacles to agreement."[28]

Such an approach could not have succeeded during the Depression, when unions were weaker and the cost of a strike to employers was smaller because they operated well below capacity. With the recovery of 1940/41, however, stronger unions could exert considerable pressure on employers anxious to avoid disrupting output. Workers, for their part, needed to support families that had endured ten or more difficult years. Thus once the contract was signed, the two sides tended to make it work or at least to try much harder than in the recent past.[29]

Throughout this period, Goldberg continued to see himself as independent of the labor movement, an attitude that, though sometimes annoying to union officials, did much to ease his dealings with employers. SWOC could not afford to pay him much, and so he still earned most of his income from other legal work. He treated the union as a client, billed it for services rendered, and never formally went on a CIO payroll as a full-time employee. "I led," he explained, "a kind of schizophrenic life. . . . I was representing lawyers and also a few small corporations and . . . the labor movement. . . . I made no commitment to them beyond handling a particular problem."[30]

Goldberg's success on behalf of SWOC soon earned him more clients, as Bittner began steering other CIO unions to him for help. Among the earliest additions were the organizing committees for the packing-house, textile, and rubber workers. Gradually, he recalled, "I started to enlarge my representation. I represented the state CIO [and] through . . . Van Bittner . . . everything from Ohio to California in the CIO."[31]

For the first time in his life, Goldberg began traveling a good deal, to the other cities of the Midwest and West Coast and to Washington, D.C. In time he amassed a string of new associates and friends in labor circles. His CIO work was, quite literally, expanding his horizons. It was increasing his personal income, too, as was the general economic recovery of 1940/41. As 1941 came to a close, the United States neared full employment for the first time in more than twelve years. Goldberg shared in the long-awaited return to prosperity as his income almost doubled from what it had been three years earlier.[32]

Goldberg's CIO clients were prospering as well. SWOC paid off the last of its debts to the UMW in 1941 and by the spring of 1942 had been formally reorganized as the United Steelworkers of America (USA).[33] By the end of the organizing drives of 1940/41, the steel union had just over a half a million dues-paying members and $1.4 million in its treasury.

Six months later, the first executive board meeting of the USA was held in Pittsburgh, at which one of the first decisions made was to purchase a large office building in Washington at Jackson Place, only a short distance from the White House. Most of that building, the new headquarters for both the CIO and the Washington office of the Steelworkers Union, USA President Murray noted ironically in his description, had been "occupied by the National Republican Committee . . . for a number of years."[34] But Murray saw only half the irony in that fact. The CIO's leaders had, in addition to displacing the Republican National Committee, also adopted as their own its concept of what a headquarters should be. The symbolism could not have been more appropriate. Organized labor was emerging as a force to be reckoned with, but in ways that resembled those it claimed to be fighting.

And there were still, also, severe weaknesses. The steel union had not been built primarily on rank-and-file activism and managed to secure the regular payment of dues by most of its members only after management agreed in 1942 to withhold them from workers' paychecks. Several thousand workers had already been inducted into the armed forces, and more would soon be drafted, leaving the union with newly hired workers who had an untested commitment to it. The big treasury, too, offered less protection than it seemed. The union was spending more than $300,000 a month, and at that rate, as Secretary-Treasurer David McDonald pointed out to the other board members, the treasury "wouldn't last very long if we were to hit upon a period of recession."[35]

The overall federation's fortunes appeared similarly mixed at that time. Murray, who assumed the additional office of CIO president following Lewis's resignation in November 1940, sounded defensive about the organization's condition at the first executive board meeting held after the Japanese attack at Pearl Harbor. He told the other board members that the

CIO is a very healthy institution. I want you to get that; I want you to get that definitely in your minds. We are altogether solvent, we have a fairly good treasury, as treasuries go, and we are paying our bills and meeting our obligations. . . . There is a lot of surreptitious backdoor talk going on here and there that a number of our unions are reaching the stage of decay and insolvency. Nothing could be further from the truth.[36]

Murray protested a bit too much to be believed. Although in a stronger position than it had been in 1938/39, the CIO was still a vulnerable organization facing an uncertain future. It was dominated by a handful of big unions, representing workers in the steel, auto, electrical, coal-mining, clothing, and textile industries. The remainder were much smaller organizing units, subsidized by the others at a total cost to the federation of approximately $20,000 per month.

What would delay a real test of the CIO's strength and give it time to increase its size was America's entry into the Second World War. The war also reshaped labor's efforts to negotiate with management, thanks to the enormous increase in government pressure against strikes, lockouts, and other actions that interfered with production. For the duration, the key bargaining usually went on in government meeting rooms and corridors, while rank-and-file discontent periodically flared on the shop floor, only to be dampened by labor leaders anxious to avoid a confrontation with employers and the state.[37]

These arrangements greatly expanded the amount of work to be done by labor economists, arbitrators, accountants, and lawyers, thus offering Goldberg the prospect of a growing role in the labor movement. His desire, however, to play an active part in the conduct of the war itself overcame any temptation he may have felt to stay with his law practice. Fairly soon after the United States entered the war, so, too, did he, for an experience that would prove the most formative of his adult life.[38]

III

December 7, 1941, ever after remained a disturbingly memorable day for Goldberg, in more ways than one. No sooner had he read about the attack on Pearl Harbor in the newspaper when the telephone rang. On the line was his secretary, a young Asian American lawyer named Elizabeth Ho. She told her boss, Goldberg later remembered, that

she . . . [had been] picked up by the FBI . . . in Chicago. . . . On that same day I called [intelligence chief William] Donovan and told him I was ready to enlist. . . . Then . . . I called the FBI and said, . . . "You're holding my secretary, on what grounds?"

"Well, you know, Pearl Harbor," [the FBI agent had replied]. So I said, "I know about Pearl Harbor, I'm the one who has enlisted, . . . what are you holding her for?" "Well, Japanese-Americans, you know . . . ," [the FBI man had answered]. So I said, "I'll tell you something. I'm going down there and you'll release her to me or I'll go into federal court and get a petition for habeas corpus. . . . "

I called a federal judge . . . and he was ready to issue the order. . . . The FBI couldn't hold her and so they released her.[39]

Although Goldberg's secretary, who later served with distinction in the U.S. Navy, had escaped the heavy hand of government repression fairly easily, the episode strongly reinforced Goldberg's inclination to get directly involved in the war effort. Unless reasonable people did so, he feared, misguided zealots like the FBI agent he had dealt with might run it and imperil in the process the very kind of freedom the country was supposed to be defending.[40]

Feeding that fear was the rapid growth in U.S. military and internal security forces that had accompanied the approach of World War II. No part of the national security apparatus had expanded more dramatically during that time than U.S. intelligence-gathering operations. A key turning point in their development had come the previous July, when FDR had issued an executive order creating an intelligence system intended to combat subversives at home and imitate their supposedly effective methods abroad.

This organization, which Roosevelt gave the nondescript name Coordinator of Information (COI), was the first civilian-run intelligence agency in modern U.S. history. To head it, Roosevelt appointed a prominent New York attorney named William Donovan, who soon assembled a group of corporate executives on leave to serve as administrators and another, subordinate one, composed of academics, to do research. They began gathering intelligence and, once the war reached the United States, also started to plan what would come to be called *covert operations*.[41]

One of Donovan's friends, a former NLRB official named Heber Blankenhorn, had proposed in the fall of 1941 creating a labor branch to develop sources of information within European trade union circles. Donovan liked the idea and became convinced that such people would be at the center of efforts to subvert Nazi rule in occupied countries.

The Nazi regime had jailed German labor leaders during the 1930s and dissolved their unions as threats to both its absolute power and fascist ideology. Hitler's government repeated that process wherever its armies conquered, which earned the Third Reich the enmity of trade unionists across the continent. Blankenhorn believed that they would readily repay the Nazis by spying on them and reporting, for example, troop movements and shipping schedules.[42]

To find someone to run the labor operation, Donovan turned to George Bowden, a onetime organizer for the Industrial Workers of the World and by then a Chicago tax lawyer, who belonged to the National Lawyers Guild and knew casually several union leaders. Bowden in turn looked around for a man more knowledgeable than he about labor and suggested to Blankenhorn that Goldberg be offered the job. To Bowden, his friend and fellow civic activist seemed well positioned to gain the trust of organized labor's European counterparts.

Goldberg, however, did not accept when, prior to Pearl Harbor, Donovan had asked him to head the labor branch. "He had been after me to join his outfit [but] at that time I said I had two children," Goldberg explained.[43] The younger of the two, his son Bob, was only an infant, and even more of a problem, Goldberg's law practice provided the family's sole income.[44]

Pearl Harbor and the incident involving the FBI together changed his mind. In joining the war effort he also made certain that, in his words, "no one could argue patriotism to me" when challenging his actions.[45] As in the case of so many others, Goldberg's wartime service helped undercut those conservative critics who hoped to paint liberals as disloyal and thereby weaken public support for New Deal programs.

Although anxious to get into the fight against Hitler, Goldberg could not enlist in the Marines, as Paul Douglas did, and actually serve in combat, because an army medical examiner determined that Goldberg was unfit for combat duty and approved his induction for desk work only.[46]

The closest Goldberg could get to the enemy was by joining the COI, which he did formally in the spring of 1942. The delay was a result of a struggle among the military service chiefs and the State Department over the COI's proper role in the intelligence field. By June Roosevelt resolved the matter by rechristening COI the Office of Strategic Services (OSS). The new agency's mission was to gather intelligence, evaluate it, and sponsor underground resistance movements in those countries under Axis domination.[47]

While waiting for the outcome of the debate over the COI's fate, Goldberg briefly considered going elsewhere and wrote to Adlai Stevenson about a possible job. Stevenson offered nothing beyond his advice to Goldberg in a letter of December 13, 1941, that "with your exceptional familiarity with industrial relations in the middle west you might be of use in the new labor situation which will evolve from conferences commencing next week."[48] Wanting to do something more directly tied to the war effort, Goldberg elected to stick with the OSS.[49]

On May 6, 1942, he officially began his work for Donovan, whom he had met casually before the war while both were working on an antitrust case in Milwaukee. Goldberg saw his new boss as a "courageous, volatile, Irishman. . . . He and I [became] great friends."[50] Donovan told him to begin his labor operation in New York, where Allen Dulles had just opened an OSS field office. Leaving his family behind in Chicago, Goldberg joined Dulles, another talented attorney turned amateur spy, who operated out of Room 3663 of the International Building at Rockefeller Center.

Dulles, Goldberg, and Ernest Cuneo, counsel to New York mayor Fiorello La Guardia, began their efforts at intelligence gathering by cooperating closely with the British, particularly their New York–based operative, William Stephenson. "We organized the New York office," Goldberg said later, "which we needed very badly because Bill Stephenson—the man called Intrepid—was right on the same floor and we really needed instruction. We [Americans] had no real intelligence service."[51]

Goldberg focused his energies on the International Transport Workers

Federation (ITWF), especially its merchant seamen members from neutral countries whose ships frequented German ports. The Belgian secretary of the ITWF, Omar Becu, told Goldberg during a visit to New York that he was willing to help, and so the two of them, in Goldberg's words, "arranged interviews . . . with the sailors" when their ships docked in New York. "We got a mineful of information . . . ," he claimed, because "when they land[ed] in a port . . . they didn't want to sit on a ship, so they wandered around Germany in various ports."[52]

Goldberg reported his findings to Whitney Shepardson, head of intelligence gathering for OSS and a former vice-president of International Railways of Central America, a corporate credential typical of those holding the senior administrative posts in the OSS. Donovan owed his appointment and his continuing budgetary appropriations to his willingness to appoint such people as the agency's managers.

Like the other important government agencies during the war, the real decision-making authority was concentrated in the hands of such men, many of whom had opposed the New Deal and still remained deeply suspicious of the activist state. They all too often proved unenthusiastic about working with resistance movements that included social democrats or those even further to the left. The administrators also got along somewhat uneasily with liberal OSS researchers and field operatives such as Goldberg.[53]

Shortly after the war, he criticized Donovan's hiring practices in a book review for *The Nation*. Goldberg wrote that the administrative appointments had been "mistakes" because the so-called dollar-a-year-men were "by background and temperament . . . unsympathetic with Donovan's conception of the necessity of unstinting cooperation with the resistance movements."[54] Much later, though, Goldberg showed that he had come to understand why his boss had picked such people. "I think he knew what he was doing," he said. "He hired a lot of those people . . . for political reasons . . . to calm down people who were asking what kind of an organization this was. . . . Maybe he hired them [also] because they were going to be future clients, I don't know. . . . Bill Donovan [had] . . . a big law firm."[55]

At first reporting directly to Shepardson, Goldberg after a year at the OSS managed to circumvent the chain of command by getting himself appointed as special assistant to Donovan. That was rather unusual, given that Goldberg already held the title of labor branch chief, but Donovan was a man who only rarely heeded organizational charts. Once Goldberg became a special assistant, he dealt personally with the OSS director, thereby increasing the influence of the labor operation. As would be the case so often in the future, Goldberg showed that he understood how to find a way to deal directly with those most likely to prove helpful.[56]

He could hardly have chosen a better place in which to meet people of future usefulness to him. Before the war, Goldberg's work had been confined mainly to the industrial centers of the Midwest and Pacific Coast, but the OSS gave him an entrée into the offices and homes of people who lived in New

York and Washington, which greatly broadened his professional and social network.

Working for Goldberg in the New York office was George Pratt, who was on leave from the NLRB, where he had been chief trial counsel. Also part of the OSS labor group was Pratt's former boss, NLRB general counsel Gerhard Van Arkel, who moved from that job to head OSS operations in North Africa. In addition to OSS people, Goldberg also came to know many who, though not on its payroll, nonetheless aided the intelligence effort.

Through friends he was introduced to Freda Kirchwey of *The Nation*, who in turn put Goldberg in touch with Alvarez del Vayo, foreign minister of the Spanish Republican government in exile. The foreign minister had been active in American leftist and émigré circles since his arrival in the United States and was therefore able to suggest the names of several people with connections to European labor groups. Goldberg also became acquainted with Jay Lovestone, a former communist who had become a close adviser to David Dubinsky, president of the AFL-affiliated International Ladies Garment Workers Union (ILGWU), and Jacob Potofsky, Sidney Hillman's deputy and heir apparent in the Amalgamated Clothing Workers Union. Both Lovestone and Potofsky helped locate sources of information and also gave Goldberg a better sense of who was who in the northeast region of the American labor movement.[57]

Helping him meet people with such diverse outlooks was labor's virtually unanimous support for the American war effort. Unlike the First World War, when American socialists had opposed their country's intervention and thereby split the union movement, after Pearl Harbor even the badly divided labor community had achieved consensus on the issue. As a result, unionists of all kinds were working together for the first time in decades, albeit often rather uneasily. The war wore down, at least temporarily, many barriers, helping give Goldberg the chance to become acquainted with a genuine cross section of that world.[58]

His first trip abroad in the late summer of 1942 widened Goldberg's horizons still further. By that time the New York office had been established and its day-to-day affairs entrusted to subordinates. Dulles left for Switzerland at about the same time to develop sources among refugees trapped there, whereas Goldberg set his sights on developing channels of communication with underground labor groups on the Continent that kept in touch with London-based governments in exile. Armed with letters of introduction from Freda Kirchwey, Jacob Potofsky, and others to help open doors for him within the British labor movement and émigré community, Goldberg flew from New York to London during the first week of September.[59]

This flight, Goldberg's first to Europe, was as exciting to him as it was routine to his army pilots. "Spanning the ocean so rapidly and with such apparent ease," he wrote to his secretary at the New York office, "demonstrates . . . better than any other way, the potentialities of aircraft both for good and evil. I recommend it particularly to those shortsighted Isolationists who are so confident about the invulnerability of our shores to attack from the air."[60]

The plane made a brief stop in Ireland, which Goldberg described in the same letter as "delightful and were it not for my name and other obvious factors, I could readily make it an adopted country. There is something about the appearance of the countryside and the people which has great appeal for me. Perhaps in my subconscious this is a reversion to high school days when I had a case on a girl recently arrived from Dublin."[61]

London's grimness posed a sharp contrast with neutral Ireland, a change Goldberg found sobering. "From the peace and quiet of an Irish Sunday," he wrote shortly after landing in Britain,

> to war-scarred England is the change which Nazi terror has brought to the world. . . . Words are inadequate to convey the impression which the nightly blackout makes upon one come recently from the States. . . . For the first few nights I felt that it was virtually impossible to venture outside, and when I did last night, it was for a very short while, made feasible only by the frequent use of the flashlight which I brought with me.[62]

Goldberg quickly settled into the routine, however, noting in the same letter that he had equipped himself with "an alien identification card, a National Registration card, a Food Rationing book, a Clothes Rationing book, and a gas mask and helmet."[63] Within three weeks he sent his first report to George Bowden in New York describing the various unions with offices in London and affiliates on the Continent. Soon he succeeded in establishing liaison arrangements with people in several countries and tried to set up contacts in foreign capitals whenever that appeared to be a useful step.[64]

Sweden, a neutral country filled with representatives of both the Axis and Allied countries, afforded a prime target. "I am impressed by the fact," Goldberg wrote Bowden,

> that it is highly important that someone be sent, or if this is not possible, that someone now in Sweden be designated to follow through such labor contacts as we have already developed, or may in future develop there. According to the information I received here in London, Sweden is apparently one of the best sources of communication through labor channels with Germany. If someone is to be sent . . . I should like to spend some time with him . . . so that I can give him a list of labor contacts available in Sweden, and outline to him the possibilities at present there.[65]

The OSS recruited Vic Shaho, a Minnesota railway union official, to serve as its representative in Stockholm, where he obtained information from Swedish transport workers and passed it along to the labor desk in London.[66]

In carrying out such missions, OSS operatives often encountered obstacles in the form of American ambassadors anxious to preserve friendly relations with neutral nations such as Sweden and Spain. Donovan usually conferred about such matters with Assistant Secretary of State A. A. Berle Jr. so that the department's representatives knew when a covert operation was under way, but sometimes the OSS chief failed to give Berle notice.

The State Department did not always keep its ambassadors informed either, which on occasion led to some bad feelings all around. More than one aggrieved ambassador, upon discovering an OSS agent planning an operation, tried to squelch it. Vic Shaho, for example, arranged in 1944 for Swedish unionists to strike a Swedish company that was secretly making ball bearings for Germany. The American ambassador to Sweden, Herschel Johnson, got wind of the scheme and threatened to have Shaho and his cohorts deported unless they dropped the idea.[67]

Goldberg's intelligence efforts in Spain created an even more explosive clash between the OSS and the State Department. His conversations while in London during the fall of 1942 with Juan Negrin, former prime minister of Spain's republican government and leader of its exile regime, suggested to Goldberg that Franco might bring Spain into the war when the Allies invaded northwest Africa. "Mr. N[egrin] believes," Goldberg wrote to the New York office for transmittal to Donovan,

> that at some time in the not too distant future there may be a front established in West Africa, and that at such time Spain will enter the war on the side of the Axis. . . . He states that his apparatus, if given the opportunity[,] would prepare for organized military . . . opposition inside Spain . . . if the resistance is to be in the form of a well-organized and internal military resistance, a preliminary period of intensive preparation will be necessary.[68]

Negrin also told Goldberg that

> in July of 1941 the entry of Spain into the war on the side of the Axis and operations were agreed upon, but that the unexpected resistance of the Russians on the Eastern Front made it necessary for Hitler to change his plans and altered General Franco's decision to bring Spain into the war at that time.[69]

Goldberg's report increased Allied worries that Franco might allow the German military to move troops through Spain and prompted U.S. military officials to ask for further OSS assistance. Concerned that German troops might strike British and American forces from the rear after they landed in Morocco, the commanders of the North Africa landings, Generals Mark Clark and George Patton, asked the OSS to find out Franco's intentions if possible.

Goldberg returned to New York in November 1942, leaving behind his associate, George Pratt, to run the London labor desk on the basis of the links already established. Once back in the States, Goldberg quickly recruited a team of Spanish republican exiles for service in Spain. Early in 1943 they were dispatched to their native country via Morocco and told to report on any signs of German activity there. For a while they performed splendidly, transmitting their findings that Franco did not intend to permit German troop movements through Spain. Eventually, however, they were captured by the Spanish security police, who tortured them until they revealed their mission. "They said everything," that "they were trained by me and where," Goldberg recalled.[70]

The matter might have ended with a simple denial by the U.S. ambassador to Spain, Carleton Hayes, of any official sponsorship of the operation, but the OSS's failure to consult either with State or Hayes beforehand led to an embarrassing confrontation. "This stupid ambassador, instead of denying everything," Goldberg commented, "sends a terrible cable to the State Department protesting this as a violation of neutrality."[71] Berle demanded an explanation from Donovan, who in turn called in Goldberg to figure out a response. He advised his boss to deny any link to the affair. Donovan instead sent Goldberg to give that story to the assistant secretary of state.

> I said [to Berle] that I knew nothing about it. He said, "How can you say you don't know anything about it? The Franco . . . secret police have . . . from these fellows . . . a statement saying you trained them and furnished them with radios and landed them by submarines."
> "What do you expect from people who have been tortured, [Goldberg replied]; they'll say anything." Berle was . . . flabbergasted.[72]

Berle thereupon sent a cable to Hayes instructing him to deny that the men were American agents, which quieted Spanish protests. Goldberg then asked Lord Halifax, the British foreign minister, in confidence, to tell his ambassador to Spain to intervene quietly so that the men would not be summarily shot. Halifax's man in Madrid did so, saving some lives, but not those of the Spanish exile ringleaders.

Hayes remained irate, convinced that the men were OSS agents. He and Berle made Donovan give his word that no more operations would be attempted in Spain. The OSS chief agreed, in part because by that time, the spring of 1943, Franco was clearly signaling his decision to remain neutral.[73]

The episode reveals both the contributions the OSS was trying to make and the disturbing precedents it was setting in the process. The agency did collect much valuable information, but the price included compromises with principles of democratic government. The lack of concern with accountability to other governmental agencies flowed from the top of the organization. Donovan himself also exuded an almost adolescent fondness for covert operations. He preferred them to the more routine, albeit highly useful, efforts to gather intelligence in other ways.

The men who ran the OSS and those elsewhere in the federal government who supported them seldom paused to worry about the pattern of conduct that was emerging: covert operations unauthorized by or even explained to the other branches of government and paid for with unvouchered funds, making futile any attempt to trace where the money actually went. Goldberg opposed the practice of using unvouchered funds and kept strict books in defiance of OSS regulations, but most OSS agents and supervisors did not. "Everyone who used any money in my operation had to account for it," he remembered, "and I gave them [the OSS] the books at the end."[74] Even he, however, understood the agency's rationale that books posed a potential threat to security. That thought was the basis for Donovan's decision not to require any detailed accounting for covert operations.[75]

OSS operatives helped establish another dangerous precedent by lying about their activities, to both members of their own government and those representing foreign ones. "They expect the denial," Goldberg explained as his reason for supporting such actions.[76] Although arguably necessary at the time, such a practice nonetheless invited abuse because it could be used to shield the agency's own mistakes as well.

In those days of the fight against fascism, right and wrong seemed so clearly distinguishable to Goldberg and his colleagues that they felt few qualms about what they were doing. But those methods would, in the years ahead, be used in contexts in which right and wrong appeared less clear, and the dangers such practices posed to democracy much more so. The World War II example, in this as in other ways, would have longer-term consequences more problematic than Goldberg, like so many other New Deal liberals, seems then to have understood.[77]

Those problems lay in the future, however, while Goldberg was still preoccupied with working toward an Allied victory. Once he had finished training the Spanish exiles in early 1943, he shifted his base of operations to OSS headquarters in Washington. He did so because Donovan had asked him to direct labor intelligence gathering and covert operations planning from there. Dorothy Goldberg rejoined him, and they rented a house for the whole family in the city's fashionable northwest section. Apart from his family's presence, though, there was little that was festive about wartime Washington's atmosphere in Goldberg's opinion. "It was a funny town in wartime," he recalled, "we really didn't do much besides work."[78]

There was still plenty of it left for him to do. Donovan recognized that and, in one of his rare efforts to create administrative order, had formally constituted the labor operation as a special intelligence branch in December 1942, shortly after the Joint Chiefs of Staff had approved the OSS charter, which guaranteed the agency's continued existence at least through the war's end.

The following May, Donovan recommended Goldberg for an army commission. The OSS board responsible for such matters recommended that he receive the rank of major, but the army approved, to his chagrin, a captain's commission. The rank mattered to Goldberg only because, as he explained in a memo written around that time, "the grade of Major would be most helpful since I will, of necessity, have a great deal of contact with high ranking officers of our own and the Allied services."[79] Donovan promised to get him the promotion before he went abroad again, but it failed to come through until November, three months after Goldberg began his next journey.[80]

This trip took him to Palestine, where Donovan wanted him to recruit an Italian Jew willing to parachute into fascist Italy and then report on political developments there after the Allies invaded the country. Captain Goldberg stopped off first in Algiers to deliver a study of Yugoslavia's rail and highway bridges to one of the senior OSS operatives in North Africa, William Eddy. Eddy was planning to infiltrate agents into the Balkans to disrupt any Nazi efforts to move through that region toward the Soviet Union.

From Algiers, Goldberg flew on across the Sahara to Jerusalem for meetings with leaders of the illegal army of the Jewish settlers, the Haganah. So complete was their distrust of the British by then that those Zionists had insisted on an American contact. Goldberg, as a Jew and Zionist who had worked with Jewish Agency officials on OSS matters in New York, was the natural choice. Reuven Shaloah, the Haganah's chief of intelligence, put him in touch with a man named Cerrano, a member of an old Italian Jewish family with extensive ties to his former homeland. Cerrano agreed to go, as Goldberg explained, "because we weren't getting good intelligence out of the part of Italy occupied by the Germans. . . . The Haganah and . . . [OSS] mounted a joint parachute mission into Italy and he did terrific for about a year . . . then someone informed on him, he was caught and . . . executed. It was a great tragedy."[81]

The visit to Palestine and work with Haganah agents reinforced Goldberg's Zionist beliefs. In his words, he had been

> a Zionist for a long time, since I was a kid . . . because I was Jewish. I didn't see how you could be a really Jewish person, proud of your ancestry, and not be a Zionist. It's not possible, logically. . . . it's like asking an Irishman . . . "Do you believe in home rule?"[82]

Goldberg's answer to a question that he phrased in such simple terms was an emphatic yes, his reasons rooted in both logic and emotion. His convictions never wavered and, indeed, grew stronger as time passed. That was in part because to be a Jew of his generation was to lose faith in the promise of Western tolerance. For most American Jews, and especially those of eastern European ancestry like Goldberg, the Holocaust would offer proof as persuasive as it was horrible of the wisdom of their early support for Zionism.[83]

After Cerrano had been sent to Italy, Goldberg first returned to Washington to report his findings and then flew to London in December. His first assignment there was to recruit anti-Nazi Germans captured in combat for use as spies when the Allies invaded France. "I . . . trained Germans, mostly from P.O.W. camps, but I didn't train Nazis or Gestapo," Goldberg explained. "Hitler was very accommodating. When he had a Social Democrat, he stamped his soldier's book 'not politically reliable.' He drafted them . . . and I checked them with Ollenhauer, the head of the German Social Democratic party [in exile], and his staff."[84] Goldberg also located Belgian transport workers willing to help out by preparing dock workers in the Channel ports to make them immediately available to the Allies upon their landing.[85]

He mounted a more elaborate effort to aid the French resistance before D-Day. With Donovan's approval, Goldberg had earlier begun sending $25,000 per month in gold to the clandestine French Confederation of Labor (CGT). The money helped the CGT reconstitute itself underground after having been forced to disband by the Nazi occupation government. A CGT underground newspaper, *Les Informations*, soon appeared. The group also fabricated thirty thousand sets of false papers and identity cards so that CGT workers could avoid the German labor draft, known as the *releve*. The CGT also used its funds to set up a communication network with members deported to Germany for work in war plants there. Goldberg acted as a liaison, sending money to the CGT and, in return, receiving intelligence that he analyzed and then transmitted to the OSS in Washington. The British had nothing like his system, which represented a real advance beyond the OSS London operation's earlier heavy reliance on exile governments for information.[86]

In the process, Goldberg met most of the Gaullist officials stationed in London, including the general himself, whom he came to admire. "De Gaulle," he reflected later, "was the symbol of courage and resistance in what was apparently a hopeless cause. . . . He rebuilt French pride."[87] Goldberg and de Gaulle took walks together to discuss covert operations, a relationship the general cultivated as part of a larger effort to win American support for his exile "government."[88]

Their friendship was cemented by Goldberg's role in supplying funds to the CGT and by his determined efforts to keep the communists in the federation from receiving any of the money directly. "At that time the split in . . . the CGT [Executive Board] was five Socialists and three Communists . . . we had to parachute in a man once a month with our allotment. . . . The Communists wanted a split. . . . I would not agree to it. I . . . was sending it to the labor movement . . . not factions."[89]

Well, yes and no. He left that to the board's socialist majority. The communists retaliated by tipping off the Gestapo about the CGT's resistance activities. "They published it in their underground press," Goldberg related, where the Nazis were sure to spot the story.[90] "So I had to stop it [the delivery scheme] and then work out a different procedure to give the socialist groups some help."[91] That was the last of the CGT communists' work for the OSS. Goldberg had distrusted them from the start because, he said, "they never gave us much information, they reported to Moscow."[92]

The issue was an important one, because financial aid helped underground movements resist the Nazi occupation, and those groups best able to do so would have the strongest claims to lead their societies once the war was won. In that sense, American aid was having the effect of boosting social democratic and socialist unionists over communist ones in their struggle for the allegiance of the Western European working class, a consequence that seems to have satisfied Goldberg completely. Unlike some liberals in those days, he understood clearly that the wartime alliance with Moscow and the Soviet people's heroic resistance to the Nazi war machine did not alter the nature of the CP program or his reasons for opposing it.[93]

Tension mounted at OSS London headquarters during the first six months of 1944. Its agents were doing what they could to prepare for the impending invasion of France amid ever worsening conditions in the city. London had a nightmarish quality to it then, with German buzz bombs laying waste to whole city blocks, air-raid sirens howling in the night, and people stumbling about in the pitch dark of the blackout.

Coping as best he could, Goldberg tried to make the Channel ports ready for their Allied liberators. He sent word through his CGT socialist friends in

January to make arrangements in all French Channel and Atlantic ports for immediate collaboration in the event of an Allied landing. In February he dispatched Eugene Ehlers, secretary of the French Transport Workers Union, to visit secretly each port and give special instructions to key CGT and other underground leaders.[94]

There was an air of unreality even in his own efforts because Goldberg did not know when or where the Allies planned to strike. Once that spring he made a wrong turn while walking down a corridor, opened a door, and entered a briefing room packed with senior officers. "Are you 'bigoted'?" an officer asked the red-faced Goldberg. "No sir," he replied.[95] He was asked to leave immediately and only later discovered that he had stumbled across a top-secret D-Day planning session. Only those "bigoted," that is, cleared to work on the landings, knew the details. All he could do in the meantime was advise his French contacts to be ready at every port, because the Allied military did not dare risk telling the Normandy harbor workers lest they unwittingly leak the news to the Nazis.[96]

These were nightmarish times in other places as well and for none so much as for Europe's Jews. In the dark and terrible year before the Normandy invasion, as the Nazis made plans to remove the last few Jews from the Warsaw ghetto and send them to their deaths, Goldberg received from a man named Samuel Zygelbojm, once head of the Jewish socialist movement in Poland, indisputable evidence that the Nazis were systematically murdering Jews. As Goldberg recounted later,

> He was a member of the Polish government-in-exile in London . . . and he produced the documents, not rumors, about what was happening in the death camps, especially Auschwitz and Birkenau. . . . Also he gave me a message from the Warsaw fighters and the Auschwitz people. They wanted the rail junction at Auschwitz bombed and . . . the Ghetto bombed. They knew they were going to be killed anyhow . . . they wanted the Germans killed. . . .
>
> I later found out where he got this information. A very brave Pole by the name of [Jan] Karski . . . went into the death camps under the guise of an Estonian soldier . . . and he got photographs, affidavits. . . . At this point there was no argument about it. We had heard reports, there had been a lot of evidence but this was cold . . . evidence. . . .
>
> I sent it to Donovan in Washington who took it up with the State Department, I don't know how high, and I got a message back that we couldn't divert our planes from the war effort. . . . I had the sad duty of telling this fellow [Zygelbojm] about it and he committed suicide the next day. That's something I'll never forget.[97]

Goldberg believed that the United States had failed European Jewry, especially in the years before America's entry into the war. He thought the Roosevelt administration's refusal to admit more than a few Jewish refugees between 1933 and 1941 was "absolutely terrible. I was a great admirer of Roosevelt and supported him in his campaigns. I thought it was a case of colossal indifference and [that] far more could have been done."[98]

Goldberg had made a brief stop in Lisbon while on OSS business and never forgot his impressions of the Jewish refugees he saw there, frantic with fear and stymied in their efforts to enter the United States. Although Goldberg openly disagreed with the U.S. government's policy, he, like many American Jews, did not come to see FDR as an enemy of the Jewish people. "I don't think Roosevelt . . . was prejudiced in the orthodox sense," Goldberg declared. "He had the concept, as far as I can figure it out . . . [that] all this is peripheral. The main thing is to defeat Hitler. . . . The concept has a certain validity but doesn't explain why we didn't take refugees. That had nothing to do with defeating Hitler."[99]

Some argued that it did, at least in the late 1930s and early 1940s. As Europeans moved inexorably toward war during those years, most Americans clung desperately to their hopes for neutrality. Those sentiments were widely shared in Congress and found expression there in its members' successful efforts to restrict drastically the president's power to aid any foreign belligerent. Roosevelt's defenders argue that he refused to risk a clash with southern conservatives on Capitol Hill over refugee policy because as the war neared he needed their votes for rearmament measures and then, once the war broke out, for Lend–Lease, both of which proved important to British and, later, Soviet military efforts.[100]

In muting their own protests against the administration's refusal to admit refugees, many American Jews showed that they, too, believed that publicizing their special interest in the conflict would only strengthen the isolationist cause.

FDR, for his part, tended to follow public opinion on the issue of intervention rather than lead it, especially after the deeply antagonistic response from leading isolationists to his 1937 "Quarantine the Aggressors" speech. That episode clearly helped persuade the president that the country would not broadly support getting mixed up in another European war. Roosevelt's subsequent caution—in hindsight, excessive—contributed to his reluctance prior to Pearl Harbor to press for admitting more Jews. Had he acted otherwise, many more might have been saved.

One can be more certain that Roosevelt was unwilling to take the risk of attempting to alter refugee policy until it was much too late to make a real difference in the number of Jews who escaped. Arthur Goldberg, like so many other American Jews, did not turn against FDR, but could never completely understand why he had failed those refugees.[101]

Although too late for European Jewry, the Allied armies landed at Normandy on June 6, 1944, with Goldberg following in their wake just three weeks later. There he met with CGT resistance fighters in Cherbourg, which the Allies had captured just hours earlier. He also spoke with CGT people from neighboring towns, where OSS plans had begun to pay off. The Cherbourg dock workers, previously alerted by the CGT, rushed to the harbor and began unloading Allied ships.

Once Patton's army broke out of the Cherbourg peninsula, Goldberg went to Rheims to establish a forward base there and receive intelligence from his

CGT contacts. His office was located in the former Gestapo headquarters, which he and some other soldiers captured upon arriving there.[102]

The rapid Allied advance during the summer of 1944 soon persuaded Goldberg that the war was all but over. "I got convinced in July," he recalled,

> erroneously, it turned out, that the war was over, it looked that way. There were no German planes in the skies, the German army was fleeing . . . and I didn't know anything about the [Far] East and [so] I went to Donovan and . . . recommended that the labor division be disbanded because none of the people I recruited knew anything about . . . Asia. . . . They had no labor unions [there].[103]

Goldberg was not alone in his belief. Patton's success persuaded many in Washington that summer to begin preparing for postwar reconversion. In August the OSS staff began to draw up reduced budget and personnel estimates so as to satisfy a cost-conscious Congress.[104]

Goldberg was anxious to get home for personal reasons as well. The Goldberg family's savings were nearly exhausted, and as he later explained, "I could not support them on a major's salary."[105] Donovan agreed to let him go, although the OSS chief continued to shower him with requests for advice once Goldberg returned to the States. "I insisted that instead of being discharged," he recalled, "that I be put on inactive duty and I told Donovan that he could get me any time he wanted."[106] By the end of August, Goldberg was back in Washington for an emotional reunion that would be repeated during the coming year in countless American homes.[107]

Like so many of his generation, Goldberg's wartime experience had a profound impact on the way he saw the world. In the course of working with European labor people while in London, he had become acquainted with a diverse group of leading figures in the trade union international, including British unionists and laborites such as Walter Citrine, general secretary of the British Trades Union Congress (TUC), and the Dockers' leader Ernest Bevin, who chaired the TUC's general council, as well as Social Democratic and Socialist Party leaders from every nation in western and central Europe and Scandinavia. Many of them had already come to embrace social democratic ideas in response to the conditions in their respective homelands, but working together on intelligence matters increased their awareness that the same intellectual currents were operating elsewhere. This exchange of ideas served to reinforce their commitment to an essentially common goal.[108]

The dream of such thinkers was to democratize, humanize, and stabilize market systems by expanding the role of the state and of labor unions in regulating economic activity. This idea rested on a number of assumptions, the first of which was that business leaders could be persuaded to make such concessions, in effect to agree to give up some of their power by sharing it with government bureaucrats and trade union officials. Inspiring faith that such a concession could be obtained was the wartime experience itself, when management seemed—at least on the surface—to have done exactly that.

Goldberg's OSS experience suggested to him just such a model. The agency's organization had offered places of importance to corporation managers, career government bureaucrats, and labor union officials. If the first group had held most of the top positions, Goldberg and his colleagues still could hope that the experience of working together constructively would in time convince management to share even more authority with the state and organized labor.[109]

A second key assumption of those thinkers was that efforts to go further in the direction of socialism would lead to disasters of either the Stalinist or fascist model. The experience of the 1930s and early 1940s appears to have convinced liberals and social democrats that efforts to wrest more power from the business community would provoke a class war, one that would lead, if the Left "won," to a highly repressive society like the Soviet Union or—and for Americans more likely—to a victory by the Right and an even less democratic set of arrangements than had existed before such a struggle took place.

Feeding that pessimism was the diminished confidence men and women such as Goldberg had come to have in the possibilities of mass politics. They saw little in recent historical experience to inspire faith in the capacity of the people to achieve a more participatory form of democratic government. By the end of the 1930s, such efforts appeared to them to lead only to the Stalinist and Nazi nightmares.

Goldberg's faith in mass politics was shaken even further by the Holocaust, the tragedy of which he and other Jews who survived it felt with much greater immediacy than did others on the Left. For them, the influential theologian Reinhold Niebuhr struck a chord when he wrote (in a book published the same year Goldberg returned from the war) of faith in humanity's beneficence as one of the conflict's principal casualties.[110]

This body of thought was not entirely new. The pessimism that informed it had been fueled by the experience of the First World War as well as that of the Second. And for Goldberg at least, the role envisioned for unions was largely congruent with ideas he had absorbed from Sidney Hillman and his associates in the Amalgamated.[111] Still, the revolution in economic thought that accompanied the Depression had underscored the need for labor unions as a critical means of maintaining high wages for workers and, by extension, aggregate consumer purchasing power. And this model had been much more developed during the 1930s, nowhere more so than in Sweden, which in the postwar period would become a source of inspiration to Goldberg and his trade union colleagues elsewhere in Europe. By the middle 1940s the Swedish model was already admired in some American intellectual and trade union circles, which learned about it from a book by journalist Marquis Childs entitled *Sweden: The Middle Way*. First published in 1936, it would go through four editions by 1948 and have a lasting influence on New Deal liberals.[112]

What remained uncertain was, first, whether those who shared that outlook could win control of working-class and state organizations in the Western industrialized societies following the war and, second, whether managerial elites would agree to such an arrangement. The latter point was not an insignificant one, especially in Goldberg's homeland. The experience of the First World War, which weighed heavily on those in American labor circles, suggested that rather than continue along the road of wartime "cooperation," managers would move quickly in the war's aftermath to win back the authority they had agreed to share for the duration. For the next five years, the outcome would remain unclear, and so too would the future direction of Goldberg's life.[113]

3

The Postwar "New Deal"

Even though Goldberg had been away during much of the past three years, the nature of his work had enabled him to keep up with the activities of his former union clients, including those of his most important one, the Steelworkers. Goldberg's tour of duty with the OSS had not harmed his standing with them, either. Union members and their leaders, deeply patriotic, had ardently supported the war effort. They therefore tended to look with favor on those who had served, especially as volunteers, and so Goldberg's absence from Chicago from the spring of 1942 through the fall of 1944 did not mean that his association with labor had lapsed.[1]

In fact, the situation was just the reverse: Goldberg's wartime experience had greatly expanded his knowledge of organized labor, which enabled him to work even more effectively on its behalf and increased the likelihood that union leaders would steer legal work his way during the immediate postwar period. Although he was still not widely known among the top leaders of American unions, he had made some important friends during his tour of duty at the OSS, and these wartime associations would prove crucial to his eventual emergence as the nation's leading labor lawyer.[2]

All that still lay ahead, however, eclipsed for the moment by his more immediate concerns, which were to return home and settle into a civilian job. Goldberg and his family went back to Chicago in the fall of 1944, where he reopened his law office and spent his spare time helping out with the Roosevelt reelection campaign. "I could not have picked a better time to come back to Chicago, arriving as I did on the eve of the election," he wrote a friend in November.

> It was a pleasure to be unhatched and to be able to lend a hand in the closing days of the campaign. I did some work with the NCPAC [the National Citizens Political Action Committee] and also with PAC [the CIO Political

45

Action Committee]. As you know, it is generally recognized that these organizations provided the margin of success for the President.[3]

Following the election, the CIO held its national convention in Chicago
during the third week of November. Among those attending was Goldberg,
who wrote that "while my law practice has prevented me from taking in all of
the sessions, I did manage to spend a little time there and to meet many
mutual friends. It was a good convention, and I suppose its most important
decision was to continue PAC on a permanent basis."[4]

Goldberg's labor clients, with whom he quickly reestablished links, had
undergone some dramatic changes during the almost three years he had spent
in the OSS. In order to understand the issues he would face in representing
them, one needs to look closely at both those wartime developments and the
debate they sparked within the unions over what their postwar objectives
should be.

First among the wartime changes was the increase in labor's size. The
Steelworkers Union, the principal union that Goldberg represented and his
power base in the labor movement throughout his association with it, reflected the overall wartime trend. The USA's membership had grown from
460,000 in the spring of 1942 to 750,000 just two years later. And when USA
members serving in the armed forces were added to the latter number, the
total reached almost 1 million.[5]

Second, the labor–management relationship had become far more regulated by government than it had been before the war. The National Defense
Mediation Board (NDMB) and its successor, the National War Labor Board
(NWLB), had been organized as tripartite bodies that included equal numbers of business, labor, and so-called public representatives, all appointed by
the Roosevelt administration. The goal of those two organizations was to
ensure maximum production for the war effort, by resolving labor–
management disputes through arbitration rather than strikes. During the war,
the influence of that administrative framework on industrial relations proved
enormous. It pushed unions and businesses to adopt the kind of stabilizing
and bureaucratic arrangements that before the war had existed only in the
garment industry. Those wartime practices also transferred a good deal of
formal authority from managers and union leaders to government bureaucrats. The result was a much more stable and predictable system of labor–
management relations, one long sought by New Dealers during the 1930s.[6]

Government supervision had been a mixed blessing for unions, whose
principal benefits had been the maintenance of membership and checkoff
provisions contained in the initial War Labor Board ruling, the "Little Steel
formula." This decree had essentially made union membership and dues
payment requirements of employment in those industries in which unions
had existed before the United States entered the war. The ruling had thereby
helped organized labor to enroll millions of new members during wartime
and to regularize the payment of dues, which in turn allowed unions to amass
large strike funds. The Steelworkers' treasury, one of the largest, grew during

that period from $1.4 million to more than $3 million. Accumulating such big war chests would in time help deter those corporate managers who sought to get rid of unions once the war ended.[7]

On the other hand, increased government supervision had greatly limited unions' freedom of action. And as the business community's influence over the federal government grew during the war, government supervision increasingly implied decisions favorable to management. The tenor of the discussions at USA Executive Board meetings suggests that its members, who belonged to a union that stood in the center of the American labor movement, had few illusions about what was happening but saw themselves as lacking constructive alternatives.[8] Even though CIO and Steelworkers' president Philip Murray's loyalty to FDR never wavered, Murray described Congress as "not only bad, but vicious" and supported in its efforts against labor by the nation's newspapers, all at the behest of management.[9]

Both the desire to support the war effort and the fear that the government would conscript strikers deterred CIO leaders for the duration from adopting a more confrontational stance. Although some more militant voices in the CIO argued that the United Mine Workers had won more by striking, Murray and other USA leaders saw the UMW's gains as having come at the expense of other unions' members, because the Mine Workers' actions had greatly increased public support for restrictive legislation against unions and did much to erode the popularity of the labor movement more generally. The managers of at least some steel companies, Murray believed, were trying to goad the Steelworkers into striking and thereby use the occasion to crush the union on the pretext of patriotism.[10]

Thus by the time Goldberg returned to Chicago in the fall of 1944, the leaders of the CIO felt increasingly beleaguered by management and the government. They were haunted, too, by the memory of the post–World War I experience, when the business community and the state had worked together to erase labor's wartime progress. Even more ominously, the unions that had suffered the most after World War I were the new industrial ones, which had collapsed completely in the face of that attack. Greatly weakening labor during that earlier period had been the postwar recession, which had lasted for two years. The USA Executive Board's members understood the link between an economic downturn and union vulnerability and viewed with foreboding the post–World War II recession that all of them expected.[11]

In addition to those external threats, there also were internal weaknesses. Potentially most troubling to the USA was what its leaders perceived as the unreliability of those union members added during the war. Those workers were mostly labor "conscripts," who joined the union as a condition of employment in accordance with the Little Steel decision.[12] Many of them seemed, at least to Murray and the other executive board members, to lack the militancy and discipline of those who had signed up during the 1930s.

At board meetings, Murray repeatedly expressed his frustration with such workers. When the USA lobbied the government for a retroactive pay increase in the spring of 1944, for example, Murray complained that

the members of the National War Labor Board have not been hearing from
the membership of the United Steelworkers of America. I have a few . . .
resolutions here . . . mostly from individuals. . . .

. . . They have been addressed to the President of the organization and
they think the President of the organization ought to be able to do the things
that they suggest should be done.[13]

Murray tended to blame the leadership for failing to mobilize the rank and
file, but the union's highly centralized governing system gave most of them
very little to do. Typical of the way the union was run was the executive
board's decision in the fall of 1943 to limit the membership of the National
Wage Policy Committee, the main unit for the formulation of contract demands, to a subset of the local presidents. Despite the group's fairly small size,
the USA leadership expected that it, in Secretary-Treasurer McDonald's all-
too-revealing phrase, could "do the basic thinking, at any rate, for the entire
organization."[14] In such a situation, worker apathy should not have been so
surprising.

Apathy was fed, too, by the lack of any real choice even over that most basic
question, membership in the union. The wartime formula more or less compelled workers to join American unions, and in the Steelworkers Union at
least, leaders made certain that those dues-paying members would have a very
hard time getting out when peace returned. Van Bittner expressed that
thought to the board members in characteristically blunt terms:

If the only way a man can become obligated as a member of this union is in
the local union meeting of the union, and if that is the only way he can get in
the meeting as a full-fledged member, I say that is the only way he should
be able to get out of the union. If he wants to get out of the union, let him
come up and say, "I have resigned as a member of the union." Somebody
might say that that is not giving the fellow a square deal. This union is not set
up to give men any sort of a deal who want to get out of the union. . . . if
that sort of a policy is carried out you won't have very many resign from the
union.[15]

This policy made a mockery of the notion that workers had freely con-
sented to join the organization, contributing still further to the kind of "passivity" about which labor leaders so often complained.

And yet at the same time Murray and other board members bemoaned
worker passivity, they also voiced their unhappiness with the increasing number of wildcat strikes, which seemed to suggest quite the opposite problem.
Some of those strikes were about pay and benefits, but others were motivated
by the rank and file's anger over issues involving governance of the workplace.
With workers barred from striking for the duration, some steel industry
managers had taken the opportunity to alter some long-established work
practices, such as the length of break periods, starting and quitting times, and
crew sizes. Such changes often angered workers who valued the older cus-
toms, many of which had originally been agreed to by managers in exchange
for other concessions from employees. At stake were issues of control of the

workplace, which in steel at least, remained highly important to the rank and file.[16]

The work stoppages that occurred over such questions disrupted relationships with employers and endangered government support for the maintenance-of-membership and checkoff provisions of the Little Steel decision, which the union had obtained by making a no-strike pledge. Murray noted that in the twelve months following September 1942 there had been "eight hundred strikes of varying degree and character throughout the industry."[17] He warned the district directors that the managers were recording them all, for use in building a case that labor was not complying with the Little Steel decision and that Congress should therefore enact a labor conscription bill. Murray's discussion of the problem revealed graphically the dilemmas that labor leaders faced, having accepted the wartime scheme of government supervision:

> Now if we go to Congress and we say . . . "We don't want conscription: we are going to fight it," then we have got to be in a position to present to Congress an alternative program. And what is that program? That we will work out our own problems with the management; that management and labor will conceive ideas designed to give this Nation the maximum of production, thereby obviating the necessity of compulsory service legislation.[18]

In some ways passive and in others unruly, the Steelworkers' rank and file was pressing its leadership to win more concessions from management in ways that undermined the leadership's ability to maintain the union's compliance with the Little Steel bargain. The lack of discipline boded poorly, USA leaders believed, for labor's prospects in the anticipated postwar clash with management.[19]

There were other divisions, too, between the leadership and the workers, none more explosive than that over the issue of race. In the Steelworkers Union, racism within the rank and file threatened to divide the union against itself. By the spring of 1944, there were roughly eighty thousand black steelworkers, a majority of whom were USA members. Many were coming under attack if they sought skilled jobs or promotions that placed them in positions senior to white workers.

At a meeting of the USA Executive Board in September 1943, after a summer with the worst race riots since 1919, Murray admonished the board to take action against racist members of the rank and file. He also noted, by way of warning, that the Fair Employment Practices Commission (FEPC) had fifteen unions on trial for refusing to admit blacks. A measure of the USA leaders' fear of racists in the rank and file could be seen in board members' behavior at that meeting.

At first, following Murray's denunciation of racism as inconsistent with the labor movement's goals, the board approved unanimously a motion to send out to all USA members a verbatim transcript of his remarks and those of the union officer charged with mediating racial disputes, Boyd Wilson. After the luncheon recess, however, at which several directors warned Murray that such a step might lead to open warfare with many in the rank and file, the board revoked its decision. The most that Murray and his brethren would do was expand Wilson's role and budget.[20]

Another weakness in the USA lay in the area of jurisdictional disputes between it and other CIO unions. The Steelworkers had clashed on occasion with the Autoworkers over such issues and had experienced fairly serious problems with the third big CIO union, the United Electrical, Radio and Machine Workers (UE). The UE was led by men sympathetic to the American Communist Party's political program, and the struggle between the UE and the more moderate Steelworkers for control of the CIO continued in muted form throughout the period of the wartime united front. The USA and UE had begun to compete for members, with the UE aided by its greater openness to organizing blacks and its lower monthly dues. USA organizing efforts were disrupted in Philadelphia, Cincinnati, and other places by the presence of competing UE operatives. Relations between the respective USA and UE district directors in those areas became deeply antagonistic, all of which strained still further the ties between the two unions' top officers. These divisions over jurisdiction, themselves partly the product of larger cleavages over political outlook, undermined the CIO's ability to push forward a coherent postwar program of its own, a problem of which Murray was acutely aware.[21]

Making matters still worse for all CIO unions was the continuing rift with the AFL, which the wartime experience had done little to mend. The war had altered the balance of power between the two federations in at least two ways. First and most important, the expansion in union membership that accompanied the wartime boom benefited both, but the AFL significantly more than the CIO. The CIO's membership rose by 2.09 million during the war, and the AFL's by 3.012 million. By war's end, the AFL had almost 7 million members, to the CIO's total of just under 4 million, thus confirming the older labor federation's status as the dominant one.[22]

At the same time, however, the growth in the membership of the CIO-affiliated steel and auto unions made them the largest in the country, ones whose relationships with management set the pace for smaller unions in both labor federations. Thus the CIO continued to exert an influence in bargaining with management and the government beyond what its overall membership might have indicated.

The CIO, too, because its leaders were much more enthusiastic about government supervision of labor–management relations than were the AFL labor chiefs, enjoyed much closer ties to those elements of the Roosevelt administration still friendly to organized labor. Squabbling between the two federations, however, weakened labor's ability to speak with one voice, which hampered them in meeting the managerial counteroffensive that union leaders expected after the return to peace.[23]

The post–World War I precedent had its limits, however. By the time Goldberg came home, the labor movement was much stronger than it had been in 1918. Roughly one-third of the nonfarm workforce had been organized by the end of 1944, and that increased size gave labor more power to resist management's efforts to destroy it. The most highly visible sign of the change was the CIO leaders' decision to create the Political Action Committee (PAC) in 1943, with the goals of helping reelect Roosevelt and diminish the number of labor's enemies in Congress. The USA, ACW, and UAW each contributed $100,000 to the PAC's budget, and their leaders viewed with enormous satisfaction FDR's success in the 1944 presidential election. Labor was aided as well by the public's heartfelt desire to avoid a return to the Depression, a mood that tended to impede management's efforts to roll back labor's gains.[24]

Goldberg had thus arrived back in the United States at a highly uncertain time for both labor and the country at large. It was a time of uncertainty for him as well. Although he had reopened his law office, for a few months in the wake of Roosevelt's reelection Goldberg toyed with the idea of returning to Washington, where he had been offered a job in the Justice Department. "I have been offered the post of . . . second ranking assistant-ship in the department," he wrote on April 12, 1945, to Carl Devoe, a lawyer with whom he planned to practice once Devoe finished his wartime service abroad. "I am very doubtful as to whether I shall accept. As you know, Washington does not appeal to me particularly, and I am reluctant to leave Chicago after returning from a period of prolonged absence."[25]

Roosevelt's death on that same day dispelled any lingering desire Goldberg had to reenter the government's employ. The news shocked him, although he had seen for himself only a few months earlier how weak and ailing the president had been. "I attended the fourth inauguration," he remembered, "and shook Roosevelt's hand. I saw . . . that he was a dying man . . . in terrible shape."[26] When writing about FDR's death to Carl Devoe a few days after it occurred, Goldberg drew a parallel made by many others about the news from Warm Springs: "I wish I had the words to describe to you the national mourning of the last few days. If you have access to Carl Sandberg's 'Lincoln — The War Years,' you will find in Volume 4 a description, which, if the name 'Roosevelt' were substituted for 'Lincoln' would apply with equal force today."[27]

Like the president and many others, the war years had aged Goldberg as well. He gave a speech about his wartime service to the National Lawyers Guild chapter in Chicago after returning home, at which an observant reporter noted the changes in his appearance and demeanor:

> Modest, almost to the point of embarrassment, above medium height, level eyed but showing the strain of day and night work on his face and the gray in his brown hair, Major Goldberg shied away from his part in the work, talking of what he had seen done by others.[28]

Slowing down only a little, the thirty-six-year-old Goldberg quickly plunged back into private practice. In the flush of wartime and immediate postwar prosperity, he and Carl Devoe were soon earning substantial incomes. After thirty months of living on an army salary that averaged about $6,000 per year, Goldberg earned more than twice that amount in 1945. That triumph of Keynesian economic theory had its drawbacks, however, as he and his associates soon discovered while looking for adequate office space. Chicago's LaSalle Street area, home of most of the city's major law firms, was filled to overflowing with returnees from government wartime service. "We had a devil of a time here," he wrote to a friend and fellow attorney in January 1946,

> but finally have been able to get additional space, and as of next month we will be occupying new quarters. I suppose that all of us should be delighted with the prosperity boom sweeping the country, but I can remember back somewhat nostalgically to the time when landlords pursued us rather than our pursuing them.[29]

The postwar expansion was having a big impact, too, on Goldberg's labor clients, for whom the year 1945 marked a major turning point. As 1944 had come to a close, labor leaders remained unsure when the war would finally end and thus when they should expect a return to prewar relations with management. For the first half of the year, Murray and other top USA leaders were content to stick with the wartime scheme, especially following the November 1944 War Labor Board ruling on the Steelworkers' demands for changes in the Little Steel formula. The union had sought a retroactive pay increase and other changes from the NWLB, whose ruling also had been awaited by the other industrial unions, because it would presumably establish a pattern governing their relationships with employers as well. The ruling had not come easily. As CIO and Steelworkers' general counsel Lee Pressman noted in his remarks about the decision, it was the product of more than a year of struggle.[30]

Although the workers won no general pay increase, the decision contained some important new provisions for vacation pay and severance pay, the principle of employer liability for unemployment created by technological innovation, a commitment to standardize wage rates throughout the industry, a somewhat opaque provision barring unilateral changes in work rules by management, and the continuation of union security through the maintenance of membership and checkoff provisions. The ruling also called for a comprehensive government study of labor's plan for a guaranteed annual wage. The study, Murray contended, showed that the Roosevelt administration was taking the idea seriously, despite fierce employer resistance.[31]

The result, in the USA leaders' view, was good enough to warrant continued support for the wartime arrangement as long as the administration was serious about price control. Otherwise, the failure to gain a pay increase would prove unacceptable to them and, more important, to the rank and file. Murray noted also that all four management representatives on the board had dissented from its ruling, which suggested that the government still supplied to labor more than business executives themselves were willing to concede.[32]

For that reason, the business community pressed for an end as soon as possible to the scheme of wartime regulation. For all practical purposes, they ceased to cooperate with it soon after the Japanese government surrendered. By the fall of 1945, Van Bittner made clear at a USA Executive Board meeting that the "War Labor Board is through—let's remember that. From now on we will have to do some collective bargaining and use the strength and power and influence of our union to get those things that we are entitled to as representatives of our membership."[33] In the aftermath of the war, the break-down in the administrative apparatus produced a period of social strife, one marked for the first three years by a failure to reach a postwar bargain or "social contract" of the sort that many labor leaders and a few business ones had sought. In part, that stemmed from divisions within labor over what its terms should be and whether to pursue such a pact at all.[34]

Many in organized labor, and particularly those who led the Steelworkers Union which stood at its center, favored an accord with business. In Murray's case, that goal owed much to the influence of liberal Catholic thought, which emphasized the dignity of labor, a rejection of class warfare in favor of recip-rocal obligations between owners and workers, and support for laborers' efforts to achieve decent working and living conditions by organizing trade unions. Those ideas had been spread to Murray as well as many of the other top CIO leaders by a group of Catholic clergy sometimes referred to as the *labor priests*. One of them, Father Charles Rice of Pittsburgh, was a close friend and counselor to Murray and had participated with him in picketing, feeding strikers, and raising bail for those who had been arrested. The social philosophy espoused by such priests resonated strongly with many industrial workers, a majority of whom were Catholic. During the 1930s and 1940s, many of them had sought to reconcile their religious faith, so integral a part of their traditions and culture, with participation in the union movement. The result was a social program that meshed well with the Sweden-inspired "Mid-dle Way" supported by many more secular American reformers.[35]

Goldberg shared that general outlook, which encompassed ideas about how best to structure labor–management relations in unionized industries, what the proper place for workers in American society should be, and the conces-sions that management and the government should offer them in return for class peace. Although in his case those beliefs were rooted in a different intellectual and religious tradition, Goldberg also established a close personal relationship with a leading labor priest, Father George Higgins, who in the late 1940s was the assistant director of the social-action department of the National Catholic Welfare Conference. Like Sidney Hillman, who had worked closely with another Catholic clergyman, Goldberg managed to con-nect his Jewish cultural traditions with those of liberal Catholicism. Those beliefs seem to have been much more in tune with working-class attitudes during the Depression than the secularized radicalism of the American Com-munist Party.[36]

After V-J Day, unionists with that more moderate outlook sought to con-tinue the tripartite wartime framework and to obtain from management a more explicit endorsement of unions as vital to the stability of a market system. This managerial support, it was hoped, would include opposition to any efforts by more conservative businessmen to win passage of new laws restricting labor's ability to organize and represent industrial workers. Such a commitment would assist the unions' efforts to expand into regions of the country where they were weakest, most notably the South. That, in turn, would both halt the movement of industry to that region, a trend based largely on the lower labor costs available there, and bolster labor's strength in the political arena, thus reducing still further the likelihood that Congress would enact legislation hostile to labor's interests. David McDonald noted to USA Executive Board members in the spring of 1946 the link between those last two objectives in explaining the reasoning behind the southern organizing drive:

> The necessity of this campaign of course cannot be over-emphasized. We all know the political situation in the South, we know how deplorable it is, and we know how very fortunate we have been in being able to beat back those reactionary forces in Congress. We have been very fortunate, in view of the makeup of that Congress, that we have not had some awfully bad legislation passed. As you know, the backbone of reaction is the South. We are firmly convinced that the only way to change that situation is by building unions.[37]

In addition to penetrating the South, labor leaders wanted to complete the organization everywhere of those workers still not in unions. Included among them were those not yet enrolled in labor organizations because they were considered to be nominally managerial employees. Mostly supervisors and foremen, they had not been legally eligible for union membership until an NLRB ruling in early 1945 opened the way for them to join. If such employees truly lacked the power to hire and fire—which for unionists was the defining attribute of management—then the USA Executive Board members believed they should be allowed in, although the discussion of the issue by USA leaders indicates that they understood that to go further would undermine any chance for a broad postwar agreement with management.[38]

The larger social agenda of such unionists included more federally subsidized housing, a federal health care program, and an expanded social security system, all of which would require further increases in the state's responsibility for the public's welfare. That program was informed by Keynesian economic theory, which premised an avoidance of a return to the Depression on the payment of good wages to a fully employed workforce, which in turn would use its enhanced purchasing power to make the economy spiral upward. Murray spoke again and again in 1945 and 1946 of the need for such a program and of his fears of a renewed slump if it were not adopted.[39]

There were opponents in the labor movement, however, of at least parts of that program. The AFL, although quite receptive to Keynesian schemes for postwar prosperity, viewed dimly Murray's enthusiasm for continuing the corporatist wartime arrangements. AFL leaders lacked confidence that in a market system like that of the United States, the government could ever achieve enough autonomy from the business community so as to police such a social bargain fairly. For the AFL leadership, the road to economic expansion lay through vigorous collective bargaining and union organization unsupervised by the various units of government. Although they shared many of the same goals as Murray and his allies, AFL leaders preferred private pacts with employers to an expanded role for the state. In large part this was a product of their unhappy experiences with the government, and especially the judiciary, before the New Deal, which had led to an AFL obsession with freedom from a state supervision that AFL leaders believed usually advanced the interests of employers and not workers.[40]

A third viewpoint was that of the vocal minority in the CIO who favored a more confrontational approach to management and the state. Most leaders of the UE, some in the UAW, and those of some smaller CIO affiliates argued that the immediate postwar period was one in which labor should try to use its accumulated power to expand into the South, win more power in the workplace as well as increases in pay and benefits, and pursue the idea of political action independent of the Democratic Party. These leaders were still seeking the larger transformation of society that had been their goal since joining the CIO in the middle 1930s. For those who advocated that more radical course, the conduct of John L. Lewis and the UMW during the Second World War had offered an example. Through militance, Lewis's miners had won more than the Little Steel formula provided, and this road seemed to CIO radicals as the one most likely to bring success.[41]

The debate over which course to pursue turned in part on managerial attitudes, and, as with labor, the business community was divided into three principal factions. The first, and by far the smallest, was composed of men such as Chamber of Commerce head Eric Johnston, automaker Paul D. Studebaker, J. D. Zellerbach of Crown Zellerbach, and Henry Kaiser of the Kaiser Companies. These businessmen sought an accord of the kind Goldberg and Murray favored, one in which managers recognized unions as valuable, and so worked with them to develop a more stable and egalitarian market system, which put sizable wages in workers' pockets in accordance with Keynesian economic theory. Although widely publicized, the group's ideas were relatively uninfluential in American business circles, most of which adamantly opposed Kaiser's call for a "people's capitalism."[42]

The second group, headed by the leaders of the biggest industrial corporations, favored a more cautious détente with labor, one in which no explicit effort would be made to break existing unions, but at the same time no new concessions would be granted, either. Their numbers included U.S. Steel's chief labor negotiator John A. Stephens, General Motors' CEO Charles "Engine Charlie" Wilson, and National Association of Manufacturers' (NAM) spokesman Ira Mosher. Business realists, they had come to understand that unions might provide some stabilizing benefits, and even more, they understood that labor's increased strength made much higher the potential cost of an all-out war against unions akin to that of 1918–22. They were leery, too, of such a course because it would increase the risk of a return to the prewar slump. Their cautious acceptance of certain Keynesian concepts moved them toward supporting the status quo, which, should labor become an obstacle to continuing prosperity or simply grow weaker, could then be followed by renewed managerial efforts to win back lost prerogatives.[43]

The third group, confined mostly to smaller and midsized firms affiliated with the NAM, consisted of unrepentant union opponents. Those with unionized workforces had lost the most power to their workers during the 1930s and 1940s, because the smaller firms, once unionized, were more vulnerable to labor pressure than were the industry leaders. Also part of this faction were the firms that feared unionization the most, such as the southern textile manufacturers. The leaders of this group, men such as Sewell Avery of Montgomery Ward, Tom Girdler of Republic Steel, and Herbert Kohler of the Kohler company, favored an all-out assault on the labor movement after the war ended. Their weapons in that struggle would be management's refusal to bargain with unions or to comply with the maintenance of membership and checkoff provisions of the Little Steel formula, combined with new federal and state laws designed to help wipe out the labor movement's gains since the early 1930s. Such legislation would enable managers to win back some of the control over the workplace that they had lost over the past decade, provide for government supervision of internal union affairs, and legalize a host of managerial tactics that could be used to combat union organization. Managers with that agenda were a militant and powerful faction in the business community, one that the leaders of the biggest firms found difficult to restrain.[44]

Those managerial cleavages were all too apparent to Goldberg, as well as to Murray and other USA leaders. Representatives of each group were to be found in the steel industry, and the discussions at USA Executive Board meetings indicated that Murray and his brethren had no illusions about their attitudes. For Henry Kaiser, there was praise; for the leaders of U.S. Steel, wariness; and for men such as Republic Steel's chairman Tom Girdler, animosity. Inland and Republic, Murray told the board in May 1945, were conducting "very vicious" campaigns.[45] Republic's behavior, Murray said, "reminds me of 1936," a year in which its executives fought with the most violent of methods CIO organizing campaigns.[46]

This faction in the business community, Murray feared, sought to destroy everything the USA had built, just as antilabor employers had broken industrial unions in the aftermath of the previous world war. One of the group's key weapons materialized by the summer of 1945 in the form of the Ball, Burton, Hatch bill. This proposed federal legislation, a forerunner of the Taft–Hartley Act, would, if enacted, have made the system of labor regulation developed during the 1930s and 1940s far more responsive to businessmen seeking to undermine unions.

The only difference between 1918 and 1945, as far as these managers were concerned, lay in the realm of tactics. In discussing the bill's provisions with USA board members, Lee Pressman noted grimly what he saw as the change:

> After the first World War the employers initiated, as you may remember, the so-called American Plan to destroy Unions in this country, and they did a

pretty effective job on the American Federation of Labor. Apparently this time it is not to be done simply through the use of their thugs and spies and the methods they used back in the '20s, it is to be done under the guise of legal sanction. They have a beautiful bill, and with the assistance of these Government agencies . . . will do the job in that fashion.[47]

This measure and another similar one, the Case bill, were viewed with such alarm because they would, among other things, have made national unions liable for the actions of every member, even those acting in defiance of union policy, and have allowed employers to recover large amounts of damages from unions for behavior not authorized by the contract. The result, Pressman warned, would be litigation so expensive as to bankrupt the union treasury, no matter how large. Also threatening was the proposed Hobbs bill, which would have made any kind of labor-related violence a federal crime, punishable by up to twenty years in prison. The chilling effect such a statute would have on picketing and the potential abuse of such a law by unfriendly judges were threats that the USA leadership took quite seriously.[48]

Pressman's warnings were predicated on his assumption that if enacted, the proposed legislation would be used by managers to the maximum extent possible. For that to happen, however, the federal government would have to become even more responsive to those elements in the business community most hostile to unions. Thus, for labor, the need to keep an administration in office that they perceived as at least nominally friendly to workers remained a prime concern. Unionists wanted one that would at a minimum refrain from using the tools that hostile businessmen were seeking to give it.[49]

This concern prompted labor to continue its support for the Truman administration during its first year in office, when Truman's policies more often than not were hostile to unions, and to beat back antilabor bills in Congress. Labor proved successful in that regard, blocking the Ball–Burton–Hatch, Case, and Hobbs bills during 1945. Helping unions achieve that result was the lack of enthusiasm for such legislation manifested by leaders of the biggest firms.[50]

Success in stopping antilabor legislation and the lack of enthusiasm for it within big business circles suggested to Murray for a brief time during 1945 that a compromise was possible. The basis for his belief was the proposed labor–management code agreed to by Murray on behalf of the CIO, William Green of the AFL, and Eric Johnston of the Chamber of Commerce on March 28 of that year. Negotiations over specifics eventually broke down, however, in part because of AFL hostility to continued government supervision and left-wing CIO members' desire for more ambitious union objectives. Also responsible for this outcome were the large sections of the business community that balked at labor's insistence on an expanded social welfare system and no new restrictive labor legislation. By December 1945, the proposed accord lay in ruins.[51]

It would take a struggle stretching over the next four years to teach both sides something about the limits of their power and eventually produce a durable postwar settlement. In the meantime, a conflict would ensue from which neither labor nor management would emerge with everything it had wanted. This contest mattered enormously to Goldberg, because the events it set in motion would carry him from the secondary role he played in the Midwest to a principal one in Washington, by far the most consequential advance of his entire career. To understand how that happened, we must now consider the broader dimensions of this conflict.

II

The fight began early in 1946, with more strikes during the first two months than the country had experienced in the preceding four years combined. Workers in the auto, steel, oil, glass, textile, trucking, railway, coal mining, meatpacking, electrical, and other industries struck, and a majority of them did so in defiance of union leadership. Most strikers were furious about the decline in their real income brought about by the postwar rise in prices and were no longer willing to wait for the government to authorize a pay increase. Together they participated in the biggest strike wave Americans had ever seen.[52]

The Steelworkers, among the first to strike, walked off the job early in January. Their four-week work stoppage was the largest in the union's history, with more than 750,000 workers involved. A settlement came fairly quickly once U.S. Steel's managers agreed to grant an 18.5-cents-an-hour pay increase, as well as to extend for one year the current contract, including the maintenance of membership and checkoff provisions that Murray and Pressman viewed as the crux of the dispute.

Despite U.S. Steel CEO Benjamin Fairless's threats to Murray that "we will wipe you out," the swiftness of the settlement indicated that managers of the industry's largest producer were not seriously inclined at that stage to try breaking the union.[53] As Pressman pointed out to the board members in the first meeting after the settlement, U.S. Steel's management had agreed to extend the union security provisions beyond the expiration of the federal administrative scheme, thereby yielding that point for the first time through collective bargaining.[54] The result, in Pressman's view, was recognition by U.S. Steel's managers that the union "was in this industry to stay."[55] The basic issue of union security, Pressman added, is one "on which there can no longer be any collective bargaining or negotiations."[56] The steel agreement established a pattern to which the other major industrial unions soon conformed.[57]

Another consequence of the 1946 contract, at least in steel, was to prolong the role beyond wartime of the whole host of arbitrators who had emerged during the negotiation of the Little Steel formula. Van Bittner noted how their role during the war had gradually expanded until they, and not union members, were doing most of the bargaining:

The four years that I was on the War Labor Board it seemed to me that somebody in this country decided that the only impartial people there were in America were college professors. . . . They had what they liked to term an open mind. Well, after those open-minded young professors were working with the National War Labor Board for anywhere from three days to three weeks they began to tell everybody, especially the representatives of labor, that we didn't really know how to protect the interests of labor. God had given them a special mission in life to do that job and they were going to do it without any advice from anybody that did any work so far as a labor union is concerned.[58]

Labor economists and lawyers such as David Cole, Archibald Cox, John T. Dunlop, Nathan Feinsinger, Clark Kerr, Wayne Morse, Sumner Slichter, George W. Taylor, and Willard Wirtz believed that the best way to promote an accord between labor and management was for both to rely on government-sponsored mediation to reach agreement. Their reasoning was based on an assumption of government neutrality that the experiences of the 1930s and early 1940s had persuaded them was realistic.

Lee Pressman had warned the USA Executive Board following the 1946 contract settlement that to give the federal government the power to approve wage increases would only expand the role of arbitrators beyond the wartime experience. In his words,

I don't think we ought to condition our wage increase on getting approval from the Wage Stabilization Board, for if you do that I can't tell you when you will get such approval . . . in talking to some members of that Board in the last two days, the public members, the Chairman of the Board, Mr. Wurtz [sic] and some of his staff people, I can already see the glint in their eye indicating that they think they have us in their grasp again. When we got out of their toils [on] August 18th they were a bunch of frustrated individuals and they could no longer say, we know what is best for labor. But in the last few days I can see the glint in their eye again.[59]

The entire administrative scheme, including the regional boards, greatly inhibited labor's freedom of action, but those who administered it saw the approach as worthy of emulation, albeit in a more limited form, following the war's end.[60]

Virtually all businessmen, however, agreed that the wartime experience should not be extended. But although most remained bitterly opposed to any formal scheme of government intervention during peacetime, by the early postwar period at least some corporation managers had come to see some value in labor's call for private arbitration schemes. Such managers placed a high value on stability and predictability in labor–management relations, something that an alternative method for resolving disputes appeared to promise.[61]

Leading the change in the steel industry were, not surprisingly, executives at the largest producer, U.S. Steel, who suggested employing a single arbitrator to resolve disputes arising under the 1946 contract. That suggestion came,

Murray noted, despite U.S. Steel management's previous pattern of having "consistently fought off any attempt on the part of the [USA] organization to have arbitration of its disputes."[62]

The union's leaders seem to have envisioned the procedure as moving a whole host of disputes out of the realm of the courts or of direct action by workers and replacing those mechanisms with a kind of private judicial system for resolving disputes between workers and managers. Although some in labor might have preferred a more corporatist model, one in which the government acted more directly as a supervisor, a privatized arrangement with management appears to have been an acceptable alternative to Murray and his supporters, as well as to the business realists running U.S. Steel.[63]

Goldberg himself noted the growing influence of the arbitrators in a 1946 review of a book on that subject. In the review he pointed out the pioneering role played by the garment industries in the arbitration area and observed that with the return to peacetime, arbitration would necessarily have to change, from a compulsory process to a more voluntary one. He made clear his preference for such a privatized system of dispute resolution, one that by mid-1946 seemed destined to replace government coercion, at least in the steel industry.[64]

Goldberg's perspective on the 1946 USA strike was that of a lawyer operating at the secondary level out of Chicago. He participated during the strike itself and in other CIO-led work stoppages that year, by trying to keep the courts and police from interfering with picketing. Once the basic contracts with managers of the leading companies were reached, he also helped negotiate the modifications needed to meet the needs of individual plants and smaller producers.[65]

The 1946 steel strike also revived for him the troublesome question of what to do about more radical members of the rank and file, who wanted more than the contract continuation and modest pay increase agreed to by the USA leadership. During the strike, violence had erupted on the South Side of Chicago when radicals clashed with supporters of Joe Germano, the Chicago USA leader, over the terms of the proposed contract. The radicals, who viewed the terms as too favorable to management, had tried to distribute leaflets attacking the proposed settlement to the rank and file. They were met with violent resistance from the Germano faction, which saw them as endangering the union's survival.[66]

That episode, and similar clashes elsewhere around the country, resulted in the first discussion ever at a USA Executive Board meeting of what to do about "communist" influence in the union. Germano claimed at the meeting that the Communist Party was behind the radicals. The party's followers, he contended, "have orders to get into the Local Unions and elect all the officers they possibly can, and I know that the Communist Party is paying the bill."[67]

Murray responded that he favored tolerance but would not permit any outside group to seek control over the Steelworkers Union. He did, however, flatly oppose any ban on party members' becoming union officers, on the ground that such a provision in the Mine Workers' constitution had been used unfairly against rivals of the Lewis machine. The board in October 1946 made its own feelings clear about denunciations of Murray's leadership that had appeared in the Communist Party's *Daily Worker* by passing a resolution, sponsored by Germano, that endorsed Murray's resignation as CIO president, should he wish to take that step in response. The uneasy alliance of the wartime popular front was beginning to come apart over the question of labor's proper place in the postwar order.[68]

The events of 1946 did much to discredit more radical voices in the CIO leadership. Although some argued then and afterward that the strikes failed to put management on the defensive because Murray and others in the CIO lacked the nerve to challenge the state, Goldberg, Murray, and other moderates tended to view such a strategy as doomed to fail. They also did not share left-wing CIO members' ardor for transforming society or the AFL's hostility to state supervision. For them the ideal of a state-supervised social contract between labor and management was the most attractive of the likely outcomes. The main result of the 1946 strikes in steel, autos, and other sectors of the economy was to mobilize the electorate behind the antilabor candidates who won control of Congress in the fall of 1946. That outcome appeared to confirm the wisdom of the labor moderates' more cautious assessment.[69]

Goldberg's conclusions about that year were drawn from both his experiences as a contract negotiator and his work in the arena of electoral politics. In 1946 he had been one of the vice-chairmen of the Illinois division of the PAC and helped direct its political action campaign. His most prominent role had been in organizing and presiding over a large rally in Chicago, which included speeches by former Vice-President Henry Wallace, Chicago Mayor Ed Kelly, Illinois Democratic Party chief Jacob "Jack" Arvey, and national PAC director Jack Kroll. Although the meeting had been sponsored by labor organizations that were ostensibly nonpartisan, its heavily Democratic makeup reflected the gradual merging of labor's political machine with that of the Democratic Party.

The disastrous defeats subsequently suffered by the Democrats both in Illinois and nationwide Goldberg saw as threatening the labor movement's continued survival. For him, the activities of radicals in the movement were not only futile but also dangerous, because they undermined labor's acceptance by those outside its ranks. For that reason, Goldberg believed the radicals were forfeiting their claims to be acting on the workers' behalf. Increasingly he would support strategies intended to oust the radicals and replace them with leaders he saw as more realistic.[70]

As in the 1930s, the struggle on the shop floor and at the factory gate gave rise to another in the halls of Congress. The so-called do-nothing Eightieth Congress actually accomplished a great deal by passing the Taft–Hartley Act, a key element in the managerial counteroffensive of 1946/47 that halted the forward march of organized labor. Even though adverse court and NLRB rulings had already whittled away at some Wagner Act protections, the Taft–Hartley law did more than merely codify those earlier changes. It closed the door to organizing foremen and supervisors, thus limiting still further labor's power to win control over the workplace. Even more disturbing, it revived the labor injunction, required union leaders to renounce the radical program of the American Communist Party by signing affidavits to that effect in exchange for access to the government's labor relations apparatus, restricted union activity in the realm of partisan politics, outlawed the secondary boycott and sympathy strike, and made unions liable for damages in lawsuits brought by employers claiming worker breaches of the union contract. Unions were deemed liable even when the offending workers acted in defiance of the leadership. The act also permitted states to pass so-called right-to-work laws that undermined labor power by abolishing the union shop.[71]

Murray, Pressman, and the other USA leaders viewed the measure as a major and thoroughly disastrous change in federal labor policy. Murray himself reacted to Pressman's discussion of Taft–Hartley at the first USA Executive Board meeting held after the Senate passed the bill, by denouncing it in the strongest terms he knew:

> Where in the name of God is our country going? You have read these stories of what is happening in Europe, you have read about them elsewhere. We have said—I have said and you have said, "Oh, these things will never visit us in this country." And yet, through the use of subtle cleverness and manipulations there has been recorded on the statute books of the Federal Congress for the first time to my own knowledge all of the dastardly, vicious provisions to which I have made reference. . . .
>   . . . I venture the assertion that if that bill becomes a law, in the course of time under its operation the lives of men engaged in this whole endeavor to organize the unorganized will not be saved, because you and I today happen to be living in a nation, whether we are inclined to believe it or not, it is nevertheless true, where the trends are and the powers have so decreed, that we should have a type of Fascist, capitalistic control over the lives of men, women and children. That statement I make in measured tones, after giving much consideration and having much experience with the problems incident to the enactment of the current anti-labor legislation in the Federal Congress.[72]

The USA Executive Board's discussion of the new law highlighted in particular the dangers created by the provisions governing political action, lawsuits, injunctions, and the so-called right-to-work laws. Those creations of the Eightieth Congress and the underlying power relationships they reflected suggested to Murray and his colleagues that labor's hopes for expanding into the South and those sectors of the economy not yet organized had been seriously diminished, if not altogether lost.[73]

The more conservative makeup of Congress also doomed, for the foreseeable future, any further advances in social welfare legislation of the sort for which Murray and others in labor had been pressing. Those developments persuaded the steel union's leaders to adopt a two-track approach to the achievement of greater insurance, pensions, and other fringe benefits, by continuing to press for such legislation, embodied in the Wagner–Murray–

Dingell bill pending before Congress, and in the interim, by bargaining with employers for a private benefits system.[74]

The USA leadership had made its first moves in that direction even before the 1946 elections, the poor results of which seemed to confirm the futility of relying solely on the enactment of a public benefits system. In so doing, labor leaders understood the risk that such a course might have of diminishing support in the working class for a more comprehensive legislative scheme but nonetheless felt compelled to respond to the demands of their own membership. David McDonald had noted this risk in arguing for the parallel course during a June 1946 meeting of the USA Executive Board:

> The organization, of course, in the advancement of a social security program is confronted with a decision which it will be required to make, and that is should the organization press for an improved social security plan for its members through negotiations, which might weaken the chances of the Wagner–Murray–Dingell Bill, or should the organization forego the former and concentrate on the latter, the prosecution of the Wagner–Murray–Dingell Bill. I am . . . of the opinion . . . that we should press for the inclusion of social security and group insurance programs in our collective bargaining conferences. At the same time we should not leave up our pressure on the Wagner–Murray–Dingell bill.[75]

The election later that year of a Congress in which for the first time since 1930 Republicans held majorities in both houses helped persuade the board that a public program might be a very long time in coming, whereas bargaining for a private scheme offered the promise of something in the immediate future.[76] The strong feelings of the membership, which had petitioned and passed resolutions in support of greater social security, appear to have been important in pushing the USA leadership to take that more cautious course. The decision reflected a narrowing of labor's vision, one that occurred in response to the managerial counteroffensive.[77]

The election of a Republican-controlled Congress in 1946 had other consequences as well, beyond the enactment of Taft–Hartley and labor's shift to emphasizing a private benefits scheme. The election results also suggested that the Truman administration would likely not endure beyond January 1949, by which time businessmen could expect a new president even more sympathetic to their wishes. The leaders of U.S. Steel appear to have been content to wait until that change occurred before reaching any kind of lasting settlement with the USA, and so they agreed in April 1947 to extend the Steelworkers' contract for two years. U.S. Steel's managers also conceded a five-point provision governing work rules which in essence barred unilateral changes unless the basis for a rule's existence had disappeared. This provision, which the union eventually obtained from executives at the other steel companies, signaled management's decision not reopen, at least for a time, the explosive issues of workplace governance. Rather than try to win back the managerial prerogatives lost during the Depression, which some business leaders called the unfettered "right to manage," the industry's leaders were moving toward an accommodation with labor that preserved the division of control between workers and managers that had emerged from the struggles of the preceding decade.[78]

Those concessions did not signal, however, steel industry managers' decision to pursue a more general accord with labor on the terms that Murray wanted. Still inclined to view a direct assault on labor's power as too costly, leaders of the biggest firms nonetheless held back to see how much the managerial counteroffensive, led by the more intransigent managers, could retrieve for business. This alliance of business realists and more conservative managers had supplied the pressure for Taft–Hartley and also for the related state laws passed once it became effective.[79]

The left wing of the CIO, which included general counsel Pressman, viewed the enactment of the law as a devastating setback, one that suggested labor would do better by abandoning its alliance with the Democratic Party and its cooperation with the state. However, Murray and others more at the center of the union movement drew a different conclusion. Besieged by management and a Republican-controlled Congress, labor, Murray and his allies decided, could ill afford to break with an administration at least nominally sympathetic to it. Murray had no illusions about the hostility of several key members of the Truman administration, but the president's growing support for labor and his decision to veto the Taft–Hartley Act—even though overridden by Congress—provided Murray with the minimum needed to support the Democratic ticket in 1948.[80]

The first clear sign of those divisions in the CIO came on May 16, 1947, shortly before Congress passed the final version of the Taft–Hartley bill. At a CIO Executive Board meeting held on that day, a resolution condemning the radical Mine, Mill, and Smelter Workers Union for actions inconsistent with overall CIO policy was approved by a vote of twenty-seven to eight. The three-to-one margin reflected the balance of forces in the federation between those unions led by men sympathetic to Murray's more cautious program of support for the Truman administration and the continued search for an accord with management, and those led by CIO radicals such as Harry Bridges of the Longshoremen's Union and Julius Emspak of the UE, who favored a more confrontational approach to both the state and management in the postwar period.[81]

A second key vote, which confirmed both the respective strengths of the two factions and the breadth of the divide between them, came in a meeting held on January 22, 1948. After a bitter argument over whether the CIO should endorse either Truman or Henry Wallace in the upcoming presidential election, the executive board voted thirty-three to eleven in favor of the former. The meeting marked the end, for all practical purposes, of the alliance between social democratic and radical trade unionists that had begun when the CIO emerged in the middle 1930s.[82]

This split over labor's political and economic strategy brought Goldberg to the top in the CIO, because the division precipitated the departure of Pressman and the search for a new general counsel who supported the more moderate course outlined by Murray. Following the January 22 meeting at which the CIO in effect endorsed Truman and the Marshall Plan, Pressman voiced his opposition to those decisions in strong terms. Murray's response was that "under the circumstances he ought to quit."[83]

The message was clear: Either support the majority's position or be gone. Pressman's formal letter of resignation was tendered on February 6, opening the way for the appointment of a new CIO and USA general counsel. Murray agonized over the decision for some time before deciding on Goldberg. The key figures in persuading Murray to make that choice were Van Bittner and Jacob Potofsky, both of whom had great confidence in Goldberg's abilities.[84]

Goldberg himself later described the events leading up to his selection in the following way:

> I know that [idea] didn't come out of Phil's head alone. David [McDonald] talked to him, [USA vice-president] Jim [Thimmes] talked to him, Van [Bittner] talked to him, Joe Germano, [district director] Jim Robb and probably others. . . . I talked to Van, and I came down to Washington very frankly determined to tell Phil that I could not do the job. . . . That was a personal decision of my own. I had been away during the war years, and I felt that in respect to my family that I ought not to undertake to leave my practice in Chicago again.
>
> You know Phil Murray. I sat down in his office in Washington. . . . Phil talked to me about three minutes to be exact, and although my mind had been made up to say no I found myself saying yes.[85]

In choosing to take the job, Goldberg knew that he was committing himself to working primarily with a group of clients who mostly had less formal education and knowledge of the world than he did, and that his effectiveness in dealing with them would depend in part on his ability to conceal his awareness of that reality. He understood, too, that such a choice would mean, at least for a time, earning an income substantially below what he could have made from a more conventional private practice. In the end, though, Goldberg said, he felt that he should say yes because "I could render a service not only to the CIO but to the country. The CIO was sort of messed up at the time . . . and we had to clean out the CIO."[86] By accepting such an important post, Goldberg reasoned, he could do much more to help labor achieve an accord with management, one that would end the conflict between the two that was so familiar to his generation of Americans.[87]

Goldberg owed his new job to his proven legal skills, his familiarity with the national and international labor movements gained from his time at the OSS, and his long-standing hostility to the American Communist Party. Most important, his support for what liberals were beginning to call "the Middle Way" located him ideologically at the point toward which the CIO leadership was gradually moving. Goldberg's appointment on March 5 as CIO and USA general counsel was one of several key developments in 1948 that signaled the rightward drift of American labor, a direction not so much the one its leaders desired but, rather, the only one they saw as likely to preserve the unions' gains of the previous decade and a half.[88]

In taking the post, Goldberg had not planned at first to move to Washington, but the large amount of work and responsibility soon dumped on him left him with no choice, a situation only made worse when Murray fell ill at the end of 1948. In Goldberg's words,

> I laid down some conditions. . . . I said to Phil: . . . I want to keep my firm in Chicago, I want to retain my identity with it, I want to be there frequently, and if that can be arranged I will come down.
>   You know Phil. He said, "fine, fine, fine." And I came down. I found . . . that the situation did not meet the conditions that I set forth. Phil worked at his job twenty-four hours a day, and anybody who had any association with him worked at his job twenty-four hours a day as well.[89]

The general counsel's job was a particularly demanding one because it combined the twin duties of top Washington lobbyist for the CIO with that of chief contract negotiator for the USA. Meeting both sets of responsibilities required constant trips between the District of Columbia and Pittsburgh, where the headquarters of the Steelworkers Union was located. Those facts soon persuaded Goldberg to move from Chicago to Washington and to reduce his connection with his Chicago firm to merely an inactive partnership.[90]

Soon after his arrival at CIO headquarters on March 4, Goldberg began using that as his base of operations. Within three weeks he was immersed in contract negotiations with the major steel companies. The principal sticking point that year was the issue of social insurance, with the union demanding pensions right away and the managers arguing that they were not yet ready to discuss the matter.

Goldberg studied the USA's master contract with steel employers and decided that its reopening clause did not give the union the right to strike over the issue. Murray, however, goaded by both the rank and file and the UMW's success in getting such a plan, told his new general counsel to "find a way."[91]

Goldberg thought it over and concluded that even though the USA had no legal right to strike for pensions that year, employers under the National Labor Relations Act had a duty at least to bargain over the issue, regardless of what action the union could take if no agreement resulted. An approach as clever as it was legalistic, Goldberg took it to the NLRB, which ruled in the union's favor.

Management promptly appealed the decision in the courts, where executives deployed a massive legal team comprising close to one hundred lawyers. The effort to overwhelm the USA's comparatively tiny staff of lawyers failed, however, because the employers' attorneys missed the fine distinction Goldberg had drawn between a union's right to strike and management's duty to bargain. The employers' briefs and oral arguments focused on the first issue and the USA's on the second, which led to a ruling by the U.S. Court of Appeals for the Seventh Circuit in September 1948 upholding the earlier NLRB decision.

Refusing to give up, steel industry managers appealed to the Supreme

Court, whose decision would not come until the following spring. Goldberg had a central role throughout the struggle, which had the effect of expanding his influence over other USA Executive Board decisions, as its members subordinated other concerns to the overriding one of gaining a private benefits system for the rank and file.[92]

His activities reflected the steadily growing importance of lawyers in labor unions, which the wartime model had done so much to foster. Taft–Hartley, with its even greater measure of government regulation of union activity, only accelerated that trend. As Pressman had noted with foresight, the new law "creates a heaven for lawyers."[93]

Following the law's enactment, the USA Executive Board had been compelled to increase substantially the size and budget of the union's legal department, which would in time give the general counsel a degree of influence that few in organized labor could have imagined during the 1930s.[94] This meant that Goldberg would play a role in the CIO and USA that increasingly resembled that of the president's deputy, one whose powers would grow over the next four years as Murray experienced recurring bouts of severe illness, and so bring with it a very large measure of responsibility.[95]

The struggle over social insurance in which Goldberg participated that year was part of a larger social process by which labor and management sought to define the terms of labor's proper place in postwar America. At the heart of that struggle with management, and of the related one going on that year in the arena of electoral politics, was the search for some kind of social contract between labor and management that would spell an end to the warfare of the preceding fifteen years. This was not an easy or harmonious process, and it continued through the fall of 1949, by which time the outlines of the postwar bargain would become clearly discernible.[96]

Several major areas were still in dispute by the spring of 1948. First among them was the extent to which the government should be allowed to intervene during major industrial strikes, together with the related issue of its proper role in supervising the labor–management agreement. Second was labor's demand for some form of employer-sponsored, privatized welfare system as an alternative to the public one that workers lacked the political power to win from Congress. Third was labor's insistence on a managerial commitment to maintain high levels of output and employment, which in the steel industry took the form of demands for building more plants and expanding production. Fourth and last was the extent to which labor leaders could win workers' support for the Marshall Plan and the emerging policy of Soviet containment, thereby overcoming the hostility to those initiatives emanating from radicals and isolationists. Implicit in all of this was business executives' insistence that the labor federations take action to restrain the radicals in exchange for a compact with management.[97]

Goldberg found himself in the middle of this process of negotiation, because on most of the key issues in dispute, the USA stood at the center of the labor movement, neither as radical as some in the UAW or as most in the UE, nor as committed to the more cautious brand of unionism that characterized most AFL affiliates. With respect to the critical question of the government's proper role in supervising the agreement, the steel union's position was the one that ultimately prevailed, over the wishes of most in the AFL and the CIO radical faction, who shared the goal of greater autonomy for unions, albeit for very different reasons.

Steel led the way, too, because of the way both the industry and its union were organized. In steel, the dominance of one company, U.S. Steel, combined with the fungibility of the product, compelled the industry's managers to act in concert when bargaining with the union. That second point was as important as it was difficult to grasp immediately. In steel, unlike autos, for example, the companies produced commodities that were essentially interchangeable. Thus steel managers could not rely on customer loyalty in the event of a strike, which persuaded them to act together to preserve their respective market shares.

Although formal industrywide bargaining did not appear officially until the mid-1950s, it had been going on covertly in steel since the early 1940s. As Pressman noted in discussing that issue at a USA Executive Board meeting in the summer of 1946, "we actually have got industry[-wide] collective bargaining, but we haven't got them in the same room. To get industry[-wide] collective bargaining will be simply putting in the open what is going on secretly."[98] That kind of coordination closely resembled the relationship among employers that had emerged in Sweden, a connection of which both management and union leaders were aware.[99]

The steel union's structure similarly enabled that industry to lead the way in reaching a labor–management pact. The USA, which represented almost all of the industry's workers, had the most highly centralized governing structure of the major industrial unions. For that reason, the Steelworkers' leaders were in the best position to forge an agreement with management that was in keeping with the Swedish model so influential in American social democratic circles.[100]

In tracing Goldberg's actions during 1948/49 and those of his principal union client during that same period, one can see how labor and management finally reached the postwar agreement that they did, one that would endure, despite challenges from dissenters on both sides, well into the 1960s. And of course, one can also discover how Goldberg emerged in the late 1940s as one of the most influential union spokesmen in America, a development with far-reaching implications for his career.

III

The CIO and USA proceeded during 1948 by tackling simultaneously those matters that required unilateral actions on labor's part, as well as those made in tandem with corporate managers. Examples of the former included formal endorsements of the Marshall Plan and the Truman administration's anti-Soviet line, both of which Murray and a majority of the CIO Executive Board had decided to support by February of that year. In a USA Executive Board meeting on February 16, Murray denounced those CIO union leaders who disagreed, declaring that they "could not have had their minds changed by reason or logic on any basis, because they were evidently and obviously aligned to vote against anything that might run counter to the wishes of the Soviet government. Now that is a simple, unadulterated fact."[101]

Murray's statement was not as unfair as it sounded, because those who had opposed his stands were committed to a differing vision of the good society, one much closer to the Soviet socialist model than to the social democratic one that Murray favored. The dissenters were thus unwilling to embrace politicians and policies that promised to undercut Communist forces abroad. For men such as Pressman, Bridges, and Emspak, Soviet-style socialism, whatever its faults, was worth preserving. They perceived correctly that the Marshall Plan and the containment policy would tend to achieve just the opposite. Thus if the Soviet government saw the Marshall Plan and Truman's overall foreign policy as threatening, the CIO radicals were inclined to agree, not because they took their orders from Moscow, but rather because they remained committed to socialism, which at that time, they believed, was to be found, albeit in flawed form, only in the USSR.[102]

Goldberg, like Murray, saw that set of priorities as a betrayal of American workers, one that subordinated their needs and wishes to the radicals' desire to support the international communist movement. For Goldberg, the solution was to get rid of the radical union leaders, whose views he believed were at odds with those of the workers they claimed to represent. By the spring of 1948, Murray had agreed with the need to expel the dissenters. The CIO radicals' stands against the Marshall Plan and Truman, combined with the decision by some to adopt the no-strike pledge supported by the American Communist Party, persuaded Murray to move against them.[103]

This last point of contention, seemingly a rather technical one, proved to be of considerable importance. The American Communist Party had been advocating since 1944 a permanent no-strike pledge once wartime controls ended, so as to ensure maximum industrial output, thus making available goods that could be used for the relief of America's war-ravaged allies, including the Soviet Union. The decision by Longshoremen's Union chief Harry Bridges, one of the leading CIO radicals, to support that plan wholeheartedly after V-J Day helped convince Murray and other key CIO moderates that Bridges and his allies in the federation leadership had to go.

Goldberg later recalled that Bridges's continuing support for the no-strike pledge constituted something of a last straw for Murray. Accordingly, by the spring of 1948, Murray began moving toward a break with Bridges and his like-minded colleagues, confident by then that most of the federation would remain intact. With the radicals out of the CIO—Murray, Goldberg, and their cohorts reasoned—one big obstacle to achieving a pact with management would be removed.[104]

A third decision made in the labor movement was to adopt a well-financed and serious political action effort in 1948, one aimed less at helping Truman, whom labor leaders saw as certain to lose, than at electing to Congress as many friends of labor as possible, thereby warding off further restrictive legislation.[105] This time, members and leaders of both labor federations endorsed political action, the extent of which constituted something of a break with AFL tradition. The catalyst for that activity was the Taft–Hartley Act, which had made so many antiunion weapons available to the government that all factions in the labor movement viewed the law as unacceptable. By the spring of 1948, the on-again, off-again federation unity talks were once again in evidence, a development inspired largely by the managerial counteroffensive of 1946/47.

Formal reunification did not come about, however, because both the Lewis faction, by then back in the AFL, and the CIO radicals, for differing reasons, opposed that course. The two wings of the American labor movement would have to divide before they could once again reunite. The managerial counteroffensive of 1946/47 pushed labor to take the first steps in that direction, but new federation leadership and the threat of yet another management drive against labor would be needed to complete that process. For the time being, AFL and CIO leaders agreed only to run parallel political action campaigns, coordinating where feasible the efforts of the AFL's newly created Labor League for Political Education (LLPE) with the CIO's PAC.[106]

The LLPE's head, Joe Keenan, had served in a government agency during the war with Goldberg's old teacher, Lillian Herstein. Through her, the two men had met. Although they respected each other, Goldberg had no illusions about the constraints under which Keenan was operating. The AFL tradition of eschewing direct political action was a deeply ingrained one, which even the threat of Taft–Hartley did not overcome at once. Friendly on a personal level with both him and Keenan's CIO counterpart, Jack Kroll, Goldberg helped coordinate their activities during this period of uneasy alliance. The experience confirmed to him that a more vigorous and united labor political action effort would pay rich dividends in the years ahead, an idea he would promote throughout his career as a union lawyer.[107]

The GOP's unwillingness to support publicly any amendments to the new labor law, and the ominous silence of its presidential candidate on the question of how the act would be used if he were elected, fueled labor's determination to contest the elections with all its by-then considerable institutional might. In so doing, labor officials were hampered by the CIO radicals, who were urging the industrial working class in particular to support Henry Wallace.

Even more infuriating to Murray than the radicals' activity in a presidential election that labor expected to lose was their opposition to Democratic senatorial candidates such as Hubert Humphrey in Minnesota and Paul Douglas in Illinois. The strongly anti-Soviet position that both had adopted by 1948 persuaded radicals that their less internationalist opponents were preferable, despite the latter's support for Taft–Hartley. The elevation of the first issue over the second enraged Murray, who saw that set of priorities as inconsistent with one's obligations as an American trade unionist. He was furious, too, because he saw senatorial candidates such as Humphrey and Douglas as having a real chance to win, unlike Truman, whose prospects as late as October 1948 Murray viewed dimly.[108]

Goldberg shared that pessimistic assessment. Through election day he remained convinced, in his words, that "it was lost," a view shared by most of his colleagues in the CIO and USA. When Jack Arvey telephoned Goldberg in the early morning hours of November 3 with the news that "Truman's got it," Goldberg commented with no little understatement that "I was surprised."[109]

Truman's astonishing triumph on election night in 1948 confirmed to Goldberg as well as Murray and his supporters that the moderate position was the right one for that time. Democrats who stood for the Middle Way were big winners in 1948, and in their ranks stood many of the most prominent political figures of the postwar era. Newly elected to the Senate were both Hubert Humphrey and Paul Douglas—who won despite the Wallace supporters—as well as Estes Kefauver of Tennessee, Lyndon Johnson of Texas, Robert Kerr of Oklahoma, and Clinton Anderson of New Mexico. Victorious gubernatorial candidates with the same basic outlook included Goldberg's colleague and friend Adlai Stevenson of Illinois, as well as G. Mennen Williams of Michigan, Frank Lausche of Ohio, and Chester Bowles of Connecticut. And riding in on their coattails was the man who had vetoed Taft–Hartley and denounced it from the first day of his campaign to the last, Harry Truman. When asked by a visitor the morning after the election how on earth he had beaten Dewey, Truman replied with characteristic forthrightness that "labor did it."[110]

The editors of *Fortune* magazine, never inclined to credit labor with influence it did not have, appeared to agree. Their report on the election result was appropriately entitled "Our 'Laboristic' President" and noted with prescience that members of the GOP would not win back the White House or Congress "until they have found a way to interest the workingman and the farmer in the Republican cause."[111]

In another concession to the by-then clear signs that labor unions would, at least for a time, be a power in the land, *Fortune*'s editors had inaugurated in the month before the election a new labor section of the magazine, written by that one-time member of the Young People's Socialist League turned mainstream journalist, Daniel Bell. The timing of the decision signaled managers' understanding that even a narrow Dewey victory would not have challenged the union movement's new status in American society.[112]

The election results appeared to confirm the salience of class issues in determining the outcome. Partisanship based on social class for once approached the levels ordinarily seen in Western European societies, which suggested a sharp polarization. But also striking about the election was the turnout, the second lowest in U.S. history and far below that recorded in Western European elections held around the same time. The turnout in many urban areas, where the industrial working class was concentrated, actually declined from the totals recorded four years earlier, despite the return of military personnel and population growth. Voters in the twelve largest cities supported Truman over Dewey, but the overall margin was almost 750,000 less than Roosevelt had received four years earlier. The total of just under 49 million votes cast nationwide was a million less than the turnout in 1940.[113]

Those numbers suggested that the American version of the Middle Way lacked the kind of powerful mobilizing appeal Goldberg and its other advocates had hoped for, and in that there should have been little surprise. The scheme reflected a retreat from a more participatory role for the working class in governing American society and, for that reason, bred more indifference than excitement in its ranks. In 1948 the faction to which Goldberg belonged had won the struggle against apathy, but only just barely. Whether its vision of social democracy would ever inspire workers in the way that republicanism had in the eighteenth and nineteenth centuries or socialism had in the twentieth remains an open question. For the next few decades, however, those who supported it would do so fairly confident that the Middle Way would prove, if not inspiring to workers, at least acceptable enough to them to be worth fighting for.[114]

At the center of those in the labor movement who thought so was another man who had arrived in 1948, Arthur J. Goldberg. Less than two months after the election, Murray fell ill, creating a vacuum that Goldberg filled while seeking to complete labor's unfinished business with management. The principal challenge facing labor in early 1949 was to finish the agreement that had begun to emerge from the struggle of the preceding three years. Many of the pieces were already in place. The ones that remained took through the fall of 1949 to hammer out, a process that posed the first major test of Goldberg's abilities as a broker for organized labor.[115]

First, there was Taft–Hartley. The statute was, in Daniel Bell's apt phrase, "essentially a definition of power, involving conflicting group interests and disagreement over principles."[116] The balance struck in 1947 proved unacceptable to labor moderates in one crucial respect, namely, the national emergency disputes provision, which revived the labor injunction in certain circumstances. Union leaders viewed the injunction weapon as too dangerous to be left in the hands of an unfriendly administration, and the election results had boosted their confidence that Taft–Hartley amendments would be forthcoming.[117]

Goldberg, however, was neither as sanguine about the prospects for such changes nor as convinced that they were essential to protect the union movement. Despite the new Democratic majorities in the House and Senate, the returns showed that members who had voted for the law made up a majority even in the new Eighty-first Congress, a hard fact that Goldberg grasped fully. He moreover had become convinced, in his words, that "while I testified against it, [and] wrote a lot . . . about it, . . . as I read the statute, as a lawyer of some experience, I didn't think it would interfere with the labor movement."[118] The new law had struck a balance between labor and management that Goldberg saw as an acceptable one. Those aspects of the act that were the most offensive could be modified, he suspected, by administrative rulings and court decisions.[119]

For those reasons, he did not share the hostility to the administration so prevalent in more radical CIO and some AFL circles. And although he and Murray felt obligated — in response to pressure from the left wing of the CIO and the Lewis faction in the AFL — to sound militant about Taft–Hartley's repeal in their public statements, both men understood the balance of power in Congress and so sought no more than a few key amendments. For that reason, radicals in the CIO, in particular, charged that Murray and Goldberg were "selling out" the working class.[120]

Murray's illness essentially incapacitated him from December 1948 through April 1949, leaving Goldberg in charge of orchestrating the fight to secure the desired amendments. With him acting as coordinator, a group of union lawyers worked closely with the administration in drafting a substitute measure. Introduced by House Labor Committee Chairman John Lesinski, it failed to pass that spring after the Lewis faction and the unions led by CIO radicals lobbied against any compromise that would have allowed government intervention during major industrial strikes.[121]

Sharing a similar aversion to such intervention, although for very different reasons, Lewis's group and the radicals were determined to head off the compromise that both Murray and Goldberg favored. The latter's proposed revision would have replaced the injunction weapon with government fact-finding boards, which would have been empowered to recommend reasonable terms for settling such strikes. But even that more modest government role proved too much for the Lewisites and the radicals, who were opposed to labor's giving its consent to such a law. If there was to be such a statute, they reasoned, better to let it be forced on workers who could continue to object to it rather than grudgingly agree and thereby be foreclosed from lobbying for its abolition.[122]

Although the Lewis faction and the radicals thus frustrated the labor moderates' efforts to arrive at a statutory accord on that issue, an agreement was achieved nonetheless by going around Congress. The Truman administration simply refused to use the injunction weapon that the act provided and over the next four years substituted for it the fact-finding-board approach that Goldberg had offered as the alternative acceptable to labor. In that fashion, by the spring of 1949 one of the few remaining areas of conflict had been resolved.[123]

Another was the expulsion of the radicals, a course along which Murray and Goldberg advanced throughout that year. The last CIO Executive Board meeting attended by both factions took place in May, at which Goldberg and the radicals clashed angrily over amendments to Taft–Hartley, verbal attacks on Murray's leadership, and a motion to censure the Mine, Mill, and Smelter Workers Union for its efforts to undermine a USA organizing campaign at a Bessemer plant in Alabama. The exchanges over Taft–Hartley were ugly, with the radicals accusing Goldberg of "selling out" the labor movement with a "phony compromise bill." He replied in turn that they were liars who had done as much to undermine Taft–Hartley repeal as the congressional conservatives had.[124]

What had heretofore been a major rift was by the end of that meeting a civil war. In telling off the radicals, Murray observed caustically that "the per capita tax of the Left Wing element that fights National CIO policy in this movement constitutes less than eleven and a half per cent of the total membership."[125] His remarks indicated to the dissidents that they were through and could expect formal ouster at the next CIO convention, thereby removing another obstacle to a postwar bargain with management.[126]

The ease with which that was accomplished calls into question the view so popular in some liberal circles of the radicals as masters of intrigue and manipulation. In fact, the radicals had been thoroughly committed to building the labor movement, albeit for their own reasons, and its success in the 1930s and early 1940s stemmed in part from the energy they had given it. Deftly used by trade union leaders and liberals, the radicals were discarded when the need for them seemed no longer to be so urgent. Although they were responsible for that outcome, it nonetheless had a price for the labor movement as a whole: With the radicals' departure came a decline in union militance and dynamism, problems from which the American labor movement has yet to recover.[127]

With the difficult debates over Taft–Hartley amendments and the labor radicals' fate at an end, the one remaining area of serious conflict was that of pensions and social insurance. In April 1949, Goldberg's earlier victory at the appellate level became final when the U.S. Supreme Court denied management's petition for review. Labor's strategy of enlisting the support of the state in seeking a private benefits system had thus paid off nicely. The NLRB and the courts had ruled that managers were obligated to bargain over the issue, and the union was legally allowed to strike if employers refused to do so. The outcome of the courtroom contest also meant that the first major confrontation over pensions in the influential manufacturing sector would come in the steel industry, one that would be watched carefully by labor leaders and managers in other parts of the economy, facts of which Goldberg, Murray, and the other USA board members were very aware.[128]

And of course, with Truman safely returned to the White House, the USA could take on management over this issue secure in the knowledge that no Taft–Hartley injunction would be forthcoming. Instead, the administration cooperated with the Steelworkers Union when management balked over the issue in July 1949. At Goldberg's urging, Truman asked the USA and steel company executives for a sixty-day contract extension so that a government fact-finding board could examine the dispute. On September 10 its report was published backing the Steelworkers on the crucial pension issue.[129]

Management, however, resisted briefly before conceding, and the result was a forty-five-day union walkout that began on October 1. Faced with government support for the USA's demand and clear signs that the rank and file really cared about the issue, management surrendered in mid-November, giving labor what all agreed was its biggest victory of the year, and perhaps several years. *Fortune* labor reporter Daniel Bell noted the event by publishing a profile of Goldberg under the heading "Pension Strategist," in which Bell called him "labor's man of the year."[130]

The precedent in steel would soon ripple outward to other unionized parts of the economy. Murray reported to the USA Executive Board in September that UAW Chief Walter Reuther's reaction to the steel board's findings was one of enormous excitement mixed with a more than a little envy. According to Murray,

> After he [Reuther] had examined it [the pension report] both he and the Ford negotiating committee, the boys from the plants who were with him, . . . said, "My God, I wish we could get this at Ford tomorrow." Mr. Reuther said it was the greatest human document ever contrived in the mind of man, it was another Magna Charta.[131]

The plan that became the model for the steel industry was the one adopted by U.S. Steel, an indication of how central the largest firms led by the business realists were in defining the terms of the postwar social contract.[132]

One other area of disagreement—the extent to which managers should commit themselves to expanding their factories' size so as to promote full employment—had receded somewhat in its urgency owing to the continuing postwar boom. In the steel industry, labor continued to press for a managerial commitment to expand plant capacity, and union leaders were assisted in their efforts by leading officials in the Truman administration and by influential members of Congress. Although pushed hard to build new plants, steel industry managers would resist until the outbreak of the Korean War in 1950, after which they would do so with the help of large subsidies provided by the federal government.

By the late 1940s, labor and management had, however, reached an accommodation on the goal of promoting high levels of output and employment, because the success of the economy since 1941 had done much to persuade leaders of the biggest firms that Keynesian economic theory held a key to continued prosperity.[133]

Thus by the time the 1949 contract in steel had been signed in November, the basic terms of the postwar agreement had been worked out. Labor had given up any further effort to wrest control over the management of large enterprises, leaving the decisions about such matters as capital investment, marketing, plant location, and overall output in the hands of the managers. Union leaders also agreed, in the main, to demand only wage increases that were tied to rising corporate profits derived from enhanced productivity. That wage restraint concession would do much to keep the overall price level from increasing very much, during peacetime at least, for the next two decades.

Union leaders also agreed to back the anti-Soviet foreign policies supported by the Truman administration and the business community and to do their best to oust radicals from leadership posts in the labor movement. Management, for its part, agreed to end its efforts to win back prerogatives lost during the 1930s and 1940s, to stop trying to break existing unions, to grant fringe benefits that supplemented the limited social welfare system provided by the state, and to pursue investment and output policies that helped promote high employment for union workers. This last concession was in exchange for labor's abandonment of the guaranteed annual wage idea that Murray had supported at the war's end, a proposal now seen as less vital in the face of continuing prosperity.[134]

The adoption of that program by one-time FDR supporters signaled a sea change in the intellectual content of New Deal liberalism. Although at least some strands of New Deal thought had embraced greater state control over the operation of major industrial enterprises, by the mid-1940s that element had been lost. What had emerged instead was a more modest commitment to social democracy, coupled with a militant hostility to Soviet-style socialism, or "communism," which New Deal liberals by then found hard to distinguish from fascism. In the spring of 1946 David McDonald had expressed that thought in the following terms:

> I believe that Communism and Fascism and Nazism and the basic philoso-
> phy of Marxianism is a revolution of the Right, it is a counter revolution,
> . . . counter to the American Revolution. I believe that firmly.
>   Communism, Fascism, or Marxianism to me is . . . something designed
> in its practical application to remove the democratic rights of the people.[135]

Arthur Schlesinger Jr. gave those ideas more elaborate expression in his book *The Vital Center*, published three years later, which the newly formed Americans for Democratic Action (ADA) took as its creed. Although committed to reform, the organization's program clearly marked a retreat from support for greater state control over corporate power. In that respect, the ADA offered American workers less hope of gaining a say in the governance of the workplace and the larger society than New Dealers had in the 1930s. In exchange, workers were promised social peace, high employment, and a much greater measure of material security and comfort than they had known during the Depression. For that generation, which had experienced the worst economic catastrophe in American history and the most destructive war ever, those concessions appeared to be a great deal. And, one should remember, Goldberg and his ADA allies hoped in the future to move further in the direction of the Swedish model, which seemed to have imposed greater limits on managerial authority.[136]

That model had influence elsewhere, too, of course. The social struggle in which Goldberg had played a leading role as negotiator was only one part of a larger, international process that played itself out in the other highly industrialized societies of Western Europe and Japan during the same period. American labor leaders were acutely conscious of developments there. They had, for example, greeted with excitement the British Labour Party's victory in 1945, and they continued to communicate with European trade unionists through the late 1940s. Murray reported to the USA Executive Board his discussions with representatives from France, Britain, China, and other countries at the San Francisco meeting that launched the United Nations about "the need for labor organizations . . . [to] buttress and implement and constructively help a friendly government in solving the manifold problems of economic and social interests."[137] Perhaps most telling was Murray's use of European labor leaders' views in advocating USA support for the Marshall Plan.[138] By November 1949, that informal network of trade unionists had withdrawn from the World Federation of Trade Unions (WFTU) and reorganized themselves as the International Confederation of Free Trade Unions (ICFTU).[139]

The Marshall Plan and other foreign-aid arrangements that ICFTU members endorsed did succeed, as their framers had hoped, in "recovering" Western Europe and Japan from the spread of Soviet-style socialism. The exact terms reached in those societies varied in response to labor's strength there, but the overall result showed its common parentage. In those countries in which American intervention was the most direct and pervasive, that is, Germany and Japan, labor–management struggle eventually produced social compacts on more or less the same terms as were reached in the United States. In other societies, such as France and Italy, where communists had built strong labor organizations before the war, the same sorts of social contracts were reached, but without the direct participation of the political parties with which those unions were affiliated. Keynesianism, with its promise of economic growth, was attractive to all but the most radical workers in postwar Europe and Japan, a fact clearly understood by labor leaders of all ideological stripes.[140]

The postwar bargain would henceforth be known in Western Europe simply as "the social contract," and in the United States, more confusingly, as "the New Deal." The latter term invited misunderstanding because it was used, then as now, to refer to both the legislative enactments of Roosevelt's presidency during the 1930s and the postwar settlement that ultimately materialized in the late 1940s. The first had surely contributed to the second, but they were not one and the same.[141]

What should be kept in mind is that the postwar "New Deal" was not designed solely by management and imposed on a powerless and victimized working class. Labor did not, as one historian has written, simply "lie down like good dogs" in the postwar period.[142] Workers in unions had fought for the continued existence of their organizations and won a class peace on terms vastly preferable to those they had known after the First World War. What emerged from the social struggle of 1945–49 was a result that neither side fully wanted, and for that reason it would prove difficult to sustain. Goldberg, like his peers in the other highly industrialized market societies, was conscious of the potential hazards but nonetheless tended to view the future with the self-confidence of those who had won both the war and the social peace that eventually followed. For a time, events would appear to justify his self-confidence.[143]

4

Containment, Domestic and Foreign

Unlike the preceding five years, which had been marked by a struggle to define the shape of the postwar order, the next eight would be characterized by a large degree of consensus in support of it. Especially in the United States, life between 1950 and 1957 appeared placid, at least on the surface, which would lead many students of social trends to conclude that such peace was both "normal" and likely to continue indefinitely.[1]

For the labor movement, those years witnessed an enormous expansion in total union membership and, at the same time, an inability to do much more than maintain its share of the steadily growing workforce. At the outset of this period, the CIO was shrinking in size as its leaders expelled the dissidents, and by its end, the federation — its membership greater than ever before — had reunited with the AFL to give the American working class the largest formal organization it had ever known.[2]

Such institutional power, and the rank-and-file solidarity on which it was based, helped give most American workers greater material prosperity and security than they had ever known. Although many of those gains were enjoyed primarily by the roughly one-third of the nonfarm workforce organized into unions, the spillover effects reached millions of workers outside them. And with the passage of time, the value of those gains appears ever greater to the workers who enjoyed them. At the same time, however, those benefits did much to dissipate working-class militancy and dynamism, without which no labor movement can be sustained indefinitely.

For labor, then, the early to middle 1950s was a period of, paradoxically, both expansion and decline. Throughout that time, organized labor remained a powerful defender of working-class interests, one that compelled business managers and the state to support the postwar New Deal. By 1957, however, the first signs of a business revolt against it would begin to materialize. The roots of that rebellion can be found in the events of those preceding years.[3]

For Goldberg, as for so many others, the early to middle 1950s were a time of steadily increasing prosperity, ambition, and expectations. At its start he was an influential assistant to one of the most powerful labor leaders in America; by its conclusion he had become a powerful labor leader himself in all but name. Making that rise possible was the changing nature of American political life.

Before the late 1940s, American labor leaders were necessarily skilled in the art of mobilizing masses of workers, but by the 1950s politics was characterized more by negotiations among leaders of labor, management, and the state. Although Goldberg lacked the oratorical gifts needed to function as a labor leader under the old order, he excelled in the new one. He stood at the center of institutional interactions, playing the role of highly self-conscious broker on behalf of the organized working class. In so doing, he observed at first hand some of the most important developments of this period. At the same time, he and other labor leaders and workers fought to defend the postwar New Deal against both business managers unreconciled to labor's place in it and the influential minority within the labor movement itself that pressed for even more managerial concessions.[4] The effort would prove exhausting for Goldberg. In 1950 and again in 1955 he would be hospitalized for nervous exhaustion brought on by the pressures of his job. But in the eight years from 1950 to 1957, he would enjoy a large degree of success in preserving the new consensus, and from his perspective one can see clearly both the reasons why the postwar New Deal worked so smoothly and the origins of the growing challenges to it.[5]

In the first half of that period, from 1950 to 1954, many, although not all, of his accomplishments would be of an essentially defensive nature. Goldberg's primary concern then was to protect labor's gains of the previous fifteen years, and the postwar social contract more generally, from its opponents both at home and abroad. Such efforts made up a distinct and highly important phase of his public life and the story with which this chapter is concerned.

II

For Goldberg, the new era of labor–management détente opened, appropriately enough, with the drive to expel its fiercest critics from the CIO, namely, those ten affiliates still under radical leadership. Although the outcome was a foregone conclusion after the spring of 1949, the actual process took almost two years to run its course. The first step, insofar as Goldberg was concerned, lay in creating the legal authority to oust a union for domination by, or conformity with the policies of, the American Communist Party. Philip Murray and other CIO leaders, however, objected at first to giving the radicals any measure of due process. He and his allies simply pushed through resolutions at the 1949 CIO convention, expelling the two most influential affiliates controlled by the radicals, the United Electrical Workers (UE) and the Farm Equipment Workers (FE).[6]

Goldberg's warning that those moves were dangerous because they could be attacked in the courts on due process grounds helped persuade the CIO leadership to adopt a more legalistic method for expelling the remaining radical-controlled affiliates. His solution was to draft, in consultation with a few other CIO union chiefs, an amendment to its constitution, which the federation then adopted at its 1949 annual convention. The next step was to give the eight unions under investigation a very modest measure of due process, something he believed appropriate in any case. The CIO leadership, however, appears to have gone along more to shield the CIO's findings from review in the courts than to provide any real procedural fairness to the accused union leaders.

Goldberg and Murray decided not to use lawyers in these proceedings, in order to strengthen their case that civil liberties were not involved and that the CIO Executive Board's actions were essentially unreviewable by the judiciary. Goldberg, however, played a major part in gathering the evidence to be used against the defendants and helped prepare the questions asked of them at their "trials." Predictably, seven of the eight unions were found "guilty" and expelled, although the entire sequence took eighteen months to complete.[7]

At least a few of the radicals tried to contest those proceedings in the courts, and although the radicals failed, their efforts touched a raw nerve. Opposition to judicial intervention into internal union affairs was one of the most deeply held tenets of American labor, and the radicals' efforts to use the courts enraged Murray and other CIO Executive Board members. In the end, a group of thirty-two CIO unions voted together to oust the remaining nine. By November 1950 the job was largely finished, and Murray was predicting to the remaining CIO Executive Board members that "I have every reason to believe and hope that before November, 1951 the old United Electrical Workers organization will be completely removed from the electrical manufacturing industry."[8] That was a crucial objective, he suggested, because the "UE was the heart of the American Communist party."[9] Murray and the other remaining CIO leaders were confident that most of the workers lost would soon be enrolled in those affiliates still in the CIO or in newly created ones such as the International Union of Electrical Workers (IUE), which was established to win over electrical workers who had been affiliated with the UE.[10]

Murray and Goldberg ultimately succeeded in ridding the federation of the radicals and in almost wiping out their unions through raiding by other CIO affiliates. The effort, however, left the CIO weaker in both numbers and other respects. By the end of the expulsion drive, the federation had roughly 4 million members, of which nearly half belonged to just two unions, the UAW and the USA. Five other unions claimed roughly another quarter of the CIO's membership, and thus what purported to be a major federation had become by 1950 a group of seven major unions and twenty-five relatively minor ones. The price of achieving a broad unity of outlook over basic CIO objectives had been high. Securing them now, without the radicals, would still prove to be very difficult.[11]

Complicating matters still further was the continuing fear of a return to Depression-era levels of unemployment. The nation's economy entered a recession in the late summer of 1949, and by early 1950 unemployment was still rising. The official estimate of those out of work in February stood at just under 4.7 million, 7.6 percent of the nation's workforce. The situation seemed so serious to Murray that he sought unity talks with the AFL in order to forge a united program for stimulating the economy. Although rebuffed by the AFL's leadership, which clung, at least publicly, to its recommendations for a reduction in government spending so as to balance the federal budget, the CIO pressed for public-works spending, a rise in the minimum wage, increased levels of unemployment compensation, and a tax cut, all in accordance with Keynesian economic thought.

The sluggish response in Congress to those demands, together with a persistently high unemployment rate, led Murray to warn the USA leadership in late March 1950 that "at the present rate of growth of unemployment it is anticipated by Mr. Keyserling, of the President's Economic Council, that if these trends continue as they have been in the past year, one can readily anticipate the possibility of 12,000,000 unemployed in 1954."[12] The USA Executive Board's discussion revealed labor leaders' enduring fear of a return to high levels of unemployment. The tentative nature of the business community's acceptance of Keynesian concepts contributed to that insecurity. More specifically, the continuing resistance of many business managers and some senior administration officials to high levels of federal government spending during peacetime boded ill to Murray, Goldberg, and other CIO leaders. Within a few months, however, this opposition would disappear, and along with it the fear among labor leaders of a return to the dreary economic conditions of the 1930s.[13]

The Truman administration's decision to fight in Korea transformed the economic and political situation. By September 1950 Murray was telling the USA leadership that

> I don't believe that even if we should win in Korea that we are going to stop with [an army of] three million men. I think there is a determination upon the part of the people, and certainly it seems to be evidenced on the part of the administration, to go through with a tremendously big armament program. . . . The world is fraught with fear and there are evidences of war, spotty in nature, but nevertheless world-wide in effect. I have been briefed on these things, and I have looked at the information with relation to the position of the Soviet Union and its satellite countries, its armies, its armament and so forth, and the dangers which beset us are more acute than we really understand. . . .
>
> So there are reasonable grounds for believing — at least I think there is, for this thing that we are in at the moment lasting a long while.[14]

Murray's prophetic words signaled a revolution in the way labor leaders thought about the needs of American workers. The "problem" now, according to Murray, was "scarcity of manpower," rather than the opposite.[15] The guaranteed annual wage idea that had seemed so important in the 1940s became, almost overnight, largely irrelevant in Murray's eyes.[16]

Along with the militarization of the conflict between market and Soviet socialist societies came a change in the way Murray spoke and apparently thought about the latter. Until the outbreak of hostilities in Korea, Murray had never compared the Soviet Union with Nazi Germany in CIO or USA Executive Board sessions. The term *fascist*, if used at all, he applied only to business managers. The Korean War, however, appears to have completed the transformation in Murray's thinking about the Soviet Union. In 1951/52, the last two years of his long career as a labor leader, Murray finally began to use in USA and CIO Executive Board meetings the cold war language and concepts that have since become so ingrained in American political discourse. With that change he achieved very much the same outlook as that of his general counsel and by-then top aide.[17]

This development helped cement an already close relationship and led Murray to delegate enormous amounts of responsibility to Goldberg once the Korean War began. Part of the reason lay in the government's expanded role in regulating labor–management relations. Mobilizing the American economy to support a military effort in Korea had produced this change. As government agencies such as the Wage Stabilization Board (WSB) were established and the Defense Production Act passed, Goldberg's role as Washington lobbyist for the CIO and USA grew in importance.[18]

The first order of business for the Steelworkers once the war broke out, however, was to secure a revision in their 1949 three-year contract to keep up with inflation. Murray and the other USA leaders had rejected, because of its unpredictability, the cost-of-living allowance (COLA) provision incorporated into the 1948 Autoworkers contract. As Murray told the USA Executive Board members in the fall of 1950, "I have not publicly discussed my own point of view with respect to the Autoworkers' contract, but I have told the [steel] companies that I don't want our organization to negotiate on a cost-of-living arrangement."[19]

The overall price level had declined in 1949 and then began rising sharply after the United States entered the Korean conflict, a back-and-forth movement that Murray and most other labor leaders viewed as unacceptable to workers, who were inclined to favor steadily increasing wages that reflected rising corporate profits. For that reason, the Steelworkers' leadership had insisted on a provision in their 1949 contract that allowed the union to reopen negotiations over wages during the second and third years of its life. Thus even though the industry and the USA negotiated three-year contracts beginning in 1946, collective bargaining went on more or less constantly during the following decade. For the USA leadership, that was the best way to ensure that workers' wages and benefits kept up with both rising living costs and growing corporate profits.[20]

The bargaining over the size of the 1950 wage increase took place during the fall and was hampered by the concurrent union-shop elections in steel.

Mandated by the Taft–Hartley Act, the elections were held to determine whether steelworkers favored a union shop. The overall margin among those eligible to vote of between 65 and 70 percent testified eloquently to the lack of dynamism in the USA that had followed from building the union so completely from the top down. Murray told the other USA leaders that the steel companies had backed away from an early wage agreement once the first set of returns were in, no doubt feeling that their bargaining position had improved as a result.

To make matters worse, workers at Weirton Steel, the one major steel company not yet organized by the USA, voted at the same time to affiliate with the Independent Steelworkers Union, which USA leaders saw as little more than a company organization. Comparing the USA's poor record with that of the UAW, which had organized more than 98 percent of the basic auto manufacturing industry, Murray noted that the UAW

> will have, as a result of its militancy and its fight and its spirit and its organizational activities, brought into its union . . . in the next sixty days 250,000 new members. . . .
>
> Now that's the picture. We have just as many organizing possibilities as the Auto Workers ever dared to have, but we are certainly not doing the work that they are doing in the field of organizing.[21]

Despite the USA's poor showing in the union-shop elections, by late November 1950, the union had obtained a new wage increase. USA Vice-President Jim Thimmes estimated the size of the increase at eighteen and a half cents an hour, which he noted was larger than that obtained by most other major industrial unions. The USA had moved quickly so as to get an increase approved before the federal government's wage stabilization machinery was fully established, thereby limiting further wage gains. Murray told USA Executive Board members as early as September that the pressures for a wage freeze order had been intense, which he opposed so long as such an order failed to include price controls as well. With the passage of the Defense Production Act in that same month, the Truman administration received the power needed to order such a freeze. That, Murray noted, "is one of the things that I have been really fighting in Washington behind closed doors in the State Department and over in the White House."[22]

In the first five months of the war, the mobilization program was modest in its reach. Significantly, the two men Truman appointed to direct it, Stuart Symington, who headed the National Security Resources Board (NSRB), and Alan Valentine, director of the Economic Stabilization Agency (ESA), were given little real power to regulate the flow of vitally needed raw materials or to control wages and prices. And even though Symington was not as overtly hostile to labor as Valentine, both turned deaf ears to the CIO's call for more labor participation in the regulatory apparatus.

Symington's effort to deal with labor characteristically contained much more in the way of public relations than substance. As Murray complained to the CIO leadership in the fall of 1950,

> I am sitting as a member of this Symington [Advisory] Committee. . . . I
> am told that as a member . . . that I am getting the inside dope, I am
> getting the top secret stuff. . . . Well, God love you, I tell you I never did
> see so many charts in all my life . . . and hours . . . is consumed while
> you are being briefed; and . . . all of the stuff I have read on the charts I
> have read in the morning papers.[23]

Goldberg had been intimately involved in both the wage negotiation and
the related wage freeze efforts. Murray's gratitude for Goldberg's help was
revealed in the praise showered on him at the USA Executive Board meeting
held shortly after the agreement was reached. Goldberg, he said, had

> provided a great deal of encouragement and inspiration and intelligent guid-
> ance to me while these [wage increase] conversations were underway with
> the United States Steel Corporation. He performed admirably, intelligently
> and constructively, as only he can, and I cannot measure in words the deep
> sense of appreciation that permeates my bosom when I say to Art Goldberg
> that he did an excellent job in these negotiations.[24]

Goldberg's role expanded even more as Murray fell ill again in 1951, leaving
Goldberg with most of the day-to-day responsibility for running the CIO
national office.[25]

Goldberg had several tasks ahead once the 1950 contract talks were behind
him. First and foremost, he sought to wrest from the Truman administration
an endorsement of the CIO-backed mobilization program, which called for
wage and price restraints, higher taxes on corporate profits, and a tripartite
labor board with powers similar to those of the World War II–era War Labor
Board. Under the existing scheme, the ESA's two principal subdivisions, the
Office of Price Stability (OPS), headed by former Toledo mayor Michael V.
DiSalle, and the Wage Stabilization Board (WSB), composed of equal numbers of employer, labor, farmer, and "public" members, lacked much real
authority to control wages and prices. Convinced that a stronger regulatory
scheme was needed, Goldberg lobbied for it in the fall of 1950 but made little
headway until after the Chinese army entered the Korean War in November.

This development, which promised to prolong the fighting far beyond
what most Americans had expected, helped persuade Murray and Goldberg to
pursue a formal alliance with the AFL that would bolster their own lobbying
efforts. It materialized one month later as the United Labor Policy Committee (ULP), whose members endeavored to win acceptance for what was essentially the CIO's mobilization program. Goldberg appeared at all the committee's meetings, which began in January 1951. By the spring of 1951, he, rather
than Murray, was reporting to the USA and CIO Executive Boards on the
progress of negotiations with the administration and Congress.[26]

Goldberg took the position in all his dealings with government officials that
the stabilization scheme established under the Defense Production Act of
1950 left the United States poorly prepared

> for the worst crisis that this country has ever been in. I think that, although
> we went through a world war last time, we have never been in a situation

where we have been faced with the threat that now confronts us, a threat that may very well last for a generation, and a threat that is a real, serious, continuing threat that may sap our resources and drive us to bankruptcy as a nation unless we equip ourselves and take the proper steps to guard against it.[27]

Goldberg regarded the Soviet threat as genuine and enormous, and in his view, the only way to meet it was to call for sacrifices from management as well as labor. This formulation did much to strengthen the popularity and legitimacy with the public of labor's demands for price controls and higher taxes on corporate profits, but only at the very high cost of reinforcing still further the cold war hysteria that grew steadily after the American military intervention in Korea.[28]

Business managers, for their part, did not agree that the military situation in Korea required such a response, and so they resisted fiercely the labor movement's mobilization program. Employers favored instead freezing wages to keep inflation in check and using Taft–Hartley to deal with labor disputes. Business leaders made certain that no new war labor board would be created under the authority of the law mandating defense mobilization. In Goldberg's words,

> They wrote a section into the Defense Production Act that says the President is authorized to create machinery to settle disputes under this statute . . . as may be agreed upon at conferences between management, labor and such persons as the President may designate to represent government and the public. . . .
>
> In other words, they tried to get themselves a veto power because they were hopeful that the instrument that would be used would be the Taft–Hartley Act. And they said that boldly before the Wage Board.[29]

The congressional elections held shortly after the act was passed only made matters worse. Of the representatives and senators elected that year, less than a third had received the CIO's endorsement. Although overall Democratic losses were modest by the standard of off-year elections, most of those defeated in the House had been New Deal liberals friendly to labor. As Jack Kroll observed in summarizing the results for the CIO leadership, "I think we had our ears pinned back because we lost too many friends."[30]

In listing the reasons for labor's poor showing, Kroll noted that the Democrats had done badly in urban areas, in part because "the Democratic party machinery in the various localities sat on their back sides and they let us do the job; they figured labor was going to do the job and therefore they could take it easy and save their dough."[31] David McDonald also acknowledged that worker apathy had contributed to the debacle. He told the USA leadership shortly after the election that in Pennsylvania only 35 percent of the rank and file had registered to vote. PAC contributions, too, lagged far behind the desired levels. Even more ominous to Kroll was the reelection of Ohio Senator and Taft–Hartley Act author Robert Taft by 430,000 votes, the largest majority ever in an Ohio Senate contest. By the spring of 1951, Goldberg was calling the new Congress "one of the worst . . . that has ever assembled on Capitol Hill."[32]

A reflection of management's increased strength lay in Truman's appointment of Charles "Electric Charlie" Wilson, the president of General Electric, to head the newly reorganized mobilization effort. Wilson, a business realist who sought to keep labor's role to a minimum, attempted to placate the union chiefs' demands for labor participation by making a few token appointments. The real decision-making power, however, he concentrated in the hands of men drawn almost entirely from large corporations. As Goldberg told CIO Executive Board members early in 1951,

> The President called in Wilson of General Electric and gave him . . . the greatest grant of authority ever given to any man in the history of this country. . . . Mr. Wilson was given by executive order the complete authority to . . . decide issues involving production, economic stabilization, which means wages and prices, manpower, and all other aspects of the mobilization program.[33]

Despite the best efforts of labor leaders to gain a share of that authority, Wilson and his subordinates repeatedly rebuffed them. "He went about his work," Goldberg noted, "and we heard nothing from Mr. Wilson."[34]

The most Wilson would do to please labor leaders was to appoint Eric Johnston, formerly head of the U.S. Chamber of Commerce, to act as the chief of economic stabilization. Johnston, who had played a leading role in negotiating the postwar New Deal, was more sympathetic to labor's demands for participation in the mobilization scheme, but as Goldberg reminded the CIO Executive Board, "under the law he is subordinate to Wilson, Wilson is the real boss in that situation."[35]

Goldberg informed the USA Executive Board in April that the best efforts of the United Labor Policy Committee, which had met almost constantly from January through April, had not yet secured an increase in corporate taxes or the creation of a tripartite board with the power to settle labor–management disputes.[36]

Wilson's decision in late January to order a general wage freeze proved to be the last straw for the labor movement. Soon after its enactment, the United Labor Policy Committee instructed all labor people participating in the mobilization effort to withdraw, resulting in a political and economic crisis for the Truman administration. The predictable response of the business community, Goldberg noted, soon materialized:

> We have been accused of striking against the Government and accused of imperiling the mobilization program. There is a simple answer. We were in no position to imperil the mobilization program because we were not in the mobilization program. . . . Altogether there were four men representing labor in the mobilization agencies.[37]

That stark admission highlighted the limits of labor's power in the postwar period, even during a period of wartime when labor's bargaining power expanded as the economy neared full employment.

But if weak when compared with the formidable resources of the business managers, workers and their leaders were far from powerless. Labor's defection from the mobilization agencies placed enormous pressure on the Truman administration to make some concessions. And labor was helped by unusually strong support from farmer representatives, furious that they, too, had been excluded from any real say in how the mobilization program was to operate.

In response to pressure from the twelve labor, farmer, and public members of the WSB, Truman issued an executive order creating a new wage stabilization board empowered to find facts in specific cases and to make settlement recommendations.[38] He did this despite the fierce resistance of business leaders and over the opposition, as Goldberg drily noted, of his own attorney general, who saw the move as beyond the authority granted to the president by Congress. The new scheme adopted was, in essence, a wartime version of the alternative to Taft–Hartley that Murray and Goldberg had advocated since the spring of 1949.[39]

The second wage board, however, proved in its first six months of existence to be as ineffectual as its predecessor in controlling wage increases. The two boards after ten months of combined operation had, Daniel Bell reported in *Fortune*, "no visible effect on the national wage level. . . . [T]he board," he concluded, "had never really proved its authority."[40] The crisis abated in the spring, however, with the slowing of inflation. Prices leveled off once the Truman administration's determination to keep Korea a limited war — even in the face of Chinese intervention — became clear. Goldberg spent a great deal of time working on WSB matters, in large part to prevent the board from issuing a ruling on incentive pay that would limit still further union wage increases.[41]

With beginning of contract negotiations in the steel industry, the board's value to organized labor became more readily apparent. Goldberg and Murray had understood the connection between the two from the outset, as had the steel companies' managers. The industry leaders had been at the center of business pressure on the government not to create such a board, in part because steel managers feared that a new version of the War Labor Board would recommend that employers grant the union shop. Goldberg told the USA leadership that "the steel industry . . . knows that they have to deal with us this year on the question of a union shop."[42]

Mindful of the boost the USA had received in 1949 from the Steel Board's recommendation that companies grant a pension plan to the union, steel managers were pressing hard to avoid a replay of government intervention that this time would support the USA's demand for greater union security. Winning the creation of the new WSB, Goldberg told the USA leadership, had been a "milestone," because "obviously a dispute between us and the industry which cannot be resolved by collective bargaining will, of course, wind up before that Board. And under . . . the action taken by the President that Board will be in a position to hear the facts."[43]

Murray and Goldberg also understood that the bargaining in steel would be carefully watched by managers and workers throughout the manufacturing sector of the economy and also by the federal government, because of the ripple effects that would follow from any increase in steel wages and prices. As Murray had reminded the USA Executive Board during the 1950 wage renegotiation,

> We happen to be in that kind of industry that is basic in nature, and whatever it does with respect to these matters affects all other kinds of industry.
>
> . . . when you hit steel you hit mining, quarrying, timber, railroads, shipping—you hit almost everything because whatever may be granted in steel has to flow to these other industries which are a part of the steel industry, and if prices go up that will naturally result in material costs going with it. The cycle of price increases will be far reaching in effect, in that it means that higher prices will come for the purchase of steel for the manufacture of automobiles, washing machines, refrigerators, and what have you—everything, in fact.[44]

Murray exaggerated only slightly. The central place of steel in the American economy of the 1950s meant that labor–management bargaining there would have widespread consequences for wages and prices in other industries.[45]

The timing of the negotiations appeared fortuitous for the USA. Its three-year contract with the industry's managers expired at the end of 1951, a record year for steel production, thanks in part to the demand for steel used in the Korean War effort. Steel producers were operating at full capacity and had begun to expand it even further, encouraged in that endeavor by pressure from the federal government. The Truman administration, which had earlier sought an expansion in steel capacity to no avail, now succeeded with a carrot-and-stick approach.

The carrot—changes in the nation's tax laws that essentially subsidized the construction of new facilities—may not have been as persuasive as the stick—the threat of regulating steel like a public utility—which Congressmen Joseph O'Mahoney and Emanuel Celler, as well as Senator Estes Kefauver, did much to keep alive. The result was steel managers' decision to build a large number of new facilities, which the USA viewed as portending ever more jobs in steel. The economy more generally was also operating at very close to full employment in response to the Korean wartime boom.[46]

This combination of circumstances strengthened the union's bargaining power, which led Murray and Goldberg to press for an ambitious set of contract objectives, notably a large pay raise to enable workers to keep up with inflation (and the UAW) as well as to win a bigger slice of the industry's record 1951 profits, improvements in fringe benefits such as holidays and pensions, and a union-shop clause to strengthen union security. The USA leadership took the position that the industry's managers could afford to make those concessions without any rise in steel prices. They made that argument for at least two reasons, first, because they believed industry profits were so large that the higher labor costs could be paid out of them without an increase in steel firms' revenues and, second, because both Murray and Goldberg understood that public support for the union's demands would erode if they appeared to be inflationary.[47]

As was so often the case in the 1940s and 1950s, the union's demands were only partially economic. The USA's two crucial goals in 1952 were a pay increase and the union-shop clause. The former demand in 1952 was at least partially connected to issues of control over the production process, because management took the position that increases in pay should be tied to changes in the incentive pay formula. The net result of that proposal would have been to require faster production to earn the same amounts of incentive pay as workers were earning under the current arrangement. But Murray opposed the idea and told the USA Executive Board that to give in to management's demands for greater control in determining work rules and incentive rates "would certainly place steel workers in a state of bondage."[48] The USA's demand for the union shop had even more to do with consolidating labor's power in the workplace than it did with matters of money.

Management, for its part, although bargaining as a group, nonetheless remained divided over its objectives. Once again, executives at the industry leader, U.S. Steel, appeared more inclined to compromise than did those at the "Little Steel" companies, which had pressed U.S. Steel's president, Benjamin Fairless, to stiffen his negotiating position. Managers of the smaller companies in particular seemed determined to win a guarantee from the federal government that any increase in steelworker compensation would be offset by a corresponding rise in steel prices.

This kind of government pledge, industry managers believed, would thereby shift the onus of inflationary price increases from them to the union and the Truman administration. In taking that stand, steel company executives also seem to have viewed themselves as spokesmen for corporation managers more generally.[49] But the Council of Economic Advisers (CEA) advised Truman in late 1951 that the enormous profits steel firms were earning meant that no large price increase was justified, essentially the same position as the union's. At the same time, U.S. Steel's managers were resistant to granting the union shop, at least right away, and executives at the smaller firms, much more so. The stage was thereby set for a labor–management confrontation of truly titanic proportions.[50]

The conflict began with managers' adoption of a rigid position in the early bargaining sessions, one that signaled their unwillingness to negotiate seriously over wages and benefits until they had received government assurances that a substantial price increase would be permitted. In their opening "offer," U.S. Steel's executives also demanded changes in the key Clause 2B of the master contract, which had codified the workplace balance of power achieved by the middle 1940s. Management now asked for the freedom to rearrange work schedules and job assignments and, as noted earlier, to reformulate incentive rates. These demands indicated, as Goldberg told USA Executive Board members in mid-December, that "the companies are not bargaining in any respect whatsoever."[51] Murray labeled the proposals "totalitarian" and unacceptable, and thus negotiations soon bogged down.[52]

With the contract expiration date of December 31 fast approaching, the federal government intervened to prevent a work stoppage that would interfere with steel production used in the war effort. Murray went along with Truman's request for a stay pending a recommendation by the WSB. In reaching that decision Murray was not worried so much about a Taft–Hartley injunction as about the consequences of a strike for soldiers fighting in Korea. Truman, Murray told the USA Executive Board, had told him over the telephone in late December that

> if the Communists and our United Nations people were unable to arrive at satisfactory understandings as of December 27th there would be a resumption of full-scale hostilities, and that that would undoubtedly lead to some discussions in the United Nations, and perhaps in Congress, that could very well lead to a declaration of war against China and . . . might lead to the development of other conditions in other parts of the world.[53]

Truman told Murray that a strike in such a context would create a "public clamor for Presidential intervention" so great as to be irresistible and that he, Truman, did not want that.[54]

Although Murray may well have believed that Truman exaggerated somewhat both the seriousness of the military situation and the likelihood of an adverse public response to a strike, he reluctantly endorsed Truman's request that the union defer a strike pending a ruling by the WSB. Goldberg's advice helped persuade Murray to follow that course. Goldberg argued that the USA should choose such an approach because the issue of steel managers' demands for price increases meant that the government would necessarily be involved in reaching a settlement. In his words, a strike made no sense until a WSB ruling because "there is no possibility—and the industry has made that very clear— . . . by strike action of getting the industry to do any bargaining. . . . Ultimately, strike or no strike, we have to go to the Wage Stabilization Board to make our case, and ultimately the Board will make a recommendation."[55]

Goldberg's remarks spoke volumes about the evolving nature of conflict between management and labor. During wartime, labor had lost the freedom to pursue its goals directly in contest with management. But that result did not trouble Goldberg, in large part because he was confident that a WSB ruling would back the union's key demands for a large pay raise and a union shop.[56]

The WSB's decision bore out Goldberg's confidence. The board's ruling on March 20, 1952, upheld the union with respect to both of its two key demands. And when Charles Wilson condemned the board's wage recommendation as too generous to labor, Truman responded with a reprimand, and Wilson then resigned.[57] The USA leadership, in contrast, endorsed the board's findings, whose principal elements had been adopted over the opposition of its management representatives, and set a strike deadline of April 8.

Industry managers, however, remained adamant. The recommended price increase they saw as too low, and the union shop, unacceptable, at least to executives at the smaller firms. Goldberg had had no illusions about the likely consequences of a WSB ruling favorable to the USA. He had told White House aide Harold Enarson two weeks before the board's ruling that "never in his experience had he seen the President, 'any President,' stand up against these pressures and that he just did not believe the Government of the United States was ready to take on the steel companies in a fight to the finish."[58]

But Truman, who agreed with the union about the fairness of the WSB recommendations, decided nonetheless to try pitting the power of the federal government against that of the steel industry's leaders. Rejecting a resort to the Taft–Hartley injunction as unfair to labor, he issued an executive order on April 8 "seizing" control of the mills. Murray expressed delight with Truman for both his action and his speech blaming the steel industry managers that accompanied it. As the USA chief noted in a board meeting held soon after the seizure was announced,

> In discussing the President's speech with the members of the Board I am quite sure you agree with me that no President in the history of our country was ever more forthright and honest in his treatment of a labor situation than was President Truman last Tuesday evening when he addressed the nation.[59]

The maneuver, however, was more symbolic than real. As Murray observed,

> There is no actual government operation of the industry. The industry today is operating like it did before Wednesday morning. The managers have complete control of the properties. They are receiving the benefits and profits of a lower wage structure and they will continue to operate them upon this basis in all likelihood until the picture is changed in some respects, and in what respects . . . I do not know.[60]

The most important consequences of the seizure order were to prevent workers from striking and to force both sides to begin bargaining seriously under the close supervision of Truman and his advisers.

Truman's special adviser for labor–management disputes, John Steelman, tried without much success to prod the two sides into reaching an agreement. At the heart of the argument, as Murray told the USA Executive Board, was "the question of prices, which definitely provides a roadblock against the possibility of agreement."[61] The steel industry's leaders contended that first they would need to know the size of the wage increase and have the government's assurance of support for steel price increases to offset it. Murray replied that he would make no offer on wages until the companies accepted a limitation on price increases independent of the new labor contract.

In essence, Murray and Goldberg were refusing to let management place the blame for inflationary price increases on the union. In their view, the lion's share of the increasing material benefits produced by the postwar New Deal should go into the pockets of workers, and not just enrich still further the industry's managers and stockholders. As long as managers went along, further price increases were unnecessary, and those that managers did impose resulted from their own greed.[62]

The managers disagreed, contending that greater profits were needed to build new and maintain existing steel plants and because they viewed the rewards flowing from increasing productivity as belonging to them and the stockholders. Although the union did have the power to win higher wages, managers during the 1950s generally could pass along the increased cost to steel consumers in the form of higher prices.

This dispute over the proper distribution of the fruits of postwar abundance lay at the heart of the 1952 confrontation in steel. The discussions held at the White House under Steelman's guidance were, as a result, tense and often angry. At one point, the minutes reveal,

> Mr. Murray and Mr. Randall [president of Inland Steel] engaged in a very acrimonious discussion, with Mr. Randall screaming "make us an offer" and Mr. Murray trying to explain why he couldn't. After about five minutes Mr. Murray finally challenged Mr. Randall to debate the issue before his employees which Mr. Randall accepted but then hastily subsided.[63]

U.S. Steel managers also remained adamant in their demands for changes in the work rules clause, and the smaller companies executives refused to budge on their opposition to the union shop. Management's stands in these areas may have been based in part on fears that the existing work rules clause and increased union security would encourage the USA to seek more control over the workplace than executives had conceded in the mid-1940s or would at least hamper steel managers in their efforts to replace skilled workers with new machinery.

The steel executives' recent decisions to build new plants in response to government pressure for more steel production had led to thorny debates about the kinds of technology to be used in operating them. Steel industry managers sought wherever possible to replace labor with machines, thereby lowering wage costs and weakening the union, a strategy that in the long run could bring even lower labor costs.[64]

The union opposed such moves and looked to the work rules clause and the union shop as the bases for their authority in doing so. In essence, the Steelworkers were seeking to preserve and perpetuate the concessions they had obtained from management in the 1930s and 1940s, and management was seeking ways to erode them. Goldberg expressed the union's view of these issues by asking rhetorically,

> Do we quarrel with the legitimate rights of management? Does this Union say that we want to take over the operations traditionally performed by management? Of course not. We have said to them that we recognize the right of management to run the plants, to discipline for proper cause, subject to the provisions of our contract, and in other ways to administer management's proper rights and responsibilities. And yet you will read in your local newspapers as sure as the sun will rise tomorrow morning that this Union is interfering with the legitimate prerogatives of management.[65]

Goldberg's statement was at least a little disingenuous, however, for he neglected to point out what he meant by legitimate managerial prerogatives.

In his mind, they were what remained of managerial authority after the concessions made to workers in the 1930s and 1940s. But in another sense Goldberg was right, because the USA was not pressing for more control than it had won during that earlier time. The rank and file's allegiance to the union was premised on its ability to protect those gains, and the USA leadership clearly understood that fact. For that reason, Murray and his colleagues spoke of these managerial demands as efforts to destroy the union.[66]

Steel managers, however, gained sympathy for their position from some key members of the Truman administration. Murray had no illusions about the reliability of many top advisers to Truman. He grimly told the USA Executive Board:

> We have found, as a result of our discussions with many people inside and outside Government in Washington, that our enemies are not necessarily confined to the leaders of the Industry. . . . [Commerce Secretary] Sawyer, of course, is an enemy. Lovett, the head of the Defense Department, is an enemy. Fleischmann, the head of the National Production Authority, is an enemy. Snyder, the Secretary of the . . . Treasury, is an enemy. [Charles] Wilson has gotten out. He was and is an enemy.[67]

Murray's long list testified to his understanding that the government, though more supportive of labor than the employers themselves, was hardly a steadfast ally. Although he was publicly committed to strong support for Truman's administration, Murray understood the limits of labor's ability to gain assistance from it.[68]

Rather than give way, the steel managers, led by those at the smaller and more intransigent companies, embarked instead on an expensive public relations campaign aimed at winning public approval for their position. Those efforts met with a good deal of success, in part because they were endorsed— Murray told the USA Executive Board with only slight exaggeration—by "95 per cent of the large newspapers, if not 99 per cent."[69]

Especially offensive to the newspaper publishers and their allies in the business community was Truman's claim of "inherent executive authority" to assume control over a vital industry. Steel executives fought the administration's action in the courts and within a month secured a Supreme Court ruling that set aside the seizure as unconstitutional. The USA's response was an immediate strike involving 560,000 workers in basic steel and iron ore mining, who walked off their jobs within a day of the Supreme Court ruling.

As in 1949, management remained unconvinced that workers cared enough about the issues in dispute to strike, and once again, it learned otherwise. And once again, government intervention ultimately helped produce a settlement favorable to labor.[70]

The strike went on for a month and a half before the parties finally reached an agreement. Fairless, Murray, and Truman made the final deal in a private meeting held at the White House on July 24. The impetus to settle came from Defense Secretary Robert A. Lovett, who had announced the day before that continuing the strike would mean "catastrophe" for the war effort. At the meeting, Fairless assented to the WSB's recommendations on wages without an explicit government promise of support for a price increase above the board's recommended level, and he also agreed to the union shop. At the same time Fairless abandoned the "demand" for changes in the work rules section of the contract, a bargaining position that he, at least, seems never to have fully supported. The conflict was largely over, although so, too, was the WSB's effective authority to make recommendations in labor–management disputes. After the terms of the new steel contract were made public, Congress simply refused to reenact the section of the law empowering the president to appoint an agency with such authority.[71]

The Truman administration's strong support for labor's key demands had greatly weakened its standing with both the other branches of government and the public more generally, but at the same time it had also helped win acceptance for the union shop at a time when managers were trying to slow labor's campaign for it. By the end of the steelworkers' 1952 strike, roughly half the one hundred biggest manufacturers had granted the union-shop clause, an achievement that helped strengthen labor's newly won status in the postwar order.

This victory had some potentially undemocratic implications, however, at least in the hands of unprincipled union leaders. The union-shop provision negotiated in steel allowed workers opposed to union membership periodic opportunities to opt out of it. USA Secretary-Treasurer David McDonald argued that workers should be obligated to inform the union, rather than management, of any desire to quit, after which his office would notify managers of the relevant companies to cease the union dues checkoff. In that way, McDonald told USA Executive Board members, "By the time I get around to telling the company, [the withdrawal period would have lapsed and] he is back in the union."[72] Goldberg objected to such dishonesty, and the result was a heated discussion, but the very fact it took place revealed how tenuously committed some USA leaders were to the principle of worker consent to union representation.[73]

Labor's success during the last three years of Truman's presidency was not confined to issues involving workplace governance. Despite managers' calls for a freeze on wages during the Korean War—a limit to be enforced, they demanded, by Taft–Hartley injunctions—union workers' wages generally kept pace with rising prices, thanks in part to the refusal of the Truman administration to use the Taft–Hartley weapon. And union workers continued to win increasing fringe benefits, including holiday pay and ever more generous pension provisions.

The relationship between organized labor and the Democratic administration during that period was not the "barren marriage" some have characterized it. Although the Truman administration never gave workers the Taft–Hartley repeal or the expanded welfare state they had been promised, those things were not Truman's to give. And in any event, labor did not come away empty-handed. The government's support for labor's collective bargaining demands and opposition to the Taft–Hartley injunction helped unions win more than they would have otherwise, and no one knew that better than the corporation managers.

By the spring of 1952, many of them would be working hard to reduce the government's intervention on labor's behalf. In so doing, they would be forced to accommodate themselves to labor's power and to cope with an emerging generation of younger labor leaders, changes that would reshape Goldberg's career in some very significant ways.[74]

III

Truman's policies had done much to alienate business managers, who looked hard during the last two years of his presidency for an appealing alternative. Conservative Republican Robert Taft appeared, on the surface at least, to be an ideal choice. He had written the Taft–Hartley Act, served as a forceful critic of the welfare state and federal government spending more generally, and showed acceptance of, but little enthusiasm for, the postwar balance of power between labor and management. In the end, however, most leaders of the largest corporations opposed his candidacy. Although some did so precisely because Taft remained hostile to the postwar New Deal they had negotiated with labor, more decisive perhaps was their sense that Taft could not be elected. The reason lay in the bitter hostility to him among American workers, who understood that Taft had the support of those businessmen most opposed to the new social contract. Labor's opposition to Taft's presidential aspirations thus helped tip the balance at the 1952 GOP convention against him and his supporters.[75]

Republicans chose instead by a narrow margin to nominate Dwight Eisenhower, the candidate of sophisticated business realists such as Thomas J. Watson Sr. of IBM. Even though the amiable general had never run for office before, he was not exactly new to politics. He had received consideration four years earlier from both Republicans, who saw a popular war hero as a possible means of regaining the White House, and liberal Democrats, who were seeking an alternative to Truman. In the end, however, Ike's support for an accord with labor had driven away GOP conservatives, and his lack of enthusiasm for campaigning deterred him from making a bid for the Democratic nomination.

In 1952, however, Eisenhower felt differently, and so did many Republican Party leaders. Desperately anxious both to end their twenty years in the political wilderness and to reduce the government's intervention on labor's behalf, those Republicans who argued for explicitly endorsing the postwar New Deal finally prevailed over the party's more conservative faction. On July 11, 1952, in the face of bitter and anguished opposition from the Taft forces, the Republican National Convention nominated Eisenhower, thereby handing over control of the party to the business realists who had recruited him. For the next four years, those self-styled "modern Republicans" would enjoy undisputed dominance in the party, and the postwar New Deal, its period of broadest elite support.[76]

Labor made its influence felt more directly at the Democratic Party's 1952 national convention. At that meeting, union support helped nominate the man who was probably the strongest of the potential candidates, Illinois governor Adlai Stevenson. Goldberg's old friend was persuaded, despite misgivings that Eisenhower could not be beaten, to accept the Democratic nomination. Although Goldberg had had some reservations about Stevenson's candidacy for governor in 1948, he strongly supported his nomination for president in 1952, out of respect for his abilities and a belief that he, unlike the other contenders, had at least a chance against the popular Eisenhower.[77]

While UAW Chief Walter Reuther backed the former U.S. ambassador to the Soviet Union and Marshall Plan administrator W. Averell Harriman, Goldberg, Murray, and most other CIO union chiefs ultimately supported Stevenson. Unlike Harriman, a wooden public speaker, Stevenson had struck them as an articulate defender of the postwar New Deal when he addressed the CIO convention in 1950. That speech had drawn a rave review in the CIO press, and Stevenson's welcoming address at the 1952 Democratic convention helped cement an already favorable impression among CIO leaders.

And while Harriman was marginally more identified with social democratic ideas than Stevenson was, Goldberg believed that in 1952 the latter better reflected what a majority of voters wanted. For those reasons he had promoted his friend's reputation among his labor associates but did not play a major role at the convention itself. Distracted by the steel negotiations, which were not concluded until the day before Stevenson was nominated, Goldberg was absent from Chicago during the crucial early balloting. He did, however, urge labor leaders there to support a Stevenson draft, and labor's backing played an important part in bringing about his nomination.[78]

The CIO leadership, with some prodding from their general counsel, strongly supported Stevenson and permitted as well the selection of his running mate, Alabama senator John Sparkman. Sparkman, unlike virtually all other leading southern Democrats, had made himself acceptable to labor by recanting his support for Taft–Hartley after the 1948 election. In the spring of 1949, he was one of only three Senate Democrats to change his vote on the issue, thereby qualifying for a place on the national ticket three years later. As Goldberg later explained, "At that time labor had the power to veto a Democratic nominee . . . and they used it."[79] As in 1944, when labor's opposition to James Byrnes helped eliminate him from contention for the job of Roosevelt's running mate and successor, so again in 1952 did labor succeed in blocking the selection of an antilabor vice-presidential nominee. The resulting ticket, though behind in the polls throughout the campaign, was a popular one with the voters, and if Eisenhower emerged as a Taftite in the fall, labor leaders had secured what they saw as a winning alternative.[80]

This strategy maintained the pressure on the Republicans to stick with their "new look," which they did. Stevenson, as a result, never really had a chance. The basic problems with Stevenson's liberalism and his campaign were that he could not persuade most workers either that Eisenhower's candidacy posed any real danger to the postwar order or that he, Stevenson, would defend their interests effectively in the event such a threat should materialize. And perhaps some workers may have reasoned that the New Deal would be safest as long as the leaders of the more conservative party strongly supported it.

Stevenson was handicapped, too, by a circle of advisers who neither understood working-class voters nor knew how to mobilize them as Truman had done four years earlier. His chief aides, William McCormick Blair Jr. and Carl McGowan, had, like Stevenson, spent their lives in an upper-class world far removed from workers. As a consequence, they had little sense of how to address workers' specific needs and perhaps no great interest in doing so. Goldberg, who tried to offer advice to Stevenson during the campaign, later described that situation as follows: "I thought Adlai did not pick realistic, knowledgeable people, but I didn't interfere. . . . They're nice people . . . but a little too fancy for my taste."[81]

Labor's expectations for the Democratic ticket remained low, and their opinion of Eisenhower, fairly high, which all but ensured Stevenson's defeat. Discussions about the two candidates in USA and CIO Executive Board meetings signaled how even the truncated left wing of the labor movement by then viewed the election. When Eisenhower hinted shortly before the GOP convention that he might have used a Taft–Hartley injunction to stop the 1952 steel strike, Murray told the USA Executive Board that

> I am quite sure if the General knew the facts — at least I hope if he knew the facts — and he had mingled with you people and been around to see what was going on and had he had a chance to participate in these conferences and see what it is that this union has done to win peaceable agreement out of this industry, he might have changed his mind.[82]

Eisenhower's choice of California Senator Richard Nixon as his running mate disturbed labor leaders, but not enough to rouse them greatly. CIO PAC director, Jack Kroll, tried, nonetheless, to point out that there was a potential risk. He told the CIO Executive Board that "the great danger is a man like Nixon. Those of you who come from California know Nixon. . . . The campaign he conducted in 1950 was a most vicious campaign, as vicious a campaign as I ever witnessed among all campaigns."[83]

The unimportance of the vice-presidency persuaded most union leaders, however, that the Nixon selection did not really matter very much, especially in view of the warm public response to Eisenhower, which suggested that the Republicans were sure to win anyway. Even Kroll was forced to admit in August that "the General has been a public idol up to three or four months ago."[84] By the middle of October, David McDonald was reduced to urging the USA leadership to work for a Stevenson victory, with the faint words that "the possibility . . . is certainly not a hopeless one."[85]

In the end, however, that is just what the election proved to be for Stevenson and his supporters. But if they suffered on election night, workers and their leaders were much less distressed, and with good reason. Although the Republicans had established control of both Congress and the White House simultaneously for the first time since 1930, the program of the GOP's dominant faction by then differed only marginally from that of its Democratic opponents. The postwar New Deal would continue undisturbed.[86]

It would do so, though, with a changing cast of leading characters. Shortly after the election that ousted the Democrats, the presidents of both labor federations died suddenly. For the AFL, the death of William Green opened the way for Secretary-Treasurer George Meany to assume the federation's presidency. Meany, a Bronx plumber of Irish Catholic origins, was, like Goldberg, an organization man who had spent most of his career in labor as a lobbyist, public relations expert, and broker among the AFL's various factions. Meany had been the AFL's permanent representative on the National War Labor Board during World War II and understood more clearly than older AFL leaders how government had helped unions grow during the conflict. Even more important was the difference in the way the new AFL president thought about economics and the government's role in maintaining prosperity. Although Green had steadfastly opposed Keynesian ideas, Meany embraced government stimulation of the economy to maintain consumer purchasing power. In keeping with AFL tradition, however, Meany remained wary of giving the state a large role in supervising labor–management relations. Despite that difference, Meany, unlike Green, strongly supported political action of the sort pioneered by the CIO's PAC.[87]

Meany differed from Green and some of the older AFL leaders in other ways as well. Like Goldberg, Meany had a close relationship with "labor priest" George Higgins and favored the new social contract with employers. Meany was also a staunch anticommunist from the beginning and was at least marginally more interested in fighting racial discrimination than Green had been. That combination of beliefs was not very different from those held by Goldberg and others at the center of the CIO. For that reason, Meany, unlike Green, would work hard for labor unity. He saw the achievement of that goal as essential to preserving labor's gains of the past two decades.

In pursuing those objectives, however, Meany remained hampered by his limited authority as AFL president. The heads of the AFL affiliates had not invested Meany's office or the federation's national bureaucracy with much power, preferring instead to keep it in their own hands. But if Meany held formally only the role of chief clerk for the AFL, he would prove fairly adept in prodding its real leaders to make peace with the heads of the other federation.[88]

Murray's death, which came within a few weeks of Green's, meant even more to the CIO, because its national office had exercised real power over federation affairs, influence that had grown steadily over the previous decade. His passing deprived the CIO of a leader who enjoyed strong support from all the remaining CIO affiliates. Murray had been able to achieve that kind of backing precisely because he sympathized deeply with those who wanted to reshape the nation's political economy still further while at the same time understanding that managerial power precluded bold steps in that direction. To Murray, workers thus faced some hard choices in postwar America, which toward the end of his life he sometimes described in very bleak terms.[89]

The only solution Murray offered to the dilemma faced by workers was the one many leading liberals found themselves left with: placing one's faith in the belief that corporation managers would act responsibly. Following the signing of the 1952 master contract with U.S. Steel, Murray announced to the board that he and Benjamin Fairless were going to undertake joint factory tours to promote understanding of, and support for, a genuine accord between workers and managers in the steel industry. In reaching those goals, Murray told the board members, "More important than even the language of contracts is faith, faith in each other, elimination, so far as we possibly can, of suspicion that one of the two groups is trying to take advantage of the other."[90]

Like so many other New Deal liberals of his generation, Murray appears to have reached that conclusion only after he became convinced of the futility of more confrontational strategies for bettering workers' lives. And if that answer seemed inadequate to some more radical workers and middle-class liberals, Murray, at least, could take comfort in the knowledge that he had spent most of his sixty-five years trying to improve conditions for workers and had reached that conclusion only out of a diminished sense of what was possible.[91]

With his demise the CIO lost a leader who balanced his enthusiasm for social democratic ideas with a hardheaded grasp of labor's place in the postwar order. Perhaps even more important, the federation would no longer have as its president someone who truly felt at home in working-class neighborhoods and keenly understood the impediments that both managerial power and certain aspects of working-class culture—such as racism, ethnic prejudice, and religiosity—posed to labor's quest for more ambitious social goals.[92]

Murray's successor as CIO president, UAW chief Walter Reuther, lacked the former's rapport with workers. Reuther felt more at ease in meetings with labor intellectuals and liberal academics than he did in a working-class tavern or at a sports event. His Protestantism, too, set him apart from many in the heavily Catholic CIO. And Reuther's manner was often intense to the point of humorless and reserved, qualities that other union leaders and workers found off-putting. Goldberg later characterized the difference between Murray and his successor in this way:

> Walter was an exceptionally bright and able labor leader, and he did well by his union. He also was a symbol of integrity which is a good thing to have in the labor movement. He was, unlike Murray, not a natural leader of a big movement to which workers would respond. [The] Auto Workers [Union] . . . [had] a kind of an intellectual milieu . . . at that time. . . . The average worker identifies more with a person like Phil Murray or John Lewis.

Murray used to sit on his porch on Sunday, he never moved out of Pittsburgh, anybody could come and talk to him. They take more to that type.[93]

Reuther also got along very poorly with David McDonald, whom the USA
Executive Board quickly chose as the Steelworkers' new president. This development created real problems for Goldberg, who in his dual role as CIO
and Steelworkers general counsel would henceforth have to serve both men.

Their mutual antagonism stemmed from a disagreement over the proper
agenda for labor in the postwar period. Reuther and the other UAW leaders
favored a more ambitious set of objectives, focusing in particular on winning
more power for labor in the operation of business organizations. More generally, the autoworkers union sought to renegotiate the postwar New Deal in
ways that increased labor's power vis-à-vis management. This was, however,
at most an influential minority position in the overall labor movement and
even in the CIO itself. Although Reuther and the UAW were, and still are,
typically depicted as having been at the center of the postwar order, they in
fact stood at the outer edge of labor liberalism.[94]

In contrast, Goldberg saw Reuther as unrealistic. Goldberg viewed business leaders as having assented to the postwar New Deal on the understanding that labor would give up efforts to restructure power relations in the
workplace still further. In his mind, the more constructive course for labor
was to shore up support for the postwar bargain in the business community.
By persuading that faction of American business still militantly hostile to the
new social contract of its benefits, unions could, Goldberg believed, secure
the gains workers had made during the 1930s and early 1940s. To press for
more managerial concessions, he feared, would only increase the risk that
business leaders who supported the New Deal would turn against it, thereby
imperiling its continuation. McDonald shared Goldberg's objectives, although less out of a sense that gaining greater control over the operation of
business enterprises was impossible than because McDonald viewed that goal
as undesirable.[95]

But after Murray's death, McDonald was not the real leader of the union, in
terms of its strategic policy. The delegation of authority to Goldberg begun
under Murray continued under McDonald's tenure as USA president and
even increased. McDonald lacked the skills and intellect needed to function as
the chief strategist for a major industrial union. His forte was in the area of
public relations, for which he had real talent. Before joining the Steelworkers
as Murray's personal secretary, McDonald had, in fact, given a great deal of
thought to becoming a Hollywood actor. He had decided to stick with the
labor movement, however, and was wise enough, once he became USA president, to let Goldberg do most of the key negotiating and decision making.

McDonald's dependence on Goldberg only grew with time, a fact that
irritated McDonald even as he understood how much he owed to his general
counsel. Both a drinking problem that grew worse over the years and increasing rank-and-file hostility to McDonald fed his growing reliance on Goldberg. Although McDonald occasionally indulged in childish maneuvers in-

tended to show who was at least formally in charge, he understood his obligation to Goldberg and showered large bonuses on him in return, which was McDonald's characteristic way of both rewarding an ally and securing his loyalty.[96]

For his part, Goldberg had been uneasy about McDonald for years, as Murray had been, because of the secretary-treasurer's fondness for rough, dishonest, and undemocratic practices in administering the union shop, supervising union elections, collecting dues, and spending USA funds. In the last year of Murray's life, McDonald also had begun jockeying for the chance to succeed him, which infuriated Murray and some other members of the USA Executive Board. They, in fact, had voted to strip McDonald of much of his authority in a meeting held only six months before Murray died, transferring certain key functions from the secretary-treasurer's office to that of the USA president. At the same time they adopted resolutions calling for outside auditors to review the union's finances regularly and for an outside organization to monitor all elections of Steelworkers' officers.

The USA convention, which was meeting concurrently, adopted these constitutional changes. Murray and the board no doubt conceived of the move as a stopgap measure, which could, if necessary, be followed by replacing McDonald and then restoring to his office its old authority. The maneuver backfired, however, when Murray died unexpectedly and McDonald succeeded him as acting president, in effect capturing control of the union's administrative machinery. McDonald had chosen not to fight Murray's move for precisely that reason, telling one of his allies that "the chances are he [Murray] won't live the year out. That's the reason why I took it. I'll inherit everything."[97]

So he did, but only by ceding much of the real authority to Goldberg and the board. Goldberg made clear at the first USA Executive Board meeting held after Murray's death that McDonald would enjoy a different relationship with his general counsel than Murray had. One measure of the difference was in Goldberg's decision to give McDonald an unsolicited, undated letter of resignation that he was free to accept at any time. The implication was clear: If McDonald found Goldberg's actions displeasing, the former could go along quietly or accept the loss of Goldberg's services.

The result of these negotiations was to elect a USA president who, though heavily promoted in the media and very visible to the public, lacked the ability to establish strategic goals and follow them up. McDonald's rather obvious limitations thus led some of his contemporaries, as well as students of the period during which he served as USA president, to underestimate the Steelworkers' leading role in the labor movement and in defining the terms of the labor–management relationship.[98]

The hostility between McDonald and Reuther and the differences in goals between the two factions they represented were reflected in the election that elevated Reuther to the CIO presidency and in other, related, ways. Reuther prevailed, but by a less-than-comfortable margin over the aging Allan Haywood, who was strongly supported by the USA and its allies in the federation.

Immediately afterward, Haywood was reelected CIO executive vice-president, a pairing that neatly reflected the dominant roles played in the federation by the UAW and USA.

Soon after Reuther's victory, the USA, which owned the building in Washington that housed the federation's headquarters, signaled its feelings toward the new CIO president by informing him that the rental "subsidy" would no longer be continued. McDonald and Goldberg gave Reuther and his UAW colleagues the choice of buying the building at a price that included a substantial profit for the USA or accepting a large increase in rent. The UAW leadership decided to purchase the building, a move that symbolized Reuther's effort to assume control over the federation it housed.[99]

The Reuther–McDonald rift also made necessary some changes in Goldberg's formal relations with the two organizations they headed. Reuther appears to have precipitated those developments at the 1952 CIO convention held immediately after Murray's death. Goldberg and Reuther quarreled there, with the latter apparently insisting that henceforth the CIO general counsel would owe his primary allegiance to the federation and not to any one union. Although Reuther soon backed down, no doubt feeling he needed Goldberg's support to function effectively as CIO chief, Goldberg responded by moving out of the federation's headquarters in Washington. The move had been planned for some time, precisely because he had expected problems once Reuther succeeded Murray as CIO president.

Goldberg promptly opened his own law office nearby, from which he thereafter handled all of his labor practice. He then negotiated a new arrangement with Reuther, under which he, Goldberg, would continue to run the CIO legal department from his own office. To preserve the impression of a presence at the CIO building, Goldberg ordered a telephone tie line installed between it and his firm. Most outside callers never even knew that he had left. In the most important ways, he never had. Willing to serve both the CIO and the USA, Goldberg had decided that establishing some formal independence from both would help him do that most easily.

For his part, Reuther signaled his understanding of Goldberg's leading role in the USA and the federation by agreeing, at his suggestion, to pay him an annual retainer of $25,000 plus expenses, more than any CIO officer, Reuther included, ever received. And so Murray's demise, instead of weakening Goldberg's ties to his principal labor clients, served to demonstrate how deeply they had come to rely on him.[100]

IV

With those changes, Goldberg entered a new period in his association with the CIO and USA. By the spring of 1953 he found himself invested with even more influence and responsibility than he had possessed during Murray's tenure. Over the next two years he continued to divide his energies between defensive efforts aimed at protecting the postwar New Deal from conservative attacks and initiatives intended to strengthen it and extend its reach. Chief among the former were continuing pressure on the federal government to abide by the terms of the Taft–Hartley agreement of 1949 and to insulate unions from the rampant anticommunist hysteria.

Eisenhower as a candidate had promised organized labor some revisions to the Taft–Hartley law, but his advisers disagreed vehemently over how far to go in keeping that pledge. Those at the center of the administration effort appear to have envisaged such amendments as a way of dividing still further the AFL and CIO, thereby weakening labor's standing in Washington and the workplace. In keeping with that objective, Eisenhower's aides had urged him to select plumber's union chief Martin Durkin as the new secretary of labor.

Durkin had been chosen precisely because he came out of the building trades section of the AFL, the faction in it most sympathetic to the Eisenhower administration and least friendly to the CIO. He prepared a set of amendments that reflected the AFL leadership's specific concerns. Durkin's "reform" package included some proposed changes in the law that would have made AFL raids on CIO unions easier, especially in the building trades area. His list also contained some things that leaders of both federations wanted badly, such as repealing Taft–Hartley's Section 14(b), which empowered state legislatures to pass so-called right-to-work laws, eliminating the act's ban on secondary boycotts, and curtailing state courts' jurisdiction in labor disputes.[101]

The AFL signaled its intention to use the amending process to its own advantage by refusing to cooperate with the CIO in drawing up a list of acceptable changes and lobbying for their enactment. That had disastrous consequences for both sides. Meany rebuffed Reuther's request for consultation, no doubt believing that the AFL would do better without his help, and so the CIO had no choice but to act alone. Soon after the election, Goldberg had called a two-day meeting in Washington of the chief lawyers for all CIO affiliates, who together worked out a list of acceptable amendments. The most important of their proposed changes dealt with the national emergency disputes provision and the role of the government in regulating labor–management disputes more generally.

Goldberg saw the change in administration as potentially dangerous to the labor movement, because Eisenhower and his aides might be more apt to use the labor injunction than Truman had been. Thus he argued that the CIO Executive Board should support an amendment that banned the injunction and authorized Congress to intervene on a case-by-case basis in any labor–management dispute that created a genuine national emergency.[102]

He coupled the two ideas together because he feared that to repeal the injunction provision without offering some other mechanism for resolving national emergency disputes might backfire. Goldberg told the CIO Executive Board that Truman's attorney general, Tom Clark, had issued an advisory opinion in 1949 indicating that in the absence of any national emergency disputes provision, the president had inherent authority to issue an injunction. Goldberg told the board that "I think that Clark was clearly wrong.

. . . [but] that isn't the point. We have an Attorney General opinion, and we cannot take the danger of that situation."[103] Although the CIO could have challenged any such injunction in the courts, the risk appeared too great. Truman's decision, made almost immediately after Clark issued the opinion, to appoint him to the Supreme Court had not helped either, for that body would ultimately decide the issue. Even though Clark could be expected to recuse himself, his influence on his fellow justices could not be ignored. The discussion on this point revealed how completely labor had become entangled in the web of federal government regulation, a problem that appeared even more serious now that the Republicans had won control of the White House and Congress.[104]

For that reason, Goldberg argued that the CIO ought to press for less government intervention more generally in negotiations between labor and management. Other alternatives, such as endorsing more use of boards, substituting for the injunction an amendment mandating "cooling off" periods, or proposing that the president be given an assortment of tools to use, he rejected as too dangerous in the hands of anyone other than a president decidedly sympathetic to labor. As Goldberg told the board, "As practical people we are confronted with a new administration. We don't know what kind of fact-finding we are going to have. We don't know who the fact-finders will be. So it seemed in our general discussion pretty dangerous to say we would invite fact-finding at the present time."[105]

As for the notion of giving the government the option of choosing among the injunction, seizure, or fact-finding boards, Goldberg reminded the board members of the same basic problem: "Well, again, we are up against some reality. We know who is going to exercise the choice now, and we came to the conclusion that perhaps in this arsenal the weapon that would be selected is the one that we would not like. So that did not seem feasible."[106]

Thus the CIO pressed for its own alternative while at the same time suggesting some other amendments to remove from the law those provisions that most hampered union organizing, such as the so-called free-speech provision and the ban on secondary boycotts. At the same time, the federation sought greater statutory protection from AFL raiding, essentially the opposite of Durkin's proposal in that area. Although not expecting to win enactment of that package, the CIO nonetheless endeavored to formulate a position that favored something, rather than simply opposing all administration bills.

Goldberg testified before the Senate Labor Committee on March 30 in favor of those ideas and added a sixty-five-page list of objections to the current law combined with suggested changes, but to no avail. As expected, senior members of the administration and congressional leaders simply ignored the CIO's program.[107]

The AFL fared little better. Business managers balked at giving even the AFL as many changes to the act as its leaders desired, which prompted Eisenhower and his advisers to backtrack on their own measure. A disgusted Durkin then quit, leaving the administration effort in disarray. The CIO leadership felt little distress over Durkin's departure. As David McDonald told the USA Executive Board once the story broke, "Mr. Durkin didn't ask us for our permission for him to take the job; Mr. Durkin didn't consult with us about these so-called 19 [Taft–Hartley revision] points. . . . We think that Mr. Durkin's . . . major points were directed more to the preservation of the AFL position on craft unions than anything else."[108]

Goldberg greeted Durkin's decision with relief, because even apart from Taft–Hartley, the appointment had made CIO communications with Eisenhower's administration quite difficult. Goldberg lacked confidence that information transmitted from the CIO through Durkin would remain secret from other AFL leaders, and thus as soon as the appointment had been announced, Goldberg began pressing for the designation of another aide in the White House to whom the CIO could report. The departure of Durkin as labor secretary therefore solved more than one CIO problem. Eisenhower, more aware by then of the difficulties created by appointing an AFL official, soon replaced him with James P. Mitchell, a sophisticated business realist with a background in personnel administration, whom union leaders from both federations liked, but an entire year had been lost in labor's campaign to win changes in Taft–Hartley.[109]

The administration's attempts to try again failed, though, because the CIO's leaders ultimately rejected the newly proposed amendments as simply favoring the AFL at their expense without eliminating those features of the law that impeded union organization and undermined the union shop. The administration's revised measure, now stripped of the changes in Section 14(b), as well as the state courts' jurisdiction and secondary boycott provisions, would, among other things, have permitted building trades unions to organize more workers in industrial settings, a move aimed at weakening CIO affiliates. At the same time the bill contained provisions intended to aid employers who sought to resist union-organizing campaigns.

In summarizing the administration bill's provisions before the CIO Executive Board, Goldberg said that the "amendments do not carry out the promises of President Eisenhower to restore justice and fairness to our Labor–Management Relations law."[110] The CIO's leaders instead pressed for the change in the law that mattered most to them, the national emergency disputes provision. But their efforts to outlaw use of the labor injunction in such instances failed miserably.

On April 6, 1954, the House Labor Committee rejected that proposal by a vote of twenty to seven. As Goldberg told the USA Executive Board that same day, the vote "pretty well illustrates our strength in the House Labor Committee."[111] Viewing as hopeless any effort to win amendments that would aid organized labor as a whole, the CIO pressed Congress hard to do nothing, preferring that to the administration's bill. The result was deadlock, which left the statute intact but did not mean the end of administration efforts to divide the labor movement.[112]

Following the collapse of efforts in Congress to amend Taft–Hartley, the administration's attention shifted to the NLRB. By 1954, Eisenhower had replaced most of its members with his own appointees. They in turn attempted to drive a wedge between the AFL and CIO by limiting a 1948 board decision that had blocked AFL unions from seeking to organize workers who already belonged to an industrial union. Legalizing *craft severance*, as it was called, would have weakened the CIO, which would have had to expend energy protecting its affiliates from AFL raids.

The NLRB's 1954 ruling in the *American Potash* case allowed such activity henceforth, but only in those industries to which the earlier board ruling had not been applied. The industries protected by earlier decisions—basic steel, basic aluminum, wet milling, and automobile assembly—included those of greatest concern to the two biggest CIO affiliates, but the NLRB ruling boded ill for the other industrial unions and for future organizing drives in newly emerging industrial sectors. Goldberg therefore viewed the decision with deep concern and warned the CIO Executive Board of the potential implications:

> The American Potash case . . . is very serious for the CIO. If there is a resurgence towards craft separatism it now has the offhand approval of the Labor Board. . . .
>
> The Board is undertaking to do a policing job for the AFL, not for us. . . . and that is a very, very bad development.[113]

Goldberg urged the CIO Executive Board to work harder at blocking Eisenhower's unsympathetic nominees to the NLRB, whom he saw as the source of the problem.[114]

But if the labor movement failed in its efforts to secure the Taft–Hartley amendments it wanted, labor prevailed with respect to its most important goal. The Eisenhower administration, at least for its first six years, intervened only rarely in disputes between labor and management. Although the government no longer did so on labor's behalf, as it had under Truman, neither did it do so against workers' organizations. This move to reduce government intervention had been supported by both labor and the industrial relations experts who had usually staffed Truman's fact-finding boards. For that reason, Eisenhower's policy cannot be seen simply as a victory for the business managers. Rather, the policy, which the administration's aides tended to describe as one of government "neutrality," reflected a compromise that satisfied neither side fully.[115]

The entire Taft–Hartley–NLRB episode reflected labor's embattled position in the early 1950s, and another problem, McCarthyism, illuminated that plight even more. When the antiradical hysteria first emerged during 1948, Goldberg had shared the concern of many New Deal liberals about what they themselves sometimes called "the communist conspiracy." The focus of that concern was, of course, Soviet espionage, a problem that grew in seriousness as relations between the United States and the Soviet Union steadily worsened in the late 1940s. Ferreting out such spies, from U.S. government offices in particular, was, of course, an appropriate precaution, but the way in which the Truman administration carried out that policy raised deeply troubling questions about the rights of those accused. Lawyers were especially aware of such issues, which confronted Goldberg as soon as he assumed his post as CIO general counsel.[116]

In fact, the first remarks he ever made at a CIO Executive Board meeting dealt with how labor should respond to Truman's proposed loyalty program. Although limited to federal government employees, the program was the first in a series of government initiatives that, though intended to secure the postwar order against Soviet spies and right-wing attacks, also had the effect of silencing those on the left who opposed the emerging social contract. Goldberg called on CIO chiefs in late 1948 to support the loyalty program while urging that it be amended so as to accord some modicum of procedural due process to government employees accused of espionage. He did so, characteristically, because he saw the creation of some such program as both necessary and inevitable. Labor, he believed, should therefore not waste its energy opposing Truman on the issue but instead work constructively to see that the new program did not go too far.

When CIO radical Abe Flaxer, who headed the Public Workers union, had objected to federation support for any loyalty program, an exasperated Van Bittner revealed in his reply the trend of liberals' thinking about the issue:

> I am tired of going before Congressional committees, when you know you are not going to get the kind of thing that you want, and especially on a question of this kind, and some Congressman asks, "Well, what would you do? What have you got as a substitute for what we are doing?" All I can say is that the man is entitled to a fair trial. The Government of the United States is going to, whether we like it or whether we don't, . . . have some rights as to whether a man in the employ of the Government is loyal to the Government. You cannot get away from that fact.[117]

Such reasoning was typical of New Deal liberals in this period. The basic problem in going along with such legislation, and indeed in sharing some of the exaggerated fears about communist activity on which such laws were based, was that liberals and labor leaders thereby did much, however unintentionally, to reinforce the antiradical hysteria.

Goldberg, and the CIO at his urging, supported the loyalty program and subsequent measures, most notably the McCarran Act of 1950. The latter required "communist and communist-front" organizations to register with the Subversive Activities Control Board, which could then investigate them and have arrested anyone suspected of subversive activity during a time of national emergency. Although labor had initially supported the McCarran bill on the understanding that it would contain procedural safeguards, the measure as enacted lacked such amendments.

When right-wing Senator John M. Butler of Maryland, who had been elected in 1950 with crucial support from McCarthy, introduced a bill four years later to outlaw "communist-infiltrated" labor organizations, the CIO repeated its earlier mistake. The federation supported a substitute version of the bill drafted by the liberal Democratic senator from Minnesota, Hubert Humphrey. In the end, however, the Communist Control Act of 1954 passed with the provisions Butler had desired. Although the measure also included a presumption in favor of AFL and CIO affiliates, the episode revealed liberals' limited success in restricting the reach of such laws by participating in their enactment.[118]

The CIO's drive to expel unions controlled by radicals, whom Murray, Reuther, Goldberg, and others denounced as "communists," also had the effect of fueling the Red scare of the late 1940s and 1950s, as did their subsequent efforts to raid the ousted affiliates. And when Senator Joseph McCarthy entered and assumed the leading role in the hysteria that now bears his name, those liberals who opposed him did so in ways that once again tended to strengthen, though often unwittingly, the forces of repression.

Seeing McCarthy as too extreme, liberals turned for more responsible leadership of the anticommunist crusade to FBI chief J. Edgar Hoover. By urging that Hoover be given the principal authority to investigate communist activity in the United States, Goldberg, like other liberals, hoped to cut off McCarthy and the members of Congress who chaired the House Un-American Activities Committee and the Senate Judiciary Committee's Internal Security Subcommittee. But Hoover, an archconservative, was afflicted with his own phobias about the alleged subversive threat, and the result of liberals' support for him was once again to encourage government repression of dissidents, at grievous cost to many innocent men and women.[119]

Unlike many other liberals, Goldberg had a special reason for acquiescing, at least in part, in the antiradical witch-hunt. As CIO general counsel he worried that the labor movement would fall victim to the McCarthyites. For that reason, too, he supported what he called "responsible" efforts to expel those union members with a Communist Party connection, as well as labor backing for government efforts to deal with Soviet espionage. In those ways he hoped to keep the campaign of repression within certain boundaries and to demonstrate to the public both that labor was committed to fighting leftists in its own ranks who were trying to undermine the postwar New Deal and that labor opposed genuine Soviet spies.

Such a position would, Goldberg reasoned, strengthen unions' legitimacy in the eyes of the public and the new social contract more generally. Typical of his thinking was his advice to the USA Executive Board that steelworkers be discouraged from invoking the Fifth Amendment when testifying before congressional committees:

> We don't want to serve the interests of the Communists in any policy we adopt. We know there are Communists who are conducting a campaign to encourage people unnecessarily to invoke the Fifth Amendment, and many innocent, misguided people who have no legitimate need to be concerned have been encouraged to invoke the Fifth Amendment unnecessarily. . . .
>
> I have watched some of these hearings, and I share your views about the type of hearings that have been conducted. But . . . I have the deep seated feeling that people have been encouraged to answer that way by the communists because it will protect them . . . when they have concern in invoking the Fifth Amendment.[120]

That position, though perhaps the most practical one in protecting workers and union officials from persecution, nonetheless reveals the extent to which Goldberg, like other leading liberals of his day, accepted some of the basic assumptions that underlay the McCarthy inquisition, most notably the view that even in the mid-1950s the American Communist Party posed a serious threat in the United States to the postwar order.[121]

In addition to counseling unionists about their testimony, Goldberg also did his best to shelter from Justice Department investigations those people he considered innocent. If the members of some union feared that an inquiry was planned, he would check with the department about the matter and find out what was going on. The effort largely succeeded in insulating CIO unions from government repression, but not, of course, the radicals by then outside the federation's ranks. In retrospect, the actions of labor union leaders and liberals appear to have endangered civil liberties and an open society even as they sought to protect them from their enemies on both right and left.[122]

By the middle of 1954, however, with McCarthy under investigation by his Senate colleagues and the worst of the hysteria behind them, the CIO leadership finally balked at going any further in the direction of accommodating the witch-hunters. The turning point came during a debate over whether to endorse a proposed wiretapping bill. The measure would have authorized the U.S. attorney general to tap the telephones of suspected subversives. Goldberg pressed the board to support a resolution condemning wiretapping but suggesting safeguards if Congress should proceed to enact such a statute. That equivocal approach proved too much for the CIO Executive Board, which voted sixteen to fifteen to oppose any wiretap law.

Maritime Union chief Joseph Curran captured the mood of the majority when he observed:

> I think it behooves the CIO to take a firm and forthright position. If it becomes necessary to compromise some place down the road, let's examine it at that time, but right now let's take a flat position—it's a dirty business, it is not designed for use in noble purposes. It is designed for use in all purposes and it can be used to destroy the labor movement and legitimate organizations in this country, and let's not kid ourselves.[123]

Increasingly confident that they could by then safely stand up to the federal government on this issue, CIO leaders opposed the wiretapping bill and supported the Senate's decision to condemn McCarthy in December 1954.

The CIO's decision to draw a line, however, came too late for many innocent people. Labor's essentially defensive struggle to protect the postwar New Deal had succeeded, but only at the high price of reinforcing an exaggerated sense of the threats to it posed by Soviet espionage and American leftists. The inquisition that fed off such paranoia damaged and sometimes even destroyed the lives of people who had done nothing more than voice their opposition to the containment policy or support for the socialist cause. Thus had labor contributed to achieving the outward appearance of what some have since celebrated as the postwar "consensus."[124]

The Taft–Hartley revision and McCarthyism experiences showed the defensive side of labor's struggle in the early 1950s to preserve its earlier gains, but labor achieved more than just that during those years. At the same time that it was fighting off those challenges, the labor movement was also taking positive steps to increase the number of workers who shared in the benefits of the postwar New Deal and to strengthen its acceptance. Goldberg, like George Meany, had come to see labor unity as a necessary prerequisite to further advances, and during 1953/54 both men pushed their respective federations in that direction. Despite the best efforts of the Eisenhower administration to divide the AFL and CIO, their leaders achieved by the end of 1954 an agreement to refrain from raiding each other's unions. The terms of the bargain had been formulated by Goldberg on behalf of the CIO and accepted by Meany without substantial revision.[125]

The no-raiding agreement itself had been modeled on an earlier CIO one that Goldberg had drawn up in 1951, in consultation with Walter Reuther, David McDonald, Joseph Curran, and Emil Rieve of the Textile Workers Union, to resolve jurisdictional disputes among CIO affiliates. The CIO agreement revealed Goldberg's fondness for arbitration, a hallmark of his generation of labor leader. Goldberg selected a leading figure in industrial relations circles, the former War Labor Board chairman George Taylor, to arbitrate CIO jurisdictional disputes, who in turn was followed in that job by Nathan Feinsinger, the former chairman of the Wage Stabilization Board.

The agreement Goldberg had worked out for the CIO established patterns that the later AFL–CIO pact would follow: an emphasis on preserving the status quo, adjudicating disputes in a formal, legalistic way, as well as giving the arbitrator a good deal of discretion. The CIO agreement also prefigured the AFL–CIO one in its ratification provisions: The accord became effective upon its acceptance by the executive board of each union, rather than at its convention. Like so many of Goldberg's other proposals, its effect was to shift the resolution of conflict away from the rank and file to forums open only to union leaders and arbitrators.[126]

At the time the CIO adopted its jurisdictional disputes agreement, at least some board members were aware that it might serve as a model for negotiating a pact with the AFL. Goldberg certainly thought in those terms. With the death of AFL president Green and the election of Meany, Goldberg became convinced that unity with the older house of labor had become a real possibility. The two federations established a joint committee to discuss the idea, which met for the first time on April 7, 1953.

To do the real work, the group established a subcommittee composed of Reuther, McDonald, and James Carey of the International Union of Electrical Workers (IUE) for the CIO and Meany, Secretary-Treasurer William Schnitzler, and Vice-President Mathew Woll for the AFL. The subcommittee's first act was to commission a statistical study of raiding over the past two years. The research staff reported that there had been about 2,400 raids in 1951/52, of which 1,245 had been followed by NLRB-supervised organizing elections. The CIO had taken the initiative in 704 cases and the AFL in 542, with a total of 366,470 workers involved. The result had been a net loss to the CIO of 8,373 and a gain to the AFL of 4,972, at a cost of approximately $1,000 per worker for organizing expenses. The study suggested that although raiding might benefit some affiliates in each federation, the two houses of labor derived no real advantage from the time and money spent in that area.[127]

At that point, Goldberg persuaded Reuther to let him draw up a proposed no-raiding agreement for discussion with the AFL leadership. A concrete proposal, he hoped, would focus what had hitherto been only meandering discussions in committee sessions. Goldberg's enthusiasm for unity stemmed from both a belief that raiding wasted labor's resources without benefiting the workers involved and because he saw a united labor movement as likely to win more from managers and the state than a divided one ever could, especially in view of the new administration's efforts to encourage still more feuding between the two labor federations. Goldberg also appears to have believed that the merger would force both the AFL and the UAW to move toward the middle position favored by the USA. In that way, the merger would strengthen labor's support both for limited state supervision of the postwar social contract and for leaving untouched any remaining managerial prerogatives. That was possible by then, he reasoned, because "ideological differences had disappeared" with the expulsion of the CIO radicals, especially in the area of foreign policy, and because the AFL showed growing support for Keynesian economic ideas and greater political action and an acceptance of some state supervision of labor–management relations. Thus a merger between the two federations, Goldberg believed, would strengthen both labor's own bargaining power as well as managerial support for the postwar New Deal.[128]

Goldberg's efforts to promote labor unity were complicated, however, by divisions within the two federations. The impetus for merger within the CIO did not come from either Reuther or the USA's nominal head, David McDonald. Reuther, the leading spokesman for the CIO minority that favored moving beyond the postwar social bargain, feared that unity would spell the end of those ambitions. In his first year as CIO president, Reuther sought to reinvigorate the federation, to expand the scope of its activities, and thereby to fashion it into an organization that would press for more concessions from managers and the state beyond what labor had won in the 1930s and 1940s. He proposed increasing PAC donations and activity, publishing a daily national labor newspaper, and creating radio and television programs intended to give labor a stronger and more independent voice in the mass media.[129]

The fate of those ideas, however, revealed how unrealistic Reuther had been in advocating them. The USA's leaders balked at contributing any more money to the PAC as long as Reuther continued to give voice to a labor agenda they saw as too ambitious. Instead, they voted to end the practice of subsidizing CIO affiliates that failed to contribute their PAC assessments. The money would be used instead to make contributions directly to candidates. In a thinly veiled reference to Reuther's UAW, David McDonald told the USA Executive Board:

> Other organizations affiliated with the CIO–PAC have down through the years reserved certain voluntary moneys, special accounts, so that they could make their private contributions to congressional and senatorial candidates. We haven't done that because we have always believed that all contributions should be made through the CIO–PAC. Despite our repeated protestations to that effect, our voice, even though we were carrying the PAC load, was not heeded. If that is the way it is to be, that is the way it is to be so far as we are concerned. If people are to get credit[,] let the United Steelworkers get credit as well as some other unions.[130]

Such hostility was not confined to McDonald. USA Executive Board member I. W. Abel, a cautious but hardworking and honest union official who served as the USA delegate to PAC, also voiced his opposition to Reuther's political program. Abel favored a more narrowly tailored agenda for the PAC that aimed at electing candidates pledged to support the postwar New Deal, rather than those who wanted to redefine it dramatically. He wanted more emphasis, too, on issues of immediate concern to unions, such as improving the unemployment compensation system, which he saw as a realistic objective. Frustrated with Reuther's more ambitious schemes, Abel told the USA Executive Board in January 1954:

> During the past year I have attended a number of [PAC Steering Committee] meetings, the most recent one a two-day meeting in Atlantic City, attended by both Vice President Thimmes and myself. I have from time to time reported to President McDonald that, in my opinion, these meetings are much more juvenile than were our political activities back in the very early days under the Non-Partisan League. I think we have gone backward rather than forward. The meetings have been an entire waste of time, in my opinion.[131]

The division over what labor's political action objectives should be was reflected, too, in the CIO's growing rift with the ADA. Its liberal membership—like Reuther, who strongly supported the organization—favored an ambitious program of expanding the welfare state, an agenda in which support for labor was only one part. Most CIO leaders, however, advocated a more cautious approach. They saw organized labor not as just one element of a reform coalition but, rather, as the essential prerequisite for reform.

Goldberg shared this view, believing that the labor movement had given the state its limited degree of autonomy from business managers. Without that independence, liberals could not hope to use government to restrict managerial power or create a more social democratic society. Goldberg expressed this thought to the USA Executive Board: "I have the basic conviction[,] which I have had for a long time[,] that the Presidency of the United States and the perpetuation of that office in a democracy depends upon the perpetuation of unions such as the Steelworkers' Union."[132] Thus political action must have as its paramount objective, he and most other CIO chiefs reasoned, the protection and expansion of the union movement. This dispute over objectives lay at the heart of both the UAW–USA rift in the CIO and middle-class liberals' growing disenchantment with organized labor.

In the face of such opposition, Reuther's more ambitious plans for the PAC came to little, as did his other ideas for broadening the CIO's range of activities. The labor-paper idea was torpedoed by the CIO Executive Board, after a pessimistic and highly revealing discussion about such a periodical's probable effectiveness in influencing workers' outlook. Although Reuther had hoped to compete with the nation's newspapers, which reflected the views of the wealthy publishers and advertisers who controlled them, the other CIO union heads argued that they did not have the money to compete with the existing mass media. Even more telling was Communications Workers chief Joe Beirne's objection that workers would not read such a periodical. As he told the CIO Executive Board,

> Our own conclusion in CWA, and my support in the Executive Committee, was that we just don't have that kind of money, the kind of time and that kind of energy. The reading habits of our people are such that it would not be a successful enterprise in my estimation.[133]

Beirne reminded the board of how even *PM*, an independent newspaper sympathetic to labor, "went broke and quite a few million dollars went down the drain."[134] In the end, the board decided against proceeding any further with the idea.[135]

The leadership also rejected the idea of a weekly television broadcast on the ground of cost. As Mike Quill, head of the Transport Workers Union, observed, "Unless you have the money to put on a first-class television show each week there is no use trying to compete with Bob Hope or Kate Smith, who are spending six millions annually in television."[136]

The most that the board would support was a weekly labor radio broadcast, and even that proved short lived. The cost proved to be fairly high and labor listeners few in number. As CIO public relations expert Henry Fleischer admitted to the CIO Executive Board, most of the letters and phone calls responding to the broadcasts came "from college campuses, from liberal business men and farm groups."[137] Even that modest effort cost the CIO just over $50,000 per month at a time when the federation was running a monthly deficit of $69,000.[138] The amounts indicated the lopsided advantage possessed by corporations, which sponsored most radio and television programming, when compared with the labor movement. Although some argued then and later that labor should have embraced a more ambitious agenda, the discussions in CIO Executive Board meetings suggests that its narrowing vision reflected less a failure of imagination than a lack of resources. Reuther's dream of using mass media to compete with business collided with the hard fact of managerial dominance in that realm, which labor was ill equipped to challenge.[139]

Reuther also alienated other CIO leaders with his sharp public attacks on the Eisenhower administration and his earlier statement at the 1949

ICFTU meeting that the masses wanted to be ruled by "neither Stalin nor Standard Oil." His speeches made some CIO union leaders uneasy, because they felt Reuther's remarks needlessly aroused business hostility to labor.[140]

No CIO union leader indicated his unhappiness with Reuther's agenda more openly than David McDonald did. One way he expressed his disagreement was to encourage rumors that the USA might withdraw from the CIO. Seeking to increase the pressure on Reuther, and perhaps seriously interested in leaving the CIO, he engaged in some preliminary discussions with John L. Lewis and Dave Beck, the head of the Teamsters Union, about forming a separate labor alliance. That "Lew McBeck" gambit, as the press soon dubbed it, was really little more than an effort to place pressure on Reuther.[141]

The Reuther–McDonald rift, which reflected the underlying divisions in the federation, was complicated still further by the system of apportioning voting power at CIO conventions. The allocation of votes did not reflect the actual distribution of members among the federation's affiliates. Even though the USA had slightly less than one-quarter of the total CIO membership, its voting strength was only about half that much.

The USA also, like a few of the other big unions, subsidized the smaller ones, many of which could not meet their annual assessment obligations. Those arrangements had worked fairly harmoniously when Murray had been CIO president, precisely because he had enjoyed broad support, but the emergence of factions after his death put the voting and financing schemes under severe stress. They inflated the strength of the Reuther faction, which helped him keep control, but at the same time undercut the legitimacy of his leadership.[142]

Internal divisions plagued the other house of labor as well. The resistance there to unity with the CIO came from the Carpenters Union and the Teamsters, by 1953 the two biggest in the AFL. Angry at Meany for his stand on the issue, the Carpenters' president, Maurice Hutcheson, threatened to withdraw from the federation in the summer of 1953. When the locals rebelled at the move, however, he was forced to reverse himself, greatly diminishing active resistance from that quarter.

The Teamsters, led by a handful of corrupt men, opposed any steps toward a merger, out of concern that those unions affiliated with the CIO would push hard for the expulsion of all affiliates dominated by racketeers. For that reason, Beck continued to talk indirectly about a possible "third federation," giving Meany serious problems in trying to win approval for the no-raiding pact. Meany, however, was a shrewd labor politician who enjoyed enough support throughout the federation to fend off Beck.[143]

To the surprise of at least some CIO leaders, Meany agreed in June 1953 to accept the no-raiding pact that Goldberg had drafted, without many changes. As Goldberg told the USA Executive Board,

> The only draft that was available for consideration was our draft, and with very few changes our draft . . . was accepted and . . . initialed by the A.F. of L. and CIO for presentation to the conventions.

That is quite a significant thing, I think. It bespeaks a great deal about George Meany's general attitude in this field. I think [it is] probably the most significant development that has come out of the labor situation in recent years.[144]

Under the terms of the agreement, both federations would have to ratify it at their upcoming annual conventions, which would then submit the pact to their respective affiliates for approval. The agreement would expire, unless renewed by both sides, on December 31, 1955, in effect conditioning its continuance on further progress toward reunification. Thus did the move toward labor unity begin to gather momentum, despite the best efforts of Reuther, McDonald, and Beck to slow it down.[145]

Their objections, however, made the road to unity a fairly bumpy one. Reuther presented Meany with a list of conditions that the AFL should meet before further steps toward merger would be taken. The demands reflected the views of the Reuther faction, which wanted explicit AFL promises to eliminate corruption and racial discrimination in its affiliates, reduce affiliate autonomy on those matters, and adopt the CIO's political action program. But the list served only to annoy Meany, who believed that Reuther's conditions would alienate AFL leaders without contributing at all to achieving those goals. McDonald, for his part, kept talking to Lewis and Beck, in the hope of finding another way out, or at least of keeping pressure on Reuther to go along with Goldberg's efforts to bargain with the AFL.

As late as March 1954, despite AFL and CIO convention approval of the no-raiding pact, no major AFL union had ratified the agreement. The USA had also failed to ratify it, although its leadership was ready to do so once a jurisdictional dispute with another union had been resolved. That spring, however, in response to pressure from Meany, the AFL's affiliates began to fall in line. By May, a majority of the AFL's membership had been committed to the agreement. Although several of the big AFL unions, such as the Carpenters and the Teamsters, had failed to ratify, Meany reminded the CIO that ratification did not require more than a simple majority.[146]

The AFL's action at last forced the CIO to go through with its part of the bargain, a course some CIO chiefs had never fully expected. When some of them expressed their reservations at a CIO Executive Board meeting held that same month, Reuther replied,

> I think that as a matter of good faith we are obligated to carry this thing out. If we didn't mean it we should not have ratified it, and if we didn't believe in it we should not have negotiated and we should not have asked our General Counsel to spend hours and hours drafting the document which represents the no-raiding agreement.[147]

The NLRB ruling that relaxed restrictions against craft severance encouraged them to go along, because the decision meant that the CIO would have even less to gain by raiding in the future. By the end of June, all but three CIO

affiliates had ratified the agreement, as had AFL affiliates, with just over half
the federation's 10 million members.[148]

The agreement, for all practical purposes, really went into effect on June 9,
1954. Following the earlier CIO precedent, the two sides agreed on an arbitrator. At Goldberg's suggestion, David Cole, the former head of the Federal
Mediation and Conciliation Service (FMCS), was selected. The following
summer, Goldberg finally managed to get McDonald to drop the third federation idea. With that last step, the success of the first big move toward
reunification had been assured.[149]

Labor also made some modest gains in the political realm in 1954. With the
end of the Korean War a year earlier, the economy had begun to slow down
and by January 1954 had entered a recession. The nation's official unemployment rate rose from an average of 2.9 percent during 1953, the last year of the
war, to an average of 5.8 percent the following year. By April 1954 David
McDonald reported to the USA Executive Board that "approximately 16% of
all of our members are currently unemployed, and approximately 24% are
working less than 40 hours a week."[150] The Eisenhower administration reacted slowly to the downturn, prompting labor to apply pressure for increased
federal spending and a tax cut.[151]

While Reuther assailed the administration's apparent indifference to the
recession, the USA took the lead in negotiating for a government response.
Goldberg, staff economist Otis Brubaker, and his assistants drew up a series of
suggestions that McDonald, Abel, and Vice-President Thimmes then presented to Eisenhower, his chief of staff Sherman Adams, and Arthur Burns,
chairman of the Council of Economic Advisers (CEA) at a meeting held on
April 8. The USA's suggestions combined an income tax cut to stimulate
consumer spending, relaxing the new administration's tight monetary policy
so as to encourage business investment and housing construction, extending
the duration of unemployment compensation eligibility, and increasing federal expenditures on public works, principally highways.

Eisenhower's response to those ideas mingled his apparent surprise at the
seriousness of the problem with enthusiasm for the USA's proposals.
McDonald told the USA Executive Board,

> It was our impression that he hadn't really been kept up to date by his
> Council of Economic Advisors as to what is really going on in America, and I
> think he was being influenced by Commerce Secretary Weeks and Treasury
> Secretary Humphrey.
> Anyway, we presented it to him and he was very kind, very friendly and
> extremely interested. He was so interested that our fifteen-minute appoint-
> ment ran on for fifty minutes.[152]

Eisenhower directed Burns to meet with the USA group to discuss their ideas
in more detail, a meeting that took place only a few days later. Goldberg and
the staff economists spent two hours explaining the USA's proposals, which
the CEA accepted in principle, save for the tax cut idea, which they opposed
out of concern for the size of the budget deficit. After exchanging a few more

clarifying memos, the two sides agreed to make a joint presentation to Treasury Secretary Humphrey and his advisers on May 12.[153]

The USA could not, however, claim all or even most of the credit for the administration's program to end the recession. Eisenhower's aides had begun to act on parts of the USA program even before the union had presented it, and thus labor contributed to its enactment only by pushing the administration in the direction that existing economic conditions and power arrangements had already inclined it to go. Those pressures eventually led to the passage of a tax cut as well, despite the administration's reluctance, although the form of the reduction did more to stimulate business investment than it did to increase consumer purchasing power. The end result, however, was a countercyclical economic program in keeping with Keynesian theory, another example of the extent to which the Eisenhower Republicans had assimilated the new economic thinking of the past two decades.[154]

Workers' unhappiness with the recession, which they tended to blame on the administration's economic policies, gave labor and the Democrats a chance to make some gains in the 1954 elections and, perhaps even more important, to reelect the Democratic senators who had won their seats six years earlier.

Although PAC collections had been quite modest in 1953 and early 1954, the recession had had an impact on the rank and file's willingness to give. Jack Kroll told the CIO Executive Board in October that collections rose sharply during the summer as the recession continued to get worse in many parts of the country. Labor, and especially the CIO, contributed to such leading liberal senators such as Douglas, Humphrey, and Kefauver, all of whom won reelection, and to electing some new governors. The most notable of the latter was liberal Democrat Averell Harriman, whose victory in the New York gubernatorial contest immediately established him as a leading contender for the 1956 Democratic presidential nomination.

The Democrats in 1954 also gained enough seats in Congress to take control of both houses, although that change had little more than symbolic effect. As Reuther told the CIO Executive Board, "There has been no basic shift in the center of political gravity in Washington — let's not kid ourselves. . . . What you are going to get basically is in place of a Republican–Dixiecrat coalition, you are going to get a Dixiecrat–Republican coalition. Those are the political facts of life."[155]

Reuther also noted that the new chairman of the House Labor Committee, North Carolina Democrat Graham Barden, was an enemy of organized labor and that labor had been unable to block his appointment. The reason, he said, was that "we have always been treated as second-class citizens in Washington."[156] But if workers had made little headway in the political arena, neither had their opponents. Union power, though not equal to that of the corporation managers, still remained formidable. With AFL–CIO unity drawing ever nearer, labor, at least in theory, could also look forward to expanding its political power, just as it kept adding new members to its rolls.

Goldberg possessed that more optimistic outlook. As 1954 drew to a close, he detected signs of a renewal in labor's fortunes. Overall membership had risen steadily since 1949 and now totaled 34.7 percent of the nonfarm workforce, roughly equal to the previous peak reached in 1945. Labor unions had more than 17 million members, a record number. There also were encouraging signs that suggested labor would be able to add substantially to its ranks. The Democrats appeared poised for a resurgence nationally; McCarthy had been condemned and the anticommunist hysteria was winding down; the war in Korea had ended without a victory by the Communists; and the benefits of nearly full employment had brought prosperity not only to managers but to many workers as well. The average weekly earnings of production workers in the manufacturing industries by 1954 virtually equaled the all-time high of 1944, and the economy more generally had begun a sustained recovery from recession in September.[157]

Perhaps most encouraging was the Supreme Court's 1954 ruling in the *Brown* case, which seemed to deal a major blow to a system of segregation that kept most black members of the working class from participating fully in the postwar social contract. Goldberg underscored the connection between this decision and the prospects of the labor movement more generally in a speech to San Francisco's Commonwealth Club in December. He entitled his address "The Future of American Labor," which he saw as threatened by the closed society of the South. Penetrating what he called the southern "Iron Curtain" was essential, he said, in order for the labor movement as a whole to move forward. Labor's progress depended, Goldberg argued,

> in large part, on our ability to break through that blockade and complete the job of organizing the South. And we find lined up on the barricades alongside the industrialists, the politicians of the South—men who have cast their lot with big business in order to maintain their feudal political dynasties.[158]

Goldberg, like many others in the CIO, had come to the conclusion that no southern organizing drive could succeed until the system of legalized segregation had first been dismantled. To that end he had written an amicus brief on behalf of the plaintiffs in the *Brown* case, which the Steelworkers Union submitted to the Supreme Court when the case had been argued earlier that year. The decision, he predicted, "will be given complete effect through all parts of the country . . . in the near future," a development that boded well for all American workers.[159]

The tone of Goldberg's address, and of his outlook at the end of 1954, was not entirely optimistic. Roughly one-third of his speech dealt with what he saw as the continuing threats to labor's place in the postwar order. Even as he claimed that labor was devoted to expanding its ranks and strengthening the postwar New Deal, he observed that

> as equally determined as we are . . . is another group in our economy—a group that is anti-union. . . .
>
> It is composed of the die-hard adherents to discredited theories—men who want a low-paid, job-hungry group of workers in our country.
>
> Just as we will spare no efforts or expense in organizing unorganized

workers, they will spare no effort or expense in resisting organization. And, their financial resources are far greater than are ours.[160]

Despite the challenge posed by that group, Goldberg remained confident that labor would continue to move forward. The two key reasons for that, he suggested, were the gains in civil rights for blacks and the steadily improving prospects for labor unity. The second he called "the subject which most immediately concerns the future of the American labor movement," and he hinted that the recently achieved no-raiding agreement would soon be followed by a merger between the two labor federations.[161] Goldberg closed on an upbeat note, saying that he saw "a bright, useful future for the labor movement—a future marked by continued growth."[162]

The evidence for those prospects was, however, mixed at best. Even though overall membership had risen steadily since 1949, the rate of union victories in organizing elections had declined, as had the total number of workers organized each year. Those statistics pointed to a loss of momentum for labor, the result of employer intimidation that the Taft–Hartley Act had legalized. For the next three years the signs of labor's overall health would continue to be mixed. At the beginning of that time, however, Goldberg remained confident that labor would do more than hold its own.[163]

5

Consensus, Real and Imagined

THE FIRST STEP in ensuring labor progress, Goldberg believed, was to bring about a merger between the two labor federations, a process that moved speedily toward completion in the winter of 1954/55. Reuther, however, remained unenthusiastic. At executive board meetings throughout the year and a half preceding the merger, he continued to defend the CIO's viability. His tone more often than not was defensive. At a March 1954 meeting Reuther attacked journalists who had written stories suggesting that the CIO might soon fall apart. He told board members heatedly that "these columnists would have you believe that the CIO is bankrupt, that it is in the last stages of disintegration, and that it is just a matter of having a formal burial ceremony and [the] CIO is out of business. Nothing could be further from the truth."[1] Reuther's claims of CIO progress did little to reassure his listeners. He admitted that the federation was now running a deficit, but he pointed out that the CIO's treasury was larger than that of the AFL and that the CIO's income would rise once the IUE finished off the UE.[2]

But the comparison between the AFL and CIO was an irrelevant one because the former's affiliates contributed very little in dues to the federation, preferring to keep the bulk of that income for themselves. By 1954, the AFL, with about 10 million members, had more than twice as many as did the CIO, and the sectors of the economy that the AFL had organized, such as construction and transportation, were yielding far more new members than were the basic manufacturing industries dominated by the CIO. The IUE campaign to displace the UE in the electrical industry also moved quite slowly, where overtly antiunion employers such as Westinghouse and General Electric profited from the deep divisions among the rank and file about which union to join.[3]

Those developments suggested to Goldberg that the CIO stood to gain from a merger with the larger AFL, because it would prevent the AFL from chipping away at the CIO's membership. Those affiliates in need of subsidies would at the same time be able to draw on a larger pool of resources, he reasoned, thus easing the burden borne by the UAW and USA. Thus despite Reuther's efforts to slow down the movement toward merger, Goldberg and the Steelworkers faction more generally had pushed the CIO in that direction during 1954.[4]

By December of that year, Reuther's tone became even more defensive. At an executive board meeting held that month, shortly after the CIO's annual convention, he remarked,

> We are not going to the American Federation of Labor with our hats in our hands; . . . if we get labor unity it will be because the American Federation of Labor is prepared to meet us on the kind of sound basis that will make honorable labor unity possible. I think that we ought to try to dispel and minimize this idea that we are really out of business now and that this is a kind of holding company that we have got here just until the AFL picks up the pieces, because frankly that is not the case.[5]

Reuther's remarks, however, suggested just the opposite of what he was saying. While he blustered about his "conditions," Goldberg did the hard bargaining with George Meany. Goldberg drafted a proposed merger agreement and presented it to the AFL chief during a private lunch, telling him,

> "If you want a merger you have to take it [the draft] as is. You could fool around, and that will play into the hands of those in the CIO who don't want it." I told him very frankly, "There are people in the CIO that will say, 'well, this is fine for us, but you'll never take it.'" When he looked at it, very superficially, . . . [he then said] "Yes, I'll take it."[6]

Meany's snap acceptance took Reuther and his supporters by surprise, but by then they had little choice except to go along with "their" proposal. At a meeting of the AFL–CIO unity committee on February 9, 1955, in Miami, the two sides ratified that bargain. To placate Reuther's faction in the CIO, the AFL "guaranteed" to eliminate corruption and racism from its affiliates. Those pledges, however, were not backed up by any enforcement mechanisms, which essentially meant that CIO leaders had agreed to take Meany's word that something would be done about those problems.

This kind of agreement was typical of Goldberg's negotiating style: Gain consensus on basic issues, and then postpone the more difficult ones for resolution later, in the expectation that having entered into a bargain, both sides would make good faith efforts to implement it. The result was a very loose reunification, one in which the various state and local organizations of the two federations would only gradually work out terms for merger. Reuther had wanted more explicit AFL promises in the civil rights and racketeering areas in particular, but in the end the Steelworkers faction in the CIO pushed him into acquiescing.[7]

The new organization's voting scheme and selection of top officers signaled the balance of power in the new and as yet unnamed labor federation. The key governing body, the executive council, was to be composed of twenty-nine members, of which ten would be drawn from the CIO. As Goldberg told the USA Executive Board, the distribution "represents the per capita relationship between the CIO and the AFL. That is, the whole structure is figured on that basis."[8]

This arrangement essentially gave the CIO veto power only over the most important decisions, including any expulsion of an affiliate, because such actions required a two-thirds vote to be adopted. The executive council would, in fact, exercise even more power than the older AFL and CIO Executive Boards, of which it was composed, because the two sides agreed henceforth to hold national conventions biennially, rather than annually. In the interim periods, the council would make all important decisions.

This change reflected a larger trend in labor organizations of reducing participation in governing to a small group of top officials, a hallmark of the entire postwar order. And under the terms of the agreement, the top two executive posts, the president and the secretary-treasurer, would go to George Meany and William Schnitzler, who already held those jobs in the AFL. The AFL had been willing to accept Reuther as the number two official, but in the end the UAW chief decided against taking a full-time job as Meany's deputy, preferring instead to remain the genuine leader of the UAW and an unencumbered spokesman for its influential minority position within the larger labor movement.[9]

The decision about which of the two top federation lawyers, the AFL's Albert Woll or the CIO's Goldberg, would be designated as AFL–CIO general counsel signaled, too, the true nature of the merger. Goldberg later claimed that he did not want the job, because the general counsel served the president, who would be Meany, and thus the structure of the job would be cast in the AFL mold. Unlike the CIO, Goldberg said, in which the "general counsel is a policy man. . . . [In the] AF of L it was different; the lawyer was a technical person who did legal things."[10] In that situation, he concluded, he did not want the position, and also because

> the AF of L was the older body and I felt that he [Meany] ought to have his own general counsel. . . . I was satisfied to be a special counsel and handle special things. . . . And he and I talked it over very frankly. . . . In fact, some suggestion was made that Al [Woll] and I combine our law firms, and I said, "No"; and I was perfectly content.[11]

Well, not quite. Even though he did not want the substance of the job, Goldberg would very much have liked the title, with Woll as his deputy or, at most, co-counsel. Meany balked at that, however, arguing that the general counsel had to serve the president. In the end Goldberg settled for the titles of special counsel and counsel to the new Industrial Union Department, and Woll was named AFL–CIO general counsel.[12]

Although Goldberg insisted that "this merger does not represent any going back to the House of Labor," the agreement's terms indicated otherwise.[13] The CIO unions returned to labor's older house grouped under an industrial union department analogous to the older AFL divisions. In effect, the AFL had recognized the reality of industrial unions where they existed and had left open the question of which approach — craft or industrial — would prevail in future organizing efforts. Goldberg hoped that the merger would make the AFL more like the CIO in terms of its outlook and agenda, but even in 1955 that looked like a very difficult task.

The plain-speaking Joe Germano described the new arrangement most candidly when he announced that "when the merger is effective, I, as president of the Illinois State CIO Council, for example, would want to immediately effectuate a deal to dissolve the Illinois State Branch of CIO and go into the Illinois State Federation [of the AFL]."[14] Although Goldberg and others insisted that "there will be a new movement created out of the CIO and AFL," the change was largely a cosmetic one.[15] To preserve appearances, however, the CIO did insist on a different name, in face of a strong AFL desire to keep its own for the "new" federation.[16]

The Steelworkers' central role in bringing about the merger agreement was reflected in George Meany's appearance at the USA Executive Board meeting held to discuss the terms: "The first time," he said, "I have appeared before any representative body of the Congress of Industrial Organizations."[17] Meany emphasized in his talk those areas in which the AFL leadership by then shared the views of their CIO counterparts, most notably political action. Meany suggested that the AFL had learned its lesson about the efficacy of political action in 1948, telling the board members wryly,

> In 1948 I went to a dinner in New York and I met a newspaper reporter whom I knew quite well, and after the dinner he invited me to have a drink with him. . . . We went into a club to which he belonged . . . and a fellow came in wearing a tuxedo suit; he had had a little too much of the spirit of the dinner that he attended, . . . and he looked at me standing at the bar and he said, "You're Meany, the laborskate." I said, "Yes, that's right." This was still in the period when Tom Dewey was President but not yet elected. . . . And . . . this fellow looked at me and said, ". . . Let me tell you[,] after this election, the fellow who puts the money into the business is going to make the rules."[18]

Meany received a friendly reception from the Steelworkers' leadership, but opponents of the new agreement could still be found elsewhere in the CIO. As McDonald admitted to the USA Executive Board,

> The discussions in our CIO group were more bitter and more difficult than were the discussions in the full joint [AFL–CIO] committee meeting. The day of the perfection of this agreement . . . was a most difficult day. At times I felt that my colleagues were doing everything in their power to prevent the consummation of an agreement.[19]

In the end, only Mike Quill of the Transport Workers Union refused to go along with signing the agreement on February 9, but once the members of the Reuther faction had agreed, Quill's position became untenable.[20]

Between the day of that meeting and November 1955, Goldberg and Meany spent a great deal of time cajoling recalcitrant affiliates of their respec-

tive federations to accept the deal. In April of that year Reuther tacitly acknowledged who had negotiated the merger by yielding the floor at an executive board meeting to Goldberg, who presented the terms to the rest of the
CIO leadership. During the summer he and Al Woll worked out a number of
quite technical changes in the proposed agreement, a process largely concluded by the end of September. The turning point for the CIO came in an
executive board meeting held on November 2, 1955, at which the faction
supporting merger finally prevailed.[21]

Goldberg observed later, without too much exaggeration, that "I made the
merger, very frankly."[22] He wrote a book in 1955 that gave the official version
of how the two sides had achieved agreement, glossing over most of the
controversial issues. A sign of which faction in the CIO had favored reunification lay in the differing responses of McDonald and Reuther to Goldberg's
request that they each write a short foreword to the book, which he called
Labor United. Goldberg included with his request to McDonald a proposed
foreword, which the latter accepted verbatim. Reuther, on the other hand,
refused to provide one, because, Goldberg believed, "He . . . had second
thoughts about the merger in general. . . . And he was caught by surprise."[23] In the end the book appeared with forewords by Meany and
McDonald, reflecting the AFL's and USA's leading roles in bringing about
the merger.

Goldberg also unsnarled the one remaining dispute, over a new name, by
suggesting a combination, the AFL–CIO, which satisfied both sides. On
November 15 he reported to the USA Executive Board that although "there
was a point within the last ten days when the discussions became so strained
and so difficult that it would have been almost a certainty to say that unity
would not come about. . . . The end of the great effort . . . is now going
to be . . . labor unity."[24] Goldberg argued that the name finally agreed on
indicated that the CIO, rather than returning to the House of Labor, would
instead become "married" to the AFL.[25] If so, the union was a quintessen-
tially 1950s one, in which the AFL played the part of the groom and the CIO
that of the bride, with all the inequality in power that analogy implied. The
federation made its new home in a large building located directly across
Lafayette Park from the White House, a setting that reflected both labor's
real institutional power and the extent to which it had become subordinate to
government regulation.[26]

George Meany's good faith in redeeming his promises about corruption
and civil rights would now be put to the test, a prospect that Reuther found
discouraging. Somberly he told the CIO Executive Board that

> by and large, the AFL has not moved in the right direction as far as we would
> like, and I look upon the Industrial Union Department as a kind of a
> place where we can keep the flame of those [CIO] ideals . . . burning
> brightly. . . .
>   . . . Make no mistake about it, there are going to be times when you are
> going to feel like you have lost all of your friends. . . .
>   . . . And make no mistake about it, we are not going to have any of

the top jobs in this labor movement, but when the bricks are made and they are thrown, they are not going to be thrown at George Meany and Bill Schnitzler. You mark my words, that the forces that are fighting the American labor movement are going to continue to concentrate their major attacks against the people sitting in this room, even though they will occupy secondary positions of leadership in the united labor movement.[27]

Time would tell whether Goldberg or Reuther had been more right about the merger. In 1955, however, those who had made it saw the step as strengthening the labor movement.

But if labor leaders were reorganizing the movement's institutional structure so as to expand workers' power, the changes did nothing to increase rank-and-file participation in governing "their" unions. In fact, labor's progress during the early and middle 1950s came at the expense of worker participation in running labor organizations. To understand the connection between the two, which was a key reason for labor's subsequent decline, one must now examine the issue in greater detail.

II

With the passing of Philip Murray had come the end of harmonious relationships between the USA locals and its national administration. Despite his increasingly overt hostility after 1947 to the radical minority in the union, Murray had never lost the enormous moral authority with the rank and file that he had accumulated from his earlier years with the organization. When McDonald assumed the USA presidency, however, the situation began to change, for two reasons: McDonald lacked Murray's common touch and deep-seated hostility to corporate power, which suggested to the rank and file that McDonald would not defend their interests forcefully enough. Even more important to arousing rank-and-file hostility was the way in which McDonald sought to run the union.

From the beginning, policymaking in the USA had been dominated by the leadership, whose power was buttressed by its tight control over union income. Unlike most other industrial unions, the dues withheld from steelworkers' paychecks flowed directly to headquarters in Pittsburgh, which then returned half to the locals. Dissident locals faced the risk of a dues cutoff, a powerful weapon the leadership used to maintain conformity with its policies.[28]

Never inclined to worry much about worker participation in decision making, McDonald encouraged a trend toward centralizing even more authority in the hands of the executive board. In part, that move stemmed from his own deep-seated insecurities as USA president. Aware that he lacked the kind of rank-and-file support Murray had enjoyed, McDonald attempted to concentrate power at the top so as to head off potential challenges to his presidency. But McDonald's support for such changes only encouraged a trend already evident in most of the major American unions by the early 1950s, one that followed from their decision to enter into the postwar social contract with management.

This bargain required the unions to perform certain policing roles, to make certain that the rank and file went along with the deals that labor leaders negotiated concerning control of the workplace, pay, and benefits. Although this was not the only function unions performed, it had become one of the most important ones. The trend toward centralized authority was encouraged, too, by the union's efforts to bargain with management on an industrywide basis and by labor's increasing dependence on the state to police the postwar New Deal. Thus did managerial and government forms of bureaucratic organization replicate themselves in organized labor. By 1953, the first signs of the problems that these changes were creating began to confront union leaders, including those of the Steelworkers.[29]

For the USA, the first serious problems stemmed from the union elections held in 1952, in which, for the first time, dissidents in some locals challenged incumbent local officers. Deciding which election protests to accept and which to throw out took up most of the time at the USA Executive Board meetings held on March 11–12 and May 28, 1953. A related problem was what to do about members of the locals who filed charges against their opponents.

Goldberg's response to those developments was to propose that the president be empowered to appoint commissions composed of district directors or international union representatives that would examine any appeal from the decision of a local. The commission would then recommend a settlement, on which the executive board in turn would vote. After some discussion, the board adopted the proposal unanimously. The procedure allowed the union's leaders to dominate the adjudication of internal grievances and would be used both to expel some union dissidents and to intimidate others. It thereby enabled the board to tighten even further its grasp on the reins of power.[30]

Symptomatic of the changes going on in the union during the first four years of McDonald's tenure as president were the steps taken to restrict the locals' autonomy. Of paramount concern was the issue of wildcat strikes. They were potentially even more serious a threat to the leadership's power than electoral challenges, because such strikes undermined managerial support for the postwar social contract. When they emerged in significant numbers during 1953, McDonald demanded that district leaders put a stop to them. The next issue at stake involved the proper scope of local authority, which a majority of the board made clear it intended to reduce.

In January 1954 the board voted to ban the practice of allowing locals to make their own bylaws. Instead, the national office prepared a model set of bylaws and henceforth required the locals to obtain the board's approval to include any others of their own. This was followed in turn by McDonald's urging board members to "discourage" locals from holding meetings with management representatives. McDonald's heavy-handed suggestion raised objections from some board members, who made clear during a long discussion that they viewed a ban on such meetings as unconstitutional.[31]

The increasingly bureaucratized nature of labor–management relations not only tended to concentrate power at the top of the union. The same forces also tended to place a greater share of that power into the hands of the legal department, which Goldberg headed. Secretary-Treasurer I. W. Abel told the board in the spring of 1954 that

> legal fees incurred in the district[s] are running us anywhere from $15,000 to $25,000 a month. That's a hell of a lot of money, and I found in investigating it that we have gotten to the place in a lot of instances where a staff fellow no longer can file a petition for an election – he has to have a lawyer do it. When it comes time for a hearing to set up the unit the staff man can no longer sit in a meeting and represent the organization in establishing a bargaining unit.
>
> When it comes to this thing of arbitration it seems the staff fellows can no longer prepare a brief or submit an argument before an arbitrator – they have to have a lawyer, and I sometimes wonder what the devil we have the staff fellows for any more.[32]

Goldberg also used his legal expertise to play an ever larger role in resolving disputes about internal union governance. In a meeting held the following summer, he ruled that the USA Executive Board could expel a member for belonging to the American Communist Party, despite the absence of any authorizing provision in the union's constitution. His reasoning was typical of the sort he employed in resolving those sorts of issues during the time he served McDonald. He justified his ruling by declaring:

> In my opinion the basis for the expulsion is the fact that holding membership in the Communist Party or other similarly subversive organization is entirely incompatible with the basic obligation of a membership in the United Steelworkers of America under the Constitution, since one of the objectives of the organization, and perhaps its primary object, is to perpetuate, in the language of the Constitution, "the cherished traditions of our democracy.["] And when we say our democracy, we refer to the democratic governments of the United States and Canada.[33]

Goldberg's "opinion" contained at least two key intellectual moves that signaled changes in the way that labor leaders viewed the movement's proper role in the postwar order. *Democracy* had been a word with more than one meaning during the 1930s and 1940s, at least to industrial workers. Goldberg now limited it to the form of democratic capitalism that had emerged in the United States and Canada, rather than also including other models of industrial democracy that at least some American workers had sought. And in a second twist of logic, defense of the North American model of democracy had been elevated to the status of a cardinal objective for the union and an essential prerequisite for membership. Although this formulation did help protect the union against managerial and state repression during the antiradical hysteria, Goldberg's reasoning assumed a uniformity of outlook among the rank and file that simply did not exist. In effect, Goldberg was arguing that the intentions of the union's leaders alone or, at most, those of a majority of the members should guide official interpretations of the union's constitution.

In addition to formulating the rules governing who could belong, Goldberg also dominated the decisions about who could run for office in the union. When USA Vice-President Jim Thimmes died in March 1955, a sharp quarrel broke out among the board members over who should be allowed to seek the job. Under an earlier ruling made by Philip Murray, no one could run simultaneously for two union offices. The timing of the election therefore became crucial. If the post were left vacant until the next set of regularly scheduled union elections in 1956, a district director would not be able to aspire to the vice-presidency without risking the position he already had. Less clear was whether incumbent district directors could seek the post without that risk if an election were held right away.

McDonald, anxious to secure a loyal deputy who would pose no threat to his tenure as president, favored naming his aide Howard Hague as acting vice-president and then waiting, so as to discourage a challenge by one of his rivals on the board, such as New York district director Joseph Moloney. This led to an angry discussion of a sort rarely seen at a USA Executive Board meeting. In the end, Goldberg resolved the dispute by ruling that if a special election were to be held, incumbent office holders could seek the post while simultaneously keeping the jobs they already had. The board then voted to hold such an election, thereby dealing a setback to McDonald.

In the end, however, the board gave him the upper hand by agreeing to name Hague acting vice-president until the special election was held. Moloney challenged Hague, producing an unprecedented contest for a major USA post, but to no avail. After a distasteful and sometimes violent campaign, McDonald's handpicked candidate won easily.[34]

The concentration of power in the hands of the leadership also gave rise to another kind of challenge. In early 1955 some members of the USA's staff indicated that they wanted to organize a union of their own. Although some members of the board expressed reluctance — sounding for once like the business managers they claimed to be fighting — Goldberg pressed hard for accepting the staff's request. In a similar situation the Teamsters had rejected such an idea, relying on a legal technicality to excuse their failing to recognize a staff union. Goldberg reminded the board of that potentially unflattering comparison and appealed to both their instincts for self-preservation and their sense of principle, by observing that the Teamsters' actions

> did not do credit to the Teamsters in the eyes of the public, and I think the Teamsters got a great deal of unnecessary adverse publicity arising out of their method of handling the matter. Now we are attempting to handle it differently . . . if it is good for the workers in the industry it is also good for the employees that work for the union.[35]

That such a debate was even necessary, though, showed how weakly some board members shared that commitment when it implied a loss in their own power.

Goldberg thus acted as a force in favor of some restraints on the arbitrary exercise of power by the union's leadership. In addition to supporting the staff's request for a union, he pushed for the adoption of a set of rules to govern contested USA elections. In the aftermath of the Hague–Moloney contest, he and Secretary-Treasurer I. W. Abel drew up an election manual to be used henceforth.[36] It received its first test in the union elections held in early 1957, when all officers came up for reelection. The incumbent slate of top officials faced a serious challenge, one that grew out of McDonald's determination to raise substantially the salaries paid to union officers and, as a result, the dues charged to the membership. At the 1956 USA convention, McDonald and his supporters rammed through a $10,000 increase in his own $40,000 salary and raised those paid to the two other top officers from $25,000 to $35,000. That same year McDonald had ordered increases in pay and benefits for other union officials, too. And to pay for all of this largesse, McDonald demanded and got from the convention an increase in dues from $3.00 to $5.00 per month.[37]

The anger aroused by both the substance of those changes and the heavy-handed way the USA leadership had pushed them through sparked the first major rank-and-file challenge to the leadership's authority. A little-known delegate to the 1956 convention, Donald C. Rarick of McKeesport, Pennsylvania, decided to mount a protest based on the issue of the salary and dues increases. At first he and his supporters organized a group they named the Dues Protest Committee (DPC) which called for a special convention to reconsider those decisions. When Goldberg ruled that their petition was unconstitutional and amounted to dual unionism — which in union parlance was equated with treason — the DPC decided to challenge McDonald and Abel in the 1957 elections.

Unable to find candidates among the district directors, the DPC offered Rarick as its candidate for president and the even more obscure William Klug for the post of secretary-treasurer. McDonald, armed with the enormous advantages that followed from incumbency, nonetheless had to fight hard to keep his job. Taking Goldberg's advice, he called a series of six regional conferences to air differences and win over wavering members of the rank and file. In the end, the incumbents prevailed, but by margins that were unimpressive given the little-known candidates who faced them and the tremendous disparity in resources between the two sides. McDonald was reelected by a vote of 404,172 to Rarick's 223,516, and Abel did slightly better, winning 420,085 to Klug's 181,264. Even Howard Hague, who ran unopposed, was embarrassed by the approximately 150,000 blank ballots cast against him.[38]

But if the insurgency failed in the sense that McDonald and Abel still held onto the key posts, it was not without benefit to the rank and file who disagreed with them. Although McDonald had been pushing the board to approve moving the USA headquarters from Pittsburgh to Washington, the DPC episode persuaded the leadership that such a step would only increase the rank and file's sense of alienation. Plans to move the USA headquarters were therefore quietly shelved at the end of 1956.

Even more important, the leadership in late 1956 decided to continue holding the district conferences that had begun during the contest with the

DPC. These sessions, held in USA districts around the country, enabled workers to voice their goals for the next contract with management directly to the USA's top leaders. Although McDonald nominally presided over the meetings, his role was confined mostly to making speeches. The key portion of the sessions—give-and-take with the leadership over what the union should seek from management—was assigned to a panel chaired by Goldberg. In effect, he really ran the meetings, attempting thereby to lessen the distance between the USA leadership and the rank and file it was supposed to be serving.[39]

Goldberg's assumption of so much power without holding the office of president led to some resentment among the board members. Most of the time this sentiment stayed beneath the surface, in part because McDonald's weaknesses rather than Goldberg's own ambition had led him to assume such an important role in the first place. But on occasion, hostility to Goldberg did appear openly. At a meeting in the spring of 1957, he pushed hard for the creation of a commission to study the needs of retired steelworkers, noting that other unions had already taken steps in that area. When some members of the board balked, Goldberg told them that the last USA convention had approved a resolution on the issue, thereby compelling the board to go along. That proved too much for New England director Martin Walsh, who opposed the idea anyway, saying that "I would suggest with the hope that it isn't going to cause any ill feelings that our General Counsel confine himself to giving legal opinions; I think you have presumed to tell us what to do beyond legal counsel."[40] Goldberg faced down the challenge, telling Walsh that "if it is presumption I would like the Board to tell me it is."[41] After some discussion, the board backed Goldberg. McDonald put an end to the bickering by stating that

> I do not need to present a bill of particulars in regard to the ability of Arthur J. Goldberg. I need his services and I need and appreciate his advice. I said when I introduced him to the last International Convention words to this effect that God has been awfully good to the United Steelworkers of America, and one of the greatest things he did for us was to give us Arthur J. Goldberg as our General Counsel. I said that and I meant it then, and I mean it now.[42]

In the end, what enabled Goldberg to keep the support of the board's majority, and the leadership its control over the union, was his and their ability to meet the fundamental objectives of the rank and file. At a minimum, steelworkers demanded that the union's leaders preserve the balance of power on the shop floor that had been achieved by the middle 1940s, provide job and income security, and obtain their share of the economic benefits that followed from the postwar social contract.

What enabled McDonald and Goldberg to defeat challenges to their control in 1956/57 was the series of concessions that they had secured from management over the past four years, especially the three-year contract the union had won in 1956. A closer look both at what the union obtained and how goes far toward explaining why the McDonald–Goldberg faction proved able to hold onto its control of the USA.[43]

III

The first test of the McDonald–Goldberg faction's leadership ability in contract talks had come four years earlier, during the spring of 1953. Although the union and the companies had agreed to a two-year contract in 1952, the agreement provided for an annual reopening clause at the option of either side. In 1953, the smaller and more antiunion firms did not at first cooperate as closely with U.S. Steel as they had in 1952. The leaders of the smaller companies had not yet forgiven U.S. Steel's management for its decision to grant a modified union shop and, more generally, for U.S. Steel President Benjamin Fairless's willingness to find a compromise wage-and-price agreement during that year. But the disproportionate size of the industry leader in the end compelled executives at the six major steel companies to continue the practice of coordinated bargaining with the USA.[44]

The union's leaders sought in 1953 to obtain a pay increase and an end to the practice of paying lower wages in the steel plants located in the Southeast. At the same time, the USA leadership also pushed for improvements in the pension plan. In formulating those demands, the USA Executive Board noted that the UAW had recently won a five-cents-an-hour general wage increase under the productivity formula contained in its contracts with General Motors and Ford, as well as a reduction in the number of years of employment needed to qualify for a pension at the latter company.

The interest in the UAW settlement appeared, however, to follow less from a desire to imitate it than from a concern that it would set a pattern with which the steel industry would be expected to conform. David McDonald expressed that thought to the USA Executive Board in late May, saying that "I don't know whether the United Automobile Workers situation has complicated things or made things a wee bit easier."[45] McDonald and the board were very much aware that the UAW contract, with its cost-of-living and productivity increase provisions, had done much to shape expectations of what constituted a "fair" wage increase in the manufacturing sector.[46]

In addition to economic gains, the USA also looked for an improvement in the seniority clause, one that would give those workers who lost their jobs when a plant was abandoned preference over newcomers when the company involved opened a more modern facility. That demand grew out of the expansion in steel plant capacity that had accompanied the Korean War. The new facilities had been equipped with machinery that reduced the need for labor and the overall cost of producing steel, and thus as the war wound down and so did orders for steel, firms began to abandon a few of the older, less profitable plants. The USA leadership's concern with what it called *technological unemployment* first emerged as a serious one during 1953. But when board members urged that some kind of preferential hiring clause be obtained,

Goldberg had to remind them that previous efforts had yielded nothing in 1952:

> It is really an aspect of seniority. In other words, we are asking for company-wide seniority as against new employees. If you remember, we asked for that last time as part of our contract proposals and we offered a contractual provision, and that was one of the things we could not get.[47]

That pattern was repeated in 1953. The union and steel managers reached an agreement on June 11 that contained no such improvement in job security. Instead, the union won a general pay increase of eight and a half cents an hour, the elimination of virtually the entire southern wage differential, and a commitment to study the pension system in preparation for next year's round of contract talks.

But if the union failed to gain the seniority provision it wanted, it did largely succeed in preventing the steel industry from using its capacity expansion program to get rid of veteran union members. Rather than construct mostly new facilities, the industry opted instead for improving existing ones. That decision to pursue *rounding out*, as it was called, was based on the greater speed and lower capital costs required when compared with building new plants from scratch, and on a desire to avoid a clash with the union over jobs that would otherwise have been lost.

The union also used its power to protect the membership's jobs when the steel companies were faced with the need to find new sources of iron ore. As existing supplies in the Great Lakes area began to run out, steel managers were faced with a choice of new sites in Brazil, Australia, Canada, and Africa. Although profits for the managers would have been higher if they had pursued the first two sites, in the end managers chose Canada, where the work would be done by USA members.[48]

If some labor leaders failed to understand and respond to the hazards that workers faced from "labor-saving" technology and, more generally, from changing conditions in the manufacturing sector, the record in steel indicates otherwise. Goldberg and his associates understood that the enormous capital investment in existing steel plants compelled industry managers to continue those facilities' operation, even though they required more workers to operate than more modern ones would have. Thus the focus of USA efforts in this area was to minimize the profitability of introducing new technology into existing plants, which is what Section 2B, the local work rules clause of the contract, essentially guaranteed. At the same time, the union used its considerable leverage with managers and the federal government to make certain that union labor would continue to provide iron ore for the industry. Thus the USA helped shape steel managers' two major investment programs of the 1950s.[49]

The 1953 contract revealed a disturbing development. Both the union and the companies had engaged in a struggle over their respective shares of the industry's steadily increasing income. Under the Truman administration, government pressure on wages and prices had restrained somewhat the upward motion of both. When the Republicans assumed control over the legislative and executive branches of the federal government in 1953, however, that effort was largely abandoned. Thus almost immediately after settling with the union, the companies raised the price of steel by $4.30 a ton, a 4.9 percent increase. That pattern was repeated in every year of the Eisenhower presidency, producing a steady rise in both steel industry wages and prices, as workers and managers engaged in a tug-of-war over the proper allocation of industry income. The net result was to preserve workers' share rather than enlarge it substantially but, at the same time, to make steel a steadily more expensive commodity. Eventually, that would prove inflationary for the economy as a whole, given steel's basic place in it and, even more ominously, make the industry's workers vulnerable to lower-wage competition from Japan.

These developments would not emerge as serious problems until the late 1950s, but having started down that road, labor and management would find turning back very difficult. And if both sides were to blame, the managers were more so, because the share to which they saw themselves as entitled yielded larger salaries and profits than did those prevailing elsewhere in the manufacturing sector. The steelworkers' income, on the other hand, remained in line with that received in those other industries, at least through 1956. The steel industry managers' conduct during the early and middle 1950s thus reveals how tenuous their commitment was to sharing the fruit of economic growth with workers, even at the height of managerial support for the postwar New Deal. But until foreign competition based on lower wages emerged in the late 1950s—which had the effect of making the market for steel more competitive—the pattern that emerged in 1953 would continue undisturbed.[50]

In the next round of contract talks, held a year later, the leadership, in response to pressure from the rank and file, sought to obtain improvements in the private benefits system and greater income security through the institution of some sort of guaranteed annual wage (GAW) plan. The 1954 recession had reactivated steelworkers' enthusiasm for greater economic security, but the rising unemployment rate weakened the union's bargaining power vis-à-vis management. In that context, the leadership concentrated on preserving its existing contract until the economy improved. Despite managerial pressure for changes in Section 2B, the union refused to make any concessions.

Management, for its part, refused even to consider the GAW idea. As Secretary-Treasurer Abel reported to the board, "They are not willing to even discuss it. They have given us a flat 'no' on the idea. They are not even willing to set up a joint committee which will study the problem, as insurance and pensions have been studied during the past year."[51] In the end, the union won only very modest concessions. Workers gained a five-cents-an-hour wage increase, together with improvements in the pension and insurance plans valued at another four cents an hour. In return, the USA agreed not to raise the GAW issue for two years. The total cost of the package was not very different from that obtained by the UAW that year under its productivity and cost-of-living-allowance (COLA) provisions. And once again, the settlement was followed immediately by a substantial price increase, which came to $3.24 a ton.[52]

The most significant change that year in steel was the openness with which the companies' managers had bargained together. When the negotiations had been completed with those at U.S. Steel, the rest of the firms' managerial representatives had arrived on the scene to close the same deal. As Goldberg told the board the next day, "We seem to be on the threshold of actual industry[wide] bargaining, and as we go down this road the whole character of bargaining may change in the industry, and what has been industry[wide] bargaining disguised may become industry[wide] bargaining in reality."[53] Goldberg advocated that approach, even though it ran the risk of greater managerial unity and bargaining power, because he believed more centralized bargaining would greatly reduce the negotiating burden on the union's leadership and at the same time enable it to tighten control over the entire collective bargaining process. For those reasons, he favored the adoption of formal industrywide bargaining and a shift toward one master contract for each firm, rather than the existing practice of separate contracts for each plant.[54]

In pursuing those goals, the leadership sought more than simply to increase its own power, although, indeed, for some that consideration apparently played a part. Goldberg and the USA's other leaders saw the removal of bargaining from the locals to the top as, first, a way of strengthening and preserving the entire postwar New Deal, a goal they believed of paramount importance to the rank and file. Master contracts with each firm would also be necessary if the union were to obtain some type of guaranteed annual wage. The complications arising from different contracts with each plant would have made impossible any actuarially sound plan unless it covered every employee of each company. Industrywide bargaining, the leadership believed, would also help the rank and file by eliminating disparities among firms in accord with the union's goal of equal pay for equal work. Such an approach would also reduce the risk that companies with less generous contract terms would, by offering lower steel prices, take business away from those firms that offered better compensation packages.[55]

But if the board believed that industrywide bargaining and master contracts would serve the interests of the workers, some of them disagreed. As District Director Paul Rusen told the board when discussing the desirability of a master contract with the steel producers, "I think we have to face some facts on corporation agreements. First of all I think we have got to get our own people in line. We have a lot of our own local unions that don't want to go along on a corporation basis."[56] Some of the opposition was based on a desire for more participation in formulating union demands, and some stemmed from a fear that standardizing wage rates and benefits payments would drive the less profitable units out of business. Despite that resistance, Goldberg and the other top union leaders pressed hard for greater centralization of collective bargaining, convinced that it would pay dividends for both the rank and file and themselves.[57]

The focus on industrywide bargaining also reflected the USA leadership's growing confidence in the attitude of senior executives at the industry leader, U.S. Steel. The postwar bargain with managers of that firm had, during its first five years, been much more of a détente than an accord. Daniel Bell expressed that thought in the vocabulary of the era when he wrote in the summer of 1952 that "for five years U.S. Steel has had its Panmunjom, too."[58]

But in 1953 and 1954, the ease with which agreement was reached and U.S. Steel executives' lack of interest in reopening difficult questions suggested to Goldberg that its managers were moving toward a more genuine accord with the union. The USA leadership saw the chairman of the board, Benjamin Fairless, himself a former steelworker, as someone who understood fully the Keynesian logic of high wages for workers in an economy based on mass production and consumption. As David McDonald told the board early in 1954, "Ben Fairless is definitely not a friend of anybody who thinks we can have prosperity through scarcity, that is, prosperity for the few and scarcity for the many. He is definitely opposed to that idea."[59]

Fairless, however, reached the mandatory retirement age in May 1955, and thus the USA leadership viewed with concern the struggle in the firm to succeed him. The two leading contenders were Clifford Hood, the president of U.S. Steel, and Roger Blough, the corporation's vice-chairman and general counsel. The USA leadership had no illusions about either of them. Hood, Abel told the executive board,

> is the typical old style reactionary industrialist. He has not changed since the days of 1941, when we gave him such a bad time in organizing the American Steel and Wire factories and he was President of that company at that time. I see no indication of any changed attitude on his part. I have a feeling that if Mr. Wood [sic] had the opportunity to do so he would attempt to crack or even break the United Steelworkers of America.[60]

Blough, on the other hand, was more closely identified with Fairless's policies but had not made very clear his own attitudes toward the union. A rather colorless lawyer who had first represented U.S. Steel during its efforts to fend off Roosevelt's antimonopoly investigation of the late 1930s, Blough seemed unlikely to emerge as a great friend of labor. But given the choice, the union favored him over Hood, albeit without much enthusiasm. In the end, Blough received the job.

For the first time, both the union and the company were led de facto by the chief legal officers, a response to the bureaucratic system of industrial relations that had emerged during the 1940s. But if Blough differed from Fairless in background and temperament, there was, during the first few years at least of his tenure, no major change in U.S. Steel management's policy toward the USA.[61]

There was, however, a slight deterioration in the next round of contract

talks, held in the spring of 1955. The industry as a whole earned record profits
that year, with an after-tax income that topped $1 billion for the first time. As
of May, the industry was also operating at 98 percent of capacity, which
greatly strengthened the union's bargaining power over the preceding year.
The only potential problem was a downturn that would follow a strike by the
UAW. The autoworkers were pressing hard that spring for the GAW, which
greatly increased the likelihood of a strike. McDonald reminded the board of
that danger, noting that

> 25.6% of last week's shipments of all finished steel went directly to the
> automobile companies. If a general strike ensues it is therefore conceivable
> that the steel industry's operating rate might drop as much as 25 or 30%. If
> only one company is struck . . . the drop will be considerably less.[62]

In the end, however, the UAW failed to get a guaranteed annual wage,
settling instead for a supplemental unemployment benefit (SUB), which only
partially achieved the objective of income security, and for improvements in
wages and other benefits. The agreement was, however, reached without a
strike. That encouraged the USA to seek a substantial increase in wages,
thereby ensuring workers their share of the income generated by economic
growth.[63]

The 1955 talks revealed a continuing trend toward more centralized bargaining. McDonald announced to a loudly applauding executive board in May
that "we have within the past two weeks practically achieved a system of
industry-wide bargaining."[64] In explaining how it would work, McDonald
noted the precedents set by the UMW and the Amalgamated Clothing
Workers, both of which had earlier established industrywide bargaining.
Many of the USA's leaders, drawn from the ranks of the Lewis machine, had
been exposed to the Mine Workers system, and Goldberg, as McDonald
observed, "has done a great deal of work with the Amalgamated Clothing
Workers down through the years."[65]

Under the terms of the USA's agreement, bargaining would be conducted
simultaneously with managers of the six largest steel companies: U.S. Steel,
Bethlehem, Youngstown Sheet & Tube, Republic, Jones & Laughlin, and
Inland. These six firms produced roughly 80 percent of the nation's basic steel
and since the early 1940s had been cooperating covertly with one another in
dealing with the union. In the past, each firm had bargained pro forma with a
local committee, usually headed by a district director. Beginning in 1955,
however, McDonald chaired each of those committees, and Goldberg led
their negotiating teams.[66]

Although that centralization seemed to mark a major change, it really only
eliminated the fiction that the firms had bargained separately in the past and
that local committees had played a major part in setting contract terms. Talks
between the USA and U.S. Steel's top leadership had in fact set the terms for
the rest of the industry since the early 1940s, and administrative practice was
at long last being adjusted to meet that reality. The change did mark a decline
in participation by the locals, but one more of form than of substance. U.S.

Steel's management, which had for many years resisted making the arrangement a public one, appears to have yielded in response to the often fierce government criticism that accompanied the annual rise in steel prices, which persuaded the firm's managers that a more public system of industrywide bargaining would shift some of the blame for those increases onto other firms' executives. In this way, union and government pressure succeeded in obtaining from steel industry managers the corporatist type of industrywide bargaining that they had resisted for so long. With that open endorsement of such an approach, managers had at last abandoned even their rhetorical opposition to that model of industrial relations.[67]

With the "new" system in place, the 1955 negotiations proceeded much as they had the year before. Unable to bargain for the guaranteed annual wage under the terms of the 1954 contract, Goldberg tried to interest the steel companies' managers in agreeing at least to a joint study of the issue in preparation for next year's talks. The steel managers, however, proved to be as resistant to the guaranteed annual wage idea as were those at the automakers, and so the union once again deferred its search for progress in that area until the following year. The USA instead focused on a large wage increase, but U.S. Steel's management proved to be a bit more reluctant this time. The firm's chief negotiator, John Stephens, argued that the USA should accept a wage increase equal to that obtained by the UAW. Goldberg, however, dismissed that idea because the UAW had also received improvements in their pension and insurance plans, topics that the USA was not free to bring up until the following spring. He rejected, too, the notion that the UAW should set the standard for other manufacturing industries.

In reporting to the board about the lack of progress with Stephens, Goldberg noted that "throughout these meetings we have always made the point that we want our own pattern; we want to establish our own wage pattern. We don't want to be tied to the patterns that are established in other industries."[68] Goldberg and a few other USA leaders consulted with both Labor Secretary Mitchell and Mediation Service Chief Joseph Finnegan, who were quite sympathetic, but in keeping with what Eisenhower's aides called a policy of *neutrality*, the federal government made no real effort to persuade the steel companies' executives to compromise.

A one-day walkout by 400,000 steelworkers resulted, after which management agreed to a wage increase almost twice what the UAW had obtained. But rather than allow the workers to increase their share of industry profits, which is what management claimed the union was seeking by 1955, the managers, led by those at U.S. Steel, simply raised prices again, this time by $7.50 a ton, so as to preserve their rate of return on the company's capital.[69]

The agreement was soon followed by another round of talks in which the trend toward centralized bargaining became even more pronounced. For the 1956 round, the industry managers appointed a four-person team consisting of two U.S. Steel representatives and one each from Bethlehem and Republic, who spoke for executives at the nation's twelve major steel companies. These men in turn bargained with a USA group composed of Goldberg and the three top elected officers of the USA. The two sides met regularly in New York from June 7 through 30, trying without success to reach agreement before the contract expired at the end of the month.[70]

This time the union explicitly tied the proper size of the annual wage increase to the gains brought by rising worker productivity. "The industry," Goldberg told the USA Executive Board in May, "is making more steel with substantially fewer employees. This is a fact that they like to minimize and try to hide."[71] In making that argument this time, however, the union was aided by federal officials, who had studied the issue in preparation for the upcoming round of steel negotiations. Endeavoring to maximize salaries and profits, industry managers pushed hard to have the government's study buried. Goldberg announced to the board that

> I told David this morning that the Department of Labor has concluded a new study of productivity of the Steelworkers and of the industry. That should have been released. We have seen it and the industry has seen it. . . . The industry is struggling desperately against the release of those figures by the Department of Labor. . . . Mind you, both of us have the figures. The government has given the figures to both of us, but it is one thing to have the figures and another thing to have them publicly released. We are going to have to continue to make a strong effort to get the figures out on the table before the negotiations start because they will serve to dispel the argument about inflation.[72]

Labor Secretary James P. Mitchell decided to hold the data as the bargaining began, apparently intending to use the threat of releasing the figures as one way of persuading management to concede a substantial wage increase. The issue proved to be a difficult one, however, because the two sides, while agreeing that some wage increase was justified, differed on how best to measure improved productivity and, by implication, how large an increase it justified. Hard bargaining with each other and the government would be needed to resolve that issue.[73]

The leadership also demanded, in response to rank-and-file pressure, improvements in job and income security. Both the workers on the shop floor and the union's leaders were increasingly disturbed by the rapid pace of technological innovation in the steel industry. That innovation followed at least in part from the high cost of union labor, which increased managerial interest in developing machines that could replace workers. Despite repeated discussions of the problem in USA Executive Board meetings, the leadership had been unable thus far to fashion any long-term response to that problem. The GAW was their only real idea, and after twelve years of talking about it, no real progress had been made in obtaining a plan from executives at any major steel company.

At stake were both economic issues and those related to power in the workplace, because the introduction of such technology tended to erode the limited amount of worker control over the production process that the union had won in the 1930s and 1940s. Unable to obtain the GAW, Goldberg and his colleagues pressed instead for a supplemental unemployment benefit of the sort that both the UAW and the USA had won in 1955, the former from the major automakers and the latter from managers in the canning industry. That would provide partial pay for laid-off workers for up to one year but offered no real solution for the long-term unemployed. Unable to get a comprehensive solution, the union fell back instead on a piecemeal approach.[74]

Also at stake were union demands for a stronger union-shop clause, increased insurance and pension benefits, longer paid vacations, elimination of remaining wage differentials, and premiums for weekend work. The union-shop demand was intended to recapture the 10 percent of the workforce that had used the annual escape clause to avoid USA membership. As Goldberg pointed out to the board,

> If we have ten percent come in, that is a lot of revenue that the International Union and the Local Unions could use, and you'd also get away from a lot of the irritations that will continue to exist so long as there are people in the mills who take a free ride on the Union.[75]

Goldberg's reasoning pointed out the difference in perspective between labor leaders and antiunion workers on the entire issue of individual consent to union representation. For labor leaders, the interest in protecting the union, which they believed benefited all workers, outweighed any countervailing concern about individual freedom of choice.

Apart from the demand for a strict union-shop clause, most of the USA's demands were economic, which reflected the leadership's growing emphasis on material benefits. Although that seemed a far cry from labor's aspirations in the 1930s, the change neither marked a defeat for labor nor was totally at odds with the rank and file's desires. Most of the union's demands in 1956 were aimed not at more disposable income but, rather, at providing a greater degree of material security for steelworkers and their families, a goal they had been seeking for many years. Increasingly forgotten, however, were any other concerns. Thus did the postwar social contract alter the direction of union efforts to extract concessions from employers.[76]

Management put up a fierce but ultimately unsuccessful struggle against the union's demands. The industry followed the banner year of 1955 with record production levels during the first half of 1956, which undercut managers' claims that they could not afford to make such concessions. Even more important, the bargaining took place during the summer of a presidential election year, one in which Eisenhower and his aides were determined to avoid any economic disruption that might imperil the expected Republican victory. For the first time then, since Eisenhower took office, managers faced pressure from the government to compromise. Unwilling at first to give in, steel company leaders held firm as the contract expiration date neared.[77]

The tone of the managers' remarks was different from what it had been for the past three years. For the first time in recent memory, senior industry officials sharply attacked the union and publicized those views in the mass media. In so doing, steel company managers were attempting to emulate the

more rigid bargaining tactics associated with General Electric and especially
its vice-president for industrial relations, Lemuel Boulware.

Boulwarism, as it was called, emphasized making an initial offer, followed
by completely refusing to bargain any further. That approach, GE's managers
believed, would help persuade workers that whatever gains they obtained
came from management and not the union. The "take-it-or-leave-it" method
was combined with massive publicity campaigns aimed both at the workers
themselves and the public at large. This more confrontational approach to
industrial relations had emerged at GE in response to the more polarized
relations between labor and management in the electrical industry. Electrical
workers had been led during the 1930s and 1940s by the radical UE, which
had rejected the terms of the postwar New Deal. Although many electrical
workers had switched to the rival IUE, which the CIO established in 1949,
much of the rank and file remained hostile to the postwar social contract. A
more intransigent management had exploited that division since 1946, giving
the electrical industry a far less harmonious industrial relations system than
existed elsewhere in the manufacturing sector of the economy.[78]

But if Boulwarism worked to management's advantage in the electrical
industry, steel managers profited little from adopting such tactics in 1956. At
that time, the USA enjoyed much more bargaining power than either the UE
or the IUE did, thanks to both the steelworkers' much greater unity and the
much greater degree of government support their union could command,
which stemmed from the USA's strong backing for the postwar social contract.

When U.S. Steel's Roger Blough attempted in 1956 to adopt GE's tactics,
Goldberg called, in a widely quoted phrase, for "more Fairlessness and less
Boulwarism." And when U.S. Steel management refused to budge, the union
began a twenty-seven-day strike on July 1. That demonstration of rank-and-
file backing for the leadership's position, combined with the federal government's support for the union's cause, in the end forced management to back
down. Managers capitulated after Eisenhower's aides warned them that rather
than use Taft–Hartley, the government would, if the walkout continued,
appoint a fact-finding board of the sort favored by the Truman administration.

The onset of the Suez crisis in late July, which revived government concerns about the availability of steel to meet military needs, only intensified the
administration's pressure on management. The steel managers — anxious to
avoid reviving a form of government intervention they saw as working only to
the advantage of labor — gave in. The union won almost everything it had
sought, including a 7.5-cent general wage increase to be followed by 7.2-cent
increases in each of the next two years, the SUB and complete union shop, as
well as improvements in vacation, holiday pay, pension, and insurance provisions.[79]

The union also gained a cost-of-living allowance clause similar to the one
the UAW had won eight years earlier. Although the USA had resisted the idea
in the past, Goldberg had become convinced by 1956 that it now made sense.

In part, this was because the annual bargaining over wages that took place in steel between 1946 and 1956 had yielded wage increases fairly close to those that autoworkers had received under their COLA and productivity arrangement. Even more important, the prospect of a decline in the price level had disappeared by 1955 and, with it, the principal objection to the idea. A COLA clause would also ease the burden on the Steelworkers' negotiating team and allow it to devote more attention to other issues, principally job and income security. Management offered little resistance, apparently assuming that the overall price level, stable since the end of the Korean War, would not increase significantly over the next three years. That turned out to be a major miscalculation.[80]

In return for all that, the union agreed to a three-year contract without any annual reopening provisions, in effect signaling the end of a decade of constant bargaining between the two sides. Management had sought this change so as to achieve greater stability in the industry, which would make possible a program of expanding steel plant capacity and renovating existing plants without fear of work stoppages. Managers wanted, too, to keep the McDonald–Goldberg faction in charge of the union and reasoned that a generous settlement would help ensure that.

For these objectives they paid a heavy price, enabling McDonald to label the new contract "the best settlement ever made by the United Steelworkers of America."[81] And like the previous settlements, it was followed by yet another increase in steel prices, this time of $8.50 per ton. For the next two years, the wage concessions contained in the agreement ensured the continuation of that pattern. Such was the nature of the postwar New Deal in steel.[82]

But if the union had won a great deal through collective bargaining and political action between 1953 and 1957, serious weaknesses remained. At first glance, the institutional strength of the USA appeared impressive: a total membership by 1957 of about 1.1 million and monetary assets of just under $27 million. But the union's dynamism, its militancy, failed to keep up with the increasing size of the membership and the union's treasury. Joe Germano, never one to mince words, made the problem clear when explaining why the search for master contracts would be difficult:

> Where we have plants of one company all over the country I think we should make every effort—I know we have been making some progress and we have been making efforts—but in some instances the efforts haven't been too great because, frankly speaking, in some instances we have no Union. We have a contract, we have some wages there, but we haven't got the Union spirit instilled into these people where they are willing to strike for the purpose of bettering themselves . . . to have a uniform contract.[83]

The trend toward concentrating all-important decision making at the top and the union's narrowed vision were the main culprits, although the events of the previous seven years were simply part of a process that had begun during the early 1940s. David McDonald made that connection when he remarked to the board that a multiemployer bargaining session to work out details of the SUB program "is beginning to look like a veritable War Labor Board proceeding."[84] Those contradictory indications of labor's overall strength in 1957 were not, of course, confined to the USA. As we shall see, the labor movement as a whole had traveled much the same road over the past few years, one that had given workers substantial gains, but only at the expense of the militancy that had energized unions in the first place.

IV

No one was more aware of those problems than Goldberg, whose influence in the labor movement had grown with the progress toward unity of 1955–57. From his perspective, the signs of labor's health remained mixed. Public approval of unions as measured by national polling organizations stood at an all-time high of about 75 percent during those years, but labor corruption, especially in the highly publicized instance of the Teamsters Union, had begun to tarnish labor's image. Total union membership had also risen in the mid-1950s, albeit by a very modest amount, but the percentage of the workforce organized by labor had not. Even more disturbing, the organizing drives of the past three years had failed to achieve breakthroughs, and by 1956, the success rate in NLRB-supervised organizing elections had reached a twenty-year low. Most of the increase in union membership had come in sectors already organized, where the prospects for further expansion appeared modest. In 1957, so-called white-collar workers, almost all of them nonunion, for the first time outnumbered blue-collar ones. This growth in clerical and service-sector employment, partly the result of labor's strength in manufacturing, confronted labor with a daunting organizational challenge, one that union leaders had thus far been unable to meet. Thus by the end of 1957, the AFL–CIO had stalled, creating a sense of crisis among the most thoughtful of its supporters. Goldberg, though concerned, remained optimistic that labor could eventually resume its forward march.[85]

Sustaining that confidence was his awareness of both labor's power and the political and economic gains that workers had made in that same period. Following the fairly mild recession in 1954, unemployment had declined from an average official rate of 5.8 percent in that year to an average over the next three of 4.3 percent. Although the real figure was no doubt somewhat higher, it was still the best peacetime rate ever achieved since the federal government developed sophisticated surveys during the 1930s. And partly as a result, workers' income after 1954 resumed its steady climb. At the same time, the private benefits system that the USA and UAW had led the way in obtaining spread to other firms in the manufacturing sector.

It should be remembered, too, that this "privatized welfare state" aided more than just those members of industrial unions who directly participated in it. Also helped were the families of those workers, who benefited from the greater material security such plans provided. Members of the working and lower middle classes outside the unions profited as well, because managers who competed with unionized industries for employees were obliged to offer similar benefits. This spillover effect reached millions more Americans and gave them a degree of security that appeared almost miraculous when compared with what they had known only a decade earlier. If these economic gains made workers more materialistic, it distressed middle-class intellectuals more than it did the workers themselves, who wanted the greater security these economic gains made possible. This, at least, was Goldberg's view.[86]

He also knew how successfully labor had exercised its power in the political arena during those years. Determined labor lobbying during 1955 won better unemployment insurance benefits in twenty-six states and better workers' compensation benefits in thirty. At the same time, new minimum wage laws were enacted in Idaho, New Mexico, and Wyoming, and lawmakers in five other states enacted or substantially strengthened fair employment practices statutes there. At the federal level, labor helped the lowest-paid members of the working class with a successful campaign in 1955–57 to raise the minimum wage.

Labor, however, did not win every round. The unions had tried to raise the minimum wage from 75 cents to $1.25 but were forced to settle instead for $1.00, and an effort to expand the law's coverage met with failure. Even more troubling, labor was unable to prevent NLRB rulings that confined its jurisdiction to large-scale employers earning at least $500,000 from interstate commerce, which in effect helped protect many small businesses from union organizing campaigns. The board also increased its protection of employers who exercised the so-called free speech provision of the Taft–Hartley Act to defeat union organizing campaigns. Not content to stop there, the NLRB diminished strikers' legal right to keep their jobs and strengthened restrictions on the secondary boycott. These rulings, though helpful to antiunion employers, did not spell a major change in the balance of power between workers and managers. Labor's still potent political strength prevented that, leading many business leaders to conclude that Eisenhower's NLRB had failed to increase substantially management's bargaining power.[87]

In the 1956 elections, labor had also used its strength to maintain the federal government's support for the postwar New Deal. During its first four years the Eisenhower administration had pursued policies that differed little from those of its predecessor, and for that reason labor did not strongly oppose the general's reelection. In the spring of that year, the state of the economy and Eisenhower's record with workers indicated to Meany that the Republican ticket was certain to prevail. For those reasons, he favored no AFL–CIO endorsement for the Democratic ticket. Goldberg, on the other hand, backed Stevenson. In Goldberg's view, the alliance between labor and the Democrats should be maintained as long as their presidential candidates were preferable, regardless of the likely outcome.

After some heated discussion, the AFL–CIO Executive Council voted seventeen to five to endorse Goldberg's choice, but most unions did not work very hard on his behalf. Labor focused its energies instead on electing a Democratic Congress, a difficult task given Eisenhower's enormous popu-

larity. One indication of the problem lay in precedent: Only four times in
U.S. history and not since 1848 had voters elected the presidential candidate
of one party while at the same time giving control of Congress to the candidates of another. In the end, however, labor succeeded in maintaining the
Democrats' congressional majorities. Although Goldberg had preferred Stevenson and pushed hard for an AFL–CIO endorsement of his candidacy, he
did not strongly oppose Eisenhower, whose administration, he believed, had
treated labor fairly well, and especially so since the Republicans had lost
control of Congress in 1954. Despite increasing restiveness among business
managers over the concessions that the unions were continuing to win from
them, labor succeeded in maintaining a federal government strongly committed to the postwar social contract.[88]

The postwar New Deal thus continued to receive support from the state,
which in tandem with organized labor had done much over the previous
decade to improve the lives of American workers. But if the postwar social
contract worked well for many, for others the benefits were far smaller. The
biggest winners among the working class were white male union members
living in urban industrial areas, with everyone else lagging behind. For blacks,
Latinos, and other nonwhites, the period witnessed a steady improvement in
income but little real progress in combating segregation in the workplace, at
school, or in the housing market.

A presidential commission on government contracts was established toward the end of 1955, but it failed to end racial discrimination in firms doing
business with the federal government. Supreme Court rulings offered more
promise of eventual progress but had little impact on the daily existence of
most nonwhites. Domestics and members of the agricultural working class,
many of whom were also black or Latino, found themselves entirely excluded
from labor unions and also denied the protection of the Fair Labor Standards
Act and the minimum wage laws. They had gained little from what labor had
won since World War II.[89]

Goldberg was aware of those failings and, like his more sympathetic colleagues in the labor movement, had made efforts to address them. From the
very beginning of his tenure as CIO and Steelworkers' general counsel, he
had made clear his opposition to discrimination in the workplace, but conditions for blacks there did not greatly improve in the eight years after the
postwar social contract had been hammered out. In steel, the USA moved
very cautiously, typically attacking workplace discrimination only when a
promotion was denied to a highly qualified black. The USA, of course, was
not solely or even mostly to blame for such discrimination. Management had
exploited racial divisions in the working class for years in an effort to
strengthen its power vis-à-vis the rank and file. But the issue of race, which
had emerged in USA Executive Board discussions during World War II when
the number of black steel workers grew substantially, did not come up again at
a board meeting until the end of 1956. And when it did, the tone of that
discussion reveals how timidly the USA was responding to the problem.

McDonald reported in November 1956 that a USA committee charged with developing a program to fight segregation had recommended making a motion picture that documented the problem. Then, in his words,

> we propose to hold a showing in a theater in New York or Chicago, to which we will invite cultural, civic and fraternal leaders. . . . We shall show them this picture and leave the big question mark, "What are you going to do about it?" in their minds.
>
> Following the picture it would be our intention to say to this group, "We are now inviting your ideas, and 30 days from today . . . there will be a panel of distinguished . . . Americans [established] who will be sitting en banc as a Court . . . and these men would hold hearings and get your ideas . . . and after those ideas are digested . . . the panel shall write a code of fair practices on this subject of segregation."[90]

Such an approach was typical of the new politics that had emerged during the 1940s, one that emphasized reform from the top down rather than tackling the issue on the shop floor. The reluctance to act in the latter fashion stemmed not so much from the leaders' bigotry as from a fear that antiunion employers would seize the chance to undermine white workers' support for the union, which would imperil the postwar New Deal. The union's leadership, Goldberg included, wanted to redefine that social bargain so as to include blacks, but not at the risk of losing it entirely.

In order for the USA to have made substantial progress at that time, the union would have needed the cooperation of employers committed both to equality and to preserving labor's power in the workplace. But during that period, few managers were so socially responsible. Thus the most that the USA Executive Board could agree on at that meeting was to work harder against discriminatory seniority agreements. Most of the other unions formerly associated with the CIO did not do a great deal more, and many of the former AFL affiliates continued to pursue blatantly racist policies in cooperation with employers.[91]

Further progress, Goldberg believed, would have to await legislative enactments and court rulings in Washington. Once the legal basis for American apartheid had been removed, then the unions would be compelled to end discriminatory practices against blacks. At the same time, organized labor would also be able to move into the South and give blacks there a fair share of the benefits that followed from the postwar social contract. Reuther had made clear to the other CIO leaders when the merger was announced that he intended the new Industrial Union Department to be the primary vehicle for bringing about the latter change. While agreeing with Reuther's objective, Goldberg believed, however, that both labor and blacks would have to wait until changes in the laws helped foster an environment in the South conducive to that transformation.[92]

A 1955 strike by the Communications Workers in nine southern states revealed the extent of the obstacles that labor faced there at that time. At issue was the union's effort to end the lower rates of pay at Bell Telephone's southern affiliates. Ending the southern wage differential was in keeping with both the labor movement's emphasis on equal pay for equal work and its goal of diminishing the incentive for employers to move plants into the lower-wage, largely nonunion South. Managers at Bell responded to that demand with tactics reminiscent of the 1930s. As CWA leader Joe Beirne told the CIO Executive Board,

> This is a bitter fight, bitter in that the newspapers have reported a lot of violence, violence that our organization has no knowledge of, violence that is contrary to the policy of our organization.
>
> As late as the day before yesterday a shoot-to-kill order was signed by the Mayor of Knoxville. Similar instructions, while not signed proclamations or orders, have been issued in other places. . . .
>
> In the town of Morristown, [Tennessee,] for example, which I am sure the Textile Workers are familiar with, where their men were beaten to bloody pulps, shot at and some of them hit, where the union was broken in the mills . . . our fifty members in that town are 100 per cent on strike in this, the latter part of the eighth week; and they have resorted to bullets, the employers have, by paid thugs.
>
> The automobiles and homes of our people are being riddled with machine gun bullets night and day, and none of the law enforcement agencies seem to be able to get any record of even the occurrence.[93]

The simple fact of militant employer opposition, abetted by the governments in those states, thus precluded, Goldberg felt, doing much more in the South until the federal government ended the basis in law for that resistance.[94]

The record for women under the postwar New Deal was mixed as well and in some ways even more complicated. Although women had comprised roughly one-fifth of all unionized workers in 1944, they had been swiftly displaced from most of those jobs by the returning veterans who had held them before the war. Unwilling or unable to leave the paid workforce entirely, most of those women had settled instead for lower-paying and less secure jobs in the service sector. By 1950 both the total number of women in the paid labor force and the percentage of all women so employed were higher than before Pearl Harbor, and for the next seven years, both figures continued to rise steadily. At the same time, the number of women earning undergraduate and advanced degrees increased, and so, too, did the number of women trained as professionals. But even though the postwar social contract yielded rewards for women, it failed to do so in proportion to their numbers. When compared with men, women actually lost ground in education and professional employment during that time, and they continued to earn substantially less than men even when doing the same kind of work. At the same time, all but a small fraction of working-class women labored in nonunion jobs, a situation the AFL and CIO did little to change.[95]

Goldberg sympathized with the plight of working women during this period. Although the USA, unlike the UE and UAW, had not enrolled very many women members even during wartime and comparatively few afterward, Goldberg nonetheless knew from personal experience some of the issues that women faced in trying to achieve outside the home. One of the most influential figures in his life was Lillian Herstein, who worked as a union official, teacher, and government bureaucrat. He also benefited from the example of his own wife, for whom painting was very much a vocation and not just a hobby. Indicative of Goldberg's outlook was his friendship with Esther Peterson, a trade union official with the Amalgamated Clothing Workers who had lived in Sweden for a few years during the 1940s. She later became a lobbyist in Washington for the ACW during the early 1950s and, after the AFL–CIO merger, one of the chief legislative representatives of the new Industrial Union Department. She and Goldberg had stood together on the two legislative questions of greatest importance to working women during the 1950s, the proposals for an equal rights amendment (ERA) to the Constitution and an equal pay law.[96]

Peterson and Goldberg, like other labor union officials, had opposed the ERA on the grounds that such an amendment would do more for the business managers who supported it than it would for working women. In particular, labor leaders viewed the ERA as a threat to the whole host of protective legislation that labor had fought for and won since the late nineteenth century, laws that had done much to reduce the exploitation of women workers. Although their well-to-do "sisters" who supported the idea might have gained from it, Goldberg and Peterson believed they would do so only at the expense of working- and lower-middle-class women. Labor's opposition to the ERA, firmly and repeatedly expressed, helped keep it from going anywhere in Congress.[97]

Instead of this approach to the problems confronted by working women, Goldberg favored an equal pay law, which would have forbidden employers to pay women less than men received to do the same work. That idea had received strong support from the CIO, but not the AFL. The latter had opposed the idea from 1947 onward, arguing that the government should not be given the power to supervise job evaluations and wage scales. Although this objection was in keeping with the AFL's tradition of preserving its autonomy from the state, the federation's support for protective laws governing wages and hours pointed to an inconsistency in its position.

With the merger in 1956, the AFL changed its policy and joined the coalition supporting the proposed equal pay act. But by the end of 1957, after a decade of lobbying, the idea had gone nowhere in Congress, largely due to the opposition of the business community, which profited from paying lower wages to its female employees. At the state level, on the other hand, women met with more success. They won equal pay laws in six states between 1945 and 1950, and in all but one instance labor's support proved crucial. By 1950, no fewer than twelve states had passed such laws, and statutes in fifteen others specifically banned wage discrimination in at least some employment categories, most notably teaching. But even those laws, like the federal bill that failed to pass, did nothing to end discriminatory hiring practices, in which both managers and unions participated. For women then, the postwar social contract had yielded benefits, but ones far less than those received by most men.[98]

Losing even more were the poor and the dissenting radicals. The former shared only modestly in the postwar abundance. The fifth of the population earning the least—which included most of the poor—saw its portion of national income decline in the decade after 1945, albeit slightly, from 5.0 percent to 4.8 percent. Denied the protection of the privatized welfare state that labor had won for itself and much of the middle class, the poor fell even further behind when sick or aged. Life for them, though not as desperate as it had been during the Depression, remained grim. Suffering in a different way were the radicals who had opposed the postwar New Deal. Throughout this period they were hounded by employers, unions, and the government, which viewed them as a threat to that social bargain. Although the dominant mood of this period was one of complacency, the fates of the poor and the radicals served as sobering reminders of how imperfectly the postwar New Deal worked, even during its heyday.[99]

The operation of the American version of the postwar social contract was connected, of course, to developments in the larger international order established during the late 1940s. Labor's fate at home was intimately connected to that of unions in Western Europe and Japan. Like other labor leaders, Goldberg clearly understood that fact and pushed hard during the early 1950s for Marshall Plan aid to help rebuild organized labor in those societies and to see that workers there benefited from American economic aid. Only in that way would the power relationships in the highly industrialized market societies continue to favor supporters of the postwar social contract. For that reason, both the AFL and CIO monitored closely how Marshall Plan funds were spent, anxious to prevent a distribution that increased managerial power at the expense of social democratic unionists.[100]

CIO leaders had few illusions about the limited nature of their role in the Economic Cooperation Agency (ECA), which administered the aid program. ECA policies had, from the very beginning, displeased Goldberg, Murray, and other CIO leaders. They remained concerned that most of the Marshall Plan aid in France and Italy, where radicals dominated working-class organizations, was flowing to business managers. The result was only to intensify workers' support in those countries for socialist policies, rather than the social democratic alternative favored by the CIO's leadership.

The onset of the Korean War, which diverted social resources from civilian goods to munitions, only further alienated workers in those societies. Without working-class support, Murray and other CIO leaders believed, efforts to halt the spread of communism would fail. Murray made this clear when he told the CIO Executive Board shortly after the Korean War broke out that "it don't make too much difference how much money you pour into armaments . . . unless you give the people the food and build up their morale and give them better standards of living they won't fight."[101]

To get that message across to their own government, Murray, Goldberg, Reuther, Jacob Potofsky, and a CIO staff man, Michael Ross, met with ECA administrator W. Averell Harriman and two of his aides on August 28, 1950. During that closed-door session held in Murray's Washington, D.C., hotel room, the CIO group "made loud protestations" against the way in which Marshall Plan aid was being distributed in France and Italy and demanded a greater role for American labor in administering the ECA.[102]

The sense of urgency engendered by the outbreak of fighting in Korea, when combined with labor pressure, did encourage Harriman and other ECA administrators to direct more of the economic aid to the French and Italian working classes. Aid alone, however, did not immediately induce most of their members to desert unions headed by communists. At least some CIO leaders understood that many workers in those societies still favored the more radical agenda that the Communist Party leaders advocated, regardless of how "fairly" American aid was distributed. As CIO Executive Board member George Baldanzi told his colleagues the day after the CIO delegation met with Harriman,

> The only reason Communism in Italy is as strong as it was five years ago is because they [the party leaders] still express the overwhelming desires of the workers of that country. We might as well make up our minds to that. It is all right to make speeches against Communism but as long as the left-wing unions emulate the desires of the people you are not going to establish the kind of unions we ought to have to combat Communism.[103]

During the early and middle 1950s, however, American labor leaders did make progress in their campaign against radical French and Italian labor organizations. In France, the fraction of workers enrolled in unions declined as workers began to shun them more generally, and in Italy substantial numbers moved from unions headed by communists to those led by social democrats. Thus the American labor movement helped bolster support abroad for the postwar social contract.[104]

In northern Europe, on the other hand, working-class organizations tended from the beginning to back the CIO's position. In West Germany, the CIO strongly supported efforts to rebuild the labor movement and to protect it once the conservative Adenauer government came to power in 1953. When Adenauer's administration attempted to weaken labor's power there by trying to split the German labor federation, the CIO protested privately to the State Department, and Reuther issued a public warning to the West German government to stay out of labor's internal affairs.

At the center of contacts between American and northern European labor groups was Goldberg, who drew on the network of friends he had developed during the war. He attended ICFTU sessions abroad, lobbied the Truman administration for increasing American labor's role in the postwar order, and argued consistently that winning the allegiance of the European working class was the key to containing communism. Goldberg and the CIO he represented mattered more than did the AFL affiliates in the international arena, because unionists in northern Europe favored the CIO's social democratic line over the AFL's more cautious brand of business unionism.[105]

The American labor movement did not confine such efforts to Europe alone. Murray, Goldberg, Green, and Meany pressed as well for U.S. aid in building Latin American labor unions and to reconstruct Japanese unions suppressed during the 1930s and early 1940s. In particular, they argued that the State Department should appoint labor attachés to the embassies in those countries, who would use American influence to press for employer acceptance of unions. Their efforts yielded only modest results in Latin America, but in Japan the labor movement did recover, although largely because the working class there would accept nothing less. In those societies then, American labor power affected the outcome only marginally.[106]

The CIO's influence was felt more strongly in shaping American foreign economic policy more generally, in part because the federation's two largest affiliates dominated industries of enormous importance to the overall economy. The greater influence of the CIO than the AFL even with the Eisenhower administration became evident when, shortly after taking office, it established the Commission on Foreign Economic Policy. The group was charged with developing a policy for increasing world trade, in line with the Republicans' 1952 campaign pledge of "trade, not aid." Eisenhower appointed Clarence Randall, Inland Steel's chief executive officer and former steel consultant for the ECA, to head the group, and added David McDonald to represent labor. Most of the other fifteen were so-called public members, drawn from both the executive branch and the staffs of the relevant congressional committees.

The Randall Commission, as it came to be called, was intended to enlist support in Congress for reducing tariffs, an idea still strongly resisted there as late as 1953. Within the steel industry itself, such sentiment was mostly confined to the smaller producers, with the notable exception of Inland, which by virtue of its midwestern location and proximity to markets there, faced little immediate prospect of foreign competition. The CIO's interest in the issue was great because its two largest affiliates manufactured steel, trucks, and agricultural implements, for which there was strong demand in overseas markets. At the same time, the revival of the steel industries of Western Europe and Japan portended increased competition for both American and overseas markets.[107]

In the end, however, the goal of reviving the economies of the other Western industrialized societies and Japan so as to contain the spread of Soviet-style socialism trumped that of protecting American industries from foreign competitors. The Randall Commission's report, although it broke little new ground in the area of tariff reductions, did help persuade a reluctant business community and Congress to maintain the present policy of modest tariffs in the face of increasing European and Japanese industrial production. Also left untouched was the program of direct U.S. economic assistance to foreign industries, most notably steel.

From the beginning of Truman's second term in 1949 through the end of 1953, when the Randall Commission submitted its report, direct American aid to foreign steel producers in Western Europe, Japan, and the newly industrializing societies of the Third World totaled $369 million, and the Eisenhower administration, rather than reversing that trend, accelerated it. Over the next four years, the U.S. government paid out another $567.5

million, not including other forms of indirect aid such as help in training managers and securing raw materials.

Labor's contribution and that of the entire commission was not to break new ground in foreign economic policy. Rather, the USA in particular and labor more generally supported the commission so as to preserve the postwar social contract while the other industrialized societies in the Western alliance rebuilt their economies.[108]

This did not mean that American labor leaders failed to grasp the potential problem of foreign competition, but only that they refused to address it through protectionist policies that most believed had contributed to the Depression. Goldberg and his colleagues instead had favored establishing a program of federal government subsidies to American industries damaged by lower tariffs. The program would provide severance pay to workers and retraining, along with loans to communities and firms to help them shift into new kinds of manufacturing. Labor failed, however, to win the Randall Commission's support for the idea, after conservative Republicans on the panel threatened to abandon it if the majority supported a subsidy program. Even without that approach, Goldberg continued to support lower tariffs as a way to increase economic growth, and seems to have thought that the best way to guard against foreign competition was to encourage the unions in the other Western industrialized countries and Japan to seek wages and benefits comparable to those won by the American labor movement. In that way, the loss of markets to low-wage and less expensive foreign competitors would be avoided.

During the early 1950s, the economies of Western Europe and Japan had been so fragile that wages there remained substantially lower than in the United States, but by 1956 conditions had so improved that Goldberg expected unions to begin pushing much harder for wages and benefits similar to those now prevalent in the American manufacturing sector.[109]

For that reason, Goldberg strongly supported international conferences between trade union leaders and led the USA delegation, which consisted of himself and two district directors, Marty Burns and C. B. Newell, to the International Metal Workers conference held in Stratford, England, in the fall of 1956. He startled the Western European and Japanese union leaders who attended, by describing in detail the recently concluded contract between the USA and executives of the major American steelmakers. When Goldberg finished his presentation, his audience responded with surprise, envy, and even apprehension that the contract might upset the economic equilibrium achieved during the past three years. In C. B. Newell's words,

> When General Counsel Goldberg presented the entire story [of the 1956 contract] he did so in great . . . detail, and the picture shocked and almost stunned some of the people, particularly the representatives from Germany. The aggressiveness, the militancy, the power of the Steelworkers in America was something they could not quite accept, they didn't understand it, and it jolted . . . them.[110]

They were shocked, too, at the disparities in wages between themselves and their American counterparts. The comparison came naturally because, as Newell explained,

> the steel industry represents a completely universal language. We went to a couple of steel mills, and after I left England I went up to Sweden and visited some of the industries in that country, and wherever I go I find I might just as well be going to a plant somewhere in the United States. The plants look alike, they smell alike, . . . the working processes are precisely the same, and the end product is the same; they sell it for the same price the American worker does. The only difference is the rate of pay paid to the guy who makes steel, and that difference is very great indeed.[111]

In reporting on the session to the USA Executive Board, Goldberg defended the need for such conferences as a way of sharing information and also because they would prod Western European and Japanese unions to seek higher wages, which in the longer run would work to the USA's own advantage. He told the board:

> In Europe and in Japan and in every steel country all over the world, every time our bosses raise the price they raise the prices over there, but they don't raise wages. But the significant difference is this: Forty percent of the sales dollar in steel in the United States goes to labor, that is the proportion of labor cost. In Europe it is 17 percent. You see what that means in terms of our own position, so we owe a big obligation to remain active in this field.
>
> I think our great contribution to this conference was summed up by Harry Douglass [of the British steelworkers union] at the end when he came to us and said, "By God, we've got to stiffen our demands."[112]

Thus did the USA attempt to strengthen the postwar social contract at home by encouraging its extension abroad to other industrialized societies.

In the meantime, if European workers earned somewhat less than their American counterparts, in other ways the former were still better off. The industrialized societies of northern and western Europe had all established the comprehensive health, old age, and employment insurance systems that had eluded American workers in the postwar period. Perhaps even more important, in Germany and Scandinavia, organized labor had achieved greater control over the direction of business organizations. In Germany, workers in some industries had won "Mitbestimmungsrecht," or "codetermination," which gave them direct representation on the boards that ran major firms. In Sweden, workers also won a greater say in the direction of economic enterprises, through a combination of worker representation on corporate boards and a highly centralized system of collective bargaining. In those societies, then, unions found themselves better able to restrain managerial efforts to replace labor with new equipment and to win schemes that eased the burden on workers when such changes did take place. The net result was to make jobs more secure for the rank and file, which was one of its primary goals.[113]

It was that achievement, and especially the German one, that Walter

Reuther sought without success to emulate in the United States. What Reuther never entirely understood was that German managers had been compelled to yield codetermination only because losing the war had done so much to demoralize and discredit them, as well as to reduce their political and economic power. In the United States, however, the war had produced the opposite result. Thus the differing consequences of the war for Western European and American workers made for somewhat different outcomes in those places. Still unclear, however, was whether those differences would persist or diminish as the Western European economy continued its steady comeback.[114]

Because he was more conscious of the limits to winning something like codetermination in the United States, Goldberg was more inclined to press for the sort of highly centralized collective bargaining system to be found in Sweden, which would leave more managerial prerogatives intact but nonetheless yield greater job security than had been obtained thus far by most American unions. Even this more modest goal he saw as one to be achieved only gradually. To attempt to move more quickly, he feared, would serve only to alienate managers and weaken their support for the existing social bargain. This concern was heightened when, during the spring of 1957, the first clear signs of a managerial revolt against it began to appear. Goldberg's efforts to turn back that challenge formed a key turning point in both his own career and the operation of the postwar New Deal with which it was so closely identified.[115]

6

The Postwar Order Under Stress, Round One

T HE YEAR 1957 would prove to be a turning point for Arthur Goldberg and organized labor, as well as for the social contract they had achieved during the late 1940s. Over the next five years, that agreement would come under growing pressure from managers seeking to win back some of the concessions they had made, from an increasingly restive rank and file who wanted more of a say in how unions and the workplace were governed, and from groups such as blacks and women who grew steadily more discontented with their disproportionately small shares of the agreement's benefits. Those pressures had existed before 1957 but until then had been largely kept in check by the groups that had earlier worked out the postwar New Deal. Despite those formidable challenges, its defenders would succeed in preserving the postwar order during this period. The contest would make Goldberg a major public figure and prove to be the high point of his career.

The single most important source of those growing divisions was an economic downturn, which began in the fall of 1957 and became the worst since the Great Depression. The subsequent recovery in 1959 and early 1960 soon gave way to yet another recession almost as deep, the effects of which persisted through the end of 1962. The immediate causes of the prolonged downturn were declines in consumer spending on durable goods and in capital investment by corporations, after a three-year boom in both areas. The underlying reason for those changes lay in the nation's growing inflation rate, which stemmed largely from the struggle between labor and management over their respective shares of the fruits of the postwar social contract, combined with the Eisenhower administration's inability to police prices. Making matters still worse were the efforts by managers in the late 1950s to win back lost prerogatives as a way of restoring price stability without endangering profits, a campaign that disrupted the economy even further. Taken together, those developments created the economic and political crisis of this period.[1]

The most visible symptoms of the emerging crisis were higher levels of inflation and unemployment. Although prices had remained fairly stable from 1953 to 1955, they climbed an average of 4.1 percent during each of the following two years. By the spring of 1957, the Eisenhower administration had begun to press for reduced government spending, on armaments in particular, and for tighter credit so as to restore price stability. Although eventually successful in reducing inflation, the new policies failed to eliminate it. From 1958 to 1962, a period in which the federal government maintained the same basic approach despite a change in administration, prices rose at an annual rate of almost 1.7 percent.

At the same time, and as a direct result of the new economic policies, the official unemployment rate increased from an average of less than 4 percent between 1950 and 1957 to just over 6 percent during the following five years. Indeed, when compared with what workers had known since the end of the Depression in 1941, the five-year period beginning in the fall of 1957 resembled a permanent recession. And unemployment among blacks living in urban areas rose to heights approaching those that whites had experienced during the worst years of the 1930s. The result was to weaken popular support for the federal government's policies, as well as for the postwar New Deal more generally, and to diminish labor's bargaining power vis-à-vis employers.[2]

The new economic policies had yet another problematic result, namely, reviving disagreement over the proper level of military spending. The public controversy over the Soviets' successful launch of the *Sputnik* satellite reflected a deeper division among the nation's leaders over Soviet intentions and capabilities.

During its second term, the Eisenhower administration pushed for a modest reduction in expenditures on armaments, believing it would reduce inflation without creating any real risk to the postwar order. But the effort was controversial with leaders from management, labor, and both major political parties, many of whom argued in favor of maintaining the status quo. The issue provoked sharp debate because it had implications not just for the military strength of the Western alliance but also because the cut would diminish the largest component of countercyclical government spending. This would have potentially severe consequences for the workers and managers in the industries directly affected, as well as for the economy as a whole. Despite the resistance the change engendered, the Eisenhower administration did reduce military spending significantly from 1958 to 1960, a change its successor essentially maintained. The shift also brought renewed wrangling over the proper nature and amount of government spending on armaments after eight years of fairly widespread agreement among business managers, labor leaders, and politicians.[3]

Making matters even more difficult was the emergence in 1958 of a large U.S. deficit in its balance of payments with its major trading partners. The deficit stemmed in part from the rising prices of American-made goods, which hampered the sale of exports and encouraged imports, and from the federal government's policy of relaxing trade barriers. After only very modest deficits between 1953 and 1956 and a surplus the following year, there came a dramatic change. The deficit in 1958 grew to more than five times the average since 1953 and was the beginning of a long-term pattern of increases. By 1960, that change had created a crisis in the foreign currency markets. Over the following two years, the system of fixed exchange rates devised at the 1944 Bretton Woods Conference came under severe pressure, as the value of U.S. dollars declined relative to Western European currencies.[4]

In all, the period stretching from the fall of 1957 through the end of 1962 marked the first serious crisis for the postwar political and economic system, one that offered neither management nor labor a decisive victory. It could best be characterized as a period of stresses and stalemate, of challenges made and contained but not eliminated. That constituted a kind of limited triumph for Goldberg and the other defenders of the postwar New Deal while their managerial opponents experienced enormous and growing frustration. The inconclusive contest and the divisions it reflected helped spark a period of social ferment, one that marked a change from the numbing blandness of the preceding eight years. The struggle between the two sides also led to the public airing of problems that had been concealed during that period, creating what some social commentators called a crisis in public morality. At the same time it offered the first serious challenge to those intellectuals who viewed consensus as characteristic of American life, both past and present.

For Goldberg, these years were filled with growing responsibility and prominence but also with increasing concern over the challenges facing the labor movement and the postwar social contract it had fought to sustain. Viewed from his perspective, one can see both how labor held its managerial opponents at bay during this time and why the effort, in the longer run, was doomed to fail. The entire period can be neatly divided into three distinct stages of approximately equal length, which this chapter and the two that follow it will address. To the first of those intervals, which makes up the story of this chapter, we now turn.[5]

II

The years 1957 and 1958 were marked by managerial efforts to regain the initiative from labor and the state in determining the shape of the postwar order. The sea change in employer attitudes developed soon after the 1956 elections, and partly in response to their result. Eisenhower had been returned to office by a huge electoral vote margin, but unlike 1952, his administration's popularity had not carried Republican congressional majorities in along with it. And unlike four years earlier, Eisenhower could never again run for reelection, the first American president barred by the Constitution from seeking a third term. The president's value to conservatives had thus clearly been reduced. The result was to weaken the administration's power to keep in check those among them who had never become genuine supporters of the postwar New Deal.[6]

At the same time, the administration came under increasing pressure to reduce labor's power, from many of the business realists who had previously supported that social bargain. For them, the emergence of inflation as a serious problem indicated the need for a return to a more confrontational approach in dealing with organized labor. Leaders of the core industrial firms, most notably U.S. Steel, sought to regain the control over production processes lost during the 1930s and 1940s and to weaken unions' power to win wage increases in accordance with the productivity formula. In that way, such managers reasoned, labor costs could be reduced, thereby eliminating the inflation and balance-of-payments problems. This program rested on an assumption that unions were to blame for the crisis and that workers therefore should bear the primary burden of resolving it.[7]

Not all business realists endorsed this view of the problem. Such a formulation struck some of them as too one-sided and potentially disruptive. Men such as Thomas J. Watson Jr. of IBM and Joseph Block of Inland Steel would instead argue during this period for a more consensual solution to the crisis, one that preserved the postwar social contract and labor's place in it. This difference of opinion led to a major rift in the ranks of leading business managers, a split that weakened still further the Eisenhower administration they had backed so strongly in its first term. During 1957/58, however, the business realists more hostile to labor would seize the initiative by launching a campaign aimed at securing their objectives.[8]

The first part of a concerted effort to win back power lost to labor and the state consisted of putting pressure on Congress to investigate and publicize corruption in the labor movement. In that way, conservatives hoped to delegitimate labor in the eyes of the public and create momentum for changes in the national labor relations act that would reduce labor's power in the workplace and the realm of elective politics. Managers pressed huge publicity campaigns through the news media and the schools to arouse hostility toward corrupt union officials.

The pressure culminated during January 1957 in the establishment of a Senate investigating committee, the Select Committee on Improper Activities in the Labor or Management Field, chaired by antilabor Senator John McClellan of Arkansas. Despite the seeming evenhandedness implied by the committee's name, the group was never intended to probe with equal effort corruption in both labor and managerial ranks. Rather, the McClellan Committee, as it soon became popularly known, was intended to expose trade union corruption on the unspoken and erroneous assumption that unions alone had such problems. The committee's composition testified to its one-sidedness: Of its eight members, five came from states that had outlawed the union shop. Using all the means perfected during earlier congressional investigations of radicals and racketeers, the committee's conservative majority quickly began gathering evidence and issuing subpoenas.[9]

Labor unions clearly shared some of the blame for this development. They had failed to take action earlier against much of the existing corruption, thereby exposing themselves to the risk of just such an attack. Goldberg had argued ever since becoming CIO general counsel that unions needed to police themselves more effectively in that area. In the USA itself, Murray's early concern with the issue had led to the creation of safeguards that prevented most of the abuses that plagued some major AFL unions, notably the Teamsters and Longshoremen.

When the emergence of large pension funds created the potential for new kinds of corruption, Goldberg had insisted that the USA assign to steel managers the sole responsibility for administering such funds. Murray, although inclined at first to push for joint administration, had agreed with Goldberg's reasoning that such an approach would likely lead to wrongdoing or mismanagement. The USA, therefore, would face no serious problems in that area.[10]

Believing that self-regulation would prove effective, CIO leaders had opposed managerial pressure for greater government supervision of the ways in which labor administered its pension and welfare funds. The AFL's chieftains had less reason to believe that such an approach would be adequate. Corruption already plagued some of their largest affiliates, principally the Teamsters, Garment Workers, building trades, and Longshoremen's unions. The older federation, however, had also opposed government supervision of such funds when they first came into being. AFL leaders' traditional hostility to intervention by a government that they still doubted would treat unions fairly had led them to assume that position.

After studying the issue for eight months, the Wage Stabilization Board in late 1951 issued a report on the pension fund issue. Over the objections of the three employer representatives, the board endorsed, with only a few modest exceptions, the self-regulation approach.[11]

It was sufficient in the Steelworkers, thanks in part to Goldberg's vigilance. Most of the other CIO affiliates, however, had paid less attention to the issue in the belief that serious corruption was essentially an AFL problem. As early as the fall of 1954, however, following a New York State probe of abuses in union administration of pension funds, Goldberg had informed CIO Executive Board members that their assumption was incorrect. At a meeting on October 5 he recounted to them the state insurance authorities' findings that local CIO union officials had, among other things, used pension funds to buy automobiles for their personal use, had taken money outright, and charged pension and welfare funds enormous fees for administration when no work of any kind was involved. Endeavoring to shatter the board's complacency, he told its members that "the disclosures in New York indicate that there is a problem within the CIO. That is not saying anything in particular against the retail union, because we cannot say that the problem is confined to the retail union. We do not know."[12] He also warned the board that "the problem of the administration of welfare funds is going to be very, very much in the

Captain Goldberg, Labor Branch, Office of Strategic Services (OSS).
Arthur J. Goldberg Papers, Library of Congress.

(*Left*) Dorothy Kurgans Goldberg. Photo courtesy of Frances S. Guilbert. (*Right*) Lillian Herstein, Goldberg's teacher and early mentor. The George Meany Memorial Archives.

(*Left*) Van A. Bittner, the CIO leader in Chicago who first brought Goldberg into the union movement. USWA / Penn State University, Historical Collections and Labor Archives. (*Right*) Joe Germano, Director of Steelworkers Union District 31 (East Chicago, Indiana), another early and important CIO colleague and supporter. USWA / Penn State University, Historical Collections and Labor Archives.

The new CIO general counsel (Goldberg, *far left*) and colleagues (*from left to right*) James Carey, Philip Murray, Jacob Potofsky, and Emil Rieve exit the White House smiling after meeting with the recently re-elected Harry Truman. Wide World Photos, Inc. / The George Meany Memorial Archives.

The United Labor Policy Committee meets with Truman in April 1951 to discuss Korean War mobilization efforts. UPI / Bettmann Archive.

Goldberg, CIO president Philip Murray (*center*), and Goldberg's secretary, Frances Simonson Guilbert, during the 1952 steel negotiations. Wide World Photos, Inc. / Frances S. Guilbert.

Goldberg with Murray's successor as Steelworkers Union president, David J. McDonald. USWA / Penn State University, Historical Collections and Labor Archives.

Retiring U.S. Steel CEO Benjamin Fairless (*right*) shakes hands with his successor, Roger M. Blough, in May 1955. USWA / Penn State University, Historical Collections and Labor Archives.

Goldberg with CIO and Autoworkers president Walter Reuther (*center*) and Machinists Union president Al Hayes. National Publishing Company / The George Meany Memorial Archives.

George Meany pins on Goldberg's official badge at the convention held in December 1955 that officially merged the AFL and CIO. The George Meany Memorial Archives.

Goldberg, Communications Workers president Joseph Beirne, and United Textile Workers president Anthony Valente meeting with Eisenhower (*left*) in January 1957 to discuss the minimum wage. Wide World Photos Inc. / Dwight D. Eisenhower Library.

Goldberg with Adlai Stevenson. Photo courtesy of Frances S. Guilbert.

Goldberg's law partners, David Feller (*left*), who succeeded him as Steelworkers general counsel, and Elliot Bredhoff. USWA / Penn State University, Historical Collections and Labor Archives.

David McDonald (*right*) with U.S. Steel chief negotiator R. Conrad Cooper (*with cigar*). USWA / Penn State University, Historical Collections and Labor Archives.

Goldberg and top Steelworkers Union officials (*from left to right*) I. W. Abel, Howard Hague, and David McDonald meet with Eisenhower during the 1959 steel strike. National Park Service / Dwight D. Eisenhower Library.

public eye in the immediate period ahead. There are obviously political implications involved. It is quite apparent that certain forces in this country want to
use this subject for political reasons."[13]

The board responded by creating an ethical practices committee composed
of Goldberg, Joseph Curran, Jacob Potofsky, and James Thimmes. They were
asked to investigate any complaints in that area, then to devise a set of rules
governing the administration of all pension and welfare funds, and to recommend any appropriate legislation. As a first step, the committee circulated a
questionnaire to all CIO affiliates to learn how each administered such funds.
Every union promptly supplied detailed answers, which the committee then
used as the basis for a two-day public hearing in New York. The two purposes
of the meeting were to solicit advice from insurance company officials and
academics on how best to guard against malfeasance while at the same time
advertising the CIO's efforts to police itself. The event achieved both objectives, drawing an audience of more than 250 such officials and academics, as
well as more than thirty journalists from major American newspapers. The
federation published a transcript of the hearings in book form and distributed
copies to those who attended and to the CIO leadership.

At the next CIO Executive Board meeting on December 1, Goldberg
reported those developments and announced that the committee's report,
which contained a set of internal union standards, would be ready for submis-
sion to the CIO National Convention planned for later that month. Seeking
to reassure the federation's top leaders about each union's autonomy, Goldberg noted, "This will be a voluntary set of standards that the CIO will
recommend to its affiliated unions."[14]

The committee's recommendations for self-regulation included a detailed,
annual audit of each fund, which would be circulated to the rank and file, and
the adoption by each union's national office of a set of rules governing the
locals' activities in that area. The latter remedy was to be combined with
giving the national office the power to audit locals suspected of wrongdoing
and to discipline any found guilty. The committee also recommended placing
some limits on the commissions paid to companies handling the contributions
to such funds and on the payments to the union officials charged with administering them. In that way, the committee hoped to put a stop to paying
inflated commissions in exchange for kickbacks and overcharging for administering the welfare fund, the two most prevalent and damaging kinds of
malfeasance it had uncovered.[15]

The CIO convention did adopt the proposed code, thereby recommending
it to all the federation's affiliates. The Ethical Practices Committee's recommendations for legislation were completed the following spring, and Goldberg presented them to the board at a meeting held in May 1955. The
committee, he reported, had concluded that federal legislation was needed,
both to prevent further corruption and to keep the states from adopting a
crazy quilt of different regulatory schemes. Goldberg presented the proposed
statute to the board that would have required each union to file an annual

report with the Labor Department explaining how pension and welfare funds were being administered. These filing requirements were to be backed by criminal penalties for failing to comply.

Although the CIO Executive Board unanimously approved the committee's recommendations, the proposal went nowhere, largely because of differences with the AFL over the issue. In adopting a similar plan that same month, the AFL's Executive Council had insisted that the Bureau of Internal Revenue receive the reports rather than the Labor Department and that the penalty for failing to file properly be limited to the loss of tax-exempt status. The CIO Ethical Practices Committee, however—in Goldberg's words—thought the AFL proposal a mistake, explaining that "we do not have confidence in the Bureau and its regulation to vest in them the enforcement of this provision. . . . We think it is much sounder to vest in the Department of Labor the operation and to provide as we have criminal sections."[16] The disagreement between the two stymied the effort for remedial legislation, leaving organized labor vulnerable when the McClellan Committee began its operation.

That vulnerability was greatly increased by the much more serious problem of AFL corruption. Although George Meany opposed corruption in principle and played a leading role soon after becoming AFL president in expelling the International Longshoremen's Association (ILA), one of the worst offenders, the weakness of the federation's national headquarters combined with Meany's own caution left other affiliates untouched. The managerial offensive and the McClellan Committee it inspired would greatly strengthen Meany's ability to oust the unions dominated by gangsters but also expose the entire labor movement during 1957 to blame for its association with such organizations.[17]

Labor's opponents made the most of those weaknesses. The McClellan Committee assembled the largest investigative staff in the history of Congress at that time, eventually employing more than a hundred people. The committee established offices in eight cities and by the end of 1957 had fifteen different investigations under way simultaneously. Over its three-year term of existence the committee would take testimony from more than fifteen hundred witnesses, which filled over fifty volumes, and at the peak of its activity would be receiving more than six hundred letters a day requesting investigations. Most harmful to labor's public standing, the fledgling television networks broadcast the committee's hearings day after day to almost every community in America.[18]

Meany and Goldberg had at first responded cautiously to the McClellan Committee's creation. Unhappy with the corruption rampant in a few major unions, both men understood that no one could argue persuasively that there was no basis for such a probe. Rather than fight the whole idea, they decided to try to work with the committee so as to prevent unwarranted investigations. Soon after the committee began its work, Goldberg and Meany met for breakfast in the Senate Office Building with McClellan; New York Senator Irving Ives, the ranking Republican on the committee; and its chief counsel,

Robert Kennedy. There they worked out a procedure for allowing Goldberg, on behalf of the AFL–CIO, to evaluate any proposed investigation before the committee moved ahead with it. In return, Meany and Goldberg agreed to urge the AFL–CIO Executive Council to cooperate with the committee's work.[19]

The screening procedure proved to be a valuable concession, in part thanks to Robert Kennedy's ignorance of the labor movement. A thirty-one-year-old moderate Democrat who had voted for Eisenhower in 1956, Kennedy's credentials for the job consisted of a law degree from the University of Virginia, a brief stint at the Justice Department, and a much longer one on the staff of the Senate's Permanent Subcommittee on Investigations. He had gone there first in January 1953 as an assistant counsel to its chairman, Joseph McCarthy, then at the height of his monstrous power. After seven months Kennedy left the job, having grown disillusioned with McCarthy's methods but not his goal of investigating radicals, and then returned the following year as counsel for the committee's Democratic members. As general counsel for the McClellan Committee, Kennedy was charged with directing all investigations. In that role he proved to be rash, overzealous, and often oblivious to the harm the committee's work could cause the labor movement as a whole.

Goldberg recalled much later one example of his troubles with Robert Kennedy at that time:

> I remember one time Bobby Kennedy wanted to subpoena a fellow from California whose only malefaction — alleged — . . . was that the union paid his moving expenses. And I said to young Robert Kennedy . . . , "You're out of your mind! You were born a rich fellow. Executives, businesses always pay moving expenses and a labor fellow transferred by his union from California to New York hasn't got the money to move his family. It's a legitimate expense."[20]

Through those kinds of exchanges, Goldberg reduced the number of proposed investigations and in the process taught both Robert Kennedy and his brother John, who was serving on the McClellan Committee, a good deal about how the labor movement worked.[21]

In addition to that essentially defensive response to the McClellan Committee's work, Goldberg also pressed the labor movement to take affirmative steps to clean its own house. Following the AFL–CIO merger, the federation had established its own Ethical Practices Committee, composed of Goldberg, Potofsky, and Curran from the CIO; George Harrison of the Railway Clerks, Al Hayes of the Machinists; and David Dubinsky of the Garment Workers. Assigning equal numbers of members from each of the two federations constituted a departure from the general two-thirds AFL, one-third CIO pattern applied to most other merged bodies, a sign of how sensitive the labor leaders believed the corruption issue to be.[22]

Along with the other two lawyers in his firm, Goldberg drafted six ethical practices codes for the new federation. They dealt with the chartering of locals; corruption in handling pension and welfare funds; infiltration by gangsters, radicals, or other "undesirables"; conflict-of-interest problems that trade union officials might encounter; the operation of union treasuries; and democratic procedures within unions. The federation soon adopted those codes, thereby making each affiliate's membership in the AFL–CIO contingent on observing their requirements. At the same time, the federation passed the codes along to the affiliates for consideration and ratification. That latter step, if taken, would obligate each member of an affiliate to obey the codes or face expulsion from his or her own union. The federation's Ethical Practices Committee would hear all such disputes, a departure from the tradition of allowing the affiliates' governing bodies to resolve such matters themselves.[23]

The codes — in essence the same as those Goldberg had earlier drawn up for the CIO — were considered by the USA Executive Board in a meeting on May 17, 1957. He made the presentation, discussing in detail the codes' provisions, including the expulsion remedy for serious offenders. The rules were novel, Goldberg observed, only in that they were now formally written down. He stated emphatically to the USA Executive Board that the Ethical Practices Codes were "not a new statement, these are not new codes — the Committee has been attempting to restate some fundamental principles of trade union morality that have always governed the trade union movement and, God willing, always will govern the trade union movement."[24]

As was true in other areas of trade union activity, the codes' creation reflected a trend during the postwar period toward replacing older, less formal procedures governing union members' behavior with steadily more legalistic ones. In his remarks, Goldberg noted that the USA's legal department had played the principal part in formulating the codes, urging the other affiliates to adopt them, and investigating corrupt affiliates. Not everyone on the USA Executive Board approved of that trend or of allowing the federation's Ethical Practices Committee to sit in judgment on the honesty of each affiliate's members. But despite District Director James Robb's impassioned attack on the proposed codes for those reasons, in the end only he voted against their adoption.[25]

While the affiliates debated whether to adopt the codes for themselves, the federation's Ethical Practices Committee moved into its investigative phase. In carrying out that task, the committee received support from its staff, which, Goldberg noted, "consists of three lawyers of the Steelworkers Union, myself, Dave [Feller], and Elliott [Bredhoff]."[26] So far, he reported, the committee had investigated three unions — the Allied Industrial Workers, the Distillery Workers, and the Laundry Workers — and found serious problems in all of them. In February 1957 the Ethical Practices Committee met in a Miami hotel to "try" those unions. All three were found guilty and ordered to rid themselves of corruption within ninety days or face expulsion from the federation. Fearful of exposing themselves to raiding if ousted, the three affiliates made efforts to reform. They were all small, however, and lacked the resources needed to survive outside the AFL–CIO.

The bigger problems lay ahead, with Goldberg noting that the committee was proceeding next to investigate the Teamsters and Bakers Unions. The disposition of those two cases would test Meany's ability to deliver on his pledge to clean house, a key CIO condition for agreeing to the merger.[27]

Strengthening Meany's hand in achieving that objective was the McClellan Committee's investigation. But the cost, as Goldberg told the USA Executive Board at that same meeting, was proving to be very high. In arguing to members of the board that labor should cooperate, he warned them,

> We are in a grave problem in this country as a result of primarily what has occurred in the Teamsters Union. We have provided the enemies of labor with tremendous ammunition which they are using at this time. . . . You can imagine what the reaction is in every [union] household when they hear that Dave Beck made a profit of $10,000 on a widow of one of his friends.
>
> The trade union movement and the AFL–CIO and this Union is in a great dilemma. We know that there are obviously enemies of the trade union movement on the [McClellan] Committee. Look at that Committee! There are a few friends and many enemies.[28]

Without illusions about the motive behind the probe or the attitudes of the McClellan Committee's majority, Goldberg nonetheless believed labor could not attack the investigation as unwarranted or unfair. As he told the board,

> We cannot say, even though we don't like the procedure, even though we quarrel with the procedure, we cannot say that there was not a legitimate basis for investigating the situation which has been disclosed with respect to the Teamsters Union. . . . Nor is it a defense for us to say that things happen on the management side that are as bad or worse, because, after all, the trade union movement is not a business enterprise, and things that businessmen take for granted are not applicable to the trade union movement which is founded on a different principle.[29]

Goldberg's response was at least somewhat disingenuous. Labor's inability to dismiss the investigation as one-sided stemmed not only from labor and management's dissimilar purposes but also from the differing degrees of influence each possessed in the United States. But his larger point about labor's inability to discredit the probe with the public by branding it unfair was essentially correct. Managerial power precluded that alternative. Confronted with that harsh reality, Goldberg argued instead for cooperating whenever possible and for using the pressure the committee's work was creating to oust the corrupt affiliates from the labor movement and to construct safeguards against any recurrence of those problems. To do otherwise, he warned, would lead to legislation establishing federal government control over union finances. The committee, he said, was laying the foundation for a law "to control the finances of the trade union movement in politics, principally, and in other areas so as to lose [us] our effectiveness."[30] The board reluctantly agreed that some cooperation would be needed to prevent that result.[31]

In another move intended to blunt the force of the congressional attack on labor, the leaders of the major industrial unions decided to use the first conference of the AFL–CIO's new Industrial Union Department (IUD), scheduled for June 1957, to respond to the committee's investigation. As District Director Al Whitehouse explained to the USA Executive Board,

> The purpose of the Conference is to direct the eyes of the nation, as much as we can, toward the abuses and wrongs that labor has suffered, and to try to change the climate somewhat to counteract the climate of this McClellan hearing, this right-to-worker that is conducting these investigations that are creating such a bad climate for us.[32]

The contest was not an equal one. Labor, lacking a strong media network of its own, could not compete with the campaign against it in the nation's magazines and newspapers, and especially on television.

But if operating at a disadvantage there, Goldberg did not see labor as utterly helpless. Unions without any serious problems would come through unscathed, he argued. The USA example was instructive. When one district came under investigation during 1957 and the entire union for its conduct during the election of its chief officers early that year, Goldberg urged and obtained cooperation. Unable to find any evidence of illegality, Robert Kennedy notified McDonald in April 1958 that the investigation had been closed. A related inquiry by the Internal Revenue Service likewise led nowhere. The committee's probe of the UAW produced the same result, although only after calling several of its officers, Reuther included, to testify. As in the case of the Steelworkers, there was no real basis for the probe of the UAW. Its position at the outer edge of labor liberalism, however, made the union more vulnerable than the USA, a fact not lost on Reuther himself. Taking no chances, he asked Goldberg to prepare his testimony before the McClellan Committee and took the latter's advice to stay away from controversial topics. In the end, of the former CIO unions, only the Textile Workers Union was found to have a serious problem. Despite strong pressure from conservative committee members Goldwater and Curtis to focus on former CIO affiliates, and especially the UAW, all of them except the TWU received a clean bill of health.[33]

Those investigations nonetheless presented dangers that union leaders deeply resented. Most disturbing was the McClellan Committee's extensive and irresponsible wiretapping. McDonald blasted that practice at an executive board meeting in the fall of 1957, as did Secretary-Treasurer Abel. Abel wanted, he himself explained,

> to try, if I can, to impress everybody with just the extent to which this sort of thing has gone and how dastardly it is and how impossible it makes the functions of an organization such as ours. . . .
> As President McDonald said, our wires have been tapped. As a matter of fact, many of you Board members know in your conversations with me in the past year that it got to the place where we could barely hear each other talk there were so many taps on the wire, and the drain was so heavy you could hardly get through. I am satisfied that there hasn't been a conversation by President McDonald over any of his phones or by myself over any of my phones in the past year that isn't recorded.[34]

The Steelworkers' experience in that area testified eloquently to the increasingly intense managerial opposition that even honest unions faced during the late 1950s.

Others that before 1956 had formed the AFL experienced much rougher treatment from the McClellan Committee. Robert Kennedy's investigators uncovered serious wrongdoing in the Teamsters, Meat Cutters, Sheet Metal Workers, Mail Deliverers, Electrical Workers, Bakers, Operating Engineers, Carpenters, Laundry Workers, and Hotel and Restaurant Workers. The investigation of the Teamsters, the largest union in the country at that time, turned out to be the most sensational undertaken by the McClellan Committee. Within six months after testifying, Teamsters President Dave Beck resigned. Soon thereafter, he was charged with larceny and income tax evasion, convicted, and sent to prison for more than a decade. Beck's testimony made for spellbinding viewing, as did that given by his lieutenant and successor as Teamsters chief, Jimmy Hoffa. Their remarks and Robert Kennedy's relentless questioning were broadcast live to a national television audience, which could only conclude that organized crime had linked itself to some of the most important unions in America.[35]

Although the unions guilty of wrongdoing made up only a small fraction of the entire labor movement, that distinction soon became lost, with most unfortunate consequences. The result of the Teamsters inquiry was to fix firmly in the minds of many Americans a picture of labor leaders as arrogant and dishonest, motivated only by a desire to accumulate money and power. The emerging medium of television thus helped create a stereotype that persists to this day, even among people too young to remember the McClellan Committee's work. Antiunion managers had indeed won a great deal by pressing for the committee's creation. Perhaps most indicative of its true purpose lay in the failure to put an end to the most pervasive forms of illegality exposed during the late 1950s. The lasting legacy of the McClellan Committee proved to be much less the elimination of corruption than the discrediting of organized labor. Public approval of unions declined significantly after the McClellan Committee set to work, never to regain the high levels that pollsters had recorded over the preceding five years.[36]

This change helped create a climate more favorable to the enactment of antilabor legislation, a development Goldberg had foreseen and tried to head off in two ways. First, he pushed the AFL–CIO to expel immediately those affiliates hopelessly infiltrated by gangsters and to suspend others until their officers cleaned house. During 1957, this campaign, with crucial support from George Meany, progressed toward those goals. In proceeding with it, Goldberg drew a parallel with the CIO's earlier expulsion of unions dominated by radicals. "This is," he told the USA Executive Board, "the same job that the CIO did with the Commie unions, wherein in the cases that we heard, we found that the Commie unions were not unions, they were Communist Party members masquerading as unions."[37] Although that reasoning was open to question with respect to both the radicals and the unions infiltrated by criminals, the accused AFL affiliates fared little better than had the radical-led CIO ones.

This time the proponents of the move to expel had a better basis for their actions. The CIO, as Goldberg reminded the USA Executive Board, had insisted that

> the merger Constitution ought to contain a provision dealing with the sub-ject of corrupt influences in the labor movement. . . . As a result, there was written into the merger Constitution an unprecedented provision which was not even contained in the CIO Constitution which . . . provided that one of the objectives of the merged movement was to keep the movement free of all corrupt influences.[38]

Armed with that provision, Goldberg—along with Meany, Reuther, and David Dubinsky, president of the International Ladies Garment Workers Union (ILGWU) and a longtime foe of labor racketeering—pressed the AFL–CIO to take action against the Teamsters in particular. The heart of the Teamsters' offense, in Goldberg's view, was their misuse of pension and welfare funds. The leaders of the Teamsters, he later recalled, "were taking their pension and welfare funds and giving it to [Paul] Dorfman [who headed an AFL–CIO local in Chicago]. . . . Well, they were taking as their per-centage [for administrative costs] . . . twenty percent. Now I had negotiated a steel contract where the companies and the insurance company were allowed only three percent."[39] In view of those findings, the Ethical Practices Committee on September 25, 1957, found that the Teamsters Union was "dominated, controlled or substantially influenced in the conduct of its affairs by corrupt influences, in violation of the constitution of the A.F.L.–C.I.O."[40] The union was ordered to reform immediately or face expulsion. At the same time, a special committee headed by Goldberg recommended expelling Dorf-man's local, a move Meany backed after some initial hesitation. So chilling was the look Dorfman gave Goldberg at their final meeting that he told his wife that same day about it, remarking, "If anything ever happens to me, you call the FBI and tell them that's the man who did it."[41]

Refusing to be intimidated, Goldberg and the others on the Ethical Prac-tices Committee pressed on with their work. The leaders of the Bakers Union were found to have embezzled their own union's funds and were similarly ordered to clean house or face expulsion. The committee saw these two types of corruption, so-called sweetheart deals with outsiders in return for payoffs, for which the Teamsters became notorious, and the outright theft of a union's funds by its officers, the Bakers' cardinal offense, as major problems that called for drastic action. Several other unions were found guilty of either one or the other offense and were also ordered to reform or face the conse-quences. The key proceeding continued to be that against the Teamsters. The fate of the other unions under investigation would turn on the federa-tion's ability either to reform or oust its largest affiliate.[42]

When the Teamsters failed to respond satisfactorily to the committee's action, the AFL–CIO leadership was forced to debate taking the final step.

Some union leaders, notably David McDonald, favored giving the Teamsters a chance to reform themselves by agreeing to outside management of their pension and welfare funds. That offer was extended to the union, but Hoffa never responded. And when McDonald suggested a different version of the same idea at a meeting of the AFL–CIO Executive Council, Meany played the decisive role in rejecting it. Although reluctant at first to expel the Teamsters, Meany became a strong supporter during 1957 of the move to oust the worst offenders. When McDonald outlined his idea for allowing the Teamsters to reform themselves, Meany, in McDonald's words, "slammed his fist down on the table and he said, 'No. Hoffa's gotta go. Hoffa's gotta go.' I said, 'Well, George, if that's the way you feel about it, I'm certainly not going to vote against you.' That was that."[43]

The council then voted, only a month after the Ethical Practices Committee had rendered its "verdict," to suspend the Teamsters, in effect denying the union voting rights on the executive council and at the upcoming AFL–CIO convention in December. The council recommended that the delegates attending vote to expel the Teamsters, the Bakers, and Laundry Workers and to place several other unions on probation or suspension pending internal reform. Despite vocal opposition from some of the building trades unions, the convention approved those recommendations. This principled if somewhat tardy act cost the federation more than a million and a half dues-paying members but won it only mixed reviews in the press. Many newspapers and magazines tended to report the story in ways that further damaged labor's public standing, a sign of the dilemma in which respectable unionists by then found themselves.[44]

The second part of labor's campaign to respond to the crisis constructively came in the area of new legislation. The best way for labor to prevent the passage of punitive laws, Goldberg reasoned, was to offer its own proposal, which would create safeguards without harming legitimate trade unions. First came a bill sponsored by Senator Paul Douglas in 1957 requiring the registration, reporting, and disclosure of employee welfare and benefit plans. Essentially the same measure the CIO had proposed in 1955, it encountered stiff resistance from conservative Republican Senators Goldwater, Mundt, and William Knowland of California, who offered a series of floor amendments to the bill. Those amendments reflected the findings of the McClellan Committee's antilabor majority, ones that revealed its paramount objective: to weaken labor's power in dealing with management and the state.[45]

The conservatives had recommended new laws to regulate and control pension, health, and welfare funds, as well as union income and expenditures more generally, provisions to reduce the degree to which the NLRB's rulings preempted state regulation, to curb the activities of middlemen in labor–management relations, and a so-called worker bill-of-rights to ensure union "democracy." All of them touched on extremely sensitive areas. The conservatives' proposed restrictions on union spending, for example, were intended partly to inhibit the AFL–CIO's Committee on Political Education (COPE), the federation's successor to the CIO's PAC. The proposal dealing with the

NLRB's preemption of state labor regulation, the so-called no-man's land provision, reflected conservatives' desire to turn over to the states the regulation of small businesses organized by unions. This would serve to strengthen labor's opponents in the South and West where unions were weakest. The restrictions on middlemen could easily interfere with the use of legitimate arbitrators, whose services labor leaders had come to value. And potentially most dangerous were the conservatives' proposals for a secret ballot in elections for union officials, for their recall, and for any strike vote.[46]

The "union democracy" provisions grew out of conservatives' desire to give greater legal protection to dissident factions within trade unions. The intended result was to weaken the rank-and-file solidarity on which union power was based, aiding those managers seeking to renegotiate the postwar social contract on terms more favorable to them. Strengthening managers in that quest were the instances uncovered by the McClellan Committee in which corrupt union leaders, mainly in the Teamsters Union, had abused their power to defeat honest locals' efforts to handle their affairs properly. One of Hoffa's favorite methods for bringing rebellious locals into line was to declare them improperly run. Under a clause in many union constitutions at that time, this finding gave a union's national leadership grounds for placing the local under the control of an administrator, who would restore the local's affairs to proper order. An appropriate and valuable safeguard in an honestly run union, administratorships proved to be a much-abused procedure in the hands of crooked ones. Teamsters leaders' blatant misuse of that power did much to diminish public confidence in the way unions governed themselves.[47]

The behavior of unions untouched by organized crime also contributed to that loss of faith. The USA's own experience in that area was typical. The emergence of rank-and-file dissent against the McDonald–Goldberg faction's leadership of the union created problems even for honest and responsible trade unionists. McDonald's campaign during late 1956 and early 1957 for reelection as USA president had brought the issue of union democracy to the forefront for the first time, and it did not disappear once that contest had ended. The dissident minority's continuing quest to reduce dues, reverse the trend toward centralization of the collective bargaining process and union governance, and adopt a more confrontational approach in dealing with management all served to keep the issue salient through the end of 1958.[48]

Although he was a believer in democratic procedures, Goldberg felt that labor unions' insecure position in American society severely limited their ability to permit internal dissent. He rejected completely the comparison that some managers, academics, and union dissidents made between union elections and those for public office. When such figures began pressing unions through speeches and articles to adopt the latter model in electing officers and deciding when to strike, Goldberg attacked the premises on which their reasoning was based. In May 1958 he spoke in that vein at a conference sponsored by the liberal Fund for the Republic in New York. At that meeting, called to air differences about the union democracy issue, Goldberg observed:

One of the fundamental assumptions upon which our political society rests is that there is a common consent that it shall continue to exist. This is so elementary that it is often ignored. Our society can tolerate extremes of factionalism because there is no question that, whichever faction receives the vote of the majority, the government will not disintegrate. Republican can denounce Democrat and Democrat can denounce Republican because all are certain that whichever is elected, the republic will survive.[49]

Unions, on the other hand, he still saw as insurgent forces in American society. In response to industrial relations expert Clark Kerr's contention that unions were "established, secure and accepted" institutions, Goldberg stated, "This is simply not true."[50] He noted that managerial resistance continued and was manifested most clearly in the enactment of state statutes outlawing the union shop. Even in states without the so-called right-to-work law, labor's position remained far from secure. The National Labor Relations Act, Goldberg pointed out, did not compel employers to enter into collective bargaining relationships unless the workers succeeded on their own initiative in organizing a union, typically in the face of fierce managerial resistance. "The plain fact of the matter is that in the United States less than 30% of all workers are organized, and . . . many of our unions are still struggling, and sometimes unsuccessfully, to become established, secure, and accepted."[51] Even where unions had been organized, he argued, continuing pressure from management precluded the adoption of governing procedures analogous to those used in the realm of elective politics. In his words,

> Even where the existence and status of a union is unquestioned—as, for example, in the basic steel industry—it is unlike political government in that it cannot legislate by itself on the matters of primary concern to it—wages, hours and working conditions. It can only demand, and its success in achieving its demands depends upon agreement of the employer and upon the economic strength of the union, should the employer refuse. If there is analogy to political government, the analogy is to a political government which may simultaneously face uncertainty as to its continued existence; i.e., a revolution, and which is periodically at war.[52]

In that situation, the full range of democratic procedures urged on labor by some managers, academics, and rank-and-file dissidents simply could not be accepted without imperiling the continued existence of organizations such as the USA. So Goldberg reasoned, and in large measure he was right.[53]

Those critical of his position and friendly to labor argued that managers had come to rely on unions and, indeed, would themselves feel the need to create them had workers not done so. Unions, they concluded, had thus achieved the degree of security needed to permit more democratic systems of government. This line of reasoning missed a crucial distinction between the kinds of unions that sophisticated business managers believed necessary and those that workers themselves had created during the 1930s and 1940s. During that time such managers had come to see the need for the rationalizing and stabilizing benefits that unions offered and the value of collective bargaining in maintaining wage levels that contributed to overall consumer spending in accordance with Keynesian theory. Absent from that conception of unions, however, was their role in transforming power relations on the shop floor, which in the USA had been codified in the key Section 2B of its master contract with U.S. Steel. That redistribution of power from managers to workers had been one of the union's most important and hard-won achievements. The rank and file's support for the McDonald–Goldberg faction's leadership of the union hinged on that group's ability to preserve the gains embodied in Clause 2B, in the face of continuing and growing managerial resistance. If not the revolutionary organizations some radicals had hoped for during the 1930s, the USA and its brethren were also not the company unions that, two decades later, embittered dissidents and leftists argued they had become. The American labor movement during that time, like the Steel-workers Union that stood at its center, served some functions sophisticated business managers had come to value, as well as others they still strongly resisted.[54]

In that context, Goldberg argued that union members were entitled in their own interest to fewer rights than they enjoyed in the realm of partisan politics. He had addressed the issue in detail at a conference held at Northwestern University the previous October. At that meeting, Goldberg contended that unions such as the USA should do more to protect the more limited set of rights already promised to their members. They were entitled, he pointed out, to the right to vote for their leaders in honestly conducted elections, to run for office subject only to fair qualifications, and to speak their minds at union meetings. Those accused of violating union rules deserved, he noted, a measure of due process. And every member was entitled as well to a union free both from criminal activity and discrimination based on race, creed, or color and to one whose leaders proved to be effective in bargaining with management. He observed that some of those rights, especially the ones dealing with discrimination, had not yet been given full effect and defined labor's union democracy obligation to be the redemption of those existing pledges. In return, Goldberg argued, members should participate in union affairs, establish and enforce ethical standards, respect civil rights, and show loyalty to the union itself, which he defined as supporting "wholeheartedly and intelligently the union's collective bargaining goals arrived at by democratic processes."[55]

In a crucial intellectual move, Goldberg went on to blame the membership for failing to meet those responsibilities, especially the key one of participation, and thus as sharing the blame for union officials' wrongdoing. "After all," he declared, "nobody 'forces' the union member to stay home [instead,] watching television."[56] True as far as that went, Goldberg, like so many of his generation, simply did not understand that the existing system of union governance bred apathy because it gave most members so little real say in making important decisions. To blame the rank and file for its own lethargy was unfair, because only a more participatory system could have inspired them to take more responsibility for the conduct of union affairs.

The trend toward centralized decision making had become so pronounced in the USA by the late 1950s that even executive board members began to complain about their lack of participation in union governance. When Goldberg urged the board to cooperate with the McClellan Committee investigation, District Director Martin Walsh complained in response that he "had been on the Executive Board for the past 20 years, and that if he were dragged before the McClellan Committee and asked about the workings of the organization, he would have to state that he doesn't know too much about it."[57] District Director Alex Kojetinksy echoed those sentiments at another board meeting, observing that "in some twenty[-]odd years [as a Board member] I haven't had the privilege of having an itemized [financial] report read to me."[58] Those comments graphically illustrated how little real say in making decisions the USA offered to most of its members.

Although much of the blame for that situation belonged to business managers still fighting to keep labor's power in check, the union's leaders deserved some as well. McDonald in particular demonstrated a disturbing lack of respect for responsible opposition to the dues increase and pay raises approved in 1956. When a leader of the Dues Protest Committee, which persisted in its efforts even after its candidates lost the 1957 USA elections, made an address urging the rank and file to continue protesting those moves, McDonald denounced it as "a Communist Party line speech, if I ever read one in my life."[59] He went on next to suggest that such dissenters were being aided and abetted by "company agents in the ranks of the local union officership and others who are just rank and file members whose job it is to stir up trouble and turmoil within our organization."[60] Determined to hang on to his job, McDonald interpreted all challenges to his authority as threats to the union's survival. Although restrained by Goldberg, who acted as the de facto president in most instances, McDonald nonetheless abused his powers to contain rank-and-file dissent. That kind of behavior even in a clean union like the USA help diminish the rank and file's enthusiasm for participating in its activities. The heavy-handed way most union leaders responded to rank-and-file challenges also eroded public support for the union movement as a whole.[61]

Tarnished by the criminality found in only a small fraction of all unions but magnified by the McClellan Committee and by their leaders' seeming disinterest in democratic procedures, labor unions faced a serious challenge by 1957 from congressional conservatives. The AFL–CIO nonetheless succeeded in beating back that threat. All the floor amendments offered to the Douglas Pension and Welfare Fund Disclosure bill by McClellan Committee members Knowland, Curtis, and Goldwater went down to defeat in the spring of 1958. Labor, with Goldberg acting as the principal lobbyist for the bill, had won the first round, but only after Senate Majority Leader Lyndon Johnson signaled that further legislation would be forthcoming, in essence giving the conservatives another chance.

With that understanding, Senator Douglas's bill passed the Senate by a wide margin. In the House, however, the measure was weakened considerably, in response to pressure from the Teamsters, whose leaders feared government scrutiny, and from conservatives who apparently preferred an ineffectual bill to one that might quiet the clamor for further remedial legislation. Told by antilabor Representative Graham Barden, chairman of the House Education and Labor Committee, to take it or leave it, Douglas and his allies yielded reluctantly. The amended bill then passed both chambers by huge margins. It proved to be inadequate, as a way of either blunting managerial pressure for legislation that would reduce union power or eliminating dishonest management of pension and welfare funds.[62]

The experience aided Goldberg in arguing with Meany and other top AFL–CIO leaders that they should support a broader reform measure of their own. Convinced at last that more legislation on the subject was inevitable, Meany and his colleagues reluctantly agreed that Goldberg should take the lead on the federation's behalf in drafting a bill that would not harm labor's legitimate interests. Armed with that lukewarm endorsement, Goldberg sought out John Kennedy and Irving Ives, the two senators on the McClellan Committee considered friendly to labor but not overly so. They were also the ranking members on the panel that had jurisdiction over labor legislation, the Subcommittee on Labor of the Senate Committee on Labor and Public Welfare. Kennedy and Ives agreed to sponsor a second, "bipartisan," labor reform bill, which would compel unions to file annual financial reports with the secretary of labor. To underscore the bill's "neutrality" with respect to the economic and political contest between labor and management, Kennedy asked Harvard Law professor Archibald Cox to organize a so-called blue ribbon panel of industrial relations experts to advise in drafting such a bill. The result of their deliberations and Goldberg's own suggestions eventually became the basis for the Kennedy–Ives bill.[63]

Cox and Goldberg played the leading roles in drafting the measure, which contained four major parts and a technical fifth one. Title I mandated a reporting and disclosure scheme for union officers; Title II, restrictions on administratorships; Title III, some modest restrictions on the way union elections were conducted; Title IV, a Code of Ethical Practices for union officers that was essentially the one the AFL–CIO had already adopted; and Title V, key definitions and some miscellaneous provisions. These reforms, Goldberg believed, would make impossible the kinds of thievery and misconduct that the McClellan Committee had uncovered while at the same time preventing managers still hostile to labor from weakening the movement as a whole. In drafting even those provisions, however, Goldberg was hampered by opposition from some of the building trades unions, the Carpenters and Hod Carriers in particular, and the Teamsters, which, as he later said, were "vulnerable" in some of those areas.[64] Joining them in lobbying against any bill was the United Mine Workers, which opposed the measure as a further and highly objectionable reduction in labor's autonomy from the state.[65]

Making matters even more difficult, David McDonald's personal assistant and USA legislative director, Nordy Hoffman, also opposed the measure. That apparent split in the USA's ranks reflected both McDonald's fears that such a law might require an audit of his own quite generous expense account and the uneasiness other USA leaders felt over where such regulation might lead. Divisions over the issue had emerged openly in debating a resolution Goldberg had drafted that curbed the practice of imposing administrators on rebellious or mismanaged locals. That power had been much abused by the Teamsters, particularly to discipline honest locals, and Goldberg favored the resolution as one way to reduce sentiment in Congress for legislation in that vein.

Goldberg argued that the best defense against government regulation of internal union affairs was regulation by the unions themselves. But what he failed to point out was that if unions felt obliged to undertake such "voluntary" regulation each time the government considered compulsory legislation, then the difference between the two would become meaningless. Joe Germano, in his typically blunt fashion, told the board that although he would vote for the resolution, the USA "must stop passing resolutions which indicate that labor recognizes its past faults and is endeavoring to do what Congress is telling it to do. . . . I think that sometime along the line we are going to have to say how far we are willing to go here."[66] McDonald added, "I certainly am completely and irrevocably opposed to the idea which Brother Germano mentions about the filing with certain people of complete statements about all of the operations of the officers of labor unions, whether they be financial operations or otherwise."[67] Despite all the grumbling, the board approved the resolution. At the same time, the USA's official position remained one of support for the Kennedy–Ives bill, but without any real enthusiasm.[68]

Faced with that situation and more active opposition from other unions, Goldberg arrived at what seemed a practical solution: to add to the Kennedy–Ives measure some Taft–Hartley amendments long sought by the unions most opposed to an anticorruption bill. Thus to the first five sections of the bill, which dealt exclusively with issues of labor corruption, Goldberg and his fellow draftsman Archibald Cox added a sixth. Formally known as Title VI, it contained three major provisions. First, it included a new definition of the term *supervisor* sought by the Communications Workers, a change that would eliminate the practice of allowing craft workers to exercise jurisdiction over their unskilled fellow employees. Second was a clause requiring the application of federal law to labor disputes involving small employers. This provision would, in effect, eliminate the "no-man's land" created by the NLRB's refusal to exercise its jurisdiction over such matters. And third, the new Title VI included a provision legalizing collective bargaining agreements in the construction industry made before an NLRB election, the so-called prehire agreements. Also included were several less important changes that would prohibit employers from making certain kinds of payments to union officials, would make their acceptance of such payments illegal, would require employers in some instances to file noncommunist affidavits, would ban picketing for personal profit, and would legalize certain kinds of pooling arrangements in the construction industry that funded worker-vacation and apprenticeship-training programs.[69]

Those "sweeteners," as they soon became known, helped secure the formal support of the building trades unions and the Communications Workers, but at the cost of increasing managerial opposition to the Kennedy–Ives bill. Even more serious, adding Taft–Hartley amendments to a labor "reform" bill meant that other such amendments would henceforth be relevant under congressional rules of order. Labor's opponents would thus have an easier time in seeking to use the debate over labor corruption to advance their larger objective of weakening unions' power. In the jargon of Capitol Hill, adding the sweeteners "opened up the bill" to the kinds of Taft–Hartley changes for which some managers had been pressing since the Eisenhower administration took office. Goldberg's decision to endorse that approach was a calculated risk: Without the sweeteners, divisions in the labor movement would likely have doomed the Kennedy–Ives bill, but their inclusion increased the odds that its final form would prove harmful to the union movement as a whole. Goldberg felt confident, however, that he, Kennedy, and Ives could muster enough votes in the Senate committee and on the floor to fight off antilabor Taft–Hartley amendments. Conscious of the risks, he nonetheless pressed ahead in his campaign for a constructive legislative response that would steal the thunder from the antilabor members of the committee.[70]

Goldberg's work on what soon officially became the proposed Kennedy–Ives Labor Management Reporting and Disclosure Act marked the first time that he had worked closely with the Massachusetts senator. The two had first met in 1948, shortly after Goldberg became CIO general counsel, but his first impression of the freshman congressman had left no sense of future greatness: "He looked like a high school graduate," Goldberg later recalled.[71] They had seen each other occasionally since then, thanks in large part to Kennedy's service on the House Labor Committee from 1947 to 1952 and the corresponding Senate panel thereafter. Although his voting record had been acceptable to labor, in all that time Kennedy had never immersed himself in the details of any major legislative proposal, earning a reputation among his colleagues on Capitol Hill as a lightweight. That changed, however, with the onset of the McClellan Committee hearings and the search for a legislative solution that would not be harmful to labor. Goldberg spent long evenings with Kennedy, answering his questions about specific provisions and educating him more generally about the labor movement. While working with Kennedy, Goldberg observed, "I gradually came to the conclusion that here was someone to be reckoned with."[72] Their relationship at first strictly business, the two men nonetheless worked together closely on the labor reform bill. It proved to be the beginning of much bigger things.[73]

Their first collaboration, like so many others in the future, soon encountered stiff resistance from managerial forces seeking to weaken labor. Even though the measure passed the Senate by an overwhelming eighty-eight-to-one-vote margin, with only Goldwater opposed, some thirty-two amendments were added in the process, which diminished the AFL–CIO's support for the bill. Convinced that labor could not hope to do better and that the amendments did not create serious problems for labor, Goldberg pressed on in the House. There the members felt the full weight of managerial power, deployed to prevent passage of the Kennedy–Ives bill. Spokesmen for the U.S. Chamber of Commerce, the NAM, the American Retail Federation, and other employer groups clearly stated their reason for opposing the measure, arguing that it did not reduce sufficiently the "monopoly power" of organized labor. Leading managers thus made plain their refusal to accept an anticorruption bill that failed at the same time to weaken labor's power in the workplace and in realm of elective politics. Tacitly supported by the Eisenhower administration, which favored a measure more hostile to labor, and by unions opposing any bill at all, managers prevailed by August 1958 in their effort to kill Kennedy–Ives. Employer groups indicated, too, that they intended to try again after the congressional elections later that year.[74]

III

While engaged in fighting off the McClellan Committee probe and the resulting pressure for antilabor legislation, Goldberg also found himself confronted with two other managerial initiatives aimed at renegotiating the postwar New Deal. The first of those, a more rigid approach to collective bargaining, reached the steel industry during 1957. Although the USA's master contract with most steel companies would not expire until 1959, Goldberg began to feel the changing attitudes among managers two years earlier.

In September 1957 a dispute arose at one of the smaller companies organized by the USA, Lone Star Steel. Its chief executive officer, Eugene Germany, had established the east Texas firm with a government "loan" from the Reconstruction Finance Corporation (RFC) yet still considered himself, as did so many other recipients of such aid, a staunch defender of the free-enterprise system. Deeply hostile to unions, he had resisted an arbitration board ruling that all temporary vacancies at the Lone Star mill be filled by union members according to seniority. Rather than accept the decision, Lone Star's managers chose their own replacements and took each case to arbitration, clearly abusing the grievance mechanism. Roughly 2,500 workers responded with an unauthorized, or "wildcat" strike, one neither permitted by the contract nor sanctioned by the USA.[75]

Even though that sort of job action was not very unusual, Germany's response this time clearly was. Spurning the union's offer of help in getting the strikers to return, he decided to fire them and operate the plant with nonunion replacements. He also announced that those strikers he eventually chose to rehire would lose all their seniority rights. Those actions precipitated violent clashes between union members and strikebreakers, producing in David McDonald's words "shootings of all kinds and descriptions" and nearly culminating in "a major riot."[76] And when District Director Martin Burns requested that Germany meet with Goldberg and McDonald to work out their differences, the steel company executive agreed to do so but refused to bend at all during the session.

In response to Goldberg's suggestion that they refer the whole dispute to arbitration, Germany said that the union had not requested it within the time allowed by the contract and so had lost that opportunity. His reply and antagonistic manner so infuriated Goldberg, as he later told the executive board, that the "meeting in New York virtually broke up as a brawl between me and Mr. Germany, because I had never seen such an attitude demonstrated in all of my experience. Dave was the conciliator at that meeting, and I must say that neither a good partner nor a bad partner could do anything with that fellow."[77] In effect Germany was signaling his intention to withdraw from the postwar social contract with the USA and to return to a strategy aimed at winning back some of the control over the firm that workers had obtained earlier.[78]

The dispute assumed even greater significance when managers at the major steel companies decided to back Germany's efforts to make his demands stick. Unwilling to risk an open confrontation with the USA, those managers apparently saw the Lone Star dispute as a way to test the waters for adopting a more confrontational strategy. None of that was lost on the union's leaders. Goldberg reported to the board that the major companies "had observers there to witness the strike, and . . . other interests were issuing special reports to the Iron and Steel Institute Industrial Relations Committee about the conduct of this situation, stating they were wondering whether or not this . . . was . . . a good technique to use."[79]

Even more serious, the major steel companies made their considerable resources available to Lone Star's executives in fighting the union's quest for a favorable arbitration ruling. At issue was, first, whether the union was entitled to use that mechanism to resolve the seniority dispute and, second, whether Germany had behaved improperly in dismissing workers for their participation in the related wildcat strike. The Lone Star case, as measured by the number of workers involved, became the largest ever resolved at that time through arbitration. Goldberg argued the union's side, and Lone Star was represented by the chief counsel of National Steel, assisted by an attorney from Jones and Laughlin. Calling those developments "very significant," Goldberg also told the USA Executive Board that "the representatives of several steel companies sat as observers in the argument on the case. I don't mean to infer that they participated, but they threw their weight around and were [there] to see what was happening."[80]

Despite that aid, Lone Star's managers failed to win a favorable ruling from the arbitrator. On May 12, 1958, he rejected their claim that the strikers had lost the right to seek arbitration and ruled instead that management was obligated to reinstate all 2,500 workers. He also held that the 1,025 temporary replacements that Lone Star managers had recruited during the strike were entitled to only the seniority they had accumulated before the work stoppage began, in effect compelling their dismissal. As a penalty for the wildcat strike, the arbitrator denied the strikers any back pay, but the overall decision marked a major victory for the union in its efforts to preserve its power in the workplace. The ruling also helped quash an Armco subsidiary's effort to use the same technique. In summarizing the result for the USA Executive Board, Goldberg observed that the dispute marked

> the first time in the basic steel industry since we got substantial recognition that the company apparently determined to fight it out with the union on the basis of its economic power and the wide interest of the steel industry in this was natural, because it was such a big case. And it was also very disturbing, because it did indicate an interest in this particular technique.[81]

Crucial to winning that victory was the arbitration system Goldberg had favored since the 1940s, which he saw as a major bulwark against managers seeking to win back lost prerogatives.

The system had been greatly strengthened less than a year earlier, when the U.S. Supreme Court had ruled on June 3, 1957, that federal courts had the power to enforce arbitration clauses in labor–management contracts. In *Textile Workers Union* v. *Lincoln Mills of Alabama* and two companion cases decided the same day, employers had refused to submit grievances to a third party as required by their union contracts. According to the law in most states at that time, such arbitration agreements were legally unenforceable, a position the U.S. Court of Appeals for the Fifth Circuit had sustained in deciding the *Lincoln Mills* case. The Supreme Court overturned that decision, however, holding that in agreeing to accept an arbitration clause, workers were, by implication, surrendering their right to strike over arbitrable issues and that as a matter of federal policy, arbitration clauses should be legally enforceable as a way of promoting industrial peace.[82]

Goldberg had represented the Textile Workers before the Supreme Court in the *Lincoln Mills* case and made exactly those arguments. Although some scholars later argued that the decision ultimately marked a defeat for unions because it restricted still further their freedom to strike, denied them resort to the judiciary in resolving many disputes, and tended to diminish shop-floor militancy, such critics missed the ruling's importance in containing employers' efforts to renegotiate the postwar New Deal in ways more favorable to them. The state's intervention in this instance tended to strengthen labor in its dealings with antiunion employers. When the USA won a favorable arbitration ruling in the Lone Star Steel dispute less than a year later, the *Lincoln Mills* decision compelled Eugene Germany to accept it. Although he continued to resist, in the end the USA prevailed. Labor's successful campaign under Goldberg's expert direction to win that decision had, in effect, foreclosed one managerial strategy for rolling back union power.[83]

Disturbed by the behavior of the major steel companies' managers in aiding Lone Star, Goldberg found even more worrisome the hardening he detected in the attitudes of executives at the smaller firms whose contracts came up for renewal in 1958. The economic decline that had begun the previous fall reached its nadir the following April, a situation that suggested to him the need for a wage increase to expand purchasing power, rather than the freeze that many managers and a spokesman for the building trades unions publicly supported. Goldberg also favored winning the cost-of-living allowance

(COLA) clause, which most of the smaller firms had not yet granted, because the rise in prices over the past two years had highlighted its importance in protecting workers' real incomes. He also decided to insist on one-year contracts with those companies, rather than the more common multiyear term. That final demand was intended as a precautionary move. Signing one-year agreements with the smaller companies meant that all USA contracts with steel firms would expire simultaneously in July 1959. That in turn would increase the USA's bargaining power should the industry's leaders seek a confrontation, as their behavior in the Lone Star Steel dispute suggested they might.[84]

The firms' response to those demands only increased Goldberg's suspicion that trouble lay ahead for the USA. Negotiations with the smaller firms located in Canada went nowhere, as the union's demands for a wage increase met with fierce resistance. Eamon Park, a USA officer who represented its Canadian membership, noted in reporting to the executive board the connection between the resulting strike and a hardening of managerial attitudes more generally in the Canadian business community. He told the board members that the strike was "forced on us by the insistence of the Steel Company of Canada as the mouthpiece of the Canadian Manufacturers Association. It is a strike of great importance not only to ourselves but to all of the members of the Canadian trade union movement."[85]

The USA encountered the same rigid response from some American firms as well during 1958, most notably Timken Roller Bearing of Ohio. There the dispute revolved around the union's effort to win improvements in the pension plan comparable to those won from managers of the major steel companies in 1956. Management refused to budge and rejected the USA's offer of a contract extension pending resolution of the dispute, thereby precipitating a strike by more than nine thousand workers. The acrimonious tone of the union's dealings with executives at Timken and the other smaller firms in 1958 indicated to Goldberg that a change was in the wind.[86]

The union's preliminary talks with U.S. Steel's managers about the 1959 contract negotiations reinforced that sense of foreboding. In August 1958 McDonald and I. W. Abel met with management's principal negotiators to discuss changes in the incentive pay and job classification provisions. "They let us know," David McDonald soon told the board, "in . . . unmistakable terms that we can expect no improvements in our labor contracts next year. It is just as simple as that."[87] Other signals pointed in the same direction, especially the prediction that same month in the industry's trade publication, *The Iron Age*, of a long strike the following year, and U.S. Steel executives' decision to replace John Stephens, chief negotiator during the more amicable years of the mid-1950s, with Conrad Cooper, who favored a confrontational approach in dealing with the union. Those developments seemed to portend a major clash in 1959, one that Goldberg believed would do neither side much good.[88]

The same general pattern also emerged in other parts of the economy's manufacturing sector, which suggested to Goldberg that the growing rigidity among steel managers was not solely the result of their unhappiness with the cost of the 1956 contract. Collective bargaining agreements between executives at the major automakers and the UAW came up for renegotiation in 1958, and this time the employers chose to bargain through a united committee that strongly resisted the union's demands for a wage increase and improvements in the supplemental unemployment benefits (SUB) plan. The same pattern emerged in talks between managers at General Electric and the Electrical Workers, developments not lost on Goldberg or the USA leadership more generally. Seeing their prospects in 1959 as dependent in part on the pattern established the previous year, the USA Executive Board voted to lend the UAW $1 million to replenish its nearly exhausted operating fund and thereby to strengthen Reuther's hand at the bargaining table. The meager gains he eventually obtained suggested that the USA would face similar problems the following year. Even more troubling, the self-conscious way in which leaders of the core industrial firms seemed to be banding together to resist labor's demands for better pay and benefits indicated that such managers had become determined to reverse the trend of the preceding nine years.[89]

All these events strengthened Goldberg's belief that the simultaneous emergence of the labor corruption controversy and the leading firms' tougher bargaining posture were no mere coincidence. The third major antiunion initiative, which materialized at the same time, confirmed his suspicions about managerial intentions. That effort, which was aimed at outlawing the union shop in states where unions were strong, gathered momentum during 1957/58 in response to heavy pressure from the business community on state lawmakers. Before that time, such campaigns had been successful only in states where labor was relatively weak. By the end of 1956, seventeen states had such a law in effect, but ten of those were in the South, four in the northern plains, and three in the Southwest. Efforts in other states had failed in the face of strong union pressure, as well as opposition from the Truman and Eisenhower administrations.[90]

The campaign achieved a breakthrough, however, during the spring of 1957, when the Indiana state legislature narrowly approved a so-called right-to-work bill. Although the state contained many small towns, it also included some large urban areas, including Gary, an industrial suburb of Chicago and a major steelmaking center. As a result, the state had 600,000 union members, whose representatives had staunchly opposed the bill to outlaw the union shop. When it passed, Goldberg became deeply concerned, because such a statute would endanger contracts involving a substantial number of USA members. He, along with other labor lobbyists, attempted to beat back the antiunion campaign by pressing for a gubernatorial veto of the bill, but to no avail.[91]

Victory in Indiana encouraged managers to expand their efforts elsewhere. During 1957/58, Senators Goldwater and McClellan pushed in Congress for a nationwide ban on the union shop, and managerial forces also pressed hard for the passage of state laws in Louisiana, Kentucky, Maryland, Rhode Island,

Delaware, Ohio, California, Idaho, Kansas, Colorado, and Washington. Labor's firm opposition blocked the move in Congress and defeated antiunion
efforts in the first five of these states. In the others, though, managers succeeded in placing the issue on the ballot, which helped turn the upcoming
1958 elections there into a referendum on the issue. Those ballot initiatives,
together with the elections for Congress and state offices with which they
soon became linked, offered the AFL–CIO's new political arm, the Committee on Political Education (COPE), its first big test. The so-called right-to-
work campaign of 1957/58 also convinced Goldberg that the first major
challenge to the postwar New Deal was brewing in the ranks of leading
business managers.[92]

Although it fought hard against all these ballot initiatives in 1958, COPE
devoted its greatest efforts to the contests in California and Ohio, the only
major industrial states of the group, and those where labor stood to lose the
most if the measure passed. Both states also featured gubernatorial contests in
which the Republican candidates, Knowland in California and O'Neill in
Ohio, supported efforts to outlaw the union shop. One indication of how the
emerging rift in the business community was weakening the Eisenhower
administration lay in its equivocal response to the Ohio and California contests. After first trying to keep silent on the union-shop issue, Labor Secretary
Mitchell finally announced his opposition to the ballot initiatives. Vice-
President Richard Nixon, dispatched by Eisenhower to campaign for GOP
candidates around the country, and especially in Nixon's home state of California, never took a clear stand on the question. The president himself publicly declared his neutrality. With Republican ranks thus deeply divided for
the first time since the summer of 1952, the Democratic Party's electoral
prospects improved dramatically.[93]

Goldberg participated in drafting the party's 1958 labor plank, which highlighted the mounting Republican attacks on unions. The draft Goldberg
submitted on behalf of the Labor Advisory Committee to the Democratic
Advisory Committee blasted the GOP for its equivocation on the union-shop
issue, noting that "the Republican Party professes its 'friendship' for labor at
the same time that its leader in the U.S. Senate, Sen. Knowland of California,
is campaigning in the state of California in support of an anti-union 'right-to-
work' law."[94] Although the Democrats were somewhat vulnerable to the same
charge, given Senator McClellan's prominent role in exposing labor corruption, the Republicans proved much more so. This was because their party's
leaders were the ones either heading the campaign to ban the union shop or
vacillating on the issue, whereas most leading Democrats opposed the measure. The more serious split in GOP ranks thus enabled the Democratic Party
for the first time in six years to pose as the only genuine champion of the
postwar New Deal. Though not entirely true, the claim did much to reinvigorate the party's electoral appeal.[95]

In addition to making those sorts of declarations, Goldberg and other labor
leaders concentrated on raising funds and mobilizing their members to defeat
the union-shop initiatives and the Republican candidates who backed them.

They were helped in this effort by the 1958 recession, which dispelled some of the complacency with which workers had come to view electoral contests. According to the formula worked out when COPE was established, the USA's obligatory contribution was $94,000 per year, which would come out of the general operating account if the membership failed to give the necessary amount. In addition, the union contributed funds on its own initiative to candidates for state and federal office, which required donations above the COPE assessment. During the first eight months of 1957 the union managed to raise only $31,374.64, which reflected the members' lack of concern over the upcoming elections. At a board meeting held in September of that year, several members grumbled about the low level of donations and the need to raise more to secure repeal of the Indiana law banning the union shop, as well as recently enacted measures in that state and in neighboring Ohio, which in effect outlawed SUB payments.[96]

The emergence of the SUB controversy in Ohio and Indiana clearly illustrated the growing split in the ranks of business leaders and politicians over labor's place in the postwar order. Goldberg noted that in Ohio a state official had ruled that SUB payments could not be used to supplement unemployment benefits paid by the government, even though the state's law on that subject was essentially the same as those in thirty-eight other states that permitted the SUB program to operate. Goldberg told the board that Governor O'Neill had "undoubtedly" told the official to make that ruling. Goldberg then went on to say that the major steel companies' executives had opposed the decision and the forces that had enacted the Indiana law outlawing SUB payments. Steel industry leaders, Goldberg told the board,

> said . . . that they have done everything within the power of the steel industry to get approval in Ohio and Indiana, and I want to say that from everything we have been able to gather that is true. . . . They have been much more cooperative, for example, than the auto industry. . . . In the auto industry Ford generally has been cooperative, but General Motors has not been too cooperative.[97]

Goldberg and the steel executives proceeded to devise a SUB provision that they believed legal under the relevant Ohio statute, and they planned to test the clause in the courts if necessary. They also enlisted Labor Secretary Mitchell to pressure Governor O'Neill to accept the new proposal. Although Goldberg told the USA Executive Board that the managers' lawyers and he all expected to win such a suit, "you never know what happens from one day to the next in Ohio, as we discovered in this area."[98] His remark reflected the confusion being created there by the emerging managerial revolt.

Several board members, and Joe Germano in particular, emphasized that the rank and file did not as yet understand the dangers posed by the SUB measure, the so-called right-to-work law, or by the McClellan Committee's investigations. Secretary-Treasurer Abel, who headed the USA's Political Action Committee (PAC), acknowledged that problem and observed that maybe a few things like that [SUB controversy] will awaken the membership to the fact that these same people who are trying to save them from the labor bosses by passing right-to-work laws will at the same time take bread out of their mouths, too. Maybe we can get a little action and support in our political action program now.[99]

In exhorting the board members to go forth and beat the bushes for contributions, McDonald pointed out the dangers the labor movement then faced, having endorsed government supervision of labor–management relations. He told the board:

We are in a tough fight in our country and we can't kid ourselves about that. We have traitors who are trying to destroy our union, who are cooperating with anti-union people. We have a tremendous anti-union sentiment as a result of certain actions in Washington which permeate the thinking of the American people. And, as somebody said, we got this union as a result of the enactment of certain laws in Washington and we can lose this union by the enactment of certain laws in Washington.

. . . If you have got money[,] get it in. If you haven't raised money[,] begin to raise the money now. . . . We are going to need a lot of money for the next congressional elections.[100]

McDonald was at most only half right. The USA owed its existence to rank-and-file militance and the original organizing committee's inspired leadership, as well as to the aid provided by the National Labor Relations Act. But his remarks revealed the extent to which labor leaders increasingly relied on the government to sustain their organizations. Although that approach had yielded important benefits since the middle 1930s, it had also made them vulnerable to the attacks they now faced.

Labor's successes in the elections held during 1957/58 tended, however, to vindicate those like Goldberg who viewed government supervision of the postwar social contract as, on the whole, beneficial to the union movement. The first portents of the likely outcome in 1958 had come a year earlier, during two special Senate elections held to fill unexpected vacancies. In April 1957, liberal Democrat Ralph Yarborough had captured a Texas Senate seat formerly held by conservative Price Daniel. And in Wisconsin later that same year, Senator Joseph McCarthy's death opened the way to a contest between Democrat William Proxmire and former Republican Governor Walter Kohler Jr., which Proxmire won easily. Both Yarborough and Proxmire campaigned as, and proved to be over the next five years, strong supporters of the postwar New Deal. Their victories, which the USA had helped create through direct contributions of money and volunteers, encouraged its leadership about labor's prospects in 1958.[101]

Aiding labor in that fight was a sea change in attitudes among the rank and file toward political action. In December 1957, Abel reported a significant improvement in PAC collections. By the following August, the USA had raised roughly $180,000 over what had been contributed by September 1957. Noting that this was still too low, Abel urged renewed efforts. The membership's increasing responsiveness to those pleas reflected more than just their unhappiness with the McClellan Committee and the campaign to ban the union shop. Just as important was the rise in unemployment that accompanied the recession of 1957/58.

By March 1958 the USA had approved a statement criticizing the Eisenhower administration's economic policy, which reported that "more than 200,000 of our members are unemployed and more than 300,000 are under-employed. . . . Thus, almost half of our total membership is suffering from this depression. The basic steel industry is operating at little more than one-half capacity."[102] The economic downturn hit the durable goods industries especially hard, because the boom in sales of those items ended abruptly during late 1957. In part this stemmed from the cyclical nature of such expansions, but the Eisenhower administration's credit-tightening policies made the decline in durable purchases even deeper. The result was to persuade many workers who had viewed Eisenhower with approval to swing back toward support for the Democrats.[103]

The USA leadership helped solidify this shift by putting forward its own antirecession program, which differed from Eisenhower's by emphasizing measures to stimulate economic growth, rather than fighting inflation. The USA plan promoted income tax cuts for the working and lower middle classes; a reduction in consumption taxes; an increase in the amount and duration of unemployment compensation; more spending on housing, education, and public works; economic aid for so-called distressed areas; a rise in the minimum wage from $1.00 to $1.25, along with an expansion of its coverage; and other fiscal policies that would reduce unemployment by accelerating economic growth. This list of solutions, which formed a major part of the Democratic Party's program for the next eight years, received its first real test at the polls in 1958. The results suggested that at least for a time, those policies and the Democrats who backed them would enjoy a large measure of public support.[104]

The lingering effects of the recession, which persisted despite the beginnings of a recovery that summer, contributed still further to a Democratic revival. So, too, did resentment against the GOP in rural areas. There the Eisenhower administration's inability to maintain agricultural commodity prices in the facing of growing domestic surpluses and declining foreign markets angered voters. The key issue in California, Ohio, Idaho, Kansas, Colorado, and Kansas, however, where the union-shop issue measure appeared on the ballot, remained the GOP's apparent retreat from its strong support for the postwar New Deal. Organized labor, faced with well-financed and sophisticated campaigns from their managerial opponents in those states, threw its still very substantial power into those contests.[105]

The results demonstrated just how potent that power still was. The so-called right-to-work measure passed only in heavily rural Kansas, and even there by a fairly narrow margin. Elsewhere the proposal lost, and in the key industrial states of California and Ohio, by a margin of roughly three to two. The depth of voter concern with the issue as well as labor's ability to mobilize its membership were reflected in the almost 80 percent turnout among registered voters in California, which set a new record for an off-year election. And riding in on that wave of voter discontent came Democratic gubernatorial candidate Pat Brown, who beat Knowland by amassing 60 percent of the vote, thereby becoming only the second Democrat to win that office in the twentieth century. Carried in along with him were Democratic candidates for six out of the seven statewide offices, as well as majorities in both houses of the legislature and the congressional delegation, giving California Democrats their most complete triumph in almost seventy years. The same tide also swept over Ohio's Republican incumbent governor William O'Neill, whose televised endorsement of the union-shop ban two weeks before election day served only to seal his fate. Democrat Michael V. DiSalle, like Brown a staunch opponent of the union-shop measure, won the governorship with 57 percent of all votes cast.[106]

The current rolled through the legislatures as well, nowhere more so than in Indiana. Labor's campaign there to oust state lawmakers who had voted to ban the union shop produced a political earthquake. Before election day Republicans had outnumbered Democrats in the Indiana legislature 75 to 25; after the ballots were tallied, the margin stood at 79 Democrats and 21 Republicans. Perhaps most impressive of all, labor's political action efforts helped give the Democrats their finest showing in the congressional elections since the New Deal zenith of 1936. What had been fairly narrow Democratic margins in the House and Senate stood, after the 1958 elections, at 282 to 154 and 64 to 34, respectively. In the face of an explicit managerial assault on the postwar New Deal, labor had rallied to score a stunning electoral victory.[107]

Those results suggested differing lessons to Democratic analysts. Some saw in them the signs of reviving public support for liberal reform. Most prominent among those who drew that conclusion was the New Deal historian and liberal activist Arthur Schlesinger Jr. His cyclical model of American politics indicated that after a time of conservative reaction, voters were now growing more receptive to the ADA's reform program. Less sanguine was Goldberg, who viewed the contest as essentially an effort to preserve the status quo in the face of a conservative attack. Although labor-backed candidates had won many key electoral contests, the Dixiecrat–GOP alliance still commanded narrow majorities in both houses of Congress.[108]

Deeply disturbed by the events of the past year and a half, Goldberg had been working during that time to formulate a response to those managers and politicians increasingly unhappy with the economic problems the postwar New Deal was creating. For the past eighteen months, labor had been reacting to the managerial revolt in essentially defensive ways. Now was the time, Goldberg decided, to do more than that, to offer a positive program to meet the problems that had stirred managers to action, yet do so in a way that preserved labor's place in the postwar order.

Immediately after the elections, Goldberg presented labor's alternative in a major address at the University of Wisconsin. Entitled "The State of Labor–Management Relations, 1958–1959," Goldberg's speech decried the growing antagonism between the two sides. Acknowledging that organized labor appeared as strong at the end of 1958 as it had for many years, he argued that just beneath the surface were persistent problems, among them the failure to organize either most of the South or so-called white-collar workers nationwide.[109]

Making matters worse, he contended, was a growing shift in managerial attitudes. Business leaders seemed, he observed, to be retreating from the more consensual approach predominant during the eight years between 1949 and 1956:

> I thought . . . about ten years ago . . . we seemed to be on the road toward achievement of mutual respect and understanding in our basic industries. . . . But in the recent past I see a hardening of attitudes, and retrogression rather than progress in understanding. . . .
>
> Throughout American industry there is a widespread movement to replace genuine acceptance of and cooperation with unions by a philosophy of labor–management relations keyed to keeping the unions at arm's length, of working with the union as little as possible, of seeking, wherever possible, to go around the union to its members rather than to deal with the union as a living institution. This philosophy treats unions as necessary evils rather than as constructive partners.[110]

Speculating on the reasons for the change, Goldberg acknowledged that there were some areas of the economy in which labor power was great and employer power much less, situations in which unions sometimes abused their influence. He went on to point out that such instances were the exception, not the rule, and, with no little understatement, observed that "the American industrial scene is not one in which poor, downtrodden, profitless business enterprises have every last penny extracted from them by powerful labor unions."[111] Trying to strike a note of moderation, Goldberg attacked business leaders who had taken to accusing organized labor of trying to "socialize America" and, indirectly, Walter Reuther, for his "nonsensical" charge that a major employer was "seeking a fascist America." These "stereotype images," Goldberg said, were "taking the place of reality," a deplorable trend, in his view, that had to be stopped.[112]

The best way to achieve that goal, Goldberg contended, was to create a forum in which labor and business leaders could meet to discuss their problems and thereby reach a mutual understanding. The previous generation of top union chiefs and managers, he said, had gained such a perspective through their service on the War Production Board and the National War Labor Board, but the present group, especially its managerial members, lacked the benefit of that experience. The latter, he said, "are more inclined to be organization men, with all the parochial characteristics of that breed." The bargaining table itself, Goldberg argued, had proved unhelpful as a forum, because the immediate need to strike a short-term bargain on wages and benefits precluded thinking in broader terms.[113]

His proposed alternative was to create a "labor–management assembly," convened under the auspices of the federal government and with the secretaries of labor and commerce acting as co-chairmen. Goldberg emphasized, however, that it would not be a government agency in the ordinary sense. Seeking to increase government supervision of the postwar social contract in ways that would help strengthen it, Goldberg said he viewed "the role of the government as providing prestige, of supplying facts, and of bringing together a secretariat for the conduct of the meeting." He went on to propose that the members of the Business Advisory Council (BAC), a private group that advised the Commerce Department, supply most of the assembly's management representatives. In view of the preponderance of big business leaders in the BAC, he suggested including in the proposed body some heads of smaller firms as well. Labor's delegates, Goldberg said, should be the members of the AFL–CIO Executive Board, together with leaders of "respectable" unaffiliated unions.[114]

Although he envisioned the assembly primarily as a place for discussion, Goldberg did say that he hoped its members would issue recommendations that reflected a genuine consensus on the problems confronting them. To achieve those goals, he called for periodic meetings, held off the record, combined with social events and small group discussions intended to foster the maximum amount of intellectual exchange. The specific subjects to be addressed, he added, must include inflation; unemployment resulting from the introduction of new technology or, as it was increasingly termed, *automation*; the union-shop issue; corruption in both labor and management circles; as well as worker education and retraining. Admitting that what such an organization could do might be limited, Goldberg argued nonetheless that the effort was worth making.[115]

In its totality, the scheme reflected both the influence of the wartime model of cooperation so influential among labor leaders of Goldberg's generation and the corporatist ideas most fully developed in Sweden. It was not, however, a warmed-over version of the "Industrial Councils" idea that Philip Murray and Walter Reuther had promoted some fifteen years earlier, which to many managers had become synonymous with German-style codetermination. Winning managerial cooperation in the effort to preserve the postwar New Deal, Goldberg believed, depended in part on labor's willingness to stop trying to win greater control over firms' strategic decisions. In his speech he had said that "American labor has not the slightest interest in co-determination" or "any joint control of industry."[116] But an influential minority in the AFL–CIO led by Walter Reuther still persisted in seeking such schemes. Goldberg's approach to the problems facing labor and management in the late 1950s reflected the thinking of the USA leadership, which stood at the center of organized labor during that time, but it did not command universal support among the former CIO unions.

Even more troubling, Goldberg's vision of a "soft" corporatism, one that laid much greater emphasis on voluntary interest-group cooperation than on government coercion, still rang alarm bells among many union leaders who before 1956 had dominated the AFL and since then its successor, as well as some of their managerial adversaries. Leery of increasing government supervision of the postwar social contract, especially at a time when managerial influence over the government seemed to be growing, Meany and his former AFL colleagues gave Goldberg's ideas only cautious and highly tentative acceptance. The plan received an even cooler reception from leaders of the core industrial firms, who feared that such an organization would only pave the way for more government intervention in corporate decision making, without providing the benefits that Goldberg suggested it might bring.

But amid the growing acrimony on both sides, Goldberg's plan suggested a peaceful and humane way out of the troubles labor leaders and business executives faced in the late 1950s. For that reason, his speech won a respectful hearing in both camps. It received nationwide attention, including front-page coverage in major newspapers. The publicity helped spark a flood of responses, more than one hundred in the first week after Goldberg had given the address. His call for moderation and negotiation struck a chord with those business leaders and politicians who had strongly supported the postwar New Deal yet saw some merit in managerial complaints.

Over the next two years, Goldberg and the center of the union movement for which he spoke would attempt to win approval for the idea, in face of strong resistance from some managers and only lukewarm support from much of the AFL–CIO leadership. Along the way he would face some of the most difficult challenges of his career.[117]

7

The Postwar Order Under Stress, Round Two

As 1959 BEGAN, the managerial offensive intensified in the realms of elective politics, collective bargaining, and the workplace itself. During the first half of the year Goldberg would spend the bulk of his time fending off the first threat, which came in the form of a campaign for new antiunion legislation. That was followed by six months of turmoil in the steel industry, as managers there attempted to roll back the USA's economic gains and its power on the shop floor. The result was a 116-day walkout that became, and still remains, the largest industrial dispute in U.S. history.

Although those events came in sequence, they were part of a single, coordinated campaign to readjust the postwar New Deal in ways more favorable to management. Indeed, while Goldberg spent much of the spring and summer of 1959 fighting for an acceptable bill to curb union corruption, at the same time he met again and again with steel company executives to negotiate a new master contract that would replace the three-year agreement scheduled to expire on July 1. Goldberg played leading roles in both struggles and in the presidential election that followed them. Taken together, they signaled a dramatic change in managerial behavior from the pattern of the preceding decade.[1]

Soon after the 1958 elections, work resumed in Congress on a new labor "reform" bill. The clamor aroused by the McClellan Committee for laws designed to combat labor corruption did not die down and, indeed, grew louder as the new year opened. The large amount of attention devoted to that issue in the mass media clearly illustrated the consequences for labor of its earlier inability to create a daily newspaper or cope with the increasing expense of radio and television programming. At a USA Executive Board meeting held early in 1959, members complained bitterly about the antiunion sentiment stimulated by the newspapers, radio, and especially the McClellan Committee's televised broadcasts.[2]

Seeking to fight back, McDonald and several board members called for increasing the USA's own publicity efforts. But television's high cost precluded heavy use of that medium at a time when its influence was growing enormously. Over the previous two years, the union had produced a monthly filmed program featuring McDonald in the role of USA spokesman. Unable to afford a network broadcast, the union instead had distributed copies of the films to local unions, libraries, colleges, and universities. The audience for those films was, not surprisingly, much smaller than for those broadcast via network television. But even this modest effort, along with newspaper and radio advertising, had cost the union $958,000 in 1958, almost 9 percent of the international union's operating budget for that year.

Some board members, dissatisfied with the very limited impact of this effort, suggested sponsoring a prime-time program, but the cost of such an experiment posed an insurmountable barrier. As McDonald explained to the board,

> *Maverick*, for God's sake, is out of sight, $40,000 a week. *The Dinah Shore Show* costs $165,000 a week to produce. . . . one of those tremendous big spectaculars that went on the air recently cost $575,000 just to produce that one show, and another $300,000 to get it on the air.
>
>   This is tremendously big league, and we can't go that big league because we don't have that kind of dough.[3]

Although the board did approve plans to increase radio programming and paid advertising in the print media, these moves proved no match for the resources of labor's opponents. Unable to resist effectively, labor leaders watched the calls for new labor legislation mount in response to the mass media's one-sided depiction of union corruption.[4]

This situation helped persuade Goldberg that a labor campaign to block any such law would fail. Moreover, he saw a real need for some remedial legislation to address the corruption problem, a step that Goldberg believed would benefit honest unions. He therefore set to work once again to draft an alternative that would address the problem of labor corruption, but not in ways that would weaken honestly run unions.

As he had in the preceding effort, Goldberg collaborated with John Kennedy in preparing such a bill, although this time it would not be offered as a bipartisan measure, at least not in the ordinary sense of that term. New York Senator Irving Ives had retired, and no other Republican on the Labor Subcommittee would agree to cosponsor the new bill. Forced to choose from among the other Democratic members, Kennedy settled on Sam Ervin of North Carolina. Representing a state with only a weak labor movement and one in which the union shop had been outlawed twelve years earlier, Ervin's support helped give what became the Kennedy–Ervin bill some semblance of objectivity.[5]

Trying to enhance that perception, Kennedy also once again requested that a "nonpartisan" panel of experts be established to provide advice on labor reform legislation. This advisory panel's members included two representatives each from labor and management and five so-called public members with expertise in industrial relations. The group this time was unable to reach any real consensus, a development that reflected the growing divisions in managerial and union ranks. Instructed by Kennedy to make its recommendations by June 1, the so-called blue ribbon panel failed to issue any report until after Congress had passed new labor legislation. The inability from the outset to achieve broad agreement signaled to all concerned that the struggle to enact the Kennedy–Ervin bill would be a bitterly divisive one.[6]

A key stumbling block lay in Title VI, the Taft–Hartley "sweeteners." Given the increasing managerial and administration pressure for a bill that reduced labor's economic and political power, Kennedy, Ervin, and Senate majority leader Lyndon Johnson now favored a reform measure stripped of Title VI. In that way, the leadership in both the House and the Senate could rule floor amendments to Taft–Hartley out of order, thereby bottling up the antilabor initiatives. And to make that palatable to both labor and management, Kennedy proposed a "two-package" approach, in which the Senate would first consider an anticorruption bill and then one dealing with Taft–Hartley amendments. But this plan foundered on the implacable opposition of the building trades unions and George Meany. Kennedy had won their support for the bill the previous year only by pledging to back the Taft–Hartley changes contained in Title VI and could not renege on that commitment without endangering the federation's support for an anticorruption measure. Meany and most other labor leaders rightly suspected that the second half of the "two-package" deal would never materialize; to leave out the sweeteners in the first bill would very likely lose them for good. For those reasons he adamantly refused to budge, leaving Kennedy with no choice but to leave Title VI in his new bill. That would prove to be a crucial mistake.[7]

Seeking to provide some kind of rationalization for a move that would still shield the bill from other Taft–Hartley changes, Goldberg argued that the Title VI provisions, having been considered the previous year and passed by the Senate, should be deemed "noncontroversial" Taft–Hartley amendments. All other proposed changes, so his reasoning went, belonged in the second bill because they would require careful consideration by the Senate Subcommittee on Labor. But this legalistic argument was more ingenious than sound. In the context of that time, almost no Taft–Hartley amendment could be considered truly noncontroversial. Furthermore, under the Senate's existing parliamentary rules, including Title VI made relevant any further proposed changes to Taft–Hartley, thereby opening the Kennedy–Ervin bill to floor amendments. Thus labor's own disunity had paved the way for a conservative onslaught.[8]

The new Kennedy measure, essentially the same as the earlier Kennedy–Ives proposal, soon encountered the first sign of impending trouble when Kennedy endeavored on February 16 to report the bill to the full Senate Committee on Labor and Public Welfare. Goldberg, along with the other lobbyists backing the measure, had planned on moving swiftly, capitalizing on the favorable mood produced by the recent elections. In that way the Senate — whose membership was more sympathetic to labor and more insulated from managerial lobbying than was that of the House — would play the leading role. So, at least, Goldberg and his colleagues had reasoned. But pressure from Senators McClellan, Curtis, and Mundt, who wanted the panel to consider other amendments, compelled Kennedy's subcommittee to delay for an entire month before sending the measure along to the full committee. There the same pattern emerged, one of the efforts by conservative Republicans and Senator McClellan to slow down the Kennedy–Ervin bill's progress.

On March 25, more than a month later than Kennedy, Goldberg, and their allies had originally planned, the Senate Committee on Labor and Public Welfare voted thirteen to two to send the measure to the Senate floor. Along the way a few amendments had been added, but none to which labor voiced strong objections. The stage was thereby set for a dramatic showdown between the supporters of the postwar New Deal and those increasingly hostile to labor's place in it.[9]

It came immediately after two key early roll calls. The first, Senator Ervin's proposed amendment to divest the bill of Title VI, failed twenty-seven to sixty-seven. So, too, did a motion by Senate minority leader Everett Dirksen to substitute the administration's proposed Taft–Hartley changes for Title VI, this time by a margin of twenty-four to sixty-seven. Following those two votes, both of which took place on April 21, Senator Ervin abandoned his cosponsorship of the Kennedy bill, in effect ending whatever appearance of conservative support it still had.

Sure at last that Title VI as drafted would remain in the bill, Goldberg and the other union lobbyists braced themselves for more amendments to Taft–Hartley. The votes on the Ervin and Dirksen motions persuaded them that they could keep such amendments from passing, but Senator McClellan proved them wrong the very next day. On April 22 he offered an amendment to Title VI that would add a so-called bill of rights for union members. A similar floor amendment had failed during the 1958 consideration of Kennedy–Ives, but this time things turned out differently. After an emotional two-hour address by Senator McClellan urging its adoption, combined with furious debate from other members, intense managerial and labor lobbying, and parliamentary maneuvering on both sides, the Senate voted to adopt it by a margin of forty-seven to forty-six. A second motion to retable failed on a tie vote broken by Vice-President Richard Nixon. All but two Republicans and five southern Democrats voting supported the move to insert the so-called union democracy provisions, despite the best efforts by unions and their allies in the Senate. Most infuriating to them, and especially to Goldberg, of the five senators absent, three were reliable labor supporters, and thus, had they been present, the outcome might have been different.[10]

Other amendments passed that limited organizational picketing and outlawed "hot cargo" agreements in the motor carrier industry. The latter referred to contracts between unions and employers in the freight business that barred the shipment of goods to or from a firm engaged in a labor dispute. The U.S. Supreme Court had ruled a year earlier that that powerful union weapon was legal, infuriating employer groups. The Senate also approved a few other provisions intended to regulate the conduct of union elections and impose stricter bonding requirements on union officials. Through it all, Senator McClellan played the leading role, capitalizing on the public exposure and moral authority he had gained through his committee's investigation of union corruption. In the end, labor staved off completely only the conservatives' proposals to prohibit all kinds of secondary boycotts and to give the states jurisdiction over labor–management relations in the area of small businesses, the "no-man's land" amendment. Goldberg and his fellow lobbyists did win changes in the wording of the other McClellan amendments, revisions that removed some of their worst features, but those victories offered only modest consolation. The final bill passed by the Senate was substantially more restrictive than the previous year's Kennedy–Ives measure, despite the Democrats' strong showing in the intervening elections.[11]

Goldberg laid most of the blame for the setback on leading business organizations and the conservative coalition in the Senate. He told the USA Executive Board afterward:

> The NAM and the Chamber [of Commerce] and the anti-labor forces of the country this time had organized themselves, such as they have never before been organized, and as a result of a demagogic appeal by Senator McClellan and by the Republicans the bill that came out of the Senate was worsened.[12]

Although all this was true, the overconfidence of some labor leaders had contributed to the setback in the Senate. Goldberg, like many of them, had assumed that the results of the 1958 elections would incline the Senate to pass the original Kennedy bill. They soon learned otherwise. Goldberg and his union colleagues had also failed to organize any grassroots lobbying effort to offset the managerial one, preferring instead to rely on bargaining conducted at the top, a costly error.[13]

But having endorsed the need for new laws to curb corruption in the union movement, Goldberg reasoned that the AFL–CIO could not now simply oppose the amended measure as totally unnecessary. The bill passed by the Senate also contained some provisions, the so-called sweeteners, that labor really wanted. Furthermore, only the enactment of some legislation that attacked the worst kinds of abuses the McClellan Committee had identified would dissipate the public hostility to organized labor that the managerial campaign had so effectively aroused. So Goldberg reasoned, in the face of angry protests from Nordy Hoffman and some USA district directors, who preferred to fight against any bill that contained the McClellan amendments, a view shared by the leaders of some other AFL–CIO unions.[14]

The debate continued in the AFL–CIO for more than a month, as its chieftains digested Goldberg's detailed legal analysis of the amendments added on the Senate floor. After a brief period in which Meany declared the federation opposed to the Kennedy bill as passed and determined to insist on the sweeteners, the mood changed. When the House Committee on Education and Labor indicated that it would report a bill similar to the Kennedy measure, Meany and the federation leadership finally came around to supporting the removal of all Taft–Hartley amendments.

They were too late. House Democratic leaders now told Goldberg and the other labor lobbyists that conservative members, increasingly confident that they would prevail, would no longer settle for a bill that did not address the organizational picketing, hot cargo, and so-called union democracy issues. Having misjudged the situation at the outset, Meany and his colleagues in the building trades had landed the AFL–CIO in a mess, from which Goldberg, Reuther, and other industrial union leaders would attempt to extricate it. Their efforts were complicated by continuing resistance from the building trades and outright opposition to any bill from the still quite powerful Teamsters, as well as the United Mine Workers.[15]

The center of the union movement, for which Goldberg spoke, pressed ahead nonetheless. It faced opposition also from management representatives who, having won an important and unexpected victory in the Senate, now renewed their calls in the House for more restrictions on secondary boycotts and organizational picketing. And most revealing of what lay behind the campaign against labor union corruption, those same forces called for the extension of the antitrust laws to resist organized labor's "monopoly power," a provision banning the union shop nationwide, a requirement that all strike votes be conducted by secret ballot, and restrictions on the use of union dues for political action. In contrast to the pattern of the previous year, business community lobbyists argued in unison for those changes, all under the tight supervision of the White House staff. Although Secretary of Labor Mitchell continued to sound unenthusiastic about these further amendments and, indeed, had publicly expressed reservations about the so-called bill of rights already adopted by the Senate, most leading members of the Eisenhower administration, responding to managerial pressure, by then strongly supported the managerial lobbying campaign. In the face of that formidable combination, and with dissident factions in the union movement itself pushing in other directions, Goldberg and his allies persevered.[16]

Matters came to a head in the House, as they had in the Senate, on the floor. There the members chose between two measures, one, the Elliott bill, which was slightly more favorable to labor than the version passed by the Senate, and the Landrum–Griffin bill, which added to the Senate version the "no-man's land" provision that management supported, bans on all hot cargo agreements and all secondary boycotts, as well as further restrictions on organizational picketing, while excluding the "sweeteners" sought by labor. Its firmly expressed opposition to the more extreme managerial demands for a national right-to-work law, a compulsory secret ballot for all strike votes, and controls over union political action and for bringing unions under the antitrust laws led to their exclusion from the Landrum–Griffin bill, but in all, the measure contained much of what management sought.[17]

After seemingly endless jockeying, the issue came to a vote on August 13.

Amid a crescendo of lobbying from all sides, some of it very heavy-handed, the House voted by the narrow margin of 229 to 201 to adopt the Landrum–Griffin bill.[18] The intensity of the pressures operating on House members can be seen in the number of them present and voting on the measure, the highest at that time for any bill in U.S. history. Goldberg afterward was furious with many of the labor lobbyists for their behavior, especially those from the Teamsters Union who had tried to block passage of any bill. In the end, their threats served only to antagonize some of the union movement's strongest congressional allies.

Disappointed with the result, Goldberg still laid most of the blame on the managerial forces that had supported the Landrum–Griffin bill. As he told the members of the USA Executive Board soon after the House bill passed, when it had reached that chamber, the managerial

> campaign started in high gear, and there was an outpouring, an avalanche of mail and communications reaching the members of the House—on one thing—we want a strong Labor Reform bill. I want to say to you frankly within our family here that every congressman got thousands of letters to this effect, and very few letters from our side.[19]

Adding to that pressure was President Eisenhower's televised address urging enactment of the Landrum–Griffin bill. Seeking to shake the generally favorable impression many board members still had of Eisenhower, Goldberg said,

> Let's not delude ourselves about the effect of that broadcast. That broadcast produced an overwhelming reaction on the American public that every member of Congress felt. It was a very deceptive broadcast, in that it had nothing to do with labor reform, nothing to do with accounting for funds[,] or investment of funds or anything of that sort. The President addressed himself to the area of the economic strength of the labor movement. . . . he talked about secondary boycotts, . . . organizational picketing, and . . . "no man's land." . . . none of these areas has a thing to do with labor reform.[20]

The combination of fierce managerial pressure and Eisenhower's endorsement had led the conservative majority in the House to support the Landrum–Griffin bill. Cementing the Dixiecrat–GOP alliance's support for the measure, Goldberg told the USA Executive Board, was an unholy bargain between the House Rules Committee chairman Howard Smith of Virginia, a leader of the southern conservatives, and the House minority leader Charles Halleck of Indiana. Halleck had promised Smith that the Republicans in the House would prevent any civil rights bill from passing in exchange for southern Democrats' support for Landrum–Griffin, an offer Smith had accepted. On the key roll call, the bill had passed with the support of 126 Republicans, 100 southern and border state Democrats, and 3 other members of the "majority" party who represented districts in Kansas, Nebraska, and New Mexico.[21]

In discussing the whole episode with the USA Executive Board afterward, Goldberg made clear that he believed Senate majority leader Lyndon Johnson deserved a large share of the blame. Johnson, Goldberg told the board, "has now over-reached himself."[22] Never a totally reliable ally of labor and lacking a real understanding of unions' role in the postwar order, Johnson in 1959 had felt the full pressure from business groups to allow the Landrum–Griffin bill to pass. He characteristically had attempted to mollify both sides, but the outcome in this case signaled his true allegiance. Johnson had meddled in the House, urging members of the Texas delegation there to support the Landrum–Griffin bill. Goldberg told the USA Executive Board at a meeting in August 1959 that

> you will notice that the Texas delegation did not support the Speaker, except [for] four fellows. They voted for the Landrum–Griffin bill. The story has come out . . . that Mr. Johnson has told the members of the Texas delegation that their political life in Texas depended upon their voting for the Landrum–Griffin bill and not following the Speaker's activities.[23]

Goldberg grimly reported that the adverse publicity and labor's protests had now turned the opportunistic Johnson around:

> There is no doubt that Johnson played a bad part in the House situation. That has been reported and not denied. However, he has gotten scared, he realizes that the word has gotten out, and now he is being very cooperative, he is trying to do a rescue job. Of course, we have been after him, we had quite a time with Senator Johnson.[24]

Johnson and Kennedy proceeded to work for the deletion of some of the most antiunion provisions during the negotiations in the House and Senate Conference Committee. Goldberg — his less rosy view of labor's prospects in the House now confirmed — won firm support from the AFL–CIO to act as its agent in working with the committee. The conservatives, although a narrow majority of that body, had acquiesced in the selection of Kennedy as chair, believing that would pose no real threat to the passage of a measure that incorporated what they wanted while at the same time identifying it so closely with the Massachusetts senator himself as to doom his emerging presidential campaign. Kennedy started out cautiously, raising first the provisions dealing with labor corruption, which aroused little real controversy among the conferees. They soon resolved those issues amicably and then began to tackle the thornier ones, the Taft–Hartley amendments. Settling those disputes would consume the bulk of the committee's time and energy and pose the greatest challenges to both Kennedy and Goldberg.[25]

The latter worked feverishly with Kennedy, Archibald Cox, and, to a lesser extent, Lyndon Johnson to repair as much as possible the damage done by the House. Goldberg believed that labor now had no other choice. Although the Senate had earlier rejected several of the House bill's provisions, its members were now wavering in the face of managerial and administration pressure. As he told the USA Executive Board in a meeting held at that same time,

This hysteria has hit the Senate, as well as the House, and whereas just a few months ago these same provisions were defeated by a vote of 60 to 30, the present count, in which Nordy Hoffman will agree with me, will indicate that probably the maximum . . . we could summon is about 40 votes. We thought we had won a great victory at the polls, but apparently we haven't won enough.[26]

The already tense mood turned ugly when an unidentified assailant pulled up his car beside one containing a House conferee and proceeded to squirt acid on him. Although the congressman escaped unharmed, the incident contributed to the general climate of fear and anger that engulfed Capitol Hill, much of it directed at the Teamsters Union lobbyists who were still fighting against the enactment of any bill.[27]

In that context, labor's leverage was limited. What Goldberg had going for his cause was uncertainty in managerial ranks over whether they could win a Senate roll-call vote on the House version. Having already won more than they had expected to, business lobbyists were unwilling to risk a loss in the Senate, one that might doom the passage of any bill that year. Goldberg and Kennedy exploited this caution to gain consideration for a set of changes that Goldberg had taken the lead in drafting and to which the AFL–CIO had given its formal endorsement. The Kennedy–Goldberg proposals weakened the House-passed restrictions on secondary boycotts and organizational picketing and gave the regional directors of the NLRB control over the "no man's land" area, in effect reversing the House vote to give the states that power. Kennedy made clear to the other conferees that they must accept all these changes or the package would be withdrawn.[28]

In the end, he and Goldberg got most of them, although not the "no-man's land" provision, but even the House version permitted the states to regulate labor–management relations in small businesses only if the NLRB did not exercise its jurisdiction. The net effect of allowing the provision's adoption was to increase the value to labor of having a more sympathetic administration elected. The same could be said for much of the reporting and disclosure requirements in the reform section of the bill. The power to oversee union compliance had been placed in the hands of the secretary of labor, once again raising the stakes for labor in future presidential elections. But the final act, which passed both houses of Congress during the first week of September, contained much that was harmful to the labor movement, especially to its capacity for future growth.[29]

Despite Goldberg's efforts to defend the result as better than nothing and "protective of the decent labor movement," no one could hide the fact that labor had suffered a serious and embarrassing defeat.[30] At the same time, however, its highly successful political action campaign in 1958 and lobbying thereafter had blocked the managerial campaign to bring labor unions under the antitrust laws, ban the union shop nationwide, hem in its political action efforts, and compel secret ballots on all strike votes. Goldberg and his allies had succeeded in staving off a major disaster, but at a heavy price. The entire experience demonstrated more vividly than ever that political action alone could not win support from the government for the union movement. In the last analysis, labor's ability to influence the government depended on the economic and political strength of the unions themselves, which clearly had begun to wane.[31]

II

During the same summer in which Congress passed Landrum–Griffin, bargaining between the USA and the major steel companies' managers over a new master contract ended in a strike, events that Goldberg saw as clearly related. The contest with the USA, which had played a leading role in working out the postwar New Deal, was intended to pave the way for similar renegotiations in other industries. As he told the USA Executive Board in August, the pressure for Landrum–Griffin "is part of the industry move throughout the country to take on the labor movement, and we are being taken on here in New York on the economic front, while in Washington the whole labor movement is being taken on, on the political and legislative front."[32] The behavior of steel industry managers, especially those at U.S. Steel, reinforced that belief. They conducted themselves throughout the 1959 confrontation in ways that suggested that they viewed themselves as defending not simply their own interests but those of the American business community more generally.[33]

As in the past, the bargaining over a new master contract in steel would have implications for the nation's entire labor–management relationship. The USA negotiations during 1959 brought to the surface conflicts that had begun to emerge in other heavily unionized industries. Clashes in those other areas of the economy tended, however, to be much less visible and divisive during the late 1950s than would be the case in steel. The USA's central position in the postwar order led to a different outcome there. The conflict in steel during 1959 would signal to managers in other industries whether a more aggressive effort to roll back labor's gains should be adopted. For that reason, the 1959 talks between the USA and steel executives would be watched closely by business, labor, and government leaders. There the managerial offensive would receive its clearest and most important early test. Goldberg acknowledged those facts in writing to I. W. Abel after the dispute had been resolved, telling him that "the steel negotiations . . . posed . . . a grave threat not only to the vitality of the Union and the benefits and protections won by it over the years for the membership, but to the entire American labor movement."[34]

The contest had begun on the shop floor even before contract talks opened that spring. Employers had been making a concerted effort there since late 1957 to reduce the rank and file's control over local working conditions. This campaign in steel and other industries was responsible for reversing an eight-year trend of decline in the total number of employer unfair labor practice cases unions had brought before the NLRB. After reaching an all-time low in

1957, the number of such cases more than doubled over the next three years.
As David McDonald told the USA leadership in January 1959, the growing

> rigidity in the positions taken by labor and management in terms of indus-
> trial philosophy, labor legislation and political activity is having harmful
> effects on the entire scope of collective bargaining. This divergence is deep-
> rooted, and to an impressive degree it is evidenced by a remarkable increase
> in unfair labor practice cases before the National Labor Relations Board.[35]

The onset of recession tended in steel and elsewhere to shift the balance of
power in management's favor. Even the subsequent recovery, which began
during the summer of 1958, worked to managers' advantage. They chose to
recall substantially fewer employees, thereby achieving unilateral reductions in the size of work crews, a practice that Clause 2B of the master
contract expressly forbade. This was only another in a series of moves aimed
at regaining more managerial control over the production process.[36]

Infuriating to workers and local union officials alike, these changes did not
go unnoticed by the international union's leaders. At a May 1958 executive
board meeting called to formulate contract demands, District Director Paul
Rusen insisted that these issues be addressed in the upcoming round of talks.
Specifically, Rusen told the other board members, "The question I am raising
is that we have job descriptions that they [Wheeling Steel] are now directly
violating, and that is going to be a great argument, the job description part of
the contract. They are doing that in all plants and I am assuming everybody
has the same problem."[37] The board's discussion of the issue revealed its
continuing failure to come up with any real answer to the decline in employment that followed from management's investment in new equipment.
Although Section 2B of the master contract placed restrictions on that substi-
tution, managers tended to use the recession-induced layoffs to escape
them.[38]

By the end of 1958, this practice had made itself felt in two areas that every
USA officer, no matter how senior, could appreciate: union size and income.
David McDonald informed the USA Executive Board the following January
that the total number of dues-paying members had slipped below the psycho-
logically important 1 million mark, from an average of 1,092,194 for the first
eleven months of 1957 to 902,302 for the same period in 1958. At the same
meeting, I. W. Abel reported that the four-year pattern of steady increases in
the USA's net worth had been broken. Still a healthy sum at a little over $33
million, the union had begun to run some worrisome monthly losses.[39]

All of these developments had persuaded Goldberg by the spring of 1959
that the USA would face a very serious challenge in its pending contract talks.
As they heated up, he would play the key negotiating role, leaving to
McDonald most of the more visible public relations work that went along
with that process. This time Goldberg would be bargaining with U.S. Steel's
newly appointed vice-president for industrial relations and personnel,
R. Conrad Cooper. Long the advocate of a more confrontational approach in
dealing with the union, Cooper had replaced the much less antagonistic John

Stephens the previous year. Cooper chaired the twelve major firms' management negotiating committee, which bargained during 1959 in the industrywide fashion perfected three years earlier. The first five months of 1959 witnessed little real negotiating, as both sides waged public relations campaigns intended to win support for their respective positions.[40]

U.S. Steel's management started the contest with an advertising campaign designed by the public relations firm of Hill and Knowlton. It ran statements in the print media that blamed the union for rising steel prices and inflation more generally. U.S. Steel's chairman of the board, Roger Blough, also publicly sounded those themes, arguing that the need to reduce inflation had forced steel producers to press both for abolishing the cost of living allowance (COLA) clause and against any general wage increase.

Steel managers such as Blough were also becoming seriously concerned about reviving foreign competition from Western Europe and Japan. Steel firms there — already at an advantage thanks to their much lower labor costs — had begun to produce large amounts of steel made with more advanced technology, the basic oxygen furnace in particular. Although total exports to the United States of such steel remained small and were confined mostly to the simplest kinds of steel products, the long-term trend could not be ignored. In order for American firms to keep up with such foreign competition, they would need to invest substantial amounts of capital in new plants and equipment, a change that would require the union's cooperation if it were to succeed.

The high cost of domestically produced steel was also beginning to incline American manufacturers to seek lower-cost substitutes, such as aluminum, concrete, and plastics, a trend that posed another long-term threat to the industry's continued prosperity. This situation, Blough and his colleagues believed, militated against any further wage increases, an argument repeated over and over in their paid advertising.[41]

Although he was aware of the long-term problems beginning to emerge in steel, Goldberg nonetheless disagreed with much of Blough's reasoning, in particular his assumption that the union deserved the blame for the failure to introduce new technology, as well as for rising steel prices and inflation. Goldberg knew that steel company profits over the previous three years had been quite large, despite the substantial wage increases workers had received during that time. In the spring of 1959 the companies reported huge profits, reflecting the economy's recovery from recession and very large increases in worker productivity, which stemmed largely from the managers' decision to rehire many fewer workers. For these reasons, Goldberg argued that the union was entitled to a wage increase in accordance with the productivity formula, one that would not necessitate any increase in steel prices. This in turn would still leave most steel producers, he contended, with ample capital to introduce new technology, thereby keeping the USA competitive in its domestic and foreign markets. Goldberg believed that the culprits responsible for past increases in steel prices were the Eisenhower administration, which steadfastly refused to make the kinds of serious efforts its predecessor had had to, to police prices, and steel company managers, who demanded more than what he saw as their fair share of industry income. And he regarded the failure to introduce new equipment as following much more from managerial short-sightedness than from obstacles erected by the union.[42]

There was some truth on both sides, but more on that of the union. Goldberg's public statements during the 1959 negotiations about industry profits were somewhat misleading. Some of the very large profits steelmakers reported during the spring and summer of 1959 stemmed from customer stockpiling in anticipation of a strike, a practice that usually preceded the expiration of the industry's master contract. Such stockpiling caused the industry to run near capacity, but obviously this practice and the profits it yielded could not be sustained for very long. Furthermore, industry profits as a percentage of stockholders' equity had fallen since 1956, to a point slightly below the average for the manufacturing sector as a whole.

Even so, the union's view that management deserved much of the blame for the emerging problems was essentially correct. Steel industry managers had insisted on financing new investment in plant and equipment mainly out of accumulated profits rather than through borrowing, the more traditional route in American industry. According to the practices common in the manufacturing sector, steel firms had earned ample funds over the past decade to finance new plants and equipment. And even though the union's Clause 2B, which protected existing work rules, did reduce investors' return on making that kind of investment, the provision did not pose an absolute bar.[43]

For those reasons, Goldberg and McDonald told Cooper that to press his demands for a wage freeze and an end to the COLA would lead the USA to support Senator Kefauver's plan to regulate steel industry pricing.

Cooper called the bluff, telling them that government regulation would include wage controls as well, which steel executives believed the union would never accept. Both sides knew that the last government effort to regulate steel industry prices, which had taken place during the Korean War, had eventually failed and that the Eisenhower administration would probably be more zealous in limiting wages than Truman's had been. Indeed, when a few of the district directors suggested that the union propose a wage freeze in exchange for the companies' agreement to cut prices, a bargain that the Eisenhower administration would likely have supported, Goldberg rejected the idea. Attractive in the abstract, the proposal, Goldberg told them, would prove to be a trap, because neither the government nor the union had the power to compel steel producers to reduce their prices. He told the board,

> If we were to make a proposal on the reduction of prices we would put ourselves in a box at this time. There is no government power, and we haven't got the power, to insist they do it. Even a warrior like President Truman couldn't force them . . . to reduce prices . . . [or even to] accept the price line that was established for all of American industry. They fought our government and they defeated our government on this issue. They were more powerful than the government of the United States.[44]

In this context, to signal any support for a wage freeze would simply under-mine the union's argument that a pay increase was appropriate, given the rising cost of living and the industry's substantial profits, without achieving the price restraint needed to reduce inflation. So Goldberg reasoned, and in large part he was right. At the heart of the dispute this time, as in the past, was a disagreement over the respective shares of industry income to which workers, managers, and stockholders were entitled. Either a wage freeze or changes in the contract that allowed managers to replace workers with new machinery more easily would simply be followed by unilateral managerial decisions about prices that increased managers' and investors' shares of indus-try income at the workers' expense. The government's inability to police prices effectively, a problem compounded by Eisenhower's unwilling-ness even to try, ensured that the tug-of-war would continue, thereby gen-erating inflation and the other related problems that all sides wished to avoid.[45]

On the other hand, the union's prospects for increases in wages and bene-fits looked dimmer in 1959 than they had at any time since the end of the Korean War. Total worker compensation under the three-year contract ne-gotiated in 1956 had risen substantially above that prevailing elsewhere in the manufacturing sector. This advance, however, was largely illusory. Steel managers had chosen in the wake of the 1954 and 1958 recessions to eliminate through automation many of the lowest-paying jobs, thereby boosting the industry's average hourly wage. This accounted for most of the steelworkers' apparent wage advantage over those in other manufacturing industries. Management's advertising campaign, however, stressed the seeming jump in hourly wages, suggesting to much of the public and many government officials that the union had won more than it deserved in its 1956 con-tract.

Goldberg and his colleagues thus knew that they would encounter more resistance to contract improvements from the public and the Eisenhower administration than in the past. At the outset of the contract talks, Eisen-hower and Labor Secretary James P. Mitchell endorsed a price freeze and wage increase in line with the productivity formula, but this time, unlike 1956, they refused even to consider the idea of direct government interven-tion to secure those terms. The business community's increasing pressure on the administration to curb labor's demands for higher wages and benefits persuaded Eisenhower and his associates to assume nothing more than a mediating role.[46]

Added to those developments was uncertainty about the economy's overall health, which would affect the union's bargaining power, and about the atti-tude of the workers themselves. The high and unusually persistent level of unemployment that had accompanied the 1958 recession took its toll on the rank and file. Few had any great enthusiasm for a strike, which would put them back out on the streets again. Indeed, had steel company executives confined themselves to their demands for abolishing the COLA and obtaining a wage freeze, Goldberg and his colleagues seriously doubted that the rank and file would have chosen to strike for more.[47]

Cooper's June 4 remark that Section 2B of the contract constituted a "roadblock to progress," followed by his announcement six days later that management would offer no wage or benefit improvements unless the union agreed to changes in Section 2B and its related provisions, transformed the situation.[48] The rank and file, already discontented with managers' efforts to achieve such changes indirectly, reacted fiercely to this explicit challenge to existing power relationships in the workplace. The demand also weakened the federal government's support for management's bargaining position.

After listening to Cooper's statement, Goldberg and the other senior USA officials retreated into a private room where they shared their jubilation. Steel company executives had handed them an issue that they knew would rouse the membership to action, thereby strengthening the leadership's hand in bargaining for contract improvements.[49]

In essence, the company's decision to raise the Section 2B issue directly reopened one of the bitterly divisive conflicts at the heart of the 1952 strike. This time, however, there were two important differences. First, executives at the smaller firms, who had shown no interest in the 2B issue during the 1952 dispute, now strongly supported U.S. Steel management's position. Even more indicative of the changed managerial mood, executives at the industry leader this time showed no willingness to yield, as they had ultimately agreed to do seven years earlier. The emerging prospects of serious foreign competition and the trend among American manufacturers to seek substitutes for ever more expensive steel had transformed managerial attitudes at the smaller firms toward Section 2B and had hardened those at U.S. Steel.

With the emergence of this issue, the tone of the talks turned nasty. Cooper's specific suggestions for changes in 2B and related clauses, delivered formally on June 10, only made matters worse. Consisting of eight provisions in all, the most important called for greater managerial freedom to rearrange work rules, draw up work and vacation schedules, revise the incentive pay formula, discipline wildcat strikers, and maintain seniority lists. Within twenty-four hours Goldberg and McDonald publicly denounced the proposals as completely unacceptable. As in 1952, the two sides had reached a total impasse.[50]

In explaining the situation to the USA Executive Board two weeks later, McDonald labeled the proposal the "8-point-break-the-union" offer. He told board members:

> We are in a fight to save the union. They are not kidding about these eight points. . . . They have presented sections for agreement which are just sickening in their contents. You may as well give up and go back and get a job as a company-union representative. You will be far better off because the Steelworkers would not exist as an important economic entity. They not only proposed it in general terms, but they spelled them out in specific terms where you [would] have not a single right left of these many things we won down through the years.[51]

McDonald also made these same charges publicly. Although quickly dismissed by steel industry managers as overblown union rhetoric, his words reflected an underlying reality. Section 2B, which had codified the transformation in power relations on the shop floor achieved during the 1930s and 1940s, was crucial to the rank and file's support for the union. Without the gains encompassed by that clause, worker support for the union itself would gradually whither away. For that reason, McDonald's seemingly hyperbolic description of Cooper's proposals had a real basis in fact.[52]

Similarly, when McDonald told the press that Cooper's plan was aimed at turning the USA into a "company union," the words in this context had a specific and accurate meaning. A union that had surrendered control over governance of the workplace, enjoying only the power to bargain collectively over wages and benefits, would more closely resemble the employee representation plans that steel executives had first sponsored during the 1920s than the industrial unions that had emerged in the following decade. Such employee organizations might succeed in providing workers with better wages and fringe benefits but would not give them any real say in how the workplace was run. Thus in 1959, the stakes were, in fact, every bit as high as McDonald's apocalyptic language suggested.[53]

Management's bargaining tactics in 1959 suggested to Goldberg that this 2B dispute would be even more bitter than the previous one had been. As the talks neared the contract expiration date of June 30, the Eisenhower administration urged both sides to extend the existing agreement and continue bargaining, as they had in 1952. In that year labor and management had observed an informal contract extension for over four months. This time, however, managers tried to add several contract modifications to the extension agreement, a step Goldberg viewed as intentionally provocative.

Similarly, when the union offered a one-year contract extension and proposals to create joint committees to study the work rules and benefits issues, Cooper rejected those ideas and then announced to the news media that "we have no offer from the union which is deemed a basis for settlement," leaving most reporters with the erroneous impression that a strike was imminent because the union had failed to make any proposals of its own.

And when the steel managers finally agreed less than forty-eight hours before the strike deadline to a fifteen-day extension on the traditional terms, they did so in ways calculated to offend the union's negotiating team. The extension itself ultimately made no difference. Cooper, on behalf of managers at the twelve major producers, insisted that the USA accept either a one-year extension of the existing contract minus the COLA clause or a modest wage increase offset by the eight-point work rules provision. And in private talks with McDonald and Goldberg, Cooper simply reiterated those terms and then released still more misleading statements to the press, all intended to suggest that the union was refusing to negotiate seriously.[54]

Believing that they had no other choice, Goldberg and his colleagues prepared for a strike. In view of the seriousness of the issues at stake, the USA leadership chose to include among the strike's targets most of the smaller steel companies as well. In that way, Goldberg reasoned, the work stoppage would produce the maximum impact on domestic steel production, for both civilian and military use.

The latter concern, even though the nation remained officially at peace, was not a minor one. With Chinese armed forces shelling the Formosa strait and tension rising in Berlin, the implications for U.S. military preparedness of a steel shortage concerned senior officials in the Eisenhower administration and on Capitol Hill. By including the smaller firms, the strike heightened that concern, which Goldberg hoped would induce the administration to intervene on the union's behalf. His foresight in demanding one-year extensions in 1958 from managers at the smaller companies had paid off. On July 15, 519,000 steelworkers walked off their jobs to begin the biggest single strike in American history.[55]

Forty days after the work stoppage had begun, the union had made no progress whatsoever in negotiating with management. At a USA Executive Board meeting on August 25, Goldberg told its members that the managers had signaled their lack of interest in bargaining by reducing their twelve-company team of representatives to just four, Cooper and Heath Larry of U.S. Steel and John Morse and H. C. Lumb, attorneys for Bethlehem and Republic, respectively. The federal mediators had told Goldberg, he said, that these four

> do not have the knowledge to develop twelve company contracts . . . also they do not know their own agreements. . . . We have said throughout and we keep repeating it that the only way this thing will ever be settled is to have the twelve negotiating committees reconvene, and when you have some basic understanding for the twelve companies, then consummate those under-standings, which has always been the case in the past.[56]

Even more frustrating, the steel company managers continued to publish advertisements proclaiming their willingness to grant improvements in wages and benefits while insisting in the bargaining sessions that the union first agree to accept changes in 2B. Thus the stalemate continued.[57]

With neither side willing to budge, the strike essentially evolved into an endurance contest, marking a real departure from the pattern established over the previous decade. During that time, steel industry managers had typically forced a strike simply to test whether the rank and file truly supported the leadership's demands. Once that fact had been demonstrated, managers had tended to settle quickly. This time, however, managers appeared to regard the confrontation as a fight to the finish. Already aware that the rank and file highly valued the work rules provisions, managers were not testing their attitudes so much as the union's overall political and economic strength.

In this contest, the USA basically stood alone. Although the entire labor movement monitored the strike and perceived its enormous importance, the AFL–CIO offered little in the way of concrete support. A meeting of the federation's leadership in August produced only symbolic gestures of solidarity, although Reuther, Carey, and Joe Beirne pledged substantial sums if they should prove necessary. Money, at least initially, was not a severe problem, given the very large war chest the Steelworkers had been accumulating over the years.[58]

More difficult was making a case to the wider public and the government that the union deserved their support. News coverage of the negotiations tended to favor management, a situation that stirred the wrath of several USA Executive Board members. District director Paul Rusen spoke for them when he stated:

> On the point Joe [Germano] makes, I go along with that, too, this public be damned. I don't mean to go out and say "Damn the public," but I don't think there is a man in this room who doesn't know that the union was never built by any public. It was built by the United Steelworkers of America. . . . When you get out here [in New York City] and get to thinking about the public and then pick up the newspapers and you see the people who are attacking this union—and we consider them the public—I don't think they are the public. I think they are just a bunch in this country who are after organized labor and everybody in this room knows who they are.[59]

Goldberg and McDonald, however, viewed public support as crucial to enlisting the government's help. Still seeing it as a potential ally, the two men continued to press the union's case through more limited advertising of its own. But Eisenhower and Mitchell offered nothing beyond mediation, which thus far had been useless.[60]

After two and a half months of stalemate came a change. The Eisenhower administration, growing ever more concerned about the declining supply of steel, finally roused itself to action. On September 28 the president called in first management's representatives and then labor's to encourage them to settle. When speaking with Goldberg and McDonald, Eisenhower signaled both his desire to stay out of the bargaining and his intention to invoke the emergency dispute provisions of Taft–Hartley in the event the impasse continued. He encouraged the two men to meet with Blough and the heads of the other major firms and hammer out an agreement.

They did see them later that same day, a meeting that foundered, as earlier ones had, on the steel executives' insistence on changes in the contract's work rules provisions. Speaking for management at that session were chief executive officers Blough, Charles White of Republic Steel, Arthur Homer of Bethlehem, Avery Adams of Jones and Laughlin, Joseph Block of Inland, as well as Conrad Cooper, and for the union, Goldberg and McDonald.[61]

Although the managers hastened to assure Goldberg and McDonald that they did not intend to break the union, the phrase meant different things to the two sides. To men such as Blough, the value of a steelworkers union lay principally in its contribution to rationalizing and stabilizing employer–employee relations and in maintaining wage levels that helped sustain an economy based on mass production and consumption. The transformation in power relations on the shop floor, however, that 2B and its related clauses codified, Blough and his associates still staunchly opposed.

This explained how Charles White of Republic, to give one example, could favor changes in 2B yet tell McDonald, as McDonald related to the board, that

> all this talk about us desiring to break the Union is a lot of bunk. We don't want to have anything like that occur. We want to get along. . . . if the Union were broken . . . he couldn't get along without the Steelworkers Union . . . if the Steelworkers Union weren't in existence they would have to form one because the men certainly have to be represented.[62]

Goldberg and McDonald, however, saw things differently. For them 2B was vital to the union's existence as an organization with some meaningful degree of independence from managerial power. They therefore found management's latest offer to be as unacceptable as the one spelled out almost four months earlier. Deadlocked over the issue, the meeting broke up, ensuring that the strike would continue.[63]

Fed up, Eisenhower appointed a board of inquiry as provided under the Taft–Hartley Act. This was not a move the union welcomed particularly, because Eisenhower limited the board's mandate to clarifying the issues in dispute and attempting mediation, rather than recommending terms for a settlement. The board did prove to have some limited value, however, for it forced management at last to make a serious offer. This turned out to be a three-year contract with some modest improvements in pay and benefits, and a proposal that the work rules dispute be resolved through binding arbitration.

Fearing that approach might commit the union to solutions that would ultimately prove quite unfair, Goldberg rejected the proposal and countered with one of his own. It consisted of a two-year contract containing slightly larger wage-and-benefit increases and a committee to examine the work rules controversy.[64]

Goldberg's committee proposal reflected his very different view of how best to resolve the long-term problems confronting the steel industry. His plan called for establishing a nine-member, tripartite study committee consisting of equal numbers of labor, management, and "public" members. The committee would study the work rules and related issues over the life of the proposed two-year contract and recommend solutions for incorporation in its successor. This was essentially the solution to the steel dispute that Goldberg had been urging since June and a miniature version of the broader corporatist scheme that he had been advocating since November 1958. The plan committed both sides to finding a consensual solution to the related problems of inflation, rising foreign competition, and the need for new technology to meet it.

Cooper, however, rejected the offer only a day after Goldberg had presented it, and although the two sides did some additional haggling, they remained far apart on October 17. That left the board of inquiry with no choice other than to file its report explaining why mediation had failed.[65]

This satisfied managers more than it did Goldberg, because the former seemed increasingly confident that the Eisenhower administration would enjoin the strike. Although that power had theoretically existed since the Taft–Hartley law was first passed, the federal government had, after 1948, refrained from using it against unions such as the USA, which had accepted government supervision of labor–management relations and the other terms of the postwar social contract. The managerial counteroffensive launched during 1957 had placed increasing pressure on the government to retreat from that earlier and highly important commitment.

McDonald warned the USA Executive Board that the danger was far from remote. He told the board in early October:

> I have a definite feeling that the time is running short. We have been advised; we know . . . that all the papers for [a] Taft–Hartley [injunction] have been prepared. . . . I am sure that if we cannot reach an agreement within a very short time, a matter of days, Taft–Hartley will be imposed upon the American steel industry.[66]

Under the terms of the law, such an injunction would compel workers to return to their jobs for eighty days, during which time the two sides would attempt to reach an agreement. If unsuccessful after the first sixty days, the rank and file would then be asked to vote on management's final offer. Confident that they would turn it down, Goldberg and McDonald were forced to ponder what would follow a resumption of the strike. The law provided that Congress would be obliged to act, an unprecedented step whose outcome they could not predict with any certainty. In view of the managerial victory there only six weeks earlier in the battle to enact Landrum–Griffin, opening the whole dispute to congressional intervention seemed an unappealing option. These prospects were evidently what persuaded managers to maintain their rigid bargaining position. For the moment, they appeared to have the upper hand.[67]

At the same time, however, Goldberg had been searching for a way to counter management's strategy. The key problem in winning congressional and administration support, he believed, had been the twelve major companies' united front. If it could be broken, then the union could argue that "responsible" managers opposed the hard line on wages and work rules taken by executives at the industry leader.

Goldberg hit on Kaiser Steel's management as the most likely to defect. Although now headed by Henry Kaiser's son Edgar, who was less deeply committed than his father to Keynesian ideas, he still followed the former's lead in negotiating with the union. Goldberg telephoned Henry Kaiser at this juncture to explain what the other companies' managers were planning and to ask whether his influence could be made to work on Edgar. His father, with whom Goldberg had maintained a very friendly relationship since becoming USA general counsel, agreed to meet with Edgar and Goldberg the following day. The three sat down for a conversation that at first consisted entirely of small talk. And then, Goldberg later recalled, the old man got up and said, "All right, now you settle this thing," and began to walk out of the room. And Edgar said, "Dad, you haven't told me what you want me to do." And the old man said, "Do whatever Arthur tells you to, he's a fair person." And we [Edgar and I] both burst out laughing.[68]

The logjam broken, Goldberg and Edgar Kaiser began serious negotiations, using as their basis the proposal Goldberg had offered to the board of inquiry. Although it issued a final report on October 19 finding that there were no significant areas of agreement between big steel's senior managers and the USA, Kaiser and Goldberg continued meeting for another week. With that step, the first real crack in managers' united front had finally appeared.[69]

Executives at the other major steel companies, however, remained adamant. Cooper, having earlier rejected the proposals Kaiser had agreed to consider, simply refused to budge. Thus, in the short run, the decision to pursue separate negotiations with Kaiser yielded no real help in dealing with the multicompany managerial bargaining committee or with the government. More specifically, bargaining separately with Kaiser failed to avert the looming Taft–Hartley injunction.

On October 19, McDonald informed the USA leadership that the attorney general would seek such an order within twenty-four hours. The debate at that meeting turned on whether to accept Cooper's final gambit, a suggestion that the work rules dispute be referred to compulsory arbitration, or face the injunction. Although several district directors spoke in favor of accepting arbitration, the board eventually rejected that option. The key reason lay in the members' increasing uncertainty over whether the two sides could agree on arbitrators who would treat the union fairly. Their faith in managerial goodwill at its lowest in more than a decade, the USA Executive Board voted unanimously to take the injunction, fight it in the courts, and refuse to surrender on 2B.[70]

The next day, Eisenhower's administration moved to obtain an injunction, an event that marked the government's first major breach of the postwar New Deal. The government's petition asserted that steel's importance to the economy and to the weapons industries in particular made reopening the mills necessary now that steel supplies had reached low levels. The attorney general's brief also argued that the steel strike's impact on unemployment elsewhere in the economy also furnished the basis for finding that a national emergency existed.[71]

Goldberg directed an arduous legal campaign to block the move, a process that began immediately in the federal district court for the western district of Pennsylvania. There he filed a brief arguing that the government had failed to demonstrate that a genuine national emergency as defined by the statute existed and that the statute required the court to make such a determination. And, Goldberg's brief continued, if the court found that the statute authorized it to issue an injunction without first making such a determination, the law's provision would be unconstitutional because it obligated the court to do something that did not constitute an exercise of judicial power. Under Article III, Section II, of the U.S. Constitution, federal courts were empowered to decide only "cases and controversies," a phrase with a specific meaning. The union's brief stated that issuing a Taft–Hartley injunction without first ruling on the merits of the government's findings would not fall into that legal category because the court's order would not follow from its resolving of a case or controversy before it. For that reason, Goldberg contended, the court should strike down Taft–Hartley's injunction provision in its entirety. A technical argument, it nonetheless had some merit. He had made it once before in an earlier case, only to lose at the U.S. Court of Appeals for the Second Circuit. Once again, Goldberg's efforts met with the same result.[72]

When the district court rejected Goldberg's arguments, he appealed to the U.S. Court of Appeals for the Third Circuit in Philadelphia and won a stay of the injunction until that court issued its ruling. In the court of appeals, Goldberg's arguments failed to sway a majority of the three-judge panel assigned to hear the case. Although he lost there by a margin of two to one, Judge William H. Hastie's dissent did support the union's contention that issuing such an injunction would merely prolong the strike rather than resolve it. In another promising sign, the full court of appeals divided three to three on whether to rehear the case. Although the tie vote allowed the existing verdict to stand, the margin signaled substantial doubt over its correctness. Encouraged, Goldberg filed a petition for certiorari, which the U.S. Supreme Court accepted, scheduling hearings for the first week of November. Once again, he obtained a stay of the injunction until the Court issued a final ruling on the merits.[73]

Preparing the union's case dramatically increased Goldberg's workload and that of his staff. Writing about this period afterward, Goldberg recalled:

> Our activities, which were hectic from the start, became even more intensified in October when the Taft–Hartley national emergency procedures were invoked and imposed massive additional responsibilities on the Legal Department. From that time on, the Legal Department devoted itself literally day and night, seven days a week to these critical matters.[74]

At the same time, Kaiser and Goldberg continued to bargain. On October 26, they reached a settlement, giving the union its first real breakthrough. The two men agreed to a twenty-month contract based essentially on the same terms Goldberg had presented to the board of inquiry. The new agreement contained most of the wage-and-benefit improvements the union had suggested, along with the tripartite study committee Goldberg had pushed as the best way to resolve the work rules dispute and related issues. Kaiser also agreed to accept Goldberg's suggestions for filling the three key slots on that committee, its trio of "public" representatives. His choices, John Dunlop, David Cole, and George Taylor, were among the most prominent industrial relations experts of that day and strongly supported the postwar social contract with which they were so closely identified.[75]

In all, the Kaiser contract constituted a powerful reminder that the managerial offensive of the late 1950s remained controversial even in business circles. Kaiser's willingness to settle, and that of executives at a few other small companies who agreed to the same terms, testified to the still substantial, if waning, sentiment in managerial ranks for a more consensual solution to the emerging problems that increasingly imperiled the postwar New Deal. Managers at the other eleven major firms refused to follow Kaiser's lead, but the agreement served a valuable purpose nonetheless. Goldberg offered it to the public as proof that the union was willing to conclude a fair agreement. The Kaiser contract for that reason gave the union its first real victory in the contest for public and government support.[76]

The Kaiser contract would eventually prove quite helpful to the union in its contest with the steel industry's other managers, but in the short run the agreement offered no escape from the Taft–Hartley injunction. Goldberg and Solicitor General J. Lee Rankin dueled with each other for four hours before the Supreme Court on November 4, but the justices' questioning signaled that they would probably uphold the appeals court's verdict. Three days later, the Court confirmed that impression when it ruled eight to one that both the injunction and the statute authorizing it were lawful. Only Justice William O. Douglas dissented against the Court's finding that the government had offered sufficient evidence of danger to the nation's health and safety, without which no Taft–Hartley injunction could be granted.

Even though Goldberg's three-week courtroom campaign to prevent the injunction had failed, his expert handling of the case had kept the outcome in doubt until the very end. The legal campaign, Goldberg later wrote, "threw the steel companies off their time table, [and] evoked much favorable public sentiment."[77] These considerations, the first one in particular, were by no means unimportant. Prolonging the strike made steel shortages more acute and raised the likelihood that the stoppage would persist into the election year of 1960. Both results increased the pressure on the government to resolve the dispute, lest it endanger military preparedness or incumbent officeholders' prospects for reelection.

With the Supreme Court's ruling on November 7, the injunction finally went into effect, ending for the moment at least what had become a 116-day walkout. Under the terms of the injunction, both sides now had to resume their essentially fruitless bargaining talks. McDonald reported to the USA Executive Board five days later that the executives of at least one firm among the remaining group of eleven, National Steel, seemed to be wavering but that at the moment the union had not achieved any real breakthrough. He and Goldberg continued to talk with Labor Secretary Mitchell and others in the administration, but none of them so far had offered any real help. Not yet persuaded that the Eisenhower administration would go down the line for the steel industry managers, the USA leadership refrained from criticizing it directly. But they viewed the injunction as a breach with labor that would not be forgiven.[78]

Sustaining the leadership throughout was the solidarity of the rank and file. Even after returning to jobs made unusually easy by managers endeavoring to win them over, the vast majority of workers remained committed to defending their power in the workplace. District Director Thomas Shane captured the nature of the membership's response to the soft treatment by reporting:

> If they [the foremen] need a crew of five they make sure they call seven or eight. The result is that pipefitters and millwrights are standing around with their arms folded and there is nothing to do yet, and as a foreman goes by they grab him by the arm and say, "What do you want me to do? I have only got 76 days left." That is their spirit. The reporters have talked to the wives and members of the family [*sic*] and didn't get one damn kick out of anybody.[79]

Resenting management for its efforts to regain lost prerogatives, the workers also increasingly blamed Eisenhower for failing to help them. After six and a half years during which many steelworkers had tended to view his administration favorably, the strike and especially the injunction produced a major shift in outlook. District Director Paul Rusen told the board how visible the change had become: "For example, the bulk of our people at Wheeling Steel are going to work with arm bands on calling themselves Ike's Slaves. They have signs up at the plant [saying] that they are returning as Ike's slaves to the plant."[80]

Fortified by that kind of worker militancy, the board debated what to do next if the injunction expired without any resolution of the issues in dispute. McDonald suggested that the executive board mull over his suggestion that they urge workers to boycott the mandatory vote on management's last offer, "on the basis that they are not going . . . to accept in any sense this slave labor law."[81]

Three days later the companies' managers presented what they called their "last offer," which gave a little ground on benefits but yielded none with respect to 2B. Cooper announced that management would, assuming no agreement had been reached by the injunction's sixtieth day of operation, submit that offer to the rank and file for a vote. Goldberg and the other USA leaders, seeing almost nothing really new in the proposal, rejected it. Rather than give in now, they chose instead to continue their strategy of trying to undermine management's apparent solidarity.[82]

During the last two weeks of November, Goldberg spent most of his time bargaining with management representatives of the aluminum and can companies organized by the USA. Those firms' contracts expired in December. Early in that month, executives at those companies agreed to improvements in wages and benefits substantially above those offered by steel management's bargaining committee. Even more important, the aluminum and can companies' managers accepted the union's demand for maintaining the existing work rules provisions.

Like Kaiser some six weeks earlier, the managers at these companies signaled by signing with the union that they disapproved of Blough's and Cooper's more confrontational approach. Winning those contracts constituted the union's second major victory in the struggle for support from the government and the public. Once again, Goldberg and McDonald could point to the terms on which the aluminum and canning firms had settled as proof that steel management had behaved unreasonably from the start.[83]

By this point, Goldberg had assumed even the outward signs of authority that McDonald had jealously guarded in the past. The latter was almost exhausted, unaccustomed as he had become to the demands of working full time on USA business. As the year neared its end, McDonald gradually turned over all major responsibilities to Goldberg. For that reason the press would later report that it was he, rather than his "boss," who had supplied "the steel in the steel union."[84] Goldberg, having played most of his cards already, but as yet to no avail, turned next for help to Congress and the administration.[85]

Congress was at the outset more receptive to his requests, and no one more so than Senator Kennedy. Goldberg had first written him back in late September, asking that Kennedy launch an immediate congressional investigation into the adequacy and fairness of the existing Taft–Hartley provisions governing so-called national emergency strikes. Kennedy had replied the same day, agreeing to hold such hearings "so that our recommendations can be formulated for action by the Congress when it reconvenes in January."[86]

This proved to be an overly optimistic timetable. The most Kennedy could do was to schedule hearings for the first week of January, when Congress returned from its recess. More important, however, Kennedy promised Goldberg that he would lead the fight in Congress at that time to amend the Taft–Hartley Act. Kennedy pledged his support for changes in the law that would broaden the number of options available to the administration. In particular, Kennedy promised to seek the enactment of a Taft–Hartley amendment legalizing the seizure procedure Truman had tried to use back in 1952. The likelihood of Kennedy's being able to redeem those commitments was not great, but his willingness to back them openly by late December contributed to managers' uncertainty about what Congress might do if the injunction were allowed to expire.[87]

The Eisenhower administration gave its aid less freely, but in the end it proved more valuable. During the last week of December and the first of the new year, Vice-President Nixon began pressuring Blough and his colleagues to make a deal along the lines of the Kaiser compromise. Increasingly nervous that the strike would weaken the economy so much as to doom his own presidential aspirations in 1960, Nixon gave Goldberg and the union their first real governmental assist.

Blough and Goldberg hammered out a preliminary three-year agreement, and then, almost overnight, Blough backed away from it, because it essentially surrendered on the key work rules issue. The draft called for one committee to study 2B and its related provisions and another long-range planning committee to examine the best ways to keep the industry competitive, a modified version of the scheme that Kaiser had accepted the previous October. Blough appeared to yield that concession and then backtracked. Having invested so much in waging this fight, he and the other steel company executives could not quite bring themselves to yield on the central issue. At this point Nixon met privately with the leaders of the eleven companies still bargaining jointly and told them in no uncertain terms that the administration's patience was exhausted.[88]

In the face of such pressure, as well as that coming from business leaders growing alarmed about what congressional intervention might mean for labor relations more generally, the steel managers finally caved in. Seven months after their representatives had first raised the 2B issue in a serious way, USA power and the government support it still commanded had beaten them on that issue. Steel industry executives did, in effect, win back at least part of the COLA provision, but only by conceding in return a pay increase and some significant improvements in fringe benefits. Although the total cost of the package was less than what Kaiser had allowed, the differences between the two contracts were ones of degree. Thus the deal Goldberg had achieved two and a half months earlier became, in the end, the basis for the industrywide settlement. Blough and his brethren had emerged the losers, and they knew it. The USA's herculean efforts had fought to a standstill one of the most important moves of the managerial offensive.[89]

McDonald acknowledged the key roles played by Goldberg and the rank and file in achieving that result. The USA's president told the executive board on January 5:

> Confidentially . . . I can say, we wrote this agreement and handed it to the Vice President, — we did, Arthur and his associates did. It comes as a recommendation from the government, but it is ours. . . . We wrote this memorandum of understanding and the Secretary of Labor and the Vice President put it over.
>
> But, of course, it was the loyalty and the determination of our people which made all this possible. This would not have been possible without them.[90]

An indication of the membership's elation can be seen in the response of those present when McDonald formally announced the settlement's terms. He described the scene for USA Executive Board members:

> Last night I was up with my friend Joe Moloney in Buffalo. It was a cold, nasty, snowy night. There must have been 10,000 people in the Municipal Auditorium up there, Steelworkers. Joe will attest to the fact that we fought our way in and it took 12 policemen, Nordie and Bob and Charlie Louis to get us out. You have never seen such a wild, enthusiastic crowd of people in all your life. They tore us, shook our hands and pounded our shoulders until we were sore.[91]

After McDonald finished his summary of the final negotiations, the board honored him, Goldberg, and the other architects of this dramatic victory with a rare standing ovation.[92]

But the triumph left its scars, both literally and figuratively. The entire struggle had worn out Goldberg completely. In early February he wrote to I. W. Abel:

> On reflection, a mere recitation of the broad areas in which we [in the Legal
> Department) were obligated to function . . . makes one wonder how we
> were physically able to do what had to be done. Negotiations, meetings with
> Government and Congressional officials, Board of Inquiry proceedings, the
> legal challenge to the national emergency injunction which . . . culmi-
> nated in the historic Supreme Court decision, the Kaiser settlement, the Can
> settlements, the Aluminum settlements and finally the Steel settlements
> themselves—these were . . . major subjects which demanded and con-
> sumed every available moment.[93]

Soon afterward, Goldberg consulted a doctor, who diagnosed him as suffering from the symptoms of what appeared to be a gastric ulcer and blood
clot. Following his doctor's orders, Goldberg entered the hospital for ex-
ploratory surgery. Although the surgeons found no evidence of permanent
damage, Goldberg developed a postoperative infection that kept him flat on
his back for another week. And after leaving the hospital, Goldberg took what
for him was a highly unusual step, a long vacation, at his doctor's insistence.
Goldberg eventually made a full recovery, but his clash with the heavy weight
of managerial power left him with a grisly souvenir, what associate general
counsel Elliot Bredhoff told the USA Executive Board was "a huge inci-
sion."[94]

Other union officials fared even worse. McDonald reported to the board in
March that

> many of our Directors are very sick people, and this is a direct result of the
> 1959 fracas in basic steel. We have had 22 heart attacks in recent weeks, and
> these I think you can trace directly to the strain and the hard work which was
> undertaken by all of us during the year 1959 and up to date in 1960.[95]

One of the directors, USA Executive Board member Carman Newell, died of
such a seizure at the age of fifty-one. McDonald told the board bitterly that
"he is a victim of the strike, no question about it."[96]

Although the managers deserved most of the blame for this tragedy, the
union's leaders had unwittingly contributed to its occurrence. They had done
much over the past seven years to concentrate the real decision-making power
in the USA in their own hands. One consequence was to increase their own
workload during contract negotiations, a burden that grew tremendously
during the 1959 confrontation. The way in which the leadership met that
challenge, however, gave the lie to those who saw it as lazy and unresponsive.
At a moment of genuine crisis in the USA's history, its leaders had thrown
themselves into the fight, and at substantial cost to their own well-being.

Also suffering were the rank and file, many of whom lost their life savings
during the strike and saw the union coffers their contributions had filled,
drain dramatically. Although the union intervened with banks to prevent
foreclosures on the membership's homes, many workers went into debt to
survive. Some would spend years recovering what they had lost, and quite a
few local unions faced similar problems. In keeping with traditional practices,
the locals, which received one-half of the dues receipts, had served as the
primary source of strike relief payments. The locals' share of such benefits

eventually totaled almost $7 million, which came on top of just over $4 million in payments from their community services funds. Many locals had spent all they had and borrowed more from the international office to meet their obligations to the rank and file. Loans from the international union to the locals came to almost $1.9 million. The former's total net worth, over $32 million when the strike began, stood at about $26 million shortly after its conclusion. The six-month struggle with management thus had cost the USA's locals almost $13 million in expenditures, and the international union, another $6 million in strike-related costs and lost income.[97]

In view of these enormous human and material sacrifices, Goldberg believed that some other solution must be found, lest the union find itself in 1962 fighting the same battle all over again and with fewer resources. Heightening that concern was Roger Blough's address to a Miami business group early in 1960. Blough indicated there that he saw the recent settlement as a truce and nothing more. Management's quest to solve the growing problems of inflation and foreign competition, he told his audience, would continue. U.S. Steel's annual report, released around the same time, elaborated on Blough's themes.

As McDonald told the board, "It is full of the same old junk—monopolistic labor unions, inflation, the whole line all over again."[98] The indications he and Goldberg were receiving suggested that management's failure to win back its lost prerogatives in 1959 had led to no fundamental change in outlook. If anything, the strike had reinforced managers' view that foreign competition demanded such changes. In 1959, thanks in large part to the four-month interruption in steel production that managers had precipitated, the total value of steel imports to the United States for the first time exceeded that of exports, the beginning of a long-term trend. Although the steel imported into the United States during 1959 consisted of the most basic and lowest-priced products, the sea change that year signaled serious trouble ahead for the American steel industry's workers and managers.[99]

Goldberg favored addressing those problems, but not as Blough and his colleagues wished. Goldberg remained committed to the consensual approach outlined in his University of Wisconsin address. The principal challenge in the wake of the strike, Goldberg believed, was to build support for that plan in labor and management circles and especially in the federal government. With Eisenhower due to retire from the presidency the following year, the need for electing someone much more responsive to labor's alternative seemed great, for without such support Goldberg had little confidence that his program could succeed. That quest would keep him as busy as ever during 1960 and lead to a major change in his career.[100]

III

Goldberg directed his attention toward the upcoming presidential election immediately after the steel dispute ended. When Richard Nixon held a so-called peace dinner for steel executives and top USA leaders on January 14, much of the conversation revolved around the subject of presidential politics. Nixon predicted that the Democrats would nominate Kennedy to oppose him. The steel industry managers present, including Blough and Cooper, indicated that they would be supporting the vice-president and expected him to win. Goldberg, the sole registered Democrat in the room, said only that he expected Adlai Stevenson to be renominated yet again.[101]

Soon thereafter, Goldberg flew to Chicago for a talk with his old friend Stevenson about his plans for that year. Although increasingly impressed by Kennedy's efforts to defend the postwar New Deal from the managerial counteroffensive and even more by his sophisticated and well-financed campaign effort, Goldberg refused to abandon Stevenson if he should choose to campaign seriously for the Democratic nomination. The former Illinois governor told Goldberg that he would not enter the primaries, at which point the latter replied:

> If you're not going to run again, I'm going to support John F. Kennedy. I think he has a chance of winning, and furthermore, I think there's an important principle behind his candidacy: we've got to break this notion once and for all that only a white, male Protestant can be elected President. This is important for our democracy, it's important for me, for my children and grandchildren.[102]

Surprised by this news, Stevenson asked why Goldberg had not chosen instead to support Hubert Humphrey. The Minnesota senator had been, as Goldberg well knew, a far more productive and articulate defender of the postwar order in Congress than Kennedy. Indeed, even Goldberg admitted that he and Humphrey "agreed on just about everything."[103] Even so, Goldberg told Stevenson that "Humphrey couldn't win" and that backing him would be pointless.[104] In view of the increasing managerial pressure on the government to readjust the postwar social contract in ways favorable to management, supporting a hopeless Humphrey candidacy would only make matters worse. Humphrey, moreover, was a Protestant, whose election could not have the impact on social barriers that limited the advancement of American Catholics and Jews that Kennedy's necessarily would. Like many others who chose to support Kennedy in 1960, Goldberg remained acutely aware from personal experience that there were systems of oppression other than the one based on class. Electing Kennedy offered the best chance of progress against all of them. So Goldberg reasoned, to the dismay of Stevenson, Humphrey, and many of their liberal supporters.[105]

Goldberg's decision also strained his relationship with some trade union officials. Leaders of the building trades, furious with Kennedy for participating in the McClellan Committee investigation and supporting legislation aimed at curbing union corruption, pressed hard for a labor veto of his candidacy. Also hostile to it, although much less so, was the faction led by Walter Reuther, who tended to view Kennedy as an opportunist lacking genuine liberal credentials.[106]

Animosity in the labor movement grew when Kennedy began his campaign in the summer of 1959 and peaked in early 1960. In February of that year, Meany called an AFL–CIO Executive Council meeting to discuss, among other things, whether the federation should publicly announce its opposition to Kennedy's candidacy. Goldberg, realizing that such a move would doom Kennedy's campaign, agreed to appear at the council meeting on his behalf. After a fairly sharp debate, the motion went down to defeat.

Even though the building trades unions would continue to oppose Kennedy openly, their leaders had failed to swing a majority of the AFL–CIO Executive Council behind their cause. Meany had played a key role in that debate. Although attracted to Kennedy, in part because he was a fellow Catholic, the AFL–CIO president at that time could not bring himself to believe that Kennedy could win. For that reason, Meany did nothing to mobilize the federation's machinery on Kennedy's behalf during the primary season. If the Massachusetts senator were to win the active support of the union movement, he would have to do so by demonstrating, on his own, real strength in the preconvention contests.[107]

Goldberg served from that time onward as Kennedy's principal liaison to the labor movement and leading promoter in its ranks. After recovering from the effects of the steel strike, Goldberg worked at building support for Kennedy in labor and liberal circles while also advising the candidate about how best to win their allegiance. Aided by a few labor colleagues, most notably Hatters Union president Alex Rose, a spokesman for New York's Liberal Party, Goldberg continued to work on Meany and other top AFL–CIO figures. His efforts began to pay off by the middle of March, when Rose wrote Goldberg to report that "George Meany is now beginning to believe that Kennedy has a chance to be elected, but he fears — and the others [William Schnitzler, David Dubinksy, and Jacob Potofsky] agreed — that he may not be able to get the nomination."[108]

The concern stemmed from their knowledge that Kennedy's standing remained fairly weak with the four key constituencies that dominated the Democratic Party: labor, southerners, middle-class liberals, and the urban machines. Humphrey enjoyed the strongest support from the first group, Johnson that of the second, and Stevenson the devoted backing of the third. Most members of the fourth group — led by such men as Pennsylvania's David Lawrence, New York's Carmine DeSapio, and Illinois's Richard Daley — favored Stevenson, Johnson, or Missouri senator Stuart Symington. Kennedy's only hope was to persuade all four factions that he, rather than their first choices, stood the best chance of beating Nixon, whom none of them wanted.[109]

Helping lay the foundation for that argument were Kennedy's proven record of electoral success and the outcome of two key gubernatorial contests in 1958. Unlike most of the other contenders for the nomination, who had won election and reelection in years when the electoral trend favored the Democrats, Kennedy had captured a House seat in 1946 and then advanced to the Senate in 1952, the two worst years for Democratic congressional candi-

dates since the 1920s. Kennedy's appeal, like that of Eisenhower, who also
carried Massachusetts in 1952, was rooted in voters' perception of him as a
supporter of the postwar New Deal but one not inclined to move much
further toward social democracy. And in 1958, when Kennedy ran for reelection to the Senate during a year in which the GOP seemed increasingly
hostile to that social bargain, he had emerged the victor by a margin of almost
875,000 votes, the largest at that time in the history of a Massachusetts
senatorial contest. Kennedy's moderation, which accounted in large measure
for his demonstrated ability to run ahead of the Democratic ticket, had done
much to persuade Goldberg that he could win in the fall.[110]

Also pointing to that same conclusion were the results in the two most
important gubernatorial races of 1958. In California and Ohio, moderate
Catholic Democrats had won landslide victories against conservatives cut
from much the same cloth as Vice-President Richard Nixon. Pat Brown's and
Michael DiSalle's moderation had appealed to middle-class voters, while their
religious affiliation helped them draw votes from the heavily Catholic, white,
industrial working class, which responded much less enthusiastically to Protestant candidates of that same ideological stripe. The combination had been
highly effective during the California and Ohio gubernatorial contests of
1958. Those portents convinced Goldberg that Kennedy could defeat the
Republicans' likely candidate. The leaders of the party's key constituencies,
however, awaited proof that Kennedy could show such strength outside his
native New England.[111]

Kennedy's victories in the Wisconsin and West Virginia primaries transformed the race for the Democratic presidential nomination. The results of
those two contests accomplished three objectives essential to his nomination:
First, they eliminated Humphrey as a rival who might otherwise have si-
phoned off enough support to produce a convention deadlock. Second, Kennedy's victory in Wisconsin on April 5 demonstrated that a northeastern
moderate could win in a midwestern state considered a hotbed of Stevensonian liberalism. And third, the outcome of the West Virginia contest on
May 10 showed that a Catholic presidential candidate could win a contested
election in an overwhelming Protestant state.[112]

The outcomes in Wisconsin and West Virginia turned the tide among
Goldberg's labor colleagues. After Humphrey's defeat in the first contest,
union leaders withdrew their support for his candidacy, seeing little to be
gained from further contests that might weaken their second choice, Kennedy. Kennedy's decisive victory in West Virginia completed labor leaders'
conversion.

Increasingly confident that Kennedy would win the nomination, Goldberg
turned after the West Virginia contest ended to fending off die-hard Stevensonians' efforts to draft their champion. Joining Goldberg in that quest were
most of the AFL–CIO chieftains, who had never been very fond of Stevenson
in the first place. As Kennedy swept the remaining primaries in Maryland,
Nebraska, and Oregon during the latter half of May, he cemented labor's
support for his candidacy. By the end of that month, Goldberg felt confident

that the bulk of organized labor would help put Kennedy over the top at the upcoming Democratic convention in July.[113]

In May Goldberg also played a leading role in drafting a statement for the Democratic Advisory Council (DAC), which functioned as the clearinghouse for suggestions relating to the party's 1960 platform. The proposed labor plank included the traditional litany of union achievements and the Democrats' role in promoting them, along with denunciations of the Landrum–Griffin Act and the larger conservative assault on the labor movement. Blasting the "coalition between reactionary Republicans and a minority group of 'Democrats' faithless to the Party and its Platform" that had passed the law, Goldberg's draft called for "a national labor policy, not a national antilabor policy."[114]

Although essentially a symbolic exercise, the statement reflected one of the few important differences between the likely Republican and Democratic presidential candidates. Democratic Platform Committee chairman Chester Bowles, to whom Goldberg sent a copy of the labor statement, acknowledged its importance by writing back in June that "this will be very helpful indeed."[115]

At the same time, along with other prominent liberal converts to Kennedy, Goldberg busied himself with combating the Stevensonians' quest for a last hurrah. Kennedy's liberal supporters published newspaper ads on June 17 voicing their reasons for backing the Massachusetts senator, a move that helped blunt the growing enthusiasm for Stevenson. Signers of the manifesto included Goldberg; Alex Rose; historians Arthur M. Schlesinger Jr., Henry S. Commager, and Allan Nevins; political scientist James MacGregor Burns; attorney Joseph Rauh; economist John Kenneth Galbraith; *New Republic* editor Gilbert Harrison; and several others. Five months of tireless efforts by Kennedy's initial handful of liberal supporters had at last born fruit. This achievement suggested to Goldberg that Kennedy's candidacy and the larger effort to turn back the managerial revolt—of which his presidential campaign was only one part—were succeeding.[116]

Also contributing to that optimistic outlook was some good news of a very different sort that Goldberg received that same month. On June 20 the Supreme Court handed down decisions in three suits brought by the USA. Dubbed the "Steelworkers Trilogy" by labor law experts, all three cases involved arbitration clauses in union contracts.

When the managerial offensive on the shop floor intensified after 1957, managers had attempted to limit unions' resort to the arbitration system. Rather than make a frontal assault of the sort attempted unsuccessfully by Lone Star Steel's managers, executives at other companies organized by the USA sought instead simply to narrow the scope of the arbitration provisions contained in the union's contracts. These clauses, and the system of arbitration more generally, managers saw as impeding their efforts to win back prerogatives lost during the 1930s and 1940s. Managerial resistance to arbitration had by 1959 given rise to several lawsuits, three of which made their way to the nation's highest court.[117]

The first, *United Steelworkers of America* v. *American Manufacturing Company*, involved a worker who had left his job after a disabling injury and then decided he could return to work. Management refused to take him back, arguing that he had received a worker's compensation award on the assumption that he was permanently disabled. The union filed a grievance on the worker's behalf, which management refused to arbitrate on the ground that the claim was frivolous. Goldberg's associate, David Feller, argued in the courts that they should enforce agreements to arbitrate, regardless of the underlying grievance's merit. Feller contended that such a finding would promote the federal policy in favor of arbitration that the Supreme Court had articulated in its 1957 *Lincoln Mills* decision.

Both the district court and the court of appeals found in management's favor, but the Supreme Court overruled the lower court's decision. Justice Douglas, speaking for a unanimous Court, agreed with the union's argument, finding that the federal policy in favor of arbitration "can be effectuated only if the means chosen by the parties for settlement of their differences under a collective bargaining agreement is given full play."[118] The arbitration clause at issue had been very broad in its scope, and in such situations, the Court held, managers should not be allowed to resist the provision's reach, even in potentially frivolous disputes.[119]

The second case, *United Steelworkers of America* v. *Warrior and Gulf Navigation Company*, proved only slightly more difficult for the Supreme Court. In this case, the company's managers contracted out work ordinarily performed by its own unionized employees. The USA filed a grievance attacking the action, arguing that it constituted a partial employer lockout barred by the union contract. The arbitration clause at issue was fairly broad but explicitly excluded from its reach "matters which are strictly a function of management."[120]

Feller contended that another clause of the arbitration provision stated that any disputes as to its meaning should themselves be referred to arbitration and that the latter provision should take precedence. Although the district court found for management and the court of appeals affirmed, the U.S. Supreme Court reversed. Once again, Justice Douglas delivered its opinion, against which only Justice Charles E. Whittaker dissented. Douglas's opinion was far-reaching in its language and implications. He found that the collective bargaining agreement "is more than a contract; it is a generalized code to govern a myriad of cases which the draftsmen cannot wholly anticipate."[121] For that reason, the courts should refrain from resolving any disputes about how to interpret such agreements unless the arbitration clause excluded areas of potential dispute in very specific terms. Douglas repeated that the Court would support the arbitration system in almost all instances because it reflected a federal policy in favor of resolving workplace disputes in that fashion, rather than by resort to the judiciary.[122]

The union also won the third and final case of the arbitration trilogy, *United Steelworkers of America* v. *Enterprise Wheel and Car Company*. In this suit, several workers had engaged in a wildcat strike, for which they were fired. The employer refused to arbitrate, and the union sued. The district court found for the union and ordered arbitration. The arbitrator found that under the contract the workers merited at most a ten-day suspension. Management refused to accept the award and won a verdict in the court of appeals on the ground that the collective bargaining agreement had expired before the arbitrator had announced his decision. Once again, the Supreme Court reversed, and Justice Douglas wrote its decision. He found that in almost all cases, the courts should defer to the arbitrator's findings, because a policy of judicial deference would best promote the federal policy in favor of arbitration. That had been the USA's argument, and the Court chose to accept it.[123]

Although some scholars later argued that those three decisions constituted a defeat for organized labor, such a view fails to take into account the challenges it faced in the late 1950s. Goldberg had favored recognizing arbitration as the preferred method for resolving workplace disputes precisely because he saw the judiciary as much more responsive to managerial pressure. Managers showed they agreed, through their efforts to narrow the reach of arbitration clauses and in their willingness to litigate the issues all the way to the nation's highest court. The stakes for both sides were high. By June 1960, when the Court handed down its verdicts in the Steelworkers Trilogy, more than 90 percent of all union contracts contained an arbitration clause. Therefore Goldberg saw the three decisions as a tremendous victory for labor, because they cut off managers' efforts to escape a grievance resolution mechanism that they found difficult to manipulate.[124]

The decisions were doubly important because they also increased union leaders' ability to ward off challenges from rebellious members of the rank and file, which the arbitration system tended to contain. This result furthered the trend toward concentrating power at the top, which Goldberg saw as a prerequisite for more coordinated bargaining with management. Greater coordination in turn increased the likelihood that his soft corporatist scheme for strengthening the postwar social contract could be made to work. Coordinated bargaining, Goldberg understood, had been one of the keys to the success of the Swedish model, elements of which he sought to replicate in the United States. And so for those reasons, too, Goldberg viewed the Supreme Court's rulings in the Steelworkers Trilogy as an important triumph for the entire labor movement.[125]

Much more so than his later scholarly critics, Goldberg was right. What he failed to understand, however, was how labor's campaign to buttress the arbitration system might eventually backfire if management gradually won back more and more control over the workplace and the state. At the time, however, Goldberg and his allies were seeking to prevent that outcome. In the face of an explicit managerial assault on labor's power in the workplace, Goldberg and his colleagues won the Supreme Court's rulings in the Steelworkers' Trilogy that served to check this offensive. As in so many other contests during this period, the union's victories in those cases helped contain the managerial revolt. Still unclear, however, was whether Goldberg and his allies could quell it entirely.[126]

The progress of Kennedy's presidential campaign encouraged Goldberg's belief that the task could be accomplished. Although liberal support for Stevenson grew during the last few weeks before the Democratic convention opened on July 10, Goldberg remained confident that Kennedy would win. Goldberg flew to Los Angeles, as did most of the AFL–CIO's other top leaders, to make certain of that outcome. Stevenson's quest there for a third presidential nomination made matters momentarily difficult for one-time supporters such as Goldberg who had switched to Kennedy earlier that year. More important, Stevenson's last-ditch effort also strained the already frayed ties that bound the labor–liberal alliance together. In the end, however, union leaders turned deaf ears to his appeals. They also blocked Lyndon Johnson's quest for a brokered nomination, thereby exacting revenge for the Texan's role in allowing Landrum–Griffin to pass. Goldberg, Meany, Reuther, and other senior labor leaders, aided by the urban bosses who spoke for essentially the same constituency, gave Kennedy's campaign bandwagon the final push it needed. On July 13, 1960, their candidate narrowly won the Democratic presidential nomination on the first ballot.[127]

No sooner had that struggle ended then another began, this one over the selection of Kennedy's running mate. Goldberg, like his labor colleagues, favored Humphrey.

Implicit in this choice was Goldberg's assumption that Kennedy should seek to carry the more urban and industrialized states and forgo trying to win most of the still rural and agricultural South. New Deal liberals such as Goldberg dreamed of liberating the Democratic Party from its southern captivity, of turning it into a vehicle that more closely resembled the labor and social democratic parties of Western Europe. A Kennedy victory and Democratic congressional coalition based on the industrial, heavily unionized states offered the promise of expanding the welfare state and the labor movement. To stick with the Democrats' existing big city–Dixiecrat alliance, in contrast, offered at best only the hope of maintaining the status quo. Alex Rose had expressed those same thoughts in a letter to Goldberg the previous March:

> Instead of relying on the heavily Democratic South and nearby states for an electoral majority, Kennedy's victory will have to come mainly through the industrial states in the North, Middle West and West, where the Catholic vote is strong and where the labor vote can be strong.
>
> From the point of view of labor interest, an electoral victory based on states that produce a normally conservative delegation to Congress is a limited victory. An electoral victory that will also produce a liberal and pro-labor delegation to Congress will make it a complete victory.[128]

For these reasons, Rose concluded, "I told George Meany, and you and I have already discussed this, that Kennedy needs Humphrey and Humphrey needs Kennedy; and that we must bring our influence to bear to unite these forces—either for a joint Kennedy–Humphrey ticket, or any other way."[129]

That vision foundered on Kennedy's unwillingness to take such a large gamble. No Democrat had ever won the presidency without carrying a majority of the eleven states of the old Confederacy. A Kennedy–Humphrey ticket would surely fail to do so, thereby forcing the Democrats to carry all of the major industrial states in order to beat Nixon. Kennedy read the electorate's shift since 1957 in those states toward the Democrats as reflecting a desire to defend the status quo in the face of conservative attacks rather than for moving beyond it. Choosing Humphrey would send a signal that the Democrats favored the latter course, making a sweep of those states unlikely. In the parlance of the time, a Kennedy–Humphrey ticket would be seen as "too liberal." For those reasons, Humphrey never really received Kennedy's serious consideration for the vice-presidency, although to maintain labor and liberal support for his campaign, Kennedy, before being nominated, repeatedly feigned interest in the idea.[130]

His thoughts about a running mate turned first to the candidate of the party's southern wing, Lyndon Johnson. Kennedy had assumed since becoming a candidate that Johnson would not surrender the powerful post of Senate majority leader in exchange for the essentially empty one of vice-president. This was why JFK, in a characteristically cynical move, had instructed his staff to tell liberals and trade unionists that Johnson would not be selected. Those groups, hostile to Johnson for his conservative record on issues of race and class, understood that statement as a promise rather than a prediction. Kennedy, however, viewed it as just the reverse. Believing both that he should try to get Johnson to take the job and that even if unsuccessful the offer would please the Dixiecrats, Kennedy telephoned him early on the morning of July 14. When Johnson unexpectedly indicated his willingness to accept, Kennedy resolved to take that course, confident that such a ticket offered the best prospects for winning in the fall.[131]

He did, however, go through the motions later that same morning of consulting with labor leaders about their choice. Present at the 11:00 A.M. meeting in Kennedy's hotel suite were the candidate himself, his brother Bobby who served as the campaign's manager, Goldberg, Alex Rose, Reuther, and his lieutenant Jack Conway. Goldberg reported to Kennedy that Humphrey was willing to take second place on the ticket. The other trade union officials then urged Kennedy to pick their man and, at Kennedy's request, discussed the merits of the other contenders, including Minnesota governor Orville Freeman and Senators Henry Jackson of Washington and Stuart Symington of Missouri.

Kennedy listened and asked for their thoughts about Johnson as a possible running mate. Simply suggesting that possibility upset Rose, Reuther, and Conway, who argued vehemently against the idea. Although Kennedy acted noncommittal, Goldberg became convinced that he intended to pick LBJ. Much later, Goldberg described the meeting in this way:

> During the course of the conversation—it never occurred to me at the beginning that he would pick Johnson, he didn't like Johnson. . . . Nevertheless, he made a remark which indicated to me that he had already made his choice. . . . The others left. . . . Walter Reuther in particular was going to get a hold of Bobby and see if . . . Hubert could be put

through but I got silent and then Kennedy said to me, "Would you mind remaining over for a while?" and [so then] I did. And he said to me, "You were pretty quiet." I said, "You've picked Johnson, haven't you?" He said, "Yes." I said, "Why?" He said, "Look, every poll says I've got to have Texas to win. Without Johnson, I can't win."[132]

Goldberg, unhappy with the choice, resigned himself to accepting it. When Kennedy offered to call Meany and explain the decision, Goldberg advised him to "stay away from Meany, he has a hot temper."[133] Goldberg telephoned instead and discovered that Meany, like himself, was disappointed but realistic. Kennedy was still preferable to Nixon, and so labor would come around to supporting the Democratic ticket, even with Johnson as part of it. Despite their outraged cries of protest from the floor and galleries when LBJ's nomination was offered for approval, in the end the labor–liberal alliance acquiesced to it.[134]

Goldberg proceeded to rationalize the result in his own mind by making light of Kennedy's decision. Reassuring himself that the vice-presidency was a powerless office and mindful that Johnson's age and heart condition made him an unlikely candidate to succeed Kennedy after what Goldberg expected would be two terms in office, he chose to ignore the setback. The entire episode, however, offered further evidence of organized labor's slipping strength. For the first time since the labor movement had emerged as a major force in the Democratic Party during the middle 1930s, union leaders had failed to block a candidate for the national ticket whom they perceived to be antilabor. And the party's nominee had chosen to stick with its traditional coalition of city dwellers and Dixiecrats, rather than strike out in the new direction labor had favored. The implications of that defeat would become fully apparent only later. For the moment, Goldberg and his colleagues basked in the glow of victory, however incomplete, at the Democratic National Convention. They left Los Angeles confident that "their" ticket would prevail.[135]

The feeling of having been let down, however, soon returned. The mood was reinforced by the failure to win passage of any of the legislation that labor had backed during the special session of Congress that August. After leaving the convention, Goldberg traveled first to Santa Barbara, California. In addition to relaxing there, he also attended an academic conference that examined the Swedish system of collective bargaining. In attendance were some of the leading industrial relations experts of that day, including Clark Kerr, David Cole, and Northwestern University law professor Willard Wirtz. The topic they discussed reflected their own notions of how best to solve the emerging problems that lay behind the managerial revolt. Viewing a Kennedy victory as likely, Goldberg had begun to think ahead about what that might mean for himself and the country more generally. Kennedy had to win, however, before he and his colleagues would have the chance to try out their ideas. Upon returning to Washington, Goldberg faced this more pressing issue and an increasingly gloomy situation in the steel industry.[136]

Employment in steel had rebounded immediately after the Taft–Hartley injunction had gone into effect on November 7, 1959, but the boom proved to be short lived. After a four-month period in which steelmakers busied themselves filling back orders, overall steel employment began to decline, a trend that continued into the summer. During May, total employment in steel dropped below 700,000, the average for the peak years of 1955–57. The layoffs only intensified over the course of the summer, reaching a total of 110,000 by August.

This disturbing development was the major topic of discussion at the USA Executive Board meeting held that month. The board approved a resolution that termed the situation in steel a *depression*, noting that in addition to those entirely without work were another 350,000 employed less than full time.[137] The union's resolution also called on employers to reduce the workweek in steel from forty to thirty-two hours and to lower the industry's retirement age, as well for Congress to raise the minimum wage, increase funding for school construction, and pass the rest of the spending bills still bottled up there.[138]

In debating the resolution's merits and the reasons for the downturn in steel, board members for the first time discussed at length the issues of excess capacity and foreign competition. Although McDonald and some district directors continued to view those problems without great concern, others disagreed. Joe Moloney cautiously voiced their sentiments:

> It well may be that we have too much capacity for steel in this country. I don't know; I am not armed with any statistics. But that may be the trouble. I read in *Steel Labor* that the importation of foreign steel is not a problem. I am not going to dispute that, David. But I do know that in Niagara Falls and Buffalo tens of thousands of tons of Italian steel have been used in the Niagara Power Project. And the reason it was used in that [is because] they can buy it so much more cheaper than we can make it. Joe Germano can tell you something about Japanese steel. I know it to be a fact Japanese pig iron is laid in Toronto just as cheaply as they can make it in [the United States] . . . so there is such a thing as foreign competition and it is my guess that this foreign competition is going to grow. Our wages are twice, three . . . or four times as high as the wages paid in Europe and Japan and in most of the free nations; and it is my guess that the importation of steel will increase. It is my guess that our export of steel will decrease.[139]

Moloney's remarks signaled the failure thus far of labor's efforts to promote stronger unions and higher wages in the other industrialized societies of Western Europe and Japan. He noted that Joe Germano had recently made a trip to Japan where he had met with the leaders of its steelworkers union. Germano had urged them to press for higher wages and benefits, but to no avail. Moloney reminded board members that "Joe had difficulty conveying to these Japanese . . . our concept of trade unions, our advocacy of high wages and short hours."[140] Moloney advocated sending more delegations there and also to Western Europe's steel-producing regions, to teach unionists in those countries the good things which we enjoy, lest some day—and it is happening now in the City of Buffalo where Allegheny–Ludlum has come to me as you well know, David, and asked me to cut the wages of their employees. And when I rejected, of course, their proposal they sought a conference with you, Mr. President, and you met with them and . . . told them that under no circumstances could they cut their wages. . . . And they tell me they will close their plant in September.[141]

To continue along the same road of insisting on better wages and benefits for American workers while paying scant attention to those granted abroad, Moloney warned presciently, would lead management to "come to us and say 'We can't compete.' They will ask for wage cuts so that they can meet the wages and bad conditions which exist abroad. That is, in my judgement, competition in degradation."[142] Canadian director Larry Sefton chimed in, warning that even in the short run, excess steel capacity posed a threat to the union's bargaining power:

> We have too much capacity in terms of keeping our industry operating in the usual way. We are into a situation now where every time we are going to come up to a bargaining situation . . . the industry can plan an inventory ahead, and we are going to be faced with a long shutdown.[143]

The board's majority's however, did not respond immediately to those warnings or to Moloney's call for sending "our men and our fortunes abroad."[144] The dangers he described still seemed fairly remote, and the remedies he offered, rather impractical. But the executive board's willingness to give Moloney's views a hearing remained significant nonetheless. For the first time at a meeting of the USA's top leaders, these sorts of questions commanded more than passing attention. The discussion marked a major turning point for the steel industry, which stood at the center of the postwar economy. Like coal mining, textiles, shipping, and railways before it, steel had reached the very first stage in what could eventually become a process of decline. Whether the industry would meet with the same fate as the others depended in large measure on addressing the problems the board had discussed. They weighed heavily on Goldberg's mind, contributing still further to his sense that the postwar order faced a genuine crisis.[145]

He and most other members of the union's leadership pinned their hopes on a Democratic victory in the presidential election that year. They voted on August 9 to ask John Kennedy to address the USA convention planned for the following month, a move tantamount to endorsement. Although David McDonald, who was friendly to Nixon, urged that the board allow both candidates to speak, Joe Germano squelched the idea. The motion to invite Kennedy alone passed after Germano gently reminded McDonald that "You can't be fish and fowl both."[146] Despite some initial grumbling, the AFL–CIO Executive Council followed suit, endorsing Kennedy later that same month, shortly after the Republican National Convention nominated Nixon. Although the building trades unions in the federation and the Teamsters outside it preferred the GOP candidate, most other unions actively supported the Democratic ticket.[147]

What had transpired at the Republican convention a few weeks earlier offered further evidence of labor's declining influence. For the first time in twelve years, the GOP leadership had chosen as its presidential nominee a man whom labor leaders distrusted. Nixon's choice for a running mate, the U.S. ambassador to the United Nations Henry Cabot Lodge Jr., also disappointed them. The union chiefs had favored Labor Secretary James P. Mitchell for the post, but his strong support for the postwar New Deal had alienated GOP conservatives, who insisted on someone more in tune with their outlook. Lodge, like Mitchell, was both from the Northeast and closely identified with Eisenhower. But the diplomat had established no real record over the past eight years regarding issues of domestic political economy. Labor's indirect influence at the GOP convention had in the end proved very modest. Thus pushed as well as pulled toward the Democratic ticket, by August most of the union movement had chosen to back it strongly.[148]

Having begun the year as one of Kennedy's few supporters in the AFL–CIO hierarchy, Goldberg took great satisfaction in its endorsement. But even he knew that the move stemmed at least as much from hostility to Nixon as it did from enthusiasm for Kennedy. Although many middle-class liberals debated during the fall the issue raised by Arthur Schlesinger's latest book, *Kennedy and Nixon: Does It Make Any Difference?* most labor leaders never seriously entertained that question. Some of them, like many liberals, disliked Kennedy's call for increased military spending and generally hawkish outlook, which seemed much more belligerent than Eisenhower's. They were bothered, too, by the Democratic candidate's seeming indifference to the segregation issue.

But even though Nixon's stands on those questions differed little from Kennedy's, on issues of class the latter struck labor leaders as vastly preferable. Nixon's vicious attacks on the CIO–PAC during his first race for Congress in 1946, his vote for the Taft–Hartley Act of 1947, his ugly campaign for the Senate in 1950 against a labor-backed candidate, and his cozy relationship with right-wing Republicans all inclined labor leaders against him. Although he had remained publicly neutral during the so-called right-to-work contests in 1958 and seemed less doctrinaire than the most conservative congressional Republicans, his tie-breaking vote for the first McClellan amendment to the Kennedy–Ervin bill served only to confirm labor leaders' earlier unfavorable impressions. Most of them would therefore do their utmost to defeat him.[149]

So motivated, George Meany announced in August that COPE would sponsor for the first time a national voter registration drive. Its aim was to register enough new voters in the key industrial states to ensure a Kennedy victory. Unlike 1948 — the last time labor leaders had felt greatly alarmed by the prospect of a Republican victory and directed their efforts toward electing a sympathetic Congress — labor in 1960 focused on the presidential race. The large Democratic majorities in Congress, which labor had done so much to elect two years earlier, had turned out to be of limited value, given the Eisenhower administration's increasing unfriendliness. Electing a president more supportive of unions, most AFL–CIO leaders believed, would doom the enactment of further antilabor bills, ensure a sympathetic administration of the new Landrum–Griffin Act, and transform the NLRB into a reliable ally in the fight against the managerial offensive.[150]

Goldberg, his major contributions to Kennedy's campaign already made, watched as labor's efforts on its behalf gained momentum in late September. Kennedy's adroit handling of the religious issue in a meeting with Protestant ministers earlier that month had heartened his union supporters. The contest between Kennedy and Nixon also sharpened that same month, highlighting the differences between the two in ways encouraging to Kennedy's labor allies. Of the three principal themes that JFK stressed, two had come directly from labor's own political program of the past two years. In addition to his call for a consensual solution to the problems facing the postwar order, Kennedy also backed labor's proposals for increasing economic growth.[151]

To those two themes, Kennedy added a third, increased government spending on armaments. This had been the nation's principal form of countercyclical government spending since 1950 and was a central element of Kennedy's solution to the problems confronting the postwar order. By stressing the Soviet "threat," Kennedy and his advisers hoped to accomplish two related goals. First, it would arrest the drop in such expenditures that Eisenhower had initiated two years earlier, a shift in policy that they believed had contributed to the economic slowdown of the preceding three years. And at the same time, the emphasis on the "crisis" facing the nation would persuade the leaders of the managerial revolt to desist for its duration. Thus the effort to defend the postwar New Deal went hand in hand with intensifying the cold war.[152]

Although labor's proposals for preserving the postwar New Deal had not originally contained this theme, by the end of the campaign they had become entwined with it. And Goldberg, along with most other labor leaders, acquiesced. In part that was because he shared that alarmist view of Soviet intentions and capacities. Goldberg and his labor colleagues also went along with Kennedy's hawkish line, much as they had with Truman's twelve years earlier, in order to achieve their paramount objective of defending American workers' well-being. This consideration appears to have been the more influential of the two, but it made no difference in the end result. Labor leaders, Goldberg included, echoed Kennedy's implicit message that attacks on the postwar social contract were not only unjust but also unpatriotic.[153]

Kennedy's support for much of their program pleased his labor supporters. What truly energized them, however, was his unexpectedly strong showing in the first televised presidential debate on September 26. Nixon, having underestimated Kennedy's abilities, allowed his opponent an opening that the latter fully exploited.

Nixon's overconfidence stemmed in part from his initial impression of

Kennedy, formed thirteen years earlier during a debate over the proposed Taft–Hartley Act. In the steel town of McKeesport, Pennsylvania, the two men had jousted over the proposed law before a local civic group. Nixon, better prepared, made clearer and more detailed arguments on behalf of the bill, but Kennedy won more favor with the audience and the press. In part this was because he, like many of them, was a Catholic Democrat. More important, however, was Kennedy's opposition to the Taft–Hartley bill, which Nixon stoutly defended.[154]

Nixon's first impression of Kennedy, formed during the McKeesport debate, was of a callow youth carried along in public life by his family's enormous wealth. Although a largely accurate view of Kennedy at the time, he had by 1960 acquired a basic grasp of the postwar New Deal. Kennedy, moreover, campaigned as one of its defenders, seeking to preserve that social bargain from its managerial foes while redefining it to include those largely excluded from its benefits. Nixon, however, persisted in seeing Kennedy as essentially the same man he had debated thirteen years earlier, thereby misjudging the challenge awaiting him in the televised debates.[155]

The Republican candidate was hampered, too, by his acute sense of the widening division in the Republican Party between the postwar New Deal's supporters and its critics. Believing he needed the backing of both factions in order to win, Nixon refused to take a clear stand on the issues that divided them. Although he had chosen to campaign on the slogan "You've never had it so good," a slightly less grammatical echo of the one used by British Conservative Prime Minister Harold Macmillan in winning reelection the year before, the two men stood far apart.

Macmillan had written a political manifesto during the late 1930s entitled *The Middle Way*, an eloquent defense of corporatist ideas and the welfare state. Even more revealing, perhaps, of his true outlook, the Conservative Party leader had lifted his 1959 campaign slogan from the speeches of George Meany. By 1960, Macmillan and Kennedy had come to share the same general worldview, even though Kennedy grasped it more loosely.

Nixon, on the other hand, had never taken a clear stand on the postwar New Deal. Indeed, his entire career since first running for Congress in 1946 had consisted of efforts to win support from both wings of his party. It was this quality that had earned Nixon the sobriquet "Tricky Dick" among his detractors. Having entered politics more to earn a living than to promote a deeply held set of ideas, Nixon in 1960, like Dewey in 1948, offered no clear answers to the most pressing issues in the presidential election. His apparent loss in the first debate with Kennedy followed as a direct consequence. Nixon's defeat there stemmed less from the way he looked than from the vagueness of his pronouncements.[156]

Kennedy's forceful performance during the September 26 debate did more than energize his labor and middle-class liberal supporters. It also won him an important convert in the ranks of the business realists. IBM chairman Thomas J. Watson Jr., whose father and predecessor had helped recruit Eisenhower for the presidency in 1952 and since then been one of his strongest supporters, watched Nixon's performance that night with dismay. Already uneasy about his managerial colleagues' increasing hostility to the postwar social contract, Watson favored a redefinition that preserved it along the lines Goldberg had been suggesting. Nixon's evasiveness during the first debate contrasted sharply with Kennedy's strong support for a more consensual approach. Their second debate only reinforced this impression in Watson's mind. Immediately following the latter contest, he wrote Kennedy to declare his support and spread the word to other business managers. Most of them greeted Watson's decision with disbelief and outright hostility. Although they strongly supported Nixon, Watson's stand, and that of a few other industrialists who backed Kennedy, gave his candidacy an important boost. Labor would endeavor to do the rest.[157]

Kennedy's success in the presidential debates, and the growing support it brought him, added to Goldberg's confidence in a Democratic victory. Seeking to make that outcome certain, he and his union colleagues proceeded to mobilize labor's still quite potent political apparatus. For the first time, COPE emerged as a truly national force, operating in all fifty states. At the center of labor's political action efforts was the new voter registration drive, supported by more than $500,000 in union contributions. Some 9,100 workers enrolled approximately 1.5 million new voters. The AFL–CIO affiliates, directly and through COPE, also invested millions more in direct contributions to sympathetic Democratic candidates. At the same time, COPE produced seven taped radio programs aimed at northern black voters in eight key urban centers. The broadcasts, carried by nineteen radio stations with predominantly black audiences, featured leading Democrats, all of whom were, with the exception of Kennedy himself, strongly identified with previous and proposed civil rights legislation. Those speakers attacked the Republican record on the racial segregation issue and urged their listeners to back the Democratic ticket. And in the South, COPE financed civil rights organizations that sought to register blacks there. Having thereby swelled the ranks of potential Kennedy voters, COPE's operatives followed through, urging them to cast their ballots on November 7. As election day approached, the union movement pulled out all the stops in an effort to get its supporters to the polls.[158]

In the end, most blacks appear to have swung to Kennedy, although more for reasons of class than race. Most of them then, as ever, were workers. They had fared the worst following the 1957 recession, as very high levels of unemployment persisted among blacks living in northern cities. Although Kennedy had shown little interest in the civil rights issue as a member of Congress and had been blacks' least favorite choice in the primaries, by late October most had come to support him, however reluctantly. Helping him attract their backing was his heavily publicized intervention on behalf of Martin Luther King Jr. after the civil rights leader was jailed on October 19. Although partly an exercise in public relations, Kennedy's action did help in getting King out of prison, to the surprise and delight of many black voters.

COPE operatives, stressing the economic issues, worked feverishly during the campaign's final days to capitalize on that fortuitous development.[159]

Inclining workers, white as well as black, to take labor leaders' advice about which candidate to support and even whether to vote at all was the worsening condition of the nation's economy. Unemployment among steelworkers had continued to grow, and at an accelerating rate that peaked in October. The downturn in steel had also begun spreading to other sectors of the economy, to the automotive industry in particular. Although Nixon tried hard to deny that a recession was beginning, voters knew better. The managerial offensive of the preceding three years, capped by the six-month disturbance in steel, had disrupted the economy's recovery from the 1957/58 recession. Republican conservatives and their managerial allies had miscalculated, with disastrous consequences for the GOP national ticket. Despite a massive advertising campaign via television during the last ten days of the campaign, their candidate came up short. In the end, labor's efforts on Kennedy's behalf proved to be just barely enough.[160]

Throughout the campaign, Goldberg's confidence had never wavered, although he later admitted that the returns "tested it to the limit."[161] In some ways, the outcome greatly resembled that of 1948, the last time labor had gone all out for the Democrats. Kennedy's 303 electoral votes and 49.9 percent of all ballots cast almost exactly duplicated Truman's totals of twelve years earlier. In other respects, however, the 1960 results differed dramatically. The Republicans, who had lost heavily in the 1948 elections for Congress, this time actually gained two seats in the Senate and twenty-two in the House. The overall voter turnout, which had been quite low in 1948, reached 62.8 percent, roughly the same as that recorded during the two previous presidential elections. The most significant difference, however, lay in the size of the combined vote for Nixon and the Dixiecrat candidate Harry F. Byrd. Unlike 1948, when the popular vote for Dewey and the States Rights Party's nominee Strom Thurmond had totaled 47.5 percent, in 1960, the ballots cast for the two conservative candidates constituted a majority, albeit the tiniest of ones.[162]

Goldberg did not find this news, or that buried deeper in the returns, very encouraging. Although the Kennedy–Johnson ticket carried seven of the ten largest states where labor was strongest, the margins in all but one were very close. Among the three such states the Democrats failed to carry were Ohio and California. Nixon's narrow victories there owed much to his earlier ambiguity during the 1958 drive to outlaw the union shop in those states. Also disappointing was the outcome in the South, where Kennedy had just barely won a majority of the old Confederacy's eleven states. Adding Johnson to the Democratic ticket had in the end been of limited, albeit crucial, value there.[163]

Goldberg rejected, however, the notion that an honest count would have favored Nixon, some of whose supporters believed that he had really won in Illinois and Texas. For Nixon to have prevailed in the electoral college, he would have needed to carry both states, and Goldberg was certain that Kennedy had won in Illinois. As Goldberg later recalled, Illinois senator "Everett Dirksen . . . told me [that] 'if we had [had] a recount, they'd have found we [Republicans] stole more votes downstate than [the Democrats did] . . . in Chicago.' There were too many observers in Chicago."[164] The narrowness of Kennedy's victory there and nationwide did suggest to Goldberg, however, that his quest to defeat the managerial offensive faced large obstacles. He consoled himself with the thought that Kennedy's victory at least gave the postwar New Deal's defenders a real chance. And he resolved to make the most of it.[165]

8

Stalemate

GOLDBERG'S EARLY AND highly valued support for Kennedy's candidacy had earned him a major post in the new administration, a move he felt increasingly inclined to make. In part this was because the struggle to enact an anticorruption law had seriously damaged some of his relationships with other trade union officials, contributing to Goldberg's sense that he had gone as far as he could in the labor movement. He was tired, too, of standing in the shadow of his ostensible boss, David McDonald, who was so obviously Goldberg's intellectual inferior. Shifting to a high-level post in the government would also give him a wider field in which to exercise his talents. For all these reasons, Goldberg was receptive to Kennedy's request that he accept such an appointment.[1]

At first Goldberg flirted with the idea of becoming attorney general, the most direct stepping-stone to his cherished goal of a seat on the Supreme Court. But when Kennedy made clear soon after the election that his brother Bobby would be receiving the top Justice Department post, Goldberg's thoughts turned next to the number two position there, that of solicitor general. Robert Kennedy's inexperience apparently suggested to Goldberg that he might well play a leading role at Justice while acting officially as Kennedy's subordinate. But even Goldberg understood that given his own expertise, the logical position for him would be that of labor secretary.[2]

Kennedy, in recognition of Goldberg's efforts to contain the managerial revolt and in return for his support, decided on him for that job by late November. As a first step, Kennedy went through the motions early the following month of consulting George Meany about the appointment. Kennedy asked the AFL–CIO chief to submit a list of acceptable candidates, expecting to find Goldberg's name among them. To Kennedy's chagrin, Goldberg's name failed to appear on Meany's list. The omission reflected opposition from the building trades, whose leaders feared that Goldberg would prove all too zealous in prosecuting corrupt union officials under the new Landrum–Griffin law, and concern among the former AFL affiliates that his administration would encroach on what remained of their jealously guarded autonomy from the state. Every union official who had previously served in a high-ranking Labor Department post had come from the AFL and had reflected its traditional outlook. It was this concern Meany was reflecting when he communicated the federation's preference for "a regular labor man."[3]

The news of Meany's reluctance "cooled me off" the whole idea, Goldberg later remembered.[4] He told Kennedy that no Democratic president could afford to start off without the labor movement's support and advised him to pick someone else for the job. Goldberg had doubts of his own about the Labor Department slot. Accepting it, he believed, would mean an irrevocable departure from the union movement. Goldberg could not expect to do his job properly without sometimes offending the AFL–CIO leadership, from whom he would need to demonstrate real independence. Meeting his responsibilities as labor secretary would, he firmly believed, make impossible a return afterward to labor's ranks. Such a career change would cost him dearly. His total income in 1960 had topped $100,000; as a cabinet secretary he would earn $25,000, and unlike many others who served in that body, Goldberg lacked a large personal fortune to sustain himself and his family.[5]

Upon learning, however, that the building trades' unions constituted the heart of the opposition to his appointment, Goldberg soon changed his mind. They, he believed, should not be allowed to decide who best represented the interests of American workers. Unwilling to accord them that power, Goldberg resolved to overcome their resistance. Kennedy, for his part, persisted in pressing for Meany's approval. The latter quickly came around, under fierce pressure from Alex Rose and David Dubinsky in particular. On December 16, Kennedy summoned Meany and Goldberg to his home in Georgetown. There the president-elect told both men that he planned to announce immediately Goldberg's appointment as secretary of labor. Meany indicated that he had no objections, and Goldberg, his feelings still quite mixed, unenthusiastically agreed to accept the job. Seeking to dispel the tension, Kennedy, Goldberg remembered, said jokingly: "Do you want to be like Adlai Stevenson? He didn't say 'yes' [to being named United Nations ambassador] until I announced his appointment to the press."[6] Aware of the obstacles facing him in labor as well as management circles, Goldberg decided nonetheless to give his utmost to the new job and the larger effort to preserve the postwar New Deal. He would find them daunting challenges.[7]

The news of his appointment drew revealing reactions from businessmen and union leaders. Those executives least identified with the managerial revolt applauded the appointment, as did the editors of the liberal *New Republic*. More cautious responses came from U.S. Steel management, in the form of a Christmas card from Conrad Cooper, and from the *AFL–CIO News*, which emphasized Goldberg's letters of congratulation from industrialists and quoted Goldberg as saying, "The Labor Department is not a class department but promotes the welfare of all Americans."[8] The *News* also carried a statement from Labor Secretary Mitchell that Kennedy "could not have made a better appointment."[9]

This pattern of genuine enthusiasm from the postwar New Deal's strongest supporters and more cautious acceptance from both the business realists and the AFL wing of the labor movement was not confined to the Goldberg appointment. Kennedy's other cabinet selections, especially for the key posts of Treasury, State, and Defense, all were more attractive to liberal Republicans than to either Roger Blough or George Meany. Indeed, Kennedy's choices to head those three departments, Douglas Dillon, Dean Rusk, and Robert McNamara, could have fit quite comfortably into the Eisenhower cabinet. Those further to the left among the Kennedy appointees were relegated to largely ceremonial or secondary positions, thereby signaling that the new administration would seek to maintain and strengthen the postwar social contract, rather than move beyond it.[10]

This continuity was reflected, too, in Goldberg's approach to staffing the Department of Labor. He had obtained the president-elect's promise not to interfere with Goldberg's selection of his most important aides. Thereby insulated from pressure to hire only Kennedy partisans, Goldberg as a first step decided to keep most of the senior bureaucrats, especially those that James Mitchell had himself selected, in their present positions. For the department's second spot Goldberg tapped die-hard Stevensonian Willard Wirtz, a Northwestern University law professor who had served on the Wage Stabilization Board during World War II and thereafter had become one of nation's leading arbitrators. And for the post of assistant secretary for labor–management relations, who was responsible for, among other things, overseeing enforcement of the Landrum–Griffin Act's anticorruption provisions, Goldberg selected James J. Reynolds. A self-described "liberal industrialist," Reynolds had served on the NLRB under President Truman.[11] Just as the decision to keep most of the senior bureaucrats where Mitchell had placed them showed the continuity in outlook between Goldberg and his immediate predecessor, so did the backgrounds of the three top officials in the Kennedy Labor Department reflect the tripartite industrial relations scheme labor had done so much to promote since the 1930s.[12]

As revealing, in different ways, were Goldberg's three other appointments to high-ranking posts at Labor. The first two went to a black, the IUE's director of political education, George Weaver, and a woman, the Industrial Union Department lobbyist Esther Peterson. Goldberg's decision to name Weaver as assistant secretary for international affairs and Peterson as head of the Women's Bureau reflected both his goal of redefining the postwar New Deal so as to enable nonwhites and women to share its benefits more fully and the secondary place that objective occupied in relation to that of preserving the gains of the working and lower middle classes.

Goldberg's one other major appointment, that of Texas AFL–CIO president Jerry Holleman to the third position in the department's chain of command, was intended to represent a different constituency. With the rest of the top jobs held either by people identified with the CIO wing of the labor movement or by those from outside its ranks, George Meany had insisted that Goldberg choose at least one person from its AFL faction for a senior post. Holleman, who had originally come from the federation's building trades department, was that man, and although Goldberg had not known him well beforehand, he, Goldberg, agreed to select him, thereby concluding a process that had yielded a very neatly balanced team of subordinates.[13]

Yet another indication of the degree of continuity between the outgoing and incoming administrations lay in the ease with which the Senate approved Goldberg's nomination as labor secretary. His January 13, 1961, confirmation hearing before the Committee on Labor and Public Welfare was both brief and friendly. The committee's liberals greeted Goldberg's candidacy enthusiastically, and his record of opposition to unions dominated by either radicals or racketeers and his strong support for an anti-Soviet foreign policy helped win him the backing even of its most conservative members, Everett Dirksen and Barry Goldwater. In eight days, both the committee and the full Senate unanimously endorsed his appointment to the cabinet.[14]

With that step, Goldberg's twenty-year association with the Steelworkers Union officially came to an end. He had attended his last USA Executive Board meeting only two weeks earlier, at which he made his valedictory remarks. Goldberg offered his old colleagues a bleak view of the challenges facing the incoming administration:

> I don't have to tell you what a critical situation the country is in. All any of us have to do is read the newspapers from day to day, and it is quite evident that both in the foreign field and in the domestic field our country is confronted with many, many grave crises.[15]

The gravest dangers he cited stemmed from "a very implacable enemy in the Soviet Union," and a level of seasonally adjusted unemployment that he correctly observed was "the largest . . . since the great depression."[16] Even more "ominous," he said, "is the fact that after each of the last three recessions the level of unemployment was higher at the end of the recession than it was previously. In other words, we came out of a recession but a considerable number of people were permanently affected by the recession."[17] Although Goldberg promised, in the vocabulary of the new administration, "very vigorous and fundamental action to change this course of events," he acknowledged that the makeup of the new Congress would make such progress very difficult.[18]

Goldberg also felt compelled to warn his listeners that he would not act in his new role simply as the union movement's agent in the administration. Unwilling to accept any benefit that might be viewed as giving the labor the power to produce such a result, Goldberg had refused the USA's offer of a pension amounting to $25,000 for every year after age sixty. For the same reason, he had also declared on being named to the cabinet post that he would never again take a union as a client. And he also advised the USA Executive Board that he would enforce fully the new Landrum–Griffin law against labor corruption. In all, the tone of Goldberg's remarks reflected his understanding

that the solutions he and Kennedy were pushing to address the current political and economic crisis called for sacrifices from labor as well as management
and that his former union colleagues should expect nothing else.[19]

Goldberg did temper his rather somber speech by acknowledging that both
the social movement that had carried him to the Labor Department and his
own working-class origins would continue to inform his view of what the
federal government ought to be doing. In that vein, Goldberg noted that he
owed his cabinet seat to the Steelworkers Union and that he would be promoting what were essentially its solutions to the problems facing American
workers. "You are," he reminded the USA's leaders,

> the closest to me of any group in the labor movement. . . . I have had
> other clients and I am proud of those associations, but the Steelworkers
> Union . . . has been intimately associated with me. . . . and . . . I am
> not oblivious of the fact that if it weren't for that association I would be in
> Chicago, whatever my capacities were, and not in the national scene, and not
> recognized . . . by this [cabinet] appointment.[20]

In much the same vein, he told the board that "while I have had a formal
education, by reason of my family and . . . background and our beginnings
there is a feeling of closer identification [among workers] with me than maybe
other members of the Cabinet. . . . and I am conscious of that, too."[21] The
board, for its part, rewarded Goldberg's candor with a highly unusual standing ovation and a unanimous resolution praising his service to the union and
expressing its best wishes for success in his new post. With that he exited, to
take up tasks even more challenging than those he had faced during his two
decades with the Steelworkers.[22]

Indicative of how difficult his mission would be was the far more skeptical
response he received from senior managers at some of the country's largest
corporations. During a closed-door meeting four days later at New York's
exclusive "21" Club, Goldberg bluntly laid down the administration's new
political and economic policies to that group. In attendance were Henry
Luce, who had arranged the session, and representatives of AT&T, Chase
National Bank, Standard Oil, the American Can Company, Olin-Mathiessen,
Macy's, and several other major firms.

Mincing no words, Goldberg told those men that the time had come to end
the managerial revolt and seek instead a compromise solution to the problems
facing workers and managers. The forum for such negotiations, he explained,
would be a labor–management advisory committee appointed by the president, the idea Goldberg had been pushing for the past two years. He went on
to say that although he would not try to force the plan on anyone present, he
thought it was a worthwhile step deserving of their support. Goldberg spoke
for an hour, to an audience that listened respectfully but without any real
enthusiasm. At the end of the session, one member of the audience came up to
offer his support, but the rest remained noncommittal. For the moment, most
adopted a wait-and-see attitude.[23]

Kennedy's decision to have Goldberg, rather than his commerce secretary-designate, Luther Hodges, brief business leaders about the new administration's policies illustrated Goldberg's prominent role in the new cabinet. He and Douglas Dillon would be the members of it most influential in determining the administration's domestic political and economic program. At the first meeting of the Kennedy cabinet on January 26, this quickly became obvious.

The new head of the Council of Economic Advisers, Walter Heller, and Harvard economist John Kenneth Galbraith proposed a so-called incomes policy that came close to outright wage-and-price controls. According to Heller's and Galbraith's initial conception, the federal government would seek to prevent any price increases, as well as any wage increases above what the productivity formula would allow. Hodges, to Goldberg's disbelief, simply sat there listening and voiced no objections.

When Goldberg's turn to speak came, he said of the Heller–Galbraith plan that "it won't go" and argued instead for what eventually became the wage–price guideposts policy, a less heavy-handed approach intended to achieve much the same result.[24] Rather than police all wage-and-price increases, the federal government would seek merely to hold the annual increase in wages for the economy as a whole to no more than 3.2 percent, an amount roughly equal to the overall growth in worker productivity. In various industries, wage increases following from improved productivity would likely vary, with some above and others below that figure, but as long as the 3.2 percent average for the entire workforce was maintained, Goldberg, Heller, and Dillon reasoned, overall prices would remain steady, thereby eliminating the inflation that had given rise to the crisis of the preceding three years.[25]

In obtaining that kind of wage-and-price restraint, Goldberg argued for so-called moral suasion, or jawboning, and other voluntaristic means, rather than trying to police prices and wages unilaterally. As he well knew, managers at the biggest corporations could frustrate at will the government's efforts to dictate a freeze on prices. And for that reason, he understood, an incomes policy rigidly enforced by the government would quickly alienate organized labor, whose leaders rightly doubted that the government would police prices with either the same zeal or effectiveness as it would wages. In sum, Goldberg called for mobilizing the federal government to win through "voluntary" cooperation what it lacked the power to demand directly, a policy only marginally different from the one Eisenhower's aides had been pursuing since 1956.[26]

A key to keeping wages and prices down, Goldberg believed, lay in minimizing strikes. Thus the Labor Department under his direction would increase its supervision of collective bargaining in an effort to head off work stoppages that led to either inflationary agreements or increased reliance on imports. Under Eisenhower, such efforts had been the primary responsibility of the Federal Mediation and Conciliation Service, with the labor secretary and his staff intervening only in the biggest disputes, such as the steel and auto industry negotiations. And in the last Democratic administration, disputes had been mediated for the most part by Truman's aide John Steelman, rather than by Labor Secretaries Schwellenbach and Tobin. But Goldberg intended to handle more of those kinds of matters personally, and he elicited a pledge from Kennedy that "there would be no John Steelman" on the White House staff.[27] Thus, soon after Goldberg and his subordinates were installed at the Labor Department, they were involved to an unprecedented degree in mediating labor–management conflicts, to advance the administration's paramount goals of wage-and-price stability.[28]

Goldberg played a highly visible part in resolving several knotty disputes, beginning only two days after being sworn in as labor secretary with a tug-and ferryboat strike in New York City. Nearly seventeen hundred workers there had walked off their jobs two weeks earlier, a strike that soon involved eleven railroads. The central issues were much the same as in the 1959 steel strike: managers insisting on changes in work rules, in particular on reducing the size of boat crews from five to three men, and the union both refusing to go along while also demanding a pay raise. Sympathy strikes in the railway industry had disrupted freight traffic as far away as St. Louis; a serious fuel shortage on the East Coast loomed in the dead of winter; and approximately 100,000 suburbanites were without mass transit to and from New York City.

New York Governor Nelson Rockefeller, frustrated by the failure of both local and federal mediators, asked Goldberg to tackle the problem personally. It took him exactly fourteen hours, spent in constant talks with both sides, to resolve it. Like the steel pact reached a year earlier, Goldberg achieved an end to the strike essentially by postponing a decision on the key work rules issue. He persuaded management to await the recommendations of an existing presidential commission, headed by James P. Mitchell, which was already studying that problem. The union, for its part, agreed to accept a very small pay increase.[29]

Goldberg repeated that performance twice more in his first six months on the job. First came a dispute in the commercial airline industry. Wildcat strikes there by pilots ended after Goldberg intervened, with both sides agreeing to the creation of another special commission to study the basic issues. The next major crisis came in the maritime industry. By mid-June 1961, matters there came to a head when eighty thousand workers belonging to five different unions struck to protest managers' increasing practice of registering ships abroad and thereby escaping the jurisdiction of U.S. labor laws. Bargaining rights on these so-called runaway ships and the unions' pressure for better wages and benefits were the principal strike issues.

When the parties initially balked at accepting a special commission, Goldberg reluctantly recommended that Kennedy use a Taft–Hartley injunction to end the strike. Unlike steel, Goldberg argued, the maritime dispute created a genuine national emergency, a distinction more convenient than persuasive. Believing, however, that he had no other choice, Goldberg succeeded in obtaining the injunction. Both management and the unions involved in the dispute eventually accepted the Taft–Hartley board's recommendations for modest pay and benefits improvements, and the key bargaining rights issue was referred to yet another special commission.[30]

In effect, Goldberg's intervention into those three major disputes bought the new administration some time, which he intended to use for pursuing a broader, more consensual solution to the problems facing the postwar order. Should his proposed Labor–Management Advisory Committee fail to reach such an agreement, however, Goldberg's mediation achievements would soon prove ephemeral. But for the moment, he appeared at least to be creating the conditions needed to make those negotiations successful.[31]

And in the short run at least, Goldberg's success in helping prevent work stoppages more generally was truly remarkable. During the first half of 1961, the United States experienced the fewest working hours lost to strikes since World War II. The number of workers involved in such actions also reached a postwar low. Goldberg's own talents helped achieve that record, but easily as important were the economic conditions bequeathed to him by the outgoing Eisenhower administration. The overall contraction in economic activity and, in particular, rising unemployment, which peaked in February at an official, seasonally adjusted rate of 6.8 percent, substantially weakened unions' bargaining power with employers. This situation inclined union leaders to settle, helping make possible Goldberg's exceptional mediation record.[32]

The managerial revolt of the preceding three years had also done much to reduce rising wages. After the Steelworkers had partially surrendered their COLA clause and agreed to quite modest wage-and-benefit increases in early 1960, the pattern had rippled outward to the other major industries facing contract negotiations that year, namely, electrical, railway, and aircraft firms. The net result was to restore almost completely by early 1961 the wage-and-price stability of the mid-1950s. The challenge facing Goldberg and the Kennedy administration more generally was to preserve that achievement while simultaneously reducing unemployment and increasing workers' real income.[33]

The concern about inflation loomed over Kennedy's advisers as they debated how best to promote renewed economic growth. Goldberg favored a combination of public-works programs; an increase in the minimum wage from $1.00 to $1.25; the broadening of its coverage to include migratory farm laborers, domestics, and other service workers; a temporary extension of the eligibility period for federal unemployment compensation from twenty-six to thirty-nine weeks; a permanent increase in the amount of the weekly benefit; the enactment of Senator Douglas's distressed-areas legislation, which would offer federal government aid to those areas most affected by long-term economic decline; and an employment program specifically targeted at young workers. These were essentially the ideas that the center of the labor movement, led by the USA, had been urging along with their middle-class liberal allies since the spring of 1958.[34]

Kennedy, however, refused to accept all of them. He told Goldberg that the total cost of his antirecession proposals would create a substantial budget deficit, in turn worsening the nation's already very serious balance-of-payments and inflation problems. When Goldberg suggested increasing taxes for the upper middle class and the rich to achieve a balanced federal budget, Kennedy demurred. He and Treasury Secretary Dillon understood that the administration lacked the power needed to extract such a measure from Congress. Requesting an income tax hike would likely lead, if successful, only to raising the amount paid by the working and lower middle classes. And that result would only take away with one hand the increased purchasing power that the other would provide through the spending programs the new taxes had financed. Without illusions about the strength of those forces that would oppose a tax bill of the sort Goldberg was suggesting, Kennedy rejected the idea as unrealistic and, for that reason, a waste of his administration's limited political capital.[35]

Goldberg at first urged Kennedy at least to make the fight so as to satisfy his union supporters but soon accepted the logic of his argument. Over labor's muffled protests, Goldberg agreed to settle for a much more limited plan. Ultimately costing about $3 billion in its first year of operation, Kennedy's antirecession package emphasized increasing the minimum wage, temporarily extending but not raising unemployment benefits, and creating very modestly financed youth-employment and distressed-areas programs. In the place of the public-works projects backed by Goldberg and organized labor, Kennedy offered only a $3 billion increase in military spending, a set of priorities essentially consistent with the federal government's policies over the previous decade.[36]

Even these proposals proved difficult to obtain from Congress. The unemployment benefits fight, which Goldberg viewed as the least controversial and therefore undertook first, proved instructive. After Kennedy warned him that the seriousness of unemployment was not matched by concern about it in Congress, Goldberg decided to publicize the problem and thereby arouse support for the administration's antirecession program. For those reasons, he embarked during the middle of February on a heavily publicized three-day tour of economically depressed areas. Seeking to increase the public's awareness of, and concern over, unemployment, he toured seven of the biggest midwestern cities, where he made several speeches; met with union leaders, employers, and politicians; and urged them to press Congress to enact the administration's unemployment benefits extension bill and the rest of the antirecession program.[37]

Upon returning to Washington, Goldberg personally directed the administration's lobbying efforts, which soon ran into unexpectedly strong resistance. Although the unemployment extension bill soon passed in the House, the Senate failed to follow suit. On March 15, the Senate Finance Committee amended the measure to give states the option of whether to accept the federally financed extended benefits. The so-called states' rights provision was intended this time, as in the past, to prevent the extension payments in those states where organized labor was weakest, thereby maintaining its bargaining power and workers' wages there at existing levels. The outcome, as Goldberg told his wife later that same day, was a reminder that "the Conservatives and the business men control this Congress. . . . The liberals do not."[38]

The vote took Goldberg by surprise, although he soon discovered what had gone wrong. The Senate Finance Committee's vote reflected opposition from both Dixiecrats and liberals. The former, led by Senator Harry Byrd of Virginia, were determined to prevent the new administration from appointing federal judges in the South who were committed to dismantling the system of legalized segregation there. Thus far, Kennedy had refused to grant southern senators approval rights on all nominees for federal judgeships in their home states, which the Dixiecrats saw as an ominous sign. Some liberals on the committee, such as Eugene McCarthy, Vance Hartke, and Clinton Anderson, also contributed to the administration bill's defeat. They did so to signal their unhappiness with an antirecession program that the labor–liberal alliance saw as far too mild.[39]

Goldberg, expecting some resistance from southern conservatives on class rather than race grounds, was caught completely off guard by the failure of some of the Finance Committee's liberal members to back the administration's bill. Furious with them for playing into the hands of the Dixiecrats and their GOP allies, Goldberg pressed for changes in the bill once it reached the Senate floor. Mobilizing the labor movement to pressure the reluctant liberals and enlisting the administration to mollify southern conservatives, Goldberg set the stage for another key vote, this time before the entire Senate. On March 25 it approved the unemployment benefits extension after defeating Senator Byrd's version of the bill by only two votes. Other victories soon followed, enabling passage of Kennedy's scaled-down antirecession program. With Goldberg playing the role of chief lobbyist, the administration won an increase in the minimum wage to $1.25 that same year; a small public-works bill costing $900 million to provide more jobs; a very modestly financed distressed-areas assistance measure, formally entitled the Area Redevelopment Act; and a small training program for the unemployed called the Manpower Development and Training Act.[40]

Even these relatively modest achievements had their price. In order to win the support of southern conservatives for its antirecession program, the administration backed off in the area of judicial appointments, in effect allowing southern senators veto power over appointments to the federal courts in their home states. Also yielded was the effort to amend the Fair Labor Standards Act (FLSA) so as to bring into its minimum wage provision the agricultural and service jobs held predominantly by blacks and Latinos.

And deferred for the moment were both the executive order banning segregation in public housing that Kennedy had promised during his campaign and a push to enact the youth employment bill. The latter measure had been intended particularly to assist urban blacks, whose high rate of joblessness Goldberg, in a memo to Kennedy written later that year, termed "social dynamite."[41] Giving in on race had enabled some modest progress against class, a very difficult choice the administration would face repeatedly throughout its tenure in office.[42]

As blacks had pushed harder during the late 1950s for dismantling the system of legalized segregation, Goldberg believed the government had failed to respond adequately. But as he later recalled, "We were at that time unable to get a statute [outlawing racial discrimination]. Congress wouldn't go for it."[43] Even the more modest approaches, such as emphasizing judicial appointments, broadening the reach of the Fair Labor Standards Act, and a youth employment program aimed primarily at blacks, had run afoul of southern conservatives in Congress. Anxious to attack the system of oppression based on race, Goldberg felt compelled to settle for less direct and smaller steps in that direction.[44]

The most notable of them was the President's Committee on Equal Employment Opportunity (PCEEO), which Kennedy created by executive order in March 1961. He assigned Lyndon Johnson to chair the group and named Goldberg vice-chairman. Although Johnson was officially in charge, Goldberg named the committee's program director and supervised much of its work. Kennedy's decision testified once again to the continuities between his administration and the preceding one. The PCEEO was "new" only in the sense that Kennedy's order creating it had consolidated two preexisting committees. The more important of them had been started by Truman in 1951, and then continued by Eisenhower, who had named his vice-president to head that group. Kennedy's choice of Johnson to chair the PCEEO proved a shrewd one in that it tended to ward off protests from Dixiecrats while giving the committee a chief who genuinely cared about the problems it was intended to address.[45]

Armed with a small budget of around $500,000, the PCEEO created one major program, Plans for Progress. Originally conceived by Robert Troutman, a southern businessman and classmate of Kennedy's at Harvard, the project was intended to use the issuing of government contracts as a lever with which to combat discriminatory hiring practices in private industry. Executives and union leaders connected with firms that received such contracts were asked to sign agreements promising to survey their current employment and union membership practices and periodically to file reports with the committee detailing their efforts to end workplace discrimination. This program, like most of Kennedy's civil rights initiatives, emphasized voluntary compliance. As Goldberg explained to PCEEO members at a meeting early in 1962,

> The President's interest is to try to lead American companies, which can exercise a great influence in these areas, to move forward, to exercise community leadership. The Vice President, of course, had this idea originally, that this ought to be done, and that we ought to do the same with the unions. I know from my experience that if a great American company will do more than give us words, but will give us some action, that this can have a tremendous impact.[46]

Such firms, Goldberg suggested, had the greatest power to fight segregation and therefore the largest share of responsibility for eliminating it. By way of example, he recalled having successfully urged Benjamin Fairless in the mid-1950s to hold an unsegregated meeting for the employees of U.S. Steel's Birmingham, Alabama, subsidiary. As he told the committee, "When U.S.

Steel made up its mind to have an unsegregated meeting in Birmingham, a lunch that was unsegregated—the Chief of Police of Birmingham throws everybody in jail if you have a private lunch that is unsegregated, let alone a public one—they through [*sic*] nobody in jail."[47]

Although the program did achieve some small breakthroughs in textile mills and aircraft plants, its overall effect on racially based workplace discrimination was minuscule. The program's lack of real teeth, most tellingly revealed by its failure to force the cancellation of even a single government contract, led most employers to pay at most only lip service to it.[48]

The record for labor unions, and former AFL affiliates in particular, was much the same, albeit for somewhat different reasons. Far less secure as social institutions than large corporations, unions faced more difficult choices in this area.

Attacking racial discrimination offered antiunion employers a weapon with which to divide workers, undermining the working-class solidarity that formed the real basis of unions' power. Not all trade unionists cared to attack discrimination even if that obstacle were removed, as Goldberg well knew. But labor's insecure position in the postwar order, one growing even more so as the 1960s opened, led him to favor pressing managers much harder than labor leaders in this area. The record for both groups remained very poor during 1961/62. Absent strong government pressure, they preferred not to address the problem seriously. Thus, like so many of Kennedy's civil rights policies, Plans for Progress was, in the last analysis, essentially an exercise in public relations.[49]

Goldberg, displeased by the PCEEO's scanty results, favored initiating more investigations of firms receiving government contracts that were suspected of practicing job discrimination, rather than merely reacting to employees' complaints. Most of the committee's work, however—in keeping with Kennedy's and Johnson's voluntaristic emphasis—consisted of the latter sorts of cases. Armed with a larger budget than its predecessors had under Eisenhower, the PCEEO did, in its first eighteen months of existence, adjudicate several hundred more cases than the two previous committees had in their six years of operation. But the greater volume apparently reflected more the growing willingness of blacks to complain openly than it did the committee's effectiveness at achieving corrective action.[50]

More meaningful steps to eradicate workplace discrimination would likely have produced a cut in the Labor Department's budget, which financed the PCEEO's operations. The committee's funding had come from this source without the congressional approval typically required for new programs. To have gone much further would have antagonized leading southern conservatives such as Senators Harry Byrd and Richard Russell. The PCEEO's vulnerability to such pressure, and consequently its limited mandate, made substantial progress against racially based job discrimination extremely unlikely. More than anything else, the committee's record revealed the weakness of a civil rights policy inhibited by Kennedy's goal of minimizing southern congressional opposition to the rest of his legislative program, which was aimed at protecting the hard-won gains of the American working and lower middle classes.[51]

Goldberg did try to make such progress in other ways, but most of them proved either symbolic or extremely limited in their reach. He did his utmost to hire and promote nonwhites in the Labor Department itself and tried to root out discriminatory practices from public-employee unions, the U.S. Employment Service, and the federal apprenticeship and training program. At a February 1962 meeting of the PCEEO, Goldberg was asked to report on the Labor Department's efforts to eliminate racial discrimination from its own ranks. In so doing, he sought to dispel the complacency engendered by many of the Plans for Progress reports, filled with upbeat language about forward steps but lacking real evidence to substantiate such claims. Goldberg told his colleagues on the committee:

> It is not an appropriate Plan for Progress to report—some, I haven't examined all of them, but a few of these plans in this report tell the committee that "We have always done well and we are going to continue to do well." That just flies in the face of the facts. Maybe there is this exemplary company that has always done well, but we are part of the company of the Federal Government and we have reported to you very candidly. We have not done well, and we would not regard it to be a satisfactory answer to this committee to give you a report that we re-affirm the fact that we have done well and we are going to continue to do well.[52]

In urging the PCEEO's members to pay more attention to these issues, closer to home and for that reason more in the administration's power to remedy, Goldberg noted that the Labor Department had by far the best record of employing nonwhites. As he told to the committee, his own survey had revealed that

> the Department of Labor . . . had quantitatively the highest number of Negro employees in the government. . . . as of April [1961] . . . 17.5 percent of the Department were non-white employees. Most of them were Negroes. I want to say to you in this room that that percentage was much higher than many other departments of the government. We have had departments of the government that have had 2.5 percent non-white employees. These have been big[,] important and larger departments of the government.[53]

The Labor Department's superior record in that regard reflected more than James Mitchell's and Goldberg's own concern about racial discrimination. This cabinet-level department, like the others, tended to take its cues in hiring from the social institutions whose interests it was intended to represent. Labor's far greater willingness to employ nonwhites than the Treasury, State, and Defense Departments—to give only three examples—offers compelling evidence that on this issue, their constituencies compared unfavorably with the Labor Department's primary one, namely, organized labor.[54]

Goldberg, however, did not take those numbers as an opportunity to engage in self-congratulation. *Where* blacks were employed, even in his own department, offered a sobering reminder of just how deeply entrenched discrimination was in the federal government. He told his fellow commissioners,

> I was not satisfied with a quantitative analysis, so I went around and had a survey made of the grades and classifications encompassed in this area. I find, those of us in government, and I am sure the same thing is characteristic of private industry, that the concentration of employment is in the lower grades, messengers, other production people, people who load on the working platform, and clerks.

Goldberg also noted, "Not all that was a result of a deliberate attempt to discriminate" on the part of individuals.[55] Institutional racism posed a persistent problem everywhere in government, he implied, just as it did elsewhere in the workforce.

Goldberg's solution was twofold. First, he began affirmative efforts to hire more nonwhites as professionals, a move that met, Goldberg reported, with "a great deal of skepticism among professional employees who are non-white about the good faith of the Federal Government, because too many of them who took this major step for determining what their future career would be ran into a dead end street."[56] He emphasized the need for such recruiting efforts, saying, "I think this is very important. You cannot in light of the justifiable skepticism in the Negro community about their opportunities in government employment just sit and wait for applications to come in."[57] And at the same time, to increase the number of such candidates from the department's own ranks, Goldberg ordered the creation of in-house training programs for black and Latino employees.[58]

In addition to these initiatives, he counseled continuing vigilance with respect to hiring and promoting such workers. Often, he pointed out, black and Latino candidates did not receive promotions because their job responsibilities failed to qualify them for advancement. Many had been hired, Goldberg told the committee's members, as "minority group consultants" and thereby denied the opportunity to broaden their work experience to meet the formal qualifications for promotion.[59]

One example involved a black man who had graduated from Cornell and compiled an excellent record at the Labor Department in that kind of job. He had applied for a higher position only to be rated lower than two other white candidates, a woman with no more than a high school diploma and a man with a fourth-grade education. Hearing about that particular incident, Goldberg said, "I refused to accept that recommendation. This weekend I am going to appoint the minority group man to the position of deputy director."[60]

Making those kinds of decisions, Goldberg admitted, was not easy. He noted that white women disliked giving preferred treatment in hiring and promotion to blacks, as did, presumably, many white men, especially those of working-class background who themselves had had to struggle against a different system of oppression. Elevating concern with race above gender and class in hiring and promotion created potentially explosive problems, but Goldberg believed the alternative would be even more socially disruptive.[61]

He did stress that such efforts should not lead to mere tokenism but to giving nonwhites a basis for believing that merit-based advancement was possible for everyone:

> The important thing always in federal employment is not to put another non-white or Negro in a spot. The important thing is to make him feel that he can advance like anybody else in the line of promotion to the top.
>
> I have tried to say consistently to our people that anybody can come into the Secretary's office. Anybody can be a job 18. . . . Anybody can be a Secretary, which is the real test of our democracy.[62]

Despite those kinds of exhortations and his other efforts to improve conditions in the Labor Department, Goldberg admitted that even there, large problems persisted. The U.S. Employment Service, which the Labor Department in theory controlled, had since its creation cooperated with employers who used racial preference systems in filling jobs. Goldberg explained to the PCEEO that like so many other supposedly federal programs, the Employment Service was in fact also partly operated by the states, which enormously complicated the federal government's efforts to reform it. He commented:

> While we call the total employment services the U.S. Employment Service, under a scheme supported by Congress, and which cannot be changed by the present lineup in the Congress, we have a Federal–State Employment Service.
>
> It is a mistake to assume that the Federal Government runs the total employment service. We give guidance, we give leadership. But on the other hand, we are dependent, under the scheme laid down by Congress, upon the State employment services to be our operational device.[63]

In late 1961, Goldberg did order all local officers of the service to eliminate racial identifications from its records. In the interstate recruitment area, which was handled directly by federal officials, Goldberg also observed that "we [now] reject job orders with discriminatory specifications."[64] He noted that the latter problem was a truly national one, that "we are just as likely to have a local employment service in New York . . . mark a card Negro or White as . . . in Texas, or perhaps even more so. And they will respond to employer requests in this area."[65] Despite progress in eliminating those sorts of racial preference systems, Goldberg admitted that "we have run into instances where, despite our order, local people have kept some kind of informal order."[66] He did, however, report some real victories, most notably desegregating unemployment offices in Florida and assigning blacks to work in important employment service jobs throughout the South.[67]

The federal apprenticeship and training program, historically segregated, proved another headache because the states and localities actually ran such activities, leaving to the federal government merely the publicity functions associated with them. Under the existing scheme, however, the Labor Department was responsible for determining whether such programs met federal standards, a lever Goldberg used fully. As he informed his PCEEO colleagues, "Without waiting for legislation, under Mr. Holleman's leadership, we have issued an order that we will not approve any apprenticeship training plan as meeting Federal specifications that is discriminatory. . . . And not only discriminatory in form but discriminatory in substance."[68] Once again, he noted, this was "not a southern problem alone," a reminder of the magnitude of the task confronting those seeking to dismantle the segregation system.[69]

In addition to attacking segregation in the government, Goldberg continued to push for amendments to the Fair Labor Standards Act (FLSA) and for a youth employment bill. Both measures were primarily addressed to the needs of nonwhites. The change in FLSA of greatest concern to him was one that would bring migrant farm workers from Latin America, or *braceros* as they were called, under the reach of the law regulating wages and hours. Early in 1962, Goldberg wrote Kennedy to report that the Committee on Migratory Labor, which brought together federal officials from all the departments concerned in some way with such workers, had united on a legislative program to improve their lot. Five bills with that goal had passed the Senate, he reported, but, like so much of the rest of Kennedy's program, remained stymied in the more conservative House.[70]

In the meantime, unilateral executive action was not possible, although some liberal members of Congress, most notably James Roosevelt of California, urged Goldberg to use his authority under the existing agreements with Latin American governments to certify a higher wage for such workers. These agreements, however, obligated employers to pay only the prevailing wage for a given job. The federal government officials who had framed the law governing such pacts had thereby hoped to protect *braceros* at least from being paid less than their American counterparts. But many of the jobs *braceros* performed were held by foreigners alone, thereby undermining that goal and leaving Goldberg without the discretion to certify a higher wage for them. The only real solution, he believed, was to amend FLSA so as to bring all farm workers under its protection.[71]

The same obstacles that impeded enactment of this measure also blocked passage of the administration's youth employment bill. Believing the latter had a better chance in Congress, Goldberg pressed much harder for it. In January 1962 he reported in a memo to Kennedy that congressional resistance remained quite strong, and two months later he informed him that "we will need to make a major drive for its enactment."[72] The key person standing in the bill's way, he told Kennedy that April, was House Rules Committee chairman Howard Smith of Virginia. Although Goldberg urged "continued quiet pressure on Judge Smith," the proposed Youth Opportunities Act, as it was called, failed to progress during 1962.[73] Even after Kennedy gave a public address strongly endorsing the measure, conservative resistance remained strong. By late August, Goldberg reported to Kennedy that the bill was still bottled up in the House Rules Committee.[74]

The administration's efforts to implement its manpower/training law in a nondiscriminatory fashion met with similar frustration. Aimed at helping retrain workers suffering from long-term unemployment, the measure had won congressional approval early in 1962 and received Kennedy's signature on March 15 of that year. Appropriations for the act soon were threatened, however, by Goldberg's intention to require that all the training conducted under its auspices be integrated. The law authorizing the program, like so many others in this area, contained a joint federal–state financing mechanism. This device, in turn, gave state governments some control over how such schemes were to operate.

By August 1962, the administration had failed to reach a consensus on whether the need for funding such programs was so urgent that it outweighed the competing concern about racial discrimination. As Goldberg himself acknowledged in a memo to Kennedy that month, a federal government ban on segregated training "will preclude participation [in the program] by nine states."[75] Once again, Goldberg and Kennedy were faced with a very difficult choice between trying to make headway against the system of oppression based on class at the expense of progress against the one based on race. For the first two years of the administration's tenure it gave priority to the former objective, but as 1962 drew to a close that commitment was clearly weakening.

The measure that raised the issue in an even more explosive fashion was Congressman James Roosevelt's proposed Equal Employment Opportunities Act. Roosevelt's bill would create a statutory commission to replace the existing PCEEO and give it subpoena and enforcement powers directed at employers and unions. To endorse such a measure would alienate southern conservatives and likely doom enactment of the rest of the administration's program, which was in enough trouble already. Roosevelt, reflecting the growing pressure from blacks on the government to attack segregation, demanded that Goldberg appear at the hearings on the bill as an administration witness.

On January 23, 1962, Goldberg wrote Kennedy:

> A Subcommittee of the House Labor Committee headed by Congressman Roosevelt is holding hearings on [the proposed] . . . Equal Opportunities Act. . . . The Committee is insisting that I testify on behalf of the Administration and have scheduled my testimony for tomorrow. Thus far I have not been able to obtain an agreed upon administration view but it is difficult to see how the Administration can fail to support this civil rights measure.[76]

As an interim move, Goldberg proposed, in time-honored bureaucratic fashion, that he say the administration was studying the idea but that he, personally, supported it in principle. The maneuver bought Kennedy some time, but little else. As Goldberg noted in his memo, pressure from northern black voters and their white liberal allies meant that the proposal would not go away. He explained to Kennedy that "Congressman Roosevelt and other northern Congressmen feel they must insist upon this bill if they are not to prejudice their chances for re-election this fall."[77] The federal government contained that demand during 1961/62, but its ability to do so was on the wane.[78]

Another indication of the sea change beginning to take place was the growing sentiment in Congress for attacking discrimination based on gender as well as race. As pressure from upper-middle-class and more elite women for enactment of the Equal Rights Amendment (ERA) grew during the late 1950s, Goldberg, like his labor colleagues and those women's groups closest to the union movement, had persisted in seeking measures such as the proposed equal pay law, which they believed would improve the lot of working- and lower-middle-class women.

Women from well-to-do backgrounds, mainly those identified with the National Woman's Party, favored attacking the problem of wage disparities in a different way, by enacting the ERA. In their view, the overall differential between the average income earned by full-time, year-round men and women workers in the paid labor force stemmed mostly from the concentration of women workers in low-skill, low-paid clerical, service, and factory jobs. A measure that promised only to eliminate wage disparities in those jobs women already held, without expanding their access to other, better-paying ones, would be, many elite feminists believed, no real answer to the larger problem of inequality in income between men and women.[79]

Persuasive as far as it went, this argument neglected the likely consequences of enacting the ERA instead. Goldberg and his labor allies feared that passing such a measure would ultimately operate to the disadvantage of most women. Even though the ERA might widen access to high-paying professional jobs, it would likely do so at the cost of weakening the protective legislation that working- and lower-middle-class women valued. Even more important, enacting elite feminists' agenda—in effect giving the struggle against gender-based discrimination priority over the one against class—threatened to alienate working-class men. To do so would likely fracture the working-class solidarity that was the prerequisite for maintaining and extending the material gains that the working and lower middle classes had won since the 1930s.[80]

Like the campaign for black equality, the reemerging women's rights movement imperiled the postwar New Deal precisely because this movement threatened to divide the working class. Elevating the struggles against race- and gender-based systems of oppression above the one rooted in class would, Goldberg feared, benefit the most privileged nonwhites and women, at the expense of others in those groups. And most women—like most blacks and Latinos—were neither rich nor upper middle class. For that reason, Goldberg viewed the ERA's elite women supporters as pursuing a self-serving course of action, one harmful to the interests of most women for whom they claimed to speak. Implicit in his view was an assumption that protecting and increasing their economic security mattered more to most women than moving faster toward equality with men.

These priorities, widely shared by his own Depression-scarred generation, were beginning to shift in the early 1960s. As the fear of a return to those kinds of hard times had receded under the operation of the postwar social contract, concern among women, as among blacks, increasingly focused on other kinds of hardships. Class, though it remained a powerful system of oppression, was not the only one. The postwar New Deal's increasing ineffectiveness from the late 1950s onward in promoting the interests of working- and lower-middle-class nonwhites and women also contributed to that sea change. But Goldberg—like so many other white men of his generation—found these developments difficult to appreciate fully.[81]

This is why he pressed instead for eradicating disparities between the wages paid to men and women in the jobs they already occupied while working more gradually at wearing down the barriers women faced in seeking higher-paid positions. Goldberg also favored accelerating economic growth in ways that benefited all members of the working and lower middle classes, women included. He reminded Eleanor Roosevelt of this in a letter, writing, "Women have made the greatest progress in overcoming barriers to employment opportunity during periods of high employment, and even of labor shortages."[82] Increasing the rate of economic growth was particularly important to women for this reason and because those already in the paid labor force had, like blacks, suffered disproportionately from the 1957/58 and 1960/61 recessions. Shortly before the beginning of the first of those downturns, the wages of full-time, year-round women workers in the paid labor force had averaged 63.6 percent those of men, but by the end of 1960 the figure stood at 60.6 percent, a decline that reflected the working- and lower-middle-class backgrounds of most such women.[83]

The center of concern in the executive branch about that problem and women's issues more generally was the Women's Bureau of the Labor Department. Goldberg's choice to head that office, Esther Peterson, shared his general outlook on such subjects. Seeking to bolster her ability to advance their own agenda for women, Goldberg soon sought congressional approval for elevating her post to the rank of assistant secretary. In arguing on behalf of this change, he wrote Senate Labor Committee chairman Lister Hill that "special attention and special emphasis will be required to plan programs relating to women workers as they enter the labor force in ever increasing numbers."[84]

The change in Peterson's status, Goldberg made clear, was intended to reflect the Labor Department's view that such workers were neither exceptional nor marginal to the economy as a whole. In his words, "Women have the same right to be in the labor force as men and to the same opportunities. We hope to enhance these opportunities through the new office which S. 1815 authorizes."[85] The bill soon went through, and thus eight months after assuming the directorship of the Women's Bureau, Peterson found herself the highest-ranking woman in the entire Kennedy administration.[86]

Goldberg and Peterson, endeavoring to mobilize women's groups in ways they viewed as constructive, suggested to Kennedy that he contain pressures for the ERA by creating a commission to examine the whole range of issues concerning women. Early in 1961, he signed an executive order that gave birth to the President's Commission on the Status of Women. Kennedy selected as the bulk of its members—in keeping with the advice he received from Goldberg and Peterson—those who shared their emphasis on aiding working- and lower-middle-class women. The commission's members were instructed to consider the ERA and other ideas and to come up with a program the administration could then present to Congress. The clear intention on the part of Goldberg, Peterson, and the president was to bury the ERA and develop instead a consensus among women's groups for legislation more in line with the administration's objectives.[87]

While the commission deliberated, Goldberg encouraged Peterson to come up with initiatives in that area. She favored first winning an equal pay law of the sort organized labor had been advocating since the mid-1950s.

In lobbying for the idea, Peterson found that the women's organizations composed predominantly of those with elite backgrounds offered no real help. Leading feminists of that stripe, such as the head of the National Woman's Party, Emma Guffy Miller, privately dismissed Peterson's project as "the so-called equal pay bill."[88] No doubt afraid that passing such a law would only dissipate support for the ERA, Miller and her cohorts offered only a hedged endorsement for equal pay legislation. The White House staff and many unions, albeit for somewhat different reasons, assumed much the same position but did not place any roadblocks in the bill's path. As Peterson recalled later, the only high-ranking administration official outside the Women's Bureau who really pushed for the idea was Goldberg. On the other side were business groups and at least one major union, which pressed for crippling amendments.[89]

Aware that the Labor Department's legislative liaison had little interest in the measure, Goldberg gave the Women's Bureau complete discretion in lobbying Congress on the bill's behalf, an unprecedented step, while confining his own role to advising Esther Peterson on how best to run that campaign. Although weakened substantially by conservatives' amendments, a narrowly tailored version of the measure did pass both houses of Congress in 1962. The Women's Bureau's quite sophisticated lobbying effort had born fruit, to the alarm of the NAM and the U.S. Chamber of Commerce. Applying the maximum amount of their formidable power, these groups succeeded in killing the bill at the conference stage. As in the case of bills aimed specifically at undermining the system of oppression based on race, the one major piece of proposed legislation intended to attack gender-based discrimination failed to emerge from the Eighty-seventh Congress.[90]

Unable to disturb gender-based discrimination outside the federal government, Goldberg was forced to settle, as in the area of race, merely for reform in it. In the spring of 1962 the President's Commission on the Status of Women had recommended that Kennedy issue an executive order banning sex discrimination in employment throughout the executive branch. Goldberg used that recommendation as the basis for suggesting to the president that he take such a step, which materialized in July 1962. The initial response was very modest, but the move betokened large changes. Thus, as in the area of race, through the end of 1962, the status quo, although increasingly under pressure, nonetheless remained essentially intact.[91]

The existing postwar New Deal thus endured during the Kennedy administration's first two years, despite pressure against it from increasingly restive business managers, as well as from some of those who had received a dispro-portionately small share of its benefits, namely, nonwhites and women. Dur-ing that time, Goldberg tried to bring about a renegotiation of this social bargain that preserved its gains for the working and lower middle classes while redefining it in ways that offered more to those who had received the least since its creation. The antirecession measures, efforts to minimize strikes, and initiatives against race- and gender-based discrimination formed only part of that larger endeavor.

Even more important was the work of the President's Advisory Committee on Labor–Management Policy, in which leading business managers, union chiefs, and several so-called public members deliberated how best to deal with the problems that had inspired the managerial revolt. Developments in that forum and in the steel industry, which stood at the center of the postwar order, offered the clearest indications of whether the effort to quash the rebellion would succeed. More than anything else, events there would deter-mine the future course of Goldberg's career.

II

Unlike much of the rest of the new administration's political and economic program, which was largely consistent with those of its two immediate prede-cessors, Kennedy's decision to establish Goldberg's proposed labor–manage-ment body marked a significant change in policy.

Even this plan, however, was not really a new idea. Other presidents had tried some form of it, but without much success. Truman's abortive labor–management conference of 1945 was the most notable precedent, but not the only one. In the last two years of the Eisenhower administration, some of his top aides had seriously considered something like the Goldberg proposal, urged on them by liberal Republican senator Jacob Javits of New York. Although Eisenhower did create a cabinet committee in 1959 headed by Richard Nixon to study the problems behind the managerial revolt, the presi-dent rejected Javits's broader scheme for a conference on this subject that would have brought together representatives from management, labor, and the federal government. When George Meany had made a similar suggestion one year later, it met with the same response. Apparently believing that the idea would be unworkable given the staunch business opposition to it, Eisenhower refused even to try. With Kennedy's victory over Nixon, how-ever, the plan would at last be put to the test.[92]

Goldberg had refined his own version of the idea somewhat since giving the speech that first proposed it. In August 1960 he had given another address on the same subject, calling for the creation of "a permanent National Council of Labor–Management Advisers," patterned loosely after the Council of Eco-nomic Advisers (CEA) and including its head as a member.[93]

In making the proposal, Goldberg understood that it would likely arouse fears among business executives and labor leaders. Both tended to suspect that any such group might acquire the power to establish a general wage-and-price policy for the economy as a whole and thereby define the content of collective bargaining agreements. This, in effect, would have meant the adoption of the corporatist approach prevalent in some Western European countries, most notably Sweden. Seeking to allay those worries, Goldberg told his listeners:

> The Council should "advise" and "recommend." It should not be a third legislative body. I am not proposing, nor would I support, any form of corporate state. The Council would not and should not have any political or legislative functions.
>
> The Council should not interfere with our established and tried methods of collective bargaining. It should not take over or infringe on the functions of either labor or management.
>
> I am suggesting an agency to assist in helping our free institutions work in these troubled times, not to displace them.[94]

In effect, Goldberg was telling business managers and union leaders, wary of where participation in such a group might lead, that the proposed council would attempt only to devise and then suggest solutions, leaving all parties free either to accept or reject them.[95]

He did, however, add cautiously that there was "one 'operational' role which the Council might very well be given," namely, resolving so-called national emergency disputes.[96] The inability of government mediators to resolve the 1959 steel strike indicated to Goldberg that some other way of handling such conflicts must be found. He told business and labor leaders, too, that this would be a more attractive alternative for all concerned than the compulsory arbitration law some were suggesting, and he emphasized that such a function would constitute only a sidelight to the council's primary activities.

These arguments helped persuade labor leaders such as George Meany and Walter Reuther to back the idea, but they were less effective with their managerial counterparts. The latter remained reluctant to participate precisely because they well knew that any policies Goldberg's group "recommended" would enjoy much greater legitimacy in the eyes of the wider public, and therefore be much harder to resist, than those put forward by organized labor alone. Business leaders, more confident than labor ones that they could get what they wanted unilaterally, or through the state via compulsory arbitration, thus remained much less willing to endorse Goldberg's proposal.[97]

In another move aimed at reassuring the plan's critics, Goldberg in his second speech had called for similar meetings in specific industries, conferences that would essentially replicate in miniature his proposed council. In that way, the larger group's proposals could be tailored to conditions existing in different areas of the economy. That was Goldberg's conception of the role to be played by the USA–Kaiser Steel long-range planning committee and the similar groups at the other major steel producers that the union had won through the 1959 strike. Although those smaller groups, like the larger one, would lack the power to command, Goldberg intended their recommendations to be influential in defining the terms of labor–management relationships throughout the country. Thus although "softer" and less "statist" than Swedish-style corporatism, there could be no mistaking the scheme's Scandinavian parentage.[98]

It was this revised plan that formed the basis for the President's Advisory Committee on Labor–Management Policy. Kennedy announced his intention early in December 1960 to create the group, and his February 16, 1961, executive order establishing it proved to be one of his administration's first major initiatives. Under Kennedy's order, the committee was to be composed of seven representatives each from labor and management, along with seven so-called public members, Goldberg, Luther Hodges, and five others drawn from the ranks of economists and industrial relations experts. In addition, CEA member Kermit Gordon was to join the group as liaison between those two bodies.

The committee was charged with examining the emergency disputes procedures to which Goldberg had referred in his speech the previous August, as well as determining how best to achieve wage-and-price stability, cushion workers against the effects of automation, and improve worker productivity.[99]

Although not quite the council Goldberg had proposed, the committee would study this idea and try to develop a consensus in favor of its adoption. The committee's more limited mandate stemmed in part from the Council of Economic Advisers' strong objections to giving the new group more power. Fearful that Goldberg's creation would usurp the CEA's own function, Kennedy's top economic advisers had succeeded in narrowing somewhat the scope of the executive order that created it.

Goldberg, however, managed to preserve the committee's authority to consider a very wide range of subjects. In theory confined to discussing specific industrial relations issues such as automation, retraining, collective bargaining, and the effect of American wages on exports, the committee would, at Goldberg's direction, consider those topics in the broadest possible fashion. As he wrote Willard Wirtz in preparing the agenda, the first topic, automation, should be considered "in the context of the entire employment situation. This will enable the members of the Committee to deal with the question of how we achieve maximum employment in light of the entire economic situation and in view of increasing automation."[100]

In addition to intruding on the CEA's turf, the group's mandate overlapped as well with that of the Business Advisory Council (BAC) to the Commerce Department. Established by Roosevelt in 1933, this body of senior corporation executives, under Eisenhower in particular, had exercised a great deal of influence over the federal government's political and economic policies. In so doing, the BAC had functioned in a highly autonomous and secretive manner, which Kennedy disliked. The group contained no small businessmen, a source of continuing irritation to them and to Luther Hodges, who sympathized with the small-business perspective.

Even more important to Goldberg and his colleagues in the labor movement, both the Commerce and Labor Departments under Eisenhower had steadfastly refused to establish a parallel labor advisory council. This lack of symmetrical participation indicated the limits of labor's power in the postwar order, its failure to achieve a real partnership with management in decision making. In winning the creation of a Labor–Management Advisory Committee that soon eclipsed the BAC, Goldberg was attempting to move closer toward that elusive goal.[101]

He used great care in selecting the committee's members, striving to find ones who would command real influence in their respective constituencies but not take positions so rigid as to preclude serious negotiations. From business circles Goldberg chose Elliott Bell, the editor and publisher of *Business Week*, chief executive officers Joseph Block of Inland Steel; Henry Ford II of Ford Motors; John Franklin of U.S. Lines Company; Spencer Love of Burlington Industries, a southern textiles firm; Richard Reynolds of Reynolds Metals; and Thomas J. Watson Jr. of IBM, the newly elected vice-chairman of the BAC. All of these men came from the center of the business community, the realists most identified with the postwar New Deal. Sensitive to criticism that the group did not represent an exact cross section of business leaders, Goldberg emphasized publicly that each member would reflect business leaders' views as a whole, rather than merely speak for the particular industry in which he worked. A clever though not entirely accurate argument, it served nonetheless to defuse the only major complaint about his selections.[102]

On the whole, the group was an impressive one, especially because all its members enjoyed an unusually large degree of influence in their respective enterprises. This reflected Goldberg's goal of getting management members who could speak with authority, who in effect carried enough weight in their own firms to make any deal they negotiated stick.

But missing from the group were representatives of the nation's core industrial firms, such as U.S. Steel, General Electric, and General Motors. The most conspicuous omission among the three was that of Roger Blough, who had recently been chosen BAC chairman. Goldberg had purposely left out him and his counterparts at those other two firms, thanks to the leading roles they all had played in the managerial revolt. Rather than trying to bargain directly with men who had taken such unyielding positions, Goldberg preferred to work with a group of business realists he believed was more open to making a deal. Whether they could persuade their more influential colleagues to accept it was a question with which Goldberg did not concern himself at that stage. For the moment he focused on the first step, which was to achieve such a social bargain.[103]

This same concern informed Goldberg's choices for the committee's labor delegation. In addition to George Meany and Walter Reuther, who along with Goldberg himself had been the movement's most important spokesmen since the late 1940s, he picked David McDonald; the ILGWU's president David Dubinsky; George Harrison, who headed the most powerful railway union; Electrical Workers president Joseph Keenan, whose union belonged to the AFL–CIO's influential building trades department; and Thomas Kennedy, John L. Lewis's handpicked successor as president of the UMW. More so than the management team, the labor group reflected the range of viewpoints in its constituency. Goldberg's selections included three from the AFL and two from the CIO wings, as well as a couple from major unions outside the federation's ranks.

As a whole, the seven represented the three major factions in the American labor movement, its social democratic, center, and traditional AFL blocs. And like their managerial counterparts, those seven labor leaders exercised, with the notable—and, given Goldberg's role, irrelevant—exception of David McDonald, a great deal of power in their respective organizations.[104]

Even the labor delegation, however, contained some glaring omissions. The two most apparent were the failure to represent either the Teamsters, the country's largest union, or the powerful Carpenters. Goldberg lacked confidence that the leaders of either would help negotiate any settlement that called for sacrifices from both sides. More specifically, both unions had shown little interest in confining their wage demands to those justified by increased productivity, which Goldberg saw as crucial to eliminating the related inflation and balance-of-payments problems. Once again, however, he preferred to choose representatives who would make a serious effort to reach a consensus before facing the difficult task of persuading their more recalcitrant brethren to accept it.[105]

The first two of the so-called public members had been designated by the executive order and were the secretaries of labor and commerce, who would rotate annually the committee's chairmanship. Goldberg's five other choices, like his labor ones, reflected an effort to represent the major factions in their constituency. Those selected were Arthur Burns, CEA chairman during Eisenhower's first presidential term and thereafter president of the National Bureau of Economic Research; David Cole, a leading arbitrator; Clark Kerr, president of the University of California; Ralph McGill, publisher of the *Atlanta Constitution*; and George Taylor, one of the most distinguished figures in the industrial relations community. Burns and Kerr tended to sympathize more with the managerial perspective, whereas Cole and Taylor sided more often with labor. McGill enjoyed a good relationship with both, thereby producing exactly the kind of balance among the public members and, therefore in the committee as a whole, that Goldberg had intended.[106]

The first meeting of the new group took place on March 21, 1961, in the cabinet room of the White House. Goldberg had chosen that site both to convey the committee's status and to reflect his own sense of its real function, that is, the administration's chief source of proposals for its domestic political and economic program. Present at the opening of the first session were both Kennedy and Johnson, a further reminder of the group's importance to their administration.

Goldberg played the leading role in addressing the first order of business, which was to lay down the ground rules for the committee's deliberations. At his suggestion, its members agreed—in a key move—to require unanimity for any recommendations they might make. Goldberg also emphasized that members would not be expected to submerge their own views in debating matters of policy, that the committee would not interfere with private collective bargaining, that opportunities for informal, off-the-record exchanges would be provided, and that the committee faced no specific deadlines, which would have placed limits on the time allowed for its deliberations. Having thereby reassured the group's somewhat skittish management members, Goldberg then yielded the floor to Walter Heller, Robert McNamara, Douglas Dillon, and Luther Hodges. Each of them spoke for about thirty minutes and then took questions in their respective areas of expertise. With the conclusion of that orientation program, the meeting adjourned.[107]

The next two sessions featured similarly general discussion. The first, which took place on May 1, dealt with the issue of automation-induced unemployment. The committee heard three presentations on that subject from the government, management, and labor perspectives, which led in turn to a meandering debate most notable for the divisions it revealed between the group's two leading labor representatives. Walter Reuther argued that market forces alone could not eliminate the long-term unemployment that had emerged in the wake of the 1957/58 recession. George Meany countered by saying that the key to solving all the various problems facing the workforce was to increase the rate of economic growth, rather than to focus on the problems of particular subsets of the unemployed.[108]

This difference of opinion led Clark Kerr to suggest that the committee study Sweden's successful experience in addressing the issue, a proposal Reuther echoed. Sweden's system of retraining and relocating workers displaced by the introduction of new technology struck the labor members as the best way to achieve automation's advantages while cushioning workers against its adverse effects. The enthusiasm among the labor and public members for retraining schemes as a solution for unemployment met, however, with some skepticism from the management representatives. IBM's Thomas Watson Jr. spoke for them when he cautioned that a lack of jobs, rather than the need for training, constituted the most basic problem that workers faced.[109]

Seeking to focus future discussions, Goldberg suggested that the group consider the effect of U.S. wages and prices on foreign competition at the upcoming June session, collective bargaining and industrial peace in July, and then ways to improve living standards and productivity in August. He also advocated calling a White House conference in the fall to address these same issues, in effect broadening the talks by bringing in larger teams of representatives from management and labor. The other members of the committee agreed to his first suggestion, but not to the second. They ruled out holding a conference until the committee had reached some specific conclusions, which could then be offered to the larger body for its own consideration. Without some initial agreement among the committee's own members, such a conference would, they believed, lead nowhere.[110]

The next session, ostensibly devoted to the first of Goldberg's three suggested topics, quickly demonstrated the impossibility of attempting to advance toward agreement without greater structure. The discussion there revolved around the issues of economic growth and the failure of the nation's economy to rebound quickly from the 1960/61 recession, rather than the subject Goldberg had mentioned a month earlier. The failure to examine how wage-and-price inflation affected foreign competition, the topic officially on the agenda, stemmed in part from Kennedy's desire to obtain the committee's endorsement of his antirecession program.

Also responsible were the very general briefing papers that CEA chairman Walter Heller had sent to committee members shortly before the meeting. The papers examined the issue of wages and prices in Heller's characteristically discursive fashion, concluding that the administration intended to bring down unemployment to an official rate of 4 percent and to achieve an average annual economic growth rate of 3.5 percent.[111]

Those twin objectives drew a heated rejoinder from Walter Reuther. He pointed out that societies in northern and western Europe had exceeded both of those targets, and he went on to complain that Heller's prescription for improving growth focused too much on increasing capital spending, rather than expanding consumer purchasing power. Reuther proceeded next to denounce the complacent attitude toward the recession implied by Kennedy's mild legislative program to combat it. Angry that Heller was apparently satisfied to let workers assume most of the hardships in bringing down inflation, Reuther told his colleagues that "blue collar workers have been carrying the main burden of depressions . . . and they are not willing to continue to bear this burden."[112] Heller then backed off a bit, stressing that these goals were only interim ones, but the CEA chairman did not go along with Reuther's call for measures that would increase consumer demand.[113]

When Goldberg attempted to obtain the committee's written endorsement of the administration's economic goals, some of the group's other leading members balked as well. Both Joseph Block and Ralph McGill indicated that they opposed issuing any statement that would appear to suggest real agreement when none as yet existed. Reuther chimed in, suggesting that the committee would achieve more by exploring fewer topics in greater detail, rather than the broad proposals the CEA papers had contained. This complaint drew a response from Goldberg, who was growing frustrated with the difficulty of addressing individually the central problems confronting the postwar order. He pointed out that "all of these problems are interrelated and . . . the Committee cannot break out a particular topic without considering its relationship to other topics." By the end of the session, the committee had agreed only that it supported "in principle" the idea of a broad worker-retraining program as one way to deal with long-term unemployment following from technological change.[114]

These meager results led Goldberg to propose a major change in its procedures at the committee's next meeting. Rather than address specific subjects in the entire committee, Goldberg suggested that it create five topical subcommittees, each to be chaired by a "public" representative, as follows: free and responsible collective bargaining and industrial peace: David Cole; economic growth and unemployment: Ralph McGill; automation, technological advance, industrial productivity, and higher standards of living: Clark Kerr;

policies designed to ensure that American products are competitive in world markets: Arthur Burns; and sound wage-and-price policies: George Taylor. Each group would, Goldberg continued, produce a working paper for the full committee's consideration, which it in turn would revise and then submit to the president. Goldberg and Hodges would serve on each of the five subcommittees, which would also contain equal numbers of labor and management members. After some debate about who should be assigned to the five groups, the full committee accepted Goldberg's proposal, a decision that promised to focus future discussions.[115]

With that matter out of the way, Goldberg sat back and let the group's other members debate the issue of wage-and-price policy, easily the most explosive subject on its agenda. The discussion grew out of a working paper prepared by the staffs of the Commerce and Labor Departments and that of the CEA.

Walter Reuther led off by attacking the paper as biased, implying, as it did, that wage increases constituted the root cause of inflation and the related balance-of-payments problem. The real culprit, Reuther argued, was managers' exportation of American capital abroad. He then went on to propose the creation of a tripartite body that could hold hearings on key wage-and-price changes. The group, Reuther said, should not be empowered to set wages or prices, but it should have the authority to compel managers and union leaders to defend their decisions in those areas and to mobilize public opinion behind a "sound" policy with respect to wages, prices, and profits. The alternative, he suggested, would likely be a compulsory government scheme aimed at achieving the same result.[116]

Reuther's comments elicited strong resistance from the committee's management members. Spencer Love called capital flight "inevitable," a sentiment shared by his fellow business executives in the group.[117] Implicit in their view was an understanding that the U.S. government, unlike its Western European counterparts, lacked the power to stop capital movements and an assumption that American managers would never agree to grant the federal government such authority. Although some management members, such as Love, Joseph Block, and Thomas Watson Jr., were willing to consider a more limited version of Reuther's proposed public agency, Henry Ford II firmly opposed the idea in any form whatsoever. He blasted Reuther's proposal, saying that "the proper place to set prices was the market place" and that the "government should stay out of labor–management relationships."[118] Ford also added that the union exemption from the antitrust laws was unfair, implying that the root cause of inflation was excessive union power, which the Sherman Act should be used to reduce.[119]

Meany weighed in at that point, saying that salary costs as a percentage of all employee compensation had risen from 23 percent in 1953 to 33 percent in 1958, whereas wages had fallen from 72.9 percent to 66.7 percent in that same period. Thus, he suggested, the rise in salaries was contributing more to overall inflation than was the increase in wages paid to unionized workers. Meany's remarks eventually drew a sharp retort from Joseph Block, who declared that "salaries . . . follow wages, up to the highest executive level."[120]

Both men were right. Meany was arguing, in effect, that managers were refusing to accept what organized labor believed to be its proper share of industry income. Instead, they had simply increased salaries in a effort to restore what in their view was the proper ratio between the incomes earned by workers and managerial employees. That, and the replacement of the least-skilled workers with machines, explained the rising share of employment costs devoted to salaries. Block, for his part, assumed that labor's efforts to win the income share it saw as fair were illegitimate and therefore constituted the real root of inflation. The differences between Meany and Block highlighted the central problem, that is, the lack of any real consensus between labor and management on the respective shares of industry income to which each was entitled.

The productivity formula—ostensibly the guide to making that allocation—had proved difficult to apply in practice, partly because of the problems associated with measuring it accurately. The committee members who supported the proposal to create a new public agency believed that helping develop such information should be the new entity's primary purpose. In Thomas Watson Jr.'s formulation, such an agency should "prepare statistics on foreign competition, finance, productivity, etc., and . . . make the data available for general use, as, for example, in wage negotiations."[121] Most committee members agreed on that at least, accepting David Cole's conclusion that the emergency boards authorized by Taft–Hartley could not play such a role. In his experience, Cole said, "an emergency board under the Taft–Hartley Act cannot be concerned with over-all policies because its functions are extremely limited and it is essentially an impotent instrument."[122]

The unanimity broke down, however, when they turned to debating the degree to which such an agency should be involved in specific collective bargaining disputes. Whether such an entity should operate publicly provoked sharp disagreement, as did the question of whether it should evaluate union contracts or price increases, either before or after they became final. Cole called for combining Reuther's suggestion for creating an agency that held public hearings with Watson's proposal that its primary function be limited to gathering data and offering it to the parties. The value of public hearings, he suggested, would be to place pressure on the parties to accept a settlement in the interest of the country as a whole. An agency with those powers, Cole continued, working in tandem with labor–management committees of the sort recently created in the steel industry, could lead to collective bargaining that was informed by the needs of the larger public. This combination of ideas was essentially what Goldberg saw as the solution to the crisis that threatened the postwar order.[123]

Although everyone on the committee supported parts of this plan, some aspects drew strong criticism. Most members seemed to favor allowing such an agency to hold public hearings, but Henry Ford II opposed the idea. Obliged to leave the meeting early, Ford had his views articulated by his subordinate, Theodore Yntema, who noted the possibility that "public hearings would become converted into a political circus," meaning that those participating would fail to act responsibly and instead simply try to bolster their standing with their respective constituencies. When Goldberg observed that "there are various types of hearings and . . . they would not necessarily be political in nature," Yntema replied that "if the fact-finding body were Congressional in character, it would be political in nature. . . . facts don't mean anything by themselves and . . . criteria are needed for interpreting the facts, which the public cannot master." In the last analysis, he concluded, giving such an agency the power to hold public hearings meant that "fact-finding may degenerate into propaganda."[124]

The second issue—whether to allow such an agency to become involved in disputes affecting wages and prices before such struggles culminated in specific decisions—provoked an equally vigorous debate. The "public" members of the committee and Walter Reuther expressed support for that idea, as did George Meany, albeit more cautiously. The management members, however, disagreed. The most that they would consider was to allow such an agency a role after the fact. Thomas Watson Jr., the management member seemingly most open to the whole agency idea, expressed their view that

> it would not be practical to have a public body make this [kind of] review before the negotiations are concluded but . . . such a review might be appropriate after wage settlements are made, with the thought that the agency would bring public opinion to bear on the problem as it developed out of review of key settlements.[125]

The impracticality of prior review stemmed, Watson implied, from business managers' unwillingness to yield any more of their managerial prerogatives to the government.

This same obstacle led to a dispute over how such an agency should acquire the data it needed to play even the more modest role management members contemplated for it. Reuther argued that a voluntary system of reporting, such as that used by the Bureau of Labor Statistics, would be inadequate because some firms would simply refuse to provide reliable information. For that reason, he favored giving the proposed agency the authority to force the release of such information to it. Although a few of the "public" members appeared receptive to that proposal, the management members refrained even from discussing it. They understood how resistant their constituency would be to that idea. To yield control over information was to give up power, something most business managers believed they had already done all too often since the early 1930s. The meeting thus ended inconclusively, with members breaking up into their respective subcommittees for detailed discussions.[126]

For the next three months, they debated specific proposals, whose limits had been decided by the full committee's initial talks. In carrying out their tasks, the subcommittees would, Goldberg had explained, be able to draw on the government's resources. He arranged to provide consulting services, data, and any other assistance they deemed necessary. During that same summer, he also invited twenty leading industrial relations experts to review the existing national emergency disputes machinery, to see what ideas those most experienced in resolving such conflicts might suggest.[127]

In the interim, Goldberg also educated himself much more thoroughly about the Swedish model of industrial relations, which appeared to offer the best hope for eliminating the problems that increasingly threatened the postwar social contract. His learning process had begun in the spring of 1961, when Goldberg started communicating with Swedish government and trade union officials. In April of that year he had written to the head of the Swedish Labor Market Board requesting information about its system for retraining and relocating workers displaced by technological innovation. At Goldberg's suggestion, the AFL–CIO's Industrial Union Department also undertook a study of the Swedish system, the results of which had been sent to him two months earlier.[128]

Goldberg's inquiries generated enthusiasm in Sweden for his policies and an invitation to visit from its prime minister. On August 21, 1961, Goldberg formally accepted the offer and scheduled a three-day trip for the following month. In preparing for that visit, Goldberg asked Esther Peterson, familiar with the Swedish language from having spent several years living in that country, to prepare translations of a few key phrases. Among them were "We think much of Sweden in America" and "We have much to learn from you," expressions that indicated the motivation behind the whole excursion.[129]

Goldberg, accompanied by his wife, son, Labor Department aides Peterson and Seymour Wolfbein, and a press officer, arrived in Stockholm on September 22. Ever conscious of the symbolic, Goldberg chose to fly coach class, a gesture that won him applause in the Swedish press. His elaboration on the themes contained in his handful of Swedish phrases delighted Goldberg's hosts, unaccustomed to hearing American government officials express such opinions. While in Sweden he also delivered an address on American economic policy, toured employment and retraining facilities, and discussed the Swedish approach to unemployment with the heads of that country's labor and management organizations. The trip proved an enormous success from the standpoint of U.S.–Swedish relations, as the American ambassador to Stockholm soon reported to the State Department. It gave Goldberg, too, a clearer understanding of both the origins and workings of the Swedish system. Buoyed by his visit, he returned home to face the difficult challenge of persuading Americans to emulate that model.[130]

With that objective in mind, Goldberg continued his communications with Swedish officials. In October 1961 he invited Torsten Nilsson, Sweden's minister of social affairs, to visit the United States. Goldberg's rationale for the trip, as he explained in his letter of invitation, was that "there should be a mutual benefit in continuing this intellectual and personal interchange between us, since many of the problems in the labor and social affairs field are similar in our two countries."[131]

Intending to visit Sweden again, so as to keep the dialogue going, Goldberg also stayed in touch with the American ambassador there. The latter wrote Goldberg that same month, suggesting that he also invite some Swedish labor and management representatives to visit the United States, where they could meet with their American counterparts. Goldberg liked the idea but decided to wait until the Advisory Committee on Labor–Management Policy had reached the point at which such a visit would do the most good.[132]

Discussions in that group resumed in October 1961, but progress remained slow. The principal item of business at that month's meeting was to discuss the papers prepared by the first and third subcommittees, which dealt with collective bargaining and automation, respectively. Unlike the other three subcommittees, which had made little headway, these two had managed to produce first drafts of their reports. Achievements in themselves, the drafts nonetheless clearly pleased neither the labor nor the management representatives very much.[133]

The labor members objected particularly to the automation subcommittee's dismissal of labor's proposal for a shorter workweek. The report's authors concluded that any such step—given its potential effect of reducing overall industrial production—would have to wait until the cold war came to an end. To reduce hours without cutting workers' incomes would also have implied increasing real wage costs by more than the growth in worker productivity, an idea Goldberg and others on the subcommittee opposed. That kind of increase in workers' incomes would only make worse the problems stemming from foreign competition.

Labor leaders, however, found these arguments less than persuasive. They favored moving very gradually toward a shorter week, an approach that would minimize the risks of reducing overall industrial production and encouraging imports. The military necessity argument bothered them even more than the one related to foreign competition. David McDonald explained why when he noted that the conflict between the United States and the Soviet Union could last a lifetime, and thus to link the shorter workweek idea to so-called national security concerns would be to defer its adoption indefinitely.[134]

The committee's management members also showed displeasure with the automation subcommittee's report. Joseph Block complained that the tenor of the document was too negative, that technological innovation was not solely responsible for unemployment, that in the long run those workers displaced by automation did find new jobs, and thus that he opposed the report's recommendation for public-works projects to employ workers idled for that reason. Henry Ford II disagreed even more vehemently with the subcommittee's draft, calling it "unacceptable . . . in its present form."[135] He objected to any suggestion that a shorter workweek might ever be desirable and demanded that the approximate cost of any new programs be calculated before receiving the committee's endorsement. When Richard Reynolds argued that the committee should make more specific suggestions for ways to reduce unemployment, Spencer Love responded by saying that "the report probably goes as far as it can go in expressing a consensus and . . . in order to achieve such a consensus it may be necessary to avoid specifics."[136]

"Public" member Arthur Burns had underscored that problem earlier by criticizing the report's lack of focus. Burns had stated that the report should make clear that it proposed remedies only for unemployment growing out of technological change, rather than joblessness more generally, and that the recommended measures were aimed at a long-term solution, as opposed merely to fighting the present recession.[137]

Love's and Burns's remarks revealed the lack of a genuine consensus between management and labor, save for vague endorsements of retraining schemes and the need for faster economic growth. Even the basic question of whether automation was desirable remained open, as the remarks by Arthur Burns and railway union leader George Harrison indicated. Burns attacked the draft report for failing to state clearly that its authors saw technological innovation as beneficial and in need of acceleration. Harrison challenged Burns's view, saying that there should be more planning in advance of automation and calling it "a cancer in certain areas."[138] Thomas Watson Jr. noted in response that all members of the automation subcommittee had agreed on the desirability of that process but the larger group clearly did not.[139]

The other draft report, which dealt with collective bargaining, elicited even stronger objections. Unlike the automation report, the one on collective bargaining contained several dissenting statements, pointing to the failure of even the subcommittee's members to reach a consensus. The dissents, chairman David Cole reported, "stemmed from a general fear of government intervention, either on the theory that it would lead to the demise of collective bargaining or that it would cause inflationary settlements."[140] Labor's fear of compulsory arbitration and management's concern over government pressure to grant wage increases had inclined representatives of both to oppose greater state supervision of the labor–management relationship.[141]

Regarding the issue as crucial, Goldberg indicated that the draft report needed first a general statement defining the appropriate roles for management, labor, and the government in the collective bargaining process before proceeding to specific proposals. In that way he hoped to quiet fears among the labor and management representatives, especially the latter. But the business executives on the committee, principally Joseph Block and Henry Ford II, would not be mollified so easily. Block called for revising the report to make clear that "the function of government is to point the way, to give general guidelines for private behavior, and not to issue orders."[142]

Even that limited endorsement of greater government activity drew criticism from Henry Ford II. Having by this point clearly assumed the role of spokesman for the more rigid business realists excluded from the committee, Ford stated that "the report appeared . . . to call for substantial government intervention and that he is opposed to government intervention of any type except for mediation."[143] Next he listed his specific objections to the report's endorsement of greater government fact-finding in advance of collective bargaining disputes. More frequent intervention prior to strikes, Ford pointed out, would increase the government's influence over the terms reached in what was supposed to be a collective bargaining system free of government coercion. By introducing larger considerations of prices and profits into such negotiations, he said, the government would force managers to release confidential information, thereby narrowing the scope of management "rights." The net effect of increased intervention, Ford concluded, would be "higher wages and therefore more inflation," the exact opposite of what the committee intended.[144]

Arthur Burns agreed with most of those objections and added some of his own. By far the most important was his complaint that the report gave the impression that the president had the authority to intervene in most major collective bargaining disputes. Burns urged that the report recommend such intervention only in those instances that truly constituted a national emergency. Goldberg dismissed the argument, saying that the president already had that power, given the demonstrated willingness of the courts to interpret broadly the relevant Taft–Hartley provision. The objection remained important, nonetheless, because Burns implied that the federal government was attempting to increase unilaterally the scope of its authority to supervise labor–management relationships, a potentially explosive issue.[145]

More than anything else, Ford's and Burns's objections signaled the lack of any real basis for an agreement between organized labor and the leading business realists. Thomas Watson Jr. hinted at that when he noted that the objections raised were disappointing precisely because those making them offered no alternatives. Although the committee proceeded next to debate whether government-sponsored tripartite boards should be used more frequently to head off strikes in key industries, this discussion also failed to produce a consensus. The most members could agree on was that the two subcommittees should prepare second drafts that would satisfy those who had raised objections.[146]

The futility of this assignment became apparent during the committee's final meeting of the year. There Henry Ford II, having read the revised automation report, urged that members of the committee be allowed to add their dissenting opinions to it. Ford's suggestion provoked a lively discussion, because everyone present understood that to include dissents — in effect overturning the earlier decision to require unanimity in making recommendations — was to acknowledge the committee's failure to reach a genuine consensus. After listening to the arguments on both sides and recognizing the reality of continuing divisions, Goldberg announced that Ford's proposal would be adopted and asked members to submit all such statements before the group's next meeting.[147]

The committee then proceeded to discuss the revised version of the automation report, a process that underscored the underlying disunity. Those present did agree to a number of changes, thereby giving rise to a sense of progress. In almost every instance, however, the revisions only watered down the existing language so as to broaden support for the report. Having thereby traded away much of the draft report's specificity in the hope of minimizing the number of dissenting statements, the committee turned over the draft to

Goldberg. He promised to incorporate the new suggestions and circulate the result before the committee's next session.[148]

In the interim, dissents arrived in his office from the labor members of the committee, Henry Ford II, and Arthur Burns. The labor group, led by George Meany, objected to the automation report's rejection of movement toward a shorter workweek as one way of addressing technologically created unemployment. This single labor complaint, though significant, did not pose a major obstacle, because even union leaders agreed that their solution was a long-term one, which could be achieved only gradually. More troubling were the lengthy dissents from Ford and Burns, which essentially restated their earlier objections.

These memoranda arrived at the Labor Department during Goldberg's absence, where they received Willard Wirtz's careful scrutiny. He wrote Goldberg immediately thereafter:

> I suspect that it will be exceedingly difficult to get either of them to retreat very far from these positions. . . . My own thought, in which [AFL–CIO operative] Stanley [Ruttenberg] concurs, is that this isn't so bad—so long as it doesn't mean a lot of other separate statements. Stanley feels confident that he can keep this from happening as far as the labor people are concerned. There seems to me good reason to believe that we can take care of it on the other two sides.[149]

Thus by January the watered-down automation report was ready for presentation to the president, but only because the labor and management members unhappy with it had been allowed to add their various dissents. For the committee's next session, Goldberg scheduled three items of business: a briefing by Douglas Dillon on the balance-of-payments problem, a meeting with Kennedy to deliver formally the automation report, and further group discussion of the collective bargaining report.

When he opened the two-day session on January 11, 1962, Goldberg tried to revive a sense of urgency and patriotism among the members of the committee, whose earlier willingness to strike a deal appeared to be eroding. Reminding them that the committee owed its existence to the problems and tensions that had arisen over the past few years, he pointed out that it was a symbol of national unity. Hodges echoed those sentiments, but the two men's exhortations failed to budge the group's more rigid members.[150]

This fact became evident during its discussion of the revised collective bargaining report. Most of the document dealt with ways to head off major strikes, either by means of government fact-finding during contract talks themselves or through greater use of government mediation boards and other tools aimed at persuading parties to accept a "fair" settlement if negotiations reached an impasse. With the memory of the 1959 steel strike still fairly fresh and aware that the industry's master contract would expire in less than six months, the report's authors had attempted to come up with government techniques more effective than those that had been used during the previous steel dispute. Although everyone on the committee recognized the need to prevent any more such strikes, in steel or other industries, they could not agree on alternative solutions.[151]

The inability to achieve a real meeting of the minds stemmed largely from managerial hostility to expanding the government's role beyond mediation. This opposition manifested itself in a series of clarifying amendments that the management members offered to the report's language, ones that removed what few teeth it still had left. Joseph Block demanded the addition of a general statement that the committee viewed free collective bargaining as the best system, a clear signal that he opposed moving to a substantially more statist one. Richard Reynolds insisted that the report make clear that it did not endorse further limiting managers' power to lock out employees. In effect, he was demanding that the report acknowledge that employers should retain the power to provoke strikes if bargaining reached an impasse. Reynolds also requested the insertion of passages stating that fact-finding boards should be confined to examining those topics that both labor and management deemed relevant, that the use of government intervention should be viewed as an extraordinary move rather than a routine one, and that the courts retained the authority to review any presidential determination that a strike gave rise to a national emergency. The last item was important because it reflected management's opposition to giving the executive branch of the federal government more authority to resolve the vast majority of labor–management conflicts. Reynolds finished by also urging that the group delete the section that endorsed giving fact-finding boards the power to make nonbinding recommendations, calling it "a move in the direction of compulsory arbitration."[152]

After Reynolds's remarks came those of Henry Ford II, who said that his earlier objections still stood, a one–two managerial punch that deeply disappointed labor members of the committee. George Meany complained that the report failed to address directly and clearly whether the injunction should be an appropriate response to national emergency disputes or to indicate that giving the president other ways to resolve such matters would not deprive either labor or management of the right to judicial review. Walter Reuther went even further, saying that the revised report was worse than the earlier one because it failed to state explicitly that the president should be given a variety of alternatives to the Taft–Hartley injunction procedure.[153]

Arthur Burns spoke out next, attacking the wording of the section that discussed how the president should constitute government mediation boards. Subcommittee chairman David Cole, attempting to reconcile all the various points of view on this touchy subject, proposed a vague statement that emergency dispute boards be established as the president "may consider best."[154] Burns argued that the Federal Mediation and Conciliation Service should be used in all except "very exceptional cases" and that its director, rather than the secretary of labor, should suggest the members of such boards. This proposal reflected a desire to keep such entities as "nonpartisan" as possible, further limiting the president's power to push a settlement that he viewed as appropriate.[155]

The meeting's other business reflected these same deep divisions. When presenting the automation report, formally entitled "The Benefits and Problems Incident to Automation and Other Technological Advances," to President Kennedy, the committee debated its findings with him. Kennedy questioned Ford and Burns at length, correctly perceiving that their dissents were the most damaging to his administration's quest for a consensual solution to one of the problems behind the managerial revolt. The two men did make their views clear to him but could only agree to disagree.

After the session, Ford signaled his unhappiness with the report's findings to the reporters present, a move that deeply disturbed Thomas Watson Jr. When the committee resumed its meeting the following day, Watson asked for the floor and then made a personal plea that all members refrain from such behavior, which, he said, "would make constructive discussions in the Committee itself more difficult."156 Watson's admonition did prompt an exchange that helped clear the air but failed to bring about any lasting change in Ford's basic outlook.157

The committee then returned to discussing the proposed collective bargaining report. Trying to breath new life into what seemed a flagging enterprise, David McDonald, Joseph Block, Clark Kerr, Walter Reuther, George Taylor, and Arthur Burns all reiterated their belief that in the future labor and management must place much greater emphasis on promoting the general public interest rather than those of the specific parties at the bargaining table. Although there was a genuine consensus in the committee in favor of that general sentiment, meaning that individual corporations and unions should — when making decisions about wages, prices, profits, and technological innovation — seek to do what would strengthen and preserve the postwar New Deal rather than simply pursue their own selfish advantage, there was no real agreement on how to do so. Goldberg emphasized that government supervision of such disputes, particularly as a fact-finder, was the key and suggested that the committee might benefit from learning more about the Swedish industrial relations systems, in which the government played that role. For that reason, he said, he had invited the heads of the Swedish employer and labor federations to meet with the committee later that year.158

The momentary sensation of widespread agreement created by these general remarks soon vanished, however, when the committee returned to discussing the specific provisions of the revised collective bargaining report. Although the group agreed that it should reaffirm the right of employers to lock out employees, the committee members failed to reach a consensus on the critical issue of how to define that term. A similarly inconclusive discussion followed over what kinds of strikes could properly be considered national emergency disputes. Debate over whether to endorse partial operation of struck industries that produced material deemed vital to the national economy also led nowhere. An important issue precisely because such a procedure promised to undercut the strike weapon, the committee concluded only that partial operation appeared practical in some situations but not in others. The members did agree that no government board should be given the power to dictate a settlement, but beyond that, they remained divided over alternative procedures. Having offered only that murky "guidance," the committee asked David Cole to try his hand at yet another draft. The group then adjourned, planning to take up other business at future meetings until Cole completed his revisions of the collective bargaining report.[159]

Goldberg opened the committee's next session, which took place on February 6, 1962, by passing out copies of a draft letter to the president, calling on him to sponsor a national economic conference. It would be attended, Goldberg's letter suggested, by labor, management, and industrial relations experts, who would examine the specific automation, collective bargaining, and economic growth issues with which the committee had been wrestling for almost a year. Having raised the idea at the last meeting and won the committee's consent to prepare such a draft, Goldberg had decided that the time had come to push hard for its acceptance. Apparently believing that calling such a conference might restore the group's fading sense of momentum, Goldberg thus offered his letter for the committee's endorsement.[160]

Henry Ford II, aware that the steel negotiations would likely be going on at the same time, opposed Goldberg's proposal on the ground that the conferees' recommendations might interfere with collective bargaining. Ford's comments drew a sharp retort from Goldberg, who pointed out that the purpose of such a conference would be to protect collective bargaining by offering the parties to specific negotiations some guidance in achieving an agreement. Goldberg pushed hard at the meeting for the idea and thereby won the committee's endorsement for it. Over Ford's lone dissent, the group agreed to send a letter to Kennedy asking him to convene such a meeting. In deference to the concerns Ford had raised, the committee voted to delete the references to specific subjects from Goldberg's earlier draft and to revise it to show that the purpose of the conference was to exchange ideas rather than to intrude on what was called "private decision making."[161] Once again, the committee had achieved something approaching consensus, but only by trading away the specificity that gave the idea most of its real value.

With that matter out of the way, the committee turned to considering the draft report of the fifth subcommittee, which dealt with wage-and-price policies. After some discussion, the committee agreed to add a statement explicitly rejecting the use in all circumstances of both compulsory arbitration and wage-and-price controls. The new passage stated that neither solution was acceptable, even in view of the inflation and related problems of the 1956–58 period. The committee's decision underscored the only real consensus in the area of wages and prices, which was opposition to government coercion. On that both Henry Ford II and George Meany could agree, although neither offered any constructive alternatives.[162]

The group weakened the draft report still further by amending two of its key passages. First came changes in the report's language that called for relating long-term productivity and wage increases in the economy as a whole to each other. The group qualified that statement, adding, "This should be a factor among others and the parties must adapt it to the particular circumstances of each bargaining situation," essentially retreating from the earlier goal of defining a more uniform wage policy. This revision was followed by another stating the committee's belief that a policy of voluntarism would eventually eliminate wage-and-price inflation. The group thereby signaled that it had backed away from even suggesting that the government's role in preventing those problems should be increased permanently.[163]

As damaging as those revisions were, even worse was the failure to reach any consensus on either the need for public hearings to review wage-and-price decisions or whether the antitrust laws should be used to reduce union power, thereby curbing wage inflation. With the committee deeply split over both issues, its members could agree only to defer decisions on them until later. Goldberg told those present to expect at the next meeting a revised draft of the entire report, at which time it would be reviewed, along with the latest version of the one on collective bargaining. Still far from any kind of real accord, the group adjourned.[164]

In the interim, Goldberg decided to give a major address with two specific purposes. First, the talk was intended to make clear just what the Kennedy–Goldberg guidelines policy was. Both men had mentioned the guidelines in speeches to the AFL–CIO convention the previous December, but their remarks had generated more heat than light. Both labor leaders and managers remained unsure whether the administration intended to try to keep all major collective bargaining agreements in the guidelines or pursue a "softer" policy aimed only at limiting the wage increase for the economy as a whole to the 3.2 percent target. The policy as stated seemed ambiguous precisely because achieving the latter, the administration's ostensible objective, depended in part on keeping the key pattern-setting wage agreements in the guidelines. In the last analysis, then, the Kennedy–Goldberg policy called for something in between policing every collective bargaining agreement and focusing only on the overall change in wages, a distinction many observers found confusing.[165]

In addition to clarifying that issue, Goldberg's upcoming speech was also intended to encourage managerial participation in the national conference planned for later that spring. Thus he chose as the forum for his address the February 23 meeting of the Chicago Executives' Club. Goldberg's speech, widely reported, discussed in detail the administration's basic industrial relations policies. With the economic recovery slowly beginning to gather steam, Goldberg told his listeners, this was the time for both management and labor to collaborate with the government. All sides, he said, had an interest in preventing a replay of the events of the late 1950s, including the disastrous 1959 steel strike. Admitting that the Advisory Committee on Labor–Management Policy had not yet come up with specific solutions, he pointed out that at least the group was still trying and that his audience should be doing so as well.[166]

This much of Goldberg's message was well received, but his efforts to define what he saw as the solution met with a different reaction. His call for government guidelines to make certain that labor unions and corporations negotiated contracts in the interest of the public as a whole offended leaders in both communities. George Meany, willing to discuss the idea privately and without reference to specific collective bargaining agreements, reacted angrily to what he saw as Goldberg's attempt to define a solution that the Advisory Committee on Labor–Management Policy had yet to endorse. On learning of Goldberg's speech, Meany attacked it in language reminiscent of Samuel Gompers. Goldberg's policies, Meany argued in the traditional AFL idiom, were "infringing on the rights of a free people and a free society."[167] For the AFL–CIO chief, agreeing to accept that much more government supervision of labor–management relationships in a country in which managerial power appeared to be growing would lead directly to disaster.[168]

The more rigid business realists shared Meany's hostility to Goldberg's speech, albeit for their own quite different reasons. Increasingly confident that they could unilaterally roll back labor's power, such executives disliked Goldberg's call for giving the government more authority to regulate collective bargaining. This approach, they believed, needlessly risked further government inroads on managerial prerogatives. Such managers therefore concluded, like their AFL counterparts, that Goldberg's proposed guidelines should be resisted. The response from the heads of the major steel firms, was typical. Of the twelve, only Joseph Block publicly endorsed Goldberg's address. Thus by the spring of 1962, the center in both labor and management circles had clearly lost much of its earlier vitality.[169]

Disheartened by the negative response, Goldberg still refused to give up. The next two sessions of the Advisory Committee on Labor–Management Policy offered, however, little reason for encouragement. The two-day March meeting began smoothly enough, with all approving Goldberg's suggestion that he appoint a five-member subcommittee to handle the basic planning for the upcoming national economic conference. The group also agreed to accept Walter Reuther's proposal that it study the growing cost of arbitration and the threat this problem posed to the future of the whole system. Matters then grew more difficult as Joseph Block and Arthur Burns requested that the committee also examine the labor monopoly issue with respect to so-called national emergency disputes. In effect, the two men were proposing that the committee decide whether it favored reducing unions' power as one way of coping with disputes such as the 1959 steel strike.[170]

There could be no clearer indication of the gulf that increasingly separated business managers and union leaders than the Block and Burns's proposal. Goldberg, along with the union leaders and most of the industrial relations experts on the committee, disagreed totally with the assumptions behind that suggestion. Goldberg saw the effort to use the antimonopoly language more generally and the antitrust laws in particular against organized labor as totally at odds with the ideas on which they were based. He understood that the antimonopoly impulse and the antitrust laws it had inspired stemmed from hostility toward power concentrated in the state and the business community rather than the labor movement. Goldberg also knew only too well that labor's power remained far less than that of the other two. Even more important, he was aware that the rise of the labor movement had reduced significantly the amount of authority placed in managerial hands. For that reason, he viewed the effort to redirect the antimonopoly impulse from its traditional targets toward unions as turning the whole idea on its head.[171]

This was not entirely true. American labor unions had, by offering their members so little real voice in making decisions, invited exactly the sort of criticism at the heart of the antimonopoly tradition. But continuing managerial resistance was largely to blame for that problem, and to have addressed it in the context of that time would have weakened organized labor. Reducing the amount of authority placed in the hands of union leaders, by either increasing rank-and-file participation in decision making or in the other ways Block and Burns were suggesting, Goldberg correctly concluded, would produce a result inconsistent with Americans' deep-seated hostility toward concentrated power.

Realizing that a study of labor's "monopoly" power would necessarily raise the most fundamental and divisive questions about unions' place in the postwar order, Goldberg sought to avoid dealing with such an explosive issue. He therefore suggested, and the committee agreed, only to undertake a special study of the issue at some unspecified later date. To placate labor members of the committee who might view even that concession as too much, the issue was defined in a way that seemed more balanced, as "the relationship of concentration of labor and management power to the development of national emergency situations."[172]

Having navigated around that obstacle, at least for the moment, Goldberg returned the committee's attention to the latest draft of the collective bargaining report. The changes that the members proposed and adopted signaled once again the deep divisions between labor and management and their joint opposition, albeit for different reasons, to increasing significantly the government's role in supervising their compliance with the postwar New Deal.

The first major revision concerned a passage in the report emphasizing that the U.S. role abroad and the health of its economy were principal areas to which labor and management should, in bargaining with each other, be responsive. Both sides opposed linking so directly the process of collective bargaining with the nation's conduct of the cold war. Instead, the committee chose to substitute language that merely recognized that so-called national security and economic concerns were "matters of vital interest."[173] In making this change, both managers and union leaders signaled a declining willingness to accept the government's claim of military necessity as a reason for deferring the pursuit of their own objectives. This linchpin holding together the postwar social contract had clearly begun to weaken.

In another important change, the committee inserted a passage into the report stating that the scheduled national economic conference should not attempt to devise formulas for application to specific collective bargaining disputes. This decision revealed the unwillingness among the management members, in particular, to accept any kind of genuine incomes policy, even if expressed in such mild terms as *recommendations* or *guidelines*.[174]

After making some modest changes in the section dealing with how emergency dispute mediation boards were to function and recommending that the last-offer provision be eliminated from the Taft–Hartley law, the committee addressed a central problem. Aware that a report riddled with footnotes would command little real influence, Joseph Block, Thomas Watson Jr., Walter Reuther, and others urged that all members agree to omit them. Block, after stating that he would drop his dissenting labor-monopoly footnote if the committee agreed to insert into the report's text a statement endorsing the proposed study, called on the others to do likewise.

Only Arthur Burns refused, saying that he disapproved of the "increasing tendencies within this Committee to exert great pressures for compromise and seeming consensus and against individual expression of views." Unwilling to budge, Burns endured an onslaught of criticism from Watson, who called dissenting footnotes "deplorable," and Walter Reuther, who attacked Burns's implication that the committee had attempted to coerce agreement from its members.[175]

Goldberg was therefore left with no choice but to recognize Burns's right to dissent. In closing the meeting, Goldberg asked for all such statements by March 21 and stated that the final collective bargaining report would be presented to the president at the committee's next meeting.[176]

In the end, Burns did not stand alone in objecting to the others' attempt to maintain at least the outward appearance of unanimity on behalf of the group's watered-down recommendations. At the next meeting, held on April 3 and 4, Joseph Block objected to the way in which Goldberg had worded the passage dealing with monopoly power. Henry Ford II, the management member whose views corresponded most closely to those heading the core industrial firms, went even further. Ford announced that he dissented "from the overall implications of the report taken as a whole," specifically because it failed to state that excessive union power was the key reason for the problems that the report purported to address.[177]

Ford's remarks reopened debate over the entire report, leading the committee to postpone its meeting with Kennedy for at least a month. George Taylor, seeking to give Ford a face-saving way to retreat, stated that he might not have understood how much time and effort had gone into the paragraph on monopoly power and that the group had agreed that the whole subject could not be addressed adequately in a footnote or dissent. Ford, however, disagreed, saying that he had "submitted footnotes on other points as well as on the basic question of monopoly power, and . . . considers this to be the proper function of a member of the Committee."[178]

Taylor replied that the other matters that had given rise to dissents were "of different magnitude" from that of the monopoly power issue but failed to sway Ford. Taylor's observation revealed starkly the divide separating the most influential business managers from their trade union and academic counterparts. The former had come to believe that the best way to eliminate the problems at the root of the managerial rebellion was to reduce the labor movement's power. Union leaders and industrial relations experts such as

Taylor understood, however, that to weaken labor would only lead to a rupture in the postwar social order, rather than to its salvation.[179]

Elliott Bell, apparently trying to prevent Ford from becoming completely alienated from the rest of the group, defended the right of any member to dissent without having to face an attack each time he did so. Goldberg, disturbed by Ford's disruptive remarks, stated that members would not be prevented from exercising their right to dissent, but he urged the auto executive to accept the existing passage promising a future study of the monopoly power issue. But the time had finally begun to run out on that strategy of deferring the explosive issues until later, when the need to handle the most pressing concerns would force both sides to compromise. This technique had worked again and again for Goldberg over the past fourteen years precisely because the differences separating those at the center of the business community and the labor movement had been fairly small. With divisions between the two steadily widening, Goldberg's method had at last begun to prove ineffective.

After listening to Goldberg's request, Ford replied firmly that "the paragraph on monopoly power . . . is not embracive enough and does not point out the significance of this issue as the basic underlying factor in the need to write a report of this nature." For that reason, Ford concluded, he "was not inclined to change his statement of dissent." Despite the urgings of management member John Franklin that Ford not undo the earlier compromise and Goldberg's offer to expand the text's discussion of the labor monopoly issue, the auto executive simply repeated his earlier refusal to reconsider.[180]

Instead of going along, Ford continued to demand the incorporation of all of his dissenting remarks. The most important of the remainder dealt with the use of government mediation, euphemistically termed *third parties*, in resolving collective bargaining disputes. Ford opposed the report's passages on that subject because they endorsed a modest expansion of what Ford believed would inevitably become coercive government intervention. When David Cole attempted to persuade Ford that the use of government mediation boards and other kinds of government entities had always been discussed in terms of complete voluntarism, Ford disagreed with the assumption underlying Cole's remarks. Ford saw more government mediation as inconsistent with voluntarism. For that reason he said that "the use of third parties leads down the road to compulsion" and demanded to the right to say so in his dissent.[181]

Seeing that the discussion was going nowhere, Goldberg called for a recess in the hope that private talks might produce some kind of compromise. The most he could come up with was a proposal that an addendum would be attached to the text of the report, stating the views of all parties wishing to comment on the labor monopoly issue. On resuming the formal committee meeting, Ford agreed to consider the addendum idea if the group would postpone its final work on the report until the next meeting. The others concurred, and so Goldberg pressed on, trying to adjust the text so as to eliminate any other dissents. George Meany had offered four such reservations, but they were mostly minor ones. The committee readily agreed to make some small changes in the text's wording, thereby leading the AFL–CIO chief to drop all of his own objections.[182]

More difficult was the task of accommodating Ford's remaining dissents. The committee agreed to dilute its endorsement of government fact-finding still further, in effect all but withdrawing it. The committee "agreed" that "fact finding approaches . . . are better left to the parties themselves in the natural development of their bargaining relationship."[183] Next came a revision in the passage dealing with government mediation more generally. Once again, the changes adopted essentially undercut the draft's call for that remedy. In the place of the existing text, the committee inserted a statement that it "did not in any sense imply that the use of a third party procedure is a preferable objective or that the use of third parties will lead to more desirable long range relationships or sounder settlements."

As if that were not clear enough, the committee also agreed to incorporate into the text Ford's view that although the report endorsed more use of government mediation, such activity "should and will continue to remain an entirely voluntary process."[184] With that, the committee turned to other business, having restored the appearance of consensus, but only by sacrificing almost every passage in the report that had called for greater government supervision of the labor–management relationship.[185]

After dispensing with some minor details related to the holding of the national economic conference, the committee moved on to consider the revised version of the report on wage-and-price policy. The one major dispute concerned the basis of the administration's entire policy, namely, the guidelines themselves. When CEA members Walter Heller and Kermit Gordon complained that the report as drafted appeared to criticize their formulation of that policy, the report's principal author, George Taylor, responded that the effect of the guidelines was proving to be inflationary. Taylor was suggesting that the council—by giving for the first time in its history a single, specific figure for the overall wage increase—had made matters worse. Unions were coming to view the 3.2 percent figure as a minimum goal, regardless of the rate of productivity growth in specific industries. The weakest unions were tending to accept nothing less, and some stronger ones felt free to demand even more. Managers, for their part, preferred to treat the figure as a maximum, with similarly unfortunate results. To address this problem, the report had stated that the guidelines were at most only one factor to be considered in arriving at individual collective bargaining agreements.[186]

Seeking to reconcile the opposing views, Goldberg stated that one of the group's goals in writing the wage-and-price policy report was to straighten out the misunderstanding created by the CEA's 3.2 percent guideline. He told the group that no single wage policy could be adopted and that the CEA had run into trouble precisely because it had sought to make its traditional role into a more meaningful one. Heller agreed with that conclusion, thereby breaking the logjam. The committee agreed to adjourn after instructing the subcommittee and the CEA to meet and redraft the section so as to clarify the content of the guidelines policy.[187]

Goldberg's comments had reflected some crucial conclusions. He, in effect, had acknowledged that the basis of the Swedish approach to controlling inflation could not be duplicated in the United States at that time. In Sweden, leading labor and management organizations kept inflation under control by negotiating and then enforcing an overall wage policy. The corresponding American "peak" organizations, Goldberg implied, lacked the strength of their Swedish counterparts. Thus even if the AFL–CIO national office and the heads of the U.S. Chamber of Commerce and the NAM could agree on a single wage policy, they lacked the power to make it stick, because both the American labor movement and business community were too loosely woven to achieve such a result. Americans' antagonism to concentrated power had helped create "peak" organizations too weak to achieve a Scandinavian type of corporatism, a problem that undermined the entire effort to preserve the postwar New Deal.[188]

After three and a half years of pushing managers and labor leaders to emulate the Swedish system, Goldberg had come to understand better the obstacles standing in the way of that quest. The heads of the core industrial firms may have grasped them all along, which would help explain their rigid refusal even to consider Goldberg's plan. Also important to motivating their negative response, however, appears to have been managers' unwillingness to surrender any more of their jealously guarded prerogatives, as their Scandinavian counterparts had done. By the spring of 1962, then, even those business realists more inclined to seek a consensual approach to restraining inflation had begun to see such an effort as futile.[189]

Even if no overall wage solution were available, Goldberg still believed that much the same result could be achieved on a piecemeal basis. Using the fact-finding and mediation approaches the committee had been studying and the specific guidelines that the CEA had announced in January 1962, he hoped to help labor unions and their managerial counterparts strike such deals. The key tests in carrying out such a policy would come in those sectors in which the most influential, "pattern" contracts were made.

The first such negotiation following Goldberg's arrival at the Labor Department had come the previous fall in the auto industry. But because the committee had not yet developed a consensus in support of that approach, or the CEA its specific guideline figures, and because the problems facing the postwar order still seemed fairly remote in the automobile sector, Goldberg did not apply his new techniques there. Instead, operating in the background, he prodded both sides to sign an agreement providing for modest increases in wages and benefits, one that kept prices stable. The two sides eventually did so, a development that increased the odds that steel industry leaders would follow suit.[190]

Greater intervention would be required there, during the negotiations scheduled for the first half of 1962. Just as the outcome of the Advisory

Committee on Labor–Management Policy's deliberations would signal whether the new administration could bring about an overall solution to the problems facing the postwar New Deal, the result of the steel negotiations that year would indicate whether the committee's prescription could be applied successfully to the specific industries where those problems appeared most acute.

President Kennedy announcing to the press that Labor Secretary Goldberg's mediation efforts had ended an airline strike. John F. Kennedy Library.

The President's Committee on Equal Employment Opportunity. The clergyman
directly behind Kennedy is Monsignor George Higgins, Goldberg's longtime
adviser and friend. John F. Kennedy Library.

The first meeting of the President's Advisory Committee on Labor-Management
Policy, March 21, 1961. The tall man behind Goldberg is Thomas J. Watson Jr., of
IBM. John F. Kennedy Library.

Assistant Secretary of Labor for International Affairs George L. P. Weaver and International Labor Organization (ILO) director general David Morse meeting with the President. John F. Kennedy Library.

Assistant Secretary of Labor Jerry Holleman, Goldberg, and Vice President Johnson report to Kennedy about efforts to eliminate employment discrimination, April 3, 1962. John F. Kennedy Library.

Goldberg with Kennedy, Assistant Secretary of Labor Esther Peterson, and Civil Service Commission chairman John Macy. John F. Kennedy Library.

Goldberg watches as Kennedy signs the executive order that led to collective bargaining between the federal government and its unionized employees. John F. Kennedy Library.

Lucien Le Breton's official Supreme Court portrait of Mr. Justice Goldberg. Photo courtesy of Frances S. Guilbert.

Justices (*rear, left to right*) Potter Stewart, William Brennan, Byron White, Goldberg; (*front, left to right*) Tom Clark, Hugo Black, Earl Warren, and William O. Douglas in 1963. Harris & Ewing / Collection of the Supreme Court of the United States.

President Johnson urging Goldberg while in flight on Air Force One to leave the Court and become Ambassador to the United Nations. LBJ Library Collection.

Goldberg is sworn in as U.N. Ambassador, July 26, 1965. At rear are Goldberg's children Robert (*left of pillar*) and Barbara (*behind Dorothy Goldberg*). LBJ Library Collection.

With Johnson and Secretary of State Dean Rusk on Goldberg's first day as U.N. Ambassador. Yoichi R. Okamoto / LBJ Library Collection.

Scenes from the May 24, 1966, Oval Office meeting where Goldberg and Johnson clashed on Vietnam policy. Both photos Yoichi R. Okamoto / LBJ Library Collection.

The Wise Men meet, March 26, 1968. Yoichi R. Okamoto / LBJ Library
Collection.

With Jacob Javits, Happy and Nelson Rockefeller. Photo courtesy of Frances S. Guilbert.

Receiving the Medal of Freedom from President Carter. At rear is Secretary of State Cyrus Vance. Karl Schumaker / Jimmy Carter Library.

Arthur and Dorothy Goldberg in front of their farmhouse in Marshall, Virginia.
William Gottlieb / Photo courtesy of Frances S. Guilbert.

9

Limited Victory

Unlike the 1956 Steelworkers' agreement, a three-year one that had given both sides a real break from bargaining, the pact ending the 1959 strike gave rise almost immediately to another round of preliminary contract talks. The tripartite study committee established at Kaiser began its work during the spring of 1960, reflecting the wish among managers at that firm as well as the USA leadership to avoid a replay of the 1959 contest. The similar groups established at the eleven other major producers, on the other hand, moved much more slowly. Conrad Cooper and Heath Larry, the most senior management members of U.S. Steel's two such panels, at first showed little enthusiasm for the whole idea. The outcome of the presidential election held later that year, however, and the resulting appointment of Goldberg as secretary of labor, brought about a change in outward behavior, if not inner conviction. By January 1961, Nordy Hoffman could relate to Goldberg that at the most recent meeting between Cooper and McDonald, "the air was different," to which Goldberg, under no illusions, replied, "It's because they [U.S. Steel's managers] know Kennedy's attitude."[1]

The Kaiser Committee, aided by greater managerial support for its work and a broader mandate, set the pace for those at the other eleven firms. Organized along the same lines as the Advisory Committee on Labor–Management Policy, the Kaiser group contained equal numbers of management, labor, and "public" representatives. Goldberg had served on it during 1960 before being named labor secretary and was succeeded by Marvin Miller, an assistant to David McDonald. Miller, McDonald, and District Director Charles Smith made up the labor team, and Edgar Kaiser and two of his subordinates represented management. The three "public" members were David Cole, John Dunlop, and George Taylor, the last of whom also chaired the committee. The goal of these nine was to devise, in the context of that company, solutions to the problems that had led to the 1959 strike. And if

279

successful in making a deal, union leaders hoped executives at the other major steel firms would also choose to adopt it.[2]

The USA–Kaiser contract called for its joint committee to examine the following subjects: speeding up the grievance procedure, improving communication between workers and managers about the firm's plans for introducing new technology as well as its sales and production goals, adjusting the incentive-pay formula to the new conditions created by automation, developing programs to cushion workers against its effects, and more generally devising procedures that would help head off another major work stoppage. All these issues were related to the central one of plant *modernization*, as managers increasingly called the process of replacing workers with machinery. In discussing these matters, the committee soon found itself hampered by the labor members' lack of authority to engage in genuine contract negotiations. Such power still formally resided in the union's Wage Policy Committee, although over the past decade, this body of local representatives had routinely rubber-stamped the leadership's decisions.[3]

Goldberg, however, wanted the Kaiser Committee to become the official forum for such negotiations, and by the end of his brief tenure as one of its members, the group's managerial representatives and the USA Executive Board had assented to that change. On January 13, 1961, the USA and Kaiser announced the signing of a supplemental agreement that gave the committee the authority to engage in collective bargaining. The "public" members of the group would participate in such talks as mediators and fact-finders and possess the power to make recommendations, first privately and then publicly if an impasse developed. In keeping with the union's traditional opposition to any form of compulsory arbitration, neither side would be obligated to accept such recommendations. This agreement reflected Goldberg's desire to move toward the more explicitly corporatist approach he had been pushing since the end of 1958 while still preserving a system of collective bargaining free of state coercion.[4]

Although the supplemental agreement was a fairly small additional step in the direction of corporatism, the plan nonetheless drew opposition from several USA Executive Board members. McDonald's request that the board ratify the agreement provoked a long and heated discussion over whether the role of so-called third parties in collective bargaining should be increased and that of the union's Wage Policy Committee reduced. Goldberg's view, articulated at that meeting by Joe Germano and David McDonald, was that the new Kaiser agreement largely recognized formally what had already become standard practice. McDonald reminded his colleagues that "in every major steel dispute . . . the final settlement was made as a result of public pressure. . . . We have had boards and boards and boards of all kinds down through the years."[5]

Several board members, most notably I. W. Abel, Martin "Mike" Walsh, James Robb, John Grajciar, and Alex Kojetinsky, nevertheless questioned the wisdom of allowing the Kaiser Committee's "public" representatives more than a mediating function in contract talks. Abel voiced those concerns in the broadest terms possible, telling McDonald:

> I am quite disturbed about the trend of things in the last few years not only as it affects negotiations and strikes but the entire labor movement. I think we had a good example with respect to the McClellan Committee investigations and now the Landrum–Griffin law.
>
> . . . I think that maybe the labor movement did itself a disservice in its willingness to recognize that something was wrong with the organizations that made up labor and that perhaps some corrective measures were needed and when we publicly said so and went through some actions which we thought would take care of the situation.
>
> Well, we all know that it didn't. . . . And in my opinion that gave the enemies of labor then the encouragement to drive even harder. . . .
>
> Now the same is true with respect to strikes. We have been under terrific attack, and especially our Union, because we shut down a basic industry. . . . Of course I agree – and I think everybody agrees – that if we can find some solution to strikes of that kind that is fine; but I am wondering if we shouldn't be a little cautious in giving the public the impression that this Union of ours lacks the ability to negotiate and represent people and exercise good judgement, that we have to bring in a third party to make decisions or to tell us what is right and wrong.
>
> We may be again encouraging the enemies of labor to try further to weaken and destroy the labor movement.[6]

These kinds of complaints led an exasperated McDonald to elaborate on his earlier statement. He told his reluctant brethren:

> Every contract that I can remember except 1958 and the original contract was done as a result of some kind of governmental action. Just go back through the contracts in your own mind and see what occurred. Look at what happened in '56 and what happened in '49. Look what happened in '44, '41, '42. Every blessed agreement Uncle Sam has got into the act. We had compulsory fact-finding in the National War Labor Board, didn't we? It was compulsory. We had those long hearings. Then in the Wage Stabilization period in the seizure thing the government was in it up to their ears all the time. . . .
>
> You know what happened in '52. My God, we were in the White House more than we were in collective bargaining.
>
> And in 1959 we were asking for it. This Board asked for fact-finding.[7]

McDonald was right. If not corporatism of the Scandinavian variety, the union over the past two decades had participated in a less statist version of the same basic system. But his critics correctly pointed out that he and Goldberg intended to move even further in that direction, a controversial step that would have the effect of reducing yet again the union's autonomy from the state.

In making his remarks, Abel, the second highest officer in the union, served notice that the executive board would only go so far in accommodating McDonald's and Goldberg's wishes. But Abel and his supporters offered no constructive alternative. By 1961 the USA simply lacked the strength to win repeated industrywide strikes of the kind that had occurred in 1959. And a continuation of the status quo would, in any event, only have ensured the steel industry's continued decline. Abel's call for the union to fight labor's foes openly rather than accept more state supervision had great emotional appeal, but in the context of that time offered the steelworkers no real hope of lasting success.[8]

The reduction in rank-and-file participation that Goldberg's plan implied also aroused alarm in the USA Executive Board. New England district director Mike Walsh, at first inclined to go along with the majority in approving the supplemental agreement, changed his mind on learning that McDonald planned to use any bargain struck by the Kaiser Committee as the model for the other major firms. Goldberg and McDonald had so intended from the start, because they understood that unless fairly uniform wage rates were maintained across the industry, wage competition would emerge, much as it had overseas, and undermine those firms that provided the best wages and benefits.

Walsh, however, focused on the consequence of that plan for the Wage Policy Committee's authority to determine collective bargaining objectives. Perceiving that such a step would erode even further the workers' participation in decision making, Walsh strenuously objected. He told McDonald, "This is something that is basic to our Wage Policy Committee's jurisdiction within our Union. We go to the people and we boast about the democracy of our Union where we have a Wage Policy Committee that comes out of the ranks which determines these things."[9]

A longtime foe of the McDonald–Goldberg pattern of concentrating decision-making power at the top, Walsh demanded that the Wage Policy Committee be allowed to approve the supplemental Kaiser agreement. When McDonald refused, Walsh voted against its ratification, but no one else followed suit. McDonald's arguments that such a step was unnecessary and that the union simply lacked alternatives more promising than the Kaiser approach persuaded all but one of the more reluctant board members to go along. Despite the lopsided nature of the official vote, the dispute preceding it remained highly significant: The discussion had revealed resistance toward Goldberg's proposed solution even in his own union, a fact that boded ill for the plan's prospects.[10]

Committed to this course at least for the next few years, the USA members serving on the Kaiser Committee had begun exploring possible terms for the next contract even before the executive board had ratified the supplementary agreement. After that step, Marvin Miller gave its members a detailed report on these preliminary conversations. The union's representatives had proposed that the Kaiser Committee come up with a formula that would satisfy both the workers' income security demands and management's automation objectives. The USA members of the committee had also stated that participation by labor and management in this new social contract should not preclude a resort to their traditional weapons, the strike and the lockout. In so doing, Miller and the others signaled that neither they nor their colleagues would ever consent to transforming the USA into some form of company union. At the same time, both Miller's team and their managerial counterparts understood that a less adversarial relationship would be necessary in order to fend off growing foreign competition.[11]

Having established those basic parameters for discussion, Miller proceeded to spell out what the union's leaders saw as the basis for such a deal: Management would be required to pledge that all workers displaced by the introduction of new machinery would eventually obtain new jobs with the company and, in the interim, be entitled to financial support from it. Management would also be required to guarantee that a share of the increased profits following from automation go to the workers and that they be protected, through a COLA clause, against inflation.[12]

In return, Kaiser's managerial representatives proposed that the union must in effect agree to amend Section 2B, thereby making the introduction of new technology more attractive to management. In a related move, the union would also be required to allow changes in the incentive-pay system. Under the existing system, the most skilled workers received a higher hourly rate if they exceeded certain production targets. In many cases, the introduction of new machinery had made meeting these goals quite easy, significantly increasing workers' income and thus discouraging managers from automating further. Kaiser's managers had proposed replacing the existing incentive-pay scheme with one in which all workers participated and establishing an absolute limit on the amount of incentive pay that any worker could receive, thereby eliminating the disincentives to automation created by the existing plan.[13]

Attractive in theory, the plan contained some serious shortcomings. All workers would likely oppose the loss of control over the production process that the scheme implied, even in return for greater economic security. The proposed changes in the incentive-pay plan also promised to arouse strong opposition. Skilled workers already receiving incentive pay might well lose income from such a change or even their existing jobs, given the new plan's cap on incentive pay and its tendency to encourage further automation. Even unskilled workers might turn against the whole idea. The only way that they could become more efficient, as Miller pointed out to the board, would be if fewer of them were assigned to perform their present tasks. In his words, "This is the first big rub. Their proposal here in effect is that they [managers] be allowed to make crew size cuts even where those cuts are now protected."[14]

Although the management representatives had hastened to add that workers displaced would be employed elsewhere, Miller acknowledged that giving way on work crews was "a tremendous problem."[15] This issue had been at the root of the 1959 strike, and so persuading workers to yield on Section 2B after having fought so hard for its preservation would not be easy.

For these reasons, Miller had emphasized in the Kaiser Committee's preliminary meetings that the union would never agree to a plan that reduced the earnings of any worker, including those receiving incentive pay under the existing system, and that the union would allow crew-size cuts only in return for an ironclad employment security commitment. As he told the USA Executive Board,

> We said, "Now if there were to be crew size cuts we would have to have an absolute employment guarantee." And what we meant by that is simply that we were to have a sharp distinction between a lay-off that would take place because of a fall in business and a lay-off that would take place because of a change in method. . . . And none of those latter lay-offs could take place.[16]

Miller had thus told Kaiser's executives that as part of its price in making such a deal, the union would no longer tolerate the managerial practice of laying off workers during recessions and then failing to recall them all when production picked up again. If management wanted to reduce crew sizes, Miller was saying, then it would have to assume responsibility for employing elsewhere in the firm those workers thereby displaced. Assuming that managers could find some other activity for such workers that would generate additional firm income, such an obligation need not interfere with automation's underlying objective, which was to increase the return on the firm's capital investment and thus its ability to compete against imported steel. Whether all that could be accomplished in the context of a single company, or even a single industry, however, appeared much less clear.[17]

There were other potential problems as well. Unless both sides could agree on how to apportion the proceeds generated by the introduction of new technology, the whole negotiation would fall apart. The management members of the committee had proposed that workers receive as their share an amount equal to the current ratio of labor cost to production value, roughly 35 percent. Miller and the other union representatives viewed that as a major concession. Miller told the USA Executive Board:

> I want to point out how important that one point is. Everyone here knows the tremendous gains this Union has made in the last 20 years. But I want to tell you that, despite those gains, labor costs as a percentage of value are less than they were 20 years ago. It has fallen despite our gains and here we are on the eve, I think, of even greater technological change in the future which could have only one effect, as you know. What does technological change do but decrease the manpower needed for a given ton of steel? And as a result of more and more technology there is no doubt that the labor cost of a particular product will continue to fall as a percentage. They have proposed that we take the present ratio and freeze it.[18]

A key stumbling block lay, as always, in the realm of pricing. If managers chose to raise prices after paying workers their portion under the new profit-sharing formula, the workers' fraction of total industry income would fall. When Miller implied that the union's willingness to practice wage restraint depended on management's willingness to hold down prices, Kaiser's executives at first demurred, saying that they alone decided such matters. When that argument failed to sway Miller and his associates, the management representatives, he reported, told him, "We don't have anything to say about steel prices. U.S. Steel determines this."[19] Pressed even harder, Kaiser's managers proposed that the formula provide that if prices rose faster than wages under the new plan, workers would receive more in pay and benefits so as to protect their overall share of the firm's income.

Although both sides remained leery about certain aspects of the plan, Miller reported that prospects for reaching a settlement on the terms they had discussed appeared good. Goldberg, for his part, supported this approach and intended to use the full power of his new office in furthering those objectives. But Kaiser management's candid acknowledgment of U.S. Steel's power to set prices for the entire industry pointed out a key weakness in the entire Kaiser Committee approach. Unless the industry's dominant firm followed Kaiser's lead, the latter lacked the ability to make the proposed social contract work.[20]

The early meetings of U.S. Steel's two joint committees offered neither Goldberg nor the union's leaders much reason for optimism. The first of the two U.S. Steel groups was a three-person, tripartite one, charged with studying the local work rules issue. The second one, the Human Relations Research Committee (HRRC), contained equal numbers of labor and management representatives, but no so-called public ones. Roger Blough and his associates, in a move consistent with their opposition to government intervention during the 1959 strike, had refused to accept a tripartite structure for the committee assigned the task of studying the larger problems facing the steel industry.[21]

The first discussions between union leaders and U.S. Steel's managers revolved around who was to be assigned to do the real work of the joint committees. Although McDonald and Conrad Cooper formally chaired both, they delegated the actual day-to-day supervisory roles to Marvin Miller and Heath Larry, each assisted by a pair of subordinates. In the first sign of trouble ahead, the two sides immediately found themselves at loggerheads over whom to chose as the work rules panel's "public" member. Heath Larry soon reported that his superiors opposed the union's suggestions of John Steelman, David Cole, and William Simkin, three of the most prominent industrial relations experts of that day. A fourth, George Taylor, told Marvin Miller not even to bother submitting his name, as he was sure that it would be rejected. Also indicative of management's uncooperative attitude was Larry's insistence that the "public" representative, who would also chair the work rules panel, be someone unfamiliar with the entire dispute.[22]

While negotiations continued over the naming of the third person, the two sides exchanged preliminary position papers, a step that underscored the gulf separating the two sides. Unlike the union's carefully documented and balanced presentation, management's, Marvin Miller had reported to the USA Executive Board in August 1960, "was a series of . . . about forty[-]odd assertions of their problems with no documentation from arbitration [decisions] . . . or anything else."[23]

When Miller suggested that the two papers would be a useful starting point for the person eventually chosen as chairman, the management members apparently realized that their tactics, if not their underlying objectives, would have to change. In Miller's words,

> Well, at this point it was as if a light had been turned on across the table . . . because I think for the first time they looked at these two papers in the way that a third party might look at them. . . . And I think they . . . decided suddenly that with a third party in there they might have more to lose than to gain.[24]

For that reason, Heath Larry opened the group's next meeting in a far more accommodating manner and proceeded to suggest that the group simply dispense with the third person entirely and seek to write a consensual report. Having accepted the committee's creation in the expectation that it could only embarrass the USA, Larry and his superiors had come to appreciate the risk of adding a "public" representative who might side with the union. Anxious to head off that possibility, Larry proposed that the two sides get together and strike some sort of deal with respect to the work rules issue. As in the case of Kaiser, the key issue involved managers' freedom to replace workers with machinery. Miller reported to his USA colleagues that Larry and his subordinates had stated:

> ["]We are not interested in solving just this [work rules] problem and this problem and this problem; what we want is . . . a free hand in the future.["] And when I say "free hand," they have been very specific. . . . they are talking about only one thing, . . . they are interested in crew sizes and crew sizes alone.[25]

Management had sounded even more rigid at meetings of the HRRC, which was expected to come up with a long-term formula for calculating workers' pay and benefits increases, as well as to study the incentive-pay, grievance, and seniority systems, all of which had come under heavy strain over the preceding three years. The management team had dismissed outright the union's suggestions that increases in the rate of worker productivity, firm profits, or wages elsewhere in the industry be used as bases for a pay-raise formula. Although Larry had sounded somewhat more open to the union's proposed cost-of-living criterion, even that concession marked a retreat from U.S. Steel managers' line during the middle 1950s, that the firm's workers were entitled to a rising real wage. By the end of his August 1960 report to the USA Executive Board, Miller had sounded quite pessimistic but said that the union intended to make a good-faith effort to reach an agreement. Whether management intended to do so, McDonald had added, still remained to be seen.[26]

In monitoring those early conversations, Goldberg and the USA's leaders were haunted by the knowledge of how much weaker the union was than it had been at the same stage three years earlier. The layoffs in steel, which had begun during the spring of 1960 and intensified thereafter, finally leveled off by the end of January 1961, but employment failed to recover quickly. This weakened the union's bargaining position in two ways, by reducing management's incentive to avoid an interruption in production and by drawing down the union's coffers still further.

The drop in dues collections, I. W. Abel reported to the USA Executive

Board in February 1961, had produced a decline in the national union's total assets over the preceding year from $26 million to $24 million, and the shrinkage was continuing. As Joe Moloney pointed out to his colleagues, because $7 million of the remaining sum consisted of loans to the locals that they could not easily repay, the union had, at most, $17 million in ready reserves. Although it was nowhere near broke, the recession-induced layoffs had weakened still further the McDonald–Goldberg faction's ability to extract improvements in wages and benefits from steel industry managers, thereby endangering its control over the union. And although the economic recovery slowly began to gather momentum during the late spring of 1961, McDonald noted at a USA Executive Board meeting held the following fall that the union was still losing money.[27]

In the meantime, Goldberg watched from his new vantage point in the Labor Department as discussions in the HRRC went nowhere. At a USA Executive Board meeting on May 18, 1961, Marvin Miller reported that the talks indicated that management's attitude "has not changed in any significant detail since 1959."[28] Trying to agree on changes in the incentive-pay system that would restore the principle of equal pay for equal work—one of the union's most cherished goals—was proving to be a major headache.

Each major steel firm had expanded its incentive-pay program differently over the past fifteen years, eventually producing a situation in which virtually every kind of worker received incentive pay somewhere in the industry. No company, however, had extended the system to include all of its employees. As a result, workers doing the same sorts of jobs at different firms were, in many cases, receiving substantially different rates of pay, recreating the kinds of wage inequities that the union had fought so hard in the past to eliminate. Under the industry's master contract, management could unilaterally decide which classes of jobs were entitled to incentive pay, a power each firm's managers had apparently used to reward their most valued workers. Although the union had the right to challenge such decisions, that remedy had proved ineffective. The issue was very important precisely because the reemergence of wage inequities posed yet another threat to the rank-and-file solidarity on which the union's power was based.[29]

Discussions about that issue with U.S. Steel's managers as well as those of the other firms had thus far met only with frustration, in part because the union's traditional goal of extending the incentive-pay system to all employees increasingly collided with another cardinal objective, employment for all union members. Granting workers incentive pay led each to produce more, thereby reducing the overall demand for labor. In an industry operating at or near capacity, this had posed no real problem for the union, but after the steel companies entered a period of prolonged stagnation during the late 1950s, the spread of incentive pay began contributing to unemployment. As Miller somberly observed to the USA Executive Board,

> We have unemployment as a major problem, lack of job opportunity, and it isn't going to get any better. We know also that the extension of incentives

has meant a reduction in job opportunities. So it seems to me that we come smack against a real problem here about which way you push.[30]

The two sides had made little more headway in other areas, most notably the problems confronting the grievance and seniority systems. The first of these was buckling under the pressures created by the managerial revolt. By the spring of 1961, Miller informed the USA Executive Board, the backlog in processing grievances was enormous, "probably . . . the largest in history."[31] The growing workload had greatly increased the expense and reduced the effectiveness of a system constructed on the assumption that good-faith relations between management and the union would continue.

The seniority system, like the incentive-pay one, had also come under stress when steel production slowed down after 1957. In the mills organized by the USA, workers did not participate in one, plantwide seniority system, the sort most likely to preserve the union's traditional objective of laying off first those with the least time of service. Instead, the locals, which controlled such matters, had helped create seniority lines based on task. This had led, in extreme cases, to the establishment of hundreds of separate seniority lines in a single plant, a majority of which consisted of only one or two people.

As a result, many of the more recently hired workers in areas of steel plants that remained active even when they ran far below capacity had retained their jobs while some of the more senior workers had been laid off. The introduction of new machinery, which sometimes led to the elimination of jobs, had undermined even further the objective of the existing seniority scheme. To a lesser degree, such problems had cropped up in the past, but the prolonged downturn of the preceding four years had strained the seniority system to the breaking point.[32]

After trying to cope with seniority problems, leaders of the locals admitted to Miller and his associates in 1961 that such conflicts could not be resolved on a local level. The issues involved had proved too explosive for the locals to handle, Marvin Miller reported to the USA Executive Board, thus raising yet another threat to the rank and file's solidarity. The USA leadership's efforts to work out those problems had met with little success thus far, in part because many locals stoutly resisted what they saw as yet another inroad on their autonomy from the national office. The leadership was hampered, too, in addressing this problem by more recently hired workers' resistance to changes that would diminish their own job security.

Although the USA leadership had looked to management for help through forums such as the HRRC, some executives had failed to cooperate. Such managers remained hostile to seniority schemes precisely because they tended to protect the older, and presumably less productive, workers from layoffs, rather than the younger, more vigorous ones. Seeing a chance both to increase worker output and weaken the union, such managers were attempting to exploit the seniority mess, rather than assist the union in addressing it. By the fall of 1961, Miller was pressing the USA Executive Board to decide whether to assume responsibility for the problem or give up altogether trying to solve it, a choice the leadership appeared reluctant to face.[33]

The lack of progress in the Kaiser and U.S. Steel Committees during their first year of operation suggested, as Miller told the USA leadership, that the union would face another industrywide shutdown in July 1962. He argued, however, that the USA should not withdraw from those two groups or the other industry committees, because they were enabling the union to establish a record of having tried to reach a settlement without a strike. The union would, he said, find that useful later, should any work stoppage take place, in appealing for public and government support. And although there were, he said, "many things wrong with the [Kaiser] company's proposal," its executives had shown genuine interest in making a deal, yet another reason for the USA to keep trying.[34]

Even if the union eventually struck a bargain with Kaiser's managers, the likelihood that it would spread appeared small by the spring of 1961. U.S. Steel management had by then rejected outright the union's proposal that it transform the HRRC into a tripartite collective bargaining forum, as Kaiser had done. Conrad Cooper sent McDonald a letter in April of that year explicitly rejecting any kind of formal corporatist approach as a vehicle for shaping the terms of the firm's labor–management relationship. Cooper stated that the use of so-called third parties was particularly inappropriate when they "have no real accountability to anyone for their actions — either to the employees, to the Companies' shareholders, or to their customers."[35] Missing, of course, from Cooper's list was the public more generally, whose interests, he implied, could not and should not be represented in such talks. In effect, U.S. Steel's leading managers rejected the notion that the larger public's interest in preserving the postwar New Deal should in any way restrict their own efforts to address the problems that imperiled it.

Formally confined to playing only an advisory role, the HRRC continue to deliberate, but without much success. At a USA Executive Board meeting on October 5, 1961, Marvin Miller told its members, "As you know, we started about 18 months ago, and we have had upwards of 100 meetings of the six subcommittees. And I suppose to the surprise of practically no one in this room, there just isn't a lot of progress to report."[36]

Management's unwillingness to share certain kinds of cost data made progress in many areas all but impossible, Miller noted. And even worse, Cooper and his associates steadfastly refused to make any effort to devise a formula for determining what the workers' share of industry profits should be. Management's view, Miller told his colleagues, was

> that there are no criteria under which we are entitled to anything at all at any time. And therefore in this area, what they are saying to us, is that we can't possibly make a meaningful study, because they are not willing to concede the fact that we are entitled to anything at any time.[37]

Miller exaggerated only slightly. Cooper had hinted to him that the union was entitled to something, but only what it could wrest from management through hard bargaining and, if need be, by striking. In so doing, the U.S. Steel official signaled that his firm remained unwilling to enter into a consensual pact aimed at preserving the postwar social contract.[38]

The heads of the other leading companies were divided over how best to bargain with the union. Miller reported to the USA Executive Board that the discussions in the HRRC and its counterparts at the other major firms revealed deep splits over the work rules issue and others. Not all managers favored U.S. Steel's hard line, a development Miller found encouraging. But at the same time, even the negotiations with Kaiser's managers—by far the most friendly of those at the twelve leading firms—were progressing very slowly. As Kaiser's executives began to grasp the implications of the union's demand that they guarantee employment for those workers displaced by technological innovation, the former's resistance stiffened. Thus by the fall of 1961, the union still stood far apart even from those managers most inclined toward a consensual solution, and the prospect of another major strike loomed large.[39]

Even so, Cooper and his colleagues, Miller told the USA Executive Board in October 1961, were still pressing for an agreement on at least a few issues. This was because, Miller believed, they feared that to fail completely would only increase the likelihood of government intervention, which management adamantly opposed. He described Cooper and his associates as

> almost pathological on the question of third parties intervening at any time, that is[,] except in the case of Taft–Hartley injunctions. . . .
>
> They are well aware that President Kennedy is in the White House; they are aware Secretary Goldberg is in the Department of Labor, and they are aware that the President has a Labor–Management Advisory Committee on which our President sits. And they are aware also that the Administration is not inclined to take a hands off attitude in labor–management matters.[40]

The implied threat of such intervention, one that Goldberg did his utmost to bring home to steel industry managers, inclined them toward making some kind of bargain, although those at U.S. Steel resisted strongly developing any kind of consensual economic formula for determining what share of automation-induced profits the workers should receive.

Having monitored the steel talks from a distance during his first eight months as labor secretary, Goldberg began urging steel managers in the fall of 1961 to change their position. Hearing rumors of impending price increases, Goldberg prompted Kennedy to write the heads of the major steel companies on September 6 requesting that they refrain from any such action. Although the steel industry managers replied in letters whose tone ranged from cold formality to outright hostility, they went along with the administration's request, at least for the moment. In a related move, Goldberg persuaded Roger Blough to appoint a three-person management committee that would act as a liaison to the Labor Department during the steel negotiations. The group, chaired by Republic Steel's president Tom Patton, met with Goldberg on September 21, the first of several such sessions.[41]

During the last three months of the year, Goldberg stepped up the pressure on both sides to begin negotiating seriously. And to lead them in what he saw as the right direction, Goldberg instructed the commissioner of the Bureau of Labor Statistics to come up with information about national productivity trends, including those in the steel industry. Contract negotiators in steel could then use that information, as Goldberg explained in a letter to David McDonald, in arriving at wage-and-benefit increases that fell within the productivity guidelines.[42]

In effect, Goldberg's approach was aimed at bringing an end to the tug-of-war in steel between the union and management that had endangered the industry's health. This would require both sides to make sacrifices. From the union, Goldberg asked for wage restraint, which would mean a lower annual increase in worker compensation. And from managers, Goldberg demanded a reciprocal agreement to practice price restraint and, by implication, their acceptance of a lower rate of profit than they had been willing to concede in the past. Those shared burdens, he reasoned, could bring a halt to the developments that had led to the 1959 strike.

This approach contained pitfalls for both labor and management. For the union, Goldberg's policy implied that even if it had the power during a specific negotiation to wring more from management than the increase in worker productivity implied, the USA should refrain from doing so. Goldberg argued that this was in the best interests of the steelworkers, because it would help preserve the long-run health of the steel industry, as well as the postwar New Deal that the USA had done so much to bring about. But Goldberg was, in effect, asking steelworkers to make short-run sacrifices in defense of their own long-term interests, as well as those of the American working and lower middle classes more generally.[43]

Such notions were at odds with the traditional bargaining posture of unions such as the USA. Influenced by the value system of competitive capitalism, they tended to fight during each contract negotiation for as much as they could get, relying on managerial resistance to keep them in the bounds of what productivity gains warranted. The union also tended, for that same basic reason, to put the interests of its own members first and foremost. And even if the USA chose to exercise the kind of restraint Goldberg was advocating, its leadership ran the risk of alienating the rank and file if the heads of other major unions acted less responsibly.

When negotiating a new master contract for the UAW the previous fall, Walter Reuther had warned Goldberg that the USA had better show similar self-discipline, or considerations of competitive advantage would doom the whole plan. For those reasons, Goldberg's proposed policy aroused resistance among both the rank and file and the union's executive board.[44]

Goldberg's approach elicited even stronger opposition from steel industry managers, especially those at U.S. Steel. Blough and Cooper continued to reject any notion that their own collective bargaining objectives should be informed by larger considerations of the sort Goldberg had in mind. Even more important, managers at U.S. Steel disagreed with the way in which the union and the government calculated the increase in worker productivity and also with the notion that as part of a mutual sacrifice, managers should accept a profit level below that achieved between 1950 and 1957. Intractable disputes over the extent to which workers were entitled to share in the fruits of automation, and more generally in the firms' income, thus led steel industry managers, even more than union leaders, to balk at accepting Goldberg's basis for a new master contract.[45]

While the government's productivity data were being assembled, Goldberg kept pushing both sides to get down to work. After three more months of stalling, contract talks finally began in earnest on January 15, 1962. Although late in the sense that the HRRC had been discussing the major issues for almost a year, formal negotiations for the 1962 contract opened three and a half months earlier than they had during the previous round in 1959. Goldberg's continuing campaign for an early settlement was, in the face of stiff resistance, nonetheless making some headway. Anxious to avoid the kind of stockpiling in anticipation of a strike that might disrupt the economy's still sluggish recovery, Goldberg pressed for a completed contract by the end of that same month.[46]

A key sticking point—even assuming that both sides could agree on work rules, incentives, grievances, and seniority—lay in the area of prices. Goldberg understood that further increases in general steel prices must be prevented, lest the problems facing the steel industry, and the economy more generally, only grow worse. He understood, too, that there was no hope of getting the union to practice wage restraint unless managers made a reciprocal pledge to keep prices down. To do otherwise risked allowing managers simply to reap the harvest of lower wages in the form of higher dividends and managerial salaries, rather than the increased gains in competitiveness needed to keep the industry healthy.[47]

Blough, Cooper, and their counterparts at most of the other major firms, on the other hand, objected to linking wage-and-price increases directly. When Goldberg arranged for Blough and McDonald to meet with Kennedy at the White House on January 23, the difference in attitude between the union leader and his managerial counterpart became quite clear. Kennedy opened the meeting by restating his view that the economy's recovery must not be disturbed by either a steel strike or the signing of an inflationary agreement. He then asked both his guests to commit themselves to negotiating a new contract that cost between 2.5 percent and 3 percent. This, Kennedy added, CEA chairman Walter Heller had assured him would be low enough to eliminate the need for any increase in steel prices, two related themes on which Goldberg elaborated.

After blustering a bit, McDonald agreed to go along, but Blough refused to follow suit. He told Kennedy that U.S. Steel management's own productivity calculations called for a smaller wage increase than the president had recommended and that its figure was the only appropriate basis for a new contract with the USA. Despite repeated prodding by Kennedy, Goldberg, and McDonald, Blough refused to commit himself to the administration's policy.

The meeting thus ended inconclusively, thereby disappointing everyone present except Roger Blough.[48]

Having failed to bring about any consensual agreement, Goldberg and Kennedy were thus left with no other way to defend their policy than by trying to coerce both sides into complying with it. Aware that managers' reluctance to make a commitment on pricing stemmed partly from their fear that such a guarantee would erode their prerogatives still further, Goldberg sought to allay those concerns as much as possible without abandoning his basic objective. He understood that if managers were to make an explicit guarantee on prices in exchange for wage restraint, they would, in effect, have agreed to share control over pricing decisions with the union and the federal government, something managers had fought bitterly in the past.

Thus Goldberg tried to extract only an implicit promise from Blough and his colleagues, that if the union agreed to a modest package of wage-and-benefit improvements predicated on the assumption of stable prices, that managers would act accordingly. And from the union, Goldberg asked for genuine restraint in formulating its economic demands, without an explicit quid pro quo on prices. The alternative, he hinted, would be the kind of government intervention that neither side wanted, especially management.[49]

Hard bargaining commenced in the third week of January and continued for the next two and a half months. When he reported to U.S. Steel's board of directors at the end of January, Blough announced that since mid-1958, wages had risen twice as fast as worker productivity and hinted that further price increases were in store. His statement, leaked to the press, irritated McDonald, who retaliated by boycotting the first two HRRC sessions in February. Goldberg responded by publicly urging both sides to stop bickering. He followed up with identically worded telegrams to the management team and McDonald, which again underscored the need for an early settlement so as to avoid disrupting the economy's recovery.[50]

In bargaining, both sides preserved the outward appearance of using the arrangements perfected during the mid-1950s. Thus the USA Executive Board and the Wage Policy Committee formally viewed the results of the HRRC's deliberations only as recommendations to them and the eleven companies' management committees. In reality, however, the HRRC subcommittees did most of the real negotiating. During February, they arrived one by one at their final "recommendations." Significantly, most of the subcommittees, like the work rules panel, failed to come up with specific solutions to the related problems confronting the incentive-pay, grievance, and seniority systems.[51]

But managers appeared disinclined to resolve these disputes with another industrywide shutdown, given the far greater likelihood this time of government intervention that would aid the union rather than management. Marvin Miller reported to the USA Executive Board in early February that all the outward signs indicated that Cooper and his colleagues were willing to settle for a continuation of the existing truce. Cooper, Miller said, had pledged that executives would not raise the Section 2B issue this time, and other management representatives called it a matter to be settled plant by plant rather than through a change in the master contract. Managers also indicated their willingness to deal with the other problems in much the same way. And even more revealing, management this time refrained from the kind of publicity campaign in the news media that in the past had signaled that they were expecting a strike.

Because the Kaiser Committee had not yet reached an agreement, USA officials felt inclined to accept the draw that managers at the other eleven firms were offering. Should the Kaiser panel subsequently arrive at a deal along the lines its members had been discussing, union leaders believed that the next step would be to press for its adoption elsewhere in the industry. But the inability, after two years of trying, to come up with any real results in the two U.S. Steel committees suggested that eventual failure was the more likely outcome.[52]

Trying to keep the effort alive at least, Goldberg pushed his former USA colleagues to accept a continued truce in the work rules, incentive-pay, grievances, and seniority areas, as well as a very modest increase in steelworker compensation. In urging them to do so, he argued that the union had no choice given the bleak situation in the steel industry. After studying conditions there at length, Goldberg's staff at the Labor Department sent him a memo on March 9 filled with pessimistic findings about the industry's short-term prospects. The memo's author concluded:

> Even assuming favorable business conditions and no strike, steel production is unlikely to maintain present levels for very long. . . . Total employment in steel, which may average about 660,000 in the current half year, is probably near its peak. Roughly 120,000 of those currently employed are non-production workers. Workers presently unemployed are not likely to be recalled in the foreseeable future.[53]

Although the available evidence suggested that investment in new plant and equipment would rise during 1962, an earlier memo to Goldberg observed that "emphasis has shifted from enlarging capacity to modernization of existing facilities and promotion of efficiency and cost reduction."[54] In the light of those circumstances and the need to keep the price of American-made steel from rising any further, Goldberg argued persuasively that the union should seek contract improvements in areas such as SUBs and employment guarantees, rather than higher hourly wages.[55]

By the end of March, Goldberg's pressure tactics appeared to yield their intended result. After a final month of seesaw negotiations, McDonald and the other USA leaders, confident that Goldberg and Kennedy would not betray their trust, agreed to accept a two-year contract containing no increase in general wage rates but, rather, some improvements in job and income security programs. The new contract increased worker compensation over the following year by about 2.2 percent, the lowest rise of the postwar period and within what Goldberg and his aides had calculated was needed to prevent any further increase in steel prices. In another crucial step, the USA leadership also abandoned its demand for a shorter workweek with no cut in pay, a move that would have greatly increased labor costs. A big concession, it was bound to prove controversial with many members of the rank and file, who had supported wholeheartedly the union's earlier call for a thirty-two-hour workweek. At the same time, Blough and Cooper ceased making statements about their right to make a general price increase unilaterally, a silence that Goldberg interpreted as a sign they had tacitly accepted his proposed bargain.[56]

Formally announced on March 31, 1962, the new master contract with eleven of the twelve major firms seemed at first a dazzling vindication of the Kennedy–Goldberg policy. Hailed in the press as a sign that the administration's economic program was succeeding, the two men basked momentarily in the glow of their apparent success. On April 3 Goldberg triumphantly wrote the president that "the settlement in steel, which has been very well received in the country, will result, if past practice is followed, in comparable settlements in iron ore, aluminum, can manufacturing, and steel fabricating."[57]

But Goldberg's memo, like the press accounts, failed to take sufficient note of the agreement's fragility. USA leaders, no doubt wary that managers might choose to raise prices anyway and that the membership might not accept a contract costing managers noticeably less than the ones other major unions were obtaining, had broken with its pattern since the mid-1950s of obtaining multiyear wage-and-benefit agreements. The new contract contained a clause allowing either party to reopen negotiations after one year. In demanding this clause, the union's leaders signaled that should either of the feared problems arise, the whole deal would soon collapse.[58]

The wait proved short indeed. Only ten days after the agreement had been announced, Roger Blough paid a now-infamous visit to the White House, during which he informed Kennedy that U.S. Steel's managers were increasing prices by $6 a ton, a 3.5 percent rise. To underscore that this was a fait accompli, Blough handed the president a mimeographed copy of a press release that management was distributing publicly as the two men spoke. Kennedy, noting tersely that "I think you have made a terrible mistake," immediately summoned Goldberg.[59]

Upon arriving in the Oval Office, Goldberg scanned the announcement and then confronted Blough over what the former regarded as the dishonesty behind the price decision. Goldberg reminded Blough that his silence about prices when reaching a wage settlement had, in that context, implied management's consent not to raise them. The union had relied on Kennedy's and Goldberg's assurances that no such rise would be forthcoming in agreeing to accept such a small increase in worker compensation, and now Blough, Goldberg stressed, having used the administration, was pulling the rug out from under it. After a tense exchange between the two, Blough departed, leaving Goldberg feeling angry and defeated.[60]

But Kennedy, having listened carefully to the confrontation between Blough and Goldberg, now grasped the full implications of Blough's action, thereby becoming deeply angry himself. Unwilling to accept this affront to both his program and himself, Kennedy proceeded to unleash a whirlwind of executive action aimed at persuading Blough to back down. First Kennedy summoned Walter Heller, Ted Sorensen, and McGeorge Bundy into his office, where they and Goldberg heatedly discussed what had just transpired. Having filled them in and listened to their suggestions for a response, Kennedy and Goldberg began making phone calls. The president telephoned Douglas Dillon first, both to sound him out for ideas and to have him convey a message to the financial community that the administration would fight the price increase.[61]

The next call went out to the steel managers' old nemesis on Capitol Hill, Tennessee Senator Estes Kefauver. Kennedy asked him to convene his subcommittee, which had jurisdiction over the antitrust laws, to investigate whether steel managers had violated them by colluding to raise prices. Kefauver agreed to do so and, more important, to issue a statement immediately to that effect, thereby giving Blough and his colleagues some indication of what they would face in trying to make the price increase stick.[62]

Getting more worked up with each such conversation, Kennedy also telephoned his brother Bobby, who listened and then vowed impetuously to use the Justice Department's power to the fullest in investigating the executives involved for wrongdoing. Goldberg, surprised and pleased by the intensity of the president's reaction, called David McDonald, who had heard nothing as yet about the price increase. McDonald agreed to make a statement blasting the move and the deceitful way in which Blough and the others had gone about it.[63]

At that point, Goldberg, Sorensen, Heller, and his CEA colleague Kermit Gordon moved to Sorensen's office, where they began to map strategy for the following day. All agreed that the estimates of wage costs needed to be rechecked, lest the president be embarrassed when arguing that no price increase was justified. Goldberg then returned to his office at the Labor Department and began studying these figures, including the union's estimate of the new contract's cost. Finding no mistakes that might justify U.S. Steel's decision, he concluded that both he and his old USA colleagues had been had.[64]

After a discouraging night, interrupted by a phone call at 1:30 A.M. from Kennedy, who was "seething with a cold fury," as Goldberg told his wife, he decided to offer his resignation to the president. At a meeting with Kennedy the next morning Goldberg did so, saying that the guidelines policy had failed and that he should take the responsibility for it. Although Kennedy objected, saying that "we're in this fight together," Goldberg understood from bitter experience that the government lacked the power to win such a confrontation. In the heat of the moment, Goldberg told Kennedy what the wisest New Deal liberals had come to understand but rarely said aloud: "Mr. President, this industry cannot be tamed, they rule this country, and even Mr. Truman couldn't take them on." The outburst proved too much for Kennedy, who fell silent for a moment and then replied merely, "My father always said[,] too, that they were a bunch of skunks." He stated that Goldberg's request to leave would be deferred while the administration continued working for a reversal of U.S. Steel management's decision.[65]

In the meantime, reports began arriving that executives at the other major steel firms were falling in behind U.S. Steel. Managers at seven of the twelve largest companies eventually went along. Only Kaiser, whose executives were still bargaining with the union; Inland, whose head, Joseph Block, remained similarly committed to finding a consensual solution to the problems facing the industry; Armco; McLouth; and Colorado Fuel and Iron held out. Kennedy, now even angrier, instructed his staff to draw up a statement denouncing the offending companies' managers, which he read at the outset of his televised press conference later that same day. There he blasted the actions of Blough and his followers as "a wholly unjustifiable and irresponsible defiance of the public interest."[66]

Seeking, as he had during his presidential campaign, to suggest that such behavior was akin to treason because it undermined the national unity required for victory in the cold war, Kennedy went on to note the specific sacrifices he had asked of other, far less privileged Americans, during what he called a time of increased international tensions. They, he said, "will find it hard, as I do, to accept a situation in which a tiny handful of steel executives, whose pursuit of private power and profit exceeds their sense of public responsibility, can show such utter contempt for the interests of 185 million Americans."[67] And then, after pointing out how vital keeping prices down was to the success of his entire economic program, Kennedy added bitingly, "Some time ago I asked each American to consider what he would do for his country and I asked the steel companies. In the last twenty-four hours, we have had their answer."[68]

Goldberg watched the performance on a television at the Labor Department, where, immediately after the press conference ended, he received a call from Kennedy, who asked, "Well, now do you feel like resigning?"[69] Heartened by Kennedy's willingness to stand behind him, Goldberg relented. Instead of quitting, he began pressing the offending steel managers even harder to retreat.

Along with Kennedy's other advisers, Goldberg decided that if the five smaller firms continued to hold out and one or two others could be persuaded to back down, U.S. Steel's managers would have no choice but to rescind the general price increase. Of the latter firms, Bethlehem, the producer with the largest amount of government-related business, appeared the most vulnerable. As the administration began pressuring its executives with thinly veiled threats to terminate the firm's lucrative military contracts, Goldberg turned up the heat on U.S. Steel's managers still further. He leaked the news that he had offered his resignation, a move Goldberg knew would alarm the business community more generally. A new labor secretary would likely be far less committed to a consensual approach than he had been, raising the possibility of a return to the kind of acrimonious relationship with the executive branch that businessmen had endured during Truman's last few years as president. Such a prospect, Goldberg knew, would turn business managers against the actions of Blough and his cohorts.[70]

In the end, this combination did the trick. While Goldberg began negotiating secretly with U.S. Steel executives, pressures began building on managers at the other producers, Bethlehem in particular. To Roger Blough's apparent shock, Bethlehem's board soon surrendered. News of Goldberg's offer to quit also produced the desired effect among business executives, leading Roger Blough—just three days after peremptorily announcing a general price increase—to eat crow, at least temporarily. At a private meeting interrupted by the news of Bethlehem management's reversal, a victorious but still bitter Goldberg assailed Blough for using what Goldberg called "cheap shyster tactics."[71]

Goldberg went on, denouncing the steel executive to his face with words intended to produce the greatest possible sting:

> ["]You acted exactly like Khrushchev did. While he was negotiating for a test ban he was making secret arrangements to blow the bomb. . . . ["] Well, he [Blough] turned white . . . [.]I said, ["]I don't see the difference. In that White House where George Washington and Abraham Lincoln had been you were standing like a shyster using the President of the United States as a lackey. . . . It was a shabby performance, Roger.["][72]

Blough, momentarily without other options, gave in. U.S. Steel management issued a press release later the same day stating that it was rescinding its price increase so as to remove "a serious obstacle to proper relations between government and business."[73]

The apparent victory, much celebrated in later liberal folklore, proved ephemeral. Although Goldberg, understanding that the government lacked the power to enforce the guidelines unilaterally, had cautioned Kennedy in the aftermath of the dispute to cool things off, their efforts to reassure the leading business managers failed. The whole episode suggested to them that Kennedy and Goldberg intended to enforce their wage-and-price guidelines, in pattern-setting industries at least, in a manner indistinguishable from wage-and-price controls. Thus business managers came to believe, at least momentarily, that the administration's call for voluntary restraint and the development of a genuine consensus in support of such a policy had given way to a more interventionist approach.

The result was the one that Goldberg had feared, namely, a hardening of attitudes among business executives that made even more difficult his quest for an accord that preserved the postwar New Deal. And investors, increasingly apprehensive about an administration policy that they believed would harm their interests, showed their lack of confidence only a month later, when the stock market took its deepest one-day slide since 1929. The decline continued steadily through the end of June, amid a crescendo of business criticism of the Kennedy–Goldberg policy.[74]

Forced on the defensive, the administration's support for the whole approach began to wane. Most telling was the way in which Kennedy and his advisers reacted as the steel industry managers announced piecemeal price increases on various products, moves that over the eighteen months following the April clash essentially restored the general price rise. Afraid to reduce stockholders' confidence in the administration still further, its leaders chose not to resist steel prices' upward climb.

Also indicative of the Kennedy–Goldberg policy's lack of success was the Kaiser Committee's inability thus far to agree on a new contract. Although the members continued to meet and talk, McDonald told the USA Executive Board on September 11, 1962, that rumors of success at Kaiser were premature. The members of the HRRC likewise continued their discussions, but without making much real progress. By the end of the summer of 1962, then, although Goldberg could publicly proclaim that the policy still remained in place, the first clear signs of its eventual failure had begun to appear.[75]

The steel industry managers' refusal to accept the wage–price bargain Goldberg had advocated stemmed from the underlying dispute between labor and management over the respective shares of industry income to which they and the stockholders were entitled. Blough and the others were determined to obtain a rate of return for investors high enough to keep capital flowing into the industry. Only this would enable managers to finance the new technology needed to fight off foreign competitors and arrest the shift toward less expensive steel substitutes. For these reasons, Blough and his associates would not agree to limit their discretion to raise prices. If the new master contract with the USA ate too deeply into firm profits, Blough and his cohorts had reasoned, the latter could be restored to their "proper" level through further price rises, essentially continuing the pattern established over the preceding fifteen years. But that, Goldberg understood, would only defeat the larger objective of protecting the industry from foreign-made steel and substitutes, because the rising cost of domestically produced steel only encouraged their use.[76]

There was truth on both sides, but Blough and his fellow business managers deserved the blame for creating that dilemma. Their determination to obtain a larger share of industry income for themselves and the stockholders than the productivity formula implied that they deserved led American steel industry managers to oppose the kinds of government controls over capital movements that other Western industrialized societies had adopted. This, more than anything else, doomed both the effort to strike a new social contract in steel and the postwar order at the center of which this industry stood. Bethlehem comptroller Frank Brugler revealed management's outlook when he bluntly told a *Fortune* reporter in the spring of 1962, "We're not in business to make steel, we're not in business to build ships, we're not in business to erect buildings. We're in business to make money."[77]

Brugler clearly implied that if steel executives could not earn the high rate of return on their firms' capital that the lack of strict controls on its mobility obliged them to, then such managers would turn to employing workers to make steel and other things in places where labor cost less. U.S. Steel, the industry leader, once again set the pace in that regard.

In 1961, for the first time in the firm's history, U.S. Steel's managers entered into a joint venture with a foreign firm to manufacture steel abroad. The following year, Blough and his colleagues consummated another, similar agreement. In 1962, the firm's managers also stepped up their efforts to diversify, by acquiring a large cement company in the Caribbean. This latter trend would accelerate sharply over the next four years and would be followed by most of the other major steel firms. This would be, of necessity, a gradual process. Having made such an enormous capital investment in U.S. steel plants, managers could not simply abandon them. But they could allow the mills to deteriorate, using the profits they generated for other investments, and eventually extricate themselves as much as possible from the domestic steel business. Such was the future portended by Goldberg's inability to achieve a new social contract in steel.[78]

II

The stalemate there signaled the overall policy's failure as well, a result clearly reflected by developments in the Advisory Committee on Labor–Management Policy. Already faltering even before the steel dispute took place, the entire effort began to unravel after the Kennedy–Goldberg clash with Blough and his associates.

Less than one month after their dramatic confrontation, the national economic conference that the committee had sponsored met in Washington. Intended both to share the ideas the group had been debating with a larger assortment of business executives, labor leaders, academics, and government bureaucrats and promote a meeting of the minds, the conference was a failure, thanks to growing managerial hostility to the Kennedy–Goldberg guidelines policy. The committee tacitly acknowledged the gulf still separating management and labor by deciding in advance that no effort should be made at the conference to sum up its findings. To do otherwise—Henry Ford II, Arthur Burns, and John Franklin had suggested at a committee meeting held shortly before the conference—would imply agreement when none in fact existed.[79]

Even more indicative of how Goldberg's efforts had met with frustration were the results of the committee's work on the collective bargaining report. At that same meeting, which took place five weeks after the steel dispute and just six days before the plunge in the stock market, the group approved the final version of its collective bargaining report and presented it to Kennedy. This document, already watered down so much as to be almost totally without bite, also contained three additional statements—one from Joseph Block and Arthur Burns, a second from Henry Ford II, and a third from the labor delegates—that reiterated their earlier respective objections. The group's decision to submit a report both vague and riddled with dissents marked the failure of Goldberg's larger quest for a consensual bargain that preserved the postwar New Deal.[80]

With that step, the committee quickly lost what little momentum it still had left. After a brief session on May 22 during the national economic conference, the group did not meet again for two and a half months. For the next year it would be chaired by Luther Hodges, whose earlier attacks on the Business Advisory Council had already undermined managerial confidence in his abilities. Even though Hodges's accession had been expected under the rotating

scheme Goldberg had devised at the outset, the move made the prospects for
real progress in the committee even dimmer.[81]

The next few sessions only confirmed the growing sense of frustration
there. On August 7, the fourth subcommittee, which had examined the nation's balance-of-payments problems, presented a draft report, and like the
ones produced by the other subcommittees, it was very vague. Apart from
general agreement that the United States needed to increase exports, the
report failed to endorse specific proposals. And when Joseph Block complained about this key weakness, the subcommittee's chairman, Arthur Burns,
told him that its members could not agree on anything further.[82]

Moving from bad to worse, the committee turned next to discussing the
proposed study of concentrated economic power. Although the group had
earlier agreed to take up the issue in the fall, George Meany attacked the
whole idea, saying that examining issues on which there was no hope of
achieving a consensus would be pointless. David McDonald echoed that sentiment and then went on to predict that such a debate would only increase
labor–management antagonism and give the impression that class conflict was
once again on the rise in the United States. Such results, he added, would
satisfy only "those who rule the USSR." After some further discussion in the
same vein, Goldberg suggested that the group once again defer its study. This
proposal, which the committee adopted, prevented a complete rupture, but
Joseph Block spoke for most managerial members of the group when he
complained that it should not keep postponing its discussion of such a central
issue.[83]

Perhaps most telling was the debate at the next meeting, held the following
month, over whether to endorse government-sponsored replicas, on an industrywide basis, of the Advisory Committee on Labor–Management Policy.
The authors of the balance-of-payments report had endorsed the creation of
such groups in those industries most threatened by foreign competition.
Henry Ford II, however, disagreed sharply with the whole idea, saying that
"the matter of establishing industry labor–management committees raises
most serious questions concerning the responsibilities of management, the
role of unions, and competition among employers in the industry."[84]

Having grasped the implications for managerial prerogatives of the corporatist scheme Goldberg had in mind, Ford opposed its further development,
at least until the Advisory Committee on Labor–Management Policy could
study the whole idea very carefully. Although Reuther spoke out in favor of
the industry committees idea, the most that the others would support was a
call for labor and management to establish such bodies voluntarily. By September 1962 Goldberg's plan for expanding the process of renegotiating the
postwar New Deal in a consensual fashion thus had come to naught.[85]

The group's next session, the last Goldberg attended, featured presentations by the Swedish experts he had earlier invited to visit the United States.
Goldberg had postponed their meeting with the Advisory Committee on
Labor–Management Policy until that fall in the hope that by then the group
would have reached a genuine consensus. Instead, the Swedish visitors spoke

to a committee whose members remained deeply divided over the desirability of moving further in the direction of corporatism. Although those in attendance listened politely as the Swedish officials explained the workings of their own system, most committee members indicated no real enthusiasm for its adoption in the United States. They evidently had come to understand the obstacles that impeded replication of that model in the United States.[86]

Indeed, the most probing questions committee members asked dealt with how the Swedes had come to adopt their own system, and the answers their guests gave offered little reason for believing that Americans could copy it at this time. When Walter Reuther asked the director of the Swedish Confederation of Employers, Bertil Kugelberg, what had persuaded employers there to accept unions and the country's corporatist arrangements, he replied that the principal reason had been a desire to avoid even more statist outcomes. Although perhaps a real possibility in Sweden during the 1930s, when its managers had turned decisively toward "the Middle Way," such a powerful impetus was clearly lacking in the United States by the early 1960s, if, indeed, it had ever existed.[87]

Similar sorts of questions elicited responses in the same vein. Arthur Burns asked Kugelberg if the Swedes had enacted any legislation similar to the American Sherman Act, which tended to block movement toward a more corporatist political and economic system. Kugelberg answered that although there were some Swedish statutes that regulated cartels, "what laws do exist in Sweden are in no way like the American anti-trust laws."[88] This, too, was a crucial difference. Americans' much greater hostility to concentrated power had both created and sustained obstacles to corporatism that did not exist in Sweden.

Burns, also interested in how Sweden's almost entirely unionized workforce had been persuaded to exercise self-restraint in making wage demands, asked the head of the Swedish Trade Union Federation, Arne Geijer, about that issue. Geijer replied that the Swedish industry's much greater reliance on selling abroad was the real reason. The need to compete in a global market, he suggested, was so great that the rank and file, as well as the leadership, had become fully cognizant of the dangers created by wage–price spirals. Once again, this critical precondition simply did not exist in the United States of the early 1960s.[89]

One other key difference lay in the realm of worker control over the production process. George Taylor noted that so-called work rules issues gave rise to many labor–management disputes in the United States, and then he asked whether that was the case in Sweden. Geijer replied that such matters typically were local ones and seldom became so divisive that they demanded the attention of the national labor and management organizations. Kugelberg elaborated on that response, pointing out that "in Sweden it is an agreed principle that the employer has the right to assign work and assign the method by which it will be done."[90] Although evidently acceptable to Swedish workers, many of their American counterparts in the early 1960s still resisted making such a large concession voluntarily. If the American working class had thus far gained less economic security than the Swedish one, that was at least partly because the former still sought more than that.

The Swedes' efforts to promote their own system thus ended, like the work of the committee itself, in failure. Looking back on the whole experience much later, Goldberg observed, "We got nowhere, and it was nobody's fault really. Our labor movement was organized in such a way that the federation heads did not have the authority to bind their membership to such a deal."[91]

Goldberg was at least partly right. The very loosely woven nature of the American labor movement was a crucial obstacle impeding progress toward Swedish-style corporatism. Those affiliates that dominated industries in which foreign competition posed no immediate problem could, unlike individual Swedish unions, successfully resist the federation's support for Goldberg's program. And many of those affiliates, seeing little in it for themselves, did in fact choose to do so.

But whether the business executives behind the managerial revolt would have gone along, even if that problem had not existed, seems more doubtful than Goldberg suggested. They had shown little interest in a compromise that would necessarily have required them to share more of their power with the state and organized labor. Although Goldberg later said of the business leaders on the Labor–Management Advisory Committee that "I think they wanted to make a deal," this appears to have been true only for them.[92] The heads of the core industrial firms, on the other hand, had behaved over the preceding five years in ways that indicated otherwise.

Thus, in the last analysis, Goldberg's proposed solution failed because organized labor lacked the power to compel employers to accept it. This was the only argument leaders of the managerial revolt fully respected. Just as labor's growing power during the 1930s and 1940s had brought men who favored the postwar social contract to the top of the core industrial firms, so did the waning of that power lead eventually to the displacement of such business leaders by a new breed of more conservative successors. By the fall of 1962 the latter, and the larger business community for which they spoke, had begun withdrawing from the postwar New Deal.

Managers pursued that objective in two different ways. In industries such as steel, in which the unions proved strong enough to resist employers' efforts to regain control quickly over the production process and reduce wages, both the movement of facilities to areas with nonunion workforces and the process of diversification accelerated dramatically. In other areas of the economy— most notably chemicals, shipping, railways, aerospace, and newspaper publishing—where unions were weaker or those other options less feasible, managers used a more direct approach. They provoked bitter, heavily publicized strikes, the first successful round in a series of contests aimed at winning back the prerogatives management had surrendered during the 1930s and 1940s.

Although a few major employers had taken steps in these directions even earlier, the large firms most supportive of the postwar New Deal did not do so until the early 1960s. And at the same time, the provisions of the Taft–Hartley and Landrum–Griffin Acts that management had won earlier blocked most of labor's efforts to expand into new industries. The result in the years ahead would be the decline of private-sector unionism and of the postwar social contract that organized labor had done so much to sustain.[93]

The managerial retreat from the postwar New Deal encouraged many labor leaders, especially those identified with the traditional AFL view, to follow suit. They saw events as increasingly vindicating their continuing hostility toward state supervision of the labor–management relationship. The federal government's enforcement of the new Landrum–Griffin law in particular tended to encourage such sentiment. Although Goldberg tried to administer the act fairly, by its very nature the law tended to strengthen the insurgent groups in the unions. In that limited sense, a step forward for democracy, one direct consequence was to weaken unions in dealing with their managerial adversaries.[94]

The act tended to undermine the USA's strength, like that of other major unions, in two different ways. Landrum–Griffin's "anticorruption" provisions contained a clause requiring that all union officials be bonded. Although ostensibly a precaution that would protect USA members against official misconduct, the resulting insurance costs proved to be substantial, some $190,000 for the first three years alone. This was a substantial drain on the union's treasury, especially so during a time when the USA was already operating in the red.[95]

As burdensome as the bonding requirements were proving to be, even more worrisome to the USA leadership were the new law's provisions governing union elections. The act required secret ballots in all contests for union office, lowered the number of nominations a candidate needed in order to run for district director or international officer, and allowed dissidents to challenge any infraction of those rules in the courts. Goldberg had drafted the required changes in the USA constitution and bylaws before leaving for the Labor Department, but the new provisions underwent their first test only after he had taken up his new duties there.[96]

Conditions in the steel industry led workers to make use of the provisions to an extent the USA's leaders found disturbing. The period of prolonged unemployment in steel bred rank-and-file dissatisfaction with the leadership's policies, especially among those laid off for an extended period. Although such dissidents still constituted a minority, they proved far more able to disrupt the McDonald faction's policies, thanks to the provisions of the Landrum–Griffin Act. It also tended to increase the rank and file's unhappiness with the USA's leaders, because the law had compelled the latter to standardize election procedures for all locals.

Many members saw that as yet another unwelcome step toward centralizing power at the top. Aware of the ways in which the act had strengthened opposition to its policies, the leadership responded by denying once again the dissidents' demands for formal due process in expelling workers and by passing a new rule that denied voting privileges to any union member jobless for more than a year. Even so, dissidents continue to pressure the leadership with potentially expensive lawsuits and election challenges, undermining further the rank and file solidarity so essential to the union's strength.[97]

By the summer of 1962, such behavior, and Goldberg's insistence that the USA and other unions comply with the law, led to an eruption at an executive board meeting. There Joe Germano, leader of the largest single local and Goldberg's patron from his earliest days with SWOC, angrily attacked McDonald's policy of going along with the act's requirements. In a thinly veiled reference to Goldberg, Germano reported that "the Secretary of this organization and myself . . . tried the best way we know how to bring this [election procedures problem] to the attention of not only the Department of Labor but to the [other] people in Washington. I didn't get too much response out of them."[98]

The only way to protect the union's continued existence, he argued, was by either overturning the law through the courts or obtaining its repeal. Mincing no words, Germano told the USA Executive Board, "You just don't do it, boys, any other way, [that is, by] trying to meet all the damn requirements because if that is the way we [had] started out in 1936 to organize the United Steelworkers of America, well, good Lord, I am telling you we would all be in jail."[99]

Although evidently sympathetic to Germano's arguments, the board nonetheless refused to adopt his proposed solution. At that time, the union's chances of overturning the law, the other board members understood, were just about nil. Director James Robb spoke for McDonald and the executive board's majority when he told Germano, "I think if we could repeal Landrum–Griffin here we would sure as the world do it and do it in a hurry. But I think it is going to be with us for quite a while."[100]

That hard reality did much to discredit labor leaders such as Goldberg and Reuther, who favored allowing the government to police labor's compliance with the postwar New Deal. The fact that even a secretary of labor friendly to them felt compelled to enforce the law only underscored the dangers of consenting to such supervision. So Meany and the other former AFL chieftains increasingly reasoned. As 1962 drew to a close, they, like the executives behind the managerial revolt, would begin moving away from their earlier cautious support for that key element of the postwar social contract.

Although Reuther resisted this trend and, unlike Goldberg, remained active for the next several years in national union affairs, the UAW chief found himself increasingly isolated in the AFL–CIO. Reduced after 1962 solely to playing the role of labor's Billy Graham, Reuther kept exhorting his brethren to set their sights higher, but with steadily less effect.[101]

By the early 1960s, this sea change was producing serious strains in the federation. It had been a rocky "marriage" right from the start. In addition to the bickering over Landrum–Griffin, debates over whether to continue disciplining those affiliates whose officers had been found guilty of wrongdoing, and jurisdictional disputes also had produced deep splits in labor's ranks during the late 1950s. Indeed, so serious were those three controversies that they had almost led to a rupture in 1959.[102]

Tensions eased somewhat when the AFL–CIO Executive Council called a halt to the work of the Ethical Practices Committee. Although it had found that officials in the powerful Carpenters Union had violated the federation's Ethical Practices Code and refused to desist from such behavior, the federation's leaders declined to vote for that affiliate's expulsion. By then very conscious of how antiunion forces were using the corruption issue to weaken the labor movement, Meany and most of his colleagues opted to return to the more traditional pattern of allowing each affiliate to handle such problems on its own. Encouraging them to do so was the demonstrated failure of the expulsion remedy to harm the largest affiliate so penalized, the Teamsters, which continued to thrive outside the federation's ranks. This example had done much to reduce the fear of expulsion among other affiliates tainted by corruption and thus the effectiveness of this means of persuading such affiliates to reform themselves. For these reasons, and to Goldberg's chagrin, the Ethical Practices Committee, after its initial burst of activity during 1957–59, failed to meet again for the next three years.[103]

This hiatus did heal divisions in the federation some what during the early 1960s, but the debates over the Landrum–Griffin Act and jurisdictional disputes continued to fester. Goldberg tried hard as labor secretary to ease those tensions, and with some success. Under his watchful eye, enforcement of Landrum–Griffin's anticorruption provisions was not allowed to provide more fodder for one-sided managerial attacks. And with his help, the federation did eventually arrive at a new agreement governing jurisdictional disputes, one that put to rest some of the most divisive such conflicts.[104]

But they were not the only ones that imperiled the House of Labor's newly restored unity. By the early 1960s, the federation's leaders also began to find themselves increasingly divided over issues of race relations and foreign policy. Although a genuine consensus did exist in favor of new civil rights legislation aimed at giving nonwhites equality before the law, agreement broke down with respect to desegregating unions and the workplace. Meany and the heads of those former AFL affiliates that practiced the most blatant forms of discrimination favored slow steps, whereas officials from the former CIO unions wanted more speed.

In some instances, the reluctance to act quickly reflected an indifference rooted in bigotry. Goldberg firmly believed, however, that Meany and most heads of AFL–CIO affiliates genuinely wanted to end Jim Crow unionism and favored caution only because they feared that swift steps toward desegregation might alienate white workers and thereby undermine labor's strength. Actions that reformed unions only at the cost of severely weakening them would hurt blacks and Latinos more than they helped them, Meany argued forcefully. But inaction offered them no real assistance either, a dilemma to which he and his allies lacked an adequate answer.[105]

Although those on both sides of that debate in the AFL–CIO kept their disagreements under control between 1957 and 1962, union officials' ability to do so was coming under growing pressure from other quarters. Black and Latino workers, joined by middle-class liberals, had begun complaining loudly about the AFL–CIO chieftains' reluctance to put their own house in order, developments that by the early 1960s began to elicit a real response. In the USA, the first sign of the changing times appeared during an October 1961 executive board meeting. There Joe Germano, angry over the way in which antiunion forces were attempting to discredit labor by labeling its leaders as racists, urged his colleagues both to fight harder against discriminatory employers and to defend the union's record in that area. He reminded his colleagues, "We have been the first organization in this whole country . . . who have given . . . minority groups . . . the opportunity to get . . . jobs in these steel mills where it was all lily white."[106]

Although this was true in some instances, the USA had made itself vulnerable to criticism by failing to follow up much on its pathbreaking achievements during the 1930s and 1940s. The union's earliest wage settlements, which had granted larger pay boosts to those holding the lowest-paid jobs, had narrowed the wage differential between whites and blacks by an impressive amount. After the early 1940s, however, the Steelworkers Union gradually retreated from that objective, a change that had soon brought an end to such gains. USA leaders had also failed to give blacks more than a handful of positions on the union payroll, the kind of action that had always been at their discretion. When Joe Germano told the USA Executive Board in October 1961 that he intended to hire more blacks to work in union offices and urged his colleagues to do the same, he testified eloquently to those earlier missed opportunities.[107]

In addition to these sins of omission, the operation of the postwar New Deal itself tended to erode blacks' and Latinos' tenuous footholds in the industry. The very fact of unionization had the effect of diminishing employment opportunities for them. Steel industry managers had hired nonwhites during the first three decades of the twentieth century either to break strikes or to keep the general wage level down. After the USA emerged during the 1930s and early 1940s, these incentives vanished and, along with them, much if not all managerial interest in employing blacks and Latinos. Save for periods of acute labor shortages during wartime, openings for them thereafter had become scarce.[108]

The industry's stagnation during the late 1950s and early 1960s, as well as the managerial revolt it spawned, made that already bad situation even worse. Managers' efforts to replace workers with machinery had the greatest initial impact on the least-skilled jobs, which blacks and Latinos held in disproportionate numbers. The lack of plantwide seniority systems in steel exacerbated the problem. The existing system, based as it was on task, frustrated blacks' and Latinos' efforts to move from the sorts of jobs disappearing in the wake of automation into the more-skilled and better-paying positions more insulated from that process.[109]

Neither Goldberg nor the union's other leaders had intended such a result. Even more important, much of the blame for black and Latino workers' plight lay elsewhere. Racism in the rank and file, compounded by managers' willingness to exploit such sentiment, constituted the root causes of the shrinking job opportunities for nonwhites in steel, as it did in other unionized industries. But the USA leadership's unwillingness to fight harder against those very large obstacles made union officials vulnerable to criticism that they, too, supported segregation.[110]

But change was in the wind. The clearest sign, one that Goldberg had long favored, came in March 1962, when the union for the first time negotiated a master contract containing a clause barring racial discrimination in the workplace. Although this, like the other steps, was still only symbolic, it portended larger, more substantial measures to come. Similar actions by the earlier 1960s were taking place at other unions, especially those affiliated with the AFL–CIO's Industrial Union Department. These developments indicated to Goldberg that the federation clearly was moving, on this issue at least, toward the more traditional CIO position rather than away from it.[111]

Labor's stand on the cold war was another, more divisive matter for the AFL–CIO leadership. While Meany and his colleagues from the AFL wing continued to mouth the stridently anti-Soviet line that had been government policy since the late 1940s, some of the former CIO leaders had begun by the early 1960s to favor a less confrontational stance. This was a disagreement of great potential importance, because it could weaken a linchpin that had held together the postwar New Deal.[112]

The simmering dispute finally erupted during the summer of 1962 when Meany tried to remove both David McDonald and James Carey from their posts as alternative delegates to the International Confederation of Free Trade Unions. When McDonald told the USA Executive Board about Meany's intentions, the news sparked an angry discussion. Understanding that Meany's move was only the latest in a series that suggested that the older AFL chieftains were coming to control the "new" federation, the USA leadership voted to authorize McDonald to take any action, including withdrawal from the AFL–CIO, should Meany refuse to back down. McDonald captured the mood of the board's members when he told them:

> There have been repeated insults to our organization, repeated insults to your President, repeated insults to other members of this Executive Board who have had occasion to call upon the President of the AFL–CIO, and I don't like it. If he doesn't want our [per capita contribution of] $60,000 a month he doesn't have to take it. That's the way I feel about it.[113]

Faced with that threat, Meany relented. He and McDonald soon smoothed over their differences, but the whole episode was a harbinger of more serious disagreements yet to come.[114]

Goldberg did his best to keep the organization together on the cold war issue. He pleased George Meany and his supporters by supporting Kennedy's ill-fated attempts to dislodge Cuban leader Fidel Castro. Although Goldberg had not been privy to the Bay of Pigs invasion plan prior to its execution and would, he told Kennedy, have opposed it as certain to fail, Goldberg did defend the effort afterward as well intentioned.

He went even further, chastising liberal critics of the administration's Cuban policy in a widely reported address. Entitled "Are We Forgetting the Past?" the speech compared Kennedy's detractors on the left with those who had favored Neville Chamberlain's policy of appeasing Nazi leaders during the 1930s. At the same time, Goldberg won favor with the federation's less hawkish faction by ordering an end to covert CIA funding for U.S. labor organizations operating abroad. Believing that the proper mission of such groups was to build labor unions rather than conduct espionage, he put a stop, at least for a while, to such subsidies.[115]

Although this sort of balancing act worked fairly well during Goldberg's first eighteen months as labor secretary, by the summer of 1962, many union leaders had privately begun to grumble, from their various perspectives, about his overall performance. Goldberg's strong support for the guidelines policy and his at least temporarily successful campaign to keep down labor's wage demands offended many union leaders. He made them uneasy, too, by using his own great knowledge of their internal affairs in carrying out those policies. Although friendly to labor's cause, his vast experience gave him a degree of influence with them unprecedented for a secretary of labor, a fact some union officials found worrisome.[116]

This uneasiness, like the disputes over Landrum–Griffin, jurisdictional issues, civil rights, and foreign policy, reflected erosion in support for the center position in the AFL–CIO with which the USA was identified. Although still highly influential by the early 1960s, the union's declining strength portended a gradual shift in organized labor away from the USA's stands on most major issues toward the more traditional AFL views. Only with respect to the electoral alliance with the Democrats, and the federation's political action effort more generally, did the House of Labor adopt the CIO's views completely. For all these reasons, many union leaders began hoping that Goldberg would move on to another office, specifically the Supreme Court.[117]

Their wish was soon granted. In the last week of August 1962, Justice Felix Frankfurter decided that his poor health would no longer allow him to continue serving on the Supreme Court. He so informed Chief Justice Earl Warren, who passed along the news to the president. Kennedy, in turn, discussed the matter with his brother the attorney general. The two men, after briefly considering Harvard Law School professor Paul Freund and Solicitor General Archibald Cox, settled on Goldberg as their first choice to succeed Frankfurter.[118]

In many respects, Goldberg was the obvious one. He had long wanted such an appointment, a fact of which both Kennedys were aware. Goldberg, too, had compiled a very distinguished record as a lawyer, and—as important to the Kennedys if not more so—he had time and again demonstrated his loyalty to them. Indeed, but for Goldberg's help during the McClellan Committee investigation and the 1960 campaign, John Kennedy might never have won the presidency. And when he accepted the cabinet post that Kennedy offered to him, Goldberg also cut his ties to organized labor. Although he had told Kennedy that the move was needed to eliminate any managerial doubts about

Goldberg's "impartiality," another consequence, perhaps intended, was to increase Kennedy's existing sense of obligation.[119]

The vacated seat had been the only one held by a Jew, and this fact, too, played an important part in Kennedy's decision. Both he and his brother wanted to continue the tradition of Jewish representation on the Court. And although Freund also was Jewish, he struck Robert Kennedy in particular as too "academic" and remote. Moreover, Freund had hurt his chances by declining John Kennedy's offer of the solicitor generalship, in marked contrast with Goldberg's decision to accept the post of labor secretary.[120]

Out of respect for his abilities, appreciation for his assistance, and a desire to select someone of the Jewish faith, Kennedy thus decided to offer Goldberg the position on the Supreme Court. The president, however, clearly would have liked him to turn down the offer, because Goldberg's key role in defining and carrying out the administration's program had made him very valuable and, in Kennedy's mind at least, indispensable. But Goldberg wanted the new assignment, which had been his dream since law school. The stalemate in the Advisory Committee on Labor–Management Policy and the larger frustration with the administration's political and economic policies likely also persuaded him to make the switch. A disappointed but understanding Kennedy thus announced on August 29 that he had named Goldberg as Frankfurter's successor.[121]

And so, after joining the Kennedy administration only twenty months earlier, he was leaving it. And at the same time, Goldberg was abandoning, too, the task he had set for himself there, one that had proved too much even for his considerable talents. At best, his efforts there had sustained the postwar New Deal for a brief period, but they had failed to reinvigorate it.

The limits of Goldberg's achievements can best be seen in the administration's inability during its first two years of office to reduce unemployment below the level experienced during the late 1950s. Although the increase in government spending on armaments had helped sustain the economic recovery that had begun during the spring of 1961, the expansion failed to accelerate quickly. In the first eleven months of that year, seasonally adjusted unemployment had remained steady at an official rate of 6.8 percent. Although it dropped to 5.6 percent over the following three months, thereafter it leveled off, and at a higher plateau than those recorded after the three previous postwar recessions. Even more disturbing to Goldberg, the number of Americans out of work for six months or more during 1961 reached 800,000, the highest in more than two decades. Thus by the summer of 1962, the Kennedy administration's overall record on unemployment showed little improvement over that of Eisenhower's during his last three years in office and, in some respects, was even worse.[122]

Goldberg was also distressed by the way in which the Council of Economic Advisers tended to accept the level of employment during that period as close to "normal" or "full" employment. On January 3, 1962, Goldberg sent to Walter Heller his comments on the CEA's draft of its annual report. Goldberg's first and most serious criticism concerned the report's declaration that the administration sought to reduce unemployment to 4 percent. Goldberg argued that the report's authors should refrain from setting any specific target, "lest the public regard it as a norm."[123]

If Heller and company insisted on the need to set a goal for the year, Goldberg wrote, then they should emphasize that the 4 percent target was just an interim goal, "to be re-evaluated as we approach closer to it." He went on to attack the report's passages suggesting that in light of experience, the administration would not be "prudent" in seeking to reduce the official rate of unemployment below that target. This was important, Goldberg told Heller, because "the effort to justify the 4 per cent rate on historical grounds adds to the impression that a 4 per cent rate is a desirable norm consistent with the meaning of full employment."[124]

In addition to these objections, Goldberg offered another, even more serious one. He attacked the CEA's tendency to define "full employment" as the level of employment consistent with overall price stability. He reminded Heller that inflation could result even when joblessness was acute. To label such conditions as a period of more than *full employment* made no sense. This point was a very important one, because the draft's wording implied that the only effective means of combating inflation was to increase unemployment, a notion with which Goldberg totally disagreed. When Heller balked at making all of Goldberg's proposed changes, he followed up with two, more sharply worded memos. Goldberg stated in the second one:

> I feel very strongly that this [CEA] message should not adopt a definition of full employment cast in terms of avoiding inflation; that this definition should be [cast], rather, in terms of eliminating all except frictional unemployment; and that nothing should be included here which even permits the interpretation that the President is accepting 4% (or any other specific figure) as a measure of full employment.[125]

To Goldberg, like his labor associates, the term *full employment* should mean what it implied on its face. To underscore how far the nation still was from that objective, he took steps to improve the accuracy of the Labor Department's unemployment statistics. This initiative was controversial, because a more honest measurement of joblessness in America gave credence to the nation's socialist critics, who rightly pointed out that the USA's enormous postwar prosperity had nonetheless left millions of people without work. Goldberg argued in response to those counseling against greater candor about unemployment that the way to silence the nation's critics was to employ its people, rather than to try to conceal their plight.[126]

Increasingly dissatisfied with the administration's failure to get unemployment down even to the 4 percent "interim" target, Goldberg in the spring of 1962 began pressing for more government stimulus to accelerate economic growth. He disagreed, however, with those in the administration, most notably Walter Heller, who advocated a tax cut as the best way to achieve that goal. Goldberg suspected that such a move would prove inadequate and inevitably lead—given Kennedy's concern with avoiding a budget deficit lest the country's balance-of-payments problems grow any worse—to more reductions in federal spending.

Instead, Goldberg preferred more government expenditures on programs aimed at alleviating unemployment and poverty, the sorts of measures that labor had pressed successfully since the middle 1930s as the best way to fight joblessness. But without a tax increase levied on the well-to-do—legislation that Kennedy understood his administration lacked the power to wrest from Congress—Goldberg's approach, in the short run at least, would have produced a budget deficit, which Kennedy refused to contemplate. The related inflation and balance-of-payments concerns ruled out, in Kennedy's mind, any recourse to the traditional economic prescriptions.[127]

The stalemate continued throughout 1962, but as Goldberg's tenure at the Labor Department drew to a close, those favoring a tax cut were in the ascendancy. Still held in check through the end of 1962, the future, at least for a time, would belong to these forces. Their first real victory, the across-the-board income tax cut of 1964, would mark a major defeat for organized labor and the first big step away from the pattern of the previous two decades, when the federal government imposed significantly higher and at least modestly redistributive income taxes.[128]

The record for labor under Kennedy's tenure as president thus was very mixed. But although there was much truth to Walter Lippmann's observation that the new administration behaved during its first few years in office "like the Eisenhower administration thirty years younger," even then labor did not come away entirely empty-handed.[129] Kennedy's victory, along with those of the other Democrats labor had helped elect to Congress and the state legislatures two years earlier, helped close the door to much of the most conservative managers' antiunion agenda. Their bid to outlaw the union shop, either piecemeal or with a national so-called right-to-work law, ground to a halt during the early 1960s.

At the same time, their calls for bringing labor unions under the Sherman Act and restricting their political action efforts similarly went unheeded. When these same forces attempted to manipulate public concern about jurisdictional strikes at military bases so as to outlaw such strikes entirely, Goldberg managed to produce through mediation a compromise formula that blocked that effort. And as noted earlier, he prevented an unfair administration of the Landrum–Griffin Act's anticorruption provisions, which might have harmed labor's standing with the public even more.[130]

Goldberg also saw to it that Kennedy appointed to the NLRB and the federal bench those who opposed the managerial revolt. Kennedy's appointees handed down a series of decisions over the next few years, whose effect was to outlaw most of the confrontational bargaining tactics collectively known as *Boulwarism* while also weakening some of the Landrum–Griffin law's most restrictive features. These accomplishments had their price, however. The new rulings substantially increased both the NLRB's and the courts' supervision over the labor–management relationship. By supporting that change, labor leaders set in motion a process that eventually would work against workers' interests. But at that time, the move marked a federal government concession to labor that management had strongly resisted.[131]

In addition to these essentially defensive achievements came another, more constructive one. In the spring of 1962, Kennedy issued an executive order at Goldberg's initiative that legalized collective bargaining between the federal government and its clerical and technical workforce. The order transformed what had been government employee organizations little different from company unions into ones of the sort that composed the AFL–CIO. This change rippled outward from the executive branch of the federal government to public employees in state and local governments. From these quarters would come millions of new union members, whose numbers would offset at least partially the decline in private-sector unionism. This was a major victory for organized labor, by far the most significant of the early 1960s, and one it would surely not have won had Nixon defeated Kennedy.[132]

The record in the larger international order at the center of which the United States stood remained similarly mixed. The forces at work behind the collapse of the postwar New Deal, would in the years immediately after Goldberg's departure from the cabinet, spread beyond the United States. The clearest sign of this phenomenon was the return of the labor and social democratic parties to power in most of these countries. Like Kennedy's election in 1960, this change reflected a withdrawal by the conservative parties there from the postwar social contract. Lacking the racial divisions that plagued the American working and lower middle classes, their counterparts in those societies were better able to resist that trend, but in the end, the outcomes would prove more similar than different.[133]

Goldberg did try hard during his tenure as labor secretary to establish programs that would strengthen trade unions in the other highly industrialized market societies, but with limited effectiveness. Like his labor brethren, he saw this goal as essential to improving the lot of workers there and to preventing gradual erosion in American workers' own wages and working conditions. Of particular concern to him was the state of labor in Japan and Latin America. Unlike Western Europe, whose growing prosperity was encouraging unions to raise their collective bargaining objectives, by 1960 the unions in those countries had proved either unwilling or unable to improve wages and working conditions very much. The former reason appears to have been decisive in Japan, where workers' organizations, despite pleas from their American counterparts, refrained from pushing for much larger increases in pay and benefits.[134]

Believing that more exposure to American trade unions' methods and achievements could persuade Japanese labor leaders to imitate them, in the spring of 1961 Goldberg ordered the creation of a labor-exchange program with Japan. Working together with officials at the State Department, he arranged for visits at the government's expense of eighty Japanese union officials to the United States and twenty American labor leaders to Japan. And to shore up support for the program, Goldberg himself visited Japan in November 1961, where he met with the Japanese cabinet and leading trade union officials.

Despite such contacts, Goldberg's Japanese initiative failed to produce its intended result. Aware that lower labor costs were creating demand among American consumers for lower-priced Japanese goods, union leaders in Japan refrained from pushing for comparable wages and benefits, lest this cost advantage be lost. Although Japanese unions did press for contract improvements, their leaders made certain that labor costs there continued to trail American ones by enough to sustain the growth of Japanese exports. At most, Goldberg's efforts encouraged Japanese unionists to narrow that differential somewhat, but not enough to prevent the continued loss of markets to Japanese competitors.[135]

Goldberg's other major initiative, aimed at strengthening the international labor movement, made somewhat more headway. The Labor and State Departments, together with officials from the AFL–CIO, worked to promote the growth of social democratic trade unions throughout Latin America. At Goldberg's initiative, the number of labor attachés assigned to embassies there was increased substantially. He also endorsed and won government support for the AFL–CIO's own efforts in that direction. The primary purpose of those actions, like the Japanese initiative, was to improve wages and working conditions throughout the region while also protecting the gains of the American working and lower middle classes from low-wage foreign competition.[136]

These goals, however, were entangled from the outset with the imperatives of the cold war. Goldberg tried to win conservative support for that plan by arguing that the alternative would likely be more Latin American revolutions on the Cuban model. Although an effective tactic in the short run, its long-term implications were very troubling. Using this argument for building unions there encouraged a continuation of the arms race and increased the risk of another armed conflict between East and West. And if the prospects for more Cuban-style revolutions were to recede, Goldberg's reasoning implied that so too would the need for building social democratic institutions abroad. Although neither of these problems was salient by the end of his tenure at the Labor Department, their emergence would ultimately contribute to the postwar New Deal's collapse.[137]

Goldberg's departure from the Kennedy administration thus came at a time when it was still committed to its initial course, but in less than a year, pressures acting on it from above and below would push Kennedy and his principal advisers in very different directions. Most of Kennedy's and Johnson's domestic achievements after 1962 would take place on the new frontiers of race and gender, rather than what by then had come to seem the older one of class. And in the area of foreign policy, the Kennedy–Johnson administration's hawkishness, though essentially consistent with its two predecessors, would soon lead to a debacle that called into question the most basic assumptions underlying the U.S. government's conduct of the cold war. And this in turn would undermine the linchpin that had held together the postwar New Deal.

Some indications of the changes in the wind can be seen in the new books that appeared during 1962/63: James Baldwin's *The Fire Next Time*, Betty Friedan's *The Feminine Mystique*, Rachel Carson's *Silent Spring*, a manifesto prepared by a group of young student radicals called "The Port Huron Statement," Michael Harrington's *The Other America*, and ultimately perhaps the most influential, one by an obscure University of Chicago economist named Milton Friedman entitled *Capitalism and Freedom*. Another sign came in October 1962, the same month in which Goldberg assumed his seat on the Supreme Court, when the editors of *Fortune* dropped the monthly labor column that had appeared regularly since October 1948. Just as the column's emergence had reflected sophisticated business managers' understanding that labor would, at least for a time, play a major role in defining the nation's political and economic policies, so did its disappearance signal their awareness that unions would no longer do so. The heyday of Arthur Goldberg, and of the postwar New Deal with which he was so closely identified, had come to an end.[138]

10

Rupture

Wʜᴇɴ Gᴏʟᴅʙᴇʀɢ ᴀssᴜᴍᴇᴅ his place on the Supreme Court in the fall of 1962, the postwar order still appeared, on the surface at least, to be fully intact. By the time of his extraordinary decision to leave the Court in the summer of 1965, this order had clearly ruptured. During those three pivotal years, the Supreme Court both responded to the increasing pressures against the postwar New Deal and helped shape them with a burst of pathbreaking decisions, many of which were made possible by Goldberg's appointment to the bench. At the same time, these pressures caused a rupture in Goldberg's former client, the Steelworkers Union, thereby ending his hopes for seeing a new social contract emerge in this centrally important industry that would preserve its long-term health.

In elective politics, this same basic disturbance helped produce the enactment of much new legislation, whose net effect contributed still more to the postwar New Deal's decline. The actions of Goldberg, his former USA colleagues, and those operating at the national level of elective politics during these three years reveal the forces at work that brought about the postwar order's collapse and also the long-term consequences of this development, for both Goldberg and the social bargain he had helped negotiate.

II

Goldberg's appointment to the Supreme Court must be viewed in retrospect as one of the most consequential in its history. He succeeded Felix Frankfurter, who had been the Court's most influential member since Roosevelt's appointments had transformed it during the 1930s and 1940s. Under Frankfurter's leadership, the Court's Roosevelt and Truman appointees had greatly reduced its interventionist role, especially with respect to reviewing legislation regulating the economy. This change followed the Court's nearly disastrous confrontation during the mid-1930s with the Roosevelt administration and Congress, when a conservative majority on the Court had struck down several important pieces of New Deal legislation.

The clash highlighted the Court's unresponsiveness to electoral majorities and greatly damaged its reputation. Only the decision by some members of the Court's conservative bloc to desist, following Roosevelt's overwhelming reelection victory in 1936, averted the passage of legislation that would have substantially weakened the Court. Frankfurter and his followers concluded from this—and other episodes in which the Supreme Court struck down laws intended to regulate the nation's economic life—that the Court, as the head of the federal government branch least responsive to popular will, should defer to Congress and the executive in the realm of political and economic policymaking.[1]

This tack did much to restore public support for the Court, but by the time of Goldberg's appointment many in the legal community had begun to grumble that Frankfurter and his supporters had learned the lesson of the 1930s all too well. While Harvard law professor Paul Freund continued to counsel against the dangers of judicial interventionism, another group, led by Yale's Charles L. Black Jr., argued that in recent years the Court had too often refused to address important social problems, out of a misguided desire to protect its own prestige. At the heart of this controversy was a debate over the extent to which the Court should use its power to contain the pressures that threatened the postwar New Deal and to aid the effort to redefine it in ways that would allow those who had benefited the least from this social bargain to share more equally in its benefits. Freund argued against such a role for the Court on the ground that it would pave the way for a return to fiascoes such as the one experienced during the mid-1930s, and Black contended that the Constitution did not permit the Court to avoid addressing important social problems out of concern for its own survival.[2]

Goldberg tended to agree with the latter view, a fact Dorothy Goldberg noted in her diary shortly before he assumed his seat on the Court. Neatly summarizing her husband's inclination with respect to this basic difference in judicial philosophy, she wrote on September 1, 1962: "Art got one book that was the Harvard point of view, Paul Freund's book on the Supreme Court, and a Mr. Charles F. [*sic*] Black, Jr.'s book on 'The People and Court.' He's on the Yale side."[3] Frankfurter had commanded a majority bloc of five justices committed to the restraintist position, and so his departure and replacement with Goldberg at one stroke deprived the Court of its most forceful proponent of judicial restraint and gave his more activist-minded brethren, most notably Earl Warren and William Brennan, a consistent fifth vote in favor of renewed judicial activism. And so with that change in personnel came a major shift in the Court's balance of power.[4]

This did not mean, in the minds of Goldberg and his allies on the Court, a return to activism in all areas. Even the *activist bloc*, as scholars came to call it, did not favor the same degree of judicial intervention in economic policy that conservative jurists had supported from the late nineteenth century through the middle 1930s. But Goldberg, Warren, and Brennan, in particular, and William O. Douglas, Byron White, Tom Clark, and Hugo Black, to a lesser degree, did not subscribe to the view, as did Justice John M. Harlan, that the reasons for judicial restraint applied with equal force in all areas. The activists sought instead to fashion a principled rationale for judicial interventionism in some instances and for restraint in others, a distinction that Harlan and like-minded jurists found more ingenious than sound.[5]

The change in doctrine related to the one in personnel soon manifested itself in a series of important decisions in the labor–management field. A close examination of those cases and Goldberg's contribution to their resolution reveals the specific ways in which labor's political action efforts from the late 1950s through the mid-1960s compelled the NLRB and the federal judiciary to use their power to buttress the postwar New Deal and expand its reach more uniformly across the United States. Viewed from Goldberg's perspective, one can see how that contest was resolved during his three pivotal years on the bench and what the consequences were for the Court and the country.

Although Goldberg knew more about the field of labor–management relations than any other member of the Court, his influence in such cases was not always felt. His two-decade-long career as a union lawyer had involved him with so many union clients that as a justice he often found himself obliged to refrain from helping decide labor cases. Of the twenty-three important such cases that the Court decided during Goldberg's three terms as an associate justice, he had to recuse himself from participating in nine.[6]

Even without his consistent participation, however, the general trend in such disputes was still in labor's favor. This was partly because labor was on the defensive in most of those cases, seeking to preserve through court rulings its place in the postwar order. Many of the cases had grown out of the managerial revolt, either from management's efforts to roll back union power directly on the shop floor or, indirectly, by using the states' regulatory powers and the Landrum–Griffin Act. In this area, then, managers were the ones challenging the status quo, and thus even the more conservative members of the Court tended to rule labor's way, although they often disagreed with their more activist brethren over the extent to which the Court should involve itself in that contest.[7]

The seven important labor cases that the Court decided during Goldberg's first term as an associate justice signaled the overall trend in that area and the concerns aroused among those on the Court still committed to Frankfurter's course of judicial restraint. In the first, *Smith* v. *Evening News Association*, the Court ruled eight to one, with Goldberg in the majority, that a worker could sue his or her employer for wrongful discharge in breach of contract even if the worker could also have challenged the action by filing an unfair labor practice complaint with the NLRB.

In so ruling, the Court greatly reduced management's ability to stall the resolution of such disputes, because the courts typically could resolve a breach of contract action far more quickly than the NLRB could adjudicate an unfair labor practice claim. The managerial revolt had greatly increased the board's unfair labor practice caseload, in turn reducing the speed with which it could process such disputes. Rather than permit employers to abuse this situation, Goldberg and seven other justices found that workers could also use the federal courts to resolve such conflicts. The ruling thus curtailed managerial initiatives aimed at winning back prerogatives lost over the preceding three decades, by giving workers more than one way to challenge such actions.[8]

The Court's decision did, however, pose a potential long-term threat to unions, because it strengthened the ability of individual workers to challenge employers' actions, even when a worker's union representatives had found that his or her complaint did not merit filing a claim with the NLRB. As long as the Court looked with favor on unions, it would address that danger by carefully limiting the scope of the worker's right to challenge an employer's actions through breach of contract. Should the Court's membership change, however, and, with it, its attitude toward unions, then the effect of the Smith ruling would be to weaken unions, by both strengthening the power of dissidents in them and alienating employers who had been persuaded to support unions at least partly because they offered the promise of containing such challenges to managerial authority.[9]

In the second important labor case of the 1962 term, *NLRB v. Reliance Fuel Oil Corporation*, the Court handed down a decision joined by eight justices, Goldberg included, which was similarly mixed in its short- and long-term consequences. The Court ruled that in passing the National Labor Relations Act, Congress had intended to vest the NLRB with the maximum jurisdiction permitted under the Constitution's interstate commerce clause. In so holding, the Court recognized the NLRB's authority to review workers' claims of employers' misconduct that management had argued were outside the scope of the board's jurisdiction. At the time, the decision clearly favored labor, because it enabled a majority on the National Labor Relations Board determined to head off the managerial revolt to broaden its supervision of managerial conduct.

Once again, however, the long-term implications were more troubling, because the ruling could also be used—should the board's sympathies change—to adjudicate a greater number of those disputes in management's favor. And like the *Smith* case ruling, the decision in *Reliance Fuel* tended to undermine support in the business community for the postwar New Deal. By increasing the extent of government supervision over managerial decision making, the ruling had the unfortunate result of encouraging second thoughts about the wisdom of that social bargain even among those executives who had most strongly favored it.[10]

In the third major labor case, *Brotherhood of Railway Clerks v. Allen*, the Court ruled seven to one, with Goldberg not participating, that when confronted with challenges from members unhappy about how their union dues were being spent on political action, unions should be allowed to develop their own mechanisms for resolving such disputes. As long as unions provided dissenters with a procedure through which they could be excused from having to pay their proportion of dues income so expended, the Court held, such dissidents were not entitled to contest such expenditures in court. Though not as protective of organized labor's political action efforts as a ruling barring all such challenges, the result aided labor. The Court's decision did so by foreclosing the possibility that disgruntled union dissidents, acting either alone or with management, could weaken unions' political action efforts by launching time-consuming and expensive lawsuits challenging union decisions on such matters, which would have been resolved by that branch of the government traditionally most hostile to organized labor's interests, that is, the judiciary.[11]

In the next important labor decision of the term, *NLRB* v. *Erie Resistor Company*, eight justices, with Goldberg among them, found that an employer could not give more seniority to workers hired as replacements for employees striking to improve wages and working conditions than such replacements had accrued during their actual time of service, in effect compelling their dismissal at the conclusion of a strike. Although once again not as valuable to labor as a ruling that hiring permanent replacements during a strike over economic issues was itself illegal, the Court's decision produced the same result in strikes that labor managed to win and helped it do so by eliminating a powerful managerial inducement aimed at recruiting potential strikebreakers and persuading wavering strikers to abandon a work stoppage.[12]

The last three major labor decisions of the 1962 term also went labor's way, although Goldberg was unable to participate in deciding any of them. In *Plumbers* v. *Borden*, the Court ruled six to two that federal labor laws had preempted the state courts' jurisdiction in disputes between workers and their unions over hiring-hall practices. This decision was followed by two others, *NLRB* v. *General Motors Corporation* and *Retail Clerks, Local 1625* v. *Schermerhorn*, both eight-to-zero rulings. In the first case the Court upheld the legality of agency-shop agreements in those states that had not explicitly prohibited them, thereby limiting the reach and effectiveness of the states' so-called right-to-work laws, and in the second case the Court ruled that federal labor legislation preempted most state regulation of labor–management relations, including restrictions on organizational picketing.[13]

Like the Court's earlier rulings that term in the *Reliance Fuel* and *Railway Clerks* cases, these three decisions aided labor in the short run, but only by opening the door to other dangers down the road. By keeping certain kinds of labor–management disputes out of state forums more hostile to unions than federal ones and by restricting the reach of antilabor legislation at the state level, the Court's rulings helped contain the managerial revolt in those parts of the country where labor was weakest. At the same time, however, the decisions exposed the union movement to new hazards should its adversaries gain greater control over the federal government.[14]

Goldberg wrote no opinions in those seven cases, although he had joined the Court's rulings in the three in which he could participate. His vote did not directly affect the result even in those three, given the Court's near unanimity in almost all of them. But beneath the surface appearance of consensus lay the beginnings of what in time would become deep rifts. Justice Black, for example, had dissented from the Court's holding in the *Smith* case, observing that to give workers more than one forum in which to challenge employers' actions would breed confusion in the industrial relations system and arguing that the Court had gone further than it had to in deciding the case, because it raised a standing issue that offered narrower grounds for a ruling. In the *Reliance Fuel* and *Railway Clerks* cases, Black again hinted at deeper disagreements by issuing short concurrences qualifying his support for the Court's conclusions.[15]

Even more significant were Justice Harlan's opinions in the *Railway Clerks* case and *Erie Resistor*. Harlan dissented in part from the Court's finding in the first of the two, that union dissidents were entitled to some remedy when dues income was spent on political action without their consent. Harlan noted that the plaintiff had not stated any particular expenditure or even class of expenditures to which he was opposed, but only that he objected to using dues income for political action. Harlan disagreed with the Court's finding that a dissident was entitled to relief when making such a general protest and complained that to grant relief in such instances would increase such litigation.

In the second case Harlan stated in a concurrence that he believed the Court had erred in finding illegal all superseniority schemes for permanent replacements, arguing that a less extreme plan might be lawful. Implicit in both of Harlan's opinions was his criticism that the Court had issued decisions broader in their sweep than the facts of the cases had called for, a tendency disturbing to supporters of judicial restraint.[16]

The Court's decision in *Plumbers* v. *Borden* revealed an even sharper disagreement. In a strong dissent joined by Tom Clark, Justice Douglas stated that to deny union members access to state courts when they wanted to resolve a dispute with their union might deprive them of a remedy altogether, indicating a division in the Court over the extent to which efforts to protect unions from the managerial revolt should be allowed to override concerns about the rights of union dissidents.[17]

These cleavages grew only slightly during Goldberg's next year of service on the Court. During the 1963 term the Court decided eight important labor cases, with Goldberg participating in five of them. The first such decision handed down that term, *Carey* v. *Westinghouse*, raised an issue similar to the *Smith* case of the previous one. In *Carey*, the Court was asked to decide whether a union could challenge through arbitration an employer's decision about how workers were to be classified, which determined the bargaining unit they fell in, even though the NLRB had traditionally resolved such disputes.

Five other justices joined William O. Douglas's opinion for the Court, holding that arbitration was available as a remedy and that if by the time the dispute reached the board, arbitration had begun, then the NLRB should defer to that process. Although valuable to labor precisely because the arbitration system tended to contain employer efforts to roll back union power, this ruling, like the one in the *Smith* case, also helped erode managerial support for the existing industrial relations system by giving workers and their organizations more than one way to challenge management's actions and thus weakening the system's capacity for containing such protests.[18]

The next major labor decision of the term was *Humphrey* v. *Moore*, in which the Court addressed the issue of whether a union's leaders fairly represented the interests of its members by agreeing to dovetail seniority lists following the amalgamation of two separate businesses both organized by the same union. Byron White's opinion for the Court, in which Goldberg and three other justices joined, held that in so doing, the union leadership had not breached its statutory duty to represent all of its members fairly, because the evidence indicated that the union's leaders acted in the good-faith belief that the contract authorized their decision, which was reached and then implemented without hostility or arbitrary discrimination.

The ruling benefited unions by blocking dissident members' efforts to challenge the results of such decision making, which would have weakened the rank and file solidarity on which union power ultimately was based. The decision also made easier the movement toward industrywide bargaining that Goldberg, in particular, saw as beneficial to organized labor. At the same time, however, the decision strengthened the sense among dissident unionists that the trend toward industrywide bargaining would come at the expense of the rank and file's already quite limited participation in union and workplace governance. The result thus tended at the same time to weaken unions, because it bred rank-and-file alienation and apathy, which sapped unions' strength.[19]

Next came *NLRB* v. *Exchange Parts, Inc.*, a case in which an employer had granted economic benefits to its employees just before an NLRB-ordered representation election, so as to persuade them to vote against unionization. In an opinion written by Justice Harlan, the Court unanimously found for the union, which had challenged the action as an unfair labor practice. The Court ruled that the National Labor Relations Act forbade not only intrusive threats and promises but also favorable conduct designed and reasonably calculated to interfere with the employees' freedom of choice in a representation election. This was an important victory for organized labor, especially in the context of the 1960s, when all industrial relations experts agreed that labor's long-run survival would ultimately depend on whether it could expand beyond its existing base.[20]

The third labor decision of the term, *United Steelworkers of America* v. *NLRB*, also constituted a victory for unions, albeit a more modest one. In this case the Court found—in an opinion joined by seven justices with Goldberg unable to participate—that the union's picketing of a railway spur track located adjacent to an employer's property was lawful, notwithstanding the Landrum–Griffin Act's ban on secondary picketing. In so ruling, the Court found that the picketing site was so closely related to the primary employer's day-to-day operations that it was essentially indistinguishable from them. In effect, the Court chose in this instance to construe narrowly the relevant Landrum–Griffin provision, an outcome that worked to labor's advantage.[21]

This was followed by the *John Wiley & Sons, Inc.* v. *Livingston* case, an eight-to-zero decision, with Goldberg once again obliged to recuse himself. Here the Court found that the duty to arbitrate survived the disappearance of the contracting employer by reason of sale and merger. In so holding, the Court sent a clear message to business managers that corporate consolidation could not be used as a strategy to escape an arbitration system that they believed worked to labor's advantage.[22]

This was followed by the term's last three important labor decisions, in all of which Goldberg participated, involving disputes over how to interpret Landrum–Griffin's secondary boycott provisions. In *NLRB* v. *Servette*, the union had struck a wholesale distributor and, as part of its strike efforts, had tried to persuade retailers to discontinue handling merchandise supplied by the offending wholesaler. The union's methods included pleas to the retail stores' managers not to carry the goods and to the stores' patrons, through handbills, not to buy them.

As it had in the *Steelworkers* case, the Court resolved this one by narrowly construing the relevant Landrum–Griffin Act provision. The Court found unanimously that the law's ban on all boycotts except those against products "produced by an employer" did not include boycotts directed at goods distributed by a wholesaler with whom the union had its primary dispute. In so holding, the Court's opinion noted that such conduct had been lawful before passage of the Landrum–Griffin Act and that the legislative history did not clearly show that Congress had intended to ban it. The result of the ruling, like the one in the earlier *Steelworkers* case, mitigated the harm that enactment of the Landrum–Griffin Act had done to labor's efforts to organize and bargain with employers.[23]

The second of these three decisions, *NLRB* v. *Fruit & Vegetable Packers & Warehousemen, Local 760 (Tree Fruits)*, also led to a victory for labor. In this case, while engaged in a strike with apple growers, the union had picketed supermarkets that carried the fruit, asking customers not to buy it. Although the Landrum–Griffin Act had outlawed certain forms of secondary consumer picketing, five justices, including Goldberg, found that the act's legislative history did not clearly indicate Congress's intent to outlaw all such picketing and that activity aimed only at urging a boycott of goods produced by the struck employer, rather than a broader plea to boycott altogether those supermarkets that carried them, was lawful. Once again, the Court's decision had the effect of whittling away at the Landrum–Griffin Act's ban on secondary boycotts, to the detriment of managers seeking to roll back labor's power.[24]

The third of these related decisions—and the last important labor ruling of the Court's 1963 term—like the two preceding cases, once again went labor's way. In *Teamsters Local 20* v. *Morton*, the Court was asked to decide whether a union could be held liable for damages under state law for engaging in peaceful secondary activity neither explicitly protected nor prohibited by the National Labor Relations Act. All nine justices found that by legislating against certain forms of secondary activity, Congress had preempted state regulation of that area and overturned a state court's award of actual and punitive damages against the union. In keeping with the spirit of the Court's decision the previous term in *Plumbers* v. *Borden*, the justices' ruling reflected a broad view of the extent to which federal labor legislation had preempted state law in that field, an outcome that at the time clearly worked to organized labor's advantage.[25]

Although most of the Court's major labor law decisions during its 1963 term, like those of the preceding one, enjoyed broad support among the justices, some serious divisions lurked beneath the surface. In the *Carey* case, three of Goldberg's brethren had expressed reservations about the wisdom of allowing arbitration as a remedy in disputes over how bargaining units should be demarcated when the NLRB traditionally had resolved such conflicts. In a concurrence, Justice Harlan acknowledged the danger of its leading to duplicative proceedings but saw it as outweighed by the value of arbitration in resolving such conflicts. In a dissent joined by Tom Clark, Hugo Black blasted the ruling and predicted that it would undermine the NLRB's ability to promote peace in the nation's industrial relations system and instead create both confusion and delay.[26]

In his first opinion in a labor case, Goldberg—while agreeing with the result reached in the term's second such decision, *Humphrey* v. *Moore*—took issue with the majority's reasoning. In a concurrence joined by Justice Brennan, Goldberg argued that the Court should have shown even greater deference to the union and the employer that had negotiated the agreement dovetailing the two seniority lists.

Although the Court's opinion stated that the negotiation was lawful because it had been authorized by the contract, Goldberg contended that even without that sanction, the union and the employer should have been immune from workers' challenges to these kinds of agreements. Although concerned about individual rights, Goldberg noted that many of them, including the seniority rights at issue in *Humphrey*, had arisen from collective bargaining. In this area at least, Goldberg believed that the courts should refrain from interfering with the results of private decision making. In a separate concurrence, Justice Harlan generally agreed with Goldberg's view, although Harlan would have allowed such a challenge when it included a claim that the employer was a party to the alleged unfair union representation.[27]

The one other labor case of the term that also produced significant disagreements was *Tree Fruits*. Justice Black's concurring opinion stated his view that the Court should have held for the union on the grounds that the statutory ban on picketing to persuade customers not to buy struck goods violated the First Amendment's freedom of speech and press clauses. He sharply disagreed, as did Justices Harlan and Stewart, with the Court's finding that the statute did not explicitly outlaw such picketing entirely. Harlan, in a dissent joined by Stewart, dismissed Black's First Amendment argument, finding that picketing was more than, and different from, simple communication and thus was not protected by that constitutional provision. Harlan reviewed extensively the legislative history at issue and found it and the statutory language much clearer than the Court's majority did. He condemned the majority for having stretched to interpret a provision that on its face meant something else, implicitly rebuking his brethren for what he saw as their unwarranted intrusion into the government's regulation of the labor–management relationship.[28]

Despite these objections to the Court's labor rulings during its 1963 term, Goldberg and his brethren continued to exhibit at least an outward appearance of widespread agreement on specific outcomes, if not on how the Court should arrive at them. As noted earlier, this was in part because in finding for labor, the Court was reinforcing the status quo in the face of a strong managerial challenge to it. But as the Court entered its 1964 term—Goldberg's last as an associate justice—there was a discernible erosion in what had been seemingly a fairly broad consensus in labor–management cases.

During the 1964 term, the Court handed down eight important decisions in the field of labor–management relations, of which Goldberg participated in six. The first was *NLRB* v. *Burnup & Sims, Inc.* In this case the employer—acting out of a mistaken but honest belief that employees seeking a union planned to use dynamite to promote their organizing efforts—fired them. The discharged employees challenged their dismissal as having violated the National Labor Relations Act, which barred the firing of workers simply for engaging in legitimate union organizing activity. The Supreme Court ruled eight to one, with Goldberg in the majority, that the dismissals were illegal, because the employer's good-faith belief that the workers had engaged in misconduct offered no legal excuse for discharging them when in fact they were engaged only in activity protected by the National Labor Relations Act. Like many of the labor decisions decided in the two preceding terms, this was a clear and even lopsided victory for labor.[29]

The next decision, *Fibreboard Paper Products Corporation* v. *NLRB*, also was important, although Goldberg found himself unable to participate in the Court's ruling. This case raised the question of whether an employer's decision to contract out work for economic reasons was one over which it was obligated to bargain with the union representing the workers idled by that decision. Contracting out was one of the key ways in which managers could reduce labor costs and roll back the unions' power. Five justices found that the NLRB had determined correctly that contracting out was a mandatory subject of bargaining under the National Labor Relations Act, thereby giving labor real assistance in resisting that practice.[30]

The Court reached its decision by broadly interpreting the statutory provision defining those subjects over which management had to bargain. The Court went on to hold that on finding that an employer had refused to bargain about contracting out, the NLRB had the power to order the employer to reinstate the former operation, to accord back pay to those employees who had been displaced by the decision to contract out, and to compel the employer to fulfill its bargaining obligations under the act. Such a ruling, Chief Justice Warren wrote for the five-man majority, was consistent with the Wagner Act's overall objective of promoting the peaceful resolution of industrial disputes, because a broad reading of the mandatory subjects of bargaining provision increased the number of matters over which both sides had a duty to negotiate, a process, the Court concluded, that helped diminish industrial conflict.[31]

The basic flaw in the Court's reasoning was that business managers had entered into the postwar New Deal with labor on the understanding that they would retain the right to make certain kinds of decisions unilaterally. The broad language of the Court's ruling in *Fibreboard*, however, increased executives' fears that their participation in that social bargain was eroding such managerial prerogatives still further, a concern that encouraged the revolt under way since the late 1950s. In that way, the Court's ruling in *Fibreboard* actually contradicted the National Labor Relations Act's overall objective of promoting industrial peace.[32]

On the other hand, the workers and their leaders rightly regarded the specific practice at issue in this case, that is, contracting out, as a violation of the postwar social contract, because it constituted an attempt by employers to escape from one of the social contract's terms, which was to employ a union-ized workforce. This was the central dilemma the Court faced during the 1960s in resolving labor cases prompted by the managerial revolt: Rulings such as the one in the *Fibreboard* case that favored labor and protected the status quo typically did so by increasing state supervision over labor–management relations, which in turn stimulated opposition in the business community to the postwar New Deal and thus increased the long-term threat to its survival. But had the Court avoided resolving such disputes, the result would only have worked to the advantage of the most antiunion firms, which were struggling during the 1960s to escape that social bargain. Once again, an important victory for labor in the short run also increased the risk of hazards further down the road.[33]

The Court's next major labor decision of the 1964 term addressed another managerial strategy aimed at escaping the postwar New Deal, that is, partial plant closings. In *Textile Workers Union* v. *Darlington Manufacturing Company*, the Court ruled seven to zero, with Goldberg and Potter Stewart recusing themselves, that an employer operating a multifacility enterprise could not partially close one or more of them for an antiunion reason. This was a victory for labor in the context of that case, although an incomplete one, because the Court also found that an employer could lawfully close its business entirely for any reason, including a desire to escape unionization, and would not be obligated to compensate the workers who consequently lost their jobs.

Justice Harlan's opinion for the Court described the latter decision as one peculiarly at management's discretion. At the same time, however, the Court found that any plant closing intended to yield a future benefit to management also violated the National Labor Relations Act. Thus a managerial decision to terminate a business enterprise completely and then reopen in another location so as to escape unionization was illegal. Only a managerial decision to cease doing business entirely rather than deal with a union was lawful. As a practical matter, managers found total shutdowns much less feasible than partial ones, given the often substantial investment in existing facilities. The net result, then, of the Court's ruling was to diminish significantly management's ability to escape unionized workforces by shutting down older plants in favor of newer ones where workers were not organized and to compel managers to compensate the idled workforce when they did so.[34]

Next came two decisions dealing with the important question of when management could legally attempt to pressure a union by refusing to allow employees to work. The first of these two cases, *NLRB* v. *Brown*, involved a multiemployer lockout undertaken in response to the union's decision to strike firms one by one, the so-called whipsaw technique. The struck employers in this instance had also continued to operate using temporary replacements and had refused to allow their unionized workers to return until a new contract had been signed. This combined lockout and use of temporary replacements the NLRB found unlawful even without a showing that the employer's intent was improper. The Court—by a vote of eight to one, with Goldberg in the majority—reversed, finding that the use of replacements in this case was no more injurious to employee rights than was the lockout itself, especially because the replacements had been hired only temporarily, and the unionized workers would regain their jobs on agreeing to a new contract.[35]

The second lockout case, *American Shipbuilding Company* v. *NLRB*, arose when management, convinced that the union was stalling contract negotiations until business picked up and thus gave the workers more leverage in bargaining, locked out its workforce. As in the *Brown* case, the NLRB found the lockout to be an unfair labor practice on its face, and the Court, by a unanimous vote, reversed. Absent any allegation or proof that management was hostile to collective bargaining or that it intended to interfere with the union's ability to represent its members, Justice Stewart's opinion for the Court reasoned, the case turned on whether the injury to collective bargaining posed by management's actions was so great and its economic justification so small as to create a presumption of bad motive on its part. And once again, the answer, the Court held, was no.[36]

Although these two decisions worked against the unions that were parties to those cases, the Court's reasoning did no serious harm to the interests of the labor movement as a whole and even worked to its advantage. The reach of the two decisions was limited to only those employers who had shown no evidence of hostility to unions as such. The effect, then, of the two lockout decisions was to signal the leaders of the managerial revolt that they could not expect to find legal sanction for using that technique to roll back unions' power in the workplace. This was one reason that the result in both cases had commanded the support not only of the Court's more conservative members but Goldberg's as well. Thus in finding employer lockouts lawful in some specific instances, he and his brethren had also taken the opportunity to place stringent limits on their use, giving labor another important, albeit limited, victory.[37]

The Supreme Court's last three major labor decisions of the 1964 term, all handed down on its final day, raised much more explosive issues. The first,

United States v. *Brown*, involved a Landrum–Griffin Act provision that barred anyone from serving as an officer, representative, or employee, other than clerical or custodial, of a labor organization who had been, during the five years preceding appointment or election to such a position, a member of the Communist Party (CP). The provision specified criminal penalties for violations, rather than Taft–Hartley's sanction of denying access to the NLRB to those unions that violated the ban on CP members serving as union officers. By a vote of five to four, with Goldberg in the majority, the Court struck down the provision.[38]

The Court reached this verdict for two reasons. First, the Court found that by enacting the provision, Congress clearly intended to exclude from union office those likely to engage in "political" strikes. Goldberg and four other justices ruled, however, that the proscribed group chosen was both smaller than the one Congress wanted to reach, because some noncommunists engaged in such strikes, and larger, because some CP members did not favor those kinds of work stoppages. Thus the Court found that the category of present and former Communist Party members was not closely enough related to the group engaged in the activity that Congress wanted to prevent. Second, the Court held that the measure as drafted subjected present and former communists to criminal penalties without a judicial proceeding and therefore violated the Constitution's ban on bills of attainder.[39]

This was the first five-to-four decision in a major labor case since Goldberg had joined the Court and the first time that his vote had been truly decisive in determining the outcome. He had argued ever since Congress passed the Taft–Hartley Act that a provision barring Communist Party members from union office had no place in a statute governing labor–management relations and that unions should be allowed to resolve such questions themselves.

The Supreme Court, however, in a decision joined by Goldberg's predecessor, Felix Frankfurter, had sustained the legality of the Taft–Hartley provision. The Landrum–Griffin measure only made matters worse from labor's perspective. Whatever its framers claimed to have intended by enacting the provision, as a practical matter it increased still further the penalty for unions that violated the ban against allowing present and former CP members to serve as officers and, more important, enhanced antiunion employers' ability to resist trade unionists, whatever their ideological commitments, by labeling all such persons *Communists*. Goldberg — no doubt thoroughly aware of what the measure portended, thanks to his background as a union lawyer and participation in the process of enacting Landrum–Griffin — had been unable to keep the provision from passing in Congress, but when it came before the Court, he was able to do something about it.[40]

Although a victory for the union movement, the *Brown* decision, like other Warren Court rulings in labor–management cases, brought with it an unwelcome long-term consequence for labor. The Court's ruling suggested that the judiciary would no longer simply acquiesce to government efforts aimed at keeping radicals out of important union posts. Although Goldberg argued that unions could take care of such "problems" themselves, the Court's decision signaled a retreat from this earlier commitment, which was one of the key elements of the postwar New Deal. For that reason, the *Brown* ruling increased support in the business community for the managerial revolt, an outcome harmful to those trade unionists seeking to preserve the existing social bargain. Management was primarily to blame for that result, because its efforts to strengthen the ban on radical participation in union governance by winning enactment of the Landrum–Griffin provision at issue had prompted the whole dispute.

The lawsuit that culminated in the *Brown* decision thus had grown out of a managerial effort to alter unilaterally the postwar New Deal's terms in a way favorable to business executives. The Court's majority, however, used the opportunity that management had created to produce the opposite result, one that worked to labor's short-run advantage, but at the cost of further weakening the already eroding support in the business community for the postwar social contract. Such was the nature of many of the Court's labor rulings during Goldberg's brief tenure as an associate justice.[41]

Although the Court's five-to-four division in the *Brown* case underscored the difficulties the Court faced in trying to preserve the postwar New Deal, the two other labor rulings handed down on the same day highlighted this dilemma even more clearly. Both decisions, which involved two companion cases, *United Mine Workers* v. *Pennington* and *Local 189, Amalgamated Meatcutters & Butcher Workmen* v. *Jewel Tea Company*, raised highly important questions about the scope of labor's exemption from the nation's antitrust laws. At stake was whether the Court would permit the leaders of the managerial revolt to use the Sherman Act to reduce labor's power and, more specifically, to use that law to resist movement toward a more corporatist political and economic system of the sort that Goldberg and the center of the labor movement had been seeking since the late 1950s.[42]

In the first of these two cases, the Court heard a petition for certiorari from a federal appellate court's finding that the UMW's efforts to obtain and enforce an industrywide contract with coal operators was not necessarily exempt from the antitrust laws when such an agreement would eliminate the smaller and less profitable firms and therefore that the trial court's award against the union for violating the Sherman Act in that way should be affirmed. In the second case, the Court heard an appeal from another federal appellate court's decision that a multiemployer contract with the Meatcutters Union limiting working hours constituted a restraint of trade in violation of the Sherman Act, because the agreement enhanced the competitive position of certain grocery stores and butchers at the expense of others.

The Supreme Court overturned both lower court verdicts, in *Pennington* by a unanimous vote and in *Jewel Tea* by a six-to-three margin, but there even the semblance of widespread agreement ended. In both cases the Court's "opinion" commanded the support of only three justices, with the remaining six split into two other blocs of equal size. In both cases the majority agreed only that the lower courts' decisions should be reversed, the first time in a major labor case since Goldberg had joined the Court that it was unable to muster at least five votes in favor of a single opinion's reasoning and not just its result.[43]

This was not, however, the first time in the term that the Court had found itself seriously divided in a labor case. In the *Burnup & Sims* case, Justice Harlan had issued an opinion both concurring and dissenting, in which he had criticized the Court's finding that an employer's good-faith belief that workers intended to dynamite his business to promote unionization was irrelevant. Harlan saw that decision as having gone too far, because it left an employer with only the unenviable choice of doing nothing, even when he or she believed such a danger to the firm existed, or of taking action and incurring penalties under the NLRA. Instead, Harlan argued for a middle position in which the employer would be expected to reinstate workers at the point at which he or she should have known that no such danger in fact existed. Implicit in this critique was Harlan's view that the Court should not go further than the statute required and that it allowed the NLRB to ignore the employer's motive only in rare instances.[44]

Another significant division had arisen in *Fibreboard*, and for a similar reason. In this case, Justices Stewart, Douglas, and Harlan all joined in a concurring opinion seeking to narrow the reach of the Court's broad language. The concurrence, written by Justice Stewart, attempted to delineate the bounds between those business decisions that he and his brethren viewed as purely managerial in nature from those in which labor rightfully should share. Once again, the waning number of justices still committed to judicial restraint criticized the Court's ruling in the case as needlessly, and therefore improperly, sweeping in its scope.[45]

A similar difference of opinion also lay behind the outward appearance of broad agreement in the two lockout cases. Whereas eight justices had supported the result reached in *NLRB* v. *Brown*, only six fully endorsed the reasoning in Justice Brennan's opinion for the Court. Goldberg filed a concurrence, in which Earl Warren joined, and Byron White offered a dissent. Goldberg's concurrence merely pointed out his view that had the employer hired permanent replacements, as opposed to temporary ones, then the NLRB would have been right in finding an unfair labor practice.

White, however, dissented sharply from this conclusion that the Court should not defer to the board's findings in this case, even without Goldberg's proviso. White argued that if those employers facing selective strikes could hire temporary replacements, then those other employers not struck had no compelling economic interest in locking out their own employees and that the NLRB's ruling to this effect should have been allowed to stand. In this instance it was White who was complaining about the Court's interventionist posture and arguing that the judiciary should defer to the NLRB's findings in such circumstances.[46]

In the second lockout case, *American Shipbuilding Company* v. *NLRB*, the Court divided once again into the same three factions. Potter Stewart's opinion for the Court commanded six votes; Goldberg and White filed separate opinions, with Chief Justice Warren joining in the former, which concurred only in the result. Goldberg favored reversal, but only because he believed that the board's decision had not been supported by the evidence uncovered by the trial examiner.

Goldberg disagreed strongly with the majority's willingness to substitute its own judgment on the legality of lockouts more generally for that of the NLRB and took pains to remind his colleagues less familiar with the realities of industrial relations that fashioning general rules regarding lockouts was a very difficult, and therefore inadvisable, task for the judiciary.

Byron White's disagreement with the majority was slightly different. For him, the problem was not so much a lack of evidence to support the board's findings, as Goldberg had argued, but rather the board's failure to articulate a rational connection between the facts found and the board's ruling. Both concurrences faulted the Court's majority for having engaged in decision making about matters outside the judiciary's competence.[47]

Such criticism intensified in the wake of the Court's ruling in *United States* v. *Brown*, although the justices divided differently in this case. Byron White's dissenting opinion—in which Justices Clark, Harlan, and Stewart joined—attacked the Court's majority for having found that membership in the Communist Party was not a characteristic closely enough related to that group likely to engage in "political" strikes to warrant the limitation on civil liberties. White and the others condemned the majority for having substituted its own judgment on this issue for that of the legislative branch, which was better equipped to make such a determination. This kind of judicial activism, the dissenters strongly implied, was just the sort that had brought about the fiasco of the mid-1930s.

White and his colleagues also dismissed the majority's conclusion that the provision in question constituted a bill of attainder, by noting that the purpose of the prohibition was to prevent future conduct, rather than punish those who had previously belonged to the Communist Party. Although there was a possibility that some of those who had recently left the party would suffer—because they were barred from holding positions of importance in the labor movement until five years after their association with the Communist Party had ended—White and the others apparently found this merely incidental. And even if such cases arose, White and the dissenters seem to have concluded that the ban's limited duration meant that the provision did not constitute a genuine bill of attainder. This view, the dissent noted, was consistent with several important earlier Court rulings that, White argued, had now been implicitly overturned. Thus the majority's conclusions in *Brown* offended those favoring a policy of judicial restraint in a second way, too, by undermining the respect for precedent that lawyers called *stare decisis*.[48]

Although the Court's ruling in *United States* v. *Brown* had clearly divided the Court into two factions, the *Pennington* and *Jewel Tea* cases fractured it even further. Apart from an agreement among all nine justices in the first case and six in the second to reverse the lower courts' verdicts, no line of reasoning enjoyed the support of more than three justices. Justice White's opinions for "the Court" in those cases, joined only by Warren and Brennan, found that the union exemption from the Sherman Act was a limited one and that a union would forfeit it upon entering into an agreement with one set of employers to impose a wage scale on other bargaining units. On the other hand, White and his two brethren also found that the union could legally seek unilaterally the same wage scale from employers throughout the industry it had organized. Thus, as a practical matter, White's opinion for "the Court" simply obliged labor union negotiators to behave discreetly when bargaining in order to be exempted from the Sherman Act.[49]

White's opinion in *Jewel Tea* followed the same basic approach, finding that labor's exemption from the antitrust laws was limited but produced a result in which union negotiators remained, for all practical purposes, free to pursue bargaining objectives that would eliminate competition based on differences in wages and working conditions. White found that the key questions in *Jewel Tea* were whether a marketing-hours restriction was intimately related to wages, hours, and working conditions and whether the bargaining conducted by the union was *bona fide* and at arm's length. If so—and White's opinion for "the Court" so found—then the contract provision was exempt from the antitrust laws.[50]

Justice Douglas's concurrence in the *Pennington* case, joined by Hugo Black and Tom Clark, differed only slightly from White's opinion. Douglas and the others contended that White's approach to the issues was sound save for the evidentiary question. More specifically, Douglas wrote that an industrywide bargaining agreement setting wages beyond the ability of some employers to pay would be, on its face, evidence of an illegal conspiracy to restrain trade.[51]

The same trio, however, differed more sharply with White's view in *Jewel Tea*. In this case, Douglas and the two others dissented, contending that the collective bargaining agreement between the multiemployer group and the union was evidence of a conspiracy among them to impose the marketing-hours restriction on another employer by a strike threat and therefore violated the Sherman Act. Thus Douglas and his allies concluded that in this case, the Court should have affirmed the finding against the union.[52]

Although both of White's opinions were clearly favorable to labor, and even Douglas's concurrence in *Pennington* worked to labor's advantage in this instance, Goldberg disliked them—and Douglas's dissent in *Jewel Tea* still more so—for bringing certain kinds of collective bargaining under the judiciary's supervision and for their tendency to encourage the parties to such negotiations to behave artificially. He therefore wrote a dissent from "the Court's" opinions in both cases, which concurred only in the reversal of the appeals courts' verdicts against the unions involved.

Goldberg's dissent, in which Justices Harlan and Stewart joined, attacked the other opinions in both cases, calling them "a throwback to past days when courts allowed antitrust actions against unions and employers engaged in conventional collective bargaining, because 'a judge considered' the union or employer conduct in question to be 'socially or economically' objectionable." This kind of judicial activism, Goldberg observed, had been thoroughly discredited in the past, a view with which the two justices most committed to a policy of judicial restraint, Harlan and Stewart, could agree.

Goldberg denounced the other opinions in *Pennington* specifically for their failure to recognize that when bargaining over wages with either a single employer or a multiemployer group, unions routinely encountered managerial concerns about a potential competitive disadvantage associated with a particular wage demand. The other opinions in that case, he noted, would only push both sides to engage in underground communications, or the union to engage in unilateral action, most likely strikes, to secure higher wages. Neither alternative, Goldberg believed, boded well for the nation's industrial relations system.

In regard to *Jewel Tea*, Goldberg's dissent attacked Justice White's opinion for arrogating to the judiciary the task of deciding which bargaining subjects were so important to workers that they merited exemption from the antitrust laws. Such decisions, he argued, were outside the courts' competence. The proper way to resolve both cases, he concluded, was to recognize Congress's intention to exempt completely from the Sherman Act all bargaining over those subjects that the NLRA had classified as ones over which management must negotiate, that is, wages, hours, and other terms and conditions of employment. Any other course, Goldberg believed, along with Harlan and Stewart, would simply open the door to judicial meddling in disputes that the courts lacked the competence to resolve.

Goldberg found troubling, too, the other opinions' implications for labor's ability to cope with automation, at a time when that process was clearly accelerating. *Pennington* raised the issue because, as Goldberg wrote, the UMW had adopted a philosophy of achieving uniform high wages, fringe benefits, and good working conditions, in return for which it had accepted the burdens and consequences of automation. Thus the union had, Goldberg noted, acted on the view that the existence of marginal operators who could not afford such wages, benefits, and working conditions did not serve the best interests of the working miners but, on the contrary, depressed wage standards and perpetuated undesirable conditions. The Mine Workers thus had opted, when necessary, for a smaller, more consolidated industry and had accepted automation as long as the workforce shared in its benefits. It was in this light, Goldberg argued, that the Court should view the union's demand for a uniform wage policy, whose negotiation should therefore be exempt from the Sherman Act.

In *Jewel Tea*, Goldberg pointed out, the same basic issue once again lurked in the background. The marketing-hours restriction sought by the Meatcutters Union, he wrote, was clearly intended to aid the smaller, less automated employers, by preventing the supermarket chains from providing self-service meat markets when the small independent operators could not do so. The union's objective in this case was to preserve its members' jobs by obtaining a marketing-hours limitation that resisted automation's tendency to drive the smaller, less efficient firms out of business. This, he contended, was the sort of topic that the Wagner Act had explicitly recognized as one over which employers were obligated to bargain, and thus such negotiations should once again be exempted from the nation's antitrust laws.

Whether collective bargaining agreements should either encourage or oppose automation was precisely the sort of economic and political question, Goldberg contended heatedly, that the courts should refrain from attempting to resolve. Such matters were best left to the parties themselves and the branches of government more responsive to electoral majorities. He wrote bitingly:

> Putting the opinion of the Court in *Pennington* together with the opinions of my Brothers Douglas and White in *Jewel Tea*, it would seem that unions are damned if their collective bargaining philosophy involves acceptance of automation (*Pennington*) and are equally damned if their collective bargaining philosophy involves resistance to automation (*Jewel Tea*). Again, the wisdom of a union adopting either philosophy is not for judicial determination.[53]

Although Goldberg's dissent did not carry the day, labor still emerged relatively unscathed from the Court's decisions in *Pennington* and *Jewel Tea*. In both cases, at least six justices, two of them Kennedy appointees, voted to overturn the appeals courts' verdicts against the unions involved and joined the opinions written by White and Goldberg that, for all practical purposes, left labor essentially unhampered by the antitrust laws. Thus the managerial campaign to use such laws to reduce labor's power met with frustration. The outcome clearly demonstrated the value of labor's political action efforts from the late 1950s through the mid-1960s, and especially during the 1960 presidential election. Had Richard Nixon filled the two Supreme Court vacancies that ultimately went to Byron White and Arthur Goldberg, the Court's decisions in *Pennington* and *Jewel Tea* would surely have been quite different.[54]

This triumph for labor was, however, an incomplete one. The two decisions, like several others the Court issued in labor cases during Goldberg's tenure as an associate justice, would eventually be watered down by subsequent rulings. And the interventionist way in which the Warren Court addressed labor–management issues also, as noted earlier, increased the danger that when the Court's composition changed, it would use its power aggressively against unions. But at this time, the Court's labor decisions served to contain the managerial revolt and kept organized labor from experiencing an even more serious decline.[55]

In addition to the labor–management relations' cases, the Court also embarked on an interventionist course during Goldberg's tenure in three other important areas: reapportionment of state and local legislative bodies, criminal law and procedure, and civil rights. Shortly before Goldberg had joined it, the Court had already issued a major ruling in the first of those areas, finding that the judiciary could hear challenges to state and local legislative apportionment schemes.

Although the jurisdictional question had thus been settled when the Court handed down its decision during the spring of 1962 in *Baker* v. *Carr*, Goldberg and his brethren thereafter faced the difficult task of deciding the merits of such claims and fashioning appropriate remedies. In three landmark rulings, *Gray* v. *Sanders, Wesberry* v. *Sanders,* and *Reynolds* v. *Sims,* the Court, with Goldberg's support, struck down laws requiring candidates for statewide office to win a majority or plurality of counties rather than votes, and it ruled that when apportioning congressional and state legislative districts, every state must do so in accordance with the principle of one person, one vote.[56]

In the area of criminal law and procedure, the Court issued many more decisions, which likewise had the result of transforming legal doctrine in several important ways. A majority, sometimes narrow, of the Court's nine members—with Goldberg consistently part of it—ruled that the government could not punish draft evaders with the loss of their citizenship;[57] overturned the conviction of a draftee who had claimed conscientious objector status, even though he subscribed to no orthodox religion;[58] held that neither the fruits of an illegal search or arrest nor a coerced confession could be used to obtain a criminal conviction without the accused's knowing waiver of his or her right to object;[59] strengthened the defendant's privilege against self-incrimination and the right to confront the witnesses against him or her in a state court's proceedings;[60] found that defendants in felony cases were entitled to court-appointed counsel if they could not afford such assistance themselves and, in some instances, even before indictment;[61] limited the use of circumstantial evidence in criminal cases;[62] widened access to the federal judiciary for those appealing a state court's conviction;[63] applied federal court standards for determining whether to allow appeals filed in state court systems;[64] reduced the ability of state and local officials, including law enforcement officers, to bring libel suits against the media or other public officials for making or publishing statements about their public duties;[65] restricted the police's power to control peaceful picketing near public property;[66] undermined the states' ability to enforce motion picture censorship laws;[67] overturned a state statute that outlawed using contraceptive devices and giving medical advice on their use;[68] weakened the federal government's ability to require certain groups to register as "Communist-front organizations";[69] struck down a federal statute requiring the postal service to detain all mail classified by the Treasury Department as "Communist political propaganda" until such time as the addressee specifically requested delivery;[70] and ruled unconstitutional a general warrant to search a person's home for "subversive materials."[71]

In the area of protecting citizens' civil rights, especially those of blacks, the Court issued yet another batch of far-reaching and highly controversial decisions. The most important included rulings that protected the National Association for the Advancement of Colored People (NAACP)'s ability to conduct civil rights litigation;[72] overturned convictions of civil rights protesters for having participated in sit-ins and other forms of protest at segregated places of business;[73] held subsequently that the 1964 Civil Rights Act abated the convictions of those who had engaged in such activity before the law's enactment;[74] found that the act's ban on racial discrimination in restaurants, hotels, and other places of public accommodation was authorized by the Constitution's interstate commerce clause;[75] ruled that a Florida statute prohibiting a black person and a white person not married to occupy habitually a room at night violated the Fourteenth Amendment's equal protection clause;[76] and struck down a Virginia statute requiring voters in federal elections either to pay a $1.50 poll tax or file a witnessed or notarized certificate of residence for violating the Twenty-fourth Amendment's ban on poll taxes in federal elections.[77] Although Goldberg did not always agree with the reasoning of the Court's decisions, he supported the result reached in every one of them.[78]

These much studied decisions aided the struggle to open the South's closed society, whose workers—white and, much more so, black—had been unable to share fully in the fruits of the postwar New Deal. By directly attacking the system of legalized segregation there and by restricting the exercise of power by southern law enforcement authorities, the Court's rulings helped create an environment in which union organization was at least a possibility. Goldberg and like-minded New Deal liberals saw this as the prerequisite for expanding the reach of this social bargain and extending its benefits more equally to the American working and lower middle classes.[79]

These rulings had their price. One consequence, experienced immediately, was to increase the divisions in these groups. Although some of the blame for that result must be laid at the feet of racist whites, much of it belongs elsewhere. Many white members of the working and lower middle classes who favored establishing equality before the law for blacks nonetheless rightly feared that to attempt to dismantle Jim Crow quickly would weaken the class solidarity that had made possible these groups' gains over the preceding three decades and thereby frustrate the goal of bringing more of these benefits to those who had shared in them the least. Whites with that point of view— whose understanding of the intractable nature of race as a social problem was perhaps more complete than that of more elite northern New Deal liberals such as Goldberg—often responded with hostility to what they saw as a misguided effort to address enormously complicated and difficult issues.[80]

The Court's efforts to help dismantle the segregation system proved divisive, too, precisely because they aroused the populace's deeply rooted fears of concentrated power and redirected them from the business community to the state. That the branch of the federal government least responsive to electoral majorities was the one taking the lead in attacking segregation only reinforced such sentiments. And as was true of the Court's rulings in other areas, the majority's efforts to involve the Court more actively in the struggle to strengthen the postwar New Deal increased the likelihood that, should extreme conservatives gain greater control over the federal government, they would use the Court, in ways reminiscent of the 1930s, to do just the opposite.[81]

Although the wisest supporters of the status quo deplored for these reasons the Court's efforts to eradicate what they euphemistically termed *localism*, this critique contained no constructive alternative. The ongoing movement of industry both into those areas of the country and abroad where unions were weakest, which was accelerating during the mid-1960s, highlighted the inability of the postwar New Deal's defenders to maintain the existing political and economic arrangement.

To preserve this kind of social bargain in the long run required, at a minimum, that its reach become truly national and that the federal government limit the movement of capital so as to arrest its flow abroad. And the only way to accomplish these objectives was to create conditions in the South that would make the widespread growth of unions there a real possibility. This the Court's rulings helped accomplish, but at the cost of undermining support, in the near term, for an already embattled postwar social order.[82]

During Goldberg's three terms as an associate justice, these same tensions also worked themselves out in the industry with which he had been so intimately involved, that is, steel. Although largely confined to the role of passive observer, Goldberg did monitor events there and understood better than most their broader implications. To appreciate the results produced by the Court's rulings and the larger effort to preserve the postwar New Deal of which they were a part—for both Goldberg and the country's political and economic system—we now turn to the developments in steel during this same three-year period.

III

When Goldberg began his tenure on the Court, his former colleagues in the USA found themselves increasingly embattled. Although the nation's economy had gradually begun to emerge from the 1960/61 recession, unemployment had failed to recede greatly, a problem most acute in basic manufacturing industries such as steel. At a USA Executive Board meeting in August 1962, David McDonald reported that 300,000 steelworkers were still out of work. By February 1963 he had to inform his colleagues that despite more vigorous organizing efforts, which had brought in 60,000 new members, the total dues-paying membership remained "well below the 900,000 mark," which itself was between 250,000 and 300,000 below the all-time high of 1.1 million reached in 1957.[83]

As a direct consequence, the union continued to operate in the red. At a board meeting in September 1962 McDonald described the problem and stated that the national office would no longer offer construction loans to the locals. If they wanted to construct new facilities for their members, he suggested, the locals would have to raise the money on their own. The following March the board decided to require the locals henceforth to bear also all arbitration-related costs, rather than continuing to share them with the national office.

Although partly motivated by a desire to eliminate waste in the arbitration system, the principal reason for the change was to cut the national union's operating costs. To achieve this objective, McDonald and his aides also reduced the number of staff positions by approximately one hundred, mostly by allowing positions to remain unfilled when incumbents retired. During that same period, the executive board moved ahead as well with plans to amend the union's constitution so as to allow the board to increase dues should the treasury fall below $20 million. A good indication of the leadership's overall mood at that time can be seen in David McDonald's response to one board member's inquiry about a salary increase. In dismissing the idea out of hand on September 12, 1962, McDonald noted that as of that same day, the salary account was overdrawn by $543,000.[84]

This underlying problem was compounded by the steadily rising number of lawsuits launched against the union, mostly by business executives seeking to reduce its power. McDonald discussed this situation in detail at an executive board meeting held in the fall of 1962. He noted that some members of the board seemed unaware of the extent of the danger posed by such suits and, in an effort to awaken them, warned that the union faced the possibility of having to pay damage awards of up to $10 million in the next few years unless it won appeals from some adverse lower court decisions.[85]

The net effect of the union's financial problems was to weaken both its bargaining position vis-à-vis management and, as a result, the leadership's ability to contain union dissidents unhappy with the postwar New Deal's terms. This was a very serious development. Throughout the 1950s, the leadership's success in winning economic gains for the rank and file had enabled the McDonald–Goldberg faction to keep control over the union's destiny, despite some substantial dissident challenges. As the industry's decline depleted the union's treasury and undermined the leadership's ability to win more economic gains for the rank and file, the potential for a successful revolt from below grew.

Thus during Goldberg's first year as an associate justice, his most important former client faced a genuine crisis, one that the USA had thus far been unable to solve either through bargaining directly with management or with the help of the Kennedy administration that the union had helped elect. These conditions persisted through the end of 1963, creating a sense of frustration among board members with a stalemate that seemed to preclude progress in any direction. At an executive board meeting held in March 1963, district director James Griffin described the dilemma:

> Everybody agrees that the No. 1 economic problem in the United States faced not only by the Steelworkers Union and its membership but by all Americans is unemployment. Now, while we all recognize that that is the No. 1 domestic problem, we can't agree on what the solution is to that problem. The American trade union movement under the leadership of Dave McDonald and George Meany say that a partial solution to that problem . . . is the short work week, extended vacations, the sabbatical leave. The Kennedy Administration and the leaders of industry and business and their reactionaries in Congress say nuts to that, that is no solution at all. The Kennedy Administration then proposes that a reduction of taxes would be the solution to the unemployment problem because it would pump purchasing power into the economy. Big business and industry say nuts to that, if it provides reduction of taxes to the working people[–]they want it to apply to

themselves and don't want any tax reforms, and they want the assurance that
the government['s] expenditures will be curtailed.

So what I am trying to illustrate is that the factors that make up society
can't get together and agree on a solution. And because we don't make up a
larger proportion of that society we alone can't institute effectively our own
programs to deal with the economic and political problems.[86]

The logjam at the national level was reflected in steel by the inconclusive
results that its industrywide negotiating committees had achieved. Bargaining
over a new contract began less than two weeks after the 1962 agreement had
gone into effect and continued constantly for the next year. Despite many
meetings, the parties made little progress in contracting out, job security,
incentive pay, grievances, and overtime pay, all highly sensitive areas. And as
managers began to push through selective price increases over the Kennedy
administration's muted opposition, some members of the USA leadership
began to lose interest in the wage-and-price restraint policy that Kennedy and
Goldberg favored.[87]

Joe Germano mirrored the executive board's changing mood when he
suggested, at a meeting held on May 14, 1963, that the price increases actually
worked to the union's advantage because they legitimated its demand for a
wage boost, which was needed to keep up with inflation and rising corporate
profits. Germano told his colleagues:

> This organization ought to consider very seriously reopening the contracts
> for the purpose of getting something for their people in 1963. I felt that
> somewhere along the line the steel industry was contemplating increasing
> the price of steel, and I am sure some of your people remember when I made
> mention of that some time ago. And certainly I am very happy that this
> organization proceeded in the manner it did by permitting the industry to
> increase the price of steel.[88]

In effect, Germano and his like-minded colleagues were suggesting that
McDonald acknowledge that the policy of mutual restraint had proved unworkable, because managers had refused to go along with it, and thus that the
union had no choice except to press for wages increases that protected the
membership's real income and its share of industry profits.[89]

But McDonald and the other board members who most strongly supported
the wage-and-price restraint policy disagreed with this conclusion. They understood that to abandon entirely the union's opposition to price increases
and begin pressing for a rise in wages would only contribute to the industry's
long-term decline, by encouraging the consumption of imported steel and the
use of substitutes such as aluminum, concrete, and plastics. For this reason,
McDonald stubbornly defended an increasingly untenable position in the face
of growing pressures against it.

As long as the economic recovery remained mild and wage increases in
other industries modest, McDonald and his supporters were able to stick with
the mutual-restraint program. But as the economy gathered steam toward the
end of 1963, other unions, principally the UAW, began pressing for larger

increases in pay, thereby encouraging the steelworkers to do the same. McDonald, however, continued to cling to the existing policy, thereby fostering a growing split in the USA's ranks.[90]

Making matters worse was McDonald's decision in 1963 to recognize the industrywide committees as the sole bargaining forums, thereby eliminating altogether participation by representatives of the locals through the larger Wage Policy Committee. Although more a decision to acknowledge formally what was already taking place than a major policy shift, it marked yet another step along the road toward centralization of the bargaining process, one resisted by both members of the rank and file and local leaders. Making this change helped insulate the wage-and-price restraint policy from its critics in those groups, but only at the cost of further alienating them from the national leadership.[91]

The leadership's failure to preserve the shop floor's balance of power represented by Section 2B of the union's master contract deepened that sense of alienation. While the industrywide bargaining committees continued fruitless talks about the so-called noneconomic issues, managers began winning back unilaterally some of the work rules concessions they had sought during the 1959 strike, to the distress of many steelworkers. Even at Kaiser, where the union and management succeeded in reaching an agreement concerning automation, many workers were unenthusiastic about the loss of workplace control that this bargain entailed.[92]

The leadership's efforts to improve job opportunities for nonwhites in steel, and to support civil rights legislation aimed at improving their treatment in society more generally, created yet another rift in the USA. In the spring of 1964, some members of locals in Alabama, Maryland, and Texas began actively supporting George Wallace's bid for the Democratic presidential nomination, a situation deeply disturbing to the USA Executive Board. At the same time, the union's black members began pressing much harder for the more-skilled and higher-paying jobs in steel from which they had been largely excluded in the past. The net result was to weaken substantially the rank-and-file solidarity that constituted the union's basic source of strength.[93]

Matters came to a head during 1964. Both the industry's health and the union's finances began to improve as the economic recovery blossomed during that year. The boom was spurred by the Kennedy–Johnson income tax cut of 1964, which the administration managed to pass only by cutting rates for everyone, rather than simply for the working and lower middle classes, as originally planned. Making the cuts across the board secured enough support in the business community to break the logjam in Congress, but the resulting expansion, spectacular by postwar standards, undercut still further McDonald's efforts to stay with the policy of wage-and-price restraint. By May he sounded increasingly defensive about the whole idea, repeatedly telling board members at a meeting held that month that the union and management members of the principal industrywide bargaining committee "are not in bed with one another."[94]

Attempting to retreat somewhat from his previous support for using this forum as the sole one for collective bargaining, McDonald told the board:

> We do not in any sense attempt to say the Human Relations Committee is the be all and do all of our problems. But at the same time we do want to say—at least I want to say— that the Human Relations Committee has proven to be a good adjunct, and I want it to continue to be a good adjunct . . . to collective bargaining; not a collective bargaining group per se, but an adjunct to collective bargaining. I do not want it to fail.[95]

McDonald's refusal to abandon the idea entirely sparked a revolt against his plans to seek another term as USA president. Under the union's constitution, he was permitted to serve one more four-year term when his current one expired in the spring of 1965. But McDonald sent a signal that he intended to remain even longer, by pushing through a constitutional amendment at the union's 1964 convention that allowed him to serve for another eight years. This move proved too much for many of his one-time supporters. Although the other board members had long disliked McDonald's inattention to details, frequent absences from headquarters in Pittsburgh, fondness for socializing with celebrities, and problems with alcohol, no such challenge had emerged as long as he and his aides supported policies that worked to the union's advantage. McDonald's unwillingness to abandon an increasingly unworkable collective bargaining policy and the highly centralized committee that had negotiated it, combined with his openly expressed intention to stay in office for at least another two terms, finally pushed many of his associates to rebel.[96]

Goldberg monitored those events from his new vantage point on the Court, assisted in so doing by occasional memos from Walter Heller that detailed both the economic conditions facing the steel industry and the progress of collective bargaining negotiations there. Had Goldberg still been USA general counsel, he would have tried to head off the incipient revolt by seeking to meet the dissidents' minimum demands without abandoning altogether the wage-and-price restraint policy. Given the larger social forces at work against it, brokering such a deal would likely have exceeded even his negotiating talents, and indeed, achieving it proved to be beyond those of his successor as general counsel, David Feller.

Facing a very difficult challenge and lacking the kind of support from the executive board that Goldberg's long service to the union had earned him, Feller was unable to hold the USA leadership together. And when Goldberg tried next to bring together George Meany, Labor Secretary Willard Wirtz, McDonald, and Secretary-Treasurer I. W. Abel, who had emerged as the revolt's leader, to discuss alternatives to an election contest, Abel rebuffed him.[97]

The insurrection began building during the summer of 1964 but remained covert until after the November presidential and congressional elections. Unwilling to risk splitting the union until Goldwater and his supporters had been routed at the polls, Abel pretended during the fall of 1964 to be uninterested in running for the USA presidency. Once the Johnson–Humphrey ticket had been safely elected to office and accompanied by greatly increased Democratic majorities in Congress, the Abel candidacy came out into the open.

Long skeptical of the McDonald–Goldberg policy of moving further in the direction of corporatist bargaining structures, Abel campaigned against them and the mutual-restraint policy that had kept steel wages more in check than it did steel prices. Using the changes in union election procedures that Landrum–Griffin had required, Abel and his slate won a close and deeply divisive contest in April 1965, thereby spelling an end to McDonald's career and the policy that he and Goldberg had supported to preserve the steel industry's long-term health.[98]

This rupture in steel rippled outward to other manufacturing industries during the mid-1960s. In the decade after Goldberg's appointment to the Supreme Court, all but one of the principal former CIO unions experienced a serious internal revolt. In some instances the rebels won by electing new leaders, in others by pushing those incumbents who survived to demand larger wage-and-benefit increases. Thus the major CIO unions moved, from the mid-1960s onward, toward a collective bargaining policy more like the traditional AFL one, which emphasized less restrained collective bargaining unsupervised by the state. Indicative of the overall trend among the former CIO affiliates was the close relationship Abel developed with George Meany and Abel's rise in the federation's industrial union department (IUD). When Walter Reuther's UAW signaled its disapproval of the federation's policies by disaffiliating in early 1968, Abel was elected his successor as head of the IUD.[99]

With the AFL–CIO's industrial unions increasingly under the command of leaders who made more vigorous demands for higher wages and benefits through collective bargaining unsupervised by the state, inflation and its related problems only intensified in the years ahead. Although Abel and his colleagues argued forcefully that there were no feasible alternatives, Goldberg and like-minded supporters of the trade union movement lamented the long-term implications for the American working class and the society as a whole.[100]

The rupture of the social contract in the steel industry during the mid-1960s was only part of a more generalized breakdown in the postwar political and economic system, one that, as we shall now see, would have direct and unfortunate consequences for Goldberg's career.[101]

IV

Although as president, Kennedy tried hard to resist the pressures at work against the postwar New Deal, from the spring of 1963 onward his administration began yielding to them. Kennedy's assassination in November and replacement with Lyndon Johnson caused this process to accelerate.

Lacking a complete understanding of labor's place in the postwar order and being more responsive to the wishes of business managers than Kennedy had been, Johnson quickly shelved the already fading Labor–Management Advisory Committee and de-emphasized the wage-and-price guidelines policy. At the same time he pushed harder to address the concerns of civil rights activists and feminists, one result of which was to divide the working and lower middle classes and to weaken their position in the short to medium run, at least, vis-à-vis the business community.[102]

LBJ pressed, too, for an even greater economic expansion than Kennedy had contemplated, which once again worked against the interests of the working and lower middle classes. Johnson's decision in the spring of 1965 to escalate enormously the United States's military involvement in the Vietnam War, combined with his refusal until late in his presidency to raise taxes and thereby reduce consumer demand, turned a robust economic expansion into an outright boom.

Although this move strengthened the unions' ability to bargain for higher wages and benefits in the short run, the boom also sapped labor's strength in the longer term. It did so in two ways, by undermining union leaders' efforts to maintain the health of the industries organized by unions and by making the organization of other sectors more difficult. Just as the harsh economic conditions of the 1930s had helped foster working-class consciousness and solidarity, so did the decade-long boom that began in 1963 tend to dissipate them. The AFL–CIO did make some serious efforts to organize new recruits during that time and enjoyed real success in the public-employee sector. Gains elsewhere proved meager, however, a result that soon led labor to abandon as unrealistic further large-scale organizing campaigns of the sort pursued during the 1930s and 1940s. At the same time, the boom brought with it renewed and persistent inflation, which soon eroded the real income of working- and lower-middle-class Americans.[103]

Johnson's decision to escalate U.S. military involvement in the Vietnam conflict also undermined the postwar New Deal in another way. Although his decision was largely consistent with the basic assumptions underlying the nation's cold war policies since their formation during the late 1940s, it soon proved highly controversial. Johnson's refusal to abandon an increasingly unpopular and unsuccessful policy eroded support in the labor movement and the business community for the containment policy, thereby weakening the linchpin that had held together the postwar New Deal.[104]

By the mid-1960s, these changes had transformed power relationships in the Democratic Party's dominant coalition. What had been from the mid-1930s through the early 1960s a labor–liberal alliance would henceforth be a liberal–labor one, a switch best symbolized by the change in the Democratic national ticket from 1960 to 1964. In 1960, labor's choice had received the top spot, and the man who ultimately won enactment of much of middle-class liberals' program had been relegated to the bottom half of the ticket. But four years later this relationship was reversed, when the Democrats nominated Johnson for the presidency and ratified his choice of longtime labor supporter and Minnesota senator Hubert Humphrey for the vice-presidential slot.[105]

The decline of the postwar New Deal to which Johnson and his aides contributed quickly revived the radical right- and left-wing movements it had held in check since the late 1940s. Although the liberal–labor alliance was able to turn back the threat posed by the 1964 presidential campaign of Senator Barry Goldwater, a longtime conservative critic of the postwar social contract, right-wing attacks against labor persisted and even intensified. At the same time, many labor leaders and much of the rank and file found themselves under fire from radicals on the left.

Understandably dismayed by the persistence of racism and sexism in much of the labor movement, disillusioned by labor's inability to eradicate poverty, and alienated by the labor leadership's support for cold war policies, left-wing radicals attacked the increasingly beleaguered union movement from another direction. One highly vocal faction simply dismissed labor's postwar achievements as having devalued workers' lives. Other new leftists, more sophisticated in their understanding of the working class and more sympathetic to its concerns about economic security, instead attacked labor's postwar social bargain for having provided so little to those who had the least. The net result of such attacks was to diminish still further the unions' standing with the public, an outcome that served the interests of the new Right far more than it did those of the new Left.[106]

The huge Democratic majorities in Congress and the state legislatures that the AFL–CIO helped elect in 1964 somewhat masked labor's declining strength. Although the Democrats from the late 1950s onward, and especially under Johnson's leadership, had greatly increased their numbers in Congress and state legislative bodies, many of the newcomers differed significantly from the New Deal liberals who had dominated the party since the mid-1930s.

The Republican Party's rightward retreat from the postwar New Deal persuaded many office seekers who shared an elite paternalist outlook to run as Democrats rather than as liberal Republicans. Such candidates lacked the working- and lower-middle-class backgrounds and consciousness of many Democratic politicians who had first won office during the 1930s and 1940s. Although not overtly hostile to labor, these "neoliberals" pursued an agenda that proved injurious to its interests, at least in the short to medium run.[107]

The change in the Democrats' legislative priorities can be seen most clearly in labor's failure to win repeal of Taft–Hartley's Section 14(b) during 1965. This provision permitted the states to pass so-called right-to-work laws; repealing it would, in effect, have struck down those statutes, thereby greatly aiding labor's organizing efforts. The AFL–CIO had made repeal a principal legislative goal following the election of 1964, but Johnson failed to make full use of his legendary parliamentary skills on the measure's behalf. Relegating the repeal bill to secondary importance, Johnson and his aides waited until the opportunity to enact it had passed, thereby handing the labor movement a major defeat.[108]

Perhaps this outcome had been unavoidable. Pushing through the repeal of Section 14(b) first might have disrupted the coalition that ultimately passed the civil rights measures that union leaders strongly supported. Although the Civil Rights Act of 1964 and the Voting Rights Act of 1965 increased divisions in the working and lower middle classes, they also helped open the South's closed society, creating conditions there in which union organization became at least a possibility. Organizing the southern working class remained the key, trade unionists understood, to winning a truly decisive social democratic victory in the United States, and thus the civil rights measures held at least the promise of large future benefits to the union movement. Even if that sort of trade-off had been necessary, the net result was to defer 14(b)'s repeal indefinitely, much to the detriment of organized labor.[109]

Even with its power on the wane, labor did manage to chalk up in 1965 a few major legislative victories strongly supported by the working and lower middle classes. The passage of legislation granting public health insurance to the elderly was the fruit of thirty years' of struggle by organized labor. The Medicare program filled the single biggest gap in the privatized health insurance system that labor had helped create during the late 1940s. And the enactment of two major education bills gave millions of Americans greatly expanded opportunities to retrain themselves as automation and the decline of manufacturing drastically reshaped the U.S. job market. Although far from a complete solution to the problem of long-term unemployment, these two measures eased it significantly. Labor leaders rightly viewed those achievements as important gains for the union movement's constituencies.[110]

Much more problematic for labor and its agenda were Johnson's so-called poverty programs. Although most union leaders supported the enactment of those measures and Johnson's call for an unrestricted war on poverty, many workers and members of the lower middle class justifiably came to resent the increasing tax burden that they were asked to bear to support them. With organized labor in decline, the overall tax structure became increasingly regressive, thereby alienating many working- and lower-middle-class Americans. This was especially the case because the so-called poverty programs offered assistance only to the poorest and thus little to those who bore most of their cost.

The inability of Johnson's War on Poverty to meet its creators' grandiose objectives only increased working- and lower-middle-class dissatisfaction with it. These groups tended to view government support for high levels of employment, a progressive tax system, and universalist programs such as Social Security and Medicare as the best ways to fight poverty in the long run, and in large measure they were right. But these more effective policies were, in view of labor's continuing decline, steadily less realizable ones at that time.

Johnson's Great Society poverty initiatives, on the other hand, proved to be politically possible and promised to ameliorate some of the hardships caused by the postwar New Deal's breakdown, especially for those to whom the postwar social contract had given the least. One unfortunate consequence of taking this course, however, was that it turned many working- and lower-middle-class Americans against the activist state, a sentiment that conservatives would soon exploit skillfully to their own ends.[111]

Trade unionists' support for the burst of legislation passed in 1965 thus did little in the short to medium run to stem labor's continuing decline and, in some ways, even encouraged it. The first clear sign of this result came in the elections held the following year, when the Republicans rebounded from the Goldwater debacle to score their largest off-year gains in the House of Representatives since 1946 and elected several new, more conservative, governors, the most notable of whom was California's Ronald Reagan. Just as Democrat Pat Brown's election as governor of California eight years earlier had signaled the emergence of an ascendant Democratic neoliberalism, so Reagan's landslide win over Brown signaled where that change had led. Those in public office who had been most supportive of organized labor suffered the most from this shift in the political and economic landscape, and among those who felt it soonest was Arthur Goldberg.[112]

On July 14, 1965, his old friend Adlai Stevenson, then serving as U.S. ambassador to the United Nations, died suddenly, thereby creating an important gap in Lyndon Johnson's cabinet. Although never really a principal in making foreign policy, Stevenson had performed an important public relations assignment during his time at the United Nations. First Kennedy and then Johnson had relied on Stevenson to use his enormous prestige with liberals in defending the administration's generally hawkish foreign policy.

Although an unenviable task for Stevenson, who privately disagreed with the belligerent line that Kennedy and Johnson had pursued, he had nonetheless performed diligently and effectively. The loss of Stevenson from the cabinet thus increased the risk of liberal disaffection from the administration's foreign policy and, in particular, Johnson's decision to escalate drastically U.S. military involvement in Vietnam. From Johnson's perspective, the timing of Stevenson's death only made matters worse. The massive U.S. troop buildup in South Vietnam had begun the preceding spring, thereby giving the administration its greatest public relations challenge yet in the area of foreign policy.[113]

Perceiving the need for a successor to Stevenson who would also command respect in liberal circles, Johnson's thoughts turned first to Harvard economist John Kenneth Galbraith, who had served under Kennedy as ambassador to India. Johnson promptly offered Galbraith the job, much to the latter's dismay. Having watched Stevenson's performance at the UN and understood the thankless nature of his assignment, Galbraith wanted no part of it.

Unwilling to risk offending Johnson by simply turning him down cold, Galbraith hit on the idea of suggesting someone else whom Johnson might prefer, as the best way to extricate himself from a difficult position. Having heard rumors that Goldberg was feeling restless and even bored on the Court, Galbraith offered his name to Johnson, who seized on the idea at once. Its attractiveness to the president stemmed in part from the dual purpose that such an appointment would serve. If Goldberg resigned from the Court to accept the UN post, Johnson at one stroke would have solved his potential problem with liberals and also created an opening on the Court for his long-time adviser Abe Fortas.[114]

Quickly resolving to try this course, Johnson telephoned Goldberg two days after Stevenson's death to broach the subject. Using all the persuasive powers for which he became justly famous, Johnson appealed to both Goldberg's sense of patriotism and his ego. Johnson told Goldberg that the country was facing two major foreign policy crises, one at the United Nations over financing that threatened its continued existence and another in Vietnam. Describing the situation as akin to a wartime emergency, Johnson went on to say that only Goldberg's proven negotiating skills could resolve both matters.[115]

Although moved by Johnson's request, Goldberg initially resisted it. Even though Goldberg had been somewhat restless with the more monastic aspects of life on the Court, he cherished his place on it and had no interest whatsoever in other jobs either in or out of government. And although he was concerned about the UN's funding crisis and perceived the enormous danger that the Vietnam conflict could pose to the already eroding postwar order, Goldberg did not view himself initially as indispensable to the administration's diplomatic efforts in either area. The most that he would agree to do was to see Johnson the following day and discuss the matter further.[116]

Arriving at the White House on the morning of July 17, Goldberg was met by Johnson's aide Jack Valenti, who escorted him to an anteroom adjacent to the Oval Office. While waiting there, Valenti, in the course of what Goldberg thought was small talk, asked whether he had any interest in being appointed secretary of health, education and welfare (HEW). Startled by the idea, which undercut the whole rationale that Johnson had given for asking him to take the UN post, Goldberg replied that he had no interest in discussing the HEW assignment with the president. Seeking to dispel any notion that he wanted to leave the Court, Goldberg told Valenti, "I'm not an applicant for any post—including the U.N. one."[117]

Valenti, perceiving at once that Galbraith's intelligence about Goldberg's "restlessness" had been at least partially faulty, went into Johnson's office to announce Goldberg's arrival and apparently warned Johnson to stick with his initial proposal and rationale. LBJ did just that, reiterating once again his belief that the country needed Goldberg at the UN. Although once again moved by Johnson's appeal, Goldberg still resisted and agreed only to give the matter more thought. Johnson kept up the pressure by inviting Goldberg and his wife to accompany him aboard Air Force One during the journey to and from Stevenson's funeral in Bloomington, Illinois.

During the return trip, Goldberg finally yielded to Johnson's pleas, although only after gaining what he, Goldberg, had believed were two important concessions. In response to his direct question about the administration's objectives in Vietnam, Johnson stated unequivocally that he was committed to negotiating a peaceful solution. Second, Goldberg insisted that as UN ambassador he would act as a principal adviser and participant in all decision making leading to such a settlement. Even though he had his doubts about

Johnson's sincerity in agreeing to these terms, Goldberg had decided, based on their discussions, that he could turn Johnson around on Vietnam and that accomplishing this task mattered more than anything he could do at present on the Supreme Court.[118]

Making that decision more bearable to Goldberg was the thought that it need not imply an irrevocable departure from the bench. He reasoned that Johnson had picked him for the UN job to resolve a few specific crises. Should he succeed in doing so, the logical next step, on Johnson's part, would have been to reappoint him to the Court. Thus in Goldberg's mind, Johnson's request carried with it an implied promise of a return to the Court once his UN mission had been accomplished. Goldberg also knew that Chief Justice Earl Warren planned to retire before the next presidential election and that Warren would likely urge the president to appoint Goldberg as his successor. If Johnson did the honorable thing, then Goldberg could end up better off than where he had started. Aware from his previous dealings with Johnson of his capacity for duplicity, Goldberg nonetheless consoled himself with the thought that his decision to leave the bench would create a sense of obligation on Johnson's part that he would eventually feel compelled to repay.[119]

And so Goldberg and his family unenthusiastically made their way to the Rose Garden on July 26, 1965, to accept his appointment as Adlai Stevenson's successor, thereby astonishing Washington's political community. Much later, Goldberg described the series of events and his decision in this way:

> Nobody can twist the arm of a Supreme Court justice. . . . We were in a war in Vietnam. I had an exaggerated opinion of my own capacities. I thought I could persuade Johnson that we were fighting the wrong war in the wrong place, [and] to get out. . . . I would love to have stayed on the Court, but my sense of priorities was [that] this war would be disastrous.[120]

Many observers, then and later, found this answer hard to accept. Some, refusing to believe that anyone would selflessly give up a seat on the Supreme Court, spread rumors that Goldberg had agreed to accept the UN post only in return for Johnson's financial advice, supposedly given in the past and from which Goldberg had allegedly profited. Such stories lacked any foundation in fact, but they persisted nonetheless. Others puzzled by Goldberg's decision speculated that he and Johnson had struck a formal deal, whose terms required Johnson to appoint Goldberg chief justice when Warren retired, which was also patently untrue.[121]

Behind this sort of gossip was a widespread belief that Johnson must have had some kind of influence over Goldberg that induced him to say yes. And maybe Johnson did. He may have acquired such a hold over Goldberg as a consequence of a party that Goldberg had thrown in Johnson's honor three and a half years earlier. At the time, Goldberg as labor secretary had been anxious to mend the rift between the then vice-president and union leaders still angry over Johnson's role in helping pass the Landrum–Griffin Act. Although sharing his one-time labor colleagues' view of Johnson's behavior during that episode, Goldberg saw little point in continuing a feud with him, especially since his influence in the Senate could be helpful in passing legislation that labor wanted and perhaps in securing its confirmation of Goldberg some day as a Supreme Court justice.[122]

This well-intentioned plan went awry when Goldberg asked assistant secretary of labor Jerry Holleman to help with it. Holleman, a former president of the Texas State AFL–CIO, knew Johnson intimately and so seemed the logical person to consult. Holleman told Goldberg that the Mexican-style food and entertainment that he wanted could not be obtained in the Northeast. When Goldberg asked where they could get such things, Holleman replied that they would have to be flown in from the Southwest. Seeing the logic behind Holleman's suggestion, Goldberg asked him to take charge of the whole matter.[123]

Anxious to avoid any criticism in the press that Labor Department funds were being spent on a private party, Goldberg asked Holleman to pass the hat for contributions to help pay for it, a move the former soon came to regret. Although Goldberg no doubt intended Holleman to solicit small contributions from reputable sources, Holleman proceeded to take a shortcut characteristic of the political culture from which he had emerged. Rather than spend time gathering a lot of small contributions, Holleman raised $3,000 from a trio of Johnson's longtime financial supporters, including the Texas developer Billy Sol Estes. When Holleman told Goldberg how he had raised the money, Holleman later recalled, "Arthur began to get awfully nervous."[124] Apparently feeling himself already committed, Goldberg went ahead with the party and used some of his own money as well to help pay for it. The Mexican ambassador to the United States also contributed, Holleman later recalled, and thus was funded a lavish and ultimately quite successful affair, which took place on January 11, 1962.[125]

But after the party, complications soon developed. First, Billy Sol Estes came under investigation for having engaged in shady business dealings, which cast a different light on what he may have intended to buy with his contribution to the party for Johnson. And in the meantime, reporters seeking a story that might embarrass the Kennedy administration began ferreting out rumors as to how the Labor Department bash had been financed. Much later, Holleman claimed that this is what happened next:

> As time passed after the banquet, Billy Sol's empire began to crumble around him. And Arthur began to get nervous. He came to me one day and he said, "Jerry, I want the records to show that I put up all of the money for this banquet." I said, "Arthur, if that's what you want, that's all right with me." I didn't know it, but he had called a press conference within thirty minutes of that time, and he got up and swore an oath that he put up all of the money for the banquet.[126]

Goldberg's press conference—during which he produced the check stubs that purported to prove he had paid the caterers out of his own bank account—persuaded reporters that none of the rumored contributions had gone to pay for the party, although Holleman later implied that all the money collected had been spent on the event. When the press finally traced the contributions to Holleman, he—rather than explain where the money had really gone—quietly agreed to resign his post at the Labor Department and returned to Texas, where he became an industrial relations consultant to a major manufacturer.

Holleman later claimed, in a thoroughly self-serving explanation, that he could have remained in Washington but chose to quit rather than harm both Goldberg and the administration that both men served. According to Holleman,

> I could have stayed in Washington, but in doing so I would have hurt the Kennedy–Johnson Administration because I would have hurt one of its sharpest, its best images, Arthur Goldberg, and I chose not to. . . . He did more traveling, more speaking; he was quoted; his picture was in the paper; he represented a very substantial image of the Kennedy–Johnson administration. To destroy that image would only have done harm to the Kennedy–Johnson administration. I knew that when I went up there [that] I was expendable.[127]

Holleman may well also have understood, although he did not say so, that his own decision to solicit a large sum from Billy Sol Estes had made Goldberg vulnerable in the first place and thus that he, Holleman, was really the one most responsible for what had gone wrong.

Holleman asserted later that he had no idea whether Kennedy or Johnson knew the whole story, although given Johnson's close ties to just about everyone involved, he almost certainly knew then, or soon found out, what had in fact transpired. The potential harm that this information could have caused was demonstrated soon thereafter, when Kennedy nominated Goldberg to a seat on the Supreme Court.

Shortly after the nomination had gone to the Senate Judiciary Committee for confirmation, Holleman later claimed that Senator McClellan, who served on that body,

> sent the word back to me, "You are the one person who could block Arthur Goldberg's appointment to the Supreme Court. We will wait three weeks for you to step forward. We cannot wait any longer." I sent word back, "Don't wait." But they waited three weeks.
> McClellan knows the whole story, all of it. He knew it then, my lawyer went to him and told him.[128]

No doubt resenting the way in which he had had to pay for Goldberg's party and perhaps wishing to remind Goldberg in a very pointed way what Holleman's silence had meant to him, Holleman flew up to Washington for the hearing. Plainly visible to all concerned, he watched but did not testify. Goldberg's confirmation went forward smoothly, but at least a few of those involved believed that the tale of the Johnson party and its funding could have derailed it.[129]

If Holleman's story, for which there is no independent corroboration, is true, Goldberg's reluctant decision three years later to accept Johnson's request that he leave the Court makes much more sense. Although there is no evidence that Johnson ever mentioned the episode during their discussions about the UN ambassadorship, he did not need to. Had Goldberg refused the job, Johnson might well have arranged to leak the story, which at the least would have severely embarrassed Goldberg and at most could have cost him his seat on the Court.

If, on the other hand, he accepted Johnson's offer of the UN ambassadorship and performed as he hoped to there, Goldberg may well have reasoned, then a grateful Johnson would likely have reappointed him to the Court, while keeping under wraps the whole story about the funds for the party. These considerations, in addition to Goldberg's concern about the harm that U.S. participation in the Vietnam War could do to the postwar order and his belief that he could persuade Johnson to reverse course there, could have been the decisive ones.

If these were the proximate causes of Goldberg's departure from the bench, a more basic one was the rupture in the postwar New Deal that he had helped negotiate. Had labor remained as strong in 1965 as it had been from the late 1940s through the early 1960s, Goldberg could have felt confident that Johnson would keep the story of the party and its financing from coming out. In that context Johnson would not have risked offending the labor movement by tarnishing the reputation of the first union lawyer ever appointed to the Supreme Court. But with labor's power clearly waning and neoliberalism in the ascendancy, the union movement no longer had the strength to protect the more vulnerable of its most loyal supporters in government, either elected or appointed.

Helping make the difference at the margin was the tragic fact of Kennedy's assassination. More supportive of labor even with its power in decline, Kennedy, had he still been president in July 1965, would surely have left Goldberg alone. Thus Johnson's accidental accession to the presidency in this instance, as in others, strengthened the forces already working against those in the middle of the labor movement, such as Goldberg. By the summer of 1965, then, he and like-minded New Deal liberals could begin to appreciate what Kennedy's untimely death had ultimately cost them. In Goldberg's case, the price included the job he had wanted for all of his professional life and the security that went with it.[130]

11

A Time of Troubles

GOLDBERG'S MOVE TO the United Nations in late July 1965 plunged him back into the maelstrom of public life, from which he would not fully emerge until the end of 1970. Although he was to score some notable successes as a diplomat, they were outweighed by more basic frustrations: his inability to bring about an end to the war in Vietnam, to continue in public life by winning elective office, and, above all, to return to the much quieter and, for him, more satisfying world of the Court he had so reluctantly left behind. Those disappointments stemmed in part from the actions of specific individuals, most notably Lyndon Johnson, and more fundamentally from the increasing decline of the postwar order with which Goldberg was so closely identified.

An examination of this period of Goldberg's life helps explain what went wrong not only for him but also for New Deal liberals more generally during the latter half of the 1960s.

II

Goldberg's arrival at the UN reinvigorated the ambassador's role in the conduct of American foreign policy. Although Goldberg's predecessor, Adlai Stevenson, had enjoyed great prominence and prestige in the liberal community, they did not translate into real influence with Presidents Kennedy or Johnson or Secretary of State Dean Rusk. As a result, Stevenson's tenure as U.S. ambassador to the United Nations was marked by slights and worse, a situation that had driven him into depression by the time of his death. Goldberg, in contrast, commanded much more influence in the Johnson administration, especially during his first year as ambassador. Even though his disagreements with Johnson over Vietnam and, even more, Goldberg's decision to express those differences forcefully soon eroded his authority, Goldberg still exercised more clout and met with more diplomatic triumphs throughout his tenure at the UN than Stevenson had.[1]

The list of successes that Goldberg achieved during his less than three years at the United Nations is impressive. First was his role in resolving the crisis over financing that imperiled the organization's very existence. The dispute had grown out of the efforts of the United States government and some of its allies during the early 1960s to give the UN more power to resolve disputes and, in particular, to strengthen its executive authority.

Those governments most opposed to such a change, the Soviet Union and France, responded by refusing to pay their budget assessments for peacekeeping operations in the Congo and Middle East, which they viewed as unauthorized by the UN charter. A large budget deficit soon developed, one that eventually threatened to paralyze the entire organization. Although the United States and its supporters managed to postpone a real showdown over the issue by engineering a bond sale, matters came to a head in the spring of 1965.[2]

By that time, both sides had seemingly backed themselves into hopelessly irreconcilable positions. The governments of France, the Soviet Union, and ten other nations had failed for more than two years to pay their assessments for the peacekeeping forces in question, on the grounds that such operations were improper. The United States and its allies on this issue had tried to retaliate by stripping those countries' governments of their General Assembly voting rights. Under Article 19 of the United Nations Charter, the General Assembly could vote to strip any member that failed to pay its assessments for two years of all voting rights in that body. But the Franco–Soviet position commanded sufficient weight in the General Assembly to frustrate efforts there to invoke Article 19. Thus a dangerous stalemate developed. It became even worse when the UN's vocal critics in the United States began using the dispute to press their case against American membership, thereby increasing the threat to the organization's survival.[3]

So serious was this now all-but-forgotten crisis that it played a significant part in Goldberg's decision to accept the UN ambassadorship. A strong supporter of the United Nations since its inception, Goldberg perceived the Article 19 crisis as having imperiled the organization's very existence and, by extension, world peace. He managed in less than a month's time to defuse the crisis by winning support from leading Democrats and Republicans in Congress for a compromise, which he announced to the UN's Special Committee on Peacekeeping Operations on August 16, 1965.

In his remarks, Goldberg reviewed the entire episode, reiterated the American government's view of the General Assembly's rights under Article 19, and then went on to say that the United States recognized the Assembly's unwillingness to impose the penalty of loss of voting rights on those governments that had failed to pay their assessments for the past two years. In closing, he cautioned the committee and, by implication, all UN members, that the U.S. government reserved the right to withhold payment should the

General Assembly at some future time authorize peacekeeping operations with which the American government disagreed. Including the latter proviso helped Goldberg persuade conservatives in Congress and former President Eisenhower to support the new American position, which effectively broke the deadlock.[4]

Although Goldberg's mediation had helped keep the UN intact, the way in which that objective had been accomplished testified to the large obstacles that stood in the way of expanding the organization's role in world affairs. The effort during the preceding five years to move the UN from what was essentially a collection of conference mechanisms into something more like a governing body had led to a decline in the General Assembly's authority in the critical realm of financing. Within a month of Goldberg's having accepted the UN ambassadorship, then, the General Assembly's limitations, and thus those of the diplomats assigned there, had been confirmed.[5]

Even with these constraints, Goldberg still managed to achieve some further diplomatic successes while UN ambassador. When war broke out in August 1965 between India and Pakistan, Goldberg, who was then president of the Security Council, performed ably in helping negotiate a cease-fire agreement. And when the white minority government in Rhodesia proclaimed that country's independence the following October, Goldberg played an important part in mobilizing U.S. opposition to that regime and in favor of majority rule there. Despite strong resistance from the Defense, Commerce, and Treasury Departments and the National Aeronautics and Space Administration (NASA), Goldberg won the Johnson administration's backing for a UN Security Council resolution banning the purchase of Rhodesia's chief imports, which passed in December 1966.[6]

In the fall of 1966, Goldberg made his mark once again in Africa by winning U.S. government support for a resolution terminating the South African regime's legal authority over what today is known as Namibia. The resolution, which formally ended the South African mandate granted by the League of Nations, was opposed by some in the Johnson administration and was greeted unenthusiastically by U.S. allies such as Britain and France, yet in the end Goldberg prevailed. Even though the move hardly brought an end to South African rule there, it did constitute the first important diplomatic step in that direction, for which Goldberg deserved a good deal of credit.[7]

Those triumphs were followed by Goldberg's single most important accomplishment while UN ambassador, his role in negotiating both an end to the Arab–Israeli war of 1967 and a formula that could serve as the basis for a comprehensive Mideast peace agreement. Goldberg shepherded two resolutions through the Security Council, the first on June 6 and the second on June 12, which called for a cease-fire and condemned all violations of it. The two resolutions soon proved instrumental in bringing about an end to the fighting. Rather than stop there, Goldberg secured the Johnson administration's backing for a resolution to spell out the requirements for a lasting peace in the region. The resulting Security Council Resolution, Number 242, which passed unanimously on November 22, 1967, was largely Goldberg's handiwork. That it remains, even today, the starting point for those seeking a Middle East peace underscores the importance of this achievement and Goldberg's abilities as a diplomat.[8]

Over the next seven months, Goldberg's last as UN ambassador, he scored four additional diplomatic triumphs. The first had to with the growing tension between Greece and Turkey over Cyprus, which brought them to the brink of war in November 1967. Goldberg's efforts helped produce a Security Council resolution that unanimously called for restraint, thereby averting an almost certain conflict. Next came a crisis caused by the North Korean government's seizure of the USS *Pueblo* in January 1968. Goldberg's effective presentation to the UN Security Council, which was televised live across the United States, contributed to a peaceful resolution of this dispute.

Later that year he guided the Nuclear Non-Proliferation Treaty (NNPT) through the General Assembly endorsement process and was instrumental in negotiating an international agreement that banned the stationing of weapons of mass destruction in outer space. Both these arms control measures contributed in significant, if limited, ways to the maintenance of world peace. So, too, in a different way did Goldberg's role in resolving the Cyprus and *Pueblo* crises. In those four areas, as in others, he showed real talent as a peacemaker.[9]

And yet despite Goldberg's demonstrated capacities as a diplomat, the settlement he had gone to the UN to achieve ultimately eluded him. The Vietnam War was by far the most important foreign policy issue facing the Johnson administration and the country during his time at the UN, and it overshadowed everything else he managed to accomplish there. Negotiating a Vietnam peace agreement was, in a very real sense, what Goldberg's assignment to the UN was supposed to have been about. His other achievements while UN ambassador clearly indicate that Goldberg's inability to obtain such a settlement did not stem from a lack of diplomatic skills. Why he was unable to achieve an end to American military involvement in Vietnam remains the most historically significant issue associated with his UN experience and the central story of that part of his long and varied career.[10]

III

Goldberg entered the high councils of the Johnson administration at a fateful time. During the previous six months, the president and his senior foreign policy advisers had deeply committed the nation's armed forces to preserving the South Vietnamese government. By the time Goldberg began sitting in on meetings that dealt with Vietnam policy, most of the contours of the escalation program had already been delineated. Between mid-March and late July 1965, when Johnson announced Goldberg's appointment as UN ambassador, the administration had begun large-scale bombing raids over North Vietnam and increased the number of American military personnel in the South from approximately 25,000 to more than 100,000. By that time, Johnson and his advisers were also planning to increase steadily the number of U.S. troops there over the next few years to as many as 600,000.[11]

Goldberg had opposed that course from the very beginning. His stand on the Vietnam issue was very similar to that of the diplomat George Kennan and the syndicated columnist Walter Lippmann, who viewed the American interest in preserving the status quo there as fairly small and the likely cost of trying to do so as very high. Unlike some of the other leading critics of the war, however, Goldberg had no illusions about the possibility of establishing some kind of durable coalition government that included representatives of the North and South, with the North as the dominant partner.

When Lippmann suggested that idea to him during a dinner table discussion, Goldberg told him, "You're foolish, Walter. You're a good newspaperman, but if North Vietnam is on top, they're going to take over the country."[12] Goldberg saw that outcome as undesirable, but one the United States and its allies could live with, given the tensions that would likely emerge between Vietnam and its socialist neighbors to the north.[13]

Persuading Goldberg to adopt this view was his acute sense of what Johnson's escalation alternative would ultimately cost the United States. Goldberg understood that the price of such an effort would surely include more than soldiers' lives and munitions. Johnson's decision to escalate American military involvement in Vietnam posed, above and beyond these considerations, a threat to the already eroding postwar order at home. The reason was that escalation could undermine support for the entire cold war policy, the linchpin that had held together the postwar New Deal. Of course, so could withdrawal, or so LBJ feared. But his decision to escalate also promised to divide the agreement's defenders, thereby strengthening the forces already at work against American-style social democracy.[14]

Even those leading New Deal liberals such as Goldberg who opposed escalation deserved some of the blame for that policy's adoption. All too often over the preceding two decades they had echoed alarmist views of the Soviet "threat" and voiced their support for the broad outlines of the containment policy even when sometimes disagreeing with its specific application. That such liberals had supported containment at least partly out of a desire to protect the hard-won gains of the American working and lower middle classes did not change the consequences for the nation's foreign policy. Johnson's decision in the spring and summer of 1965 to go to war in Vietnam had followed directly from the basic assumptions underlying the containment policy, which liberals had endorsed in the late 1940s and reemphasized during the early 1960s. One consequence was to jeopardize almost immediately some of liberalism's most valuable achievements. Thus Goldberg and other prominent New Deal liberals found themselves hoist at last on their own petard.[15]

He distinguished himself from many of his liberal peers, however, by indicating from the outset his opposition to Johnson's ill-advised Vietnam strategy. During a meeting held at Camp David in late July 1965, shortly before Goldberg formally resigned from the bench, Defense Secretary Robert McNamara urged Johnson to call up the reserves, which would, in effect, have

placed the nation on a full wartime footing. Goldberg objected, telling Johnson in front of McNamara, "You do that and you don't get my letter of
resignation [from the Court]."[16] Johnson, who very likely would not have
taken the step McNamara had suggested, in any event, ruled it out, thereby
placating his UN ambassador to be.[17]

Goldberg immediately made his position clear in another way as well.
Understanding from that incident and their earlier conversations that he
opposed escalation, Johnson asked him to assume formally the role of devil's
advocate during internal debates over Vietnam policy. But Goldberg refused,
saying that he wanted Johnson and everyone else at such meetings to understand that he truly believed what he was saying, rather than merely playing an
assigned part, which would have undercut the force of his arguments. Undersecretary of State George Ball, who had doubts of his own about the wisdom
of the military buildup, agreed to take the role Johnson suggested, leaving
Goldberg free to challenge the existing policy openly should he wish to do
so.[18]

Despite these early disagreements, which had been illuminating for all
involved, Goldberg maintained cordial relations with Johnson and his other
top foreign policy advisers for the next ten months. He did so by moving
cautiously during that time. Anxious to turn the administration around, Goldberg appears to have tried at first to win the Johnson team's confidence in his
ability as a diplomat before pressing hard for a change in the basic Vietnam
policy.

Johnson, for his part, seems to have made a sincere effort during this time
to keep Goldberg happy. LBJ allowed Goldberg to consult with him frequently about a wide range of foreign policy matters and gave Goldberg a
prominent seat at meetings of the cabinet and National Security Council. His
success at the UN in dealing with other issues, restrained opposition to the
escalation policy during this period and willingness to defend it before liberal
audiences seemed to have persuaded Johnson of Goldberg's value to the
administration and so inclined the president to accommodate him.[19]

A turning point during this period of more or less peaceful coexistence
came in late December 1965 and early January 1966, when the Johnson
administration's first major "peace initiative" quickly fizzled out. The reason
for its failure stemmed in large part from the unwillingness of Johnson and his
hawkish advisers to make any real concessions. LBJ had settled early on a
peace "formula" that in effect precluded negotiations. First clearly articulated
in December 1965, the administration's fourteen-point peace proposal called
for an end to the bombing only after the North Vietnamese government took
steps to de-escalate. Similarly, the Johnson administration's "peace" proposals stipulated that it would withdraw U.S. military forces only after the two
sides reached a political settlement that preserved a South Vietnamese government independent of both the North and the indigenous rebels in the
South, the so-called Viet Cong.

Such an approach could more accurately be described as a formula for
continued war rather than peace, given how unacceptable those terms were to

the Hanoi government and the Viet Cong. LBJ and his advisers admitted as
much even as they ordered a thirty-seven-day bombing pause and dispatched
Goldberg, National Security Adviser McGeorge Bundy, Ambassador-at-
Large Averell Harriman, and Vice-President Hubert Humphrey around the
globe to proclaim the nation's willingness to negotiate. The heavily publicized "peace mission" that took place over the Christmas holiday that year
was partly intended by Johnson and his aides to legitimate even more fighting,
by "demonstrating" the North's unwillingness to come to the bargaining
table.[20]

For Goldberg, the "peace mission" was a disillusioning experience. Accompanied by his wife, Dorothy, Goldberg traveled to Rome for an audience with
the pope and then on to Paris for a private meeting with the French president,
Charles de Gaulle. In both meetings Goldberg explained the administration's
view and his own support for peace negotiations. The fruitlessness of the
whole effort, however, soon began to weigh heavily on him. The pope and de
Gaulle had nothing to offer besides advice to pursue negotiations and their
best wishes for success.

Once the bombing pause and peace mission came to an end in late January,
Goldberg, as he later described the situation, "increasingly got the impression
I was being used."[21] What had seemed in late December, to Goldberg at least,
as a real effort by Johnson to start negotiating, all too quickly came to look
like what it really was, an exercise in public relations that eased the transition
to an even more intense round of fighting.[22]

As the United States's military involvement in the war deepened during the
late winter and early spring of 1966, Goldberg moved toward an open challenge to the existing Vietnam policy. Having apparently decided that he had
done enough by then both to establish his own credentials as a diplomat and
to win Johnson's confidence, Goldberg that spring made his first serious
effort to nudge the president to reverse course.

On May 13, 1966, he wrote Johnson a four-page letter in which he cautiously called for halting the trend toward ever greater escalation. After congratulating Johnson for his May 11 address at Princeton University, in which
the president had proclaimed his determination to keep the U.S. military role
in Vietnam a limited one, Goldberg warned against giving into pressures for
using more force:

> From my conversations with leading Americans around the country, and
> with leading representatives of other governments in New York, the one
> factor in the present situation which I find is more disturbing than any other,
> is the danger that the war in Viet Nam will escalate beyond its present
> bounds.
>
> I am sure you will continue to get all sorts of advice over the coming
> months on what else we should do in Viet Nam.
>
> Some will argue — and it will sound tempting — that the other side needs a
> more convincing demonstration than they have yet had that they cannot win
> the war before they can ever be brought to negotiate an acceptable settle-
> ment. I can well imagine that our military experts may conclude that in

pursuit of a military "victory," we should expand our operations beyond their present level. In situations where we are spending vast sums and losing hundreds of men, it is easy for impatience to triumph over patience and for the urge to win to prevail over a willingness to live, for a time, with a stalemate, as a prelude to an acceptable political settlement.

These pressures are difficult to resist. But I believe you must resist them. The great danger, it seems to me, is that a series of unconnected decisions to step up the scale of hostilities, each adopted in reaction to a specific military problem or difficulty, may have a snowballing effect beyond what any single step might itself be expected to produce.[23]

Having addressed what he saw as the danger posed by increasing escalation, Goldberg proceeded next to underscore his own opposition to that policy:

I know how carefully you weigh every decision of this kind. But in the face of what I anticipate will be growing pressures for more drastic action, I feel compelled to add my voice to what I sense to be the majority of American opinion, and most certainly that of American liberal opinion, in expressing the earnest hope that you will find it possible to avoid further escalation of our military operations in North Viet Nam, and let the already heavy pressures we are applying against the Communists exert their full weight over time.[24]

Goldberg then listed the specific reasons he saw as arguing against some of the changes in military strategy that Johnson's most hawkish advisers were considering, such as expanding the bombing of the North to purely civilian targets, attacking Haiphong harbor, and expanding U.S. military operations to the major industrial centers of the North. Although the first of these ideas Goldberg attacked both as inhumane and likely to produce an adverse response from neutral countries, the second and third he saw as positively dangerous. Attacking Haiphong harbor, he warned, could provoke a reciprocal strike against the river channel leading to Saigon, and an assault against the North's major population centers might well induce the Chinese to enter the war.

Apparently concerned that Johnson might provoke a Chinese response just as General Douglas MacArthur's recklessness had in Korea, Goldberg warned him that "extending the area of our military operations to include the critical industrial and supply centers in the North is, I think, almost certain to produce an equal and opposite reaction by the Chinese Communists and perhaps the Soviet Union."[25]

He noted that only one week earlier—for what he believed to be the first time—Chinese fighter planes had crossed into North Vietnam as part of a defensive maneuver against American attacks, and Goldberg warned that if Johnson gave in to the hawks' demand for

taking the war to the North, I would expect to see this [Chinese fighter plane] development multiplied many times over. And if we begin to lose planes to enemy fighters based in Communist China, whether North Vietnamese or Chinese . . . I can see us becoming quickly engaged in military operations on Chinese territory. In short, escalation can only beget escalation.[26]

Goldberg closed his carefully worded and evidently quite heartfelt letter by urging Johnson to reject as futile any effort to achieve a decisive military victory, the search for which seemed to lie behind the steadily increasing U.S. military effort.

Trying to minimize the challenge to Johnson's policy by emphasizing that he, Goldberg, was calling only for what the president had from the beginning stated it to be, Goldberg wrote:

> I believe you would agree with the proposition which we hear so often that there can be no "military victory" in Viet Nam in the usual sense. And we ourselves, of course, have foresworn an effort to defeat the regime in Hanoi. Our efforts have been confined, and most properly in my judgement, to preventing North Viet Nam from overwhelming the South. Even our air operations in the North, as I suggested above, have been explainable in that context. To go beyond that will give rise to serious doubts that our objectives are genuinely limited—as you have so wisely stressed in your speeches. No matter what we then say, it will be more and more difficult to cope with the accusations of those who believe that we are, intentionally or unintentionally, heading for war with China.[27]

Goldberg ended by writing that "I wanted you to have my views on this matter" and noted that he had sent a copy of the letter to Dean Rusk as well.[28]

Some nine and a half months after joining the administration as UN ambassador, Goldberg had clearly, if cautiously, stated his opposition to the policy of increasing military involvement. The die had been cast.

In light of how consequential this letter proved to be, one should keep in mind not only what it called for but also what it did not. Goldberg had not pressed Johnson to withdraw U.S. troops already in Vietnam, to begin de-escalating unilaterally, or even to abandon strategies and tactics already in use there. The letter had simply urged the president to halt the trend toward ever deeper involvement, which Goldberg saw as the necessary first step toward a peaceful solution. Although Goldberg later claimed to have favored de-escalation strongly from the beginning, he apparently did not dare go so far as to suggest that course in his first open dissent, lest he alienate Johnson completely. For what seems to have been the same reason, Goldberg appears to have couched his more limited plea in terms he believed sufficiently cautious as to incline LBJ to listen. The net result was, in retrospect, as striking for its mildness as for the disagreement it signaled with a Vietnam policy supported by almost all of Johnson's top foreign affairs advisers.[29]

Even so, Johnson's response proved swift and severe. First came a telephone call from cabinet secretary Robert Kintner, who told Goldberg, "The President would like you to withdraw the memorandum."[30] Apparently afraid that Goldberg would leak his letter to the press and publicize the division over Vietnam policy, Johnson had ordered his aide to persuade Goldberg to back down. The "request" infuriated Goldberg, who told Kintner that LBJ could tear up the memo if he liked but that he, Goldberg, had a copy in his UN files and would not withdraw it. Kintner's call was soon followed by one from Johnson's press secretary, Bill Moyers, who told Goldberg he had "misunderstood" the president. Goldberg berated Moyers for his dishonesty in suggesting that Johnson had not meant for him to eat his words, retorting, "He [Johnson] goddamn did mean it and you shouldn't be a party to it."[31] Goldberg then told Moyers, "Part of the trouble with the whole Vietnam business is that responsible administration officials give the President the advice he wants to hear rather than what he needs to hear."[32]

Dissatisfied, to say the least, with Goldberg's response, Johnson decided to take up the issue at their next meeting. The midday session on May 24 had been scheduled to discuss the People's Republic of China's latest effort to gain entry into the United Nations, but Goldberg's Vietnam letter altered the agenda. The Oval Office meeting focused at first on Goldberg's dissent and soon degenerated into a furious argument, complete with raised voices and finger-pointing on both sides. Goldberg's decision to express his views in writing and open defiance when asked to recant had antagonized Johnson, but it was the letter's suggestion that Goldberg spoke for American liberals more generally that enraged the president.

Goldberg stuck to his guns, telling Johnson that his policy of ever greater escalation was alienating liberals across the country. For a president who had purposefully surrounded himself with talented and intelligent people whom he could, and did, turn into sycophants and yes men and who interpreted disagreements with administration policies as personal attacks, Goldberg's actions bordered on the intolerable. Although the two men managed to put aside their differences after almost fifty minutes of wrangling, when several aides joined them to discuss the Chinese representation issue, the end of the earlier conversation had also terminated a once-cordial relationship.[33]

It went from bad to worse when Goldberg chose to voice his dissent at the next two meetings of the National Security Council (NSC). At issue there was whether to expand the U.S. bombing to industrial targets such as oil storage facilities in the major urban centers of the north, principally Hanoi and Haiphong.

During the first of those sessions, held on June 17, 1966, Goldberg attacked the idea and tried to make arguments against it that would carry weight with Johnson and his hawkish advisers. First he objected to the idea as likely to prove fruitless, saying that "the Communist bloc is not going to let this outfit go down the drain. They see the Vietnam war as a confrontation. With minimum risk, they can make up for the damage we [would] do to the North Vietnamese petroleum supplies."[34] Next he listed the other likely consequences of the proposed move for the conduct of American foreign policy. The world reaction, he noted "would be strongly adverse—even Canada would oppose our action."[35]

Reminding those present that Mao's government had almost enough votes to win representation in the UN General Assembly, Goldberg suggested that widening the bombing might alienate enough allies so as to tip the balance there in favor of recognition. Another possible consequence, he observed, might be China's entry into the war. And even if none of those scenarios came to pass, Goldberg concluded, to escalate further without decisive results would surely produce a dangerous shift in American public opinion. "The domestic reaction will be very adverse if we strike these . . . targets and then this act does not end the war. The reaction domestically will be to demand stronger military action by the President."[36]

Implicitly urging a move toward de-escalation, Goldberg predicted that "the country's mood will turn at election time if the war is still going on" and, in closing, tried to buttress this argument by noting that it was based not on polls but, rather, on his conversations with influential people around the country.[37]

Apparently offended by Goldberg's suggestion that those favoring the bombing proposal had failed to think through its potential consequences, Johnson replied tersely, "No one has been reckless. Had we been, we would have struck these targets already."[38] The most Johnson would do was postpone a final decision until the next NSC meeting, which took place five days later.[39]

There Goldberg restated his earlier objections more briefly, telling Johnson, Rostow, and the others that "I am still opposed. I do not think it will bring them [the North Vietnamese government] to the conference table." Trying once again to make an argument that would sway his hawkish listeners, he stated the alternative as follows:

> Don't withdraw. I think we are doing well. Beef up our forces, go after more successes and pressure of that type. Don't convert this to an extension of the war even to Hanoi. It is tougher and painful to absorb, but it will hopefully lead to an agreed solution to let the people in the South alone.[40]

In the end, even this approach, which traded away most of what Goldberg later said he had ultimately wanted, failed to move Johnson, who elected to widen the bombing as his other advisers had urged. And Goldberg's open dissent at these two NSC meetings damaged beyond repair whatever remained of his earlier rapport with Johnson. To have quarreled with Johnson privately had been bad enough in LBJ's eyes, but to confront him in front of his other senior foreign policy advisers, as Goldberg had done, compounded the offense.

When as part of his argument against the bombing proposal Goldberg had said to Johnson, "You can't do that," Johnson visibly stiffened and snapped back, "I'm the President of the United States and of course I can do it."[41] Goldberg, determined to hold his ground, replied, "I made a mistake. Of course you can do it, but you must not."[42] By choosing to disregard this admonition, Johnson gave his answer. By this point, the two men's working relationship with respect to Vietnam policy had broken down completely.

As an exercise in persuasion, then, Goldberg's letter and subsequent defense of the views it contained proved to be a failure, in the short run at least.

For this result, he perhaps deserved a measure of the blame. Some of his mannerisms injured his advocacy, both with Johnson and his other foreign policy advisers. Several of them complained then and afterward that Goldberg tended to be long-winded, and in truth he loved to talk, which sometimes exasperated those forced to listen. Even more problematic was a pompous quality that had crept in following his resignation from the Supreme Court. Intending to rejoin the Court on completing his UN assignment, Goldberg appears to have adopted a public persona he thought fitting for a once-and-future justice. Whatever it may have contributed to his quest for reappointment to the bench, such self-importance served him poorly in debates over Vietnam policy.[43]

Goldberg was also criticized for his decision to represent himself to Johnson as a spokesman for the liberal community at large, a charge that deserves some attention. In suggesting that his views about the war more accurately reflected liberal attitudes than administration policy, Goldberg antagonized Johnson. But Goldberg never intended such a result. In fact, he had wished only to buttress his argument by making clear to Johnson that the views contained in his May 13 letter were not simply the musings of one individual but, rather, a summary of what many other liberals were thinking and so deserved greater weight than what his views alone should have had.

And furthermore, Goldberg was right. Many liberals did, by the spring of 1966, increasingly oppose the administration's continuing escalation policy. The blame for Johnson's reaction to this particular assertion lies with him, rather than the UN ambassador, who had simply told him the truth. Those so-called doves who ruled out making such a direct challenge to Johnson's view of himself and his policies failed to accomplish more than Goldberg had. In the last analysis, then, more muted dissents served little purpose other than to protect the careers of those who chose to go that route.[44]

Goldberg had taken the harder road, of which he was soon made painfully aware. Immediately following the June NSC sessions, Johnson sharply diminished the frequency of his contact with him. In fact, the president did not meet with his UN ambassador at all during the summer of 1966. Their paths sometimes crossed at social events, and Goldberg continued to attend cabinet meetings, but no real communication took place between the two men, other than on routine matters. In another clear sign of his displeasure, Johnson excluded Goldberg from meetings with the so-called Wise Men, the group of senior foreign policy advisers outside government on whom LBJ relied for counsel about Vietnam policy.[45]

And so began one of the unhappiest times of Goldberg's long and distinguished career. To have resigned, as George Ball quietly did in September 1966, would likely have meant a complete break with Johnson and the end of Goldberg's hopes for a return to the Court. Nor could he have returned at that point to his old law firm, in view of his earlier pledge upon being named secretary of labor, never again to represent a labor union. Although he could easily have gone into private practice with a major firm in New York or Washington, that option had no great appeal for him. And so he stayed, hoping against hope that LBJ would eventually see the wisdom of his forth-right advice about Vietnam.[46]

Unwilling to accept Johnson's silent treatment in the interim, Goldberg complained to him about it in late September 1966, saying that rumors about the rift between the two were undermining his effectiveness as UN am-bassador. Johnson promptly backed off, unwilling to prompt a resignation that might publicize the split in the administration over Vietnam policy. Direct communication between the two men therefore resumed on a regular basis in October and continued, save for a brief interruption, for the rest of Goldberg's time at the UN.[47]

Even that state of relations fell short, however, of a return to the relatively amicable period before May 13, 1966. Although Goldberg regularly attended cabinet and NSC meetings, Johnson continued to exclude him from Wise Men sessions and from another elite group of foreign policy decision makers known informally as the Tuesday Cabinet. To keep even this uneasy peace, Goldberg toned down his objections, apparently having concluded that fur-ther stridency was pointless, given that Johnson and his other senior aides by then understood Goldberg's basic outlook.[48]

After sixteen months of that depressing situation came at last a major change. The Tet offensive launched on January 30, 1968, transformed think-ing in Washington and the United States more generally about the Vietnam War. Although Tet proved to be a tactical defeat for the North Vietnamese and Viet Cong, by bringing the fight quite literally to the door of the U.S. embassy in Saigon, Tet undermined the American public's confidence in Johnson's rosy predictions of impending victory. By the end of the first wave of the Tet offensive in late February, domestic opposition to Johnson's con-duct of the war had mushroomed. In that sense at least, Tet had been a spectacular, if terribly costly, North Vietnamese–Viet Cong victory.[49]

Goldberg watched these events unfold in February and March with an increasing sense of vindication. Two events he found particularly gratifying were the Senate Foreign Relations Committee's grilling of Dean Rusk on March 11 and 12 and the New Hampshire primary results announced on the second of those two days. Rusk's admission during his testimony that the administration was reviewing the entire Vietnam policy Goldberg rightly viewed as a belated concession that escalation was not working. And antiwar presidential candidate Eugene McCarthy's astonishingly strong showing in the New Hampshire Democratic presidential primary held on March 12 seemed to demonstrate exactly the kind of liberal dissatisfaction with John-son's Vietnam policy that Goldberg had warned of almost two years earlier. Yet, concurrent with Rusk's remarks and McCarthy's "victory," Goldberg heard alarming rumors that Johnson and his advisers were seriously thinking about responding to Tet with another major troop buildup. Convinced that further escalation would be a terrible mistake, Goldberg decided that the time had come to send the president another long memorandum about Vietnam.[50]

On March 15, 1968, he sent a cable to Johnson through Rusk at the State Department. Like Goldberg's earlier memo of May 1966, this remarkable message merits extensive quotation. Apparently wanting to offer a rationale for sending the telegram that would not unduly offend either the president or his secretary of state, Goldberg noted first Rusk's recent remarks before the Senate Foreign Relations Committee:

> Secretary Rusk has made clear in his statement to the Senate Foreign Relations Committee that the entire situation with regard to Vietnam is under review from A to Z. It is my understanding this review encompasses not only military aspects but also possible moves toward a political solution. It is on the latter question that I should like to advance the following thoughts for the consideration of those engaged in this policy review.[51]

Having established a reasonable basis for providing unsolicited advice, Goldberg continued by listing the specific events of the past month and a half that had called into question the basic assumptions on which the escalation policy had been based:

> Recent developments in our country have demonstrated that there is grave concern among the American public whether the course we have set in our Vietnam policy is right or holds promise of results commensurate with the cost—concern which has been deepened by the reverses we and the South Vietnamese suffered during the Tet offensive, by the apparent lack of energy, effectiveness and appeal of the South Vietnamese government, by the mounting rate of American casualties, by the extent of the destruction of life and property in Vietnam, and by reports that requests have been made of the President for substantial troop reinforcements in South Vietnam. This concern reflects a growing public belief that the war in South Vietnam is increasingly an American war, not a South Vietnamese war which the US is supporting, and, further, that the war cannot be won on this basis without ever-mounting commitments not worth the cost.[52]

These considerations were compounded, Goldberg suggested, by declining public support for the escalation policy, as measured by recent polls and especially by the New Hampshire primary results. Anxious to get Johnson to listen, Goldberg alluded to this very sensitive subject only indirectly: "As I see it, under our democratic processes, if public support is permanently and substantially eroded, we will not be able to maintain let alone intensify the level of our military efforts in Vietnam."[53]

Goldberg acknowledged that "major presidential decisions cannot and should not be made on the basis of a day-by-day reading of the public's temperature" but then implied that the shift in public opinion over the past month and a half had been so dramatic as to compel a correspondingly fundamental change in Vietnam policy.

Trying hard to move Johnson, Goldberg couched his argument in terms that the president might respect in an election year: "It is my considered opinion that the very best way to prevent further erosion of public support from taking place is to make a new and fresh move toward a political solution at this time." Lest Johnson think that Goldberg favored such an initiative only for that reason, he stated firmly, "Moreover, and independently of this, I believe on the merits that a fresh move toward a political solution should be made now."[54]

The "only . . . feasible step" toward such a solution, Goldberg argued, was a unilateral halt in the bombing without prior assurances from the North Vietnamese government that it would not seek to exploit such a move militarily.[55] Its purpose, Goldberg explained, would be to determine whether the North Vietnamese government was willing to negotiate in good faith. Trying, in effect, to give Johnson a face-saving rationale for announcing what would have been a significant change in policy, Goldberg performed some legalistic acrobatics to "prove" that such a move would not involve a departure from the president's previous statements.[56]

To ease the sting of that step for Johnson and the hawks around him, Goldberg listed the various military means that would remain unaffected by a unilateral halt in the bombing. Then he described four specific initiatives the administration should take "in addition to and concurrently with the bombing cessation," the first and most controversial of which was to "go privately to the Soviets and the bloc countries to enlist their strong support toward ensuring that, on the one hand, Hanoi does not take military advantage of the bombing cessation and, on the other, that Hanoi will promptly begin negotiations which will be fruitful."[57]

Trying to anticipate the likely objections to the new path he was suggesting, such as the possibility of resistance from the South Vietnamese government or the view that the present was an inopportune time for negotiations, Goldberg stated:

> I realize fully the course I am proposing would have repercussions and implications for the government in Saigon, particularly at this time. But a growing erosion of support by the American people for our present policies would have far greater repercussions and implications for that government.
>
> In the Vietnam situation, like almost all potential negotiating situations, there can never be an ideal time for negotiations. If things are going well militarily, the natural inclination is to look upon negotiations as unnecessary. If, conversely, things are going badly militarily, then the disposition is to look upon negotiations as disadvantageous. In light of our past experience in Vietnam, there will not be, in the foreseeable future, an ideal time for negotiations. Were we to decide upon a substantial military build-up, I see no reason to believe that our adversaries are incapable, given the support they are receiving, of stepping up their military response, rather than being forced within practical time limits into negotiations under circumstances more advantageous to us than the present.

In closing, Goldberg tried to emphasize the importance of the need to move quickly, stating, "My strong conviction about the need for a move toward negotiations now is based upon these considerations. No foreseeable time will be better for negotiations than the present, and never has a serious move toward a political settlement been more necessary."[58]

And so, for the second time in less than two years, Goldberg sent Johnson a written message filled with advice its author knew was far more needed than wanted. Given Johnson's antagonistic response to the previous message, Goldberg's decision to try again showed a strength of character unique among Johnson's top foreign policy advisers. Still unclear as he sent the memo off for transmission to Rusk in Washington was whether Johnson this time would really listen.[59]

After leaving the UN that same day, Goldberg caught the 7:00 P.M. air shuttle to Washington, where he planned to press his case further with Rusk and the president. En route he encountered historian Arthur Schlesinger Jr. on his way to a meeting at Robert Kennedy's home in northern Virginia, where a final decision was to be made about whether the New York senator should enter the presidential race. The two Arthurs soon fell into a conversation about the advisability of Kennedy's running as an antiwar alternative to McCarthy. Goldberg had never enjoyed the same rapport with RFK as he had with his older brother, but he saw the logic of what Schlesinger, an early critic of the war and Kennedy intimate, was saying. McCarthy lacked the resources needed to defeat either Johnson for the nomination or Nixon, who had emerged in New Hampshire as the GOP's leading candidate, in the general election. Despite lingering doubts about the younger Kennedy from their earlier dealings, Goldberg told Schlesinger, "Bobby should 'tell the truth' — say he was the best candidate and go ahead."[60]

Kennedy declared the next day, thereby stepping up the pressure on Johnson to develop a plan for peace negotiations. Although Goldberg viewed Kennedy's candidacy as potentially constructive for that reason, even if for no other, he nevertheless stayed away from it. Understanding that Johnson would view Goldberg's support for an opponent of the administration he was serving as an act of supreme disloyalty, Goldberg took no active role in the presidential primary contests.[61] In any case, he had other, potentially far more useful, work to do.

At first, however, the response to his memo proved discouraging. It infuriated Johnson, who at that point still strongly favored staying the course. Goldberg later recalled, without exaggeration, that "that memo created an explosion. He [LBJ] didn't call me for three days."[62] What Goldberg did not know when he sent it was that Rusk had simultaneously been pushing a more limited version of the same idea, albeit for a very different reason. Rusk favored a partial bombing halt apparently as a public relations maneuver, whose failure the administration could use to legitimate further escalation. To promote that scheme, which was similar to the December 1965 bombing pause and "peace mission," Rusk gathered support among Johnson's advisers for a de facto bombing halt north of the twentieth parallel, rather than Goldberg's more comprehensive proposal.[63]

Rusk's idea and its underlying rationale persuaded Johnson to go through the motions of "debating" the two alternatives at a meeting held on March 20. On the day before, Johnson called Goldberg and invited him to attend, their first communication since the March 15 memo arrived at the White House. Goldberg dutifully appeared the next day and pressed his case, first to Johnson privately and then at a meeting that Rusk, Rostow, and others also attended. Goldberg later recalled that Johnson behaved quite civilly toward him during those sessions but did not take his advice. At one point, an exasperated Johnson told Goldberg, "Every time I want to do anything, you give me 14 reasons against it," to which Goldberg calmly replied, "When you are considering an ill-advised course, it's my duty to tell you, whether you like to hear it or not."[64]

Goldberg stood his ground, but to no avail. In a second meeting held over lunch two days later, to which he was not invited, the others discussed the two proposals more extensively and then decided in favor of Rusk's plan. In so doing, Johnson's advisers made clear to him that they doubted it would actually lead to peace negotiations. So, as late as midday on Friday, March 22, Johnson, Rusk, and Rostow—the administration's three top foreign policy decision makers—while planning a gesture of peace, still favored and expected a further widening of American involvement in the war.[65]

Before taking such an important step, Johnson agreed, at the suggestion of his new defense secretary, Clark Clifford, to consult with the so-called Wise Men, the group of senior foreign policy experts that LBJ sometimes called on for advice and support. He invited Goldberg to participate, after having excluded him from the group for years, a gesture that annoyed Goldberg even as it pleased him. Goldberg later said that he had been unaware of the Wise Men's role and was unhappy to learn that he had been kept out for so long of such an important advisory group. He would make the most of his unexpected opportunity.[66]

On the evening of March 25, 1968, Goldberg made his way to the State Department for dinner with the other members of what was formally known as the Special Advisory Group. They included former secretary of state Dean Acheson; former undersecretary of state George Ball, by then with a major financial house in New York; former Joint Chiefs of Staff (JCS) chairman General Omar Bradley; former national security adviser McGeorge Bundy; former Korean War peace negotiator Arthur Dean; former secretary of the treasury Douglas Dillon; Associate Justice Abe Fortas, Goldberg's successor on the Supreme Court and a close personal adviser to Johnson even while on the bench; former senator, UN ambassador, and ambassador to Saigon Henry Cabot Lodge Jr.; former assistant secretary of war and high commissioner to West Germany John McCloy; former State Department career diplomat Robert Murphy; former Korean war commander and NATO chief General Matthew Ridgway; former JCS chairman and ambassador to South Vietnam General Maxwell Taylor; and former deputy secretary of defense Cyrus Vance.[67]

As recently as November of the previous year, these thirteen men had voiced strong support for the escalation policy, and Johnson's aides expected a repeat of that earlier performance. Over dinner, such administration spokesmen as Rusk, Rostow, Clifford, Averell Harriman, and William Bundy gave their view of the military situation in Vietnam and the state of the South Vietnamese government. After the meal ended, the Johnson aides left, their informal "orientation" thereafter followed by three briefings given by

Bundy's deputy, Philip C. Habib; Major General William E. Dupuy, special assistant to the JCS; and George Carver, a CIA analyst. The purpose on the part of Johnson and his advisers of both the informal conversations over dinner and the more formal briefings that followed it was to "educate" the group as to the correctness of continued escalation.[68]

This plan, however, soon went awry, for which Goldberg deserved some of the credit. The first deviation from Johnson's script came as Habib delivered an unusually frank description of the situation in South Vietnam post-Tet. Already disturbed by this new and more pessimistic assessment, the other members of the group proved receptive to Goldberg's assault on General Dupuy's optimistic estimate of the current military situation. As Goldberg listened skeptically, Dupuy used casualty statistics to "prove" that Tet had in fact constituted a major North Vietnamese–Viet Cong defeat, a conclusion that was at most only half right.

Reminiscent of what Goldberg saw as all too many earlier briefings, with their false precision and breezy optimism, he decided to challenge Dupuy's presentation. As he later recalled,

> It just did not hold up in my mind. The briefing indicated that the enemy had lost 80,000 men killed in the Tet offensive. I asked the general what the normal ratio of killed to wounded would be. He said, as I recall, ten to one. And I said that was a big figure and that, assuming that the [North] Vietnamese [and Viet Cong] were not as solicitous about their wounded as we were, and would not treat their slightly wounded or would put them back into combat when we would not, could we consider three to one to be a conservative figure for those rendered ineffective by wounds? And he said yes. And then I asked the question, "How many effectives do you think they [had when Tet started] . . . in the field?" And he said something like 230,000. And I said, "Well, General, I am not a great mathematician but with 80,000 killed and with a wounded ratio of three to one, or 240,000 wounded, for a total of 320,000 [North Vietnamese and Viet Cong casualties], who the hell are we fighting?"[69]

The question left Dupuy speechless. During the long silence that followed, the response from the other Wise Men was palpable.[70]

When the discussion finally resumed, the group's changing outlook became manifest. As the evening wore on, skepticism replaced confidence in Johnson's Vietnam policies. Dean Acheson also appears to have played a key role in that transformation. A hawk's hawk and one of the principal architects of the containment policy, Acheson by mid-March had become convinced that escalation was not working. Given his immense prestige in the group, Acheson's defection proved as influential as it had been surprising. By the time the meeting broke up, then, the carefully planned Johnson–Rusk–Rostow script for it lay in tatters.[71]

Johnson got the news over lunch the next day. There the assembled Wise Men gave the president some unwelcome but long-overdue advice. McGeorge Bundy acted as spokesman, followed in turn by Acheson, Dean, Dillon, and Ball. Then, in a development that delighted Goldberg and jolted

Johnson, General Ridgway read aloud a statement of his views that he had written the night before, backing Goldberg's position to the hilt. After that bombshell, Lodge, Bradley, and Vance echoed the view that U.S. military objectives in South Vietnam must be reduced. Even though three members of the group—Fortas, Murphy, and Taylor—disagreed and endorsed the existing policy, the balance of power in the Wise Men had clearly passed to the other point of view. Johnson's policy of increasing escalation had at last been repudiated by a large majority of his own most trusted outside advisers.[72]

Goldberg let the other supporters of de-escalation do most of the talking, given that their views were the ones that had changed, not his. By the end of the meeting, he felt thoroughly vindicated, although still uncertain how exactly Johnson would respond to the Wise Men's new outlook. Much later he recalled that Johnson seemed "very disturbed" by what he was hearing, as an awareness began to dawn on him for the first time that "he had to cut back the bombing and lay the groundwork for starting a negotiation."[73]

Despite some final blustering, Johnson concluded shortly after the meeting that he had no other choice than to do what Goldberg had been pushing for over the past few years. LBJ did not, however, accept his call for a total bombing halt, preferring instead the more limited Rusk proposal. What had changed, however, was Johnson's rationale for such a move. Whereas he had earlier envisioned it as a prelude to further escalation, after the Wise Men's session of March 25–26 he had come to see the limited bombing halt as the necessary first step toward serious peace negotiations, as Goldberg, rather than Rusk, had urged. And in a move that stunned both of them and much of the rest of the country, Johnson followed his televised announcement on March 31, 1968, of what had become a genuine peace initiative, by taking himself out of the race for reelection.[74]

Goldberg had won his battle against the escalation policy, but it proved a very costly victory. Johnson, still angry with Goldberg for standing up to him and ambivalent about the de-escalation course that his UN ambassador had advocated so forcefully, used the televised address to name Averell Harriman as the administration's chief negotiator should peace talks begin in earnest. With that move, what remained of Goldberg's official rationale for staying at the UN disappeared. Once the debate in the administration had finally been resolved in favor of de-escalation, the time for peace negotiations had arrived. Based on Johnson's earlier promise when naming him to the UN post, Goldberg had expected to act as the principal bargainer for the United States in any such talks. Thus when Johnson announced on March 31 that Harriman instead had received that assignment, Goldberg felt deeply disappointed. Having lost the debate with Goldberg over escalation, Johnson had chosen to deny him the fruits of that hard-won victory.[75]

With that final indignity, Goldberg decided that the time to leave had at last arrived. Understanding by then that his relations with Johnson had become too strained to expect reappointment to the Court, Goldberg no longer had any real reason to stay. On April 23, 1968, he submitted his letter of resignation. In listing the reasons for his decision, Goldberg noted pointedly that "neither the UN [n]or the Secretary General will be a focal point for Vietnam peace talks" and that "I don't want the impression to be created that I am hanging around for a Supreme Court appointment. This is not good for the country, Mr. President, nor is it personally dignified for me."[76]

Two days later, Johnson announced that he had accepted Goldberg's resignation. In deference to Johnson's request that he stay until work on the Nuclear Non-Proliferation Treaty had been concluded, Goldberg agreed to remain at the United Nations through June, when the ongoing session of the General Assembly would conclude.[77]

At the April 25 press conference at which his resignation was announced, Goldberg chose not to air publicly the dispute over Vietnam that had precipitated it. Instead, he said only that he was leaving for personal reasons. Through the end of Johnson's administration, Goldberg remained a private rather than a public critic of its escalation policy. Leading him to take that course was his belief that more explicit opposition might be counterproductive and also extinguish whatever still remained of his hopes for reappointment to the Court. Unappeased by Goldberg's discreet remarks about Vietnam policy at the press conference, Johnson communicated his displeasure with him in a way immediately noticed by the journalists in attendance. This sort of session typically featured an avuncular Johnson heaping extravagant praise on the departing subordinate, but not this time. Instead, Johnson coolly acknowledged the resignation, without saying so much as one good word about Goldberg's service at the UN. Thus LBJ signaled how chilly relations between the two men had become.[78]

The full measure of what Goldberg's defiance had cost him became clear only during his final month as UN ambassador. Chief Justice Earl Warren, by then seventy-seven years old, had watched with mounting concern as the 1968 presidential race unfolded. Having long despised Richard Nixon and strongly opposed the forces behind him, Warren was anxious to prevent the possibility that Nixon would name the next chief justice. For that reason, Warren had begun toying early that year with the idea of resigning at the end of the Court's current term, so as to make sure that Johnson would have the chance to name a like-minded successor.[79]

By mid-March, Johnson's growing weakness in the polls had increased Warren's concern about who would eventually replace him so much that he had decided to raise the subject with Goldberg, whom he viewed as the logical choice. At lunch on March 21, Warren confessed his concerns about the Court's future should Nixon name his successor and told Goldberg that if he were in line for his place, Warren would willingly resign that spring. Goldberg, moved almost to tears by Warren's gesture, objected at first, telling his longtime friend and former colleague that he should not even think about quitting.

When Warren persisted, Goldberg told him that his recent memo to Johnson about Vietnam had eliminated whatever possibility there might once have been for reappointment to the Court. When Warren, in response, berated himself for failing to raise the matter sooner, Goldberg told him that given his earlier disagreements with Johnson over Vietnam policy, more notice would very likely have made no difference and that, in any event, sending the memo had been the right thing to do.[80]

His first plan stymied, Warren had backed off when Robert Kennedy entered the presidential contest and gained ground steadily toward the Democratic nomination. Convinced by June 1 that Kennedy would duplicate his older brother's earlier success against Nixon and that a second President Kennedy would appoint justices of Warren's own persuasion, his concern about the Court's future temporarily receded. But after Kennedy's assassination on June 4, these worries returned with a vengeance. Apparently reasoning that anyone Johnson might name would be far preferable to a Nixon nominee, Warren went to see Johnson nine days later and announced his intention to resign once a successor had been named and confirmed by the Senate. Telling Johnson that age and a desire to see a like-minded successor named had led him to take this step, Warren advised the president to pick Goldberg for the job and shortly afterward told him what he had done. Touched, Goldberg had thanked Warren and waited to see how Johnson would choose to respond.[81]

LBJ soon did so, and with characteristic vindictiveness. On June 26, just two days after George Ball was sworn in as Goldberg's successor at the UN, Johnson nominated his old friend and die-hard hawk Abe Fortas to succeed Warren. In a second move even more galling to Goldberg, the president named another longtime crony, former Texas congressman Homer Thornberry, to fill the seat Fortas would be vacating. Thus did Johnson bring to a close Goldberg's deeply frustrating and unhappy experience with him.[82]

And yet, for all of that, Goldberg's UN interlude remains in some ways his finest hour in government. From the beginning, he had rightly perceived the folly of escalation. And unlike Johnson's other top aides, so many of whom prided themselves on their toughness even as they quailed in the face of his displeasure, Goldberg had not flinched from telling him the unwelcome truth about Vietnam. Such behavior had cost Goldberg the return to the bench he had wanted so dearly but had left intact his reputation for good judgment and integrity. None of Johnson's other senior foreign policy advisers could say the same.[83]

IV

The time had come to consider new ventures. During the first month of the turbulent summer of 1968, Goldberg holed up at his farm in Marshall, Virginia, a retreat he had purchased while an associate justice. He used the time for rest and reflection, pondering in particular what his next career move should be. As an interim step, Goldberg accepted a senior partnership with the prominent New York law firm Paul, Weiss, Rifkind, Wharton and Garrison. Even in taking that highly paid position, however, he continued to think about other possibilities for the longer term. His first preference remained a return to the Court, a hope that had not entirely died, even then. And in the latter half of that year, two such chances quickly came and went.[84]

The first opportunity arose when Abe Fortas's nomination for chief justice collapsed in early October. In trouble from the very beginning, Johnson's bid to install Fortas as Warren's successor had run into heavy Senate opposition as early as July. Conservatives there in both parties had fiercely assailed the nominee for having supported the innovations in judicial doctrine that the Court had been making since the late 1950s. Fortas, strongly identified with those changes and vulnerable on other grounds as well, never really had a chance. Johnson, however, stubbornly refused to acknowledge this until a procedural vote in the Senate on October 1 indicated that Fortas lacked the votes needed for confirmation. Later that same day, Fortas asked Johnson to withdraw his nomination, a request the president reluctantly granted three days later.[85]

With Fortas finally out of the running for the chief justiceship, Goldberg's prospects for that post momentarily revived. Johnson, anxious to see the position go to a liberal, toyed with the idea of naming the man Warren had earlier suggested. Deciding at least to discuss the matter with Goldberg, LBJ summoned him to the Oval Office for an early afternoon meeting on October 10. There Johnson asked him whether he would be willing to accept appointment during the current congressional recess. Under a procedure seldom used, Goldberg would have begun serving as Warren's successor at once, before being confirmed and would go through that process once Congress returned. Goldberg—anxious to get the job and confident, based on his three previous rounds of Senate confirmation hearings that he could pass muster yet again—told Johnson that "I will take my chances. I've always been confirmed unanimously."[86]

The hour-long conversation eventually closed with Johnson's saying that he wanted to give the matter a bit more thought. The next morning, he called Goldberg and told him that his aides had discovered an earlier statement that he (Johnson) had made against recess appointments, which he felt obliged to honor. For Goldberg, who at the least could have expected a last hurrah as chief justice during the 1968/69 term even if the Senate had ultimately rejected his appointment, Johnson's decision must have come as a bitter disappointment.[87]

It was followed by another less than one month later, when what seemed to be the last real chance for reappointment also came to naught. This opportunity revolved around the presidential candidacy of Vice-President Hubert Humphrey, whom Goldberg ultimately supported. As Humphrey's campaign, which had been grievously wounded at the outset by his equivocation on the peace issue, gained ground steadily that fall, Goldberg's hopes for a return to the Court rose with it. Knowing full well that Humphrey had never entirely forgiven him for having supported Kennedy in 1960, Goldberg understood that even a Humphrey victory would not ensure reappointment to the Court. Still, the opportunity seemed momentarily alive, until buried by the Nixon victory on November 5 that pollsters had long predicted.[88]

In retrospect, these two seemingly missed opportunities, like the earlier one stemming from Johnson's decision to pass over Goldberg in favor of Fortas, surely had been more illusory than real. Appointments to the Court during presidential election years were unusual precisely because experience had shown them to be risky propositions, especially when motivated, as in 1968, by a desire to deny the opposition party the sort of choice that its candidate favored. In that case, Senate Republicans of all ideological stripes would surely have opposed a Goldberg nomination, as they ultimately did Fortas's.[89]

Even without that obstacle, Goldberg would have encountered the kind of conservative resistance in both parties that, more than anything else, had led to Fortas's defeat. Like him, Goldberg had strongly supported and been identified with the Warren majority's innovations in criminal law and procedure in particular that had aroused the ire of conservative Republicans and Democrats. Although Goldberg had been unanimously confirmed by the Senate for his previous presidential appointments, he had last run that gauntlet in the summer of 1965, just as the postwar order was coming apart. Had the former justice and Warren enthusiast faced a fourth confirmation process in 1968 or 1969, he doubtless would have felt those changes, just as Fortas did.[90]

Perhaps Goldberg could have prevailed had Johnson moved swiftly and decisively to nominate him when Warren had first told LBJ of his intention to retire. Goldberg did lack the other albatrosses that ultimately weighed down Fortas's nomination. Fortas also suffered from his decision to continue advising the president and attending White House meetings even while serving as associate justice. Many senators found that breach of tradition troubling, as they also did Fortas's efforts to supplement his income while on the bench through means of suspect propriety. The nominee's hawkish views on Vietnam had, as well, diminished enthusiasm for his appointment among such natural allies as Senate liberals. None of those liabilities would have dogged a Goldberg nomination.[91]

One cannot know for sure whether those differences would have been sufficient to have produced a different outcome. That Senate conservatives would have fought Goldberg's nomination just as hard as they did Fortas's remains the only real certainty. In the final analysis, both Fortas and Goldberg were problematic candidates to succeed Warren precisely because they shared his views at a time when opposition to them, both inside and outside Congress, was growing rapidly. The Warren "revolution" in legal doctrine, like many of Johnson's so-called Great Society legislative initiatives and, in a different way, the Vietnam War all had deeply divided supporters of the postwar New Deal. The result was to hand its right-wing opponents an opening they soon exploited. This, above all else, explains why Goldberg's hopes for a return to the Court after leaving the UN ultimately met with frustration.[92]

And so, as 1969 opened, Goldberg found himself still searching for another long-term billet. Eager to find useful and interesting work to do, he began seriously considering a run for public office. Although he had never before given the idea much thought and, indeed, had repeatedly dismissed it when others had suggested such a thing to him, Goldberg began to see its merits once a return to the Court finally seemed beyond his reach.[93]

The two leading possibilities were a run for U.S. senator or governor in New York during the upcoming election year. The first would have involved a race against neoliberal Republican Charles E. Goodell, who had been appointed to fill the remainder of Robert Kennedy's Senate term following his assassination. This option had real appeal for Goldberg, for it would have meant a return to Washington and the governmental milieu he knew best. Goodell, however, proved to be an outspoken neoliberal and a leading critic of the Vietnam War, which undercut the rationale for a Goldberg campaign against him. As the events of 1969 unfolded, Goldberg gradually came to the conclusion that by then, too little separated his own views from Goodell's to justify running against him and would have made winning highly unlikely in any event.[94]

Having ruled out that option, Goldberg also gave serious thought to running against New York's governor, Nelson Rockefeller, who planned to seek an unprecedented fourth term in 1970. At first glance, this race seemed to afford Goldberg more of an opening. Rockefeller's long tenure and its consequences, especially higher taxes, had, by the latter half of the 1960s, created considerable public dissatisfaction, particularly among upper working- and lower-middle-class whites. Many of them had vented their growing anger against Rockefeller's policies during his previous reelection race in 1966. Only strong support from neoliberal Jews and blacks had saved him then, and Goldberg rightly believed that he could win much more backing from those groups than Rockefeller's previous opponent had. The results of an extensive poll taken in September 1969 seemed to bear out that optimistic assessment. Commissioned by influential New York Democrats anxious to see Goldberg make the race, the poll results indicated that if the election had been held that same month, Goldberg would have trounced Rockefeller by twenty-five points.[95]

But other, more reliable, factors pointed toward a very different outcome. First was the governor's reputation as the living embodiment of liberal Republicanism. Animated by the same basic worldview as Johnson's Great Society program, Rockefeller's policies on the state level had proved, if anything, even bolder than Johnson's had in Washington. Rockefeller's record as governor had thus given him enormous prestige among liberals in both parties, which his unsuccessful presidential race against new-right zealot Barry Goldwater in 1964 had only enhanced. That Rockefeller had emerged from that fight as a defeated martyr only heightened liberals' sympathy for him. Like Goodell, then, Rockefeller seemed a formidable opponent precisely because he appealed to so many of the same constituencies whose support Goldberg would need to win.[96]

Two other obstacles compounded that more basic one. First, by 1969 Rockefeller had become a deeply entrenched incumbent, with all the usual resources plus his own family's truly extraordinary wealth. The more than $6 million he and his backers had poured into his previous campaign had set the record for spending in a state race. Goldberg could expect even more of the same in 1970. Second, Rockefeller had proved over the years to be something of an opportunist, a poll reader whose surprisingly narrow victory in 1966 inclined him away from increasingly controversial neoliberal stands. His gradual retreat toward a more conservative position promised to make him less vulnerable in 1970 than he had proved to be four years earlier.[97]

In the face of these less than promising portents, Goldberg wavered. After debating the issue with himself and others for almost a year, he issued a statement on December 9, 1969, announcing that he would not run against either Goodell or Rockefeller in 1970. That same winter, however, friends kept urging him to run anyway, and the lack of appealing alternatives gradually moved him in that direction. The combination finally bore fruit for his backers as the winter came to a close.

On March 19, 1970, Goldberg announced that he would challenge Nelson Rockefeller in the upcoming gubernatorial contest. Goldberg knew even in announcing that his would be a long-shot campaign, but to forgo it would have meant conceding that his long and impressive career in public life had at last come to an end. Determined to avoid that result if at all possible, he set out on a final quest to regain the kind of position and sense of purpose that had by then slipped away from him.[98]

Goldberg's gubernatorial campaign quickly got off to a rocky start, from which he and his supporters never fully recovered. Although the strong favorite of the party leadership, Goldberg immediately found himself under fire from other Democratic aspirants, such as Nassau County executive Eugene H. Nickerson, former undersecretary of commerce Howard J. Samuels, and Queens district attorney Thomas J. Mackell. That trio attacked him as the candidate of "the bosses" and mounted a spirited effort to deny him the party's endorsement at the upcoming Democratic state convention, held in Grossinger, New York, on April 2.

Although Goldberg garnered enough support to win the party's endorsement, the fierce infighting there greatly diluted its value. Understanding that he needed to project an image of greater legitimacy than the convention could provide, Goldberg told the assembled delegates that he would waive the endorsement and seek to place his name on the ballot via the petition route that the other contenders would have to use. But this attempt to steer a middle ground satisfied no one and momentarily threw the convention into chaos. In the end, state party chairman John J. Burns ruled that Goldberg's action precluded a party endorsement for any other gubernatorial aspirant, in effect allowing the leadership's candidate to have it both ways. The net result was to infuriate some of his rivals for the nomination and spark a divisive primary contest.[99]

The eventual primary result on June 23 augured poorly for the general election. Goldberg managed to persuade all but one of the other major contenders to withdraw, but even this fell short of preventing a bruising primary battle. In the end, Goldberg eked out a narrow victory over Howard Samuels, his lone remaining opponent, but at the price of having divided the party's most stalwart supporters. Goldberg won with strong support from neoliberal Jews and blacks, whereas Samuels took most of the votes from working- and lower-middle-class whites. Samuels's supporters apparently opted for him out of a concern that Goldberg would support the same neoliberal policies that Rockefeller had inaugurated and, with them, the steadily rising taxes that had hit such voters the hardest. They had suffered, too, from ever-increasing crime, about which Goldberg, like Rockefeller, seemed likely to do little. This factor also seems to have inclined such voters to support Samuels's surprisingly strong campaign. Thus New York Democrats found themselves deeply at odds with one another on primary night in 1970, to Goldberg's great dismay.[100]

The primary contest also exposed Goldberg's weaknesses as a campaigner. For most of his adult life an organization man, he lacked the kinds of public speaking skills most useful to politicians. Goldberg spoke in a nasal monotone, which audiences found uninspiring. His by-then almost legendary long-windedness also bothered them, as did his "judicial" demeanor. Mindful of his former office and determined above all else to preserve his dignity in seeking a new one, Goldberg came across to many as pompous, vain, and dull. Although his genuine warmth and decency sometimes managed to overcome this impression, it nonetheless persisted. These factors, though in themselves not decisive, contributed to his weak showing among working- and lower-middle-class voters.[101]

The lessons of the Democratic gubernatorial primary were not lost on Goldberg's GOP rival. Having carefully assessed the electoral situation, Rockefeller and his aides rightly concluded that he would need strong support from working- and lower-middle-class whites in order to win. Conceding, in effect, the bulk of neoliberal Jewish and black votes to Goldberg, the formidable Rockefeller organization chose to aim its message at so-called white ethnics. Instead of the neoliberal pledges of campaigns past, Rockefeller emphasized his determination to fight drug abuse and crime more generally, to preserve "traditional values of home and family," and to keep taxes from rising any further. In another break with precedent, the one-time darling of neoliberal Republicans spent most of his time campaigning in predominantly working- and lower-middle-class neighborhoods populated by people of Irish, Italian, and Polish ancestry. To amplify the message Rockefeller carried to such places, the born-again candidate and his advisers spent between $6 million and $10 million on television and radio advertisements, billboards, buttons, and all the rest, far more than the roughly $1 million to $2 million that Goldberg managed to raise. Underscoring Rockefeller's enormous electoral advantages and, unwittingly perhaps, his determination to do whatever was necessary to win, his seemingly ubiquitous broadsides proclaimed that "Rocky has never lost an election."[102]

By promising leaders of the building trades unions that Rockefeller would continue his ambitious construction program if reelected, rather than spend more on poverty programs as Goldberg was advocating, the governor and his aides even managed to wrest the New York State AFL–CIO endorsement for their candidate. Goldberg had hoped New York's trade union leaders would decide to back one of their own, rather than a Republican named Rockefeller, but it was not to be.

With the traditional AFL wing and its worldview by then in the ascendant, the majority of trade union leaders found Rockefeller's plans for state government spending more appealing than Goldberg's. The Republicans at least promised jobs for the membership, increasingly troubled by the consequences of the postwar New Deal's breakdown. Goldberg's pledge to spend more on programs intended to alleviate poverty struck such leaders as a less effective way of achieving that objective and one that offered little to labor's rank and file. And so, in a thoroughly cynical power play, the leaders of the building trades unions packed the state AFL–CIO convention held that September and rammed through an endorsement of the GOP incumbent, to the wonderment of many outside observers.[103]

None of it came as any great surprise to Goldberg, who had always viewed Rockefeller as something of an opportunist. Goldberg's first encounter with the governor shortly after his election in 1958 had left just such an impression. Rockefeller had asked him for help then in crafting labor reform legislation, a campaign promise. Goldberg, receptive to that request, had asked him to explain what he would like to accomplish with such a bill. Expecting at least a general statement of objectives, Goldberg had been startled and put off by Rockefeller's cavalier response: "Oh, I don't care what you put in it, as long as I can call it labor reform."[104]

The same sort of calculation informed Rockefeller's 1970 reelection effort, which by election day had overwhelmed Goldberg's more principled but much less formidable campaign. Rockefeller won on November 3, 1970, by a margin of almost 700,000 votes out of just over 3.5 million cast, the largest of his four races for governor. For Goldberg, the result was an embarrassment but not a humiliation. He had preserved his dignity, both in his own mind and in those of the voters. Election-day surveys indicated that the electorate actually had more respect for him at the end of the campaign than they did for Rockefeller. Goldberg, unlike his victorious rival, had not stooped to win.[105]

In all, the 1970 New York governor's race spoke volumes about the changing nature of American politics. Like the congressional elections of 1966, in which the GOP had made major gains, and the presidential election of 1968, which had put Richard Nixon in the White House, the Goldberg–Rockefeller contest and its outcome signaled the rightward drift of the American economic and political system. The travails that had accompanied Goldberg's nomination, and even more the unequal general election contest that followed, showed how the decline of political parties and their "bosses" had contributed to this conservative resurgence. Defended by some as making the political process more participatory, those so-called reforms nonetheless contributed to its corruption, as money became ever more decisive in determining winners and losers.[106]

In that respect, the Goldberg–Rockefeller contest constitutes a case study in what had gone wrong for New Deal liberals and the Democratic Party from the early 1960s onward. The themes that Rockefeller had used in winning a fourth term and the techniques for communicating them would become all too familiar over the next twenty years, as would their unfortunate results. And at the center of this story stood the continuing decline of organized labor and the ever more cautious positions its leaders consequently felt compelled to take.

Labor increasingly appeared, to neoliberals and new leftists in particular, as a "conservative" force, more opposed to social reform than behind it. Oddly reminiscent of the charge that some laborites had earlier leveled at the kinds of social movements that grew stronger during the 1960s and 1970s, this view was at most only half right. If labor proved increasingly cautious from the early 1960s onward, it was because its adherents found themselves and their values ever more on the defensive. The increasingly conservative results that accompanied unions' steady decline would in time provide the most persuasive rebuttal to this quite misleading characterization.[107]

These changes more than Goldberg's limitations as a campaigner explained why he was unable to stage a comeback during 1970. When his gubernatorial campaign ended on November 3, so too did his prominent role in public life. This central chapter of Goldberg's story was finally over. Like New Deal liberalism itself, of which he had been such an influential exponent, Goldberg's hour had passed.

12

Return to Private Life

SOON AFTER THE New York governor's race ended, Goldberg moved back to Washington, where he returned to the practice of law. He supplemented his work by serving from time to time on government commissions, mediating international disputes, writing newspaper columns, teaching at law schools around the country, and participating in many Jewish causes.

Unlike some of his former colleagues in the labor movement, during the 1960s Goldberg had come to understand the increasing unworkability of New Deal liberal approaches to many of the nation's most acute social problems. For that reason, he lent his name and energies over the next two decades to many of the reform movements that had blossomed during the 1960s, such as the quests to outlaw the death penalty, promote arms control and disarmament, and secure equality before the law for women. Among Goldberg's most important accomplishments in this final phase of his career was chairing a committee that studied the wrongs done to Japanese Americans during World War II. Under his leadership, the committee recommended to Congress that through their government, the American people formally acknowledge their error and establish a system of reparations for those incarcerated during World War II on the ground of national security. Congress eventually adopted those recommendations, to Goldberg's great satisfaction.[1]

During the latter half of the 1970s Goldberg also enjoyed a final tour of duty as a diplomat, as President Jimmy Carter's ambassador to the Belgrade Conference on Human Rights in 1977/78, where he performed very effectively. At the conclusion of his service there, Carter awarded him the Medal of Freedom, the highest honor the U.S. government can bestow on a civilian. In presenting the award, President Carter noted that it was in recognition of Goldberg's many contributions to his country, both in and out of government.[2]

Yet for all of his activity, Goldberg never really regained the influence or prominence he had enjoyed from the late 1940s through the end of his ill-fated race for governor. Like many other liberals closely identified with the postwar New Deal, he became a very dated figure during the 1970s and 1980s, who lived on in Washington as an aging reminder of an earlier and quite different era in American politics. By June 24, 1988, the twentieth anniversary of his departure from the Johnson administration, he had returned to relative obscurity outside Washington's political community.

Sustaining him during those years were the work he continued to do and the support of his many friends and loving family, especially his wife Dorothy. He and she had been always been devoted to each other, and so when she died of cancer on February 13, 1988, Goldberg never fully recovered from his loss. He had suffered a heart attack during her illness and then had a second, fatal, one on January 19, 1990. Three days later, Goldberg was laid to rest beside her in Arlington National Cemetery, only a short distance from the grave of his old friend and colleague, Earl Warren. In recognition of Goldberg's service to the republic in war and peace, his funeral ceremony on that unseasonably warm and sunny winter's day included full military honors. Like so much of his long and varied career, he would have wanted it no other way.[3]

That career and the worldview that informed it left behind a somewhat mixed historical legacy. As the nation's economic and political system moved further away from the social democratic vision Goldberg and New Deal liberals like him had embraced, some tended to see their achievements as fatally flawed and forever repudiated. And there were, without question, some serious drawbacks to that vision. Its excessively fearful view of Soviet military intentions and capabilities was a central weakness. Even though this militant hostility to socialism had helped hold together the postwar social contract, such hawkishness had also contributed to an arms race that imperiled the gains of that social bargain and all of humanity as well. New Deal liberals' endorsement of the containment policy and the assumptions that underlaid it contributed, too, to the emergence of a national security apparatus at home and an antiradical hysteria that endangered the very kind of freedom Goldberg and other New Deal liberals claimed to hold most dear. And by making the maintenance of the social democratic order dependent on the Soviet "threat," New Deal liberals made this order vulnerable once the cold war receded.

Goldberg's political philosophy had other shortcomings as well. New Deal liberalism's emphasis on economic security—in itself highly important to the working and lower middle classes—led the exponents of that view to underestimate the importance of trying to redress the wrongs stemming from other systems of oppression, especially those based on race and gender. Although they were related to the problems of class with which New Deal liberalism was principally concerned, they were not one and the same. And indeed, the nation's experience with the postwar New Deal suggests that no such social bargain could be made to work in the long run unless all members of the working and lower middle classes participated more or less equally in its benefits.

This same political philosophy could also be faulted for its insensitivity to concerns about popular participation in decision making, to which the postwar system had proved largely unresponsive. New Deal liberalism's emphasis on achieving social improvement through economic growth proved problematic, too, for it threatened, as did the preoccupation with containing "Soviet" socialism, to extinguish with its environmental side effects the very benefits it was intended to produce. Above and beyond those specific issues, Goldberg, like so many other New Deal liberals, had erred in assuming so confidently during the golden hour of the Middle Way that it would endure and expand indefinitely during his own lifetime. As we have seen, it was not to be so.

If this is, indeed, a story that seemingly ends in failure, it was by no means a complete one. The postwar social contract with which Goldberg was so closely identified enabled the American working and lower middle classes to do better in many important ways than they had before or have since. And when this social bargain broke down, workers and their allies were able to prevent as complete a rollback of those gains as the postwar New Deal's most conservative critics would have liked.

One should keep in mind, too, that the failure to preserve that social bargain by no means demonstrates that no similar one could ever be resurrected. The decline of the postwar New Deal over the past three decades has recreated many of the same problems that gave rise to it in the first place, a result its architects, Goldberg included, fully expected. He believed that some form of corporatism was the most that the American working and lower middle classes could realistically expect and that an economy based on mass production and mass consumption would not work without it. Whatever the other weaknesses in his worldview, Goldberg's support for these ideas had been right in his own time. It still is.

Notes

Abbreviations Used

AFL–CIO MOHC–AFL   CIO Merger Oral History Collection

AJG   Conversations between Goldberg and the author, 1981–1989

CHS   Chicago Historical Society

CIO–EBP   CIO Executive Board Proceedings

DDEL   Dwight D. Eisenhower Presidental Library

DKGD   Dorothy K. Goldberg Diary

FSG   Conversations between Frances Simonson Guilbert and the author, 1988–1994

GMMA   George Meany Memorial Archives

HCLA–PSU   Historical Collections and Labor Archives, Pennsylvania State University

HFG   Conversation between Henry F. Graff and the author, 17 June 1992

HSTL   Harry S. Truman Presidential Library

JFKL   John F. Kennedy Presidential Library

LBJL   Lyndon B. Johnson Presidential Library

LC   Library of Congress

MC–SL, YU   Manuscripts Collection-Sterling Library, Yale University

MFP   Memorandum for the President

ML–CUA   Mullen Library, Catholic University of America

MTP   Memorandum to the President

OHC   Oral History Collection

PACLMP–CM   President's Advisory Committee on Labor-Management Policy-Confidential Minutes

RBML–CU   Rare Book and Manuscript Library, Columbia University

SLRF   Secretary of Labor's Reading Files

TP–PCEEO   Transcript of Proceedings-Presidnet's Committee on Equal Employment Opportunity

USA–EBP   USA Executive Board Proceedings

WPRL   Walter P. Reuther Library

Chapter 1. Beginnings

1. See "Famed Shopping Street Is Fighting for Survival," *New York Times*, January 3, 1990; Leo Lerner's column, *Chicago Booster*, September 23, 1962.

2. AJG.

3. Robert Shaplen, "Peacemaker," *New Yorker*, pt. 1, April 7, 1962, 58–60; AJG.

4. "Famed Shopping Street"; Lerner's column.

5. *In Memoriam: Honorable Arthur J. Goldberg: Proceedings of the Bar and Officers of the Supreme Court of the United States* (Washington, D.C.: U.S. Supreme Court, 1990), 22; Shaplen, "Peacemaker," 58; AJG.

6. *In Memoriam*, 22.

7. Ibid.; Shaplen, "Peacemaker," 58–60.

8. Shaplen, "Peacemaker," 58–60. Goldberg's wife noted his feelings about his childhood encounters with bullies and anti-Semites in DKGD. See the entry for June 1967 in which she wrote that her husband had been "schooled from childhood in rock-throwing self-defense against Jew-hating Poles and Irish who waylaid him en route to school." Arthur J. and Dorothy K. Goldberg papers, LC; AJG.

9. AJG; *In Memoriam*, 22; Shaplen, "Peacemaker," 58–60.

10. AJG.

11. Ibid.

12. Shaplen, "Peacemaker," 60; *In Memoriam*, 22.

13. The details of Herstein's biography are from a 1978 interview with her in the OHC, Program on Women and Work, Institute of Labor and Industrial Relations, University of Michigan and Wayne State University. Goldberg's thoughts about her influence on him are contained in Shaplen, "Peacemaker," 60.

14. Shaplen, "Peacemaker," 60–63; *In Memoriam*, 22; AJG.

15. Shaplen, "Peacemaker," 52–60; *In Memoriam*, 22; AJG.

16. Shaplen, "Peacemaker," 60–63; AJG.

17. John Bartlow Martin, *Adlai Stevenson of Illinois* (Garden City, N.Y.: Doubleday/Anchor, 1977), 80, also 79, 81–83.

18. Shaplen, "Peacemaker," 63; AJG.

19. Ibid.; *In Memoriam*, 22–23.

20. Shaplen, "Peacemaker," 63; *In Memoriam*, 23; AJG.

21. Lester Tanzer, *The Kennedy Circle* (New York: Van Rees Press, 1961), 274.

22. Shaplen, "Peacemaker," 63; *In Memoriam*, 23.

23. Roy F. Basler, Marion Dolores Pratt, and Lloyd A. Dunlap, eds., *The Collected Works of Abraham Lincoln* (New Brunswick, N.J.: Rutgers University Press, 1953), vol. 4, 438.

24. Shaplen, "Peacemaker," 63; AJG.

25. Shaplen, "Peacemaker," 58–63; AJG. For a discussion of the worldview of immigrant Jews in the late nineteenth and early twentieth centuries, see Irving Howe, *World of Our Fathers* (New York: Simon & Schuster, 1976). On the emergence of the nation's dominant economic and political tradition in the latter half of the nineteenth century, see Eric Foner, *Free Soil, Free Labor, Free Men: The Ideology of the Republican Party Before the Civil War* (New York: Oxford University Press, 1970), 11–39. The change in this worldview wrought by the emergence of large industrial corporations is discussed briefly by Eric Foner in "Class, Ethnicity and Radicalism in the Gilded Age: The Land League and Irish America," in Eric Foner, *Politics and Ideology in the Age of the Civil War* (New York: Oxford University Press, 1980), 150–200; and more extensively in Samuel Hays, *The Response to Industrialism, 1885–1914* (Chicago: University of Chicago Press, 1957); Gabriel Kolko, *The Triumph of Conservatism: A Reinterpretation of American History, 1900–1916* (New York: Free Press, 1963), esp. 280–87; Robert H. Wiebe, *The Search for Order, 1877–1920* (New York: Hill and Wang, 1967), esp. 145–63; James Weinstein, *The Corporate Ideal in the Liberal State, 1900–1918* (Boston: Beacon Press, 1968); Louis Galambos, "The Emerging Organizational Synthesis in Modern American History," *Business History Review* 44 (1970): 279–90; Alfred D. Chandler, *The Visible Hand: The Managerial Revolution in American Business* (Cambridge, Mass.: Harvard University Press, 1977); Ellis W. Hawley, "The Discovery and Study of a 'Corporate Liberalism,'" *Business History Review* 52 (1978): 309–20; Thomas K. McCraw, *Prophets of Regulation* (Cambridge, Mass.: Harvard University Press, 1984).

26. Shaplen, "Peacemaker," 63.

27. AJG.

28. Draft of Goldberg's letter to *The Nation*, 7, in file marked "1945 correspondence," Goldberg papers.

29. AJG.

30. Martin, *Adlai Stevenson of Illinois*, 182; AJG.

31. AJG. See also Irving Bernstein, *Turbulent Years: A History of the American Worker, 1933–1941* (Boston: Houghton Mifflin, 1969), 72.

32. Bernstein, *Turbulent Years*, 72. See also David Montgomery, *The Fall of the House of Labor* (Cambridge: Cambridge University Press, 1987), esp. 370–464, for a more comprehensive study of labor's retreat during the 1920s from more radical objectives.

33. Bernstein, *Turbulent Years*, 66–75; Ronald Radosh, "The Corporate Ideology of American Labor Leaders from Gompers to Hillman," in James Weinstein and David Eakins, eds., *For a New America* (New York: Random House, 1970), 138–47; Steve Fraser, "Sidney Hillman: Labor's Machiavelli," in Melvyn Dubofsky and Warren Van Tine, eds., *Labor Leaders in America* (Urbana: University of Illinois Press, 1987), 207–33; AJG.

34. Steve Fraser, "Rehearsal for the New Deal: Shop-Floor Insurgents, Political

Elites, and Industrial Democracy in the Amalgamated Clothing Workers," in Michael H. Frisch and Daniel J. Walkowitz, eds., *Working Class America: Essays on Labor, Community, and American Society* (Urbana: University of Illinois Press, 1983), 216.

35. Ibid., 214–41; Steve Fraser, "From the New Unionism to the New Deal," *Labor History* 25 (1984): 405–30; Sanford Jacoby, "Union–Management Cooperation in the United States: Lessons from the 1920's," *Industrial and Labor Relations Review* 57 (1983): 18–33; Nelson Lichtenstein, "Great Expectations: The Promise of Collective Bargaining and Its Demise, 1935–65," paper presented at the Conference on Industrial Democracy sponsored by the Wilson Center Program on American Society and Politics, Washington, D.C., March 28–30, 1988.

36. AJG.

37. Fraser, "Rehearsal for the New Deal," 218–23.

38. Shaplen, "Peacemaker," 66; Dorothy Cassel, "The Chicago Chapter of the National Lawyers Guild: Fifty Years of Fortitude," *Chicago Reader*, October 23, 1987, 10; interview with Walter Fisher, August 1984; AJG.

39. Shaplen, "Peacemaker," 66; Cassel, "The Chicago Chapter of the National Lawyers Guild," 10; Walter Fisher interview; AJG.

40. Shaplen, "Peacemaker," 65–66; AJG.

41. Herbert Harris, *American Labor* (New Haven, Conn.: Yale University Press, 1939), 173–79; Walter Galenson, *The CIO Challenge to the AFL* (Cambridge, Mass.: Harvard University Press, 1960), 548–49; Bernstein, *Turbulent Years*, 127–34.

42. Harris, *American Labor*, 179–91; Galenson, *The CIO Challenge*, 547–54; Bernstein, *Turbulent Years*, 134–37; Barry Kritzberg, "An Unfinished Chapter in White-Collar Unionism: The Formative Years of the Chicago Newspaper Guild, Local 71, American Newspaper Guild, AFL–CIO," *Labor History* 14 (1973): 398–99; Rodney Carlisle, "William Randolph Hearst's Reaction to the American Newspaper Guild: A Challenge to New Deal Labor Legislation," *Labor History* 10 (1969): 74–77, 87–90.

43. Galenson, *The CIO Challenge*, 550–57; Bernstein, *Turbulent Years*, 135–37, 352–431.

44. Kritzberg, "An Unfinished Chapter," 400. See also Galenson, *The CIO Challenge*, 558.

45. Kritzberg, "An Unfinished Chapter," 403, also 402; Carlisle, "Hearst's Reaction," 77.

46. Kritzberg, "An Unfinished Chapter," 406. See also Galenson, *The CIO Challenge*, 558.

47. *The Guild Reporter*, December 15, 1938, 1, 3–4, January 1, 1939, 1–4; *Editor and Publisher*, December 17, 1938, 6, December 24, 1938, 12; Shaplen, "Peacemaker," 65–66; William E. Leuchtenburg, *Franklin D. Roosevelt and the New Deal* (New York: Harper & Row, 1963), 239–44; AJG.

48. Kritzberg, "An Unfinished Chapter," 407. See also *The Guild Reporter*, January 1, 1939, 1–4; *Editor and Publisher*, December 24, 1938, 12, January 7, 1939, 18; AJG.

49. *The Guild Reporter*, February 15, 1939, 1–4, March 1, 1939, 1–4; *Editor and Publisher*, February 11, 1939, 23.

50. *The Guild Reporter*, January 15, 1939, 1–4, April 1, 1939, 1–5, May 1, 1939, 1, 3–4.

51. Kritzberg, "An Unfinished Chapter," 410. See also Galenson, *The CIO Challenge*, 558.

52. Kritzberg, "An Unfinished Chapter," 407–8.

53. Ibid., 406–9; AJG.

54. *Editor and Publisher*, September 23, 1939, 28.

55. Kritzberg, "An Unfinished Chapter," 408; *Editor and Publisher*, September 16, 1939, 38, December 2, 1939, 38, January 20, 1940, 38.

56. AJG.

57. Ibid.

58. Ibid.

59. This is not meant to suggest that workers received the legislative changes that they wanted or competed more or less equally with management in the struggle to enact the National Labor Relations Act, but only that rank-and-file activity compelled the state to respond in ways that were opposed by the overwhelming majority of employers. See Theda Skocpol, "Political Response to Capitalist Crisis: Neo-Marxist Theories of the State and the Case of the New Deal," *Politics and Society* 10 (1980): 155–201; the articles contained in Peter B. Evans, Dietrich Rueschemeyer, and Theda Skocpol, eds., *Bringing the State Back In* (Cambridge: Cambridge University Press, 1985); Nicos Poulantzas, *Political Power and Social Classes* (London: Verso, 1978).

60. Bernstein, *Turbulent Years*, 635–81; Leuchtenburg, *Roosevelt and the New Deal*, 107–14, 150–52, 231, 236; Arthur M. Schlesinger Jr., *The Coming of the New Deal* (Boston: Houghton Mifflin, 1959), 385–419.

61. Irving Bernstein, *The Lean Years: A History of the American Worker, 1920–1933* (Boston: Houghton Mifflin, 1960), 195. See also Edwin E. Witte, *The Government in Labor Disputes* (New York: McGraw-Hill, 1932).

62. Quoted in Bernstein, *The Lean Years*, 393.

63. Bernstein, *The Lean Years*, 195–202, 393–415; AJG.

64. AJG.

65. Entry for Van Bittner in Gary M. Fink, ed., *The Biographical Dictionary of American Labor Leaders* (Westport, Conn.: Greenwood Press, 1974), 26; AJG.

66. AJG.

67. Robert R. R. Brooks, *As Steel Goes* (New Haven, Conn.: Yale University Press, 1940), 183; Galenson, *The CIO Challenge*, 560–64; AJG.

68. AJG.

69. Ibid.

70. *The Guild Reporter*, October 15, 1939, 3.

71. AJG.

72. Kritzberg, "An Unfinished Chapter," 408.

73. *The Guild Reporter*, December 15, 1939, 1, 3, 5.

74. *The Guild Reporter*, March 1, 1940, 2, March 15, 1940, 1, April 1, 1940, 1, 3, April 15, 1940, 1, May 1, 1940, 1–2, May 15, 1940, 1–2, 4.

75. Kritzberg, "An Unfinished Chapter," 408, also 409–12; the sources cited in the preceding note; Galenson, *The CIO Challenge*, 558.

76. Kritzberg, "An Unfinished Chapter," 412.

77. Galenson, *The CIO Challenge*, 558–59.

78. AJG.

79. Ibid.

80. Leuchtenburg, *Roosevelt and the New Deal*, 318–19; Shaplen, "Peacemaker," 68; AJG.

81. Shaplen, "Peacemaker," 68.

82. Bernstein, *Turbulent Years*, 783, also 104, 122–23, 149–55, 432–634; Bert Cochran, *Labor and Communism: The Conflict That Shaped American Unions* (Princeton, N.J.: Princeton University Press, 1977), 82–155; Harvey A. Levenstein, *Communism, Anti-Communism, and the CIO* (Westport, Conn.: Greenwood Press, 1981), 36–77.

83. Bernstein, *Turbulent Years*, 695–99; Cochran, *Labor and Communism*, 82–155; Levenstein, *Communism, Anti-Communism, and the CIO*, 36–123.

Chapter 2. The Crucible of Wartime

1. James M. Burns, *Roosevelt: The Lion and the Fox* (New York: Harcourt Brace & World, 1956), 388–400; AJG.

2. John Bartlow Martin, *Adlai Stevenson of Illinois* (Garden City, N.Y.: Doubleday/ Anchor, 1977), 3–163; AJG.

3. AJG.

4. Martin, *Adlai Stevenson of Illinois*, 103, 114, 140–42, 146, 150, 157–59; AJG.

5. Adlai Stevenson to Ellen Borden Stevenson, Wednesday [July ? 1933], quoted in Martin, *Adlai Stevenson of Illinois*, 105.

6. Martin, *Adlai Stevenson of Illinois*, 126.

7. AJG. See also Jerome E. Edwards, *The Foreign Policy of Colonel McCormick's Tribune* (Reno: University of Nevada Press, 1971), 128–56; Martin, *Adlai Stevenson of Illinois*, 164–81.

8. Martin, *Adlai Stevenson of Illinois*, 164–81; AJG.

9. Burns, *The Lion and the Fox*, 408–37; Irving Bernstein, *Turbulent Years: A History of the American Worker, 1933–1941* (Boston: Houghton Mifflin, 1969), 715–17; AJG.

10. Draft of Goldberg's letter to *The Nation*, 1, file marked "1945 Correspondence," Goldberg Papers. See also Paul H. Douglas, *In the Fullness of Time* (New York: Harcourt Brace Jovanovich, 1971), 85–100; John M. Allswang, *A House for All People—Ethnic Politics in Chicago 1890–1936* (Lexington: University of Kentucky Press, 1971); Martin, *Adlai Stevenson of Illinois*, 99–102.

11. Draft of Goldberg's letter to *The Nation*, 1–2.

12. AJG.

13. *New York Times*, October 30, 1940. See also Martin, *Adlai Stevenson of Illinois*, 166–80; Burns, *The Lion and the Fox*, 437–42.

14. Quoted in Edwards, *Colonel McCormick's Tribune*, 203, also 156–62.

15. Douglas, *In the Fullness of Time*, 105. See also William E. Leuchtenburg, *Franklin D. Roosevelt and the New Deal* (New York: Harper & Row, 1963), 321–22; Martin, *Adlai Stevenson of Illinois*, 169.

16. Burns, *The Lion and the Fox*, 431–58; Edwards, *Colonel McCormick's Tribune*, 159–70.

17. Martin, *Adlai Stevenson of Illinois*, 169–88; AJG.

18. Adlai Stevenson to M. J. Spiegel, November 15, 1940, quoted in Martin, *Adlai Stevenson of Illinois*, 177, also 181–82, 187–88.

19. See Martin, *Adlai Stevenson of Illinois*; also John Morton Blum, *V Was for Victory* (New York: Harcourt Brace Jovanovich, 1976), 172–81; AJG.

20. AJG. See also Martin, *Adlai Stevenson of Illinois*, 184–93.

21. Adlai Stevenson to Arthur J. Goldberg, July 18, 1941, reprinted in Walter Johnson, ed., *The Papers of Adlai Stevenson* (Boston: Little, Brown, 1972), vol. 1, 560.

22. Martin, *Adlai Stevenson of Illinois*, 193–95; Douglas, *In the Fullness of Time*, 106–9.

23. Robert R. R. Brooks, *As Steel Goes* (New Haven, Conn.: Yale University Press, 1940), 46–189; Walter Galenson, *The CIO Challenge to the AFL* (Cambridge, Mass.: Harvard University Press, 1960), 75–238; Bernstein, *Turbulent Years*, 40–66, 432–

571; David Brody, "The CIO After 50 Years: A Historical Reckoning," *Dissent* 32 (1985): 457–72; David Brody, "The Origins of Modern Steel Unionism: The SWOC Era," in Paul F. Clark, Peter Gottlieb, and Donald Kennedy, eds., *Forging a Union of Steel: Philip Murray, SWOC and the United Steelworkers* (Ithaca, N.Y.: Cornell University Press, 1987), 13–29; Arthur M. Schlesinger Jr., *The Coming of the New Deal* (Boston: Houghton Mifflin, 1959), 385–419; Leuchtenburg, *Roosevelt and the New Deal*, 243–54, 286–87, 299–300, 318–19.

24. Brooks, *As Steel Goes*, 183–84; Galenson, *The CIO Challenge*, 114–16; Irving Bernstein, *The Lean Years: A History of the American Worker, 1920–1933* (Boston: Houghton Mifflin, 1960), 117–26, 362–66; Melvyn Dubofsky and Warren Van Tine, *John L. Lewis: A Biography* (New York: Quadrangle, 1977), 3–299; Ronald W. Schatz, "Philip Murray and the Subordination of the Industrial Unions to the United States Government," in Melvyn Dubofsky and Warren Van Tine, eds., *Labor Leaders in America* (Urbana: University of Illinois Press, 1987), 234–46; Karl Klare, "The Judicial Deradicalization of the Wagner Act and the Origins of Modern Legal Consciousness, 1937–41," *Minnesota Law Review* 62 (1978): 265–339; Matthew W. Finkin, "Revisionism in Labor Law," *University of Maryland Law Review* 43 (1984): 23–92; Christopher L. Tomlins, *The State and the Unions; Labor Relations, Law and the Organized Labor Movement in America, 1880–1960* (Cambridge: Cambridge University Press, 1985), 99–243.

25. Galenson, *The CIO Challenge*, 116–17; Bernstein, *Turbulent Years*, 727–29; David J. McDonald, *Union Man* (New York: Dutton, 1969), 143–50; Klare, "The Judicial Deradicalization of the Wagner Act"; Tomlins, *The State and the Unions*, 99–243.

26. "Labor's Plenipotentiary," *Fortune*, March 1960, 224.

27. Quoted in ibid.

28. Dorothy Goldberg, *A Private View of a Public Life* (New York: Charterhouse, 1975), 46.

29. See, on this last point, Irving Bernstein's description of a 1934 strike in Minneapolis in which trading precision for agreement failed because of the low demand for labor, which made both sides unwilling to compromise. The account is in Bernstein's *Turbulent Years*, 239–41.

30. AJG.

31. Ibid.

32. The exact amounts were $7,349 in 1938 and $13,840 in 1941. These figures are from the files marked "Income Tax Returns—1932–45," Goldberg Papers.

33. The exact amount paid in cash was $601,000. See Murray's remarks in CIO–EBP, March 23, 1942, 130, WPRL. The acronym USA is used for the Steelworkers Union because it is what its leaders selected for the organization. But the news media refused to use that term, preferring instead to abbreviate the union's name with the initials USW. Whether that was done merely to avoid confusion or to avoid linking unionism with the name of the nation itself is unclear. The connection between the steel union and the nation was certainly one that those who came up with the USA label were trying to establish in the public's mind.

34. USA–EBP, June 22, 1942, 22, HCLA–PSU. The data on the USA's size and assets are from Murray's remarks at the CIO Executive Board meeting held on March 23, 1942. See CIO–EBP, March 23, 1942, 129–30. In addition, 540,000 dues-paying members had been enrolled in the Steelworkers Union by the end of 1941.

35. USA–EBP, June 22, 1942, 144, also 143, 145; McDonald, *Union Man*, 146–47. Of the 540,000 dues-paying members enrolled by the end of 1941, almost 90,000 net

had been lost to conscription by the spring of 1942, leaving the USA by March of that year with a total membership of about 460,000, which rose to 472,000 by June (CIO–EBP, March 23, 1942, 129; USA–EBP, June 22, 1942, 147).

36. CIO–EBP, March 23, 1942, 127–29; Bernstein, *Turbulent Years*, 721–26. The size of the treasury was around $300,000 (CIO–EBP, 129).

37. CIO–EBP, March 23, 1942, 128; Bernstein, *Turbulent Years*, 769; Nelson Lichtenstein, *Labor's War at Home* (Cambridge: Cambridge University Press, 1982), 26–202.

38. AJG.

39. Ibid.

40. Ibid.

41. Richard Harris Smith, *OSS: The Secret History of America's First Central Intelligence Agency* (Berkeley and Los Angeles: University of California Press, 1972), 1–35; Bradley F. Smith, *The Shadow Warriors* (New York: Basic Books, 1983), 3–94; Joseph E. Persico, *Piercing the Reich: The Penetration of Nazi Germany by American Secret Agents During World War II* (New York: Viking Press, 1979), 5–8; William Casey, *The Secret War Against Hitler* (Washington, D.C.: Regnery Gateway, 1988), 3–20.

42. Smith, *OSS*, 12; Persico, *Piercing the Reich*, 18–19.

43. AJG. See also Smith, *OSS*, 12; Persico, *Piercing the Reich*, 19; Robin W. Winks, *Cloak and Gown: Scholars in the Secret War, 1939–61* (New York: Morrow, 1987), 174–75.

44. AJG.

45. Ibid.

46. Goldberg had very high blood pressure. The precise details can be found in the report of his army physical examination, located in the file marked "Military Record and OSS," Goldberg Papers. See also Douglas, *In the Fullness of Time*, 105–6, 109–24.

47. Smith, *The Shadow Warriors*, 95–139.

48. Adlai Stevenson to Arthur J. Goldberg, December 13, 1941, file marked "1941 Personal and Confidential Correspondence," Goldberg Papers.

49. AJG.

50. Ibid.

51. AJG. See also Smith, *OSS*, 208.

52. AJG. See also Persico, *Piercing the Reich*, 20; Winks, *Cloak and Gown*, 174.

53. Smith, *OSS*, 14–19; Smith, *The Shadow Warriors*, 212; Lichtenstein, *Labor's War at Home*, 67–232; Blum, *V Was for Victory*, 117–46; Paul A. C. Koistenen, "Mobilizing the World War II Economy: Labor and the Industrial–Military Alliance," *Pacific Historical Review* 42 (1973): 443–78; Richard Polenberg, *War and Society* (Philadelphia: Lippincott, 1972), 5–36, 154–83, 215–37.

54. Quoted in Smith, *OSS*, 17.

55. AJG.

56. Ibid.

57. Persico, *Piercing the Reich*, 19; AJG.

58. David Kennedy, *Over Here* (New York: Oxford University Press, 1980), 26–29; Bert Cochran, *Labor and Communism* (Princeton, N.J.: Princeton University Press, 1977), 156–247; Harvey A. Levenstein, *Communism, Anti-Communism, and the CIO* (Westport, Conn.; Greenwood Press, 1981), 156–83; AJG.

59. File marked "Military Record and OSS," Goldberg Papers; Smith, *OSS*, 206–22.

60. Arthur J. Goldberg to Mildred Goodstein, September 9, 1942, 1, copy in the file marked "Military Record and OSS," Goldberg Papers.

61. Ibid.

62. Ibid., 1–2.

63. Ibid., 2.

64. Memos from Arthur J. Goldberg to George Bowden, September 24 and 29 and October 2, 1942, copies of which are in the file marked "Military Record and OSS," Goldberg Papers.

65. Arthur J. Goldberg to George Bowden, October 2, 1942, 1. See also the two other memos to Bowden, September 24 and 29, 1942.

66. Smith, *OSS*, 200.

67. Ibid.

68. Arthur J. Goldberg to Donald C. Downes, October 20, 1942, 2, copy in the file marked "Military Record and OSS," Goldberg Papers.

69. Ibid.

70. AJG. See also Smith, *OSS*, 74–81; Winks, *Cloak and Gown*, 199–202.

71. AJG. See also Winks, *Cloak and Gown*, 202.

72. AJG. See also Smith, *OSS*, 81; Winks, *Cloak and Gown*, 207.

73. Smith, *OSS*, 81–82; Smith, *The Shadow Warriors*, 219; Winks, *Cloak and Gown*, 202; AJG.

74. AJG. See Smith, *OSS*; Smith, *The Shadow Warriors*, generally on the problems caused by excessive secrecy and the use of unvouchered funds.

75. AJG.

76. Ibid.

77. Smith, *OSS*, 361–83; Smith, *The Shadow Warriors*, 390–419.

78. AJG. See also the file marked "Leases" in the Goldberg Papers, which contains the lease for the house on Albemarle Street in northwest Washington, D.C.

79. Arthur J. Goldberg to Colonel G. Edward Buxton, July 1, 1943, copy in the file marked "Military Record and OSS," Goldberg Papers.

80. See the memo cited in n. 79, the memo from William Donovan to the director of the Office of Procurement Service in the War Department, May 6, 1943, and the one entitled "Job Description—Captain Arthur J. Goldberg," copies of which are in the file marked "Military Record and OSS," and the memo labeled "Curriculum Vitae of Arthur J. Goldberg," copy in the file marked "1943 Personal Correspondence," Goldberg Papers; Smith, *The Shadow Warriors*, 165–67.

81. AJG. Details of the report Goldberg delivered to Eddy can be found in the transmittal letter from Brigadier General John Magruder, deputy director of OSS, August 27, 1943, a copy of which is in the file marked "Military Record and OSS," Goldberg Papers.

82. AJG.

83. Irving Howe, *World of Our Fathers* (New York: Simon & Schuster, 1976), 205–10, 623–26; AJG.

84. AJG.

85. Ibid.

86. Details of Goldberg's CGT operations are from a long memo summarizing them written sometime in the fall of 1944 and from a receipt for funds sent to the CGT. Both items are in the file marked "Military Record and OSS," Goldberg Papers. See also Smith, *The Shadow Warriors*, 247.

87. AJG.

88. Smith, *The Shadow Warriors*, 185; Smith, *OSS*, 166–71; AJG.

89. AJG.

90. Ibid.

91. Ibid.
92. AJG. See also Smith, *OSS*, 182.
93. Ibid.
94. See the memo summarizing the activities of Goldberg's CGT operations in the file marked "Military Record and OSS," Goldberg Papers.
95. Smith, *OSS*, 184.
96. Ibid.; AJG.
97. AJG. See also Maciej Kozlowski, "The Mission That Failed: An Interview with Jan Karski," *Dissent* 34 (1987): 326–34; Persico, *Piercing the Reich*, 22.
98. AJG.
99. Ibid.
100. See Burns, *The Lion and the Fox*, 390–468; Leuchtenburg, *Roosevelt and the New Deal*, 275–325; Blum, *V Was for Victory*, 172–81. The refusal to admit refugees earlier was at least partly the result of Depression-era unemployment. In view of that situation, public enthusiasm for letting in newcomers of any kind was doubtless not very great (Leuchtenburg, *Roosevelt and the New Deal*, 286).
101. Burns, *The Lion and the Fox*, 390–461; Herbert L. Feingold, *The Politics of Rescue: The Roosevelt Administration and the Holocaust, 1938–1945* (New Brunswick, N.J.: Schocken Books, 1970); David S. Wyman, *Paper Walls: America and the Refugee Crisis, 1938–1941* (Amherst: University of Massachusetts Press, 1968); David S. Wyman, *The Abandonment of the Jews: America and the Holocaust, 1941–1945* (New York: Pantheon Books, 1984); AJG.
102. AJG. See also Persico, *Piercing the Reich*, 23; Casey, *The Secret War Against Hitler*, 178.
103. AJG. See also Persico, *Piercing the Reich*, 23.
104. See Smith, *The Shadow Warriors*, 270, for details of the congressional move to cut the OSS budget in 1944.
105. AJG.
106. Ibid.
107. Ibid.
108. Peter B. Evans, Dietrich Rueschemeyer, and Theda Skocpol, eds., *Bringing the State Back In* (Cambridge: Cambridge University Press, 1985); Charles S. Maier, *Recasting Bourgeois Europe: Stabilization in France, Germany and Italy in the Decade after World War I* (Princeton, N.J.: Princeton University Press, 1975); Charles S. Maier, *In Search of Stability: Explorations in Historical Political Economy* (Cambridge: Cambridge University Press, 1987); Philippe C. Schmitter and Gerhard Lehmbruch, eds., *Trends Toward Corporatist Intermediation* (Beverly Hills, Calif.: Sage, 1979); Philippe C. Schmitter and Gerhard Lehmbruch, eds., *Patterns of Corporatist Policymaking* (Beverly Hills, Calif.: Sage, 1982); W. J. Mommsen, ed., *The Emergence of the Welfare State in Britain and Germany, 1850–1950* (London: Croom Helm, 1981); Suzanne Berger, ed., *Organizing Interest Groups in Western Europe* (Cambridge: Cambridge University Press, 1981); Alain Touraine, "Management and the Working Class in Western Europe," *Daedalus* 93 (1964): 304–34; Ronald W. Schatz, "From Commons to Dunlop and Kerr: Rethinking the Field and Theory of Industrial Relations," paper presented at the Conference on Industrial Democracy sponsored by the Wilson Center Program on American Society and Politics, Washington, D.C., March 28–30, 1988; AJG.
109. AJG. For the view that the corporatist system of political economy emerged out of a wartime model, see Kennedy, *Over Here*, 141–43, who argues that the decisive shift in the United States toward corporatism seems to have begun during the mobili-

zation effort accompanying the United States's entry into World War I. See also William Leuchtenburg, "The New Deal and the Analogue of War," in John Braeman, Robert H. Bremner, and Everett Walters, eds., *Change and Continuity in Twentieth Century America* (Columbus: Ohio State University Press, 1964), 81–143, which contends that the expansion in state power that accompanied the New Deal was inspired by the set of institutional arrangements developed during World War I.

110. Reinhold Niebuhr, *The Children of Light and the Children of Darkness, a Vindication of Democracy and a Critique of Its Traditional Defense* (New York: Scribners, 1944); AJG.

111. Missing by then, however, was the hope of achieving greater state control over the operation of corporate enterprises, a goal expressed since the late nineteenth century in the vocabulary of the antimonopoly tradition, one with deep roots in American political culture. The idea had gained strength in social democratic circles during the 1930s, but the wartime experience appears to have cut off other paths for its development. See Alan Brinkley, "The New Deal and the Idea of the State," in Steve Fraser and Gary Gerstle, eds., *The Rise and Fall of the New Deal Order, 1930–80* (Princeton, N.J.: Princeton University Press, 1989), 85–121. See also Kennedy, *Over Here*, 88–92; AJG.

112. Marquis Childs, *Sweden: The Middle Way* (New Haven, Conn.: Yale University Press, 1936); Marquis Childs, *Sweden: The Middle Way on Trial* (New Haven, Conn.: Yale University Press, 1980); Robert Heilbroner, "The Swedish Promise," *New York Review of Books*, December 4, 1980, 33–36; John Kenneth Galbraith, *Economics in Perspective: A Critical History* (Boston: Houghton Mifflin, 1987), 223–25; AJG.

113. Kennedy, *Over Here*, 245–95; Bernstein, *The Lean Years*, 47–189; Maier, *Recasting Bourgeois Europe*.

Chapter 3. The Postwar "New Deal"

1. Nelson Lichtenstein, *Labor's War at Home* (Cambridge: Cambridge University Press, 1982), 82–83, 145–46; Mark Reutter, *Sparrows Point: Making Steel: The Rise and Ruin of American Industrial Might* (New York: Summit Books, 1988), 303–21; AJG.

2. AJG.

3. Arthur J. Goldberg to M. B. Wolf, November 25, 1944, 2, copy in the file marked "Military Record and OSS," Goldberg Papers. See also AJG.

4. Arthur J. Goldberg to M. B. Wolf, November 25, 1944, 2.

5. USA–EBP, May 5, 1944, 5.

6. Lichtenstein, *Labor's War at Home*, 51–53, 67–81, 178–82, 207–10.

7. USA–EBP, June 22, 1942, 141–44, September 21, 1943, 73; Lichtenstein, *Labor's War at Home*, 67–81. By the spring of 1943, 80 percent of the dues paid to the Steelworkers Union came through the checkoff method (USA–EBP, May 19, 1943, 181–82).

8. Those concerns were discussed openly at a meeting held to decide whether or not to cancel all existing contracts and push for a wage increase above that allowed by the Little Steel formula (USA–EBP, September 22, 1943, 257–66). At a later board meeting, Clint Golden, an assistant to the Steelworkers president who served as a labor vice-chairman of the War Production Board, described the pattern that had emerged by the spring of 1944: "I have learned as a result of . . . associations in

Washington . . . that whenever a constructive and concrete proposal comes from labor, immediately, as if almost by some sort of centralized direction, the forces of government are set in motion, not to analyze it, not to appraise it in the light of its relation to the national welfare, but rather they are set in motion to discredit it in one form or another" (USA–EBP, June 13, 1944, 71).

9. USA–EBP, September 22, 1943, 258, also 259–63. For Murray's view of FDR, see USA–EBP, June 22, 1943, 184, where Murray said that the "greatest comfort that labor has in the United States is the fact that it has today and has had for the past ten years a labor President. He has given labor more than any other leader of any government anywhere in the world during the past ten years." See also Ronald W. Schatz, "Philip Murray and the Subordination of the Industrial Unions to the United States Government," in Melvyn Dubofsky and Warren Van Tine, eds., *Labor Leaders in America* (Urbana: University of Illinois Press, 1987), 242–49.

10. USA–EBP, September 22, 1943, 261–63, 342–60; Lichtenstein, *Labor's War at Home*, 76–78, 157–61, 165–71.

11. The fear was first expressed openly at a USA Executive Board meeting held on May 19, 1943. Murray told the board that "with all of the increased efficiencies that have been developed since 1940, if they are applied in 1946 when the war is over, you can produce what was produced in 1940 with 8,000,000 less people, and there will be actual unemployment of 9,000,000 assuming that you have that situation on your hands in 1946" (USA–EBP, May 19, 1943, 89–90). See also Irving Bernstein, *The Lean Years: A History of the American Worker, 1920–1933* (Boston: Houghton Mifflin, 1960), 83–143; Lichtenstein, *Labor's War at Home*, 27–28.

12. Lichtenstein, *Labor's War at Home*, 182.

13. USA–EBP, June 13, 1944, 46–47. See also John P. Hoerr, *And the Wolf Finally Came: The Decline of the American Steel Industry* (Pittsburgh: University of Pittsburgh Press, 1988), 101–4.

14. USA–EBP, November 8, 1943, 60, also 58–59; Lichtenstein, *Labor's War at Home*, 186–88.

15. USA–EBP, December 1, 1944, 105–6. The matter was discussed at length by several members of the board, who echoed similar thoughts (104–9).

16. On the issue of grievances relating to working conditions, see Murray's remarks in USA–EBP, September 22, 1943, 266–67, where he expressed his belief that work stoppages at Bethlehem were "attributable, not so much to a demand for a wage increase as . . . [they were] to a demand on the part of the workers to secure for themselves a correction of all the abuses to which they have been subjected since the beginning of the war, by that corporation." See also Hoerr, *And the Wolf Finally Came*, 324–29.

17. USA–EBP, September 23, 1943, 343.

18. Ibid., 350. See 342–78 for the complete discussion of the wildcat strike problem.

19. USA–EBP, June 13, 1944, 65–82.

20. USA–EBP, September 23, 1943, 303–42, May 14, 1944, 94–104; Reutter, *Sparrows Point*, 346–52; Hoerr, *And the Wolf Finally Came*, 174–75; John Morton Blum, *V Was for Victory* (New York: Harcourt Brace Jovanovich, 1976), 199–207. In asking it to reverse the earlier decision, Murray told the board that "a number of the Directors came to me during the noon recess and said, 'If you send those speeches out, you are going to have a war on your hands; it is all right to tell the Board Members these things in the room here, but don't convey them to the local unions'" (USA–EBP, September 23, 1943, 341).

21. USA–EBP, September 23, 1943, 378–87, USA–EBP, May 14, 1944, 102; Lichtenstein, *Labor's War at Home*, 157–216.

22. U.S. Bureau of the Census, *Historical Statistics of the United States: Colonial Times to the Present* (bicentennial ed.) (Washington, D.C.: U.S. Government Printing Office, 1975), pt. 1, 177. The CIO's increase had been diminished in part by the loss of the UMW, which had approximately 563,000 members when it left the CIO in 1942. See Lichtenstein, *Labor's War at Home*, 80.

23. The extent to which the USA and UAW established collective bargaining patterns followed by other unions is a matter of some dispute, but the basic point that they did so is not. See Nelson Lichtenstein, "Great Expectations: The Promise of Collective Bargaining and Its Demise, 1935–65," paper presented at the Conference on Industrial Democracy sponsored by the Wilson Center Program on American Society and Politics, Washington, D.C., March 28–30, 1988, 1–34. See also Schatz, "Philip Murray," 239–49.

24. USA–EBP, September 21, 1943, 54–61; James Caldwell Foster, *The Union Politic: The CIO Political Action Committee* (Columbia: University of Missouri Press, 1975). Pressure from unions increasingly unhappy with Roosevelt and seeking instead to establish an independent labor bloc in politics also contributed to the PAC's formation. On that point, see Lichtenstein, *Labor's War at Home*, 171–77.

25. Arthur J. Goldberg to Carl Devoe, April 12, 1945, copy in the file marked "1945 Personal Correspondence," Goldberg Papers.

26. AJG.

27. Arthur J. Goldberg to Carl Devoe, April 16, 1945, 1, copy in the file marked "1945 Personal Correspondence," Goldberg Papers.

28. *Chicago Daily News*, October 17, 1944, clipping in Goldberg Papers.

29. Arthur J. Goldberg to Mortimer Kollender, January 31, 1946, copy in the file marked "1946 Personal Correspondence," Goldberg Papers. See also Goldberg's federal income tax returns, copies of which are in the file marked "1941–46 Income Tax Returns," Goldberg Papers.

30. USA–EBP, November 26, 1944, 129. See also Lichtenstein, *Labor's War at Home*, 170–71.

31. USA–EBP, November 26, 1944, 8–151; E. Robert Livernash, *Collective Bargaining in the Basic Steel Industry* (Washington, D.C.: U.S. Department of Labor, 1961), 243–46; Hoerr, *And the Wolf Finally Came*, 326; A. D. H. Kaplan, *The Guarantee of Annual Wages* (Washington, D.C.: Brookings Institution, 1947).

32. USA–EBP, November 26, 1944, 8–151.

33. USA–EBP, September 10, 1945, 86–87. See also Lichtenstein, *Labor's War at Home*, 203–28; Barton J. Bernstein, "The Truman Administration and Its Reconversion Wage Policy," *Labor History* 6 (1965): 214–31.

34. Lichtenstein, *Labor's War at Home*, 203–45; Bernstein, "The Truman Administration and Its Reconversion Wage Policy," 214–31.

35. On liberal Catholic thought and the American labor movement, see Ronald W. Schatz, "American Labor and the Catholic Church, 1919–1950," *International Labor and Working Class History* 20 (1981): 46–53; Schatz, "Philip Murray," 236–49; "The Labor Priests," *Fortune*, January 1949, 150–52.

36. FSG; Schatz, "American Labor and the Catholic Church," 46–53; Melvyn Dubofsky, "Not So 'Turbulent Years': Another Look at the American 1930's," *Amerikastudien* 24 (1979): 5–20; David Brody, "The CIO After 50 Years: A Historical Reckoning," *Dissent* 32 (1985): 457–72; Lizabeth Cohen, *Making a New Deal: Industrial Workers in Chicago, 1919–1939* (Cambridge: Cambridge University Press, 1990).

37. USA–EBP, April 1, 1946, 82. The board responded by approving a donation of $200,000 for the organizing drive (74–103). On labor moderates' postwar objectives, see Lichtenstein, *Labor's War at Home*, 203–32; Nelson Lichtenstein, "From Corporatism to Collective Bargaining: Organized Labor and the Eclipse of Social Democracy in the Postwar Era," in Steve Fraser and Gary Gerstle, eds., *The Rise and Fall of the New Deal Order, 1930–80* (Princeton, N.J.: Princeton University Press, 1989), 122–33; Alan Brinkley, "The Concept of New Deal Liberalism, 1937–1945," unpublished manuscript, 63–75.

38. On the issue of organizing foremen and supervisors, see USA–EBP, May 24, 1945, 69–90. Lee Pressman told the board members bluntly that "whoever is going down this road [of] organizing the foremen must anticipate that insofar as the big corporations are concerned, you will get recognition only in the event that the United States Supreme Court some day says you are entitled to it. . . . It is to the death as far as they are concerned, before they recognize the foremen's union" (85–86). See also Christopher L. Tomlins, *The State and the Unions; Labor Relations, Law and the Organized Labor Movement in America, 1880–1960* (Cambridge: Cambridge University Press, 1985), 264–66.

39. Murray remarked at a meeting of the USA Executive Board on June 13, 1944, that the Steelworkers' postwar program was one based on "higher wages, [and] greater purchasing power, thereby enabling industry to provide the necessary things to keep the working population going, to keep them at work. . . . Substantially that is the answer . . . to provide that sort of wage level and guarantee post-war employment" (USA–EBP, June 13, 1944, 84–85). For other examples of Murray's support for such ideas, see USA–EBP, May 24, 1945, 10–32, December 10, 1945, 15–23, 133–48. See also Brinkley, "The Concept of New Deal Liberalism," 31–98; Alan Brinkley, "The New Deal and the Idea of the State," in Steve Fraser and Gary Gerstle, eds., *The Rise and Fall of the New Deal Order, 1930–80* (Princeton, N.J.: Princeton University Press, 1989), 85–121; Lichtenstein, *Labor's War at Home*, 203–32; Lichtenstein, "From Corporatism to Collective Bargaining," 122–33.

40. The AFL's hostility to the state is well documented in Tomlins, *The State and the Unions*. On the AFL's opposition to the wartime regulatory apparatus, see Lichtenstein, *Labor's War at Home*, 161.

41. Lichtenstein, *Labor's War at Home*, 203–32.

42. Ibid., 216–21; Howell Harris, *The Right to Manage: Industrial Relations Policies of American Business in the 1940's* (Madison: University of Wisconsin Press, 1982), 95–158; Robert M. Collins, *The Business Response to Keynes, 1929–1964* (New York: Columbia University Press, 1981), 115–41; David Brody, *Workers in Industrial America: Essays on the Twentieth Century Struggle* (New York: Oxford University Press, 1980), 175–82.

43. See the sources cited in n. 42.

44. See the sources cited in n. 42, esp. Harris, *The Right to Manage*, for a detailed discussion of this influential and vocal section of the business community.

45. USA–EBP, December 10, 1945, 37. See also AJG. For Murray's thoughts about Kaiser and Stephens, see USA–EBP, June 13, 1944, 84–85, May 24, 1945, 23–24, July 30, 1945, 306–12.

46. USA–EBP, December 10, 1945, 37. See also Irving Bernstein, *Turbulent Years: A History of the American Worker, 1933–1941* (Boston: Houghton Mifflin, 1969), 432–98; Reutter, *Sparrows Point*, 259–65.

47. USA–EBP, July 30, 1945, 237. See also Arthur F. McClure, *The Truman Administration and the Problems of Postwar Labor, 1945–48* (Cranbury, N.J.: As-

sociated University Presses, 1969), 101–23; Tomlins, *The State and the Unions*, 255–58.

48. See Pressman's discussion of the Case and Hobbs bills' provisions in USA–EBP, June 25, 1946, 353–55. In discussing the consequences of making unions financially responsible for wildcat strikes, Pressman told the board that defending one such suit during the late 1930s, at a time when it had no basis in federal or state law, had cost the USA between $100,000 and $150,000 in legal fees. The nuisance suit had been initiated by management at Republic Steel as one part of a larger strategy aimed at defeating the union's organizing campaign (USA–EBP, July 2, 1947, 91). See also McClure, *The Problems of Postwar Labor*, 124–39.

49. Lichtenstein, *Labor's War at Home*, 203–32; McClure, *The Problems of Postwar Labor*, 101–35.

50. Lichtenstein, *Labor's War at Home*, 203–32; Alonzo Hamby, *Beyond the New Deal: Harry S. Truman and American Liberalism* (New York: Columbia University Press, 1973), 53–85; Robert J. Donovan, *Conflict and Crisis: The Presidency of Harry S. Truman, 1945–48* (New York: Norton, 1977), 3–218; McClure, *The Problems of Postwar Labor*, 101–35; Harris, *The Right to Manage*, 105–25.

51. In explaining to the USA Executive Board the causes of the breakdown in the labor–management conference, which met in Washington in November 1945, Murray highlighted the AFL's hostility to government supervision and its unwillingness to seek an agreement on the appropriate size of a general wage increase (USA–EBP, December 10, 1945, 15–24). At an earlier meeting he had noted the NAM's desire for restrictive labor legislation and its opposition to expanding social security programs as key sticking points in reaching an agreement with the employers represented by that organization (USA–EBP, May 24, 1945, 25–27). Labor historian David Brody argues that the key obstacle "was labor's refusal to agree to any listing of specific functions that were exclusively management's," which would have narrowed the scope of future bargaining between the two sides (Brody, *Workers in Industrial America*, 175). Information about the failed conference was also drawn from the records of its sessions, entitled *The President's Labor–Management Conference*, 2 vols., copies of which are in box 5 of David H. Stowe Papers, "Proposed Agenda, Representation and Procedures for the National Labor–Management Conference" and other related material in the folder marked "General File – Labor," box 136, Harry S. Truman Papers, all in HSTL; McClure, *The Problems of Postwar Labor*, 45–66.

52. Lichtenstein, *Labor's War at Home*, 221–32.

53. For the Fairless threats, see Murray's remarks to the Board, USA–EBP, February 21, 1946, 52–53. Pressman explains the central importance of union security issues on pp. 4–15. See also Irving Bernstein, "The Truman Administration and the Steel Strike of 1946," *Journal of American History* 52 (1966): 791–803; Livernash, *Collective Bargaining in the Basic Steel Industry*, 249–54.

54. How fully U.S. Steel's executives understood that fact is unclear. After the contract was signed, Murray told the board he had "got Jack Stephens by the shoulder and I whispered in his ear, 'Well John, instead of canceling your contract you have for the first time in your history recognized now, through the processes of collective bargaining, maintenance of membership and the checkoff.' And I thought John was going to fall through the floor" (USA–EBP, February 21, 1946, 56–57). Pressman, however, contended that "when the corporations accepted [the contract extension] . . . they knew what they were doing" (13–14).

55. Ibid., 14–15.

56. Ibid., 15.

57. Lichtenstein, *Labor's War at Home*, 229–30.

58. USA–EBP, June 26, 1946, 198.

59. USA–EBP, February 21, 1946, 38–39. Despite Pressman's warning, the Wage Stabilization Board did supervise wage increases granted under the contract. See Bernstein, "The Truman Administration and the Steel Strike of 1946," 800–3. On the emergence of the industrial relations experts, see Ronald W. Schatz, "From Commons to Kerr: Rethinking the Field and Theory of Industrial Relations," paper presented at the Conference on Industrial Democracy sponsored by the Wilson Center Program on American Society and Politics, Washington, D.C., March 28–30, 1988, 1–26.

60. See USA–EBP, April 1, 1946, 27, where Pressman noted that "we are coming into a phase now of where these Regional Boards are going to try to re-institute the practice under the National War Labor Board of scrutinizing wage adjustments. You can see that already beginning." See also Schatz, "From Commons to Kerr."

61. Lichtenstein, *Labor's War at Home*, 178–82; Harris, *The Right to Manage*, 105–25; Bernstein, "The Truman Administration and Its Reconversion Wage Policy," 214–31.

62. USA–EBP, June 25, 1946, 116.

63. The USA Executive Board discussed at length whether the locals or the national organization would control worker access to the process and which would pay the costs. In keeping with the union's highly centralized governing structure, the board decided that the locals would have to accept most of the costs while it retained the power to decide which grievances were deemed worthy of arbitration (USA–EBP, June 25, 1946, 104–38). See also David A. Peach and E. Robert Livernash, *Grievance Initiation and Resolution: A Study in Basic Steel* (Boston: Harvard University Business School Press, 1974).

64. A draft of Goldberg's review of [?] Updegraff and [?] McCoy, *Arbitration of Labor Disputes* (Chicago: Commerce Clearing House, 1946) can be found in the file marked "1946," Goldberg Papers.

65. AJG.

66. USA–EBP, April 1, 1946, 114–15; AJG.

67. USA–EBP, April 1, 1946, 115, also 103–14.

68. USA–EBP, April 1, 1946, 151–64, May 12, 1946, 26–28, October 4, 1946, 237–47.

69. Lichtenstein, *Labor's War at Home*, 221–32; Bernstein, "The Truman Administration and the Steel Strike of 1946," 791–803, Schatz, "Philip Murray," 241–52; AJG. Conservative candidates in 1946 were helped by the large sums contributed by the business community to their campaigns, resources that labor could not match. For a discussion of that problem, see USA–EBP, April 2, 1946, 87–88. The 1946 strikes also pushed Congress even before the fall elections in the direction of enacting new laws restricting labor. As Pressman explained to the USA Executive Board in a meeting held on June 29, 1946, Truman's veto of the Case bill had been sustained by a margin of only five votes in the House of Representatives (USA–EBP, June 29, 1946, 351–53). After that veto was sustained, Congress quickly passed the far less comprehensive Hobbs bill, which Truman signed into law (McClure, *The Problems of Postwar Labor*, 133–37).

70. File marked "1946 Personal Correspondence," Goldberg Papers, which includes a copy of his speech to the rally and a letter from the Illinois PAC director; AJG.

71. Archibald Cox, Derek Bok, and Robert Gorman, *Cases and Materials on Labor Law*, 9th ed. (Mineola, N.Y.: Foundation Press, 1981), 81–87; Lichtenstein, *Labor's War at Home*, 238–41; Tomlins, *The State and the Unions*, 282–316. Lichtenstein

contends that the act "proved less of a break with the past than a rigid codification of many of the key policy goals towards which sophisticated business leaders and state industrial relations managers had been moving since the early 1940's" (*Labor's War at Home*, 238). Christopher Tomlins qualifies Lichtenstein's argument in *The State and the Unions*, 298–300. He found that "while remaining in the mainstream of institutional development of labor relations law, however, the Taft–Hartley Act was not just an elaboration of past policy" (299).

72. USA–EBP, May 19, 1947, 171–76, also 127–70; Schatz, "Philip Murray," 249–50.

73. USA–EBP, May 19, 1947, 104–80, November 18–19, 1947, 17–18, February 16, 1948, 16–21, May 4, 1949, 192–93; Lichtenstein, *Labor's War at Home*, 239–41.

74. The Wagner–Murray–Dingell bill, which would have created a national employment service, as well as national unemployment, health, and old-age insurance systems, had first been introduced in 1943. It was inspired in large part by the British Beveridge Report of 1942, which the Labour Party adopted in 1945 (Hamby, *Beyond the New Deal*, 7–8).

75. USA–EBP, June 24, 1946, 53, also 41–52, 54–66.

76. By May 1947 the board saw the congressional route as hopeless. See the discussion in USA–EBP, May 21, 1947, 389–402.

77. The board first explicitly endorsed the two-track approach in a meeting held on June 24, 1946. David McDonald observed that "the membership wants something; they don't know what they want exactly, but they do want something and some better form of insurance than they now possess" (USA–EBP, June 24, 1946, 52). Murray noted that based on the resolutions and petitions he had read that the union should press employers for "such things as [insurance against] hospitalization, retirement, sick benefits, death and kindred matters" (43). The question of specifics was referred by the board to a committee to draw up recommendations. For the entire discussion of that issue, see 41–65. Other references to rank-and-file demands for social insurance of some kind are found in the minutes of the meeting held on May 21, 1947, 411–12. See also Lawrence S. Root, *Fringe Benefits: Social Insurance in the Steel Industry* (Beverly Hills, Calif.: Sage, 1982), 29–47.

78. Paul A. Tiffany, *The Decline of American Steel: How Management, Labor and the Government Went Wrong* (New York: Oxford University Press, 1988), 42–63; USA–EBP, April 20, 1947, 17–18, 131–32; Hoerr, *And the Wolf Finally Came*, 326; Livernash, *Collective Bargaining in the Basic Steel Industry*, 254–58; Harris, *The Right to Manage*, 95–158.

79. Tiffany, *The Decline of American Steel*, 42–63; Harris, *The Right to Manage*, 95–158; R. Alton Lee, *Truman and Taft–Hartley: A Question of Mandate* (Lexington: University of Kentucky Press, 1966), 22–105; Tomlins, *The State and the Unions*, 282–316; Lichtenstein, *Labor's War at Home*, 238–41; Reutter, *Sparrows Point*, 324–34. Murray appears to have understood which segment of the business community was pressing hardest for antilabor legislation. He noted that Senator Robert Taft "does not speak for truly big business" in reviewing how the act was passed (USA–EBP, May 19, 1947, 179–80).

80. For examples of Murray's views of senior administration officials, see his description of Attorney General Tom Clark as a man who "wanted to indulge himself in a widespread campaign of persecution" against the CIO, Murray's denunciation of reconversion chief John W. Snyder as "an enemy of organized labor," and his oft-repeated complaint that the problems with Truman come from "the Snyders that are around him" (USA–EBP, May 24, 1945, 120–21, December 10, 1945, 120). See also USA–EBP, July 30, 1945, 12, 79–80; Schatz, "Philip Murray," 252–53.

81. CIO–EBP, May 16, 1947, 206–33.

82. CIO–EBP, January 22, 1948, 27–245. The vote technically was over whether or not to support a third party, but both sides understood that rejecting a third party ensured a formal endorsement of the Democratic ticket later that year. See esp. 26–132.

83. USA–EBP, February 16, 1948, 29, also 21–28; Harvey A. Levenstein, *Communism, Anti-Communism and the CIO* (Westport, Conn.: Greenwood Press, 1981), 225.

84. There had been other contenders for the general counsel post. According to one journalist, Murray "was finding it hard to choose from among four candidates when Jacob Potofsky and Van A. Bittner, both key CIO leaders, urged him to pick a fifth—Goldberg." See the profile of Goldberg by A. H. Raskin, "Troubleshooter on the New Frontier," *New York Times Magazine* February 12, 1961, 19. See also USA–EBP, February 16, 1948, 21–29.

85. USA–EBP, November 15, 1952, 36. Goldberg's reminiscence was part of an informal eulogy he delivered to the board at its first meeting after Murray's death.

86. AJG.

87. Ibid.

88. On the larger significance of Pressman's ouster and replacement with Goldberg, see Hamby, *Beyond the New Deal*, 216–17.

89. USA–EBP, November 15, 1952, 36–37.

90. Lester Tanzer, *The Kennedy Circle* (New York: Van Rees Press, 1961), 276; "Labor's Plenipotentiary," *Fortune*, March 1960, 224; AJG.

91. AJG. See also USA–EBP, July 15, 1948, 6–12, 55–58, November 15, 1952, 38.

92. Goldberg, for example, counseled the union's officers not to sign the noncommunist affidavits until the courts finished with the pension matter, because acting on the former issue might strip the courts of their jurisdiction over the pension question (USA–EBP, June 9, 1948, 45–46; "Groundwork Laid for Test Case," *Steel Labor*, June 1948, 3). See also USA–EBP, May 6, 1948, 25–26, July 15, 1948, 6–8, 10–12, 55–58, November 15, 1952, 38; Livernash, *Collective Bargaining in the Basic Steel Industry*, 258–60; AJG. Information about the NLRB ruling is from those sources and from Goldberg's two memos on that subject, both dated April 13, 1948, to Murray and the USA district directors and staff representatives. See the folder marked "Legal Department File—1948," Philip Murray Papers, ML-CUA.

93. USA–EBP, July 2, 1947, 19.

94. Ibid., 19–20; AJG.

95. AJG; Daniel Bell's profile of Goldberg, "Pension Strategist," *Fortune*, January 1950, 151. Goldberg, Bell wrote, had emerged as "Murray's chief of staff." See also "Labor Lawyers Walk a Tightrope," *Business Week*, September 4, 1954, which reported that Goldberg "virtually ran the CIO in Murray's later years—all problems were funneled through Goldberg before reaching Murray" (51); "Exit Goldberg," *New York World-Telegram and Sun*, November 19, 1953. Goldberg later described himself as Murray's "alter ego" (Arthur J. Goldberg Memoir, AFL–CIO MOHC, GMMA 5).

96. The term *social contract* is used to mean, as political scientist Peter Hauslohner has defined it, "a set of norms, constituency benefits, and political–economic institutions which elite and public . . . [regard] as legitimate means of regulating their mutual relations." For Hauslohner's use of that concept in a very different context, see his article "Gorbachev's Social Contract," *Soviet Economy* 3 (1987): 54–89.

97. See the USA–EBP for the 1948–49 period, passages of which pertaining to each specific area of dispute are cited in the following discussion; Lichtenstein, *Labor's War*

at Home, 233–45; Tomlins, *The State and the Unions*, 252–316; Tiffany, *The Decline of American Steel*, 21–63.

98. USA–EBP, June 26, 1946, 311. See also Hoerr, *And the Wolf Finally Came*, 229–31.

99. USA Vice-President Clinton Golden reported to the executive board that in speaking with management economists during a conference held in September 1946, "one of these fellows in the bunch said, 'Of course, then we have got to contact the matter around us on an industrywide basis.' . . . it appeared that in some capacity he had been in Sweden and in Sweden he painted a glowing picture of how lovely and beautiful the relationships were in that country, and according to him the whole thing could be traced back to the fact that a number of years ago they determined upon some sort of pattern on an industrywide basis. . . . What I am trying to point up is . . . that there is apparently a good deal of discussion going on about some industrywide collective bargaining but without, I feel, any clear [agreement about] . . . what the industry consists of and just how you do the thing" (USA–EBP, October 2, 1946, 138–40). Golden noted at an earlier meeting that the needle trades and the ACW had already established a precedent in the United States for coordinated bargaining (USA–EBP, June 24, 1946, 62–63).

100. The highly centralized governing structure of the USA is described in Lloyd Ulman, *The Government of the Steel Workers' Union* (New York: Wiley, 1962). See also Lichtenstein, *Labor's War at Home*, 25. The connection between concentrating power at the top of labor organizations and reaching a social compact with management is made in Robert Salisbury, "Why No Corporatism in America?" in Phillippe C. Schmitter and Gerhard Lehmbruch, eds., *Trends Toward Corporatist Intermediation* (Beverly Hills, Calif.: Sage, 1979), 213–30. See also Graham Wilson, "Why Is There No Corporatism in the United States?" in Phillippe C. Schmitter and Gerhard Lehmbruch, eds., *Patterns of Corporatist Policy-Making* (Beverly Hills, Calif.: Sage, 1982), 219–36.

101. USA–EBP, February 16, 1948, 138. Murray was referring to the eleven CIO Executive Board members who had voted against the Truman and Marshall Plan endorsements in the meeting that led to the ouster of Pressman.

102. Levenstein, *Communism, Anti-Communism and the CIO*, esp. 219–29.

103. Ibid., 219–29; AJG.

104. Lichtenstein, *Labor's War at Home*, 213–14; Levenstein, *Communism, Anti-Communism and the CIO*, 219–29; AJG.

105. At that point Murray still remained unenthusiastic about Truman, regardless of his prospects. As he told the USA Executive Board in early 1948, "Now I think almost every member of this Board knows that I am not in love with Harry Truman. . . . But I do love America and . . . its labor organizations" (USA–EBP, February 16, 1948, 144). Goldberg also counseled Murray to stay with Truman because the rank and file would do so anyway, thereby undercutting Murray's claim to speak on their behalf if the CIO chief backed someone else. Goldberg Memoir, AFL-CIO MOHC, 12; AJG.

106. Murray reported to the USA Executive Board that the unity talks had broken down on the AFL side because of Lewis. The meeting between the AFL and CIO chiefs had taken place during the same month in which Taft–Hartley had been enacted, and Murray explicitly connected the two events (USA–EBP, May 20, 1947, 370–80). The role of the LLPE in the 1948 campaign is recounted briefly in Donovan, *Conflict and Crisis*, 417. See also McClure, *The Problems of Postwar Labor*, 224–27; Brody, *Workers in Industrial America*, 217–18; Robert H. Zieger, "George Meany:

Labor's Organization Man," and Melvyn Dubofsky and Warren Van Tine, "John L. Lewis and the Triumph of Mass Production Unionism," both in Melvyn Dubofsky and Warren Van Tine, eds., *Labor Leaders in America* (Urbana: University of Illinois Press, 1987), 332–33 and 204–5, respectively.

107. AJG. See also the letter from Lillian Herstein to Goldberg, May 19, 1946, in which she discussed Keenan in response to Goldberg's query about what the AFL official would do after the war. The letter is in the file marked "1946 Personal Correspondence," Goldberg Papers.

108. McClure, *The Problems of Postwar Labor*, 213, 218–32; Hamby, *Beyond the New Deal*, 241–65; USA–EBP, February 16, 1948, 144–47. In the middle of October Murray told a group of USA officials engaged in political action work nationwide that they were "crazy" to think that Truman was going to win (David J. McDonald Memoir, AFL-CIO MOHC, 16).

109. AJG.

110. Donovan, *Conflict and Crisis*, 438. Truman had opened his fall campaign with a speech in Detroit to an audience of around 100,000, most of whom were auto-workers. The centerpiece of his address was a slashing attack on Taft–Hartley, which Truman said would "enslave totally the workingman" if it were carried "to its full implication." He closed with a speech in St. Louis that echoed the same theme. See Harry S. Truman, *Public Papers of the Presidents of the United States: Harry S. Truman, 1948* (Washington, D.C.: U.S. Government Printing Office, 1964), 479; Donovan, *Conflict and Crisis*, 417, 431; Hamby, *Beyond the New Deal*, 235, 244, 249–50. On the newly elected liberals of 1948, see Donovan, *Conflict and Crisis*, 418. Note that of the new senators, those from southern and western states where unions were weakest publicly favored a much more confrontational approach to labor, but privately they supported the postwar agreement that appeared to be emerging. Their position was close to that of the business realists. Johnson, for example, had voted for Taft–Hartley as a congressman but privately did not favor an assault on unions. See Robert Caro, *The Years of Lyndon Johnson: Means of Ascent* (New York: Knopf, 1990), 15, 125, 223–28, 253, 275–76, 283–84, 287–92; Robert Dallek, *Lone Star Rising: Lyndon Johnson and His Times, 1908–1960* (New York: Oxford University Press, 1991), 159–348. See also the remarks of LBJ's chief legislative aide George Reedy, who had studied indus-trial relations under Paul Douglas at the University of Chicago during the 1930s, in George Reedy Memoir, OHC, LBJL, pt. 9, 6, and more generally throughout. As for the benefit Truman received from Democratic candidates running for Congress and state office, see Richard S. Kirkendall, "Election of 1948," in Arthur M. Schlesinger Jr. and Fred L. Israel, eds., *History of American Presidential Elections*, vol. 4 (New York: McGraw-Hill, 1971), 3137–45. Kirkendall noted that before 1948, winning Demo-cratic presidential candidates "had led their congressional tickets, with the margin since 1896 averaging 7.5 per cent. Truman, however, ran behind his congressional ticket. This can be explained in part by the appeal of Wallace and Thurmond to some Democrats; but in some places, other candidates in Truman's party, or the active supporters of those candidates, above all, organized labor, carried him to victory" (3143).

111. "Our 'Laboristic' President," *Fortune*, December 1948, 84.

112. In the same *Fortune* article about the outcome of the election, its editors showed their understanding of that reality: "Well, what did we expect from Dewey? He would have done many or most of the things the Democrats are going to do" ("Our 'Laboristic' President," 84).

113. Information about voting behavior along class lines can be found in Richard

404   Notes to pages 72–73

Oestreicher, "Urban Working-Class Political Behavior and Theories of American Electoral Politics, 1870–1940," *Journal of American History* 74 (1988): 1285–86; Arthur C. Wolfe, "Trends in Labor Union Voting Behavior, 1948–1968," *Industrial Relations* 9 (1969): 1–2. On voter turnout, see Kirkendall, "Election of 1948," 3137–45, who concluded that "many former Roosevelt supporters in the big cities, including wage-earners, stayed at home and thereby helped Dewey carry Maryland, Pennsylvania, Connecticut, and New Jersey with only slightly larger votes than he had received when he lost them in 1944, and to carry New York and Michigan even though larger totals in those states had failed to carry them for him in 1944" (3143–44).

114. On the appeal to Americans of republicanism and socialism, see Bernard Bailyn, *Ideological Origins of the American Revolution* (Cambridge, Mass.: Harvard University Press, 1967); Eric Foner, *Free Soil, Free Labor, Free Men: The Ideology of the Republican Party Before the Civil War* (New York: Oxford University Press, 1970); Eric Foner, *Politics and Ideology in the Age of the Civil War* (New York: Oxford University Press, 1980); Nick Salvatore, *Eugene V. Debs: Citizen and Socialist* (Urbana: University of Illinois Press, 1982); James Weinstein, *The Decline of Socialism in America, 1912–1915* (New Brunswick, N.J.: Rutgers University Press, 1984).

115. "Pension Strategist," *Fortune*, January 1950, 151; "Labor Lawyers Walk a Tightrope," *Business Week*, September 4, 1954, 51; "Exit Goldberg," *New York World-Telegram and Sun*, November 19, 1953; AJG.

116. The Taft–Hartley Fumble," *Fortune*, May 1949, 190.

117. Lee, *Truman and Taft–Hartley*, 155–64.

118. AJG. See also Goldberg's explanation of why the lobbying effort failed, in USA–EBP, May 3–4, 1949, 123–41, 173–76; Lee, *Truman and Taft–Hartley*, 155–207.

119. AJG.

120. See USA–EBP, May 3–4, 1949, 123–41, 173–76; CIO–EBP, May 18–19, 1949, 279–379, 645–879, where Goldberg, Murray, and the radicals debated the issue heatedly and at great length. See also "The Sell-out on Taft–Hartley," memo dated May 9, 1949, in folder 21, box 48, AFL Legislative Department Papers, GMMA; "Goldberg Gets Ovation on This: We Want the Wagner Act Back," *CIO News*, November 29, 1948, 20.

121. The Railway Brotherhoods, unions affiliated with neither the AFL nor CIO, also opposed Goldberg's compromise, for reasons essentially the same as Lewis's. On that point, and for information about the failure to secure repeal of the act more generally, see Lee, *Truman and Taft–Hartley*, 155–207; USA–EBP, May 3–4, 1949, 123–41, 173–76; CIO–EBP, May 18, 1949, 279–370; "The Taft–Hartley Fumble," *Fortune*, May 1949, 189–91; "The Sell-out on Taft–Hartley"; "Union Chiefs Help Truman on Message," *Philadelphia Inquirer*, December 25, 1948; the copy of Goldberg's testimony before the Senate Labor Committee, February 9, 1949, in Goldberg Papers; Dubofsky and Van Tine, "John L. Lewis," 204–5; AJG.

122. Lee, *Truman and Taft–Hartley*, 155–207; USA–EBP, May 3–4, 1949, 123–41, 173–76; CIO–EBP, May 18, 1949, 279–370; "The Taft–Hartley Fumble," 189–91; "The Sell-out on Taft-Hartley"; "Union Chiefs Help Truman on Message"; the copy of Goldberg's testimony before the Senate Labor Committee, February 9, 1949; Dubofsky and Van Tine, "John L. Lewis," 204–5; AJG.

123. Truman did order Taft–Hartley injunctions three times after winning the 1948 election, against the UMW; the radical Mine, Mill, and Smelter Workers Union; and a steelworkers' local whose strike was impeding the production of atomic weapons. The first two instances involved unions that had opposed the Taft–Hartley

bargain and thus were not assured of its protection, and the third did not seriously offend the USA leadership, which opposed strikes that impaired nuclear weapons production. See "Picking up the Pieces," *Fortune*, December 1952, 84; "Labor Notes," *Fortune*, January 1953, 68; "Memorandum from Harold Enarson to John Steelman," February 13, 1951, folder marked "Memos of White House Assistant," box 4, Harold L. Enarson Papers, HSTL; CIO–EBP, February 5, 1953, 113–14.

124. CIO–EBP, May 18, 1949, 279–318.

125. CIO–EBP, May 17, 1949, 171. The UE leadership's refusal by that point to pay its per capita dues had reduced the radicals' share of the overall CIO dues-paying membership from what had been perhaps one-third to the figure Murray gave. On the UE leaders' decision to withhold the union's per capita contribution to the CIO, see Levenstein, *Communism, Anti-Communism and the CIO*, 292–94.

126. See CIO–EBP, May 17, 1949, 172. The USA leadership had already acted with respect to its own membership. At the USA annual convention held in May 1948 the delegates had approved a change in the union's constitution. Members found to be "consistent supporters" of the Communist Party were now barred from holding a union office, thereby reversing the executive board's decision of three years earlier. See Reutter, *Sparrows Point*, 352.

127. Goldberg himself later acknowledged that some of the radicals on the CIO Executive Board had proved in the 1930s and early 1940s to be "pretty able fellows." AJG.

128. "Pension Strategist," 151; USA–EBP, May 3, 1949, 144–45; Livernash, *Collective Bargaining in the Basic Steel Industry*, 216–17, 261–69; Cyrus Ching, *Review and Reflection* (New York: B. C. Forbes, 1953), 73–75, 130–31; David McDonald, *Union Man* (New York: Dutton, 1969), 204–9; Brody, *Workers in Industrial America*, 192–94; Hoerr, *And the Wolf Finally Came*, 79–80, 104; AJG.

129. The board had conducted hearings, the published transcripts of which took up twenty volumes. Dorothy Goldberg, who attended the board's sessions, wrote later in her diary that "I remember how dull the Steel Hearings were in the beginning . . . and then they took on more clarity later so that during the excitement of the big strike I could finally begin to understand that a contest was taking place that had elements of extraordinary drama behind all that stuffy terminology" (DKGD, entry for August (?), 1962). See also Tiffany, *The Decline of American Steel*, 84–86; Livernash, *Collective Bargaining in the Basic Steel Industry*, 216–17, 262–69; I. W. Abel, *Collective Bargaining–Labor Relations in Steel: Then and Now* (New York: Columbia University Press, 1976), 46–48. Truman's telegram to Goldberg notifying him of the Steel Board's findings is in Goldberg Papers.

130. "Pension Strategist," 151. The strike was technically over management's refusal to bargain over pensions, not its refusal to yield them, but the end result was the same (USA–EBP, May 3, 1949, 144–45, July 13, 1949, 8–10, July 25, 1949, 22–54, September 12, 1949, 6–68, November 18, 1949, 15–21). See also "Steel Trap," *Fortune*, July 1949, 178; "As Steel Goes . . ." *Fortune*, October 1949, 191–92; "Those Pensions," *Fortune*, December 1949, 209–10; "Steel Town Puts Hopes on Truman," *New York Times*, October 3, 1949; Livernash, *Collective Bargaining in the Basic Steel Industry*, 216–17, 258–69; Ching, *Review and Reflection*, 73–75, 130–31; McDonald, *Union Man*, 204–9; Brody, *Workers in Industrial America*, 192–94; Hoerr, *And the Wolf Finally Came*, 79–80, 104; AJG.

131. USA–EBP, September 12, 1949, 68. See also Brody, *Workers in Industrial America*, 193; Livernash, *Collective Bargaining in the Basic Steel Industry*, 143–45.

132. On the last point, see USA–EBP, November 18, 1949, 21, where Goldberg

urged the district directors to treat the U.S. Steel plan as the basic one for the industry.

133. On the capacity expansion issue in steel, see Tiffany, *The Decline of American Steel*, 21–102. Information about the acceptance of Keynesian ideas in the business community comes from Collins, *The Business Response to Keynes*, 115–41; Blum, *V Was for Victory*, 323–32.

134. Many of those ideas were summarized in a report issued by the labor committee of the Twentieth Century Fund, entitled "Partners in Production: A Basis for Labor–Management Understanding." The report's authors included representatives from the War Labor Board, the NAM, and the CIO, as well as a leading arbitrator and a prominent publisher. It was reviewed in "Industrial Relations: A Twentieth Century Fund Report Holds up a Signpost," *Fortune*, February 1949, 172. A similar review, "Industry Partners?" appeared in *Business Week*, February 26, 1949, 132. The report's recommendations had emerged from a survey undertaken in 1948 by the Twentieth Century Fund's staff. Its findings are collected in "Labor and Management Look at Collective Bargaining: A Canvas of Leaders' Views." A copy of this very interesting volume is available at the HSTL. Other sources used in arriving at conclusions contained in this paragraph are AJG, CIO–EBP, USA–EBP, and the secondary sources cited throughout this book.

135. USA–EBP, May 12, 1946, 51–54. See also Brinkley, "The Concept of New Deal Liberalism," and "The New Deal and the Idea of the State," 85–121.

136. On the emergence of the ADA and the content of its program, see Steven M. Gillon, *Politics and Vision: The ADA and American Liberalism, 1947–1985* (New York: Oxford University Press, 1987), esp. 3–130; Arthur M. Schlesinger Jr., *The Vital Center, The Politics of Freedom* (Boston: Houghton Mifflin, 1949). By virtue of his ties to the labor movement, Goldberg was not formally connected with the ADA because the CIO had adopted a policy barring affiliation with such organizations, so as to preserve unity within its ranks. But even though Goldberg did not belong to the ADA, he was representative of its membership. See Gillon, *Politics and Vision*, who concluded that the "'typical' member was a Jewish man, 'somewhat under forty years of age, a professional holding a bachelor's degree, married with just under two children per family' who lived in a single home which he owned or was purchasing" (23). Most ADA members were not working class in either status or origin, although much of the ADA's program had been supplied to it by the labor movement. See Karen Orren, "Union Politics and Postwar Liberalism in the United States, 1946–1979," in Karen Orren and Stephen Skowronek, eds., *Studies in American Political Development* (New Haven, Conn.: Yale University Press, 1986), vol. 1, 215–52.

137. USA–EBP, May 24, 1945, 111–14. On the Attlee victory, see USA–EBP, July 30, 1945, 85, when the board responded to the news by sending congratulatory telegrams to Attlee and TUC chairman Ernest Bevin. For an early expression of the AFL's interest in rebuilding the European labor movement, see the letter dated May 28, 1946, from AFL Vice-President Matthew Woll to Truman, in which Woll, who chaired the AFL Committee on International Labor Relations, urged federal government support for "the restoration of free trade unions and consumer cooperatives." A copy of the letter is in the folder marked "General File—Labor," box 136, Truman Papers. See also Anthony Carew, *Labour Under the Marshall Plan: The Politics of Productivity and the Marketing of Management Science* (Manchester: Manchester University Press, 1987), 59–79.

138. At the USA Executive Board meeting at which the decision to support the Marshall Plan was made, Murray noted that "for the information of our Executive

Board . . . the T.U.C., that is, the British trade union movement, is in wholehearted accord. . . . The Belgian trade union movement likewise is supporting our position, and the unions from the Netherlands, the low countries. . . . There is a divided opinion among the labor leaders of Italy. . . . Manifestations of opposition . . . are coming largely from the eastern countries which, for the moment, are satellites of Russia. The Czech labor movement has given no expression yet to what its convictions might be . . . although many of its leaders have, by indirection, communicated to me their thoughts, and that is that if they are free they want to support the Marshall Plan" (USA–EBP, February 16, 1948, 158–59).

139. "Labor's Two Worlds," *Fortune*, February 1950, 38a; Peter Weiler, "The United States, International Labor, and the Cold War: The Breakup of the World Federation of Trade Unions," *Diplomatic History* 5 (Winter 1981): 1–22; Carew, *Labour Under the Marshall Plan*, 70–79; Michael J. Hogan, *The Marshall Plan: America, Britain, and the Reconstruction of Western Europe, 1947–1952* (Cambridge: Cambridge University Press, 1987), 135–51.

140. One key difference in outcome between the United States and Western Europe was in the social insurance area. Western European workers succeeded in winning what American workers had not, namely, a public system that covered almost everyone. On the instances of Germany and Japan, see Volker R. Berghahn, *The Americanisation of West German Industry, 1945–1973* (Leamington Spa: Berg, 1986), esp. 40–259; Sheldon Garon, *The State and Labor in Modern Japan* (Berkeley and Los Angeles: University of California Press, 1987), esp. 187–249. See also Hogan, *The Marshall Plan*, esp. 135–237, 427–45; Charles S. Maier, *In Search of Stability: Explorations in Historical Political Economy* (Cambridge: Cambridge University Press, 1987), 121–84; the articles contained in Schmitter and Lehmbruch, *Trends Toward Corporatist Intermediation* and *Patterns of Corporatist Policy-Making*; James Miller, *The United States and Italy, 1940–1950: The Politics and Diplomacy of Stabilization* (Chapel Hill: University of North Carolina Press, 1986), esp. 131–274; John H. Goldthorpe, "Problems of Political Economy After the Postwar Period," in Charles S. Maier, ed., *Changing Boundaries of the Political* (Cambridge: Cambridge University Press, 1987), 179–99; Alain Touraine, "Management and the Working Class in Western Europe," *Daedalus* 93 (1964): 304–34.

141. For a discussion of the differences between New Deal policies in the 1930s and the New Deal liberals' postwar program, see Brinkley, "The Concept of New Deal Liberalism," and "The New Deal and the Idea of the State," 85–121.

142. The phrase is from Tomlins, *The State and the Unions*, 245.

143. AJG.

Chapter 4. Containment, Domestic and Foreign

1. Some social critics deplored the new consensus even as they argued that it was deeply rooted in American political culture. For that perspective, see Richard Hofstadter, *The American Political Tradition and the Men Who Made It* (New York: Knopf, 1948) and *The Age of Reform: From Bryan to F.D.R.* (New York: Knopf, 1955). Others, such as the historian Daniel Boorstin, chose instead to celebrate the absence of visible social discord. See, for example, his *The Genius of American Politics* (Chicago: University of Chicago Press, 1953). Despite increasing challenges to the postwar order in the late 1950s, as perceptive a social analyst as Daniel Bell could conclude at the decade's end that the United States in particular and Western industrialized societies more

generally had come to "the end of ideology" or, at least, of competing ones. See Daniel Bell, *The End of Ideology: On the Exhaustion of Political Ideas in the Fifties* (Glencoe: Free Press, 1960). For a more extensive discussion of that trend in American social thought, see John Patrick Diggins, *The Proud Decades: America in War and Peace, 1941–1960* (New York: Norton, 1988), 247–57.

2. With respect to the growth and decline in the size of organized labor, see Nelson Lichtenstein, *Labor's War at Home* (Cambridge: Cambridge University Press, 1982) 80; Christopher L. Tomlins, *The State and the Unions; Labor Relations, Law and the Organized Labor Movement in America, 1880–1960* (Cambridge: Cambridge University Press, 1985), 317; Irving Bernstein, "The Growth of American Unions, 1945–1960," *Labor History* 2 (1961): 135; John T. Dunlop, Eli Ginzberg, Frederick Meyers, Julius Rezler, and Leo Troy, "Comments: Bernstein's Growth of American Unions, 1945-1960," *Labor History* 2 (1961): 374.

3. The material gains of that period are summarized in Diggins, *The Proud Decades*, 177–88. The view that unions benefit workers outside organized labor's own ranks is argued persuasively in Richard B. Freeman and James L. Medoff, *What Do Unions Do?* (New York: Basic Books, 1984), 150–61.

4. This is not meant to suggest that labor engaged in an equal contest with management for control of the state or in enacting legislation, but only that organized labor exercised power that limited what the business community could achieve for itself by acting alone or together with the state. See, on that point, the sources cited in Chapter 1, n. 59. Recent scholarship dealing with labor's power in this period has tended to emphasize its weakness rather than its strength. For examples, see Tomlins, *The State and the Unions*, 317–28; Nelson Lichtenstein, "From Corporatism to Collective Bargaining: Organized Labor and the Eclipse of Social Democracy in the Postwar Era," in Steve Fraser and Gary Gerstle, eds., *The Rise and Fall of the New Deal Order, 1930–80* (Princeton, N.J.: Princeton University Press, 1989), 139–40; David Brody, *Workers in Industrial America: Essays on the Twentieth Century Struggle* (New York: Oxford University Press, 1980), 173–257. For a highly influential if older work that sounds that theme, see C. Wright Mills, *The Power Elite* (New York: Oxford University Press, 1956), 262–68.

5. On Goldberg's illnesses in 1950 and 1955, see his note to David McDonald and his wife, May 25, 1950, in box 60, David J. McDonald Papers, HCLA–PSU; his letter from Jacob Weinstein, Goldberg's rabbi, October 18, 1955, in Jacob Weinstein Papers, CHS; his letter to George Meany, February 1, 1956, in folder 23, box 29, AFL–CIO President's Papers, GMMA.

6. Mary Sperling McAuliffe, *Crisis on the Left: Cold War Politics and American Liberals, 1947–54* (Amherst: University of Massachusetts Press, 1978), 51–62; Harvey A. Levenstein, *Communism, Anti-Communism and the CIO* (Westport, Conn.: Greenwood Press, 1981), 299–307; Bert Cochran, *Labor and Communism: The Conflict That Shaped American Unions* (Princeton, N.J.: Princeton University Press, 1977), 248–344; Robert Shaplen, "Peacemaker," *New Yorker*, pt. 1, April 7, 1962, 78.

7. McAuliffe, *Crisis on the Left*, 51–62; Levenstein, *Communism, Anti-Communism and the CIO*, 299–307; Cochran, *Labor and Communism*, 248–344; Shaplen, "Peacemaker," 78. On Goldberg's role in drafting the constitutional amendment that authorized the expulsions, see the notes from the CIO Executive Board meeting of October 25, 1949, which are in the folder marked "Exec. Bd. Meeting, Oct. 25, 1949," box 1, CIO Secretary-Treasurer's Papers, WPRL, 4, where that official noted that "Curran, Reuther, Rieve, [and] Goldberg prepare constitutional amendment."

8. CIO–EBP, November 16, 1950, 8. The UE's membership, which had stood at

almost 400,000 before the split in the CIO, had by 1962 dwindled to just 55,000 (Lichtenstein, *Labor's War at Home*, 80). The one union that the CIO majority at first proceeded against before relenting was the Furniture Workers, whose radical leaders were voted out of office before the hearings began. Some of the unions facing expulsion tried to fight it in the courts, but all were ultimately ousted (Levenstein, *Communism, Anti-Communism and the CIO*, 302–3). See also CIO–EBP, November 16, 1950, 10–11; William E. Forbath, "The Shaping of the American Labor Movement," *Harvard Law Review* 102 (1989); 1111–32, 1202–33.

9. CIO–EBP, November 16, 1950, 9.

10. Ibid., 8–9.

11. The exact CIO membership is difficult to determine, given the tendency of the federation's leaders to inflate the size of each affiliate. The CIO leadership claimed that the overall CIO membership after the expulsions was just under 5 million (CIO–EBP, November 16, 1950, 10–11). The figure of 4 million members is from "Labor Unity – Chapter Six," *Fortune*, July 1950, 31. More reliable figures for 1946 and 1953 can be found in Lichtenstein, *Labor's War at Home*, 80. See also "Box Score on Communist Influence in U.S. Labor" and "The Thin Red Line," *Fortune*, June 1952, 71–76; "The Thinning Red Line," *Fortune*, February 1954, 82; "Curtains for the C.P.," *Fortune*, March 1956, 206, 208; Ronald W. Schatz, *The Electrical Workers: A History of Labor at General Electric and Westinghouse, 1923–60* (Urbana: University of Illinois Press, 1983), 188–243.

12. USA–EBP, March 24, 1950, 107, also 105–6, 108–12; "Labor Unity – Chapter Six," 31–34; William O. Wagner Jr., *The Politics of Economic Growth: The Truman Administration and the 1949 Recession* (Columbia: University of Missouri Press, 1970), 97–99, 174, 179; Murray's letter, June 24, 1949, to the presidents of all CIO affiliates and industrial union councils summarizing the antirecession program that the CIO Executive Board had adopted, a copy of which is in Goldberg Papers; Steven M. Gillon, *Politics and Vision: The ADA and American Liberalism, 1947–1985* (New York: Oxford University Press, 1987), 63–64.

13. Treasury Secretary John W. Snyder led the effort in the Truman administration against more federal spending to combat the 1949/50 recession (Wagner, *The Politics of Economic Growth*, 96). The result of business pressure against government spending, combined with Snyder's quest for a balanced federal budget, led to a steady decline in government spending as a percentage of the nation's GNP from 10.3 percent in the second quarter of 1949 to 6.9 percent in the third quarter of 1950, a level never again reached to this day (Wagner, *The Politics of Economic Growth*, 171). For the next twelve years, military spending alone ranged from 9 to 13 percent of the GNP, a proportion comparable to that of the German national budget during the late 1930s. See Marty Jezer, *The Dark Ages: Life in the United States, 1945–1960* (Boston: South End Press), 119–23; Robert O. Paxton, *Europe in the Twentieth Century* (New York: Harcourt Brace, 1985), 459, n. 11.

14. USA–EBP, September 21, 1950, 130.

15. Ibid., 131.

16. See USA–EBP, October 4, 1950, 8, for Murray's comment about the guaranteed annual wage. On the difficult question of whether the military buildup was consciously planned in order to achieve a permanently high level of federal government spending that would be acceptable to business managers and their allies in government, no conclusive answer is as yet available. At least some government officials in the spring of 1950 were thinking in those terms. On that point, see Wagner, *The Politics of Economic Growth*, 181–82. On the other hand, one scholar who studied

this issue extensively concluded that the business community before the Korean conflict still thought that private spending alone would be adequate to maintain high levels of production and employment. See William S. Hill Jr., "The Business Community and National Defense, 1943–50" (Ph.D. diss., Stanford University, 1979), 321–81, 407–15.

17. Ronald Schatz suggested that Murray had thought in those terms all along. See his "Philip Murray and the Subordination of the Industrial Unions to the United States Government," in Melvyn Dubofsky and Warren Van Tine, eds., *Labor Leaders in America* (Urbana: University of Illinois Press, 1987), 244. But Murray's conduct over the years indicates an evolution in his thinking. Although he remained an unswerving opponent of fascism from the 1920s onward, he worked closely with radicals during the 1930s and 1940s, indeed as late as 1947 (Schatz, "Philip Murray," 252). The contrast suggests that Murray did not, until quite late in life, consider Soviet socialism, which he called *communism*, to be as repugnant as fascism. An illustration of this difference can be seen in the warm welcome he gave to a Soviet delegation of steelworkers when they attended a USA Executive Board meeting in 1945 at his invitation (USA–EBP, July 30, 1945, 367–97). Six and a half years later, however, Murray linked the Soviet government to words such as *Nazism* and *totalitarian* (USA–EBP, December 17, 1951, 28, January 2, 1952, 36–37). Murray, it should be noted, made those remarks while denouncing steel company executives, whom he described in the same terms.

18. AJG.

19. USA–EBP, October 4, 1950, 16. This hostility to the COLA was typical for American labor unions in the late 1940s and early 1950s. Not until the early 1960s did a majority of union contracts contain a COLA provision (Lichtenstein, "From Corporatism to Collective Bargaining," 141–42).

20. For Murray's thoughts about those issues, see USA–EBP, October 4, 1950, 16–36. On the unending nature of collective bargaining in steel, see John P. Hoerr, *And the Wolf Finally Came: The Decline of the American Steel Industry* (Pittsburgh: University of Pittsburgh Press, 1988), 101–4. Hoerr noted that "the two sides went to the bargaining table in ten of the eleven years between 1946 and 1956. No sooner would one round be over, it seemed, than a new one would start" (101). On the early opposition among union leaders to the COLA idea, see Lichtenstein, "From Corporatism to Collective Bargaining," 141. The fears of a decline in the COLA index and thus of a reduction in pay did not end with the beginning of the Korean War in 1950. As that conflict neared its conclusion, such concerns resurfaced among labor leaders. On this point, see "Battle of the Index," *Fortune*, February 1953, 80–84.

21. USA–EBP, September 21, 1950, 173. See also "Counting out the C.I.O. at Weirton," *Fortune*, December 1950, 47; USA–EBP, November 29, 1950, 15, 25–26; "The Closing Price in Steel," *Fortune*, May 1952, 78; "Practice and Principle," *Fortune*, August 1952, 64–66.

22. USA–EBP, September 21, 1950, 132. See also USA–EBP, November 29, 1950, 30–31; "Bringing Home the Bacon," *Fortune*, October 1950, 45; E. Robert Livernash, *Collective Bargaining in the Basic Steel Industry* (Washington, D.C.: U.S. Department of Labor, 1961), 269–71.

23. CIO–EBP, November 16, 1950, 62–63. See also USA–EBP, September 21, 1950, 119, 129–30; Alonzo Hamby, *Beyond the New Deal: Harry S. Truman and American Liberalism* (New York: Columbia University Press, 1973), 415–18.

24. USA–EBP, November 29, 1950, 14. See also CIO–EBP, October 31, 1951, 76–77, where Murray noted that even though Goldberg "is not an elected officer . . . I

delegate to Brother Goldberg the performance of certain duties. . . . At every stage of every important situation that develops . . . in the city of Washington I usually take occasion to call Art over the telephone, and he talks to me and out of those discussions we resolve that he should follow through at the direction of the President to perform those duties. They are many . . . and extremely important in nature."

25. USA–EBP, April 19, 1951, 80–81. Murray appears to have delegated so much responsibility to Goldberg, rather than to anyone else, in part because he was confident that Goldberg had no ambitions to lead either the USA or the CIO, and thus his growing influence would not threaten members of either group's executive board (McAuliffe, *Crisis on the Left*, 46).

26. Robert J. Donovan, *Tumultuous Years: The Presidency of Harry S. Truman, 1949–53* (New York: Norton, 1981), 324–26; Hamby, *Beyond the New Deal*, 415–18, 446–54; USA–EBP, April 19, 1951, 80–148; Archie Robinson, *George Meany and His Times* (New York: Simon & Schuster, 1981), 158–59. Local units of the two federations had pooled their lobbying efforts even before the ULP emerged. On that point, see "Labor Unity – Chapter Six," *Fortune*, July 1950, 31–34.

27. USA–EBP, April 19, 1951, 87.

28. Eric F. Goldman, *The Crucial Decade – And After: America 1945–1960* (New York: Vintage Books, 1960), 202–18; Hamby, *Beyond the New Deal*, 466–80; Diggins, *The Proud Decades*, 110–17, 147–76.

29. USA–EBP, April 19, 1951, 103–4. See also "Memo for Mr. Steelman," from Harold Enarson, November 1, 1951, file marked "Memos of H. L. Enarson," box 4, Enarson Papers; Maeva Marcus, *Truman and the Steel Seizure Case: The Limits of Presidential Power* (New York: Columbia University Press, 1977), 22–25.

30. CIO–EBP, November 16, 1950, 34. The CIO's PAC had endorsed 237 candidates for Congress, of whom 131 were elected (CIO–EBP, March 15, 1951, 19). See also Hamby, *Beyond the New Deal*, 421–22; Donovan, *Tumultuous Years*, 297–98; "Labor's Failure," *Fortune*, December 1950, 47, where Daniel Bell concluded that labor "was massacred in the November 7th elections."

31. CIO–EBP, November 16, 1950, 37.

32. USA–EBP, April 19, 1951, 87, also 188–93; CIO–EBP, November 16, 1950, 36; "Labor's Failure," *Fortune*, December 1950, 47.

33. CIO–EBP, March 15, 1951, 62–63. Goldberg's remarks were part of a long and quite revealing report to the board about labor's frustrations with the mobilization scheme (45–100). Murray described the situation in even more drastic terms. Truman, he said, "for all practical purposes, had abrogated the Presidency of the United States and had yielded to Wilson the power to operate the domestic economy of the nation" (USA–EBP, April 19, 1951, 131).

34. CIO–EBP, March 15, 1951, 64.

35. Ibid., 66.

36. See USA–EBP, April 19, 1951, 81–127.

37. CIO–EBP, March 15, 1951, 77. Goldberg told the CIO leadership that the employers had behaved so intransigently because they were trying to goad unions into striking and then compel the federal government to use the Taft–Hartley injunction to break such strikes (68–69). See also "Political Bargaining," *Fortune*, April 1951, 53–54; "Dispute over 'Disputes,'" *Fortune*, May 1951, 49–52.

38. The order came after Murray, along with other labor leaders, met with Truman at the White House. Murray gave Truman's advisers a list Goldberg had prepared of proposed amendments to the Defense Production Act (USA–EBP, April 1951, 138–40). Goldberg testified on May 31 before a subcommittee of the Senate Labor Com-

mittee in favor of giving the WSB power to resolve labor–management disputes. A copy of his testimony is in the file marked "1951 Legal Department," in Murray Papers. See also in the same file the press release, July 6, 1951, that Goldberg wrote about the reconstituted WSB; USA–EBP, April 19, 1951, 116–19; Donovan, *Tumultuous Years*, 324–27; Hamby, *Beyond the New Deal*, 446–54; "Stabilizing the Stabilizers," *Fortune*, September 1951, 57–58; John H. Kaufmann, "The Problem of Coordinating Price and Wage Programs in 1950–53," pts. 1 and 2, *Indiana Law Journal* 29 (1954): 499–537, and 30 (1954): 18–58; Bruno Stein, "Wage Stabilization in the Korean War Period: The Role of the Subsidiary Wage Boards," *Labor History* 4 (1963): 161–77.

39. USA–EBP, April 19, 1951, 116–19, 138–40; Donovan, *Tumultuous Years*, 324–27; Hamby, *Beyond the New Deal*, 446–54; "Stabilizing the Stabilizers," *Fortune*, September 1951, 57–58; Kaufmann, "The Problem of Coordinating Price and Wage Programs in 1950–53," pt. 1, 499–537, and pt. 2, 18–58; Stein, "Wage Stabilization in the Korean War Period," 161–77. Goldberg saw the NAM as at the center of business opposition to giving the WSB the power to find facts and make recommendations. On this point, see "Memo to Mr. Murphy" from Harold Enarson, April 16, 1951, 1–2, file marked "Memoranda—White House Assistant," box 4, Enarson Papers.

40. "Stabilizing the Stabilizers," *Fortune*, September 1951, 57. The WSB, Bell noted, had "confined itself mostly to clucking sympathetically over the painful problems brought to it by manufacturers that had to attract manpower, unions whose members suffered from inequities, and union–management combinations warning of strikes and disruptions if increases were not granted." See also on this point, Stein, "Wage Stabilization in the Korean War Period," 161–77. Stein concluded that despite the WSB's existence, "all but a few key wages were set by collective bargaining or by the operation of the labor market" (177).

41. Incentive pay provisions in the Steelworkers' 1949 contract enabled workers to win increases in pay above the ceiling on basic pay raises. On the workings of those provisions, see "Stabilizing the Stabilizers," *Fortune*, September 1951, 57–58; USA–EBP, June 28, 1951, 160, where Murray discussed the issue, noting that "Art Goldberg spends fifty percent of his time on these stabilization cases before the board." Goldberg also spent a good deal of time negotiating who was to be appointed to the new WSB. On that point, see "Memorandum for Dr. Steelman," from Harold Enarson, March 31, 1952, file marked "Memos of H. L. Enarson," box 4, Enarson Papers, where Goldberg's role in suggesting and vetoing prospective appointees was discussed.

42. USA–EBP, April 19, 1951, 117.

43. Ibid., 119. See also "The Main Event," *Fortune*, November 1951, 49, where Daniel Bell observed that "steel negotiations will be a stabilization turning point."

44. USA–EBP, October 4, 1950, 35–36.

45. Some historians have tended to view steel's labor–management relationship as distinctive because it involved a great deal of state scrutiny and intervention. See, for example, Richard W. Nagle, "Collective Bargaining in Basic Steel and the Federal Government, 1945–1960" (Ph.D. diss., Pennsylvania State University, 1978), 1–5. Such a conclusion misses the point. Labor–management negotiations in steel involved state actors to a greater degree precisely because the agreements reached in steel had such important consequences for other industries. The author of the most recent comprehensive study of the steel industry during the 1950s concluded that the large degree of state scrutiny was "justified insofar as the steel sector was an important part of the national economy whose behavior had repercussions beyond its immediate participants." See Paul A. Tiffany, *The Decline of American Steel: How Management,*

Labor and the Government Went Wrong (New York: Oxford University Press, 1988), 137. For a discussion of the existing and very large literature on this subject, see 138–52 and the accompanying notes. And see Richard W. Kalwa, "Collective Bargaining in Basic Steel, 1946–83" (Ph.D. diss., Cornell University, 1985), 1, who contends, on the basis of careful research, that the "case of basic steel is both an essential component of the story of postwar labor relations and a paradigm for other manufacturing industries over this period." On that point, see also Donald F. Barnett and Louis Schorsch, *Steel: Upheaval in a Basic Industry* (Cambridge, Mass.: Ballinger, 1983), 7.

46. American steel production in 1950/51 was enormous by any standard. In the former year, the total output of raw steel was estimated at 45 percent of overall world production. See Barnett and Schorsch, *Steel*, 13, also 22–26; Tiffany, *The Decline of American Steel*, 21–41, 83–102, 155–56. Steel managers' sensitivity to pressure from Kefauver is discussed in Roger M. Blough, *The Washington Embrace of Business* (New York: Columbia University Press, 1975), 36. They were no doubt mindful of the British steel industry's narrow escape from nationalization in the early 1950s, an example that inclined them to cooperate with the Truman administration. See Arthur Marwick, *British Society Since 1945* (Harmondsworth: Penguin Books, 1982), 33, 104.

47. "The Main Event," *Fortune*, November 1951, 49–50; Tiffany, *The Decline of American Steel*, 94–96; Kalwa, "Collective Bargaining in Basic Steel," 27–28; Livernash, *Collective Bargaining in the Basic Steel Industry*, 272–76; USA–EBP, April 19, 1951, 116–23.

48. USA–EBP, January 2, 1952, 37–38. See also USA–EBP, June 13, 1952, 15–17, 50–51.

49. Tiffany, *The Decline of American Steel*, 91–97, 100; Livernash, *Collective Bargaining in the Basic Steel Industry*, 275; Kalwa, "Collective Bargaining in Basic Steel," 27; Marcus, *Truman and the Steel Seizure Case*, 254.

50. See "Memorandum for the President," November 15, 1951, President's Secretary's File, box 136, Truman Papers, in which the CEA members argued that "current and prospective steel profits are high enough to absorb such wage increases as are desirable." An indication of Truman's attitude is found in his handwritten note to labor troubleshooter John Steelman at the bottom of a memo, that "Jack Kroll and Arthur Goldberg came in to see me on Friday October 19, '51 to assure me that they wanted no work stoppage, that they were ready to bargain and that they want to do the right thing. I believe them." See "Memorandum for the President Re: 'The Steel Case,'" October 19, 1951, box 136, President's Secretary's File, Truman Papers, 2. See also Tiffany, *The Decline of American Steel*, 91–97, 100; Livernash, *Collective Bargaining in the Basic Steel Industry*, 275; Kalwa, "Collective Bargaining in Basic Steel," 27.

51. USA–EBP, December 17, 1951, 3. See also Kalwa, "Collective Bargaining in Basic Steel," 27; Livernash, *Collective Bargaining in the Basic Steel Industry*, 275.

52. USA–EBP, December 17, 1951, 28–29.

53. USA–EBP, December 27, 1951, 5–6. See also Goldberg's remark on 36–37 that "I know that Phil has not been bothered, although I have been trying to get him bothered, in the slightest degree about the Taft–Hartley Act. He told me that from the start. I know that is his view. I am a lawyer and I often feel differently. But that has not entered into this recommendation as far as I know, not one iota."

54. Ibid., 6–7.

55. Ibid., 37, also 25–36. Goldberg had a difficult time persuading Murray to go along and at one point threatened to quit unless Murray spoke with Truman about the matter. See Goldberg Memoir, AFL–CIO MOHC, 10; Shaplen, "Peacemaker," 84.

56. USA–EBP, December 27, 1951, 37.

57. Pressure from the USA helped produce that result. The union had blasted Wilson for criticizing the WSB decision. Goldberg, according to White House aide Harold Enarson's "Memo for the Files," March 25, 1952, 1, "refused to believe Wilson had said what he had until he saw the full text of Wilson's remarks. Goldberg went to work on a statement promptly . . . which said approximately as follows (1) Mr. Wilson has wrecked the Stabilization Program; (2) Wilson has wrecked the WSB; (3) Murray will attend no meetings with Wilson; (4) Mr. Wilson by his own acts brought about a strike. . . . [WSB Chairman] Feinsinger called Goldberg and as a result the statement was toned down somewhat." See the memo in the folder marked "Steel Strike—Memos and Statements," box 5, Enarson Papers.

58. Enarson's "Memo to Files," 2, March 5, 1952, file marked "Steel Negotiations Memos, 1951–52," box 5, Enarson Papers. According to Enarson, Goldberg had said also "that [WSB Chairman] Feinsinger was in danger of being 'intimidated' in the steel case, that he was just plain scared. . . . The industry campaign against the Board, as expressed by letters and by the Allen resolution, was pressuring Feinsinger on the one hand, and Wilson was pressuring him on the other" (1). See also Livernash, *Collective Bargaining in the Basic Steel Industry*, 277–78; Tiffany, *The Decline of American Steel*, 98. Although some students of this period later suggested that Goldberg and his colleagues underestimated business influence in the postwar order, his remarks indicated a keen awareness of the existing power relationships. On this point, see, for example, Katherine Van Wezel Stone, "The Post-War Paradigm in American Labor Law," *Yale Law Journal* 90 (1981): 1509–80, who argues that Goldberg and his fellow labor leaders believed that management and labor shared power equally in the workplace and did so independently of the larger political order. The evidence presented throughout this manuscript indicates that the leading "industrial pluralists," as Stone calls them, shared at most a hope that such a world could be constructed. Goldberg and his USA colleagues, however, appear never to have believed that they lived in one.

59. USA–EBP, April 11, 1952, 12. See also Schatz, "Philip Murray," 234–35. The use of a Taft–Hartley injunction was considered by White House staffers, but Truman remained adamantly opposed. See Harold Enarson's "Memo to Files," March 5, 1952, and "For Goldberg," April 8, 1952, Enarson's handwritten notes on the arguments for using Taft–Hartley, in the files marked "Steel Strike—Memos and Statements" and "Steel Negotiations Memos, 1951–52," respectively, box 5, Enarson Papers; Tiffany, *The Decline of American Steel*, 99.

60. USA–EBP, April 11, 1952, 12–13. See also Goldberg Memoir, AFL–CIO MOHC, 11–12.

61. USA–EBP, May 7, 1952, 9.

62. On the issue of a steel price increase, see Truman aide David Stowe's minutes of a White House bargaining session held in the first week of May between labor and management. The notes, entitled "Meeting with the Labor Group" [not dated], and the ones entitled "Joint Session of Labor and Management Representatives, 2:45 P.M." [not dated], are in the folder marked "Steel Strike—1952-1," box 4 of David H. Stowe Papers, HSTL. The memos were two in a series written by Stowe that I used for the account of the steel negotiations in this section.

63. "Joint Session of Labor and Management Representatives, 2:45 P.M." [not dated], 3, folder marked "Steel Strike—1952-1," box 4, Stowe Papers. See also Stowe's notes from the other bargaining sessions, also in that same file; Tiffany, *The Decline of American Steel*, 83–102.

64. On the union-shop point, see David Stowe's minutes of a White House bargaining session held in the first week of May between labor and management: "Industry was adamant that there would be no union shop and the unions were equally as adamant that there would be [a] union shop." Joint Meeting, 9:20 P.M. [not dated]," 1, file marked "Steel Strike – 1952-1," box 4, Stowe Papers. See also Tiffany, *The Decline of American Steel*, 21–41, 61–63, 65–66, 81–82, 91–94, 128–37, 142–44.

65. USA–EBP, June 13, 1952, 49–50, also 14–17, 51–52; December 17, 1951, 20–29; January 2, 1952, 36–37; February 12, 1952, 71–73.

66. "Labor's Coming of Middle Age," *Fortune*, October 1951, 114–15, 137–38, 140, 142, 144, 149–50; Howell Harris, *The Right to Manage: Industrial Relations Policies of American Business in the 1940's* (Madison: University of Wisconsin Press, 1982), 95–104; "Sleeper Issue in Steel," *Fortune*, April 1952, 55–56.

67. USA–EBP, May 7, 1952, 29–30.

68. Murray, like Goldberg, appears never to have believed that labor's influence with the government was equal to that of management's. See the discussion of that point in n. 58. Goldberg saw Congress as containing many supporters of the steel managers, although such sympathizers, he concluded, proved to be more vocal than influential (CIO–EBP, February 5, 1953, 122–25).

69. USA–EBP, April 11, 1952, 24. See also Tiffany, *The Decline of American Steel*, 100, where he noted that "industry appeals to mass opinion for repudiation of Truman's 'sad mistake' came primarily from representatives of the other firms, whom Fairless was under pressure to appease in order to maintain his industrywide coalition."

70. Marcus, *Truman and the Steel Seizure Case*, esp. 58–101, 195–235, 249–60; Harold Enarson's summary of the major events as seen from the perspective of a senior White House aide, entitled "The Steel Strike – A Modern Tragedy," in the file marked "Steel Strike – Memos and Statements," box 5, Enarson Papers; Livernash, *Collective Bargaining in the Basic Steel Industry*, 278–81; Tiffany, *The Decline of American Steel*, 99–100; Donovan, *Tumultuous Years*, 382–91; Hamby, *Beyond the New Deal*, 454–58; "Hard Bargaining," *Fortune*, August 1952, 64.

71. USA–EBP, July 25, 1952, 3–10; "Memorandum for Dr. Steelman" from Harold Enarson, July 28, 1952, folder marked "Memos of H. L. Enarson," box 4, Enarson Papers; Livernash, *Collective Bargaining in the Basic Steel Industry*, 283–84; Tiffany, *The Decline of American Steel*, 101; Kalwa, "Collective Bargaining in Basic Steel," 28. Murray had hinted at Fairless's greater flexibility in discussing the negotiations at a meeting of the USA Executive Board on May 7, 1952 (USA–EBP, May 7, 1952, 19–24). Although U.S. Steel's management had pushed throughout the 1952 negotiations for changes in Clause 2B, in the end the company's leaders abandoned this demand, thereby signaling that the industry's core firm continued to support the labor–management détente achieved between 1945 and 1949. On that point, see Murray's summary of his meeting with Fairless at the White House on July 24, 1952, when a final settlement was reached, in USA–EBP, July 25, 1952, 6–10. Lovett's remark at a news conference that the steel strike was doing more harm to the American military effort than "the worst possible enemy bombing raid could have done" appears to have broken the logjam. Only that statement by a sympathetic member of the administration finally helped dissolve managerial opposition to accepting the WSB recommendations. See Tiffany, *The Decline of American Steel*, 101, quoting Lovett; A. H. Raskin, "Steel Strike Is Settled with Increases in Pay and Prices," *New York Times*, July 25, 1952. And see also "The Disputed Disputes," *Fortune*, June 1952, 71–72; "Caretaker Board," *Fortune*, September 1952, 69–70.

72. USA–EBP, July 25, 1952, 68, also 67; Schatz, "Philip Murray," 254–55; "Union-Shop Issue," *Fortune*, February 1952, 62; "Big Business Is Organized – By Labor," *Fortune*, June 1952, 74; "Hard Bargaining," *Fortune*, August 1952, 62; "The Union Shop in Steel," *Fortune*, December 1952, 90.

73. USA–EBP, July 25, 1952, 67–68.

74. Schatz, "Philip Murray," 251–55; the sources cited in n. 39–40; Donovan, *Tumultuous Years*, 382–409; Hamby, *Beyond the New Deal*, 454–80. For the argument that labor's alliance with the Democrats in these years had been almost totally devoid of accomplishment, see Mike Davis, "The Barren Marriage of Labour and the Democratic Party," *New Left Review* 124 (1980): 76–78; Mike Davis, *Prisoners of the American Dream* (London: Verso, 1986), 52–101. One measure of the CIO's appreciation for what Truman's administration had done for labor can be found in the executive board's decision in 1954 to contribute $150,000 to the Truman Library Foundation. The USA Executive Board approved at the same time an additional contribution of $100,000 (CIO–EBP, May 10, 1954, 41–46). Some indications of business hostility to the Truman administration for its policies toward labor can be found in Tiffany, *The Decline of American Steel*, 59–63, 83–105, 128–29; Robert W. Griffith, "Dwight D. Eisenhower and the Corporate Commonwealth," *American Historical Review* 87 (1982): 96–100.

75. See "The Next President," *Fortune*, May 1952, 80, where Daniel Bell reported that the AFL would "sit this campaign out" if the Republicans chose Eisenhower, but if Taft received the G.O.P. nomination, "the A.F. of L. will go all out in opposition." Taft blamed his defeat on the New York financial community, the publishers of most influential newspapers identified with the Republican Party, and most GOP governors, who formed the core of Eisenhower's support. See Barton J. Bernstein, "Election of 1952," in Arthur M. Schlesinger Jr. and Fred L. Israel, eds., *History of American Presidential Elections*, vol. 4 (New York: McGraw-Hill, 1971), 3231–32, also 3224–30; Robert M. Collins, *The Business Response to Keynes, 1929–1964* (New York: Columbia University Press, 1981), 142–72; Harris, *The Right to Manage*, 129–58; Griffith, "Eisenhower and the Corporate Commonwealth," esp. 88–109; Schatz, "Philip Murray," 253–55; Tiffany, *The Decline of American Steel*, 5–105; Goldman, *The Crucial Decade*, 219–20; Diggins, *The Proud Decades*, 122–25; Stephen Ambrose, *Eisenhower: Soldier, General of the Army, President-Elect, 1890–1952* (New York: Simon & Schuster, 1983), 464–542.

76. Bernstein, "Election of 1952," 3224–34; Ambrose, *Eisenhower: Soldier*, 458–549; Donovan, *Tumultuous Years*, 392–401; Goldman, *The Crucial Decade*, 202–36; Hamby, *Beyond the New Deal*, 481–93; Collins, *The Business Response to Keynes*, 142–72; Harris, *The Right to Manage*, 129–58; Griffith, "Eisenhower and the Corporate Commonwealth," 87–122; Diggins, *The Proud Decades*, 122–36; David C. Plotke, "The Democratic Political Order, 1932–1972" (Ph.D. diss., University of California at Berkeley, 1985), 689–90; Eli Ginzberg's Memoir, OHC, DDEL, esp. 5–14, 100–8.

77. Goldberg explained his reservations about Stevenson's run for governor as follows: "I told him [in 1948] to run for the Senate. It was Jack Arvey who engineered the deal making him the governor, for which I thought he was not suitable, and for making Paul Douglas the senator, and Paul Douglas would have made a better governor. The machine thought that they could do more business with Adlai . . . and less with Paul Douglas. Adlai was a friend of mine, but he was more malleable than Paul Douglas" (AJG). Stevenson and Estes Kefauver showed the greatest strength in the polls published around the time of the Democratic convention. The polls indicated that Kefauver was more popular, but the Tennessee senator was unacceptable to the

party's leadership, without whose support he could not hope to be elected (Bernstein, "The Election of 1952," 3229, 3234–36).

78. Bernstein, "Election of 1952," 3237–40; Stevenson's letter to Goldberg, December 23, 1952, thanking him for "everything you did for me and for the Democratic cause," in Goldberg Papers; Gillon, *Politics and Vision*, 83–89; "The Next President," *Fortune*, May 1952, 80; "The Economics of Seven Democrats," *Fortune*, July 1956, 74–77, 188, 190, 192, 195–96; AJG.

79. AJG. See also R. Alton Lee, *Truman and Taft–Hartley: A Question of Mandate* (Lexington: University of Kentucky Press, 1966), 176–78. The two other Democratic senators who changed their votes in 1949 were Scott Lucas of Illinois and Kenneth McKellar of Tennessee (177).

80. Bernstein, "Election of 1952," 3234–40, 3250–55; John Bartlow Martin, *Adlai Stevenson of Illinois* (Garden City N.Y.: Doubleday/Anchor, 1977), 351–765; Goldman, *The Crucial Decade*, 202–36; Hamby, *Beyond the New Deal*, 481–503; Donovan, *Tumultuous Years*, 397–401; Gillon, *Politics and Vision*, 83–93; Diggins, *The Proud Decades*, 122–28; Leon Friedman, "Election of 1944," in Arthur M. Schlesinger Jr. and Fred L. Israel, eds., *History of American Presidential Elections*, vol. 4 (New York: McGraw-Hill, 1971), 3025–28; James Caldwell Foster, *The Union Politic: The CIO Political Action Committee* (Columbia: University of Missouri Press, 1975), 45–48.

81. AJG. Gillon, *Politics and Vision*, 89, suggests that Stevenson was hampered in winning working-class votes by "his suspicion of unions, his sympathy with Taft–Hartley, and his belief of that Keynesian economics amounted to little more than a rationalization for poor management." A study by the University of Michigan's Survey Research Center found that in the 1952 presidential election, 56 percent of union households supported the Democratic ticket, compared with 80 percent four years earlier. See Arthur C. Wolfe, "Trends in Labor Union Voting Behavior, 1948–1968," *Industrial Relations* 9 (1969): 2. Voter turnout increased substantially among all groups in 1952. Overall it was 63.3 percent of those registered, the highest since 1908. On that point, see Bernstein, "Election of 1952," 3258–59. And see also 3251; "The 1952 Elections," *Fortune*, February 1952, 59–60; "The Unions and the Election," *Fortune*, October 1952, 89–90; "Picking up the Pieces," *Fortune*, December 1952, 83–84; Martin, *Adlai Stevenson of Illinois*, 161, 449–50.

82. USA–EBP, June 13, 1952, 29. According to Goldberg, Murray had been enthusiastic about Eisenhower as a Democratic candidate four years earlier. Goldberg had told him then "to knock it off" because Eisenhower was "a conservative. He would never be a Democratic candidate" (AJG). See also Goldberg Memoir, AFL–CIO MOHC, 12; McAuliffe, *Crisis on the Left*, 154, n. 8; CIO–EBP, August 14, 1952, 82–101. Schatz contends that Murray feared Eisenhower and was deeply discouraged by his election ("Philip Murray," 255–56). But Goldberg disagreed, as did his secretary, Frances Guilbert. She was with Murray and his wife in the days just after the election and before his death and detected no such depression (AJG); see also FSG; CIO–EBP, November 14, 1952, 17, where CIO Vice-President Allan Haywood dismissed the notion that Murray had been discouraged, saying that Murray had, on the night before he died, told Haywood exuberantly that "our boys have worked. This is an Eisenhower victory, not a Republican victory."

83. CIO–EBP, August 14, 1952, 105.

84. Ibid.

85. USA–EBP, October 13, 1952, 31.

86. Wolfe, "Trends in Labor Union Voting Behavior," 1–9; Bernstein, "Election of 1952," 3258–66; the sources cited in n. 81.

87. AJG; Goldberg Memoir, AFL–CIO MOHC, 13; "Labor's New Men of Power," *Fortune*, June 1953, 151–52; "Let George Do It," *Fortune*, May 1951, 50; Craig Phelan, "William Green and the Ideal of Christian Cooperation," and Robert H. Zieger, "George Meany: Labor's Organization Man," both in Melvyn Dubofsky and Warren Van Tine, eds., *Labor Leaders in America* (Urbana: University of Illinois, 1987), 134–59 and 324–37, respectively; Robinson, *George Meany*, 162–84.

88. AJG; Goldberg Memoir, AFL–CIO MOHC, 13; "Labor's New Men of Power," *Fortune*, June 1953, 151–52; Zieger, "George Meany," 324–37; Robinson, *George Meany*, 162–84; "Father George," *Fortune*, April 1955, 80–82; Phelan, "William Green," 134–59.

89. See, for example, USA–EBP, April 19, 1951, 129–30, where Murray during the darkest period of the 1951/52 clash with steel industry managers told USA board members that "the struggle that has gone on within the country in the past few months is evidenced by the control that big business has taken over the people of the United States. The system of control which they have at the moment here in the United States is almost as terrifying as is the Communist policy of aggression. You have got to make a choice, a difficult choice, between a system of Fascism which is enveloping the nation due to these controls that big business has over the nation, and the heavy hand of Communist totalitarianism." See also 193–94, where Murray noted with great apprehension the warm response of conservatives to the recently dismissed General Douglas MacArthur. He told the executive board that MacArthur had become "the instrumentality through which these wicked people can impose their will upon America. That is your danger."

90. USA–EBP, July 25, 1952, 9. For an example of a leading liberal thinker in the 1940s and 1950s who found himself left only with that faith, see Richard Fox, *Reinhold Niebuhr: A Biography* (New York: Harper & Row, 1985), 193–223.

91. For darker views of Murray's legacy, see Lichtenstein, *Labor's War at Home*, 216–45; Tomlins, *The State and the Unions*, 188–89, 241–43, 247–51; Schatz, "Philip Murray," 234–57.

92. See Schatz, "Philip Murray," 234–39, 248–56, for details of Murray's personality.

93. AJG. These impressions of Murray and Reuther were also based on conversations with Goldberg's secretary, Frances Guilbert, who knew all three during the 1940s and early 1950s. See also "Labor's New Men of Power," *Fortune*, June 1953, 148–51; Nelson Lichtenstein, "Walter Reuther and the Rise of Labor Liberalism," in Melvyn Dubofsky and Warren Van Tine, eds., *Labor Leaders in America* (Urbana: University of Illinois Press, 1987), 280–87, 298–99; John Barnard, *Walter Reuther and the Rise of the Auto Workers* (Boston: Little, Brown, 1983), 109–10, 177–80; McDonald Memoir, AFL–CIO MOHC, 13.

94. This is not to suggest that the pay and benefits provisions of the UAW's collective bargaining agreements were not influential in shaping the postwar social contract, for indeed they were. But the UAW's larger social agenda and its efforts to obtain more union influence over corporations' strategic decision making, goals that Reuther gave such eloquent expression, were more ambitious than those favored by most unionists. What sustained the image of Reuther's centrality were the business critics of the postwar New Deal, who sought to weaken managerial support for it by arguing that the entire labor movement advocated "Reutherism," and the Stevensonian liberals, who hoped that promoting the UAW president would increase labor's support for their own social agenda. On Reuther's agenda during the 1950s, see "Where Does Labor Go from Here?" *Fortune*, December 1957, 153–55, 256–62;

Barnard, *Walter Reuther*, 132–69. For examples of managerial efforts to depict "Re-utherism" as organized labor's agenda, see Totton J. Anderson, "The 1958 Election in California," *Western Political Quarterly* 12 (1958): 285–300; Gilbert S. Gall, *The Politics of Right to Work: The Labor Federations as Special Interests, 1943–79* (West-port, Conn.: Greenwood Press, 1988), 107–21. See also Eisenhower Labor Secretary James P. Mitchell's personal and confidential memo, October 6, 1956, to White House Chief of Staff Sherman Adams, which advised GOP attacks on Reuther only, and not on "big union leadership" more generally, in the file marked "1956 — White House — Confidential," box 159, James P. Mitchell Papers, DDEL. An example of the Stevensonian tendency to overrate Reuther's influence is in Arthur M. Schlesinger Jr., *Robert Kennedy and His Times* (Boston: Houghton Mifflin, 1978), 205. This combined campaign to promote Reuther, albeit for very different reasons, has also misled his critics on the left, who, like the others, tend to portray Reuther's program as at the center of the postwar order. For an example, see Lichtenstein, "Walter Reuther," 287–301, in which he depicts Reuther's more ambitious agenda with great clarity but suggests that it was at the center of politics from the late 1940s through the middle 1960s. This presentation of Reuther's views and importance is restated in Lichten-stein, "From Corporatism to Collective Bargaining," 122–52. For AFL attitudes to-ward Reuther, see Robinson, *George Meany*, 251–75.

95. AJG; David J. McDonald, *Union Man* (New York: Dutton, 1969), 230–325.

96. For evidence of Goldberg's leadership role, see John Herling, *Right to Chal-lenge: People and Power in the Steelworkers Union* (New York: Harper & Row, 1972), 27–28, who quoted one board member as saying that "while we often criticized Arthur, as we later criticized David Feller, his associate and successor, to an even greater degree for assumption of power, in many ways that charge was unjust. . . . They were really filling a vacuum. McDonald just couldn't make any damned decisions. For a long time Arthur influenced the destiny of the union more than anyone realized." Stephen Wexler, a young lawyer whom McDonald hired in 1965 to help him fend off a challenge to his control of the union, expressed the same thought more simply: "I read every single line of the Steelworkers minutes of the Executive Board from the time of SWOC. They're good minutes. Talk about interesting read-ing! One thing that did come out, actually from the time Phil Murray died until 1960, I think that if anybody ran the union, it was probably Arthur Goldberg" (149). My reading of those minutes (see also 33–148, 150–300) and the other sources cited in this manuscript points to the same conclusion; McDonald, *Union Man*, 15–89; "A Suit That's Right for the Job," *CIO News*, November 23, 1953, 16; Goldberg Memoir, AFL–CIO MOHC, 5–6; "He's Called 'McDonald's Brain,'" *Newsweek*, November 2, 1959, 86; "Dave McDonald's Flub," *Fortune*, April 1953, 92–94; "The Next American Labor Movement," *Fortune*, April 1953, 202–4; "Labor's New Men of Power," *For-tune*, June 1953, 155–62; "The Decline of Dave McDonald," *Fortune*, August 1958, 169–70; Philip W. Nyden, *Steelworkers Rank-and-File: The Political Economy of a Reform Movement* (New York: Praeger, 1984), 17–42; AJG. By the late 1950s Gold-berg was profiting handsomely from McDonald's "generosity." In 1958, for exam-ple, McDonald gave his general counsel a "holiday season" bonus of $10,000. See McDonald's accompanying note to Goldberg, December 22, 1958, in box 60, McDonald Papers. McDonald apparently gave Goldberg a large bonus every year. See, for other examples, the cover letter for the 1954 gift from McDonald to Gold-berg, December 17, 1954, and Goldberg's reply, December 21, 1954, and a similar letter, January 2, 1958, from Goldberg regarding a gift in December 1957, and another such note, December 22, 1960, all of which are in the same file.

97. Quoted in Herling, *Right to Challenge*, 18, also 9–17, 19–28; "No Dirty Linen," *Fortune*, May 1952, 80; McDonald, *Union Man*, 143–97.

98. USA–EBP, November 15, 1952, 40–47; Goldberg Memoir, AFL–CIO MOHC, 4; Herling, *Right to Challenge*, 24–26.

99. Goldberg personally favored Reuther as better qualified but did not interfere when the USA supported Haywood for CIO president (Goldberg Memoir, AFL–CIO MOHC, 4–5). Haywood died soon after taking office and was replaced by John Riffe, who was also identified with the USA faction in the federation. See "C.I.O.'s Quiet Man," *Fortune*, June 1953, 78; also "Every Man a Dark Horse," *Fortune*, November 1951, 54–56; "C.I.O. Leaders Fail to Agree on Chief," *New York Times*, November 25, 1952; "Why Reuther?" *Fortune*, January 1953, 66, 68; "The Next American Labor Movement," *Fortune*, April 1953, 201–2; "Labor's New Men of Power," *Fortune*, June 1953, 148–66; McDonald Memoir, AFL–CIO MOHC, 8–9.

100. Reuther sent Goldberg a letter of regret saying that the "last thing in the world that I would want to do is to jeopardize the continuation of our relationship which I believe is more important in terms of the future of [the] CIO than ever before." See the letter from Reuther to Goldberg, December 13, 1952, folder 3, box 290, Walter Reuther Papers, WPRL. After talking the matter through over the telephone, the two agreed that Goldberg would continue to head the CIO legal department in all respects even after he removed himself from the federation's headquarters, where some of the legal staff continued to be housed. See, for the details, Goldberg's memo to Reuther, March 3, 1953, summarizing the new arrangement, in the folder marked "Legal Department, 1953–54," box 74, CIO Secretary Treasurer's Papers. Reuther's response, April 7, 1953, is in folder 3, box 290, of Reuther Papers, and the press release announcing Goldberg's decision to remain with the CIO, January 15, 1953, is in folder 7, box 60, of Reuther Papers. See also Goldberg Memoir, AFL–CIO MOHC, 5; USA–EBP, November 15, 1952, 44–45; the memo entitled "Lee Pressman," in the folder marked "Legal Department, 1948–1952," box 74, CIO Secretary Treasurer's Papers; "Labor Lawyers Walk a Tightrope," *Business Week*, September 4, 1954, 51.

101. "Mr. Taft Proposes," *Fortune*, January 1953, 63–66; "Eisenhower's Labor Liaison," *Fortune*, March 1953, 77–80; Gerald Pomper, "Labor Legislation: The Revision of Taft–Hartley in 1953–1954," *Labor History* 6 (1965): 143–49; Stephen Ambrose, *Eisenhower: The President* (New York: Simon & Schuster, 1984), 24, 116–17.

102. CIO–EBP, February 5, 1953, 106–31. A copy of the handwritten notes of the CIO general counsels' conference, which were labeled "Legal–Legislative Conference, January 14 & 15, 1953," is in folder 21, box 48, AFL–CIO Legislative Department Papers, GMMA.

103. CIO–EBP, February 5, 1953, 116–17. See also on that point, "Teeth and Injunctions," *The Nation*, February 12, 1949, 173–74.

104. Liberal outrage at the Clark appointment is recounted in Hamby, *Beyond the New Deal*, 336–38.

105. CIO–EBP, February 5, 1953, 117. See also "Legal–Legislative Conference, January 14 & 15, 1953," folder 21, box 48, AFL–CIO Legislative Department Papers.

106. CIO–EBP, February 5, 1953, 121. The Massachusetts legislature in 1947 had enacted a law, drafted by Harvard law professor Archibald Cox and modeled on an idea of Harvard economist Summer Slichter, that mandated exactly this approach. Labor's acceptance of it after initial opposition probably reflected a belief that in a major industrial state such as Massachusetts, the governor would necessarily adopt a friendly

attitude toward unions. The governor who signed the act into law was Democrat Maurice Tobin, whom Truman appointed secretary of labor just one year later ("Boston Roulette," *Fortune*, February 1961, 190, 193).

107. CIO–EBP, February 5, 1953, 78–131; "Tension with the GOP," *Fortune*, May 1953, 73–76. An indication of Goldberg's central role in the Taft–Hartley revision debates lay in his department's preparation of Reuther's testimony before Congress on that issue (CIO–EBP, February 5, 1953, 131). A copy of the press release summarizing Goldberg's own testimony is in folder 21, box 48, AFL–CIO Legislative Department Papers.

108. USA–EBP, September 17, 1953, 128–29; "Tension with the GOP," *Fortune*, May 1953, 73–76; "Durkin's Troubles," *Fortune*, September 1953, 67; the chart entitled "Summary Analysis of White House Draft of Taft–Hartley Amendments," a copy of which is in the file marked "1953-Taft–Hartley Revisions–(3)," box 106, Mitchell Papers.

109. By June 1953, Goldberg was telling the CIO Executive Board that no action on Taft–Hartley would be forthcoming until late that year or early in the next (CIO–EBP, June 4, 1953, 45). See also Ambrose, *Eisenhower: The President*, 24, 116–18; "Labor Notes," *Fortune*, April 1953, 98; "Labor Tension with the G.O.P.," *Fortune*, May 1953, 73–76; "Labor Secretary or Chief of Staff?" *Fortune*, December 1953, 61–64; "Mitchell – Man in the Middle," *Fortune*, February 1955, 61–64; CIO–EBP, February 5, 1953, 86–87, 96–97, 106–31; "Eisenhower's Labor Liaison," *Fortune*, March 1953, 77–80.

110. CIO–EBP, February 5, 1953, 79.

111. USA–EBP, April 6, 1954, 199.

112. See the discussion in USA–EBP, April 5, 1954, 5–23, where Goldberg described both the House and Senate versions of the administration bill as bad and voiced his fears that Eisenhower would sign whatever Congress enacted, thus underscoring the need to prevent any bill from reaching his desk. On the critical roll call in the Senate, every Democrat voted to recommit the bill. They were joined by a few liberal Republicans representing states where labor was strong, thus ending efforts to change the law. See Pomper, "The Revision of Taft–Hartley," 152–58; "Down the Middle," *Fortune*, February 1954, 75–76; "Jobs and Taxes," *Fortune*, April 1954, 76–78; "Memo to Robert Oliver from Goldberg Re: Building Trade Department Bill," June 18, 1954, in folder 8, box 25, CIO Washington Office Records, WPRL.

113. CIO–EBP, March 22–23, 1954, 106–7, also 72–75; Archibald Cox, Derek Bok, and Robert Gorman, *Cases and Materials on Labor Law*, 9th ed. (Mineola, N.Y.: Foundation Press, 1981), 288–91; "Balkanization of Labor," *Fortune*, May 1954, 53–54; "What Kind of Board?" *Fortune*, February 1953, 81–84; "The New NLRB," *Fortune*, November 1953, 76–78; "Ike's Board," *Fortune*, October 1954, 67, 70; Reuther's memo to Goldberg, January 14, 1954, in folder 7, box 60, Reuther Papers. Business managers themselves were far from united on the advisability of allowing craft severance. Some saw the potential benefits to business of allowing it as outweighed by the workplace disruptions that would accompany AFL competition with the CIO. For that reason, management as well as labor in the *American Potash* case had opposed craft severance. See "Balkanization of Labor," *Fortune*, May 1954, 53.

114. CIO–EBP, March 23, 1954, 104–6; Seymour Scher, "Regulatory Agency Control Through Appointment: The Case of the Eisenhower Administration and the NLRB," *Journal of Politics* 23 (1961): 667–88; "The New NLRB," *Fortune*, November 1953, 76–78; "Government Policy," *Fortune*, January 1954, 68–70; "Ike's Board," *Fortune*, October 1954, 67, 70.

115. "Away with Labor Laws?" *Fortune*, June 1953, 73–74; "Down the Middle," *Fortune*, February 1954, 75–76.

116. John Lewis Gaddis, *The United States and the Origins of the Cold War, 1941–1947* (New York: Columbia University Press, 1972), 282–352; Goldman, *The Crucial Decade*, 34–40, 100–37; CIO–EBP, November 27, 1948, 361–91; AJG.

117. CIO–EBP, November 27, 1948, 380–81, also 361–79, 82–91; McAuliffe, *Crisis on the Left*, 27–29; William J. Keller, *The Liberals and J. Edgar Hoover: Rise and Fall of a Domestic Counter-Intelligence State* (Princeton, N.J.: Princeton University Press, 1989), 28–71; Hamby, *Beyond the New Deal*, 170–72, 190; Gillon, *Politics and Vision*, 72–82; AJG.

118. The Communist Control Act of 1954 did, in effect, exempt AFL and CIO unions from prosecution, thereby undercutting Butler's antiunion objective, but with the resulting consequence that some radical unions attempted to affiliate with one of the two federations. On that point, see Goldberg's memo to all CIO affiliate presidents, February 11, 1955, in box 60, McDonald Papers; "The Blow of T-H," *Fortune*, March 1956, 208. See also McAuliffe, *Crisis on the Left*, 134–38; Diggins, *The Proud Decades*, 110–21; Hamby, *Beyond the New Deal*, 466–80; Gillon, *Politics and Vision*, 106–11; Richard M. Fried, *Men Against McCarthy* (New York: Columbia University Press, 1976), 122–53.

119. Keller, *The Liberals and Hoover*, 28–71; Richard Gid Powers, *Secrecy and Power: The Life of J. Edgar Hoover* (New York: Free Press, 1987), 275–323, 336–52.

120. USA–EBP, March 3, 1955, 170–71.

121. On the liberal response to McCarthyism, see Hamby, *Beyond the New Deal*, 466–80. Goldberg had been one of the founding members of the ACLU, and its own agonizing over civil liberties issues is described in McAuliffe, *Crisis on the Left*, 89–107.

122. AJG. The principal targets of Justice Department investigations were radicals in the expelled UE, Longshoremen, and Mine and Mill Workers unions. On that point, see "'Subversives' in Industry," *Fortune*, February 1954, 76–80; "The Blow of T-H," *Fortune*, March 1956, 208.

123. CIO–EBP, May 10, 1954, 75, also 66–74, 76–100.

124. Republican Senator Everett Dirksen denounced the CIO for having joined in the attack on McCarthy. Dirksen said that the federation had, along with the ADA and other groups, allied itself with the Communist Party by supporting the Senate's move to condemn McCarthy (Fried, *Men Against McCarthy*, 296). See also CIO–EBP, May 10, 1954, 66–100; AJG.

125. AJG; Robinson, *George Meany*, 162–69; Shaplen, "Peacemaker," 96.

126. CIO–EBP, October 31, 1951, 85–160, November 9, 1951, 212–13, August 14, 1952, 30–35, April 6, 1953, 28–29.

127. On the possibility of using the CIO agreement as a model for an AFL–CIO one, see CIO–EBP, October 31, 1951, 159–60. Goldberg said later that "the impetus for the No-Raiding Agreement came from the CIO" (Goldberg Memoir, AFL–CIO MOHC, 1). Meany later claimed that the survey was his idea, but there is no other evidence to support that claim. For Meany's view, see Robinson, *George Meany*, 165–66. See also USA–EBP, May 28, 1953, 203–4, September 17, 1953, 95–98; "Economics of Raiding," *Fortune*, August 1953, 60, 62.

128. AJG; Goldberg Memoir, AFL–CIO MOHC, 1–3; USA–EBP, May 28, 1953, 203–5, September 17, 1953, 98–109.

129. Reuther had stated his intention to expand the CIO's activities soon after being elected CIO president. See his remarks in CIO–EBP, December 5, 1952, 45–46, February 5, 1953, 6.

130. USA–EBP, September 17, 1953, 77–78. See also USA–EBP, October 23, 1953, 9, January 26, 1954, 53–56.

131. USA–EBP, January 26, 1954, 54–55.

132. USA–EBP, November 15, 1952, 34. Symptomatic of the growing split with liberal groups was the shrinking size of labor contributions to the ADA's coffers. On that point, and the nature of the rift more generally, see Gillon, *Politics and Vision*, 57–82. McDonald had proposed very early in his presidency that the USA subsidy to the ADA, which had ranged from $2,000 to $500 a month since 1948, be eliminated, a sign of labor's growing unhappiness with the organization's agenda (USA–EBP, March 11, 1953, 27). See also Lichtenstein, "Walter Reuther," 292–93.

133. CIO–EBP, February 5–6, 1953, 195, also 68–71, 192–94, October 31, 1951, 37–56.

134. CIO–EBP, February 6, 1953, 194.

135. Ibid., 192–96.

136. CIO–EBP, November 12, 1953, 20. The USA did make an effort to use television, making some programs that featured McDonald as the spokesman (USA–EBP, June 27, 1955, 15–16). The UAW used television even more actively in the realm of political action, only to be indicted for violating the Taft–Hartley Act (CIO–EBP, July 20, 1955, 90).

137. CIO–EBP, November 12, 1953, 16. Even this modest effort concerned business managers. Fleischer reported that the public relations firm Hill and Knowlton had undertaken two audience surveys for corporate clients and that "at least 20 surveys" had been made by corporations (CIO–EBP, July 20, 1955, 13). See also CIO–EBP, August 20, 1953, 6–8, November 12, 1953, 12–20, March 23, 1954, 331–32, July 20, 1955, 12–16, 90.

138. The data on program costs and CIO budget deficits come from CIO–EBP, March 23, 1954, 249, 331–32. Information also comes from Fleischer's memos to Reuther. See those dated April 20, 1953, May 15, 1953, and June 1, 1953, in folder 11, box 27, CIO Washington Office Records.

139. For the argument that labor should have embraced a wider agenda, see Davis, *Prisoners of the American Dream*, 52–117.

140. USA–EBP, April 5, 1954, 180; "Deals and Dickers," *Fortune*, August 1953, 59–60; "Labor's New Men of Power," *Fortune*, June 1953, 151; CIO–EBP, March 22, 1954, 10–24; Lichtenstein, "Walter Reuther," 292, 298–99.

141. David McDonald discussed the feelers to Beck and Lewis with the USA Executive Board and denied that they were intended to do anything more than put pressure on Reuther (USA–EBP, September 17, 1953, 109–21). He also denied at a meeting of the CIO Executive Board any effort to negotiate with the two men, although he hinted at the same time that if CIO affiliates stood in the way of unity talks with the AFL, the USA would reduce its subsidy to the federation (CIO–EBP, August 20, 1953, 80–82; USA–EBP, September 17, 1953, 111–12). See also "New Lineups, New Loyalties," *Fortune*, August 1953, 60, 62; "McDonald's Straws," *Fortune*, April 1954, 75–76; "Lew McBeck's Contact Man," *Fortune*, August 1954, 48–50; "End of the Feud?" *Fortune*, September 1954, 60–62; McDonald, *Union Man*, 241–42; McDonald Memoir, 2–3, and Goldberg Memoir, 6, both in the AFL–CIO MOHC.

142. The CIO's voting strength and union membership figures can be found in CIO–EBP, November 12, 1953, 32–33. The USA was allotted 36 delegates to the annual convention out of a total of 296, and it paid membership dues on 1.1 million members out of the CIO's total of 4.6 million. The seven largest CIO affiliates had roughly half of the total membership, and the remaining twenty-eight, the rest.

143. Robinson, *George Meany*, 162–68; "New Lineups, New Loyalties," *Fortune*, August 1953, 60, 62; "The Next American Labor Movement," *Fortune*, April 1953, 120–21; "Labor's New Men of Power," *Fortune*, June 1953, 152–55; "Beck's Big Wheels," *Fortune*, August 1953, 62, 64.

144. USA–EBP, September 17, 1953, 99, also 95–98, 100–9.

145. Ratification by the conventions only restrained the national labor federations from raiding. The real source of the problem was not them so much as the affiliates. On that point, see Arthur J. Goldberg, *AFL–CIO: Labor United* (New York: McGraw-Hill, 1956), 76–83. McDonald received the ratification forms for the USA on December 2, 1953. See Goldberg's letter to him, December 1, 1953, in box 60 of McDonald Papers. See also Goldberg's letter to McDonald, September 29, 1955, explaining the procedures for ratifying the merger agreement in the same box of McDonald Papers; "The Politics of Labor," *Fortune*, January 1954, 70–72.

146. A draft of a letter from Meany to the heads of the various AFL affiliates attacked the CIO's apparent stalling and urged them to speed up ratification. The letter was sent on March 31, 1954. The draft is in folder 26, box 62, AFL President's Papers, GMMA. See also CIO–EBP, April 6, 1953, 55–58, May 10, 1954, 46–55; Robinson, *George Meany*, 168–70; Shaplen, "Peacemaker," 96, 98.

147. CIO–EBP, May 10, 1954, 59, also 12–58, 60–66.

148. McDonald had expressed concern about the American Potash case even before the NLRB had issued its decision. He told the USA Executive Board that if the NLRB legalized craft severance in all industries, "I fear that you are going to be confronted in your respective districts with some serious attempts on the part of A.F. of L. unions to raid you" (USA–EBP, January 26, 1954, 44). See also Goldberg, *Labor United*, 83; Robinson, *George Meany*, 168–69.

149. Immediately after the agreement went into effect, Goldberg sent out a memo advising the CIO union presidents on how the plan would operate. See "Memorandum to the Presidents of All CIO Affiliated Unions," June 16, 1954, box 60, McDonald Papers. See also CIO–EBP, June 29, 1954, 49–50. On getting McDonald to support unity publicly, see McDonald Memoir, 3–4, and Goldberg Memoir, 5–6, both of which are in the AFL–CIO MOHC; Goldberg, *Labor United*, 83–85; "Unity in '55," *Fortune*, December 1954, 63; Shaplen, "Peacemaker," 100, where Shaplen quotes a CIO official as saying that "Arthur pointed out to McDonald that Lewis was old and isolated, and Beck was a curious character, and that if McDonald really wanted to be effective he shouldn't be playing around with those fellows."

150. USA–EBP, April 5, 1954, 175. See also Henry C. Kenski, "The Impact of Unemployment on Presidential Popularity from Eisenhower to Nixon," *Presidential Studies Quarterly* 7 (1977): 120.

151. "Jobs and Taxes," *Fortune*, April 1954, 76–78; McDonald, *Union Man*, 246.

152. USA–EBP, May 6, 1954, 12. The USA memo dated April 5, 1954, containing the union's proposals for fighting the recession is in the file marked "Labor – United Steel Workers (2)," box 113, Arthur F. Burns Papers, DDEL. See also "Jobs and Taxes," *Fortune*, April 1954, 76–78; McDonald, *Union Man*, 246.

153. USA–EBP, May 6, 1954, 11–14; McDonald, *Union Man*, 246; the USA memo cited in the preceding footnote and the other items in that same file, and the one marked "Labor – United Steel Workers (1), box 113, all in Burns Papers.

154. For the similarities in the way the federal government responded to the recessions of 1949 and 1954 – despite the change in control of Congress and the White House from the Democrats to the Republicans – see A. E. Holmans, "The Eisenhower Administration and the Recession, 1953–5," *Oxford Economic Papers*

(1958): 34–54. Holmans concluded that "the differences between their policies were slight indeed" (50). See also Collins, *The Business Response to Keynes*, 152–58.

155. CIO–EBP, December 1, 1954, 69. See also CIO–EBP, October 5, 1954, 105–6; "Labor and the Eighty-fourth Congress," *Fortune*, December 1954, 64; James C. Foster, "1954: A CIO Victory?" *Labor History* 12 (1971): 392–408; Wolfe, "Trends in Labor Union Voting Behavior," 1–9.

156. CIO–EBP, December 1, 1954, 65. The new chairman of the Senate Labor Committee, also a southerner, was Lister Hill of Alabama, from labor's perspective, only slightly better than Barden. See "Labor and the Eighty-fourth Congress," *Fortune*, December 1954, 64.

157. See "The Future of American Labor," a speech that Goldberg gave at the Commonwealth Club of San Francisco on December 3, 1954, where he claimed that "the American trade union movement stands at its peak strength in terms of membership, in terms of stature, in terms of accomplishments" (8). A copy of the address is in Goldberg Papers. See also Paul Weiler, "Promises to Keep: Securing Workers' Rights to Self-Organization Under the NLRA," *Harvard Law Review* 96 (1983): 1771–72; Holmans, "The Eisenhower Administration and the Recession," 51–53; Diggins, *The Proud Decades*, 178–81; Jezer, *The Dark Ages*, 201–3. Jezer concluded that the period should be viewed as one of failure for workers because there was no great redistribution of personal income shares between 1945 and 1955. But during that decade of very rapid economic growth, the three middle quintiles more than held their own, and the bottom and top quintiles saw their shares of national income decline slightly. A very large majority of working- and lower-middle-class Americans belonged to those three middle groups, which experienced a steady rise in their disposable income during the decade after World War II. In view of what those kinds of Americans had experienced before that time and, indeed, what they have faced since the postwar New Deal came apart completely in the early 1970s, the notion that workers and the lower middle class lost economically between 1945 and 1955 seems steadily less persuasive.

158. Goldberg, "The Future of American Labor," 17.

159. Ibid., 27. See also AJG. On the failure of the labor movement to attack workplace discrimination against blacks more forcefully in this period, see Robert Korstad and Nelson Lichtenstein, "Opportunities Found and Lost: Labor, Radicals and the Early Civil Rights Movement," *Journal of American History* 75 (1988): 786–811. They argue that in the 1940s there was an opportunity to unionize the South and dismantle legalized segregation and that labor was partly to blame for the failure to do so. Given the conditions existing in the South at that time, their argument is not persuasive. The failure of the southern organizing drive is chronicled by Barbara S. Griffith in *The Crisis of American Labor: Operation Dixie and the Defeat of the CIO* (Philadelphia: Temple University Press, 1988). Griffith concluded that such an opportunity never really existed (161–76). This is not to suggest that the CIO's antiradical policy from 1948 onward did not make organizing in the South more difficult, for it surely did, but only that even without such a split in the CIO's ranks, that task still could not have been accomplished. For evidence of the harm done by the CIO antiradical policy to the southern organizing drive, see Griffith, *The Crisis of American Labor*, 139–60. For the result in the USA's largest southern local, see Robert J. Norrell, "Caste in Steel: Jim Crow Careers in Birmingham, Alabama," *Journal of American History* 73 (1986): 682–85.

160. Goldberg, "The Future of American Labor," 9–10.

161. Ibid., 26.

162. Ibid., 31.

163. Weiler, "Promises to Keep," 1775–77, supplied the NLRB election data. See also "Notes of the Month," *Fortune*, July 1954, 35. The economic expansion that accompanied the United States's entry into the Korean conflict contributed to labor's ability to organize new workers. Immediately before the war's outbreak, organizing drives had been yielding paltry results ("Organizing—The Cream Is Off," *Fortune*, April 1950, 51–54). Even during the war, however, the results were not that impressive ("Unionism on a Plateau," *Fortune*, November 1952, 78–80). The steel industry was fairly typical, with the decline in organizing success so pronounced by 1953 that McDonald made one of his rare pleas for the USA Executive Board to work harder in that area (USA–EBP, September 17, 1953, 133–34). One union that bucked the trend was the Teamsters ("Beck's Big Wheels," *Fortune*, August 1953, 62, 64). On the reason for the decline in union organizing victories, see Weiler, "Promises to Keep," 1777, who concluded that it was in large part attributable to "coercive antiunion employer tactics that the NLRA [Wagner Act] was supposed to eliminate." Once Eisenhower's appointees assumed control of the NLRB, it allowed employers greater latitude in fighting union organizing campaigns. See Cox, Bok, and Gorman, *Labor Law*, 141–43.

Chapter 5. Consensus, Real and Imagined

1. CIO–EBP, March 22, 1954, 25.

2. Ibid., 25–27, 247–58.

3. The CIO in 1953 had 4.8 million members. See "The AFL Inflates," *Fortune*, October 1953, 118, 120; Nelson Lichtenstein, "From Corporatism to Collective Bargaining: Organized Labor and the Eclipse of Social Democracy in the Postwar Era," in Steve Fraser and Gary Gerstle, eds., *The Rise and Fall of the New Deal Order, 1930–80* (Princeton, N.J.: Princeton University Press, 1989), 131; Nelson Lichtenstein, *Labor's War at Home* (Cambridge: Cambridge University Press, 1982), 80. See also Ronald W. Schatz, *The Electrical Workers: A History of Labor at General Electric and Westinghouse, 1923–60* (Urbana: University of Illinois Press, 1983), 225–240; "Carey vs. Boulware," *Fortune*, October 1952, 92–93.

4. AJG; Goldberg Memoir, AFL–CIO MOHC, 1–13; Robert Shaplen, "Peacemaker," *New Yorker*, pt. 1, April 7, 1962, 98–100.

5. CIO–EBP, December 10, 1954, 36–37.

6. Goldberg Memoir, AFL–CIO MOHC, 15. McDonald had "authorized" Goldberg to present the draft in January 1955. See the exchange of letters between Goldberg and him, dated January 25 and January 27, respectively, in box 60 of McDonald Papers. A copy of the draft, entitled the "Report and Recommendations of the Joint AFL–CIO Unity Committee," February 1, 1955, is in box 60, McDonald Papers. See also Archie Robinson, *George Meany and His Times* (New York: Simon & Schuster, 1981), 169–72.

7. USA–EBP, March 2, 1955, 6–24; Goldberg Memoir, AFL–CIO MOHC, 15–18; Robinson, *George Meany*, 172–76; Shaplen, "Peacemaker," 98, 100; "Bigger and Bigger Unions," *Fortune*, April 1955, 75–76; "Unity, Ouch," *Fortune*, November 1955, 67–68, 70; "Merger: Personnel & Policies," *Fortune*, December 1955, 62, 64; "Upcoming Mergers," *Fortune*, January 1956, 186, 188; "'Let George Do It,'" *Fortune*, July 1956, 179–82; "A 'Moige' But No Marriage," *Fortune*, November 1957, 242–46; "Who's Raiding Whom?" *Fortune*, May 1957, 252–57.

8. USA–EBP, March 2, 1955, 15.

9. Ibid., 6–24; Goldberg Memoir, AFL–CIO MOHC, 14; Robinson, *George Meany*, 173; Robert H. Zieger, "George Meany: Labor's Organization Man," in Melvyn Dubofsky and Warren Van Tine, eds., *Labor Leaders in America* (Urbana: University of Illinois Press, 1987), 334–35; "The Powers of Meany," *Fortune*, August 1956, 189.

10. Goldberg Memoir, AFL–CIO MOHC, 3. See also "Labor Lawyers Walk a Tightrope," *Business Week*, September 4, 1954, 50–51; "Man of Many Connections," *Fortune*, April 1957, 234.

11. Goldberg Memoir, AFL–CIO MOHC, 17.

12. Evidence of Goldberg's unhappiness at not receiving the title of general counsel is in his letter to Meany, February 1, 1956, in folder 23, box 29, AFL–CIO President's Papers. Reuther had suggested the co-counsel idea in a letter to Meany, November 10, 1955. A copy is in folder 5, box 22, CIO Washington Office Records. Goldberg's secretary, Frances Guilbert, suggested that he was annoyed mostly because he would like to have been offered the job, even if he could not, for his own reasons, have accepted it. FSG. See also Shaplen, "Peacemaker," 102.

13. USA–EBP, March 2, 1955, 7.

14. Ibid., 26. By the end of 1955 Reuther told the CIO Executive Board that Western European trade union officials feared the consequence of the merger would be just the opposite, that the CIO would become more like the AFL (CIO–EBP, November 2, 1955, 106).

15. USA–EBP, March 2, 1955, 7.

16. For Reuther's discussion of the struggle for a name other than the AFL, see CIO–EBP, July 20, 1955, 17–23. He made clear that the UAW would not accept the AFL name even if every other CIO union did so (21).

17. USA–EBP, March 2, 1955, 47.

18. Ibid., 54, also 47–53, 55–64.

19. Ibid., 40.

20. CIO–EBP, November 2, 1955, 47–49; USA–EBP, March 2, 1955, 7; Robinson, *George Meany*, 176–79; Joshua B. Freeman, *In Transit: The Transport Workers Union in New York City, 1933–66* (New York: Oxford University Press, 1989), 333–34.

21. Goldberg explained the proposed merger agreement to the CIO Executive Board at a meeting held on May 7, 1955 (CIO–EBP, May 7, 1955, 24–123). A copy of his memo, September 21, 1955, detailing the minor changes in the agreement is in folder 4, box 54, CIO Washington Office Records.

22. AJG.

23. Goldberg Memoir, AFL–CIO MOHC, 16. Goldberg's letter of request to McDonald, September 16, 1955, together with the proposed forward, is in box 60, McDonald Papers. The book appeared the following year and received a good deal of publicity. See "New Book on Labor Merger Brings Debate," *Business Week*, November 24, 1956, 60–68.

24. USA–EBP, November 15, 1955, 19–20. See also Arthur J. Goldberg, *AFL–CIO: Labor United* (New York: McGraw-Hill, 1956), ix–xi. The struggle to bring the merger about wore so heavily on Goldberg that he was hospitalized for sheer exhaustion in the fall. See the letter to him from Jacob Weinstein, October 18, 1955, in Weinstein Papers; Goldberg's letter to George Meany, February 1, 1956, in folder 23, box 29, AFL–CIO President's Papers; Shaplen, "Peacemaker," 100–2. Goldberg's invention of the AFL–CIO rubric is noted in David J. McDonald, *Union Man* (New York: Dutton, 1969), 247; Shaplen, "Peacemaker," 100. Meany also claimed to have

invented the name, but there is little evidence to support that contention (Robinson, *George Meany*, 176).

25. See USA–EBP, November 15, 1955, 21. Goldberg went on to say that "we hope it will be a happy marriage that will last throughout the lifetime of the American labor movement."

26. Zieger, "George Meany," 338; "The Power and the Glory," *Fortune*, July 1956, 180.

27. CIO–EBP, November 2, 1955, 94–101.

28. John Herling, *Right to Challenge: People and Power in the Steelworkers Union* (New York: Harper & Row, 1972), 1–32; Lloyd Ulman, *The Government of the Steel Workers' Union* (New York: Wiley, 1962), 1–137; Philip W. Nyden, *Steelworkers Rank-and-File: The Political Economy of a Reform Movement* (New York: Praeger, 1984), 1–39; Mark Reutter, *Sparrows Point: Making Steel: The Rise and Ruin of American Industrial Might* (New York: Summit Books, 1988), 344–45, 359–60.

29. On the trend toward centralization of power at the top of the USA, see Ulman, *The Government of the Steel Workers' Union*, 1–137; John P. Hoerr, *And the Wolf Finally Came: The Decline of the American Steel Industry* (Pittsburgh: University of Pittsburgh Press, 1988), 199; Nyden, *Steelworkers Rank-and-File*, 33–39. The changes were being felt by other unions and even by the federations. For an example of the latter development, see CIO–EBP, April 6, 1953, 40–55, where the board discussed and then approved restrictions on fund-raising by the locals. Lichtenstein, *Labor's War at Home*, 241–45, and Christopher L. Tomlins, *The State and the Unions; Labor Relations, Law and the Organized Labor Movement in America, 1880–1960* (Cambridge: Cambridge University Press, 1985), 317–28, note the pervasive nature of these trends throughout organized labor during the 1950's. Labor's agreement to police the shop floor as part of its larger bargain with management is discussed in David Brody, *Workers in Industrial America: Essays on the Twentieth Century Struggle* (New York: Oxford University Press, 1980), 198–211.

30. USA–EBP, March 11–12, 1953, 32–178, May 28, 1953, 4–176, September 17, 1953, 127–28; Nyden, *Steelworkers Rank-and-File*, 41; Reutter, *Sparrows Point*, 342–60; Ulman, *The Government of the Steel Workers' Union*, 165–69.

31. USA–EBP, September 17, 1953, 130–33, January 26, 1954, 49–50, 61–67; Brody, *Workers in Industrial America*, 198–211.

32. USA–EBP, April 5, 1954, 123–24. See also Ulman, *The Government of the Steel Workers' Union*, 73–77.

33. USA–EBP, August 19, 1954, 46, also 43–45, 47.

34. USA–EBP, March 2, 1955, 118–39; "Joe Moloney of Steel," *Fortune*, May 1955, 60; Ulman, *The Government of the Steel Workers' Union*, 137–140; Herling, *Right to Challenge*, 33–40. The lack of much competition for union offices extended even to the post of district director. Between 1945 and 1961, the USA had between twenty-nine and thirty-nine directors, elected every four years. Incumbents were defeated exactly eight times during that period (Ulman, *The Government of the Steel Workers' Union*, 129). The absence of a tradition in the USA of contested elections was not very unusual. Such contests were relatively rare in the American labor movement during the first half of the twentieth century. See C. Wright Mills, *The New Men of Power: America's Labor Leaders* (New York: Harcourt Brace, 1948), 62–67.

35. USA–EBP, November 15, 1955, 117, also 113–16, 118–29.

36. The idea of drawing up a set of principles to govern elections had first surfaced when the vice-presidential slot became vacant in March 1955 (USA–EBP, March 3,

1955, 328–29). The election manual that Goldberg and Abel devised was submitted to the board and approved one year later (USA–EBP, April 18, 1956, 5–20).

37. See Herling, *Right to Challenge*, 43–48. According to USA–EBP, September 11, 1956, 29–45, Larry Sefton, a district director from Canada, voiced doubts about the whole idea at that meeting, arguing that higher dues would hamper organizing efforts, but the board's majority supported the plan. McDonald claimed, not very convincingly, that he had opposed a pay raise for himself (*Union Man*, 253–55). His new salary of $50,000 was the highest by far for any CIO union chief, and large even by AFL standards ("$25,000-a-Year Men," *Fortune*, July 1957, 207). The leadership's unwillingness to give locals a greater say in formulating contract demands may have contributed to the challenge it faced in 1956. On that point, see USA–EBP, March 3, 1955, 336, where the board rejected a petition in that vein from two locals. Nyden, *Steelworkers Rank-and-File*, 39, contends, however, that it was administrative centralization rather than work rules or wage issues that contributed to the insurgency of the mid-1950s.

38. Herling, *Right to Challenge*, 48–54; "Revolt in Steel," *Fortune*, February 1957, 205–6; Nyden, *Steelworkers Rank-and-File*, 40–41; Ulman, *The Government of the Steel Workers' Union*, 140–44. McDonald tended to view rank-and-file protests of all kinds as disguised efforts by communists, managers, or both to destroy him (USA–EBP, March 8, 1956, 7–23, November 27, 1956, 124–31). On the dissidents' efforts to challenge some of the election results, see USA–EBP, January 14, 1957, 4–178, where the board, at Goldberg's direction, rejected their appeals. The difficulties that insurgents faced in contesting a USA election are depicted graphically in William Kornblum, *Blue Collar Community* (Chicago: University of Chicago Press, 1974), 112–32, 220–23. See also Ulman, *The Government of the Steel Workers' Union*, 153–65. And in one important respect, the USA was more democratic even than its supposedly more enlightened rival, the UAW. In the former, the rank and file elected the union's top officers, and in the latter, the convention did so, which was even more easily manipulated than were rank-and-file contests (Hoerr, *And the Wolf Finally Came*, 199).

39. McDonald raised the idea of moving the USA headquarters to Washington at an executive board meeting held on March 3, 1955 (USA–EBP, March 3, 1955, 364). The board rejected the idea at a meeting held on November 27, 1956, during the middle of the McDonald–Rarick contest (USA–EBP, November 27, 1956, 56–57). See also USA–EBP, May 15, 1957, 65–68. McDonald outlined the new plan for holding regular district conferences at the November 1956 meeting (USA–EBP, November 27, 1956, 95–119).

40. USA–EBP, May 15, 1957, 89.

41. Ibid.

42. Ibid., 93, also 87–92.

43. The decisive role of the 1956 contract in securing McDonald's reelection is noted by Ulman, *The Government of the Steel Workers' Union*, 153–54.

44. USA–EBP, May 28, 1953, 179–89.

45. Ibid., 185, also 186–91.

46. On the UAW contract's influence over collective bargaining in the manufacturing sector, see Lichtenstein, "From Corporatism to Collective Bargaining," 140–44.

47. USA–EBP, April 27, 1953, 11, also 8–10, 12; Paul A. Tiffany, *The Decline of American Steel: How Management, Labor and the Government Went Wrong* (New York: Oxford University Press, 1988), 65–82, 91–94; Donald F. Barnett and Louis

Schorsch, *Steel: Upheaval in a Basic Industry* (Cambridge, Mass.: Ballinger, 1983), 22–26.

48. Managers had been encouraged to select the Canadian site by the federal government, which in 1954 enacted legislation, strongly supported by the USA, mandating the construction of a series of canals now known as the St. Lawrence Seaway. The seaway was intended to reduce the cost of shipping iron ore from Labrador to steel plants in the Midwest. See Kenneth Warren, *The American Steel Industry, 1850–1970: A Geographical Interpretation* (Pittsburgh: University of Pittsburgh Press, 1973), 250, 302. See also USA–EBP, June 12, 1953, 7–11; E. Robert Livernash, *Collective Bargaining in the Basic Steel Industry* (Washington, D.C.: U.S. Department of Labor, 1961), 284–87; Richard W. Kalwa, "Collective Bargaining in Basic Steel, 1946–83" (Ph.D. diss., Cornell University, 1985), 29; Tiffany, *The Decline of American Steel,* 128–37; Barnett and Schorsch, *Steel,* 26–30.

49. Tiffany, *The Decline of American Steel,* 128–37; Barnett and Schorsch, *Steel,* 26–30. Barnett and Schorsch faulted the industry's investment policies in this period for their "disappointing commitments" (30). McDonald appears to have had no real understanding of the forces driving technological innovation, but as noted, he was never the union's real strategist. His lack of understanding is evident in remarks he made during a USA Executive Board meeting held on September 17, 1953 (USA–EBP, September 17, 1953, 118–20). Labor's worries about the "automation" issue are recounted in "Push-Button Labor," *Fortune,* August 1954, 50–52; "Technological Alarms," and "Beyond the Annual Wage," *Fortune,* May 1955, 59–60 and 92–94; "The First 'Automation' Strike," *Fortune,* December 1955, 57–58; "Work Under Automation," *Fortune,* July 1956, 182.

50. The most recent study of the steel industry in this period concluded that it borrowed much less to finance new construction than did other firms in the manufacturing sector (Tiffany, *The Decline of American Steel,* 239, n. 41). Bethlehem Steel and, to a lesser extent, Republic, National, and U.S. Steel also offered their chief managers incomes substantially in excess of those earned by other senior corporation executives. See the study of steel management's income and cover letter from Steve Horn to WCW, August 10, 1959, in the file marked "1959 Steel Strike (August 1–15) 1," box 92, Mitchell Papers. Donald Barnett and Louis Schorsch also noted the industry's high profits during this period but blamed the government and, by implication, the union also for pressuring managers to build expensive and unneeded plants (Barnett and Schorsch, *Steel,* 30–32). Note that both management and the unions discounted the danger of foreign competition because of the expectation that it would come from Europe and that steel prices would rise there at the same rate as in the United States. And that, in fact, happened. Not foreseen, however, was the emergence of Japanese steel made with much cheaper labor and marketed at much lower prices (Tiffany, *The Decline of American Steel,* 144).

51. USA–EBP, June 22, 1954, 21, also 5–6; USA–EBP, April 5, 1954, 94; "Steel the Money or the Glory" and "Downwind Bargaining," *Fortune,* January 1954, 65–70; "McDonald's Straws," *Fortune,* April 1954, 75–76; "Guaranteed Surprise," *Fortune,* June 1954, 63–64, 68.

52. Livernash, *Collective Bargaining in the Basic Steel Industry,* 287–91; Kalwa, "Collective Bargaining in Basic Steel," 29–30; Tiffany, *The Decline of American Steel,* 147–49. The steel contract was in line with others in the manufacturing sector ("The Wage Trend Levels Off," *Fortune,* August 1954, 47–48; "Wage Trickle," *Fortune,* October 1954, 74, 76).

53. USA–EBP, June 29, 1954, 5–6, also 7–17, 20–25.

54. Ibid., 20–25.

55. USA–EBP, May 6, 1954, 22–28, June 29, 1954, 20–25, May 11, 1955, 21–30. Goldberg explained the need for master contracts in order to establish a GAW or supplemental unemployment benefits (SUB) plan at a USA Executive Board meeting held on May 14, 1956 (USA–EBP, May 14, 1956, 23). The board's view that more uniform contracts would increase the union's bargaining power emerged also from the long discussion of the issue, which took place at a meeting held on June 11, 1957 (USA–EBP, June 11, 1957, 14–64).

56. USA–EBP, May 6, 1954, 23, also 22, 24–28.

57. On the opposition based on a desire for more participation by the rank and file, see Nyden, *Steelworkers Rank-and-File*, 36–39. Directors Paul Rusen and Joe Germano expressed fears that industrywide bargaining would eliminate marginal producers (USA–EBP, May 6, 1954, 24–26).

58. "Behind the Steel Strike," *Fortune*, July 1952, 55.

59. USA–EBP, January 26, 1954, 79. Goldberg later said that "by 1956, I felt that a high point of understanding existed between the union and the industry, and I had hopes that we were going to enter upon a new period of relations, which would be what I call a period of maturity" (quoted in Shaplen, "Peacemaker," 84).

60. USA–EBP, June 22, 1954, 25; Roger M. Blough, *The Washington Embrace of Business* (New York: Columbia University Press, 1975), 7.

61. USA–EBP, June 22, 1954, 23–27; Blough, *The Washington Embrace of Business*, 7–8; Tiffany, *The Decline of American Steel*, 149; Roger M. Blough Memoir, OHC, LBJL, 1–27.

62. USA–EBP, May 11, 1955, 14, also 13, 15–19; Tiffany, *The Decline of American Steel*, 149.

63. "Labor—Set to Go," *Fortune*, January 1955, 47–50; "Bargaining Calendar," *Fortune*, March 1955, 49; "McDonald Dissents," *Fortune*, April 1955, 82; "Beyond the Annual Wage," *Fortune*, May 1955, 92–94; "After Ford," *Fortune*, July 1955, 47–50; "S.U.B.: A Slow Start," *Fortune*, June 1956, 237–38; "The Disappointing S.U.B.," *Fortune*, September 1957, 235; Brody, *Industrial Workers in America*, 193–94; Tiffany, *The Decline of American Steel*, 149.

64. USA–EBP, May 11, 1955, 22.

65. Ibid., 28, also 27.

66. Ibid., 21–29; Hoerr, *And the Wolf Finally Came*, 229–31; Livernash, *Collective Bargaining in the Basic Steel Industry*, 291–92; Kalwa, "Collective Bargaining in Basic Steel," 30.

67. Hoerr, *And the Wolf Finally Came*, 229–31; Livernash, *Collective Bargaining in the Basic Steel Industry*, 291–92; Kalwa, "Collective Bargaining in Basic Steel," 30.

68. USA–EBP, June 27, 1955, 12, also 9–11, 13–17; Livernash, *Collective Bargaining in the Basic Steel Industry*, 291–94; Kalwa, "Collective Bargaining in Basic Steel," 30; Tiffany, *The Decline of American Steel*, 149.

69. USA–EBP, June 27, 1955, 9–17; Tiffany, *The Decline of American Steel*, 149; Livernash, *Collective Bargaining in the Basic Steel Industry*, 291–94; Kalwa, "Collective Bargaining in Basic Steel," 30.

70. Kalwa, "Collective Bargaining in Basic Steel," 30–31; Livernash, *Collective Bargaining in the Basic Steel Industry*, 294–97; Hoerr, *And the Wolf Finally Came*, 230–31; Tiffany, *The Decline of American Steel*, 149–50.

71. USA–EBP, May 14, 1956, 9–10.

72. Ibid., 10–11. The study, a copy of which is in the file marked "1956 Steel Strike (1)," box 91, Mitchell Papers, concluded that from 1947 to 1955, steel "prices in-

creased significantly more than unit labor costs." For the way in which the figures were calculated, see the memo from Ewan Clague to Charles D. Stewart, July 13, 1956, entitled "Summary Report on the Steel Industry," and the supplemental memo to John J. Gilhooley from Stewart, July 20, 1956, both of which are in that same file. Mitchell sent copies of the study to Eisenhower and George Humphrey. A copy of Mitchell's cover letter to the former is also in that file. Eisenhower sent Mitchell a reply thanking him for "sending me that highly interesting chart." See the letter, April 3, 1956, in the file marked "1956–White House Confidential," box 159, Mitchell Papers. U.S. Steel executives met with a senior official at the Labor Department and vehemently expressed their opposition to its conclusions. See Ewan Clague's memo to Mitchell reporting on that meeting, entitled "Conference on Steel," May 7, 1956, in the file marked "1956 Steel Strike (1)," box 91, Mitchell Papers.

73. Tiffany, *The Decline of American Steel*, 149–52.

74. USA–EBP, May 11, 1955, 30–32, April 18, 1956, 22–33, May 14, 1956, 12–18; "Annual Wage–Cont.," *Fortune*, April 1952, 64; "Stumbling Blocks to the G.A.W.," *Fortune*, August 1955, 55–56; "Tin Can to the Annual Wage," *Fortune*, November 1955, 67; "1956 and Beyond" and "Which Kind of S.U.P.?" *Fortune*, January 1956 184–86; Kalwa, "Collective Bargaining in Basic Steel," 30–32; Livernash, *Collective Bargaining in the Basic Steel Industry*, 294–300; Tiffany, *The Decline of American Steel*, 149–51; Hoerr, *And the Wolf Finally Came*, 76–77; Lichtenstein, *Labor's War at Home*, 240.

75. USA–EBP, May 14, 1956, 21, also 18–20, 22–23; "Steel–Coming Up," *Fortune*, May 1956, 215; Kalwa, "Collective Bargaining in Basic Steel," 30–32; Livernash, *Collective Bargaining in the Basic Steel Industry*, 294–300; Tiffany, *The Decline of American Steel*, 149–51; Hoerr, *And the Wolf Finally Came*, 76–77.

76. On the narrowing of labor's vision in the postwar period, see Lichtenstein, *Labor's War at Home*, 203–45; Lichtenstein, "From Corporatism to Collective Bargaining," 140–45; Brody, *Workers in Industrial America*, 190–91. Even radical unions such as the UE emphasized economic gains from the mid-1940s onward (Schatz, *The Electrical Workers*, 150–60).

77. See the chronology of negotiations entitled "Pre-Strike," in the file marked "1956 Steel Strike (2)," box 91, Mitchell Papers; Kalwa, "Collective Bargaining in Basic Steel," 30–31; Livernash, *Collective Bargaining in the Basic Steel Industry*, 294–98; Tiffany, *The Decline of American Steel*, 149–50.

78. On the emergence of Boulwarism, see Schatz, *The Electrical Workers*, 170–74; "Carey vs. Boulware," *Fortune*, October 1952, 90–91; Mike Davis, *Prisoners of the American Dream* (London: Verso, 1986), 117–21.

79. "Steel's Strangest Strike" and "Steel's Bargain Package," *Fortune*, September 1956, 125, 246, and 207, respectively; Kalwa, "Collective Bargaining in Basic Steel," 31–32; Livernash, *Collective Bargaining in the Basic Steel Industry*, 297–300; Tiffany, *The Decline of American Steel*, 149–51. The potential candidates for a steel fact-finding board were discussed in a memo from George Strong to Joseph F. Finnegan, July 12, 1956, entitled "1956 Steel Dispute," a copy of which is in the file marked "1956 Steel Strike (1)," box 91, Mitchell Papers. When word leaked to the press of the heavy pressure that Mitchell had put on steel company executives to settle, he wrote U.S. Steel President Clifford Hood explaining that the disclosures had been unintentional. A copy of the letter, July 28, 1956, and of the news story that prompted it are in the file marked "1956 Secretary's Personal File–Confidential–Miscellaneous (3)," box 36, Mitchell Papers. For evidence of the business community's hostile response to Mitchell's intervention in the 1956 dispute, see the letters from business executives in the file

marked "1956 Federal Mediation and Conciliation Service—Steel Strike (1) & (3)," box 91, Mitchell Papers.

80. Kalwa, "Collective Bargaining in Basic Steel," 31–32; Livernash, *Collective Bargaining in the Basic Steel Industry*, 299–300; Tiffany, *The Decline of American Steel*, 148–51. McDonald had strongly resisted the COLA idea, but Goldberg talked him into it. On that point, see Herling, *Right to Challenge*, 42. By June 1957, McDonald was telling the board that "the cost of living adjustment provision is something new insofar as our written policy is concerned, but we believe it is necessary to negotiate these clauses in our new agreements because of what is continuing to happen . . . [to] . . . the cost of living" (USA–EBP, June 11, 1957, 14).

81. USA–EBP, July 27, 1956, 7. See also "The Trend to Longer Contracts," *Fortune*, August 1956, 185; Kalwa, "Collective Bargaining in Basic Steel," 32; Livernash, *Collective Bargaining in the Basic Steel Industry*, 299–300; Tiffany, *The Decline of American Steel*, 151.

82. In the three years governed by the 1956 contract, total hourly employment costs in steel rose almost 30 percent, and its basic price rose approximately $21 per ton. On that point and for details of the 1956 settlement, see Livernash, *Collective Bargaining in the Basic Steel Industry*, 299–300.

83. USA–EBP, June 11, 1957, 35. See also USA–EBP, September 9, 1957, 31; Leo Troy, *Trade Union Membership, 1897–1962* (Cambridge, Mass.: National Bureau of Economic Research, 1965), 19.

84. USA–EBP, September 9, 1957, 2–3.

85. The public's approval of unions, as measured by the Gallup Poll, stood at 75 percent in 1953 and did not change until the latter half of 1957. See Michael Goldfield, *The Decline of Organized Labor in the United States* (Chicago: University of Chicago Press, 1987), 35. Unions had won 82 percent of NLRB-supervised organizing elections in 1945, after which had come a steady decline. By the first quarter of 1956, the rate was 64 percent ("New Low at the NLRB," *Fortune*, July 1956, 179). On the slowing in union growth, see "White-Collar Lag," *Fortune*, April 1955, 76, 79–80; "A Little Wagner Act" and "Beyond the Annual Wage," *Fortune*, May 1955, 60, 62, 64, 94–95, 205–10; "No Boom for Unions," *Fortune*, June 1956, 136–37, 174, 186; "No Sale," *Fortune*, September 1956, 210–12; "Where Does Labor Go from Here?" *Fortune*, December 1957, 153–55, 256–62; "Labor's Slipping Strength," *Fortune*, December 1957, 229; Lichtenstein, *Labor's War at Home*, 244.

86. AJG. Goldberg headed a CIO committee that in 1954 had calculated how many union members were covered by the private benefits system. In that year 4.5 million were enrolled in life insurance plans, 4.6 million in hospitalization plans, and 3.2 million in pension plans (CIO–EBP, December 1, 1954, 98–99). See also "The Steady Push for Pensions," *Fortune*, June 1959, 209–10; Lawrence S. Root, *Fringe Benefits: Social Insurance in the Steel Industry* (Beverly Hills, Calif.: Sage, 1982), 57–227; Richard B. Freeman and James L. Medoff, *What Do Unions Do?* (New York: Basic Books, 1984), 61–77, 150–61; Henry C. Kenski, "The Impact of Unemployment on Presidential Popularity from Eisenhower to Nixon," *Presidential Studies Quarterly* 7 (1977): 120; "Characteristics of the Unemployed," *Fortune*, October 1956, 238; "Labor's 'Real' Wage Gains Under Two Administrations," *Fortune*, April 1956, 229; "Real Wages—The Breakthrough," *Fortune*, June 1956, 237; "The Ten-Cent Year," *Fortune*, December 1956, 227; "Major Economic Indicators 1947–57," *Fortune*, January 1958, 208. The term *privatized welfare state* was taken from Lichtenstein, "From Corporatism to Collective Bargaining," 140.

87. "Government Policy," *Fortune*, January 1954, 68–70; "State Labor Scores,"

Fortune, August 1955, 60; "Wage-Hour Prospects," *Fortune*, April 1957, 239; "Schism in the NLRB," *Fortune*, October 1955, 64–69; "The Hot Issue of Picketing," *Fortune*, February 1956, 193–98; "Politics and the NLRB," *Fortune*, October 1956, 237–40; "Lawless Territory," *Fortune*, May 1957, 257; "Federal Minimum Wage and Hour Laws," *Fortune*, September 1959, 222. Mitchell's support for an increase in the minimum wage as early as December 1954 is detailed in his letter to the White House chief of staff, Sherman Adams, December 6, 1954, a copy of which is in the file marked "1954—White House—Confidential," box 159, Mitchell Papers.

88. AJG; Robert M. Collins, *The Business Response to Keynes, 1929–1964* (New York: Columbia University Press, 1981), 152–58; Robert W. Griffith, "Dwight D. Eisenhower and the Corporate Commonwealth," *American Historical Review* 87 (1982): 100–22; Stephen Ambrose, *Eisenhower: The President* (New York: Simon & Schuster, 1984), 13–370; Eric F. Goldman, *The Crucial Decade—And After: America 1945–1960* (New York: Vintage Books, 1960), 237–306; John Patrick Diggins, *The Proud Decades: America in War and Peace, 1941–1960* (New York: Norton, 1988), 122–53, 306-7; Malcolm Moos, "Election of 1956," in Arthur M. Schlesinger Jr. and Fred L. Israel, eds., *History of American Presidential Elections*, vol. 4 (New York: McGraw-Hill, 1971), 3341–54; Arthur C. Wolfe, "Trends in Labor Union Voting Behavior, 1948–1968," *Industrial Relations* 9 (1969): 1–9; Steven M. Gillon, *Politics and Vision: The ADA and American Liberalism, 1947–1985* (New York: Oxford University Press, 1987), 99–103; John Bartlow Martin, *Adlai Stevenson and the World* (Garden City: Doubleday, 1977), 232–398; McDonald, *Union Man*, 252–53; "In Political Battle," *Fortune*, January 1956, 188; "Labor in the '56 Elections," *Fortune*, April 1956, 225–26, 229; "Getting Ready for '56," *Fortune*, August 1956, 189; "Labor in the 1956 Campaign," *Fortune*, November 1956, 231–36.

89. "How Big a Stick?" *Fortune*, November 1955, 70–72; Harvard Sitkoff, *A New Deal for Blacks: The Emergence of Civil Rights as a National Issue* (New York: Oxford University Press, 1978); Harvard Sitkoff, *The Struggle for Black Equality, 1954–1980* (New York: Hill & Wang, 1981), 3–65; Goldman, *The Crucial Decade*, 12–66, 182–87, 264, 293–94; Diggins, *The Proud Decades*, 275–96; Marty Jezer, *The Dark Ages: Life in the United States, 1945–1960* (Boston: South End Press, 1982), 155–59, 296–303.

90. USA–EBP, November 27, 1956, 92–93. For Goldberg's views on the issue of racial discrimination, see his speech to the Jewish Labor Committee on February 26, 1955, entitled "Civil Rights—Cornerstone of Our American Freedoms," a copy of which is in Goldberg Papers. McDonald's limited commitment to desegregation was evident from his enthusiasm for holding a USA convention in Miami, a locale favored by the AFL but shunned before the merger by the CIO unions, which refused to accept segregated facilities for their members. See his remarks on that subject in USA–EBP, March 3, 1955, 365–66, and the discussion in CIO–EBP, November 20, 1953, 183. The nature of workplace discrimination during this period and the USA's response are captured in Robert J. Norrell, "Caste in Steel: Jim Crow Careers in Birmingham, Alabama," *Journal of American History* 73 (1986): 685–89; Reutter, *Sparrows Point*, 346–52; Herling, *Right to Challenge*, 219–22. See also "Revolt in the South," *Fortune*, May 1956, 215–16; "Bias in Unions," *Fortune*, June 1957, 245–46.

91. USA–EBP, November 27, 1956, 91–95, September 10, 1957, 149–50; Norrell, "Caste in Steel," 685–89; Reutter, *Sparrows Point*, 346–52; Herling, *Right to Challenge*, 219–22; "Revolt in the South," *Fortune*, May 1956, 215–16; "Bias in Unions," *Fortune*, June 1957, 245–46.

92. CIO–EBP, July 20, 1955, 28–44; AJG.

93. CIO–EBP, May 7, 1955, 10–11, also 8–9, 12–19; "The Hot Season," *Fortune*, June 1955, 61–62; "Equal Pay for Southerners," *Fortune*, January 1957, 183–84.

94. AJG.

95. Jezer, *The Dark Ages*, 219–34; Diggins, *The Proud Decades*, 211–19; Elaine Tyler May, "Cold War–Warm Hearth: Politics and the Family in Postwar America," in Steve Fraser and Gary Gerstle, eds., *The Rise and Fall of the New Deal Order, 1930–80* (Princeton, N.J.: Princeton University Press, 1989), 153–81; William Chafe, *The American Woman: Her Changing Social, Political and Economic Roles* (New York: Oxford University Press, 1972), 135–225; Cynthia Harrison, *On Account of Sex: The Politics of Women's Issues, 1945–68* (Berkeley and Los Angeles: University of California Press, 1988), 3–65; Susan M. Hartmann, *The Home Front and Beyond: American Women in the 1940s* (Boston: Twayne, 1982), 53–120; Eugenia Kaledin, *Mothers and More: American Women in the 1950's* (Boston: Twayne, 1984), 43–80.

96. Dorothy Goldberg, *A Private View of a Public Life* (New York: Charterhouse, 1975), 3–4; Hartmann, *The Home Front*, 53–75; Reutter, *Sparrows Point*, 360–78; Esther Peterson Memoir, OHC, JFKL, 38; Esther Peterson Memoir, OHC, LBJL, 1.

97. Both the Chamber of Commerce and the National Association of Manufacturers supported the ERA (Harrison, *On Account of Sex*, 3–38; Hartmann, *The Home Front*, 128–34; Kaledin, *Mothers and More*, 67–72).

98. Harrison, *On Account of Sex*, 39–51; Hartmann, *The Home Front*, 134–38; Kaledin, *Mothers and More*, 71–73.

99. Jezer, *The Dark Ages*, 77–106, 200–14; Diggins, *The Proud Decades*, 110–17, 157–76; "'Subversives' in Industry," *Fortune*, February 1954, 76–80; Dwight McDonald's review, "Our Invisible Poor," of Michael Harrington's *The Other America*, which appeared in the *New Yorker*, January 19, 1963, 82–132.

100. For the need to view the postwar social contract in an international context, see Ronald W. Schatz, "From Commons to Dunlop and Kerr: Rethinking the Field and Theory of Industrial Relations," paper presented at the Conference on Industrial Democracy sponsored by the Wilson Center Program on American Society and Politics, Washington, D.C., March 28–30, 1988, 2–12. On the Marshall Plan and labor's response to it, see Anthony Carew, *Labour Under the Marshall Plan: The Politics of Productivity and the Marketing of Management Science* (Manchester: Manchester University Press, 1987), 80–130; Michael J. Hogan, *The Marshall Plan: America, Britain, and the Reconstruction of Western Europe, 1947–1952* (Cambridge: Cambridge University Press, 1987); William Diebold Jr., "The Marshall Plan in Retrospect: A Review of the Recent Scholarship," *Journal of International Affairs* 41 (1988): 421–35.

101. CIO–EBP, August 29, 1950, 102. See also Carew, *Labour Under the Marshall Plan*, 80–130.

102. CIO–EBP, August 29, 1950, 96–100. On the subject of labor pressure to improve conditions for French workers, see Victor Reuther's memo to his brother Walter entitled "Wage Problem in France," October 2, 1950, in folder 13, box 379, Reuther Papers.

103. CIO–EBP, August 29, 1950, 104. Murray agreed that workers in Italy and France still opposed the postwar social contract. He told the CIO Executive Board at that same meeting that "the right-wing labor movement in France is dead, it has no power, it has no strength, it has no influence" (100). The attitudes of workers in those countries are summarized in Carew, *Labour Under the Marshall Plan*, 19–39, 111–30.

104. "Labor's Role Abroad," *Fortune*, January 1957, 186–88; Carew, *Labour Under the Marshall Plan*, 101–7; Ronald L. Filipelli, *American Labor and Postwar Italy, 1943–1953* (Stanford, Calif.: Stanford University Press, 1989).

105. CIO–EBP, August 20, 1953, 56, 110–20; November 12, 1953, 132–34; "Rift in I.C.F.T.U.," *Fortune*, April 1952, 64; "A. F. of L. Scoreboard," *Fortune*, November 1954, 73; "Who Is an Anti-Communist?" *Fortune*, February 1955, 62; "Labor's Role Abroad," *Fortune*, January 1957, 186–88; Carew, *Labour Under the Marshall Plan*, 80–91, 111–30; Shaplen, "Peacemaker," 102; Gerd Hadach, "The Marshall Plan in Germany, 1948–1952," *Journal of European Economic History* 16 (1987): 433–85; Klaus Migeld, "As the Iron Curtain Descended: The Co-ordinating Committee of the Nordic Labour Movement and the Socialist International Between Potsdam and Geneva (1945-55)," *Scandinavian Journal of History* 13 (1988): 49–63; David Childs, "The Cold War and the 'British Road,' 1946–53," *Journal of Contemporary History* 23 (1988): 551–72.

106. The CIO's pressure for greater use of labor attachés is noted in a "Memorandum of Conversation" February 17, 1950. The memo was of a meeting held on that day between Secretary of State Dean Acheson and Murray, Goldberg, Potofsky, and Ross. The memo is in Dean Acheson Papers, HSTL. See also the memo entitled "Inter-American Labor," May 14, 1953, in the file marked "Latin American Labor," box 4, Philip Kaiser Papers, HSTL. Labor Secretary James Mitchell encountered resistance to the attaché program from the State Department but prevailed in his efforts to preserve the program. See three letters on that subject from Mitchell to John Foster Dulles, February 26, June 23, and November 6, 1953, in the file marked "1953 Office of International Labor Affairs," box 63, Mitchell Papers. On how Mitchell intended the program to work, see the memo from Burton A. Zorn to James P. Mitchell entitled "Labor Attaché Program," July 28, 1955, in the file marked "1955 Secretary's Personal File — Confidential — Miscellaneous (2)," and the memo entitled "Ten New Labor Attaché Positions," in the file marked "1956 Secretary's Personal File — Confidential — Miscellaneous (2)" both of which are in box 36 of Mitchell Papers. See also Sheldon Garon, *The State and Labor in Modern Japan* (Berkeley and Los Angeles: University of California Press, 1987), 187–248.

107. On the work of the Randall Commission and the key role of Clarence Randall, see his journals in DDEL; Tiffany, *The Decline of American Steel*, 109–14; McDonald, *Union Man*, 239; "Lip Service to Foreign Trade," *Fortune*, May 1953, 74; "Clarence Randall: Statesman from Steel," *Fortune*, January 1954, 120–22, 132, 134, 136, 138, 143.

108. Tiffany, *The Decline of American Steel*, 109–27; McDonald, *Union Man*, 239; "Lip Service on Foreign Trade," *Fortune*, May 1953, 74; "Clarence Randall: Statesman from Steel," *Fortune*, January 1954, 120–22, 132, 134, 136, 138, 143. The continuing weakness of the Japanese economy was noted in the memo entitled "Japanese Tariff Negotiations–A Summary," a copy of which is in the file marked "1954 — White House — Confidential," box 159, in Mitchell Papers. See also on that point the *Randall Journals*, vol. 2, entry for November 20, 1953, 3.

109. AJG. Labor's failure to win the Randall Commission's backing for subsidies intended to cushion the blow of greater foreign competition is detailed in the *Randall Journals*, vol. 2, entries for December 23, 1953, 18–19, January 6–7, 1954, 7–12.

110. USA–EBP, 27 November 1956, 69.

111. Ibid., 72.

112. Ibid., 80, also 63–79, 81; Livernash, *Collective Bargaining in the Basic Steel Industry*, 309–17; Tiffany, *The Decline of American Steel*, 121–27; Barnett and Schorsch, *Steel*, 23–26.

113. Volker R. Berghahn, *The Americanisation of West German Industry, 1945–1973* (Leamington Spa: Berg, 1986), 40–259; "Mitbestimmungsrecht," *Fortune*, April

1951, 54–58; Robert Heilbroner, "The Swedish Promise," *New York Review of Books*, December 4, 1980, 33–36; Alain Touraine, "Management and the Working Class in Western Europe," *Daedalus* 93 (1964): 304–34; Charles S. Maier, *In Search of Stability: Explorations in Historical Political Economy* (Cambridge: Cambridge University Press, 1987), 121–84; Philippe C. Schmitter and Gerhard Lehmbruch, eds., *Trends Toward Corporatist Intermediation* (Beverly Hills, Calif.: Sage, 1979); Philippe C. Schmitter and Gerhard Lehmbruch, eds., *Patterns of Corporatist Policy-Making* (Beverly Hills, Calif.: Sage, 1982).

114. The war's impact on German managerial power is discussed in Berghahn, *The Americanisation of West German Industry*, 40–259; "Mitbestimmungsrecht," *Fortune*, April 1951, 54–58. For the ways in which World War II strengthened American management, see Howell Harris, *The Right to Manage: Industrial Relations Policies of American Business in the 1940's* (Madison: University of Wisconsin Press, 1982), 105–58; Alan Brinkley, "The Concept of New Deal Liberalism, 1937–1945," unpublished manuscript, 31–63, 75–98; John Morton Blum, *V Was for Victory* (New York: Harcourt Brace Jovanovich, 1976), 90–146, 301–32.

115. AJG.

Chapter 6. The Postwar Order Under Stress, Round One

1. On the 1957–58 and 1960–61 recessions, see Raymond J. Saulnier Memoir, OHC, DDEL, 26–65; John Patrick Diggins, *The Proud Decades: America in War and Peace, 1941–1960* (New York: Norton, 1988), 178–81, 321, 345; Stephen Ambrose, *Eisenhower: The President* (New York: Simon & Schuster, 1984), 460.

2. "The Cost of Living 1947–57: How the Essentials Fared" and "Major Economic Indicators 1947–57," *Fortune*, January 1958, 206, 208; Henry C. Kenski, "Inflation and Presidential Popularity," *Public Opinion Quarterly* 41 (1977): 88; Henry C. Kenski, "The Impact of Unemployment on Presidential Popularity from Eisenhower to Nixon," *Presidential Studies Quarterly* 77 (1977): 120; Saulnier Memoir, OHC, DDEL, 26–32; "The 'Invisible' Unemployed," *Fortune*, July 1958, 105–11, 198, 200, 202, 204; "Labor's 'Race Problem,'" *Fortune*, March 1959, 191–92, 194; William H. Harris, *The Harder We Run: Black Workers Since the Civil War* (New York: Oxford University Press, 1982), 130–37; "Chronic Unemployment," *Fortune*, November 1958, 241–42, 246; "What's Happened to Real Wages?" *Fortune*, December 1958, 183; "How Much Help for the Unemployed?" *Fortune*, May 1959, 217. One key alteration in policy following the change of administration in 1961 was to increase the money supply. From 1957 to 1960 it grew at an average annual rate of 0.8 percent, but in the next seven years the increase accelerated to more than 5 percent per year (Saulnier Memoir, 60).

3. U.S. military spending as a percentage of the nation's GNP declined from just over 10 percent in 1958 to just under 9 percent in 1960 and rose only slightly over the following two years. Spending in each year after 1958 was less than for any year since 1950, although it remained enormous by historical standards for any major industrialized society ostensibly at peace. At the same time, U.S. spending on foreign aid, which included foreign military assistance, shrank from approximately 1.1 percent of GNP to 0.75 percent ("U.S. Military and Foreign Aid Spending," *Wall Street Journal*, February 21, 1989). See also Ambrose, *Eisenhower: The President* 388–406, 423–60, 590–92; Eric F. Goldman, *The Crucial Decade—And After: America 1945–1960* (New

York: Vintage Books, 1960), 307–12; Diggins, *The Proud Decades*, 312–18; Stephen E. Ambrose, *Nixon: The Education of a Politician, 1913–62* (New York: Touchstone, 1987), 442–46.

4. The growing balance-of-payments crisis and its causes are discussed in Saulnier Memoir, OHC, DDEL, 45–48. Saulnier, a Columbia University economist who chaired the Council of Economic Advisers from 1957 to 1960, observed that "as we moved through 1960, this problem became even more critical. Indeed, a crisis developed in the London Gold market" (45). See also Peter J. Katzenstein, "Introduction: Domestic and International Forces and Strategies of Foreign Economic Policy," in Peter J. Katzenstein, ed., *Between Power and Plenty: Foreign Economic Policies of Advanced Industrial States* (Madison: University of Wisconsin Press, 1978), who noted that "one of the first serious crises of the Bretton Woods system . . . [occurred when] 300 million dollars were converted into Swiss francs in a four-day period in March 1961" (13).

5. See Peter J. Katzenstein, "Domestic Structures and Strategies of Foreign Economic Policy," in Katzenstein, ed., *Between Power and Plenty*, 295; Richard H. Pells, *The Liberal Mind in a Conservative Age: American Intellectuals in the 1940's and 1950's*, 2nd ed. (Middletown, Conn.: Wesleyan University Press, 1989), 346–99; Marty Jezer, *The Dark Ages: Life in the United States, 1945–1960* (Boston: South End Press, 1982), 253–309; Diggins, *The Proud Decades*, 247–72; Goldman, *The Crucial Decade*, 315–25.

6. AJG; Barry Goldwater Memoir, OHC, DDEL, esp. 1–12; Ambrose, *Nixon*, 421–22; "In Political Battle," *Fortune*, January 1956, 188.

7. Nelson Lichtenstein, *Labor's War at Home* (Cambridge: Cambridge University Press, 1982), 242–43; Mike Davis, *Prisoners of the American Dream* (London: Verso, 1986), 121–23.

8. Lichtenstein, *Labor's War at Home*, 242–43; Davis, *Prisoners of the American Dream*, 121–23; Thomas J. Watson Jr. Memoirs, OHC, JFKL; PACLMP-CM, JFKL; Joseph L. Block Papers, LBJL.

9. Jezer, *The Dark Ages*, 213; Goldman, *The Crucial Decade*, 315; "The Shadow of McClellan," *Fortune*, April 1957, 233; R. Alton Lee, *Eisenhower and Landrum–Griffin: A Study in Labor–Management Politics* (Lexington: University of Kentucky Press, 1990), 50–54; Alan K. McAdams, *Power and Politics in Labor Legislation* (New York: Columbia University Press, 1964), 36–39; Robert F. Kennedy, *The Enemy Within* (New York: Popular Library, 1960), 15–33; Samuel C. Patterson, "Labor Lobbying and Labor Reform: The Passage of the Landrum–Griffin Act," carbon copy in folder 28, box 31, AFL–CIO Legislative Department Papers, 1–2. The *Fortune* piece noted that "this special Senate committee plainly portends a lot of trouble for union racketeers; the question is whether the trouble can be confined to them." On the publicity campaigns, see also USA–EBP, August 11, 1958, 61, where David McDonald denounced the committee as "a frontal assault on organized labor" prompted by "millions of pieces of literature being distributed throughout the colleges and to civic groups and to clubs of all kinds and description by the National Association of Manufacturers and the Chamber of Commerce and the Committee on Constitutional Education and the Right-to-Work Committee—and . . . National Retail Association." On the unfairness of a corruption investigation that focused on labor unions alone, see "The Scandals in Union Welfare Funds," *Fortune*, April 1954, 202; "The Kennedy Operation," *Fortune*, June 1957, 242; Richard B. Freeman and James L. Medoff, *What Do Unions Do?* (New York: Basic Books, 1984), 213–17. Daniel Bell noted in "The Kennedy Operation" that "at one point . . . Senator McClellan indi-

cated he would be interested in looking into business expense-account practices. But this investigation never got underway." Freeman and Medoff reported that surveys conducted by *Fortune* and the American Management Association indicate that "business crime far exceeds union crime" (215). Furthermore, labor corruption in the strictest sense was much less prevalent by 1957 than it had been twenty-five years earlier, although the rise of the private benefits system had contributed to some new problems in that area ("A Modest Housecleaning," *Fortune*, September 1956, 208).

10. AJG. Murray had imposed stringent controls during 1952, in part to curb then Secretary-Treasurer David McDonald's misuse of USA funds. On that point, see Chapters 4 and 5; the letter from Goldberg's rabbi, Jacob Weinstein, to Senator Paul Douglas, which discussed Goldberg's views on union corruption and urged Douglas to work on that problem. The letter, May 26, 1956, is in Weinstein Papers. The example of joint administration that Murray had had in mind was that pioneered by the UMW. Its mismanagement of that fund pointed out the pitfalls inherent in such an approach. See George Reedy Memoir, OHC, LBJL, pt. 12, 44–45; "Labor Notes," *Fortune*, April 1953, 96; "The Miners' Hospital Chain," *Fortune*, March 1954, 70; "The Scandals in Union Welfare Funds," *Fortune*, April 1954, 141; "The Gentlemen of Coal," *Fortune*, October 1955, 70. Joint administration did have one attractive aspect for labor, namely, giving it a say in how pension funds were invested. Labor leaders' desire to use that influence against antiunion business managers is discussed in "Unionizing the Market," *Fortune*, February 1955, 64, 66.

11. Labor opposed a subsequent effort by congressional conservatives to require stricter government scrutiny of pension plans. The proposal had been part of the package of Taft–Hartley amendments that Congress rejected in 1954. The plan, first introduced by Senator Robert Taft, is noted in "Mr. Taft Proposes," *Fortune*, January 1953, 64. See also "Notes of the Month," *Fortune*, December 1951, 52; "Labor Airs Some Dirty Linen," *Fortune*, August 1952, 81, 190, 192; "The Ghost of Lepke," *Fortune*, September 1952, 70, 72–73; "Waterfront Mess," *Fortune*, April 1953, 94, 96; "The Scandals in Union Welfare Funds," *Fortune*, April 1954, 140–42, 196, 198, 200, 202, 205–6; "Beck's Bad Boys," *Fortune*, May 1954, 54, 58 60, 62; "Beck's Bad Boys (cont.)," *Fortune*, December 1954, 61, 64, 66; "Welfare-Fund Follies," *Fortune*, October 1955, 70, 72, 76; "Racketeering—Something New?" *Fortune*, May 1956, 218, 220; "A Modest Housecleaning," *Fortune*, September 1956, 208, 210.

12. CIO–EBP, October 5, 1954, 66, also 67–72; "Labor's Unhealthy Welfare Plans," *Fortune*, May 1951, 75–76; "The Scandals in Union Welfare Funds," *Fortune*, April 1954, 140–42, 196, 198, 200, 202, 205–6; "Welfare-Fund Follies," *Fortune*, October 1955, 70, 72, 76. In 1954 a Senate subcommittee also began investigating the administration of pension and welfare funds, finding many of the same problems. See Lee, *Eisenhower and Landrum-Griffin*, 74–75; "A Modest Housecleaning," *Fortune*, September 1956, 207–8. The CIO had also experienced some corruption even before the pension and welfare funds came into existence, principally in the form of in-plant gambling ("Labor Airs Some Dirty Linen," *Fortune*, August 1952, 81, 190, 192). For the impact of the unfavorable publicity following from such practices, see "The Moral Capital," *Fortune*, January 1954, 72, where Daniel Bell noted that organized labor was beginning to suffer a serious decline in its prestige as a result of the corruption issue.

13. CIO–EBP, October 5, 1954, 65–66, also 67–72. The new evidence of union corruption prompted increases in the number of federal investigations and prosecutions aimed at eliminating it. The Justice Department opened approximately fifteen hundred such probes in 1954 and the first half of 1955. They were undertaken,

however, with a minimum of publicity ("Labor Racketeering," *Fortune*, July 1955, 50, 52).

14. CIO–EBP, December 1, 1954, 107, also 94–106, 108–14.

15. Ibid., 107–15. See also "Labor's Unhealthy Welfare Plans," *Fortune*, May 1951, 75–76; "The Scandals in Union Welfare Funds," *Fortune*, April 1954, 141–42, 196, 198, 200, 202, 205–6; "Welfare-Fund Follies," *Fortune*, October 1955, 70, 72, 76.

16. CIO–EBP, May 7, 1955, 103, also 98–102, 104–18; "Goldberg Hits Ohio Labor 'Reform' Bill," a copy of which is in Goldberg Papers; "Welfare-Fund Follies," *Fortune*, October 1955, 72, 76.

17. Archie Robinson, *George Meany and His Times* (New York: Simon & Schuster, 1981), 179–80, 185–99; Albert J. Woll Memoir, AFL–CIO MOHC, 10–11; "New York's Waterfront," *Fortune*, December 1949, 210, 213; "Labor Airs Some Dirty Linen," *Fortune*, August 1952, 81, 190; "Waterfront Mess," *Fortune*, April 1953, 94, 96; "The Lonely Doghouse of Joe Ryan," *Fortune*, November 1953, 78; "The Polluted Port," *Fortune*, December 1953, 64, 66, 68; "Welfare Funds – The Best Foot Forward" and "The Scandals in Union Welfare Funds," *Fortune*, April 1954, 76, 140–42, 196, 198, 200, 202, 205–6; "Welfare-Fund Follies," *Fortune*, October 1955, 70, 72, 76; "Racketeering – Something New?" *Fortune*, May 1956, 216, 218, 220.

18. Kennedy, *The Enemy Within*, 160–61, 171, 297; Lee, *Eisenhower and Landrum– Griffin*, 54–73; McAdams, *Power and Politics*, 11–12; Patterson, "Labor Lobbying and Labor Reform," 2–3; "The Shadow of McClellan," *Fortune*, April 1957, 233; "The Kennedy Operation," *Fortune*, June 1957, 241–42, 245; "A.F.L.–C.I.O. on the Block," *Fortune*, July 1958, 222.

19. AJG; Robert Shaplen, "Peacemaker," *New Yorker*, pt. 1, April 7, 1962, 108; Kennedy, *The Enemy Within*, 204–5, 268–9; USA–EBP, May 17, 1957, 194–95; "The Shadow of McClellan," *Fortune*, April 1957, 233.

20. AJG. See also Arthur M. Schlesinger Jr., *Robert Kennedy and His Times* (Boston: Houghton Mifflin, 1978), 3–182; Lee, *Eisenhower and Landrum–Griffin*, 50; "The Kennedy Operation," *Fortune*, June 1957, 241-42, 245.

21. AJG. At least one labor leader believed that both John and Robert Kennedy had accepted roles with the McClellan Committee to promote the former's presidential ambitions (Alexander Christie Memoir, OHC, JFKL, 7–8).

22. "Labor's Ethics," *Fortune*, July 1957, 207–8, 210; Shaplen, "Peacemaker," 108.

23. USA–EBP, May 16, 1957, 147–211; "Labor's Ethics," *Fortune*, July 1957, 207–8, 210, in which Daniel Bell reported that Goldberg had been "the principal author of all the codes" 208).

24. USA–EBP, May 17, 1957, 170. In keeping with that view, the Ethical Practices Committee ruled that the code would be given retroactive application. Goldberg's draft of a letter, April 4, 1957, for McDonald's signature to the USA Executive Board explaining the proposed code and urging its adoption is in box 60, McDonald Papers.

25. USA–EBP, May 17, 1957, 147–211; "Labor's Ethics," *Fortune*, July 1957, 208, 210.

26. USA–EBP, May 17, 1957, 195; "Labor's Ethics," *Fortune*, July 1957, 241.

27. USA–EBP, May 17, 1957, 171–77; Lester Velie, "Labor's Two-Front War Against the Rackets," *Reader's Digest*, June 1957, 37–42, clipping in Goldberg Papers; "A Modest Housecleaning," *Fortune*, September 1956, 207–8, 210; "A.I.W. House Cleaning," *Fortune*, September 1957, 241; "Labor's Ethics," *Fortune*, July 1957, 208, 210.

28. USA–EBP, May 17, 1957, 190–91. When first formed, the McClellan Committee consisted of four Democrats (McClellan, Kennedy, Sam Ervin of North Carolina, and Pat McNamara of Michigan) and four Republicans (Joseph McCarthy of Wisconsin, Karl Mundt of South Dakota, Irving Ives, and Barry Goldwater). McCarthy, however, soon fell ill and left the committee. He was replaced by Carl Curtis of Nebraska. Of those eight, the two more senior Democrats, McClellan and Ervin, and three of the four Republicans represented states that had outlawed the union shop. And this was despite a Democratic majority, albeit narrow, in the Senate and even though only thirty-six of its then ninety-six members came from such areas. See McAdams, *Power and Politics*, 36–39; Kennedy, *The Enemy Within*, 32–33, Schlesinger, *Robert Kennedy*, 153–54, 185–86.

29. USA–EBP, May 17, 1957, 191–92. See also "The Scandals in Welfare Funds," *Fortune*, April 1954, 204.

30. USA–EBP, May 17, 1957, 192, also 193–98. Senators Curtis and Goldwater had introduced a bill in the spring of 1956 to bar unions with contracts containing union-shop clauses from using their political action funds in elections for federal government office. A senior member of the AFL–CIO's legal department summarized the proposed law in a memo noting that the "bill in general resembles bills which were introduced last year in the legislatures of Ohio, Michigan, and Indiana. These proposals probably have some central origin, possibly the NAM or Chamber of Commerce." See the memo entitled "The Curtis–Goldwater Bill (S. 3074)," March 7, 1956, from Thomas E. Harris to Robert Oliver and William Hushing, in folder 95, box 84, Staff Working Files, AFL–CIO Legislative Department Papers.

31. USA–EBP, May 17, 1957, 147–211.

32. USA–EBP, May 16, 1957, 70–71.

33. USA–EBP, May 17, 1957, 192–98, August 12, 1958, 281–302. Copies of the correspondence between McDonald and Robert Kennedy are in USA–EBP, September 10, 1957, 122–26, May 14, 1958, 3–4. See also John Herling, *Right to Challenge: People and Power in the Steelworkers Union* (New York: Harper & Row, 1972), 58; Goldberg's draft of Reuther's testimony and a cover letter, March 10, 1958, in folder 5, box 418, Reuther Papers; Goldberg's revised draft and cover letter, March 13, 1958, in the same file; Reuther's eleven-page letter defending the UAW's patriotism to Senator Barry Goldwater, March 7, 1958, also in that file; "McClellan in a Kohler," *Fortune*, February 1958, 212, 214; Joseph L. Rauh Jr.'s Memoir, OHC, JFKL, 19; Kennedy, *The Enemy Within*, 177, 205, 218, 302.

34. USA–EBP, September 10, 1957, 156, also 150–55.

35. "The Kennedy Operation," *Fortune*, June 1957, 241–42, 245; "A.F.L.–C.I.O. on the Block," *Fortune*, July 1958, 222; Goldman, *The Crucial Decade*, 315; Lee, *Eisenhower and Landrum–Griffin*, 50–73; Schlesinger, *Robert Kennedy*, 147–95. See also generally, Kennedy, *The Enemy Within*, for discussions of each investigation.

36. Goldman, *The Crucial Decade*, 315; Lee, *Eisenhower and Landrum–Griffin*, 50–73; McAdams, *Power and Politics*, 39–40, 69-70; Alexander Christie Memoir, OHC, JFKL, 8; Freeman and Medoff, *What Do Unions Do?* 214–15; "A Modest Housecleaning," *Fortune*, September 1956, 208. The decline in public approval of unions is discussed in Michael Goldfield, *The Decline of Organized Labor in the United States* (Chicago: University of Chicago Press, 1987), 35–36, who noted that "favorable opinions toward unions, as measured by the Gallup polls, dropped from 75 percent before the McClelland [*sic*] hearings to 68 percent afterward." From February 1957, when the committee began its work, to September, when its activity peaked, the

approval rating slumped from 76 percent to 64 percent (35). Union leaders had feared this consequence almost from the outset of the committee's organization ("The Shadow of McClellan," *Fortune*, April 1957, 233).

37. USA–EBP, May 17, 1957, 171. See also AJG; Benjamin Aaron, "Amending the Taft–Hartley Act: A Decade of Frustration," *Industrial and Labor Relations Law Review* 11 (1958): 336–38; "Labor's Ethics," *Fortune*, July 1957, 207–8, 210.

38. USA–EBP, May 17, 1957, 168. The new clause appeared in huge type on the front page of the March 1957 issue of the *American Federationist*, a signal of Meany's seriousness about the issue. See also Woll Memoir, AFL–CIO MOHC, 4, 10–11. The clause itself was so vague that even the Teamsters did not object to it. As Woll noted, those agreeing to its inclusion in the constitution "didn't know what was actually meant by corrupt influence" (4).

39. Goldberg Memoir, AFL–CIO MOHC, 19–20. See also "The Ghost of Lepke," *Fortune*, September 1952, 72; "The Scandals in Welfare Funds," *Fortune*, April 1954, 196, 198, 200, 205; "Welfare-Fund Follies," *Fortune*, October 1955, 72, 76; "Racketeering—Something New?" *Fortune*, May 1956, 218; "McClellan in a Kohler," *Fortune*, February 1958, 214; "The Revolving Crisis," *Fortune*, May 1957, 251–52.

40. See the text of the AFL–CIO suspension notice, which was reprinted in the *New York Times*, October 25, 1957; Velie, "Labor's Two-Front War," 37–42.

41. AJG. See also Goldberg Memoir, AFL–CIO MOHC, 19, where Goldberg said that the move to oust Dorfman was handled "by a special committee. . . . He was an evil influence in the AFofL. He had this little local and he was the Mafia inside of the AFofL. George [Meany] had been advised, I don't know by whom, that he could not legally get rid of him, and then he talked to me and I said, 'Don't you worry. You can get rid of him. He's a crook, well known, and we will demonstrate by evidence that he's using that little local of 600 people as his credential for larger things,' which turned out to be the case."

42. Goldberg Memoir, 18–20, and McDonald Memoir, 7, 10–12, both in AFL–CIO MOHC. The Teamsters Union's power stemmed not just from its size but also from its strategic location in the American economy. Given the union's firm grip on the transportation system, Teamsters' backing often determined whether other unions' strikes succeeded or failed (Reedy Memoir, pt. 12, 45, OHC, LBJL).

43. McDonald Memoir, 12, also 7, 11, Goldberg Memoir, 20, and Albert J. Woll Memoir, 16–20, all in AFL–CIO MOHC; "Labor's Ethics," *Fortune*, July 1957, 207–8, 210; "Where Does Labor Go from Here?" and "Can the Teamsters Clean House?" *Fortune*, December 1957, 154, 230; Robinson, *George Meany*, 196–98.

44. AJG; Velie, "Labor's Two-Front War," 37–42; Robinson, *George Meany*, 197–202; McAdams, *Power and Politics*, 40; Patterson, "Labor Lobbying and Labor Reform," 3; USA–EBP, May 17, 1957, 169–71; Goldberg Memoir, 17–20, Woll Memoir, 16–20, and McDonald Memoir, 6–7, 10-12, 15, all in AFL–CIO MOHC. The ouster of the Teamsters alone also cost the federation $790,000 in annual dues, which had been intended to finance a major organizing campaign ("The Revolving Crisis," *Fortune*, May 1957, 251).

45. Shaplen, "Peacemaker," 108; Lee, *Eisenhower and Landrum–Griffin*, 75–78; McAdams, *Power and Politics*, 40–42; CIO–EBP, May 7, 1955, 99–102; USA–EBP, August 25, 1959, 73–75; "Welfare Fund Code," *Fortune*, April 1956, 230, 232; "Controlling the Money," *Fortune*, June 1957, 241; "A New Labor Law?" *Fortune*, November 1957, 241–42; "The Legislative Impasse," *Fortune*, June 1958, 201. A summary of the Douglas bill and a covering letter from Goldberg to McDonald,

November 29, 1957, is in the Steelworkers Papers. Goldberg noted in it that "I state on your behalf that you support the draft legislation."

46. Lee, *Eisenhower and Landrum–Griffin*, 75–78; McAdams, *Power and Politics*, 41–42; "The Legislative Impasse," *Fortune*, June 1958, 201. The Supreme Court in March 1957 had created the "no-man's land" when it ruled that states could not regulate labor–management disputes that fell within federal jurisdiction, even if the federal government had refused to exercise it ("Lawless Territory," *Fortune*, May 1957, 257). The Court one year later slightly narrowed the scope of its preemption doctrine ("Back to the States, *Fortune*, July 1958, 221–22). An earlier bill, sponsored by Senator McClellan in 1956, would have permitted state regulation of all areas of labor relations not specifically preempted by Congress. That much broader so-called states' rights measure had gone nowhere ("On the Legal Calendar," *Fortune*, April 1956, 229).

47. Goldberg noted, in urging the USA Executive Board to pass a resolution requiring some safeguards against abuse of the administratorship power, its value in helping combat racial discrimination in the locals, embezzlement of union funds, and abuse of power more generally by local officials. The resolution was adopted (USA–EBP, March 17, 1958, 131–37). On the Teamsters' misuse of administratorships and the McClellan's Committee's exposure of that problem, see Lee, *Eisenhower and Landrum–Griffin*, 56–57. The McClellan investigation also appears to have encouraged dissidents to seek aid from the federal government in opposing union leaders. See "Workers Are Complaining—To the NLRB," *Fortune*, December 1958, 188, which reported that workers' complaints against the unions rose to an all-time record that year. Conservatives had sought to include a so-called bill of rights in the original Taft–Hartley bill. The provision had been dropped as too controversial during the House–Senate conference. See Christopher L. Tomlins, *The State and the Unions; Labor Relations, Law and the Organized Labor Movement in America, 1880–1960* (Cambridge: Cambridge University Press, 1985), 290.

48. Herling, *Right to Challenge*, 43–69; Lloyd Ulman, *The Government of the Steel Workers' Union* (New York: Wiley, 1962), 140–75; Philip W. Nyden, *Steelworkers Rank-and-File: The Political Economy of a Reform Movement* (New York: Praeger, 1984), 40–42; John P. Hoerr, *And the Wolf Finally Came: The Decline of the American Steel Industry* (Pittsburgh: University of Pittsburgh Press, 1988), 252–57; "The Decline of Dave McDonald," *Fortune*, August 1958, 169–70.

49. Arthur J. Goldberg, "Labor in the Free Society: A Trade Union Point of View," speech delivered at a conference sponsored by the Fund for the Republic, New York, May 3, 1958, 4, a copy of which is in Goldberg Papers. One of the leading USA dissidents, Nicholas Mamula, had made that analogy when he told the 1958 USA convention that "if we are dual unionists, fellow Steelworkers, then the Republicans and Democrats are dual Americans" (Ulman, *The Government of the Steel Workers' Union*, 174). Sociologist Seymour Lipset drew a similarly inappropriate comparison at the New York conference. Lipset contended that the "arguments of the union people [against union democracy legislation] . . . are the very arguments that conservatives and corporations used in the early Thirties, in an effort to ward off the SEC and other regulatory bodies" (quoted in "End of the Affair?" *Fortune*, July 1958, 224). In that same article, Daniel Bell noted the growing disenchantment with labor among liberal academics and bureaucrats over the corruption and union democracy issues. See also Steven M. Gillon, *Politics and Vision: The ADA and American Liberalism, 1947–1985* (New York: Oxford University Press, 1987), 123. Gillon noted that union contributions to the leading liberal group, the ADA, dropped significantly after 1954. Twenty-

six percent of the organization's income had come from labor groups in that year, but by 1959, the figure had dropped to less than 10 percent.

50. Goldberg, "Labor in the Free Society," 7, also 1–6, 8–15; "End of the Affair?" *Fortune*, July 1958, 222–24.

51. Goldberg, "Labor in the Free Society," 8. Goldberg observed that "I need only point . . . to a great segment of the American textile industry, to many sections of the oil and chemical industries, to the communications industry, to retail trade and to almost all of the service industries" as places where employers continued to fight unionization tooth and nail (14).

52. Ibid., 6.

53. See Arthur J. Goldberg, "Rights and Responsibilities of a Trade Union Member," speech delivered at the Conference on Freedom and Responsibility in the Industrial Community sponsored by the Northwestern University Law School, Chicago, October 23, 1957, 17–18, a copy of which is in Goldberg Papers; Goldberg, "Labor in the Free Society," 1–22. Goldberg did acknowledge that unions were far more secure in some areas and industries than in others and that the range of rights should be greater where unions were strongest. "Our real problem," he concluded, "is that we have a very mixed society" ("Labor in the Free Society," 10).

54. Those who believe that managers influenced by Herbert Hoover's associationalist ideas were the true creators of the postwar order have missed that critical distinction. Hoover's hostility to the CIO stemmed from not only his disappointments as president but also his opposition to the redistribution of power in the workplace that CIO unions had brought about. The most sophisticated New Deal liberals understood that only those kinds of unions could give the state a meaningful degree of autonomy from the business managers, which was the key prerequisite for its pursuit of policies that would stabilize and preserve a market system. For evidence of Hoover's support for labor organizations, but not for the CIO, see David Burner, *Herbert Hoover* (New York: Knopf, 1979), 173–78; and Herbert Hoover, *The Memoirs of Herbert Hoover: The Great Depression, 1929–1941* (New York: Macmillan, 1952), 433–39, *Addresses upon the American Road, 1933–38* (New York: Scribners, 1938), 296–97, *Further Addresses upon the American Road, 1938–41* (New York: Scribners, 1941), 52, 55, 56, *Further Addresses upon the American Road, 1941–45* (New York: Van Nostrand, 1946), 227–29, *Further Addresses upon the American Road, 1945–48* (New York: Van Nostrand, 1949), 34–35, 51, 55–57. Hoover's "associationalist vision," is described in Ellis Hawley, "Herbert Hoover, the Commerce Secretariat, and the Vision of the 'Associative State,' 1921–28," *Journal of American History* 61 (1974): 116–40. On Goldberg's view of unions such as the USA as providing the state with autonomy from the business managers, see Chapter 4. For the liberal critique of labor leaders' opposition to "democratizing" union governance, see "End of the Affair?" *Fortune*, July 1958, 222, 224.

55. Goldberg, "Right and Responsibilities," 17, also 1–16, 18; Goldberg, "Labor in the Free Society," 16–22; Herling, *Right to Challenge*, 58.

56. Goldberg, "Rights and Responsibilities," 15.

57. USA–EBP, May 16, 1957, 91.

58. USA–EBP, August 26, 1959, 122.

59. USA–EBP, August 11, 1958, 57. See also Herling, *Right to Challenge*, 54–69; Hoerr, *And the Wolf Finally Came*, 252–57; Ulman, *The Government of the Steel Workers' Union*, 144–75; Nyden, *Steelworkers Rank-and-File*, 41–42.

60. USA–EBP, August 11, 1958, 57. See also Ulman, *The Government of the Steel Workers' Union*, 154.

61. One example of abuse was to expel members deemed guilty of disloyal acts. When some locals petitioned for a change in the constitution that would have required the executive board to notify them within a prescribed period when a member was expelled, the board voted against submitting the petition to the USA convention for consideration. See USA–EBP, January 6, 1959, 224; Ulman, *The Government of the Steel Workers' Union*, 171–72; Nyden, *Steelworkers Rank-and-File*, 2–3; "The Decline of Dave McDonald," *Fortune*, August 1958, 169–70. On the effect of the USA's efforts to restrain dissidents even on those friendly to the union, see the petition entitled "Formula to Assure Harmony in United Steelworkers of America," in McDonald Papers. Produced by a commission composed of George Meany, the director of the Social Action Department of the National Catholic Welfare Conference, a former director of the Federal Mediation and Conciliation Service, and a former vice-president of the USA, the petition noted that "a large segment of the public press and others . . . have interpreted the [1958 USA] Convention's Special [DPC] Resolution . . . as retribution against an opposition group of office-seekers" (4). Goldberg passed along the petition with a note to McDonald, October 2, 1958.

62. McAdams, *Power and Politics*, 41–43; Lee, *Eisenhower and Landrum–Griffin*, 75–81; "The Legislative Impasse," *Fortune*, June 1958, 201; "Jim Mitchell: Looking for a New Job," *Fortune*, June 1960, 246.

63. USA–EBP, August 25, 1959, 73–75; AJG; Shaplen, "Peacemaker," 108, 110; George Meany Memoir, 3–9, and Albert Zack Memoir, 8–9, both in the OHC, JFKL; Patterson, "Labor Lobbying and Labor Reform," 5–7; McAdams, *Power and Politics*, 43–46; Lee, *Eisenhower and Landrum–Griffin*, 81–83; Schlesinger, *Robert Kennedy*, 197; "The Legislative Impasse," *Fortune*, June 1958, 201–2; "End of the Affair?" *Fortune*, July 1958, 222, 224; George Reedy Memoir, OHC, LBJL, pt. 15, 10–12; the two memos from Reedy to Johnson, February 20, 1958, and June 3, 1958, which are in the files marked "Reedy: Labor— 1 of 2" and "Reedy: Labor–2 of 2," respectively, box 428, LBJ Senate Papers, LBJL. Schlesinger argues that the initiative for the law came from Kennedy but gives no evidence to support that claim. George Reedy, Senate Majority Leader Lyndon Johnson's chief legislative aide, in a memo dated June 3, 1958, noted that "Senator Kennedy has produced a labor bill . . . which was written largely in the office of Arthur Goldberg" (1).

64. AJG; Patterson, "Labor Lobbying and Labor Reform," 5–7; McAdams, *Power and Politics*, 44–46; Lee, *Eisenhower and Landrum–Griffin*, 81–83; Schlesinger, *Robert Kennedy*, 197; "The Legislative Impasse," *Fortune*, June 1958, 201–2; "End of the Affair?" *Fortune*, July 1958, 222, 224; George Reedy Memoir, OHC, LBJL, pt. 15, 10–12; the two memos from Reedy to Johnson dated February 20, 1958, and June 3, 1958. The building trades' opposition to the bill rested in part on their desire to include in any labor "reform" measure the Taft–Hartley amendments they had sought since the beginning of Eisenhower's presidency. See the memo and attached documents from Goldberg to the heads of the major industrial unions, March 22, 1957, in Steelworkers Papers.

65. Patterson, "Labor Lobbying and Labor Reform," 7; McAdams, *Power and Politics*, 46; Lee, *Eisenhower and Landrum–Griffin*, 82.

66. USA–EBP, March 17, 1958, 137, also 138–42; Patterson, "Labor Lobbying and Labor Reform," 7; Lee, *Eisenhower and Landrum–Griffin*, 81–83; McAdams, *Power and Politics*, 45–47.

67. USA–EBP, March 17, 1958, 139. George Meany also opposed any legislation that would require union officers to file personal expense statements with the Department of Labor. See the letters to the editors of the *New York Times* and the *Washing-*

ton Evening Star from Andrew Biemiller, which clarified Meany's position. Copies of the letters, dated April 1, 1958, are in folder 19, box 85, Staff Working Files, AFL–CIO Legislative Department Papers.

68. USA–EBP, March 17, 1958, 137–42; Patterson, "Labor Lobbying and Labor Reform," 7; Lee, *Eisenhower and Landrum–Griffin*, 81–83; McAdams, *Power and Politics*, 46.

69. Patterson, "Labor Lobbying and Labor Reform," 7; Lee, *Eisenhower and Landrum–Griffin*, 81–83; McAdams, *Power and Politics*, 44–45.

70. AJG; USA–EBP, March 17, 1958, 131–43; McAdams, *Power and Politics*, 44–48; Lee, *Eisenhower and Landrum–Griffin*, 81–84; George Reedy Memoir, OHC, LBJL, pt. 15, 8–9; three memos from Reedy to Lyndon Johnson, two dated January 4 and 23, 1959, and the third, which is not dated and bears the title "Meeting with Meany." All are in the folder marked "Reedy: Memos–January 1959," box 428, LBJ Senate Papers.

71. AJG.

72. AJG. See also USA–EBP, August 25, 1959, 73–75; Albert Zack Memoir, 8, and James Reynolds Memoir, 2–4, both in OHC, JFKL. Theodore Sorensen, Kennedy's senior legislative aide from 1952 onward, later wrote that the latter's work on the Kennedy–Ives bill was "the first time in his Congressional career . . . [in which] he concentrated intensively and almost exclusively for a period of years on a single piece of legislation." See Theodore Sorensen, *Kennedy* (New York: Harper & Row, 1965), 52. On Kennedy's service on the House and Senate Labor Committees, see p. 51. Labor leader Alexander Christie noted that the much more knowledgeable Oregon senator Wayne Morse played a major role in conducting the hearings on the Kennedy bill (Christie Memoir, 5, OHC, JFKL).

73. DKGD, entry for September 1, 1962; Dorothy Goldberg, *A Private View of a Public Life* (New York: Charterhouse, 1975), 132–33; my interview with Theodore Sorensen, July 21, 1993.

74. Lee, *Eisenhower and Landrum–Griffin*, 81–90; McAdams, *Power and Politics*, 45–48; Patterson, "Labor Lobbying and Labor Reform," 5–7; USA–EBP, March 17, 1958, 137–38, August 25, 1959, 74–75; the memo entitled "Position on Labor Legislation," marked "Confidential," August 6, 1958, in the file marked 1958 Secretary's Personal File–Confidential Misc–(2)," box 37, James P. Mitchell Papers. Lyndon Johnson characteristically attempted to play both ends against the middle with respect to Kennedy–Ives. See the memo to him from George Reedy, July 29, 1958, which suggested that Johnson tell business leaders pressing him to block the bill that they should support Kennedy–Ives because the Democrats would gain seats in the upcoming elections. The new Congress thus would be less likely to pass a bill more attractive to management. The memo, marked "Confidential," is in the file marked "Reedy: Labor–1 of 2," box 428, LBJ Senate Papers. See also Reedy's Memoir, OHC, LBJL, pt. 13, 2–3. Missouri congressman Charles Brown observed shortly before the key roll call in the House: "Never have I seen such a supercharged, pressurized atmosphere as that surrounding the Kennedy–Ives bill. On all sides there is hate, fear and retaliation" (quoted in Lee, *Eisenhower and Landrum–Griffin*, 87). The eventual outcome came as no great surprise. Daniel Bell had correctly predicted in April 1958 that the deep divisions in labor and management circles would likely prevent the enactment of any such measure that year ("The Legislative Impasse," *Fortune*, June 1958, 201–2).

75. Lyndon Johnson had helped Germany secure the RFC loan, thereby earning his lasting gratitude. See Eugene B. Germany Memoir, OHC, LBJL, 27–29, 54; Kenneth Warren, *The American Steel Industry, 1850–1970: A Geographical Inter-*

pretation (Pittsburgh: University of Pittsburgh Press, 1973), 248, 280; USA–EBP, May 14, 1958, 5–19; the arbitrator's final report in the *Lone Star* case, a copy of which is in Goldberg Papers.

76. USA–EBP, May 14, 1958, 18, also 5–8. Between 1956 and 1958 there were 788 wildcat strikes in steel, which cost companies an estimated 729,200 tons of production. See David Brody, *Workers in Industrial America: Essays on the Twentieth Century Struggle* (New York: Oxford University Press, 1980), 204.

77. USA–EBP, May 14, 1958, 8, also 5–7; the arbitrator's final report in Goldberg Papers.

78. District Director Martin Burns, whose jurisdiction included Lone Star, re-counted to the USA Executive Board a series of provocative actions that managers there had taken even before the arbitration controversy arose. Those actions were of such a nature, he said, that "in recent years there was no doubt in my mind that the company was trying to destroy our union" (USA–EBP, May 14, 1958, 15, 16–17).

79. Ibid., 9.

80. Ibid., 10–11.

81. Ibid., 12–13, also 14–19.

82. See *Textile Workers Union* v. *Lincoln Mills*, 353 U.S. 448 (1957); Lee Modjeska, "Labor and the Warren Court," *Industrial Relations Law Journal* 8 (1986): 512–14; David Brody, "Workplace Contractualism in America: An Historical/Comparative Analysis," 14–15, and James B. Atleson, "The Continuing Impact of Wartime Regulation of Labor," 33–34, papers given at the Conference on Industrial Democracy sponsored by the Wilson Center Program on American Society and Politics, Washington, D.C., March 28–30, 1988; Archibald Cox, Derek Bok, and Robert Gorman, *Cases and Materials in Labor Law*, 9th ed. (Mineola, N.Y.: Foundation Press, 1981), 553–60; Douglas L. Leslie, *Labor Law* (St. Paul: West, 1979), 273–76. Goldberg's associate, David Feller, argued one of the two companion cases before the Supreme Court. The third, which involved the radical-led United Electrical Workers, was argued by one of its own lawyers. See "High Court Backs Arbitration Pact," *New York Times*, June 4, 1957, a copy of which is in Goldberg Papers. The Court's decision, supported by seven of its members, drew a very sharp dissent from Justice Felix Frankfurter. His eighty-six-page opinion criticized the Court for making an interventionist ruling on the basis of a very murky legislative history. See 353 U.S. 448, 460–546 (1957).

83. For the view of arbitration and the *Lincoln Mills* decision as harmful to labor, see Katherine Van Wezel Stone, "The Post-War Paradigm in American Labor Law," *Yale Law Journal* 90 (1981): 1509–80, esp. 1523–35; Tomlins, *The State and Unions*, 321–22; Joel Edward Rogers, "Divide and Conquer: The Legal Foundations of Post-war U.S. Labor Policy" (Ph.D. diss., Princeton University, 1984), 288–332, 355–64. Those critics of the *Lincoln Mills* doctrine tend to assume that access to the courts would benefit labor in its struggles with management, but throughout U.S. history, the judiciary has been the branch of the government most hostile to labor's cause. See generally, William E. Forbath, "The Shaping of the American Labor Movement," *Harvard Law Review* 102 (1989): 1111–256. In *Industrial Workers in America*, Brody argues that the arbitration system discouraged rank-and-file dynamism, but he also notes that many managers resisted such schemes because they also tended to expand workers' rights (198–211). See also "Judging the Judges," *Fortune*, April 1959, 199, which reported that "labor has generally been more enthusiastic about arbitration than management—principally because most arbitrable issues fall into the area once considered the exclusive prerogative of management." Lone Star management's con-

tinuing but ultimately fruitless efforts to resist the union are noted in USA–EBP, January 10, 1962, 154–58, July 12, 1962, 196.

84. For the discussion of the USA's contract demands in 1958, see USA–EBP, December 3, 1957, 20–24, May 14, 1958, 19–44. According to USA–EBP, May 14, 1958, 20, the contracts open in 1958 covered 18 percent of the union's membership, some 214,631 workers. Goldberg's draft of the 1958 wage policy and his attached letter to McDonald, May 7, 1958, are in McDonald Papers. Goldberg's draft was adopted verbatim by the union's Wage Policy Committee one week later.

85. USA–EBP, August 12, 1958, 229, also 227–28.

86. Ibid., 230–37; "3 Timken Plants Shut by Walkout," *New York Times,* July 25, 1958.

87. USA–EBP, August 11, 1958, 60, also 59.

88. Ibid., 59–63; "Steel: It's a Brand-New Industry," *Fortune,* December 1960, 249–50, 254, 256; the draft of a letter from Dorothy Goldberg to her son, July 15, 1959, in which she wrote that Arthur's "antennae [had been] . . . remarkably perspicuous." The letter is in DKGD.

89. USA–EBP, May 14, 1958, 44–55, August 11, 1958, 60–62; "End of the Quiet Time," *Fortune,* January 1958, 205–6, 208; "No Strike in Autos," *Fortune,* May 1958, 203–4, 206; "Wage Scoreboard," *Fortune,* August 1958, 170; "Between Contracts," *Fortune,* October 1958, 202; "Chronic Unemployment," *Fortune,* November 1958, 241–42, 246; "After Boulware, What?" *Fortune,* December 1958, 184; "Employer Solidarity," *Fortune,* January 1959, 158. The UAW eventually won a new three-year contract, but one with the smallest wage-and-benefit increases for autoworkers since the end of World War II. The new Electrical Workers' contract was similarly unimpressive ("Chronic Unemployment," *Fortune,* November 1958, 246).

90. Gilbert S. Gall, *The Politics of Right to Work: The Labor Federations as Special Interests, 1943–79* (Westport, Conn.: Greenwood Press, 1988), 1–96; "In Political Battle," *Fortune,* January 1956, 188; "The Fire Is Spreading," *Fortune,* April 1957, 240; "The Right-to-Work Laws," *Fortune,* September 1957, 235–36, 241. USA legislative director Nordy Hoffman had voiced his concern over the union-shop legislation issue at an executive board meeting in the fall of 1953. The CIO's vigorous efforts during the election of 1954, especially in gubernatorial contests, had stemmed in part from that concern. See USA–EBP, September 17, 1953, 80–86, and CIO PAC director Jack Kroll's comments in CIO–EBP, October 5, 1954, 104. The Eisenhower administration was divided over whether to oppose the states' so-called right-to-work laws. Labor Secretary Mitchell publicly opposed them and pressed state legislators not to enact them, a position resisted by other leading figures in the administration. See "Mitchell—A Man in the Middle," *Fortune,* February 1955, 64; the memo in the file marked "1955 Secretary's Personal File—Confidential—Miscellaneous (1)," box 36, Mitchell Papers. The memo, marked "Confidential," reported to Mitchell that Vice-President Nixon had told business leaders in a private session at the Commerce Department that Mitchell's view was his "own opinion and did not represent the thinking of the administration."

91. Gall, *The Politics of Right to Work,* 96–100; "The Fire Is Spreading," *Fortune,* April 1957, 240; "The Right-to-Work Laws," *Fortune,* September 1957, 235–36, 241; "Union Shop Foes to Widen Fight," *New York Times,* March 4, 1957; USA–EBP, May 14, 1958, 45-47. On Mitchell's staff's opposition to the Indiana measure, see the memo from Walter Wallace to John Gilhooley, dated March 5, 1957, suggesting that Mitchell enlist White House chief of staff Sherman Adams in the effort to secure a gubernatorial veto. That memo, and another one from Millard Cass to Mitchell, dated

the same day and suggesting arguments he might make to the Indiana governor, are in the file marked "1957 Secretary's Personal File—Confidential Misc. (2)," box 37, Mitchell Papers.

92. Gall, *The Politics of Right to Work*, 97–128; Totton J. Anderson, "The 1958 Election in California," *Western Political Quarterly* 12 (1958): 276–300; Alan Draper, *A Rope of Sand: The AFL–CIO Committee on Political Education, 1955–67* (New York: Praeger, 1989), 68–73; "Union Shop Foes to Widen Fight," *New York Times*, March 4, 1957; "The Fire Is Spreading," *Fortune*, April 1957, 240; "The Right-to-Work Laws," *Fortune*, September 1957, 235–36, 241.

93. Draper, *A Rope of Sand*, 60–73; Gall, *The Politics of Right to Work*, 97–128; Anderson, "The 1958 Election in California," 276–300; Ambrose, *Nixon*, 488–89. On the significance of the California contest, see William Knowland's Memoir in OHC, DDEL, 98. Knowland said, "I think . . . the labor leadership of the country was fearful that if a big industrial state like California enacted it [a union-shop ban], it would then almost inevitably probably sweep the country, in the other big industrial states." See also Albert McDermott's memo to Walter Wallace, September 18, 1958, which reported that Knowland's legislative assistant had called to protest Mitchell's statement against the ballot measures. The memo is in the file marked "1958 Secretary's Personal File—Confidential Misc. (2)," box 37, Mitchell Papers. See also the letter from Charles R. Hook, president of the Ohio-based Armco Steel Company, which complained about the harm that Mitchell's remarks were doing to the campaign for the union-shop ban and GOP candidates in that state. Mitchell promptly replied, telling Hook, "I must state honestly that I do not believe that 'right-to-work' laws are wise or desirable." Hook's letter, October 28, 1958, and Mitchell's reply, November 1, 1958, are in the file marked "1958—Political (Nov.–Dec.)," box 190, Mitchell Papers.

94. "Proposed Statement of the Democratic Advisory Committee on Labor Policy," May 22, 1958, 5. A copy of that document, along with Goldberg's cover letter to members of the Labor Advisory Committee, May 23, 1958, is in Steelworkers Papers. Goldberg was the secretary for the group and drafted its statements after consulting with the labor leaders who served as members. Knowland had first aroused the ire of labor leaders in 1950, when he had sponsored a bill that would have compelled unemployed workers to accept jobs as strikebreakers or lose their unemployment benefits (CIO–EBP, June 15, 1950, 163–66). Knowland had become a gubernatorial candidate in 1958, when he forced the liberal Republican incumbent, Goodwin Knight, who opposed outlawing the union shop, to run for the Senate rather than for reelection as he had intended. See Knowland's Memoir, OHC, DDEL, 78–103; Anderson, "The 1958 Election in California," 276–83; Ambrose, *Nixon*, 446–47.

95. See Gall, *The Politics of Right to Work*, 97–98, 104–7, 215–21, who concluded after an exhaustive study of roll calls in Congress and the state legislatures on the issue that Democrats, save for those from the South, mostly opposed such measures, whereas Republicans typically supported them. The GOP official most strongly identified with the campaign to ban the union shop was Arizona Senator Barry Goldwater who, like Knowland, held an important leadership post in the Republican Party. From 1953 through 1958, Goldwater headed the Republicans' Senate Campaign Committee. During the six years in which he held that post, Goldwater succeeded in raising $6.5 million for GOP senatorial candidates (Goldwater Memoir, OHC, DDEL, 9–12).

96. USA–EBP, September 9, 1957, 41–62; "Mutual Partners," *Fortune*, May 1958, 206; USA–EBP, December 3, 1957, 8–9, March 18, 1958, 192–97, August 12, 1958, 264–65; Gall, *The Politics of Right to Work*, 107–9; Draper, *A Rope of Sand*, 64; "The

Layoff Mood," *Fortune*, March 1958, 221; "The 'Invisible' Unemployed," *Fortune*, July 1958, 105–11, 198, 200, 202, 204.

97. USA–EBP, September 10, 1957, 131, also 127–30, 132–40; "Mutual Partners," *Fortune*, May 1958, 206. An earlier effort to eliminate that obstacle in Ohio by passing a referendum had been a dismal failure. That approach, pressed by Reuther and the UAW in 1955, had gone down to defeat even in such industrial centers as Cleveland and Dayton. Leading the fight against the proposal were the Ohio Manufacturers' Association and the state's Chamber of Commerce ("In Political Battle," *Fortune*, January 1956, 188).

98. USA–EBP, September 10, 1957, 132, also 133–40; "Mutual Partners," *Fortune*, May 1958, 206.

99. USA–EBP, September 9, 1957, 47, also 41–46, 48–62; Gall, *The Politics of Right to Work*, 107–8.

100. USA–EBP, September 9, 1957, 59–60. On managers' use of alienated union members in the campaign to ban the union shop, see Gall, *The Politics of Right to Work*, 100–1.

101. The USA contributed $5,000 each to Proxmire and Yarborough (USA–EBP, September 9, 1957, 50). Yarborough defeated conservative Democrat Martin Dies and Republican Thad Hutcheson. The Texas labor movement's strong support for Yarborough and its rapidly growing size were apparently major factors in his election. Union gains there over the preceding two decades were by far the largest among the southern states. See "Texans to Choose Senator Tuesday," *New York Times*, March 31, 1957; "Texas G.O.P. Fails to Elect Senator," *New York Times*, April 3, 1957. In "Surprise in Texas," *Fortune*, March 1955, Daniel Bell reported that unions "have been growing faster in Texas than anywhere else in the U.S., with the possible exception of California" (52). On the Proxmire victory, see George Reedy's memo to Lyndon Johnson, August 27, 1957, which noted that it was the first victory by a Democrat in a Wisconsin Senate race since 1932 and that Proxmire had swept every county in the state except the central dairy belt, a feat Reedy called "amazing." Reedy attributed Proxmire's victory to the administration's tight money and farm policies, as well as "Republican labor relations (the Kohler Strike)" and the GOP foreign policy. He also observed that the Proxmire victory pointed to Democratic gains in 1958. The memo is in the file marked "Reedy: Memos, August 1957," box 420, LBJ Senate Papers. Although identified with Eisenhower's policies during the latter's first term, Kohler was the nephew of militantly antiunion Herbert V. Kohler, who headed a large manufacturing firm based in Sheboygan. The long and violent strike by its workers to obtain union recognition became a cause célèbre in labor and liberal circles during the 1950s. See "Winners in Wisconsin," and "Proxmire to Face Kohler on August 27," *New York Times*, August 1, 1957, 14.

102. A copy of the statement is reprinted in USA–EBP, March 17, 1958, 95–96, see also 97–100; USA–EBP, December 3, 1957, 8–9, August 12, 1958, 264–65. From March through August 1958, seasonally adjusted unemployment averaged 7.2 percent, the highest since 1941 (Draper, *A Rope of Sand*, 67). Just over a million of those unemployed in August of that year had been without work for more than twenty-six weeks, the maximum unemployment benefit period in most states ("How Much Help for the Unemployed?" *Fortune*, May 1959, 217).

103. Saulnier Memoir, OHC, DDEL, 37; "The 'Invisible' Unemployed," *Fortune*, July 1958, 105–11, 198, 200, 202, 204; "Chronic Unemployment," *Fortune*, November 1958, 241–42, 246; "What's Happened to Real Wages?" *Fortune*, December 1958, 183. On the layoffs in the automobile industry, which had reached about

300,000 by the end of April, see "No Strike in Autos," *Fortune*, May 1958, 203. Daniel Bell had surveyed workers' outlook early in 1958 and predicted that "if no business upturn develops by midyear, there may be a significant shift in the mood of U.S. labor." See "The Layoff Mood," *Fortune*, March 1958, 221; "The 'Invisible' Unemployed," *Fortune*, July 1958, 105.

104. A copy of the antirecession program, which the USA Executive Board approved unanimously without discussion, is in the USA–EBP, March 17, 1958, 95–100. See also Andrew Biemiller's letter to Senator John F. Kennedy, September 11, 1958, a copy of which is in AFL–CIO Papers, JFKL; "Andrew Biemiller – Labor's Man on the Hill," *Fortune*, February 1959, 196; Robert M. Collins, *The Business Response to Keynes, 1929–1964* (New York: Columbia University Press, 1981), 176–77; Ambrose, *Eisenhower: The President*, 460–61; Ambrose, *Nixon*, 484–85.

105. Diggins, *The Proud Decades*, 132–33, 322–23; Goldman, *The Crucial Decade*, 242–43, 281–82; Jezer, *The Dark Ages*, 154–75; Ambrose, *Eisenhower: President*, 299–301, 460–61; Ambrose, *Nixon*, 485, 488–89, 496; Anderson, "The 1958 Election in California," 276–300; Gall, *The Politics of Right to Work*, 93–128; Draper, *A Rope of Sand*, 60–73; Kent M. Beck, "What Was Liberalism in the 1950s?" *Political Science Quarterly* 102 (1987): 258, n. 69; "The 'Invisible' Unemployed," *Fortune*, July 1958, 105–11, 198, 200, 202, 204; "Chronic Unemployment," *Fortune*, November 1958, 241–42, 246; "How Much Help for the Unemployed?" *Fortune*, May 1959, 217. See also USA–EBP, January 6, 1959, 89–91, where Abel reported that the USA's Political Action Committee had raised during 1958 alone some $211,340.48, of which $192,091.21 was spent on that year's elections. Rank-and-file contributions to the AFL–CIO's national political apparatus, COPE, were a much less impressive $20,000 (91). A flyer listing the major business organizations backing the union-shop ban in Ohio is in the file marked "UOLO Fact Book," box 1, Samuel Pollock Papers, WPRL. See also the material in the file marked "Home Front" and the six folders marked "Right to Work, 1953–67," box 9, UAW Region Three Papers, WPRL.

106. In the 1958 California election 79.46 percent of all registered voters cast ballots. An indication of the union-shop issue's centrality to the gubernatorial race lay in the almost identical divisions recorded in both contests. The ballot initiative lost 59.6 percent to 40.4 percent, and Brown beat Knowland 59.8 percent to 40.2 percent. Even more revealing, the highly regarded Field Poll of California surveyed likely voters shortly before the election and found that those who called themselves upper class preferred Knowland, 60 percent to 40 percent, whereas those who considered themselves working class preferred Brown, 79 percent to 21 percent. Self-styled middle-class voters also preferred the latter, but by the substantially lower margin of 59 percent to 41 percent. See Anderson, "The 1958 Election in California," 277, 291, 300, also 276 and, more generally, 277–300; Gall, *The Politics of Right to Work*, 119–20; Draper, *A Rope of Sand*, 70–71. Draper noted that DiSalle carried every county that voted no on the union-shop measure, whereas O'Neill carried sixteen of the nineteen counties that voted yes (70). A list of the vote breakdown by county and a copy of O'Neill's televised address about the union-shop issue are in the files marked "UOLO-Campaign Tactics and Analysis" and "O'Neill, William – Speech," boxes 1 and 3, respectively, Samuel Pollock Papers. In both California and Ohio, the same issue also led to the defeat of GOP candidates for the U.S. Senate.

107. On the Indiana results, see James Robb's report to the USA Executive Board in USA–EBP, January 6, 1959, 225. In Ohio, the margins in the state legislature shifted after the election from GOP majorities of 55 and 10 in the House and Senate, respectively, to Democratic ones of 19 and 8 (Draper, *A Rope of Sand*, 70). In Massa-

chusetts there was a similar shift, with Democrats increasing their numbers in the other New England state legislatures (USA–EBP, January 6, 1959, 93). According to a study conducted by the University of Michigan's Survey Research Center, 78 percent of those union voters calling themselves working class voted Democratic in the 1958 congressional races, up from 64 percent in 1956. The figures for those labeling themselves middle class were 77 percent and 57 percent, respectively. Among union households, the percentage voting Democratic rose from 62 percent in 1956 to 78 percent in 1958. See Arthur C. Wolfe, "Trends in Labor Union Voting Behavior, 1948–1968," *Industrial Relation* 9 (1969): 1–6. See also Diggins, *The Proud Decades*, 324–25; Goldman, *The Crucial Decade*, 326; Draper, *A Rope of Sand*, 68; and Patterson, "Labor Lobbying and Labor Reform," 8, who observed that "particularly encouraging [to labor] was the defeat of three right-wing Republicans who served on the House Education and Labor Committee: Gwin[n] (N.Y.), Nicholson (Mass.), and Haskell (Del.)." Abel told the USA Executive Board that of the twenty-six candidates for the Senate and ninety-eight for the House to whom the USA had given funds, twenty-one and sixty-seven, respectively, prevailed. He also noted that five out of the six gubernatorial candidates who received money from the USA had won. Only in New York did the union back a losing candidate for governor, and he was beaten by liberal Republican Nelson Rockefeller, whom labor leaders saw as friendly to their cause (USA–EBP, January 6, 1959, 92).

108. Schlesinger's analysis of the voters' mood in the late 1950s is in his *A Thousand Days: John F. Kennedy in the White House* (Boston: Houghton Mifflin, 1965). Schlesinger refers there to a memo he wrote during the first half of 1959 entitled "The Shape of National Politics to Come," which predicted that "the approaching liberal epoch would resemble the Progressive period of the turn of the century more than it would the New Deal. The New Deal had taken its special character from the fight against depression; but the Progressive revolt grew out of spiritual rather than economic discontent; and this seemed the situation in 1959" (25–26). For a more recent analysis in the same vein as Schlesinger's, see Pells, *The Liberal Mind*, 395–96. Andrew Biemiller, another major labor lobbyist who headed the AFL–CIO's legislative department, shared Goldberg's more pessimistic conclusions about the 1958 election results ("Andrew Biemiller, Labor's Man on the Hill," *Fortune*, February 1959, 196).

109. "The State of Labor–Management Relations, 1958–1959," Sidney Hillman Address delivered by Arthur J. Goldberg on November 5, 1958 at the University of Wisconsin at Madison, 1–8. A copy of the address is in Goldberg Papers.

110. Ibid., 8–9.

111. Ibid., 10, also 11. Profits in the manufacturing sector did decline significantly in 1958, in part because unions pressed for wage-and-benefit increases during a slack year or were entitled to them automatically under multiyear contracts. See "Wage Scoreboard," *Fortune*, August 1958, 170; Davis, *Prisoners of the American Dream*, 121–25.

112. "The State of Labor–Management Relations," 10–11.

113. Ibid., 11–12.

114. Ibid., 16, also 11–15.

115. Ibid., 16–22. On the emergence of the "automation" issue, see "Push-Button Labor," *Fortune*, August 1954, 50, 52; "Technological Alarms," *Fortune*, May 1955, 59–60; "Work Under Automation," *Fortune*, July 1956, 182; "Rough Track," *Fortune*, November 1957, 246, 248; "Chronic Unemployment," *Fortune*, November 1958, 241–42, 246; "Longshore Woes," *Fortune*, March 1959, 194; Robert Lekachman, *The Age of Keynes* (New York: McGraw–Hill, 1966), 226–45.

116. "The State of Labor–Management Relations," 14; AJG. The influence of the wartime model in inspiring what eventually became the President's Advisory Committee on Labor–Management Policy is noted in Davis, *Prisoners of the American Dream*, 125.

117. AJG; "New Try at Keeping Labor Peace," *Business Week*, November 29, 1958, 105, 107; "Labor's Plenipotentiary," *Fortune*, March 1960, 220, 224. Clippings of the various news articles are in Goldberg Papers.

Chapter 7. The Postwar Order Under Stress, Round Two

1. See USA–EBP, August 25, 1959, 73–74.

2. Alan K. McAdams, *Power and Politics in Labor Legislation* (New York: Columbia University Press, 1964), 158–60, 174–78; Samuel C. Patterson, "Labor Lobbying and Labor Reform: The Passage of the Landrum–Griffin Act," carbon copy in folder 28, box 31, AFL–CIO Legislative Papers, 8, 47–54; R. Alton Lee, *Eisenhower and Landrum–Griffin: A Study in Labor–Management Politics* (Lexington: University of Kentucky Press, 1990), 97; "Labor Polishes Its Image," *Fortune*, January 1960, 179, 182, 184; USA–EBP, January 7, 1959, 228–79. The union had experienced problems during the 1958 elections in getting media organizations to run its material even when money was not an issue (USA–EBP, August 11, 1958, 300–2). Although the 1958 election results led to an increase in Democratic representation on the McClellan Committee, its new members supported this group's one-sided objective of investigating only labor corruption. On the committee's membership during 1959, see the memo on that subject from George Reedy to Johnson, January 17, 1959, in which Reedy urged Johnson to select a Democratic majority "*which would crack down* hard on racketeers." The memo is in file marked "Reedy: Memos—January 1959," box 428, LBJ Senate Papers.

3. USA–EBP, January 7, 1959, 274, also 228–73, 275–79; John Herling, *Right to Challenge: People and Power in the Steelworkers Union* (New York: Harper & Row, 1972), 56, 72–73.

4. USA–EBP, January 7, 1959, 228–79; McAdams, *Power and Politics*, 158–60, 174–78; Patterson, "Labor Lobbying and Labor Reform," 47–54; Lee, *Eisenhower and Landrum–Griffin*, 97. Goldberg recounted the scope of the managerial campaign to influence members of Congress in USA–EBP, August 25, 1959, 73–75. His remarks were part of a larger report on the entire effort to block antilabor legislation that year. The USA ultimately spent over $3 million on media during 1959, more than a fifth of its total operating budget. By the end of that year, the drain on the union's budget caused by the McDonald show led the union to abandon it (Herling, *Right to Challenge*, 72–73). Of the $3 million spent on media that year, approximately one-third was spent on advertising connected with the union's collective bargaining efforts ("Labor Polishes Its Image," *Fortune*, January 1960, 179).

5. AJG; USA–EBP, August 25, 1959, 75–76; Patterson, "Labor Lobbying and Labor Reform," 9, 14–15; McAdams, *Power and Politics*, 56–59, 64–65, 87–89; Lee, *Eisenhower and Landrum–Griffin*, 102. Doubtless contributing to Goldberg's sense that more legislation would be needed to defuse the corruption controversy was the McClellan Committee's ample supply of new cases, which *Fortune* reported in January 1959 "would enable it to continue investigating suspect union leaders for [another] three years" ("Ethics or Carpenters?" *Fortune*, January 1959, 158).

6. Kennedy's letter inviting Goldberg to serve on the advisory committee, Decem-

ber 30, 1958, is in folder 452, Senate Correspondence Files, Pre-Presidential Collection, John F. Kennedy Papers, JFKL. See also Kennedy's follow-up letter, January 31, 1959, folder 459, same collection; Patterson, "Labor Lobbying and Labor Reform," 14–15; McAdams, *Power and Politics*, 56, 285–86; Lee, *Eisenhower and Landrum–Griffin*, 99.

7. Patterson, "Labor Lobbying and Labor Reform," 8–20; McAdams, *Power and Politics*, 49–88; Lee, *Eisenhower and Landrum–Griffin*, 97–108; three memos from Reedy to Johnson, January 4, 17, and 23, 1959, all in file marked "Reedy: Memos, January 1959," box 428, LBJ Senate Papers. Reedy warned Johnson in the January 4 memo that "despite the Democratic victories of this Fall, it would be a mistake to attempt to 'beef it [Kennedy–Ives] up' with any more pro-labor provisions. Under the circumstances, *there may be too many in it already*." See also undated memo entitled "Meeting with Meany" in same folder. In that memo, Reedy informed Johnson that *"only Title VI opens up the field of labor–management relations. . . . If any aspect of labor–management relations is opened up, it will be difficult to prevent all aspects from being opened up*." He reiterated that warning in the January 23 memo.

8. Patterson, "Labor Lobbying and Labor Reform," 8–20; McAdams, *Power and Politics*, 49–88; Lee, *Eisenhower and Landrum–Griffin*, 97–108; the three memos from Reedy to Johnson cited in n. 7.

9. Senators Dirksen and Goldwater cast the two dissenting votes (McAdams, *Power and Politics*, 63). See also 49–62, 64–86; Patterson, "Labor Lobbying and Labor Reform," 15–22; Lee, *Eisenhower and Landrum–Griffin*, 97–108; USA–EBP, August 25, 1959, 75–77; "Andrew Biemiller—Labor's Man on the Hill," *Fortune*, February 1959, 196.

10. Patterson, "Labor Lobbying and Labor Reform," 23–30; McAdams, *Power and Politics*, 87–104; Lee, *Eisenhower and Landrum–Griffin*, 108–13; George Meany Memoir, OHC, LBJL, 4. The missing reliable senators were Hubert Humphrey, Paul Douglas, and Theodore Green of Rhode Island. The first two were away from Washington on business, the third ill. See McAdams, *Power and Politics*, 95–97; Patterson, "Labor Lobbying and Labor Reform," 28; Lee, *Eisenhower and Landrum–Griffin*, 110–11. Lyndon Johnson apparently encouraged Montana Senator James Murray, a labor supporter, to go home before the motion to retable was voted on, by assuring him that his vote would not be needed. Although Johnson himself voted against the McClellan amendment, his now-legendary parliamentary skills helped ensure its passage. See McAdams, *Power and Politics*, 90–97; Joseph Keenan Memoir, OHC, LBJL, 5–6. Having alienated labor in the process, Johnson tried to backpedal the following day. Apparently trying to weaken support for the McClellan amendment among southern senators, Johnson circulated a memo suggesting that the measure would outlaw segregated unions. The memo is in file marked "Labor Legislation," box 409, LBJ Senate Papers.

11. McAdams, *Power and Politics*, 104–12; Patterson, "Labor Lobbying and Labor Reform," 29–31; Lee, *Eisenhower and Landrum–Griffin*, 113–16; Douglas L. Leslie, *Labor Law* (St. Paul: West, 1979), 158–75. Some signs of the passions aroused by the whole subject of labor "reform" legislation can be seen in the response to the successful effort to modify the McClellan provisions. When Senator Thomas Kuchel, a moderate Republican from California, rose to offer his compromise amendment, conservative GOP Senator Henry Dworshak of Idaho began booing him loudly. When he finished his remarks, Kuchel entered the cloakroom, only to have the enraged and drunken Dworshak take a swing at him. See McAdams, *Power and Politics*,

106–12; Patterson, "Labor Lobbying and Labor Reform," 30–31; Lee, *Eisenhower and Landrum–Griffin*, 112–15.

12. USA–EBP, August 25, 1959, 77.

13. AJG; USA–EBP, August 25, 1959, 75–77; McAdams, *Power and Politics*, 87–141; Patterson, "Labor Lobbying and Labor Reform," 11, 31–40, 57–59; Lee, *Eisenhower and Landrum–Griffin*, 96-116; "Labor Polishes Its Image," *Fortune*, January 1960, 184.

14. AJG; USA–EBP, August 25, 1959, 75–77; McAdams, *Power and Politics*, 87–141; Patterson, "Labor Lobbying and Labor Reform," 31–40; Lee, *Eisenhower and Landrum–Griffin*, 117–19. An indication of the results produced by the managerial campaign against labor corruption and the McClellan Committee's work can be seen in the results of a survey, which were sent to all House members in June 1959. The poll, conducted by the reputable Opinion Research Corporation, indicated that 65 percent of those surveyed believed "the labor laws (should) regulate unions more closely than they have in the past." The margin in union member families was even higher, at 67 percent. The survey's findings are given in Patterson, "Labor Lobbying and Labor Reform," 48–49. The study revealed a substantial increase (from 49 percent) in public support for more state regulation of unions than an earlier survey had detected in January. The findings of the earlier poll are summarized in Lee, *Eisenhower and Landrum–Griffin*, 97.

15. McAdams, *Power and Politics*, 87–173; Patterson, "Labor Lobbying and Labor Reform," 35–47; Lee, *Eisenhower and Landrum–Griffin*, 117–46; Joseph Keenan Memoir, OHC, JFKL, 9–10.

16. AJG; McAdams, *Power and Politics*, 68–75, 119–21, 133, 174–83, 192–93, also more generally, 128–220; Patterson, "Labor Lobbying and Labor Reform," 33–47; Lee, *Eisenhower and Landrum–Griffin*, 117–46; Joseph Keenan Memoir, OHC, JFKL, 9–10. The U.S. Chamber of Commerce, the National Association of Manufacturers, the American Retail Federation, the American Farm Bureau Federation, and the National Small Businessmen's Association all worked together to pass the bill in the House (Patterson, "Labor Lobbying and Labor Reform," 51).

17. McAdams, *Power and Politics*, 128–206; Patterson, "Labor Lobbying and Labor Reform," 48–65; Lee, *Eisenhower and Landrum–Griffin*, 138–47. A third measure, the Shelley bill, was never seriously considered. Sponsored by a California congressman who had once been a union official, it reflected labor's desires even more closely than had the original Kennedy bill. The Shelley bill was offered mostly to create the appearance that the Elliott bill was a "compromise" measure.

18. A key preliminary vote had been even closer: 215 to 200. See McAdams, *Power and Politics*, 230–31; Patterson, "Labor Lobbying and Labor Reform," 64–65; Lee, *Eisenhower and Landrum–Griffin*, 146–47.

19. USA–EBP, August 25, 1959, 77–78. For details of the Landrum–Griffin bill's passage in the House, see McAdams, *Power and Politics*, 207–238; Lee, *Eisenhower and Landrum–Griffin*, 147–50; Patterson, "Labor Lobbying and Labor Reform," 47–67; Joseph Keenan Memoir, OHC, JFKL, 9–10; "Labor Polishes Its Image," *Fortune*, January 1960, 184.

20. USA–EBP, August 25, 1959, 78–79. Goldberg also noted the key roles played by Vice-President Nixon, Postmaster General Arthur Summerfield, and Attorney General William Rogers in lobbying House members before the final roll call (108–9). See also Patterson, "Labor Lobbying and Labor Reform," 65, 54–55; McAdams, *Power and Politics*, 193–98; Lee, *Eisenhower and Landrum–Griffin*, 138–50. McAdams

notes that Robert Kennedy's plea for the enactment of some labor "reform" law on the nationally televised *Jack Paar Show* contributed to arousing popular support for the House's action and suggested to Eisenhower's staff that a speech by the president could produce a similar, if not greater, effect.

21. "There is no doubt about it," Goldberg said, "the President's speech plus a deal that Halleck made with the Southern Democrats on civil rights, brought about the vote that took place in the House of Representatives" (USA–EBP, August 25, 1959, 79–80). See also McAdams, *Power and Politics*, 202–3, 232–35; Patterson, "Labor Lobbying and Labor Reform," 63–65; Lee, *Eisenhower and Landrum–Griffin*, 138–39, 144–45, 148. The author of the most recent study of Landrum–Griffin's enactment concluded that "northern Republicans joined forces with those southerners to support a law that would retard unionization of the South and thus help maintain a pool of low-cost labor to attract new industry to the region" (Lee, *Eisenhower and Landrum–Griffin*, 172). The one freshman Democrat from the South who voted against Landrum–Griffin, Erwin Mitchell of Georgia, was denied renomination the following year by the Georgia Democratic leadership (Lee, *Eisenhower and Landrum–Griffin*, 148).

22. USA–EBP, August 25, 1959, 81.

23. Ibid. See also McAdams, *Power and Politics*, 164–65, 170–71, 197, 201–2, 205, 233–35; Patterson, "Labor Lobbying and Labor Reform," 41, 55–57; Lee, *Eisenhower and Landrum–Griffin*, 126–27, 137, 149, 172. The Texas delegation had voted sixteen to four to back the Landrum–Griffin bill. Leading the majority in casting its ballots for the measure was Representative Homer Thornberry, a Johnson intimate. The most complete study of the law's enactment concluded that "the Texas delegation was the key to the loss on the vote to substitute Landrum–Griffin" (McAdams, *Power and Politics*, 234). See also Lee, *Eisenhower and Landrum–Griffin*, 148–49; Joseph Keenan Memoir, OHC, JFKL, 7. On Johnson's ignorance of labor law and of the role that the unions played in the postwar order more generally, see George Reedy's Memoir, OHC, LBJL, pt. 15, 9, where he said that "this was one field of legislation where Johnson had no understanding whatsoever. I think the man had some sort of a psychological block to it, because most legislation he understood thoroughly. This he did not." This, Reedy said, was particularly true with respect to craft, as opposed to industrial, unions (10).

24. USA–EBP, August 25, 1959, 107.

25. McAdams, *Power and Politics*, 238–66; Patterson, "Labor Lobbying and Labor Reform," 67–73; Lee, *Eisenhower and Landrum–Griffin*, 152–53. McAdams observed that after the committee had finished with the union reform issues, "the real battle, the battle to determine future economic power relations between management and labor, was yet to be waged" (McAdams, *Power and Politics*, 251). George Reedy stated that Johnson could not have helped in conference by appointing a set of Senate conferees more friendly to labor, because, in Reedy's words, "there's no question" that more senators favored Landrum–Griffin than the measure earlier passed by the Senate (Reedy Memoir, OHC, LBJL, pt. 15, 18–19).

26. USA–EBP, August 25, 1959, 86. See also McAdams, *Power and Politics*, 239–59; Patterson, "Labor Lobbying and Labor Reform," 69–73; Lee, *Eisenhower and Landrum–Griffin*, 152–54.

27. Representative Frank Thompson of New Jersey, a Democrat friendly to labor but determined to support a law that curbed union corruption, was the victim of that attack. The acid burned holes in his clothes, but Thompson's instinctive move to cover his face with his arm prevented any serious injury. The incident is described by

Patterson, "Labor Lobbying and Labor Reform," who observed that it "introduced an element of fear which is seldom evident in the legislative process in this country, and was exaggerated far beyond its importance" (71–72). See also 34–35, 38–45, 69–70, 73–77; McAdams, *Power and Politics*, 145, 161–69, 199, 224, 238–63; Lee, *Eisenhower and Landrum–Griffin*, 125–28, 150, 155.

28. McAdams, *Power and Politics*, 251–54; Patterson, "Labor Lobbying and Labor Reform," 67–73; Lee, *Eisenhower and Landrum–Griffin*, 153–55. See George Reedy's memo to Johnson summarizing the Kennedy–Goldberg proposals, August 19, 1959; memo, August 18, 1959; and one without a date, all addressing the conferees' proposals and in folder marked "Reedy: Memos—August 1959," box 430, LBJ Senate Papers. See also memo from Reedy to Johnson, August 17, 1959, in folder marked "Reedy: Memos—July 1959," box 429, LBJ Senate Papers.

29. McAdams, *Power and Politics*, 254–83; Patterson, "Labor Lobbying and Labor Reform," 67–77; Lee, *Eisenhower and Landrum–Griffin*, 154–74; Frank McCulloch Memoir, 15–16, Samuel V. Merrick Memoir, 116–18, Joseph Keenan Memoir, 7, all in OHC, JFKL. Keenan observed that during the conference "there were some changes, but the things that amounted to something, the real restrictive sections were kept. Whatever we got was just . . . some little concessions here or there. The big issues, the things that really are now proving to cripple us . . . were passed."

30. AJG. See also McAdams, *Power and Politics*, 267–83; Patterson, "Labor Lobbying and Labor Reform," 78–80; Lee, *Eisenhower and Landrum–Griffin*, 168–74; Archie Robinson, *George Meany and His Times* (New York: Simon & Schuster, 1981), 213–14.

31. McAdams, *Power and Politics*, 267–83; Patterson, "Labor Lobbying and Labor Reform," 78–80; Lee, *Eisenhower and Landrum–Griffin*, 160–74.

32. USA–EBP, August 25, 1959, 73–74.

33. Richard W. Kalwa, "Collective Bargaining in Basic Steel, 1946–83" (Ph.D. diss., Cornell University, 1985), 33; Richard W. Nagle, "Collective Bargaining in Basic Steel and the Federal Government, 1945–1960" (Ph.D. diss., Pennsylvania State University, 1978), 220–33; E. Robert Livernash, *Collective Bargaining in the Basic Steel Industry* (Washington, D.C.: U.S. Department of Labor, 1961), 300–1; George J. McManus, *The Inside Story of Steel Wages and Prices 1959–1967* (Philadelphia: Chilton, 1967), 8–13; Paul A. Tiffany, *The Decline of American Steel: How Management, Labor and the Government Went Wrong* (New York: Oxford University Press, 1988), 153–63; Mike Davis, *Prisoners of the American Dream* (London: Verso, 1986), 122–23; David J. McDonald, *Union Man* (New York: Dutton, 1969), 264–65; Mark Reutter, *Sparrows Point: Making Steel: The Rise and Ruin of American Industrial Might* (New York: Summit Books, 1988), 413–23. On the sense among leading steel industry managers that they spoke for the business community more generally, see Roger Blough's note to Labor Secretary Mitchell, August 19, 1959, in file marked "1959 Steel Strike (August 16–31) (2)," box 92, Mitchell Papers. Blough had sent Mitchell a copy of a *Wall Street Journal* article published the previous day noting that steel managers' struggle to win back prerogatives lost during the 1930s and 1940s was part of a larger campaign in other industries. Blough's appended note observed tersely that "this could hardly be the 'fetish' of one man." See also first Thomas J. Watson Jr. Memoir, OHC, JFKL, 14–15. In discussing steel management's outlook during the early 1960s, Watson stated, "I think that steel as an industry had sort of felt that they had a right to—how am I going to get out of this statement?—sort of had an ability to be autocratic because of the size of their industry and the length of time that they had been in business and so forth. Steel for so long was the kingpin industry in

America. . . . In days gone by steel could do pretty well what it wanted to do in America and the country had to follow. I think they were pretty statesmanlike about it. I don't think they abused the power, but they were the sort of kingpin in industry." See also Kalwa, "Collective Bargaining in Basic Steel," 142, 144, where Kalwa wrote that in the late 1950s, "U.S. Steel . . . claimed to speak for all of American business in its bargaining posture, thus harmonizing its industrial relations policy with considerations at the highest strategic levels."

34. Arthur J. Goldberg to I. W. Abel, February 9, 1960, 1, in Steelworkers Papers. See also Nelson Lichtenstein, *Labor's War at Home* (Cambridge: Cambridge University Press, 1982), 242–44; Davis, *Prisoners of the American Dream*, 121–23; Kalwa, "Collective Bargaining in Basic Steel," 33, 142–44; Nagle, "Collective Bargaining in Basic Steel," 220–33; Livernash, *Collective Bargaining in the Basic Steel Industry*, 300–1; McManus, *Inside Story of Steel Wages*, 8–13; Tiffany, *The Decline of American Steel*, 153–63; McDonald, *Union Man*, 264–65; Reutter, *Sparrows Point*, 413–23; "Chronic Unemployment," *Fortune*, November 1958, 241–42, 246; "Steel: It's a Brand-New Industry," *Fortune*, December 1960, 123–27, 249–50, 254, 256, 261–62, 264; "Labor and Management," *New York Times*, August 16, 1959. On managers' concern about keeping wages down, see "What's Happened to Real Wages?" *Fortune*, December 1958, 183, which reported that manufacturing workers' real weekly earnings by the end of September 1958 had rebounded to where they had stood in mid-1956. The article noted that conditions favored "a major breakthrough in real wages soon." The centrality of the 1959 steel negotiations to the overall wage level in manufacturing is also noted in "Bargaining Timetable – 1959," *Fortune*, January 1959, 157; "The Squeeze on Rubber," *Fortune*, August 1959, 173–74; Saulnier Memoir, OHC, DDEL, 32.

35. USA–EBP, January 7, 1959, 233. See also "Labor–Management Attitudes Found Hardening," *New York Times*, November 9, 1958; Lichtenstein, *Labor's War at Home*, 242–43; "Workers Are Complaining – To the NLRB," *Fortune*, December 1958, 188; Paul Weiler, "Promises to Keep: Securing Workers' Rights to Self-Organization Under the NLRA," *Harvard Law Review* 96 (1983): 1778–79. Weiler notes there that during the eight years after 1957, the number of employer unfair labor practices cases brought before the NLRB increased by 200 percent. For the first time since 1943, such disputes constituted a majority of the NLRB's caseload. Goldberg a year earlier had also detected a rise in the number of large damage awards that courts were entering against labor unions (USA–EBP, April 18, 1956, 42).

36. See USA–EBP, May 14, 1958, 31–34; Lichtenstein, *Labor's War at Home*, 242–43; Davis, *Prisoners of the American Dream*, 121–23; John P. Hoerr, *And the Wolf Finally Came: The Decline of the American Steel Industry* (Pittsburgh: University of Pittsburgh Press, 1988), 327; Kalwa, "Collective Bargaining in Basic Steel," 85–86; Livernash, *Collective Steel Industry in the Basic Steel Industry*, 300. Employment in basic steel dropped from just over 500,000 immediately before the 1957/58 recession to a little over 400,000 at its nadir. By the spring of 1959, more than six months after the economic recovery had begun, fewer than half the workers laid off had regained their jobs (Kalwa, "Collective Bargaining in Basic Steel," 86, fig. 4.1). The same problem also emerged elsewhere in the manufacturing sector ("Chronic Unemployment," *Fortune*, November 1958, 241–42, 246).

37. USA–EBP, May 14, 1958, 34, also 32–33.

38. Ibid., 32–34, January 6, 1959, 18–20, April 13, 1959, 66–67; Hoerr, *And the Wolf Finally Came*, 327; Kalwa, "Collective Bargaining in Basic Steel," 85–86; Livernash, *Collective Bargaining in the Basic Steel Industry*, 300; William T. Hogan, *Eco-*

nomic History of the Iron and Steel Industry in the United States (Lexington, Mass: Lexington Books, 1971), vol. 4, 1637–38; "Chronic Unemployment," *Fortune*, November 1958, 241–42, 246.

39. See USA–EBP, August 12, 1958, 261–62; January 6, 1959, 77–79. The union continued to claim a total membership of about 1.25 million. This figure was predicated on the rather optimistic assumption that all those laid off, and hence not paying dues, would eventually once again find employment in the industries organized by the USA. Other major industrial unions also experienced similar declines in the number of dues-paying members ("Chronic Unemployment," *Fortune*, November 1958, 241–42, 246).

40. USA–EBP, January 6, 1959, 2–20, April 13, 1959, 3–101, June 4, 1959, 4–16. McDonald told the board at the first of those two meetings that the change from Stephens to Cooper was even more significant than it seemed at first because Cooper possessed more formal authority than his predecessor ever had. "Conrad Cooper," McDonald said, "occupies a loftier job than John Stephens did. . . . Conrad is an Executive Vice President . . . , also a member of the Executive Committee of the corporation, and Stephens was never a member of that committee, although they would call him in for counsel and advice" (USA–EBP, January 6, 1959, 3). See also "Big Steel's New Negotiator," *Fortune*, March 1959, 192; Kalwa, "Collective Bargaining in Basic Steel," 33–35; Nagle, "Collective Bargaining in Basic Steel," 220–31; Livernash, *Collective Bargaining in the Basic Steel Industry*, 300–2; McDonald, *Union Man*, 260–67; McManus, *Inside Story of Steel Wages*, 12–15; Davis, *Prisoners of the American Dream*, 123; Tiffany, *The Decline of American Steel*, 153–62; Reutter, *Sparrows Point*, 423.

41. USA–EBP, January 6, 1959, 5–7, April 13, 1959, 3–9, June 4, 1959, 4–16; Kalwa, "Collective Bargaining in Basic Steel," 33–35; Nagle, "Collective Bargaining in Basic Steel," 220–21, 226–30; Livernash, *Collective Bargaining in the Basic Steel Industry*, 300–2; Donald F. Barnett and Louis Schorsch, *Steel: Upheaval in a Basic Industry* (Cambridge, Mass.: Ballinger, 1983), 13–35, 107–68; McDonald, *Union Man*, 260–67; McManus, *Inside Story of Steel Wages*, 12–15; Tiffany, *The Decline of American Steel*, 128–62; Davis, *Prisoners of the American Dream*, 121–23; Reutter, *Sparrows Point*, 413–24; "Labor Polishes Its Image," *Fortune*, January 1960, 179. The first signs of the industry's impending decline, visible by 1958, are described extensively in "Steel: It's a Brand-New Industry," *Fortune*, December 1960, 123–27, 249–50, 254, 256, 261–62, 264; Anthony Libertella, "The Steel Strike of 1959: Labor, Management and Government Relations" (Ph.D. diss., Ohio State University, 1972), 1–38.

42. See USA–EBP, April 13, 1959, 3–17, 67–82; McDonald, *Union Man*, 260–67; "Inflation: The Union View," *Fortune*, March 1957, 233–34, 236; Livernash, *Collective Bargaining in the Basic Steel Industry*, 300–2; Tiffany, *The Decline of American Steel*, 128–63; Kalwa, "Collective Bargaining in Basic Steel," 33–35; Nagle, "Collective Bargaining in Basic Steel," 220–21, 223–31; Barnett and Schorsch, *Steel*, 26–35. Barnett and Schorsch noted that "total productive investment in the steel industry averaged 2.6 billion dollars (in 1981 dollars) during the 1950s—a level little different from the depressed levels of the late 1970s. Relative prosperity in the immediate postwar period was therefore not associated with a corresponding commitment to the reinvestment of earnings" (27).

43. See USA–EBP, April 13, 1959, 3–17, 67–82; McDonald, *Union Man*, 260–67; Livernash, *Collective Bargaining in the Basic Steel Industry*, 300–2; Tiffany, *The Decline of American Steel*, 128–63; Kalwa, "Collective Bargaining in Basic Steel," 33–35; Nagle, "Collective Bargaining in Basic Steel," 220–21, 223–31; Libertella, "The Steel

Strike of 1959," 1–38; McManus, *Inside Story of Steel Wages*, 15–17; Reutter, *Sparrows Point*, 413–23; Barnett and Schorsch, *Steel*, 26–35; Hoerr, *And the Wolf Finally Came*, 324–29; "The New Labor Market," *Fortune*, July 1959, 202; "Steel: It's a Brand-New Industry," *Fortune*, December 1960, 123–27, 249–50, 254, 256, 261–62, 264; "Steel: 2B or Not 2B," *Fortune*, August 1959, 173; "What Work Rules?" *Fortune*, December 1959, 215–16, 218. The USA and the other major unions in the manufacturing sector did, perhaps, contribute to inflation in indirect ways. One theory advanced by *The Economist*'s editors laid the blame for growing inflation on the wage-and-benefits increases in the service and distributive sectors. Although productivity gains were typically much smaller there than in manufacturing, workers in those sectors tended to take their cues in formulating wage-and-benefit demands from the major unions in manufacturing ("Inflation: The Union View," *Fortune*, March 1957, 233–34, 236). A senior economist at the Federal Reserve Board also noted that in all industries organized by labor, the increase in productivity over the preceding decade among so-called white-collar workers, most of whom were not union members, had been much smaller than that among unionized production workers. At the same time, salaries in the former group had increased more than wages paid to the latter one ("The 'Mystery' of Wage Costs," *Fortune*, June 1958, 202, 204). Unionized workers' wage gains appear to have influenced nonunion employees' expectations about salary increases, despite the two groups' differences in productivity increases.

44. USA–EBP, April 13, 1959, 77, also 67–76, 78–83. Kefauver's pressure during the late 1950s for government supervision of steel pricing and his fellow Tennessee senator Albert Gore Sr.'s support for regulating the steel industry like a public utility are described in Tiffany, *The Decline of American Steel*, 153–61. More modest pressure in the form of threatened price-fixing investigations also emanated from the Justice Department ("Bargaining Timetable—1959," *Fortune*, January 1959, 157). McDonald described his threat to Cooper to support Kefauver's plan in USA–EBP, April 13, 1959, 12–13. In the past, the union had favored only continuing congressional fact-finding ("Inflation: The Union View," *Fortune*, March 1957, 233–34, 236).

45. For Goldberg's views on those issues, see the discussion in USA–EBP, April 13, 1959, 75–83. The economic implications of the work rules issue are discussed briefly in handwritten notes that appeared on stationery used in the office of the secretary of labor. The notes read, "I wonder if you can call those working rules 'non-economic issues.' Maybe so, unless it means the guy is out of a job & it certainly means an attempt to increase the efficiency (money) of the plant from the other viewpoint." The notes are in file marked "1959 Steel Strike (August 16–31) (2)," box 92, Mitchell Papers. See also the other one-page note on that subject, same file. Further evidence of the steel managers' at least partial responsibility for rising prices lies in the salaries they awarded themselves, which were significantly higher than those paid to other senior executives of major corporations. By far the worst offender was Bethlehem. Ten of the firm's top managers were paid more in 1958 than were the heads of Ford, Chrysler, AT&T, Dupont, Standard Oil of New Jersey, and the New York Central Railroad Company. Bethlehem's chairman, Eugene Grace, "earned" a staggering $809,011 in 1956, which was more than half a million above what the very well paid Roger Blough received two years later. The salary data appear in a memo from Labor Department aide Steve Horn to his colleague Walter C. Wallace, August 10, 1959. In passing it along to another member of the staff, Wallace observed: "The Secretary found this interesting." The memo is in the file marked "1959 Steel Strike (August 1–15) (1)," box 92, Mitchell Papers.

46. Tiffany, *The Decline of American Steel*, 161–63; Livernash, *Collective Bargaining in the Basic Steel Industry*, 133–41, 300–1; Kalwa, "Collective Bargaining in Basic Steel," 32, 86, 108; Nagle, "Collective Bargaining in Basic Steel," 220, 223–25, 228, 230, 234–36; Libertella, "The Steel Strike of 1959," 125–32, 141, 152–53; McDonald, *Union Man*, 267; Hoerr, *And the Wolf Finally Came*, 327; Reutter, *Sparrows Point*, 423–24. The impact of layoffs on average hourly wages in steel was noted in a confidential memo from the head of the Bureau of Labor Statistics, Ewan Clague, to James P. Mitchell, April 15, 1959, entitled "Automobile and Steel Wages," which reported that "the obvious conclusion is that the more rapid increase in average hourly earnings in the steel industry during the past 10 years is due mostly to the changing structure of the steel labor force. There must have been a substantial elimination of lower-rate jobs in that industry." The memo is in file marked "1959 Secretary's Personal File—Confidential—Misc.," box 38, Mitchell Papers. On the other hand, the labor cost per unit of output had risen over the preceding six years at a faster rate in the United States than in Japan or the eight major steel-producing countries of Western Europe (memo, "Indexes of Unit Labor Cost for Production Workers in the Iron and Steel Industry in Ten Countries, 1950–1960," 1–2, February 20, 1962, SLRF, roll 56, Labor Department Papers, JFKL).

47. Tiffany, *The Decline of American Steel*, 161–63; Livernash, *Collective Bargaining in the Basic Steel Industry*, 300–1; Nagle, "Collective Bargaining in Basic Steel," 225–26, 233; Libertella, "The Steel Strike of 1959," 101–6; McDonald, *Union Man*, 267; Reutter, *Sparrows Point*, 423–24; "The 'Invisible' Unemployed," *Fortune*, July 1958, 105–11, 198, 200, 202, 204; "Chronic Unemployment," *Fortune*, November 1958, 241–42, 246; "How Much Help for the Unemployed?" *Fortune*, May 1959, 217.

48. USA–EBP, June 4, 1959, 7; Nagle, "Collective Bargaining in Basic Steel," 231–33; Kalwa, "Collective Bargaining in Basic Steel," 35–36; Libertella, "The Steel Strike of 1959," 101–6; Reutter, *Sparrows Point*, 423–24; McDonald, *Union Man*, 267- 69; McManus, *Inside Story of Steel Wages*, 15–17; Tiffany, *The Decline of American Steel*, 162–63, 65; "Steel: 2B or Not 2B," *Fortune*, August 1959, 173–77.

49. USA–EBP, June 4, 1959, 4–16; Nagle, "Collective Bargaining in Basic Steel," 231–33; Kalwa, "Collective Bargaining in Basic Steel," 35–36; Libertella, "The Steel Strike of 1959," 101–6; Reutter, *Sparrows Point*, 423–24; McDonald, *Union Man*, 267–69; McManus, *Inside Story of Steel Wages*, 15–17; Tiffany, *The Decline of American Steel*, 162–63, 65; "Steel: 2B or Not 2B," *Fortune*, August 1959, 173–77. Libertella concluded that the managers' early public relations campaign against any wage increase was effective but that their decision to raise the work rules issue lost them that early advantage. The last Gallup Poll completed before the work rules issue was raised in a serious way showed a 51 to 30 percent preference for management's position, as opposed to labor's. After the work rules dispute emerged, however, Gallup reported that sentiment had become much more evenly divided at 32 to 27 percent ("The Steel Strike of 1959," 103). See also "Union Is Now Firm in Backing Walkout," *New York Times*, July 16, 1959.

50. USA–EBP, June 4, 1959, 7–8, 14–15, June 25, 1959, 2–8; Nagle, "Collective Bargaining in Basic Steel," 231–33; Livernash, *Collective Bargaining in the Basic Steel Industry*, 302–3; Kalwa, "Collective Bargaining in Basic Steel," 33–36; McDonald, *Union Man*, 267–69; Tiffany, *The Decline of American Steel*, 162–63; Hoerr, *And the Wolf Finally Came*, 302; McManus, *Inside Story of Steel Wages*, 15–17; Reutter, *Sparrows Point*, 423–24; "Steel: 2B or Not 2B," *Fortune*, August 1959, 173, 177.

51. USA–EBP, June 25, 1959, 35–36, also 5.

52. The importance of 2B and the union's efforts to defend it are discussed in Chapters 3–5; "Union Is Now Firm in Backing Walkout," *New York Times*, July 16, 1959; "Steel: 2B or Not 2B," *Fortune*, August 1959, 173, 177.

53. For McDonald's statement that the Steelworkers were not going "to be turned into a company union," see Nagle, "Collective Bargaining in Basic Steel," 233–34; McDonald, *Union Man*, 267–68; Livernash, *Collective Bargaining in the Basic Steel Industry*, 302; Tiffany, *The Decline of American Steel*, 163. For an example of the tendency even among students of this episode to miss the real meaning of his remark, see Tiffany, *The Decline of American Steel*, 163. On the emergence and demise of employee representation plans (ERPs) in the United States, see Irving Bernstein, *The Lean Years: A History of the American Worker, 1920–1933* (Boston: Houghton Mifflin, 1960), 157–89; Irving Bernstein, *Turbulent Years: A History of the American Worker, 1933–1941* (Boston: Houghton Mifflin, 1969), 456–57, 460–65, 475, 477, 493; David Montgomery, *The Fall of the House of Labor* (Cambridge: Cambridge University Press, 1987), 330–464, esp. 344, 349–50, 412–20, 425–6, 438; David Montgomery, *Workers' Control in America* (Cambridge: Cambridge University Press, 1979), 156–68. For details about ERPs in the steel industry, see Walter Galenson, *The CIO Challenge to the AFL* (Cambridge, Mass.: Harvard University Press, 1960), 87–101, 112–13; Livernash, *Collective Bargaining in the Basic Steel Industry*, 73–83; Ronald L. Filipelli, "The History Is Missing Almost: Philip Murray, the Steelworkers and Historians," and David Brody, "The Origins of Modern Steel Unionism," both in Paul F. Clark, Peter Gottlieb, and Donald Kennedy, eds., *Forging a Union of Steel: Philip Murray, SWOC and the United Steelworkers* (Ithaca, N.Y.: Cornell University Press, 1987), 1–12 and 13–29, respectively; Reutter, *Sparrows Point*, 148–54, 179–80, 241–65, 280–99.

54. USA–EBP, June 25, 1959, 22, also 2–21, 23–50, June 27, 1959, 7–25, June 29, 1959, 11–15, July 13, 1959, 6–26, July 14, 1959, 3–5; Livernash, *Collective Bargaining in the Basic Steel Industry*, 275–81, 302–3; Nagle, "Collective Bargaining in Basic Steel," 234–37; McDonald, *Union Man*, 268–69; Tiffany, *The Decline of American Steel*, 162–63; "Steel Outlook Brightened by Hint of Money Offer," *New York Times*, July 11, 1959; "Steel: 2B or Not 2B," *Fortune*, August 1959, 173, 177.

55. USA–EBP, July 13, 1959, 6–26; July 14, 1959, 3–5; Kalwa, "Collective Bargaining in Basic Steel," 36; Livernash, *Collective Bargaining in the Basic Steel Industry*, 303; Tiffany, *The Decline of American Steel*, 161–63; McDonald, *Union Man*, 268–69. The strike idled 87 percent of the nation's rated steel capacity (Livernash, *Collective Bargaining in the Basic Steel Industry*, 303).

56. USA–EBP, August 25, 1959, 5. See also Livernash, *Collective Bargaining in the Basic Steel Industry*, 302–3; Tiffany, *The Decline of American Steel*, 163–64; McDonald, *Union Man*, 269–73.

57. This tactic is discussed in USA–EBP, August 25, 1959, 6–8. See also Livernash, *Collective Bargaining in the Basic Steel Industry*, 302–3; Tiffany, *The Decline of American Steel*, 163–64; McDonald, *Union Man*, 269–73.

58. See USA–EBP, August 25, 1959, 32–71. Abel reported at that meeting that USA assets totaled $32.304 million, of which $3.1 million was in cash and most of the rest in securities. See also McDonald, *Union Man*, 269–73; Tiffany, *The Decline of American Steel*, 163–64; Davis, *Prisoners of the American Dream*, 123; Livernash, *Collective Bargaining in the Basic Steel Industry*, 303.

59. USA–EBP, June 25, 1959, 38–39, also 30–37, 40–46; McDonald, *Union Man*, 271–72.

60. Livernash, *Collective Bargaining in the Basic Steel Industry*, 303; Tiffany, *The Decline of American Steel*, 163–64; McManus, *Inside Story of Steel Wages*, 17;

McDonald, *Union Man*, 269–73; "Mitchell Holds Secret Talk Here," *New York Times*, October 9, 1959, 20; USA–EBP, January 6, 1959, 5, June 25, 1959, 39–41, August 25–26, 1959, 2–12, 112–18; Libertella, "The Steel Strike of 1959," 125–32, 141, 152–53.

61. For the details of the meetings with Eisenhower and the company heads, see USA–EBP, October 4, 1959, 3–33; McDonald, *Union Man*, 272–73; Livernash, *Collective Bargaining in the Basic Steel Industry*, 303; Tiffany, *The Decline of American Steel*, 163–64. Helping prompt the change in the administration's behavior was a September 22 memo from Labor Department aide Aryness Wickens to Secretary Mitchell. Wickens reported that if the strike were to continue until the end of October, the nation "could be virtually out of steel . . . by the end of November, even with the mills reopened by October 31. . . . We have to plan for at least a whole month's lead time on supplies. This strike has to be settled *soon* or the repercussions will be felt for a long time." Wickens also noted that executives at one of the major automakers, concerned about its steel supplies, were already pressuring steel managers to "get this settled." The memo is in file marked "1959 — Steel Strike (September 15–30)," box 93, Mitchell Papers.

62. USA–EBP, October 4, 1959, 7–8, also 5–6, 9–17.

63. See ibid., 6–34. The board voted unanimously to reject the offer (33–34). See also Livernash, *Collective Bargaining in the Basic Steel Industry*, 303; Tiffany, *The Decline of American Steel*, 164; McDonald, *Union Man*, 273.

64. See USA–EBP, October 15, 1959, 1, October 17, 1959, 1–3, October 19, 1959, 1–6; Libertella, "The Steel Strike of 1959," 213; Livernash, *Collective Bargaining in the Basic Steel Industry*, 303–4; Tiffany, *The Decline of American Steel*, 164; McDonald, *Union Man*, 273–74; Kalwa, "Collective Bargaining in Basic Steel," 36; "Steel Union Cuts Pay-Rise Demand; Talks to Resume," *New York Times*, October 16, 1959; "What Work Rules?" *Fortune*, December 1959, 215–16, 218.

65. USA–EBP, October 15, 1959, 1, October 17, 1959, 1–3, October 19, 1959, 1–6; Livernash, *Collective Bargaining in the Basic Steel Industry*, 303–4; Tiffany, *The Decline of American Steel*, 164; McDonald, *Union Man*, 273–76; Libertella, "The Steel Strike of 1959," 213; "Union and Industry Spurn Each Other's New Offers," *New York Times*, October 18, 1959; "What Work Rules?" *Fortune*, December 1959, 218.

66. USA–EBP, October 4, 1959, 32. A memo to Labor Secretary Mitchell from one of his senior aides reviewed the administration's six options and concluded that using a Taft–Hartley injunction was the "only acceptable alternative" given steel management's strong resistance to other forms of presidential intervention. The memo is in the file marked "1959 Steel Strike — Walter C. Wallace's Material (Sept. 26)," box 93, Mitchell Papers. See also Libertella, "The Steel Strike of 1959," 125–32; Tiffany, *The Decline of American Steel*, 164; McDonald, *Union Man*, 276; "Big Steel's Assumptions in the Strike," *New York Times*, December 13, 1959.

67. USA–EBP, October 19, 1959, 1–6; Archibald Cox, Derek Bok, and Robert Gorman, *Cases and Materials on Labor Law*, 9th ed. (Mineola, N.Y.: Foundation Press, 1981), 489–91; McDonald, *Union Man*, 277. Labor Department officials shared the union leaders' assessment of how the rank and file would respond in the event the federal government secured a Taft–Hartley injunction. Industrial relations expert George Shultz, in evaluating whether the government should make that move, pointed out that it had done so twelve times in the past and that in five of those cases the matter had culminated in a vote on the employer's last offer. Shultz reported: "In all five cases the union rejected the management's last offer. All five votes were overwhelming." This intelligence was conveyed to Labor Secretary Mitchell in a memo from his aide

Allen Wallis, September 28, 1959. Wallis went on to say that "without any exception, everyone I have talked with who had any qualifications in this field has felt completely certain that the members will vote against accepting the management's last offer if the union so recommends." The memo is in file marked "1959 – Steel Strike (September 15–30)," box 93, Mitchell Papers.

68. AJG. See also USA–EBP, October 15, 1959, 1, October 17, 1959, 1–3, October 19, 1959, 1–5; Libertella, "The Steel Strike of 1959," 210–11; Livernash, *Collective Bargaining in the Basic Steel Industry*, 304; Kalwa, "Collective Bargaining in Basic Steel," 36; McDonald, *Union Man*, 274–75.

69. AJG; USA–EBP, October 15, 1959, 1, October 17, 1959, 1–3, October 19, 1959, 1–5; Libertella, "The Steel Strike of 1959," 210–11; Livernash, *Collective Bargaining in the Basic Steel Industry*, 304; Kalwa, "Collective Bargaining in Basic Steel," 36; McDonald, *Union Man*, 274–75; "Steel Union Cuts Pay-Rise Demand; Talks to Resume," *New York Times*, October 16, 1959, 1; "Union and Industry Spurn Each Other's Offers," *New York Times*, October 18, 1959, 1, 55. Even as Kaiser began to bargain seriously, Blough pressured him not to break ranks ("Kaiser Discounts Hints of 'Pressure,'" *New York Times*, October 20, 1959).

70. See USA–EBP, October 19, 1959, 1–6. See also McDonald, *Union Man*, 277; Livernash, *Collective Bargaining in the Basic Steel Industry*, 304.

71. Livernash, *Collective Bargaining in the Basic Steel Industry*, 304; McManus, *Inside Story of Steel Wages*, 17–18; "Steel Strike Injunction Is Asked by Eisenhower; Union Fights Move Today," *New York Times*, October 20, 1959.

72. Livernash, *Collective Bargaining in the Basic Steel Industry*, 304; McManus, *Inside Story of Steel Wages*, 17–18; "Court to Get Plea," *New York Times*, October 20, 1959; "Steel Injunction Argued in Court; Ruling Due Today," *New York Times*, October 21, 1959. The earlier case, *United States* v. *United Steelworkers of America*, 202 F. 2d 132 (1953), involved an injunction issued against a USA local that had struck a plant involved in nuclear weapons production (for the details of the earlier dispute, see Chapter 3, n. 123). The injunction had expired before the union could launch an appeal, thus the Supreme Court had no opportunity to rule on the issue ("Steel Union Gets Injunction Stay Until Next Week," *New York Times*, October 23, 1959).

73. Livernash, *Collective Bargaining in the Basic Steel Industry*, 304; McManus, *Inside Story of Steel Wages*, 17–18; "Court to Get Plea," *New York Times*, October 20, 1959; "Steel Injunction Argued in Court; Ruling Due Today," *New York Times*, October 21, 1959; "Steel Union Gets Injunction Stay Until Next Week," *New York Times*, October 23, 1959; "High Court Bars U.S. Bid to Speed Ruling on Steel," *New York Times*, October 29, 1959; "High Court Takes Steel Dispute," *New York Times*, October 31, 1959. Judge Hastie's dissent echoed the position that Goldberg and McDonald had taken since the administration first began to consider seriously obtaining a Taft–Hartley injunction ("T–H Can't Make Steel Peace, Says McDonald," *New York Daily News*, October 13, 1959, copy in Goldberg Papers).

74. Arthur J. Goldberg to I. W. Abel, February 9, 1960, 1–2, in Steelworkers Papers. See also USA–EBP, October 23, 1959, 2–14, November 12, 1959, 3–38.

75. See USA–EBP, October 15, 1959, 1, October 17, 1958, 1–3; Libertella, "The Steel Strike of 1959," 210–13; Kalwa, "Collective Bargaining in Basic Steel," 36; McDonald, *Union Man*, 274–75; Livernash, *Collective Bargaining in the Basic Steel Industry*, 304; "Kaiser Gives 22.5 Cts an Hour in Steel Pact" and "Kaiser–Union Joint Statement and Company Discussion of the New Steel Contract," *New York Times*, October 27, 1959. The tripartite long-range planning committee idea had implications for other industries, a fact not lost on others in the labor movement. Walter

Reuther's aide Nat Weinberg sent his boss a memo summarizing the Kaiser contract. Weinberg's covering note stated: "You will probably be particularly interested in point 6," which outlined the committee idea. The memo is in folder 17, box 351, Reuther Papers.

76. AJG; Robert Shaplen, "Peacemaker," *New Yorker*, pt. 1, April 7, 1962, 90. See also USA–EBP, October 15, 1959, 1, October 17, 1959, 1–3; Libertella, "The Steel Strike of 1959," 210–13; Livernash, *Collective Bargaining in the Basic Steel Industry*, 303; Kalwa, "Collective Bargaining in Basic Steel," 36; McDonald, *Union Man*, 274–77. Eisenhower stopped short of endorsing the Kaiser contract as the proper basis for an industrywide settlement. See the transcript of his press conference of October 28, 1959, in *New York Times*, October 29, 1959.

77. Arthur J. Goldberg to I. W. Abel, February 9, 1960, 2, in Steelworkers Papers. See also *United Steelworkers of America* v. *United States*, 361 U.S. 39 (1959); USA–EBP, October 23, 1959, 2–14, November 12, 1959, 3–38; Livernash, *Collective Bargaining in the Basic Steel Industry*, 304; McDonald, *Union Man*, 277; Tiffany, *The Decline of American Steel*, 164; Libertella, "The Steel Strike of 1959," 214, 241; "He's Called 'McDonald's Brain,'" *Newsweek*, November 2, 1959, 89; "High Court Takes Steel Dispute" and "Excerpts from Supreme Court Arguments by Union and U.S. on Steel Injunction," *New York Times*, October 31, 1959; "High Court Hears Steel Arguments, Defers Its Ruling," *New York Times*, November 4, 1959; "Supreme Court, 8–1, Upholds Taft–Hartley Act Injunction, Ends Stay Immediately," *New York Times*, November 8, 1959.

78. See USA–EBP, October 23, 1959, 2–14, November 12, 1959, 3–38; Libertella, "The Steel Strike of 1959," 214, 241; Livernash, *Collective Bargaining in the Basic Steel Industry*, 304–5; McManus, *Inside Story of Steel Wages*, 18; McDonald, *Union Man*, 277. Even getting a Supreme Court ruling on the validity of Taft–Hartley's injunction provision constituted a partial victory. Labor had been trying without success to obtain such a test ever since the law had gone into effect ("High Court Takes Steel Dispute," *New York Times*, October 31, 1959).

79. USA–EBP, November 12, 1959, 23, also 25; Libertella, "The Steel Strike of 1959," 106, 217–21; Reutter, *Sparrows Point*, 424–25; McDonald, *Union Man*, 267–77; McManus, *Inside Story of Steel Wages*, 16–18; Tiffany, *The Decline of American Steel*, 165; Livernash, *Collective Bargaining in the Basic Steel Industry*, 305; "Workers Expect to Strike Again," *New York Times*, October 20, 1959, 31; "Hope for Steel Pact in Eighty Days Dim," *New York Times*, November 15, 1959; "Deep Shadow over Our Factories," *New York Times Magazine*, November 29, 1959, 20, 127–29.

80. USA–EBP, November 12, 1959, 26.

81. Ibid., 31, also 3–30, 32–38.

82. See Livernash, *Collective Bargaining in the Basic Steel Industry*, 305; Libertella, "The Steel Strike of 1959," 215–16.

83. Kalwa, "Collective Bargaining in Basic Steel," 36; Livernash, *Collective Bargaining in the Basic Steel Industry*, 305; Libertella, "The Steel Strike of 1959," 215–16; Reutter, *Sparrows Point*, 425.

84. "Labor's Plenipotentiary," *Fortune*, March 1960, 219. On McDonald's fatigue, see USA–EBP, November 12, 1959, 15; George Reedy's memo to Lyndon Johnson, March 16, 1960. Reedy's memo, intended to brief his boss before meeting with McDonald, reported that "MacDonald [*sic*] is still rather dazed over what happened to him during the steel strike." Reedy went on to observe that "he [McDonald] supposedly reposes great confidence in Arthur Goldberg and in the closing weeks of the steel negotiations practically turned over the union to Goldberg." The memo is in file

marked "Reedy Memos—1960 1 of 2," box 430, LBJ Senate Papers. McDonald's account of his activities during this period is in *Union Man*, 277–80.

85. AJG.

86. John F. Kennedy to Arthur J. Goldberg, September 23, 1959, 2. A draft copy of the letter, and of Goldberg's to Kennedy, are in folder marked "Labor Legislation File, 7/21/59–9/23/59," Senate Files General, 1958–60, box 544, Pre-Presidential Collection, JFK Papers. See also "Inquiry Is Urged in Steel Strike," *New York Times*, September 25, 1959.

87. Goldberg called for giving the president a greater variety of devices for resolving industrial disputes in "Top Union Strategist Slaps Steel and the Law," *Life*, November 9, 1959, 43. For details of Kennedy's efforts in this area, see Robert Novak, "Kennedy Likely to Lead Democratic Drive for Government-Imposed Steel Settlement," *Wall Street Journal*, December 31, 1959. A copy of the clipping is in file marked "Labor–Kennedy–Ives Bill," box 93, Stevenson Campaign Series, Willard Wirtz Papers, JFKL. Novak notes that Lyndon Johnson "is likely to oppose the Kennedy seizure proposal." See also Libertella, "The Steel Strike of 1959," 221–27; memo from UAW research staff member Nat Weinberg to the union's head lobbyist, Jack Conway, November 24, 1959, "Possible Action by Senator Kennedy in Relation to Steel Dispute," folder 17, box 351 Reuther Papers; "U.S. Considering New Strike Curb," November 18, 1959, *New York Times*.

88. AJG. For the discussion of Nixon's role and the final round of talks, see USA–EBP, January 5, 1960, 3–8, 38–39, February 16, 1961, 24–28; Tiffany, *The Decline of American Steel*, 164–65; Livernash, *Collective Bargaining in the Basic Steel Industry*, 305–6; McDonald, *Union Man*, 279–80; Davis, *Prisoners of the American Dream*, 123; Reutter, *Sparrows Point*, 425; "Big Steel's Assumptions in the Strike," *New York Times*, December 13, 1959; "Session on Steel Abruptly Put Off," *New York Times*, December 23, 1959; "2 Steel Sessions Report No Gains," *New York Times*, December 28, 1959; "Steel Board Sees Hope Dim for Now," *New York Times*, December 29, 1960; "Steel Peace Move by Nixon Rejected; Industry Adamant" and "Mitchell Sees Unionists," *New York Times*, January 1, 1960; "The Rout of Big Steel," *New York Times*, January 6, 1960; "Jim Mitchell: Looking for a New Job," *Fortune*, June 1960, 246; Libertella, "The Steel Strike of 1959," 221–27; Robert Myers's memo to Mitchell, November 3, 1959, in file marked "1959—Steel Strike (Nov. 1–14)," box 94, Mitchell Papers; memo to Mitchell from Aryness Wickens, November 16, 1959, in same collection, file marked "1959—Steel Strike (Nov. 15–30)"; December 8, 1959, Wickens's memo to Mitchell in same collection, file marked "1959—Steel Strike (Dec. 1–10)"; "Compulsory Arbitration Is Favored," *Washington Post*, December 4, 1959; Millard Cass Memoir, OHC, DDEL, 42.

89. See USA–EBP, January 5, 1960, 3–8, 17–38; Livernash, *Collective Bargaining in the Basic Steel Industry*, 306–7; Tiffany, *The Decline of American Steel*, 164–65; Reutter, *Sparrows Point*, 425; McManus, *Inside Story of Steel Wages*, 18–19; McDonald, *Union Man*, 279–80; "The Rout of Big Steel," *New York Times*, January 6, 1959; Libertella, "The Steel Strike of 1959," 210–11, 221–54. Libertella observed that the heads of the other core industrial firms had applauded steel managers' efforts to win changes in 2B and lamented their failure to do so (254). Thus the Eisenhower administration's role during the strike in the end displeased management as well as labor (241). The COLA compromise, a formula so complicated that even Goldberg had trouble making it clear to the board, essentially allowed managers to deduct from the annual increases it mandated any amounts paid for insurance plan improvements above the union's original cost estimate (USA–EBP, January 5, 1960, 25–28; I. W.

Abel Memoir, OHC, LBJL, 12). Total employment costs under the industry's new master contract rose 3.7 percent. The increase under the Kaiser settlement came to 5 percent (Hogan, *Economic History of the Iron and Steel Industry*, vol. 4, 1641).

90. USA–EBP, January 5, 1960, 7–8. See also DKGD, January 23, 1961; Shaplen, "Peacemaker," 95; Hogan, *Economic History of the Iron and Steel Industry*, vol. 4, 1640–41.

91. USA–EBP, January 5, 1960, 9–10. See also Libertella, "The Steel Strike of 1959," 253–55; Herling, *Right to Challenge*, 68–69; Livernash, *Collective Bargaining in the Basic Steel Industry*, 306–7; Philip W. Nyden, *Steelworkers Rank-and-File: The Political Economy of a Reform Movement* (New York: Praeger, 1984), 41.

92. USA–EBP, January 5, 1960, 3–10.

93. Arthur J. Goldberg to I. W. Abel, February 9, 1960, 2, in Steelworkers Papers.

94. USA–EBP, March 15, 1960, 6, also 5, 7; letters from Samuel Smith to George Meany, March 2 and April 6, 1960, in file 23, marked "Arthur J. Goldberg, 1956–1960," box 29 of collection entitled "Miscellaneous Correspondence VI.," in AFL–CIO President's Papers; Smith's letter to David McDonald, May 25, 1960, in McDonald Papers; Goldberg's letter to James P. Mitchell, March 12, 1960, in file marked "1960 – Secretary's Personal File–G," box 34, Mitchell Papers; Goldberg's letter to Jacob Weinstein, March 12, 1960, in Weinstein Papers.

95. USA–EBP, March 15, 1960, 130, also 3–5; USA–EBP, November 12, 1959, 3.

96. USA–EBP, April 28, 1960, 95.

97. The total figure would be still higher if lost income to the locals were included. Abel's financial report, which gives the details, is in USA–EBP, April 28, 1960, 33–36. See also Hoerr, *And the Wolf Finally Came*, 101–4.

98. USA–EBP, March 15, 1960, 138, also 131–37; "Steel: It's a Brand-New Industry," *Fortune*, December 1960, 256. Conrad Cooper elaborated on those themes in a speech to the American Iron and Steel Institute given in May 1960. A copy of the speech, entitled "The Problem," is in Steelworkers Papers. The master contract hammered out in the first week of January 1960 was a three-year agreement, retroactive to July 1, 1959 (Livernash, *Collective Bargaining in the Basic Steel Industry*, 306).

99. See USA–EBP, March 15, 1960, 131–38; "Steel: It's a Brand-New Industry," *Fortune*, December 1960, 123–27, 249–50, 254, 256, 261–62, 264.

100. AJG.

101. The "peace dinner" is described in Victor Reisel's column entitled "Inside Labor," January 14, 1960. A copy of the column is in file marked "1960 – Steel Strike (January 14)," box 95, Mitchell Papers. See also McDonald, *Union Man*, 282.

102. AJG. See also Theodore White, *The Making of the President 1960* (New York: Atheneum, 1961), 53–63; Theodore Sorensen, *Kennedy* (New York: Harper & Row, 1965), 95–121.

103. AJG. When Stevenson had given the delegates to the 1956 Democratic National Convention a free hand in selecting his running mate, Goldberg had supported Humphrey rather than Kennedy or the man who prevailed, Estes Kefauver. See Goldberg's remarks in George Meany Memoir, OHC, JFKL, 11.

104. AJG.

105. Ibid. Some indication of Goldberg's resentment of the discrimination practiced against Jews, Catholics, and others by elite Protestants can be found in his remarks to Nordy Hoffman on January 11, 1961, which Dorothy Goldberg recorded in her diary entry for that day. Goldberg told Hoffman that "I bet that Duquesne Club in Pittsburgh just sits and looks at each other[:] white-Protestant Americans. If there are three Catholics in it, I'll eat my hat."

106. AJG. Reuther and the national UAW maintained a pose of neutrality during the 1960 Democratic primaries, largely because they expected Kennedy to win, but Reuther and most UAW officials favored Humphrey (Joseph L. Rauh Jr.'s Memoir, 55–56, and Leonard Woodcock's Memoir, 2–3, both in OHC, JFKL). In addition to resistance from the building trades and the Reuther faction, Kennedy by early 1960 had engendered hostility even in the federation hierarchy for his role in passing the Landrum–Griffin Act (Joseph Keenan's Memoir, OHC, JFKL, 10). Keenan at that time was a senior lobbyist for the AFL–CIO.

107. AJG; Joseph Keenan Memoir, 10, George Meany Memoir, 2–18, and Albert Zack Memoir, 13, all in OHC, JFKL. Meany considered Kennedy's early voting record in Congress "sympathetic" but not "pro-labor." The union official did not get to know Kennedy well until 1957, when Kennedy began to work on the Kennedy–Ives bill and on another bill to raise the minimum wage (Meany Memoir, 2–6).

108. Alex Rose to Arthur J. Goldberg, March 14, 1960, 1, in file marked "Labor Legislation, 12/12/59–8/30/60," Senate Files General 1958–60, box 544, Pre-Presidential Collection, JFK Papers. See also White, *The Making of the President 1960*, 87, n. 1, 105; Shaplen, "Peacemaker," 110; Esther Peterson Memoir, OHC, JFKL, 20.

109. Theodore Sorensen, "Election of 1960," in Arthur M. Schlesinger Jr. and Fred L. Israel, eds., *History of American Presidential Elections*, vol. 4 (New York: McGraw-Hill, 1971), 3451–54, 3456–57; White, *The Making of the President 1960*, 28–87; Sorensen, *Kennedy*, 122–26; Steven M. Gillon, *Politics and Vision: The ADA and American Liberalism, 1947–1985* (New York: Oxford University Press, 1987), 131–32; Arthur M. Schlesinger Jr., *A Thousand Days: John F. Kennedy in the White House* (Boston: Houghton Mifflin, 1965), 14–33; Arthur M. Schlesinger Jr., *Robert Kennedy and His Times* (Boston: Houghton Mifflin, 1978), 206–12.

110. AJG; Schlesinger, *A Thousand Days*, 15–33, and *Robert Kennedy*, 8–70, 101–3; Sorensen, *Kennedy*, 11–92; White, *The Making of the President 1960*, 39–40, 53–63.

111. AJG; Sorensen, "Election of 1960," 3456–57; White, The *Making of the President 1960*, 53–63. See also the discussion of the 1958 elections and the sources cited in Chapter 6.

112. White, *The Making of the President 1960*, 85–125; Sorensen, "Election of 1960," 3458–59; Sorensen, *Kennedy*, 127–47; Schlesinger, *A Thousand Days*, 33–34; Schlesinger, *Robert Kennedy*, 209–18. Kennedy's margin of victory in Wisconsin came from conservative Catholic voters, drawn to him as a new face, a celebrity with a completely unfocused public image. Such voters drifted back to Nixon in the fall as Kennedy's stands on issues of political economy became clearer, giving the Republican candidate a victory in the state. These conclusions are based on the discussions of the Wisconsin primary in the works just cited and on a conversation with Franklin Wallick, then editor of the *Wisconsin CIO News*. Humphrey campaign operative Joseph Rauh later stated that Kennedy had won in Wisconsin with three issues: He had worked to get Hoffa behind bars, an argument Robert Kennedy repeated throughout the primary campaign; Humphrey's efforts to alter the primary voting system showed his unfairness; and Humphrey was not a serious candidate but only a stalking horse for Johnson, for whom he, Humphrey, would make a logical running mate. Above and beyond those specific issues in explaining the outcome, Rauh said, was Kennedy's Catholicism: "The religious issue was murderous. Workers, union workers, UAW union workers for whom Hubert had been the champion long before John Kennedy became a champion of these workers, went in overwhelming droves . . . for John Kennedy" (Joseph Rauh Memoir, OHC, JFKL, 40–41, also 38–39, 42). The religion

issue also swayed some UAW officials. One who backed Kennedy partly for that reason was the union's vice-president, Leonard Woodcock. See his Memoir, 2, same collection.

113. AJG: White, *The Making of the President 1960*, 104–63; Sorensen, "Election of 1960," 3458–60; Sorensen, *Kennedy*, 147–51; John Bartlow Martin, *Adlai Stevenson and the World* (Garden City, N.Y.: Doubleday, 1977), 491–513; Schlesinger, *Robert Kennedy*, 212–18.

114. "Proposed Statement on Labor Policy by the Democratic Advisory Council," 4–5. A copy of the statement, May 5, 1960, is in McDonald Papers.

115. Chester Bowles to Arthur J. Goldberg, June 23, 1960. See also Goldberg's letter to Bowles, June 10, the attached copy of his final version of the labor plank, and Goldberg's letter to Philip Perlman, June 30, 1960, all in Chester Bowles Papers, MC–SL, YU; Schlesinger and Israel, *History of American Presidential Elections*, vol. 4, 3483–86; Hobart Rowen, *The Free Enterprisers: Kennedy, Johnson and the Business Establishment* (New York: Putnam, 1964), 24–33.

116. AJG; White, *The Making of the President 1960*, 130–63; Gillon, *Politics and Vision*, 132–33; Martin, *Adlai Stevenson and the World*, 513–21; Schlesinger, *Robert Kennedy*, 218–19; Schlesinger, *A Thousand Days*, 29–38.

117. Cox, Bok, and Gorman, *Labor Law*, 565–75, 594–97; Leslie, *Labor Law*, 277–87; Lee Modjeska, "Labor and the Warren Court," *Industrial Relations Law Journal* 8 (1986): 514–15; Joel Edward Rogers, "Divide and Conquer: The Legal Foundations of Postwar U.S. Labor Policy" (Ph.D. diss., Princeton University, 1984), 296–310; "The Douglas Doctrine," *Fortune*, October 1960, 271–72; *United Steelworkers of America* v. *American Manufacturing Company*, 363 U.S. 564 (1960); *United Steelworkers of America* v. *Warrior and Gulf Navigation Company*, 363 U.S. 574 (1960); *United Steelworkers of America* v. *Enterprise Wheel and Car Corporation*, 363 U.S. 593 (1960). Managerial pressure on the arbitration system sharply increased its costs, which were shared by management and labor. Trade unionists' unhappiness with rising arbitration fees is noted in "Judging the Judges," *Fortune*, April 1959, 199–200.

118. *United Steelworkers of America* v. *American Manufacturing Company*, 363 U.S. 564, 566 (1960). Eight justices joined in the Court's decision. The ninth, Hugo Black, recused himself from participating in the case.

119. *United Steelworkers of America* v. *American Manufacturing Company*, 363 U.S. 564, 567–73 (1960). See also the discussion of this case in Leslie, *Labor Law*, 277–78; Rogers, "Divide and Conquer," 297–99; Katherine Van Wezel Stone, "The Post-War Paradigm in American Labor Law," *Yale Law Journal* 90 (1981): 1528. Douglas's conclusion that "the 'no strike' clause . . . is the *quid pro quo* for the other [grievance clause]" drew support from only three of his brethren. Justices Frankfurter, Whittaker, Brennan, and Harlan noted in concurrences that they found no basis in law for such a conclusion. See 363 U.S. 564, 569–73 (1960); also "The Douglas Doctrine," *Fortune*, October 1960, 271–72.

120. Quoted in *United Steelworkers of America* v. *Warrior and Gulf Navigation Company*, 363 U.S. 574, 576 (1960).

121. Ibid., 574, 578.

122. Ibid., 574, 578–85. See also Leslie, *Labor Law*, 278–82; Rogers, "Divide and Conquer," 299–301; Stone, "The Post-War Paradigm," 1528–29; "The Douglas Doctrine," *Fortune*, October 1960, 271–72.

123. *United Steelworkers of America* v. *Enterprise Wheel and Car Corporation*, 363 U.S. 593 (1960); Leslie, *Labor Law*, 284–87; Rogers, "Divide and Conquer," 301–4; Stone, "The Post-War Paradigm in American Labor Law," 1529; "The Douglas

Doctrine," *Fortune*, October 1960, 271–72. Seven justices joined in the Court's decision. Whittaker dissented and Black once again recused himself. See 363 U.S. 593,
599–602 (1960).

124. Rogers, "Divide and Conquer," 305–8; David Brody, *Workers in Industrial
America: Essays on the Twentieth Century Struggle* (New York: Oxford University
Press, 1980), 201–6; Stone, "The Post-War Paradigm," esp. 1528–80; Christopher L.
Tomlins, *The State and the Unions; Labor Relations, Law and the Organized Labor
Movement in America, 1880–1960* (Cambridge: Cambridge University Press, 1985),
320–22; Davis, *Prisoners of the American Dream*, 124–27. The works by Stone and
Tomlins, in particular, harshly criticize labor's support for making the arbitration
system the preeminent mechanism for resolving worker grievances. For these authors'
specific objections to the Court's decisions, see Chapter 6. Rogers is somewhat more
balanced in his assessment, conceding that the arbitration system and the Supreme
Court's decisions bolstering it served labor's "short run interests" ("Divide and Conquer," 305–6). Brody similarly argues that the arbitration system limited managerial
discretion in the workplace but that its legalistic aspects "ate at the vitals of the shop-
floor impulse" (*Workers in Industrial America*, 204–7). On the way in which arbitration limited managers' ability to impose the ultimate penalty, that is, dismissal, see
"The Dwindling Right to Fire," *Fortune*, August 1960, 204.

125. AJG; Davis, *Prisoners of the American Dream*, 126, n. 26. The need for strong
"peak organizations" in order to make possible the kind of corporatist bargaining
prevalent in Sweden is discussed in Chapters 3 and 5.

126. On the longer-term consequences of the Supreme Court's rulings in the
Steelworkers Trilogy, see Rogers, "Divide and Conquer," 305–8; Brody, *Workers in
Industrial America*, 201–6; Stone, "The Post-War Paradigm," esp. 1528–80; Tomlins,
The State and the Unions, 320–22; Davis, *Prisoners of the American Dream*, 124–27.

127. Shaplen, "Peacemaker," 110; White, *The Making of the President 1960*, 130–
88; Sorensen, "Election of 1960," 3459–60; Sorensen, *Kennedy*, 154–62; Martin, *Adlai
Stevenson and the World*, 517–28; Gillon, *Politics and Vision*, 123–33; Schlesinger, *A
Thousand Days*, 36–45; Schlesinger, *Robert Kennedy*, 219–21; Albert Zack Memoir,
OHC, JFKL, 13–14; Joseph Keenan Memoir, OHC, LBJL, 6–12; George Reedy's
memos to Johnson, in files marked "Reedy: Memos, October 1957" and "Reedy:
Confidential Memos 1959–60," boxes 420 and 430, respectively, LBJ Senate Papers;
Reedy's Memoir, OHC, LBJL, pt. 15, 19–20, 22–24; memo from Johnson aide Jerry
Siegel to his colleague Walter Jenkins, April 10, 1959, in file marked "Labor Legislation," box 409, LBJ Senate Papers. On the role of labor in dashing Johnson's hopes,
see Robinson, *George Meany*, 219; "Early Win by Kennedy Is Predicted," *Washington
Post*, July 10, 1960. The article reported that Kennedy's endorsement by North Carolina governor-elect Terry Sanford had dealt a blow to Johnson's campaign, and "a
second blow, perhaps even more grievous, was dealt him by top labor leaders. They
vetoed a Johnson nomination."

128. Alex Rose to Arthur J. Goldberg, March 14, 1960, 2, in file marked "Labor
Legislation 12/12/59–8/30/60," Senate Files General 1958–60, box 544, Pre-
Presidential Collection, JFK Papers.

129. Alex Rose to Arthur J. Goldberg, March 14, 1960, 2.

130. Those conclusions about Kennedy's reasoning are from White, *The Making of
the President 1960*, 53–63, 148–63, 188–93; Sorensen, *Kennedy*, 162–63; Schlesinger,
A Thousand Days, 22–55; Schlesinger, *Robert Kennedy*, 206–25; George Reedy Memoir, OHC, LBJL, pt. 16, 57–58, 68. None of those accounts supports them in their
entirety, and sometimes the sources conflict, but taken together they indicate that

Kennedy made his choice in the way described. Schlesinger, in particular, argued that Kennedy seriously considered Humphrey for the vice-presidential position, but that seems most unlikely. Reedy's account appears to be by far the most accurate. He later said that "I think Jack had correctly assessed the situation and had realized that without Johnson on that ticket he didn't stand much of a chance, which he didn't. He could never have carried any part of the South without Johnson, and he needed to carry some of the South because Nixon . . . already had some of the fat northern states all sewed up" (Reedy Memoir, 57). On Kennedy's hopes for winning in the South, see "Early Win by Kennedy is Predicted," *Washington Post*, July 10, 1960. It reported that in endorsing Kennedy, Terry Sanford predicted that he could "carry a majority of the Southern states."

131. AJG; DKGD, March 2, 1968; Joseph Rauh Memoir, 86–95, and David McDonald Memoir, 5–8, both in OHC, JFKL; George Reedy Memoir, OHC, LBJL, pt. 16, 56–58; White, *The Making of the President 1960*, 188–91; Sorensen, "Election of 1960," 3460–61; Sorensen, *Kennedy*, 163–65; Schlesinger, *A Thousand Days*, 50–55; Schlesinger, *Robert Kennedy*, 222–25. Readers should bear in mind that those accounts of Kennedy's decision to select Johnson conflict in some respects. I based my account on discussions with Goldberg, Goldberg's recollection as recorded in his wife's diary, and a review of the existing primary sources and secondary accounts of how those events came to pass. Theodore White told Goldberg several years later that he had run into Robert Kennedy at 7:00 A.M. that morning and asked him, "What's going on?" at which point Kennedy had replied, "Jack wants Johnson" (DKGD, March 2, 1968). Most of the scholarly disagreement over this episode is on the finality of Kennedy's decision early that morning to choose Johnson. Schlesinger, in particular, believes that Kennedy had not fully made up his mind until later that day, but the evidence indicates otherwise. George Reedy argued persuasively that "the version that Kennedy later put out was that it was offered to Johnson with the expectation that he would turn it down, but that he fooled everybody and accepted. I don't think that that was true. I don't think Jack meant it to be turned down" (Reedy Memoir, 57). Reedy also noted that Johnson enjoyed support outside the South — in the mountain states of the West and in the Jewish community — two areas in which Kennedy needed bolstering (Reedy Memoir, pt. 10, 8, pt. 14, 36–44, pt. 16, 68–71).

132. AJG. See also White, *The Making of the President 1960*, 191; Schlesinger, *A Thousand Days*, 55–60; Schlesinger, *Robert Kennedy*, 225; Joseph Beirne's Memoir, OHC, LBJL, 10–11; Joseph Keenan's Memoir, 15–16, and Albert Zack's Memoir, 14, both in OHC, JFKL. Dorothy Goldberg reported in her diary that Kennedy and her husband had retreated into a bathroom for their private discussion, leaving behind the other labor representatives. Goldberg, according to his wife's diary, remarked years later: "You remember in labor negotiations, where are all the final decisions made? In the bathroom" (DKGD, March 2, 1968).

133. AJG. See also DKGD, March 2, 1968.

134. AJG; White, *The Making of the President 1960*, 191–93; Gillon, *Politics and Vision*, 133; Schlesinger, *A Thousand Days*, 56–61; Schlesinger, *Robert Kennedy*, 225–27; Sorensen, *Kennedy*, 165–66; Robinson, *George Meany*, 219–20; Leonard Woodcock Memoir, 13–15, Albert Zack Memoir, 9–11, and Joseph Keenan Memoir, 14–17, all in OHC, JFKL; Joseph Beirne Memoir, 10–11, David Dubinsky Memoir, 10–11, and Joseph Keenan Memoir, 6–12, all in OHC, LBJL. Joseph Rauh later recalled that opponents of the Johnson nomination enjoyed a momentary moral victory when Florida governor LeRoy Collins, the convention chairman, having asked for a voice vote approving the decision, paused when the "no's" sounded so loud. Collins, Rauh

remembered, "couldn't make up his mind how to call it. And there was [Sam] Rayburn . . . and you could just read his lips. 'Yes, you damn fool. Yes, you damn fool.' . . . Collins finally ruled that it had passed. . . . but the moment of glory we had, at least for the few seconds there, was Collins' indecision. . . . It showed the latent hostility in that room" (Rauh Memoir, OHC, JFKL, 95–96). Crucial to saving Johnson's vice-presidential nomination were the leaders of the urban machines. They, like Kennedy, favored Johnson on the grounds that such a pairing offered the best possible chance for victory in November and for boosting the fortunes of candidates further down the Democratic ticket (Joseph Keenan's Memoir, OHC, JFKL, 15–16).

135. AJG; White, *The Making of the President 1960*, 191–96; Sorensen, "Election of 1960," 3461; Schlesinger, *A Thousand Days*, 61–64; Schlesinger, *Robert Kennedy*, 225–27.

136. AJG; Joseph Keenan Memoir, 15–17, Leonard Woodcock Memoir, 14, and Albert Zack Memoir, 10–12, all in OHC, JFKL; DKGD preface and entry for January 6, 1961.

137. USA–EBP, August 8, 1960, 93. On the decline in steel employment, see memo, "Employment and Unemployment in the Steel Industry Since 1959," SLRF, roll 56, Labor Department Papers, JFKL. The memo notes that employment had peaked in February 1960 at 731,000, slipped by 38,000 from March through May, and then more sharply by another 72,000 between June and August. Average hours worked per week had begun falling even earlier. The memo's author termed the one-month decline from January to February as "quite spectacular." See also "Steel's Sick City," *Wall Street Journal*, June 20, 1960, copy in 1960 press clippings scrapbook, Mitchell Papers; "Steel: It's a Brand-New Industry," *Fortune*, December 1960, 123–27, 249–50, 254, 256, 261–62, 264. The industry operated for all of 1960 at slightly over 50 percent of capacity (123).

138. See USA–EBP, August 8, 1960, 92–98. The UAW had also demanded a shorter workweek in 1958, albeit unsuccessfully. See "The U.A.W.'s Forward Look," *Fortune*, January 1957, 183.

139. USA–EBP, August 8, 1960, 100–1, also 92–99, 102–128; "Steel: It's a Brand-New Industry," *Fortune*, December 1960, 123–26, 256.

140. USA–EBP, August 8, 1960, 102. See also Germano's remarks about this trip, in USA–EBP, August 9, 1960, 174–77. For information about the Japanese labor movement generally during this period and the cautious policies pursued by its Federation of Iron and Steel Workers Unions, see Sheldon Garon, *The State and Labor in Modern Japan* (Berkeley and Los Angeles: University of California Press, 1987), 237–48.

141. USA–EBP, August 8, 1960, 102–3. On steel industry managers' plans to close many older plants during the early 1960s, see "Steel: It's a Brand-New Industry," *Fortune*, December 1960, 256.

142. USA–EBP, August 8, 1960, 103, also 101, where Moloney told the board, "I have been running up and down the State of New York carrying out the policy of this organization advocating a 32-hour week, advocating the reduction of the age at which a man could and should take his pension. I believe these are good things in themselves, but when we accomplish these things we add again to the price of a ton of steel and we encourage the Europeans and . . . the Asiatics and the free part of the world to increase their capacity and export their cheaper steel into our country."

143. Ibid., 106, also 104–5, 107.

144. Ibid., 103.

145. Some district directors openly disagreed with the bleak assessment offered by

Moloney and Larry Sefton. See, for example, Thomas Shane's remarks in USA–EBP, August 8, 1960, 107- 111, and David McDonald's, 124–27. Even Shane admitted, however, that "my good friends on the other side of the table there have [made] some very good points" (108). See also "Steel's Sick City," *Wall Street Journal*, June 20, 1960; "Steel: It's a Brand-New Industry," *Fortune*, December 1960, 264; "Foreign Flags," *Fortune*, May 1950, 56, 58; "John L. at Bat," *Fortune*, March 1952, 52–53; "Coal: The Dwindling Domain," *Fortune*, September 1953, 61–62, 66; *Fortune*, March 1954, 69; "The Gentlemen of Coal," *Fortune*, October 1955, 69–70; "The End of Textile Unionism?" *Fortune*, December 1957, 230, 232; "Rough Track," *Fortune*, November 1957, 246, 248; "Chronic Unemployment," *Fortune*, November 1958, 242; "A Protectionist Push in Labor," *Fortune*, September 1960, 251–52, 254, 259; "A New Agenda for Labor," *Fortune*, November 1960, 249–50.

146. USA–EBP, August 9, 1960, 234, also 233, June 25, 1959, 48–49; David McDonald Memoir, OHC, JFKL, 1–8; McDonald, *Union Man*, 282–91.

147. "Limited Victory," *Fortune*, January 1961, 171; Sorensen, *Kennedy*, 170; Robinson, *George Meany*, 220–21.

148. See White, *The Making of the President 1960*, 225–26; Stephen Ambrose, *Nixon: The Education of a Politician, 1913–62* (New York: Touchstone, 1987), 553–54; Stephen Ambrose, *Eisenhower: The President* (New York: Simon & Schuster, 1984), 22, 39, 79–80, 192, 221, 470, 598, 604; "Jim Mitchell: Looking for a New Job," *Fortune*, June 1960, 243–44, 246, 250.

149. AJG; Sorensen, "Election of 1960," 3450, 3461–62; Gillon, *Politics and Vision*, 133–36; Schlesinger, *A Thousand Days*, 65–71; Schlesinger, *Robert Kennedy*, 227–31; Martin, *Adlai Stevenson and the World*, 539–51; Roger Morris, *Richard Milhous Nixon: The Rise of an American Politician* (New York: Henry Holt, 1990), 257–866; Ambrose, *Nixon*, 117–555; Richard H. Pells, *The Liberal Mind in a Conservative Age: American Intellectuals in the 1940's and 1950's*, 2nd ed. (Middletown, Conn.: Weslayan University Press, 1989), 396–99; Albert Zack Memoir, 9, and Joseph Keenan Memoir, 17, both in OHC, JFKL; "Jim Mitchell: Looking for a New Job," *Fortune*, June 1960, 246.

150. George Meany Memoir, 18, OHC, JFKL; "Text of Andrew J. Biemiller Speech Before [the Industrial Relations Research Association] IRRA December 1960," 1–13, copy in folder 28, box 85, Staff Working Files, AFL–CIO Legislative Department Papers. Conservative pressure on the NLRB to endorse policies less favorable to labor intensified during the late 1950s, but the board's increasingly unfriendly policies toward labor encountered resistance in the federal judiciary. In three instances during the late 1950s, the board found that economic weapons used by unions to strengthen their position at the bargaining table violated the duty to bargain in good faith that the Taft–Hartley Act had imposed on them. In each of the first two cases, the NLRB's ruling was overturned by a federal appellate court. The third dispute reached the Supreme Court, which in February 1960 ruled unanimously in favor of the union. Six justices joined in the Court's opinion, written by Justice Brennan, which stated that the board lacked the power to decide which pressure tactics the unions could use and which they could not. The broad nature of the ruling elicited a concurrence from Justice Felix Frankfurter, joined by Harlan and Whittaker, which reached the same result but on much narrower grounds. Frankfurter's opinion contended merely that board had not shown any factual basis for its conclusion that the tactics in question conflicted with the duty to bargain in good faith. See *NLRB* v. *Insurance Agents International Union*, 361 U.S. 477 (1960); Leslie, *Labor Law*, 195–96.

151. Albert Zack Memoir, OHC, JFKL, 9; Shaplen, "Peacemaker," 110, 112;

White, *The Making of the President 1960*, 267–87; Rowen, *The Free Enterprisers*, 24–33; Sorensen, "Election of 1960," 3461–63, 3466–68; Sorensen, *Kennedy*, 168–95; Schlesinger, *A Thousand Days*, 65–71; Schlesinger, *Robert Kennedy*, 227–38.

152. For evidence of Kennedy's hawkish line in the 1960 general election, see Sorensen, "Election of 1960," 3465–66; White, *The Making of the President 1960*, 281–82, 315, 318; Schlesinger, *A Thousand Days*, 74–75. The leader of the liberal Republicans, Nelson Rockefeller, shared Kennedy's enthusiasm for that general approach. He had pressed Nixon, who proved all too willing to go along, to adopt much the same call for increasing military spending, although without adding the other themes that labor had been sounding since 1958. For Rockefeller's views on the cold war and the debate in the GOP, see White, *The Making of the President 1960*, 197–227. According to Ambrose, Eisenhower viewed all three men as irresponsible in advocating more expenditures on weapons (Ambrose, *Nixon*, 535–36, 548–53, 562, 589–90, and *Eisenhower: The President*, 598–99, 625–26). On the tendency of the business community to behave more responsibly during times of military emergency, see first Thomas J. Watson Jr. Memoir, OHC, JFKL, 8, where he observed that "the Business [Advisory] Council in times of peace without great stress on the country, I don't think really worked on national problems with really constructive and valid results."

153. On Goldberg's embrace of Kennedy's hawkish policies, see Goldberg's address delivered at Roosevelt University, Chicago, August 17, 1960, 5–10, copy in Goldberg Papers. The conclusions about other labor leaders' reasons for endorsing that program, especially those heading former CIO affiliates, are from FSG; "Let George Do It," *Fortune*, July 1956, 179–80; "Labor's Role Abroad," *Fortune*, January 1957, 184, 188; John Barnard, *Walter Reuther and the Rise of the Auto Workers* (Boston: Little, Brown, 1983), 125–26, 168–71; Robinson, *George Meany*, 122–40, 227–30.

154. Albert Zack Memoir, OHC, JFKL, 9; White, *The Making of the President 1960*, 194–95, 283–86, 306–22; Sorensen, "Election of 1960," 3463–64; Sorensen, *Kennedy*, 195–202; Schlesinger, *A Thousand Days*, 71; Morris, *Richard Milhous Nixon*, 357–58; Ambrose, *Nixon*, 144, 558, 570–76. Both Kennedy and Nixon had served on the House Labor Committee during the session in which Taft–Hartley had passed. Nixon had played a fairly important role in working on the bill, whereas Kennedy, who showed little real interest in the subject, had repeatedly voted against it. See James Reynolds Memoir, OHC, JFKL, 3; Morris, *Richard Milhous Nixon*, 343–44.

155. AJG; White, *The Making of the President 1960*, 194–95, 306–22, 283–86; Rowen, *The Free Enterprisers*, 24–33; Sorensen, *Kennedy*, 11–92; Schlesinger, *A Thousand Days*, 20–26, 65–71; Schlesinger, *Robert Kennedy*, 68–70, 77, 206–22, 227–38; Morris, *Richard Milhous Nixon*, 357–58; Ambrose, *Nixon*, 144, 558, 570–76; Alexander Christie Memoir, 4–7, James Reynolds Memoir, 3, Robert R. Nathan Memoir, 1, 21–24, Leonard Woodcock Memoir, 3, and Council of Economic Advisers Memoir, 1–483, all in OHC, JFKL.

156. The two were, of course, related. Nixon, unwilling to take a clear stand on the central issues, came across as evasive and uncomfortable. Kennedy, on the other hand, struck viewers as cool and confident, precisely because he articulated his position clearly and without equivocation. My conclusions are based on both viewing the debates in their entirety and the following secondary sources, which emphasize the surface issues of style and appearance in explaining the outcome: Ambrose, *Nixon*, 570–83; White, *The Making of the President 1960*, 288–347; Sorensen, *Kennedy*, 195–202; Sorensen, "Election of 1960," 3463–64. On the other points raised, see Ambrose, *Nixon*, 446–47, 457–59, 483–515, 535–63, 570–83; White, *The Making of the Presi-*

dent 1960, 64–84, 197–227, 288–347; Morris, *Richard Milhous Nixon*, 257–337; "Jim Mitchell: Looking for a New Job," *Fortune*, June 1960, 246; Alistair Horne, *Harold Macmillan* (New York: Viking Press, 1989), vols. 1 and 2, 103, 107–9, and 138–71, 280–97, respectively; Piers Brendon, "An Anachronism in His Own Time," *New York Times Book Review*, November 26, 1989, 11–12; "Text of Speech by Andrew J. Biemiller Before IRRA December 1960," 2. For an example of Nixon's unwillingness to take a clear stand on the issue of labor's place in the postwar order, see "Candidates' Replies to Our Questions: The Great Debate," *Washington Daily News*, October 10, 1960. Asked whether the government should be "empowered to proceed against union monopolies as it does against business monopolies," a goal sought by the business managers most hostile to the postwar social contract, Nixon's reply was, "I would have this intensively studied by a non-partisan, widely representative grouping." Kennedy's answer, in contrast, was, "When a labor union concerns itself with wages, hours and other terms and conditions of employment. . . . its actions are not comparable to business and the anti-trust laws are not applicable." See also "The Two Men," *New York Herald Tribune*, October 18, 1960, 28; Rowen, *The Free Enterprisers*, 24–33.

157. See first Thomas J. Watson Jr. Memoir, OHC, JFKL, 2–3, 10–12. Watson, who had succeeded his father as IBM's chief executive officer in 1956, recalled that shortly after he declared his support for Kennedy, "business people who began to know that I leaned in this direction thought I had lost my mind. . . . before Election Day, there was a Business [Advisory] Council meeting which my wife and I attended. And we found it difficult even to engage anyone in conversation, I think the people were so sort of exercised by our position" (2–3). See also the copies of Watson's letters of support written to Kennedy, October 14 and 20, 1960, and Kennedy's reply, October 18, 1960, all of which are appended to that interview; second Thomas J. Watson Jr. Memoir, 15, same collection; White, *The Making of the President 1960*, 78–81; Rowen, *The Free Enterprisers*, 24–33. Kennedy's strong showing in the first presidential debate also helped reassure prominent Southern Democrats that he could win. The eleven southern governors had watched the debate together, and immediately afterward ten of them sent a joint telegram of congratulations, which implied as well their full support (White, *The Making of the President 1960*, 319).

158. AJG; Alan Draper, *A Rope of Sand: The AFL–CIO Committee on Political Education, 1955–67* (New York: Praeger, 1989), 76–92; "Limited Victory," *Fortune*, January 1961, 171; "Text of Speech by Andrew J. Biemiller Before IRRA December 1960," 8, 10–11.

159. Draper, *A Rope of Sand*, 78–81, 92–93; "Text of Speech by Andrew J. Biemiller Before IRRA December 1960," 7–9; White, *The Making of the President 1960*, 251–59, 345, 351–53; 385–86; Sorensen, "Election of 1960," 3466; Carl Brauer, *John F. Kennedy and the Second Reconstruction* (New York: Columbia University Press, 1977), 42–60; Schlesinger, *A Thousand Days*, 75–76; Schlesinger, *Robert Kennedy*, 233–35; Sorensen, *Kennedy*, 49–51; Ambrose, *Nixon*, 596–97; Joseph Rauh Memoir, 54, and Esther Peterson Memoir, 1, both in OHC, JFKL. On unemployment among urban blacks, see "The 'Invisible' Unemployed," *Fortune*, July 1958, 105–11, 198; "Labor's 'Race Problem,'" *Fortune*, March 1959, 191–92, 194; William H. Harris, *The Harder We Run: Black Workers Since the Civil War* (New York: Oxford University Press, 1982), 130–37.

160. See memo to Goldberg, "Employment and Unemployment in the Steel Industry Since 1959," 1–3, SLRF, roll 56, Labor Department Papers, JFKL. The memo's author noted that "the downtrend in steel employment during early 1960, along with that of the auto industry, was a precursor of the general business recession"

(1). In the six months before the steel strike, the economy had been recovering steadily from the 1957/58 recession. In the summer of 1959, *Fortune's* labor columnist reported that overall unemployment was falling so rapidly that by "the end of this year, it now seems that many areas in the U.S. will be faced with an actual labor shortage" ("The New Labor Market," *Fortune,* July 1959, 199). See also 202; "Text of Speech by Andrew J. Biemiller Before IRRA December 1960," 2–13; White, *The Making of the President 1960,* 324–75; Rowen, *The Free Enterprisers,* 23; Sorensen, "Election of 1960," 3466; Sorenson, *Kennedy,* 217; Ambrose, *Nixon,* 600–4; "Labor's Lean Year," *Fortune,* December 1960, 219–20. For details of the Nixon campaign's final burst of televised advertising, see White, *The Making of the President 1960,* 312–13, and 336, where White noted the broad support for Nixon in the print media as well.

161. AJG.

162. White, *The Making of the President 1960,* 9–26, 381–97, 421- 22; Sorensen, "Election of 1960," 3469; Sorenson, *Kennedy,* 211–23; Draper, *A Rope of Sand,* 92–93; "Text of Speech by Andrew J. Biemiller to IRRA December 1960," 6–10; Ambrose, *Nixon,* 606–7. Even more ominous for Kennedy's labor supporters were the respective shares of the vote received by the GOP and the Dixiecrats. Byrd's campaign in 1960 showed much less strength than Thurmond's had twelve years earlier, as many southern voters shifted from the Dixiecrats to the Republicans. In contrast to 1948, when Dewey had won only 26.8 percent of the southern vote, Nixon received 47.7 percent, a total almost identical to that amassed by Eisenhower in 1952 and 1956 (White, *The Making of the President 1960,* 383, 391–93, 421–22). On labor's rather poor showing in the congressional races, see "Limited Victory," *Fortune,* January 1961, 171–72.

163. AJG. The overall margins in the ten largest states, where most of the union vote was located, were breathtakingly close. Labor's pivotal role in electing Kennedy and Johnson can be seen in the results there. The Democratic ticket carried seven of the ten, or roughly two-thirds. Except for Kennedy's home state of Massachusetts, which he won easily, his total vote in those states ranged from 52.5 percent to 49.9 percent. In the three that Kennedy lost—California, Florida, and Ohio—he polled 49.5 percent, 48.5 percent, and 46.7 percent, respectively. In the nineteen states that had outlawed the union shop, the pattern was reversed. Kennedy and Johnson carried seven in all, which was just above one-third. Data from the University of Michigan's Survey Research Center indicate that in union households, the number voting for the Democratic presidential ticket rose from 53 percent in 1956 to 63 percent four years later. See Arthur C. Wolfe, "Trends in Labor Union Voting Behavior, 1948–1968," *Industrial Relations* 9 (1969): 2–9. See also White, *The Making of the President 1960,* 9–26, 381–97, 421–22; Sorensen, "Election of 1960," 3468–69; Sorenson, *Kennedy,* 211–23, Draper, *A Rope of Sand,* 92–93; "Limited Victory," *Fortune,* January 1961, 271–72; "Text of Speech by Andrew J. Biemiller to IRRA December 1960," 6–10. GOP strategists and Nixon himself publicly blamed labor for the Republican defeat. Nixon said shortly after the election that "it was the work of the unions that made the difference" (Draper, *A Rope of Sand,* 92).

164. AJG. See also Schlesinger, *Robert Kennedy,* 237; Ambrose, *Nixon,* 606–7.

165. AJG.

Chapter 8. Stalemate

1. DKGD, January 5 and 7, 1961; Albert Zack Memoir, OHC, JFKL, 20; Robert Shaplen, "Peacemaker," *New Yorker,* pt. 1, April 7, 1962, 49, and "Peacemaker," *New Yorker,* pt. 2, April 14, 1962, 62, 64.

2. DKGD, January 5 and 7, 1961; Albert Zack Memoir, OHC, JFKL, 20; Shaplen, "Peacemaker," pt. 1, 49, and pt. 2, 62, 64; Arthur M. Schlesinger Jr., *A Thousand Days: John F. Kennedy in the White House* (Boston: Houghton Mifflin, 1965), 127; Theodore Sorensen, *Kennedy* (New York: Harper & Row, 1965), 273. Seeking to quiet any rumors that Goldberg felt miffed about not getting the attorney generalship, Kennedy asked him to join the two Kennedy brothers for the announcement of Robert Kennedy's appointment. See Arthur M. Schlesinger Jr., *Robert Kennedy and His Times* (Boston: Houghton Mifflin, 1978), 244–54; David J. McDonald, *Union Man* (New York: Dutton, 1969), 293.

3. AJG. See also Albert Zack Memoir, 20, and Millard Cass Memoir, 8, both in OHC, JFKL; Schlesinger, *A Thousand Days*, 127; Schlesinger, *Robert Kennedy*, 244–45; Sorensen, *Kennedy*, 275; Dorothy Goldberg, *A Private View of a Public Life* (New York: Charterhouse, 1975), 1–2, 3–5; "Meany Rates Goldberg Acceptable Labor Chief," December 14, 1960, unidentified newspaper clipping in Goldberg Papers; "New Legal Eagle," *Newsweek*, December 26, 1960, 19–20; "Secretary of Labor," *Time*, December 26, 1960, 13; Shaplen, "Peacemaker," pt. 1, 49, and pt. 2, 62–67.

4. AJG.

5. AJG; DKGD, December 26, 1960; Schlesinger, *Robert Kennedy*, 244–45; Goldberg, *A Private View*, 1–2, 3–5; "New Legal Eagle," *Newsweek*, December 26, 1960, 19–20; "Secretary of Labor," *Time*, December 26, 1960, 13; Shaplen, "Peacemaker," pt. 1, 49, and pt. 2, 62–67.

6. AJG. See also DKGD, January 5, 1961, where Dorothy Goldberg recorded that her husband "did not ask for this [job], nor go out of his way to seek it. Only when there was building trade opposition, did his lower lip set and his jaw stiffen and [he say] . . . 'I'll see it through, now, just because they don't think me part of the labor movement.'" See also entry for January 15, 1961; Albert Zack Memoir, OHC, JFKL, 20; Schlesinger, *A Thousand Days*, 127; Schlesinger, *Robert Kennedy*, 244–45; Goldberg, *A Private View*, 3–5; "Meany Rates Goldberg Acceptable Labor Chief"; Shaplen, "Peacemaker," pt. 2, 64–67.

7. AJG.

8. "Goldberg to Stress Growth, Labor Peace," *AFL–CIO News*, December 31, 1960, 1. See also "Secretary of Labor Goldberg," *New Republic*, December 26, 1960, 5–6; "New Legal Eagle," *Newsweek*, December 26, 1960, 19–20; "Secretary of Labor," *Time*, December 26, 1960, 13; DKGD, December 26, 1960.

9. "Goldberg Chosen as Labor Secretary," *AFL–CIO News*, December 17, 1960, 1, 12.

10. See Hobart Rowen, *The Free Enterprisers: Kennedy, Johnson and the Business Establishment* (New York: Putnam, 1964), 15–33; Schlesinger, *A Thousand Days*, 115–48; Schlesinger, *Robert Kennedy*, 238–46; Sorensen, *Kennedy*, 251–90; Steven M. Gillon, *Politics and Vision: The ADA and American Liberalism, 1947–1985* (New York: Oxford University Press, 1987), 136–37; Jim F. Heath, *John F. Kennedy and the Business Community* (Chicago: University of Chicago Press, 1969), 2–9; Albert Zack Memoir, 20, Joseph Keenan Memoir, 20–21, and Robert Nathan Memoir, 21–22, 29, all in OHC, JFKL. In evaluating Kennedy's cabinet appointments, Richard Strout of the *New Republic*, wrote in his "T.R.B. from Washington" column that "the three top men could all have sat with Eisenhower, ideologically speaking: Dean Rusk (State), Robert McNamara (Defense) and Douglas Dillon (Treasury). Two of them are Republicans and one, Dillon, actually was on the Eisenhower team, as Undersecretary of State" (December 26, 1960, 2).

11. James J. Reynolds Memoir, OHC, JFKL, 2, also 1, 3, 24, 39–41; Millard Cass

Memoir, 8–9, same collection; James J. Reynolds Memoir, OHC, LBJL, 4–5; DKGD, January 6 and 11, 1961; Goldberg, *A Private View*, 47.

12. See James J. Reynolds Memoir, OHC, JFKL, 24, where Reynolds observed that "the three of us were all, in a sense, professionals of the [industrial relations] business: I, from the management side; and Goldberg, from the labor side; and Bill Wirtz in the middle as one of the country's foremost arbitrators." See also the Millard Cass Memoir, 8–9, same collection.

13. Millard Cass Memoir, 8–9, and Esther Peterson Memoir, 1, 37–38, 44–45, both in OHC, JFKL; DKGD, January 6 and 11, 1961; Goldberg, *A Private View*, 47.

14. See U.S. Senate, Committee on Labor and Public Welfare, *Hearings on the Nomination of Arthur J. Goldberg for Secretary of Labor*, 87th Cong., 1st sess., 1961, 1–7; *Congressional Record*, "Proceedings of the 87th Congress" (Washington, D.C.: U.S. Government Printing Office, 1962), vol. 107, 1038–40; Shaplen, "Peacemaker," pt. 2, 67–68; Goldberg, *A Private View*, 19–20.

15. USA–EBP, January 6, 1961, 4.

16. Ibid., 5–7. The official unemployment rate in December 1960 reached 6.8 percent, the highest for that month since 1940. See Goldberg's testimony before the Senate Labor Committee in U.S. Senate Committee on Labor and Public Welfare, *Hearings on the Nomination of Arthur J. Goldberg for Secretary of Labor*, 7.

17. USA–EBP, January 6, 1961, 7–8.

18. Ibid., 8, also 7, 9.

19. Ibid., 9–10, 12–13; DKGD, January 5, 1961; Shaplen, "Peacemaker," pt. 2, 67–68; Goldberg, *A Private View*, 18–19.

20. USA–EBP, January 6, 1961, 11.

21. Ibid., 16, also 14–15.

22. Ibid., 16–20.

23. On the details of this meeting, see DKGD, January 10, 1961. Dorothy Goldberg recorded her husband's report that "all the 'blueblood' of American business was there." Managers' attitude toward the incoming administration is discussed in Frederick Kappel Memoir, OHC, JFKL, 16–17.

24. AJG; DKGD, January 26 and 28, 1961, March 25, 1961; George Meany Memoir, OHC, LBJL, 13; Millard Cass Memoir, 24, James J. Reynolds Memoir, 4–7, and Council of Economic Advisers Memoir, 204–6, all in OHC, JFKL; Shaplen, "Peacemaker," pt. 1, 49–50, 52, 54, and pt. 2, 49–50, 52, 54, 57, 60. Cass noted that "Goldberg was consulted by the president in a far wider range of activities and programs than would be normal for a secretary of labor, before or after Secretary Goldberg."

25. DKGD, January 26 and 28, 1961, March 25, 1961; William Simkin Memoir, OHC, JFKL, 55.

26. DKGD, January 26, 1961; Goldberg, *A Private View*, 71–73; Sorensen, *Kennedy*, 434–37; Raymond Saulnier Memoir, OHC, DDEL, 26–28. Saulnier noted that in 1957 the Eisenhower administration had rejected even a wage-and-price-guidelines approach as too interventionist.

27. AJG. See Goldberg, *A Private View*, 51, 71–74; Shaplen, "Peacemaker," pt. 1, 49–50, 52, 54, 57–58, and pt. 2, 49, 70, 72, 74, 77–78, 80, 82, 84, 86. Kennedy's decision not to place a competing industrial relations troubleshooter on the White House staff was consistent with the pattern established under Eisenhower (Millard Cass Memoir, OHC, JFKL, 16–17). Cass observed, "I liked the other people [who had served as secretary of labor since the 1930s] but I think [James] Mitchell and Goldberg were in a class by themselves." They were, Cass also noted, "too big and too strong for any bureau director to challenge them. The relations of a Jim Mitchell with President

Eisenhower or an Arthur Goldberg with President Kennedy were not to be defeated by an[y] combination of bureau directors and their constituencies." See also William Simkin Memoir, 8, 43, same collection.

28. AJG; William Simkin Memoir, OHC, JFKL, 2, 5, 8–9, 43; Goldberg, *A Private View*, 51, 71–74; Shaplen, "Peacemaker," pt. 1, 49–50, 52, 54, 57–58, and pt. 2, 49, 70, 72, 74, 77–78, 80, 82, 84, 86; Sorensen, *Kennedy*, 440–41.

29. See DKGD, January 23, 1961; "As the Good News Came," *New York Post*, January 23, 1961; Shaplen, "Peacemaker," pt. 2, 70, 72; Goldberg, *A Private View*, 21–22.

30. See Goldberg's letter to Kennedy, June 28, 1961, requesting the injunction and Goldberg's MFP, July 11, 1961, both in SLRF, roll 8, Labor Department Papers, JFKL; "Kennedy Uses Taft–Hartley Act He Fought," *Washington Evening Star*, July 3, 1961, 1; Shaplen, "Peacemaker," pt. 2, 72, 74.

31. AJG.

32. See Goldberg's letter to JFK, August 3, 1961, SLRF, roll 8, Labor Department Papers, JFKL; Sorensen, *Kennedy*, 434–36, 440–41; Schlesinger, *A Thousand Days*, 574–77. Sorensen noted that during Kennedy's tenure as president, working hours lost to strikes "were the lowest in any three peacetime years since the war" (440–41).

33. Raymond Saulnier Memoir, OHC, DDEL, 32; "Bargaining Timetable — 1960," *Fortune*, January 1960, 182; "Labor's Lean Year," *Fortune*, December 1960, 219–20; Sorensen, *Kennedy*, 434–36; Schlesinger, *A Thousand Days*, 574–77. Saulnier observed that "the steel strike of 1959 was . . . the trauma that helped reestablish cost and price stability." The one major union that won substantially higher wage-and-benefits improvements was the radical-led Longshoremen's and Warehouse-men's Union (ILWU). But in return the ILWU traded away its work rules limiting the introduction of new technology, a surrender of power in the workplace that the USA and the other unions had refused to make ("Labor's Lean Year," *Fortune*, December 1960, 220).

34. See DKGD, January 28, 1961; USA–EBP, February 18, 1961, 232–33; James J. Reynolds Memoir, OHC, JFKL, 41; Sorensen, *Kennedy*, 393–421; Rowen, *The Free Enterprisers*, 34–45; Robert M. Collins, *The Business Response to Keynes, 1929–1964* (New York: Columbia University Press, 1981), 177–78; Gillon, *Politics and Vision*, 138–39, 142; Schlesinger, *A Thousand Days*, 574–80. The distressed-areas measure was essentially the same proposal that labor had backed during the Randall Commission's negotiations. See David McDonald's remarks in USA–EBP, February 18, 1961, 232–33; McDonald, *Union Man*, 293.

35. DKGD, January 28, 1961; Council of Economic Advisers Memoir, OHC, JFKL, 289–98, 338–41; "Limited Victory," *Fortune*, December 1960, 171–72, 174, 176,; Sorensen, *Kennedy*, 393–421; Rowen, *The Free Enterprisers*, 34–45; Collins, *The Business Response to Keynes*, 177–78; Gillon, *Politics and Vision*, 138–39, 142; Schlesinger, *A Thousand Days*, 574–80.

36. Also added were a small aid program for the children of the unemployed, an increase in social security payments to encourage earlier retirement, a relief program for feed-grain farmers, and a modest rise in funds for public housing construction (Sorensen, *Kennedy*, 397). See also 393–421, 602–5; DKGD, January 28, 1961; Rowen, *The Free Enterprisers*, 34–45; Collins, *The Business Response to Keynes*, 177–78; Gillon, *Politics and Vision*, 138–39, 142; Heath, *Kennedy and the Business Community*, 99–102; Schlesinger, *A Thousand Days*, 574–80.

37. DKGD, March 15, 1961, and one not dated that recorded Goldberg's conversation with Walter Reuther about Goldberg's midwestern tour; Council of Economic

Advisers Memoir, OHC, JFKL, 292–93; Goldberg, *A Private View*, 51–58, 63–64; Shaplen, "Peacemaker," pt. 2, 102, 104.

38. DKGD, March 15, 1961, "Senator Kerr and Unemployment Compensation"; Goldberg, *A Private View*, 60–64; Shaplen, "Peacemaker," pt. 2, 102, 104. See also Samuel V. Merrick Memoir, OHC, JFKL, 56–59, 88. Merrick, who headed the Labor Department's Legislative Liaison Office under Goldberg, recalled that "during those first two Congresses under the Kennedy Administration, every New Frontier program had a wild time getting through the House. We just had [no votes] . . . to spare." See also "Limited Victory," *Fortune*, January 1961, 171–72, 174, 176; "The House Confronts Mr. Kennedy," *Fortune*, January 1962, 71–73, 168, 171–72, 174; Millard Cass Memoir, 9–10, 26–27, OHC, JFKL. Cass noted that "more than any secretary, as far as I know in the history of the [Labor] department, he [Goldberg] was his own legislative liaison" (9).

39. DKGD, "Senator Kerr and Unemployment Compensation." She recorded there that Senator Kerr of Oklahoma had informed Goldberg that the reason the administration's bill had been blocked was that "there's considerable sentiment in the Senate that they are being overlooked by the Executive with regard to patronage. If I can't get a marshall appointed in Tulsa, Oklahoma, because Bobby Kennedy thinks only Harvard Graduates should be appointed, then the President is going to have trouble with the unemployment compensation bill, and others. It's as simple as that." See also entries for January 31 and March 15, 1961; Goldberg, *A Private View*, 60–68; Shaplen, "Peacemaker," pt. 2, 102, 104.

40. DKGD, March 15, 1961; "Retraining for Jobs," *Fortune*, April 1962, 219–20; Goldberg, *A Private View*, 60–70; McDonald, *Union Man*, 293; Shaplen, "Peacemaker," pt. 2, 102, 104. The act temporarily extending unemployment benefits was for one year only. Less than a year later, the administration found its efforts either to make the extension permanent or simply to renew it for another year blocked by House Ways and Means Committee Chairman Wilbur Mills. See Goldberg's MFP, March 13, 1962, his MTP, and his telegram to Vincent J. Pignato, all three dated April 10, 1962, his MFPs dated May 1, 1962, June 5, 1962, July 17, 1962, August 21, 1962, and August 28, 1962, SLRF, rolls 11, 15, and 18, Labor Department Papers, JFKL.

41. MFP, October 17, 1961, 1, SLRF, roll 10, Labor Department Papers, JFKL. See also William H. Harris, *The Harder We Run: Black Workers Since the Civil War* (New York: Oxford University Press, 1982), 130–37; memo from Goldberg to Kennedy, July 18, 1961, and Dorothy Goldberg's attached notes, in Goldberg Papers; James J. Reynolds Memoir, OHC, JFKL, 41. Reynolds stated that "Goldberg felt that the failure to extend the act to many areas, for instance, major farm operations, to many employees of laundries and so forth, was a shocking situation. He felt that the . . . employees . . . who had very little protection vis-à-vis their employer in some of the peripheral service industries were the ones that needed the protection of the act the most. But the pragmatics of thing were that you had to go rather slowly. Many of these industries, collectively, had great influence in Congress, although individually they'd be fairly small." Kennedy's reluctance during 1961/62 to issue an executive order banning segregation in federally financed housing is discussed in Schlesinger, *A Thousand Days*, 857–58; Schlesinger, *Robert Kennedy*, 334–35; Sorensen, *Kennedy*, 480–81. Jacob Weinstein informed Goldberg in a letter, January 14, 1962, that "I have my worst time here [in Chicago] among the liberal Democrats in explaining the President's failure to sign the bill [*sic*] to end discrimination in public housing" (Weinstein Papers).

42. Kennedy appears to have understood the trade-offs involved, but many liberals

did not. See Joseph Rauh Memoir, 101–7, and the Robert Nathan Memoir, 22–23, both in OHC, JFKL; Sorensen, *Kennedy*, 475–77; Schlesinger, *A Thousand Days*, 847–50; Carl Brauer, *John F. Kennedy and the Second Reconstruction* (New York: Columbia University Press, 1977), 61–62, 87–88. At a meeting with leading liberals early in his administration, Kennedy had urged them to press the government hard for a stronger antirecession bill. According to Rauh, Kennedy turned to Robert Nathan after he argued for such a measure and said, "I want you to keep this up. It's very helpful now for you to keep pushing me this way." At that point, Rauh, who was also present, piped up, saying "'Well, Mr. President, I hope that the spirit with which you have treated Bob's pressure from the left, on the issue which he speaks for the ADA, will go equally for the issue on which I speak for the ADA—civil rights.' I've never seen a man's expression turn faster. He said, 'Absolutely not. It's a totally different thing'" (Rauh memoir, 101–2). Nathan recalled the meeting in similar terms, saying that "the President said he was being subjected mostly to conservative pressures and that he welcomed liberal pressures. In effect he said, 'Come on, fight and give me support, because I will have much more pressure on me, Congressional, business and so forth, from the conservative side. I need labor and the liberals to push and complain, press and propose, because otherwise the pressures will all be from the conservatives and they're very strong and articulate.' But he did not want pressure on civil rights. He said very firmly that he welcomed the pressure of the liberals and wanted it on economic matters, that it would be useful, but on civil rights he thought greater pressure would aggravate the nation's problems" (Nathan Memoir, 23).

43. AJG; Goldberg's letters to Thurgood Marshall, A. Philip Randolph, and Martin Luther King Jr., October 4, 1961, October 5, 1961, and May 14, 1962, respectively, SLRF, rolls 11 and 16, Labor Department Papers, JFKL.

44. AJG.

45. Ibid. Goldberg, in a similarly cagey move, gave Texan Jerry Holleman an influential role in supervising the PCEEO's work. Holleman took the lead in working out an affirmative action plan for the awarding of air force contracts. Goldberg reported to Johnson that the plan, in effect by the end of 1961, was "the most encouraging single development since the issuance of the [executive] Order [creating the PCEEO]" (Goldberg's letter to Johnson, November 24, 1961). See also Goldberg's October 3, 1961, memo to Jerry Holleman. Both items are in SLRF, rolls 11 and 12, Labor Department Papers, JFKL. See also "No Barriers," and "How Big a Stick?" *Fortune*, November 1955, 70, 72; Goldberg, *A Private View*, 71; Brauer, *Kennedy and the Second Reconstruction*, 79, 82; Sorensen, *Kennedy*, 474; Schlesinger, *Robert Kennedy*, 311, 335–36.

46. TP–PCEEO, February 15, 1962, roll 71, Labor Department Papers, JFKL, 109.

47. Ibid., 109–10.

48. Sorensen, *Kennedy*, 474; Brauer, *Kennedy and the Second Reconstruction*, 79–82; Schlesinger, *Robert Kennedy*, 311, 335- 37, 360–62. Goldberg favored focusing the committee's efforts on those arms contractors that were among the country's hundred largest employers, but their record remained very poor. See his memo to Lyndon Johnson, February 22, 1962, SLRF, roll 13, Labor Department Papers, JFKL.

49. Joseph Rauh Memoir, OHC, JFKL, 106–8; "Bias in Unions," *Fortune*, June 1957, 244, 246; "Labor's 'Race Problem,'" *Fortune*, March 1959, 191–92, 194; Sorensen, *Kennedy*, 474; Brauer, *Kennedy and the Second Reconstruction*, 79–82, 147–51; Harris, *The Harder We Run*, 140–45, 156–63; Schlesinger, *Robert Kennedy*, 311, 335–37, 360–62. Goldberg had implied as much at the February 15, 1962, PCEEO meet-

ing. See his closing remarks at that session, in TP–PCEEO, February 15, 1962, 108–9. For a summary of the committee's limited achievements with respect to unions, see Lyndon Johnson's report on that subject in TP–PCEEO, February 15, 1962, 1–7; Goldberg's memo to Kennedy, August 7, 1962. See also Goldberg's letter to Justice William 0. Douglas, January 8, 1962. The last two are in SLRF, rolls 18 and 13, Labor Department Papers, JFKL. The effect of attempting to eradicate race-based discrimination on working-class consciousness and solidarity is discussed in Bob Blauner, *Black Lives, White Lives* (Berkeley and Los Angeles: University of California Press, 1989), 122–25; and, less directly, in William Julius Wilson, "Race-Neutral Programs and the Democratic Coalition," *American Prospect* 1 (1990): 74–81.

50. The committee processed just under 1,000 cases between 1961 and 1963, of which 72 percent led to some remedial action (Goldberg, *A Private View*, 71). But by the end of that period, Willard Wirtz found that two-thirds of the companies holding federal government contracts still employed no blacks (Schlesinger, *Robert Kennedy*, 335–36, 360–62). The committee's meager achievements are also detailed in Sorensen, *Kennedy*, 474; Brauer, *Kennedy and the Second Reconstruction*, 79–82.

51. Sorensen, *Kennedy*, 474; Brauer, *Kennedy and the Second Reconstruction*, 61–88.

52. TP–PCEEO, February 15, 1962, 108. Goldberg recounted the steps taken by the Labor Department to attract more black employees in a memo to Lyndon Johnson, March 9, 1961. The memo also reported that Goldberg had issued a statement to Labor Department employees reminding them that discrimination on the basis of race or religion would not be tolerated. Goldberg went on to inform Johnson that "subsequent statements of increasing severity will be issued if and as the need arises." On public-employee unions, see Goldberg's July 14, 1961, letter to all department and agency heads on that subject. The letter informed them that the president had recently issued an order instructing management officials to "maintain relationships only with those employee organizations which are free of restrictions or practices denying membership because of race, color, religion, or national origin." See also Goldberg's July 20, 1961, letter to Adam Clayton Powell, chairman of the House Education and Labor Committee, which relayed this same information. All three items are in SLRF, rolls 4 and 8, Labor Department Papers, JFKL.

53. TP–PCEEO, February 15, 1962, 17–18. The total number of nonwhites employed by the Labor Department rose during Goldberg's first year as secretary, from 1,322 to 1,500, with an even more pronounced increase at the senior level. See also Goldberg's letter to Harlem congressman Adam Clayton Powell, October 12, 1961, SLRF, roll 11, Labor Department Papers, JFKL.

54. See Millard Cass Memoir, OHC, JFKL, 9. Cass noted that James Mitchell had appointed the first black to a post at the subcabinet level and that Goldberg's appointment of George Weaver as an assistant secretary of labor made him the highest-ranking black in the Kennedy administration. For the numbers of nonwhites employed in the other cabinet agencies at that time, see Brauer, *Kennedy and the Second Reconstruction*, 82–83.

55. TP–PCEEO, February 15, 1962, 18.

56. Ibid., 20. The concentration of blacks in the least-skilled jobs throughout the executive branch is noted in Brauer, *Kennedy and the Second Reconstruction*, 82–83.

57. TP–PCEEO, February 15, 1962, 26.

58. Ibid., 21–23.

59. Ibid., 23, also 20–22.

60. Ibid., 24, also 23–25.

61. See ibid., 24. A sign of the uneasiness that these sorts of decisions aroused

among the committee members can be seen in the discussion following Goldberg's admission that the department had begun keeping employment records listing each jobholder's race (55–56).

62. Ibid., 32–33.

63. Ibid., 33–34.

64. Ibid., 34. See also Goldberg's letter to Adam Clayton Powell, December 4, 1961, SLRF, roll 12, Labor Department Papers, JFKL.

65. TP–PCEEO, February 15, 1962, 34.

66. Ibid., 35, also 34.

67. Ibid., 35–36.

68. Ibid., 36–37. See also Goldberg's letters, October 12 and December 4, 1961, to Adam Clayton Powell, SLRF, rolls 11 and 12, Labor Department Papers, JFKL.

69. TP–PCEEO, February 15, 1962, 37.

70. See Goldberg's letter to Kennedy, January 17, 1962, SLRF, roll 11, Labor Department Papers, JFKL. The files for 1961/62 also contain much related correspondence on that issue, a clear sign of both Goldberg's interest in it and employers' resistance to bringing such workers under FLSA's protection. See also "Braceros," *Fortune*, April 1951, 58, 60, 65; "Migrant Workers' Plight," *Fortune*, November 1959, 274, 276; "The House Confronts Mr. Kennedy," *Fortune*, January 1962, 71–73, 168, 171–72, 174, 176.

71. See Goldberg's letter explaining the prevailing wage rate problem to California congressman James Roosevelt, April 12, 1962, SLRF, roll 15, Labor Department Papers, JFKL; "Braceros," *Fortune*, April 1951, 58, 60, 65; "Migrant Workers' Plight," *Fortune*, November 1959, 274, 276.

72. MFP, March 13, 1962. See also Goldberg's letter to Kennedy, January 17, 1962, 2. Both are in SLRF roll 11, Labor Department Papers, JFKL.

73. MFP, April 10, 1962. See also Goldberg's letter to Kennedy, January 17, 1962, 2, his MFP, April 3, 1962, and his MTP, May 8, 1962. All four documents are in SLRF, rolls 15 and 11, Labor Department Papers, JFKL. The May 8 memo noted that the NAM constituted the center of resistance to the measure.

74. See MFP, August 21, 1962, 1, SLRF, roll 18, Labor Department Papers, JFKL.

75. MFP, August 7, 1962, 1. See also MTPs, January 23 and February 27, 1962, and MFPs, March 13 and July 17, 1962, SLRF, rolls 18 and 11, Labor Department Papers, JFKL.

76. MTP, January 23, 1962, 1, SLRF, roll 11, Labor Department Papers, JFKL.

77. Ibid.

78. See Brauer, *Kennedy and the Second Reconstruction*, 126–51.

79. See Goldberg's letter to Eleanor Roosevelt, June 15, 1962, SLRF, roll 16, Labor Department Papers, JFKL; Esther Peterson Memoir, OHC, JFKL, 37–57; Cynthia Harrison, *On Account of Sex: The Politics of Women's Issues, 1945–68* (Berkeley and Los Angeles: University of California, 1988), 61–88. Divisions between the two sets of women's organizations were reflected in the Kennedy campaign managers' decision to establish not one but two women's groups, the Committee of Labor Women and the Women's Committee for New Frontiers. The latter organization was composed mostly of upper-middle-class and wealthy liberals who were inclined to support the ERA (74–75). The kinds of jobs that most women held and their growing numbers in the paid labor force are discussed in "The Great Back-to-Work Movement," *Fortune*, July 1956, 90–93, 168, 170, 172.

80. On the danger posed to existing protective legislation by the ERA, see Chapter 5; Harrison, *On Account of Sex*, 109–37. Goldberg never took a public stand on the

ERA during his tenure as labor secretary. See the "Memorandum for Esther Peterson," May 17, 1961, written by Goldberg's assistant Stephen Shulman, which reported that "the Secretary has decided against making a statement on the Equal Rights Amendment." In reply to a letter from the California chair of the National Woman's Party asking Goldberg for his view of the ERA, he said only that "I, of course, support the President and the Democratic Platform in their advocacy for equality for women." See his letter to Marjorie R. Longwell, May 4, 1961. Both items are in SLRF, rolls 5 and 6, respectively, Labor Department Papers, JFKL.

81. For evidence of the way in which Goldberg and Esther Peterson linked the women's and civil rights movements, see her memoir, 56, 66, in OHC, JFKL; Harrison, *On Account of Sex*, 126–30.

82. Arthur J. Goldberg to Eleanor Roosevelt, June 15, 1962, 1, SLRF, roll 16, Labor Department Papers, JFKL; Esther Peterson Memoir, OHC, JFKL, 37–57; Harrison, *On Account of Sex*, 73–91.

83. Esther Peterson Memoir, OHC, JFKL, 37–57; Harrison, *On Account of Sex*, 73–91.

84. Arthur J. Goldberg to Lister Hill, June 5, 1961, 1, SLRF, roll 6, Labor Department Papers, JFKL. See also Esther Peterson Memoir, OHC, JFKL, 38–44; Harrison, *On Account of Sex*, 73–88. Betty Friedan later acknowledged the importance of the Women's Bureau, calling its staff the "midwives" of the women's movement that emerged during the later 1960s. See Deirdre English's review of Harrison's book in *New York Times Book Review*, September 4, 1988, 20.

85. Arthur J. Goldberg to Lister Hill, June 5, 1961, 2, SLRF, roll 6, Labor Department Papers, JFKL.

86. Ibid.; Esther Peterson Memoir, OHC, JFKL, 38–44; Harrison, *On Account of Sex*, 73–88.

87. Esther Peterson Memoir, OHC, JFKL, 37–44; Harrison, *On Account of Sex*, 109–65. Harrison notes Kennedy's opposition to the ERA and his failure to appoint more than a handful of women to positions in the federal government, although she fails to explain clearly the real reason for those decisions, namely, Kennedy's primary concern with issues of class rather than gender. For her analysis, which blames "Kennedy's search method" for that result, see 73–81. Harrison does point out that Kennedy's record of appointing women to high positions was only very marginally worse than his two predecessors. Women held 2.4 percent of the executive positions overall in the Kennedy administration, the same as under Truman and Eisenhower (78).

88. Quoted in Harrison, *On Account of Sex*, 95. See also 89–94; Esther Peterson Memoir, OHC, JFKL, 37–47. Peterson later recalled that in working for the equal pay law that women's groups with members from elite backgrounds "would work on equal rights but not on what I thought was the substantive thing. So we weren't able to get some of them [to help] which we should have had" (47).

89. See Esther Peterson Memoir, OHC, JFKL, 37–48; Harrison, *On Account of Sex*, 95–98. Union and White House staff resistance to the idea stemmed partly from a sense that the bill would not make a real difference, because the problem's roots lay not in wage differentials so much as in women's not being permitted to apply for higher-paying jobs, essentially the view of elite women's organizations (Harrison, *On Account of Sex*, 92–93). Such opposition may also have reflected a sense that such a measure might weaken support for the administration and the postwar New Deal more generally among working- and lower-middle-class men. Disappointed with Willard Wirtz's coolness to gender issues, Peterson later described the difference between him and Goldberg: "Arthur had a more positive attitude[,] . . . I think,

really understood the issues more. I think it's partly because his wife was sort of a professional woman. I think those things make a difference and added up. Bill did very well with it, but I always felt that it was not from deep conviction as much as it was from, you know, carrying out what he believed to be the right thing politically and for the times" (44–45).

90. Esther Peterson Memoir, OHC, JFKL, 48–54; Harrison, *On Account of Sex*, 95–98. Of Goldberg's contribution to helping pass the equal pay bill, Peterson later said, "Arthur was awfully helpful, very, very good. I used to talk with him, and he'd help me and instruct me and give me real, real assistance" (48).

91. Esther Peterson later recalled that the executive order against sex discrimination produced "more foot dragging . . . than on almost any issue I've worked on in government" (Peterson Memoir, OHC, JFKL, 66). See also Harrison, *On Account of Sex*, 115, 142–46.

92. See "Address by Arthur J. Goldberg at Roosevelt University," 10; USA–EBP, February 16, 1961, 33–36; Joseph Keenan Memoir, OHC, JFKL, 21–22; PACLMP–CM, August 7, 1962, 19, roll 72, Labor Department Papers, JFKL; memo, "Suggested Activities of the [Nixon] Cabinet Committee," February 19, 1959, in file marked "1959 Cabinet Committee on Price Stability"; memo from Undersecretary of Labor James O'Connell to Edward A. McCabe, February 12, 1960, in file marked "1960 – White House Labor–Management Conference on Productivity (Proposed)," in boxes 136 and 142, respectively, Mitchell Papers. Despite the Nixon committee's formal name, which suggested that it was concerned with inflation alone, the first of these two memos makes clear that the group planned to address the entire range of problems that imperiled the postwar New Deal. David McDonald had reported business executives' uneasiness with the committee's activities to the USA Executive Board early in 1959 (USA–EBP, April 13, 1959, 16–17).

93. "Address by Arthur J. Goldberg at Roosevelt University," 11.

94. Ibid., 11–12. For evidence of labor leaders' concern that Goldberg's plan might lead to government dictation of contract terms, see I. W. Abel's remarks in USA–EBP, February 16, 1961, 37–39.

95. See also "Address by Arthur J. Goldberg at Roosevelt University," 13–15.

96. Ibid.

97. Ibid., 14–15; USA–EBP, February 16, 1961, 58–60; memo from Arthur J. Goldberg to Willard Wirtz, March 25, 1961, SLRF, roll 4, Labor Department Papers, JFKL. Goldberg's memo to Wirtz instructing him to prepare the agenda for the first meeting of the Advisory Committee on Labor–Management Policy's testified to the greater wariness among its business representatives. Goldberg cautioned Wirtz that "the formal agenda sent to the members should be carefully worded so as not to frighten the industry members about the breadth of the discussion."

98. See "Address by Arthur J. Goldberg at Roosevelt University," 13. On the relationship between the steel industry committees and the larger group, see David McDonald's remarks in USA–EBP, February 16, 1961, 33–36. The earlier Javits proposal had also called for combining a larger labor–management body with local groups. See memo to Edward A. McCabe from James T. O'Connell, February 12, 1960, in file marked "1960 – White House Labor–Management Conference on Productivity (Proposed)," box 142, Mitchell Papers. For evidence of Goldberg's explicit reliance on the Swedish model, see generally SLRF, Labor Department Papers, JFKL. These files contain a great deal of correspondence concerning Sweden, much more than for any other foreign country and perhaps more than for all other foreign nations combined.

99. See Goldberg's memo to Walter W. Heller, March 10, 1961, and his memo to W. W. Wirtz, March 25, 1961, 1–2, both in SLRF, roll 4, Labor Department Papers, JFKL; PACLMP–CM, March 21, 1961, 1; Council of Economic Advisers Memoir, 204–6, 256, Millard Cass Memoir, 19, and James J. Reynolds Memoir, 6–7, all in OHC, JFKL; DKGD, January 26, 1961; "Kennedy Plans Labor Board in Bid to Bar Strife, Push 'Sound' Wage, Price Policy," *Wall Street Journal*, not dated, copy in Goldberg Papers.

100. Arthur J. Goldberg memo to W. W. Wirtz, March 25, 1961, 1, SLRF, roll 4, Labor Department Papers, JFKL. See also "Kennedy Plans Labor Board in Bid to Bar Strife, Push 'Sound' Wage, Price Policy"; James J. Reynolds Memoir, OHC, JFKL, 6–7. The CEA's objections to giving the committee such a broad mandate are noted in Council of Economic Advisers Memoir, OHC, JFKL, 206, 256. One of its members, Kermit Gordon, later recalled that "Goldberg's first draft . . . setting up the Labor–Management Advisory Committee, in effect, made it into another Council of Economic Advisers. It prescribed responsibilities practically coextensive with the Employment Act of 1946. We compromised it down and got the executive order to focus . . . on manpower and labor relations and wage policy, the narrower questions. Goldberg quite obviously was making a move through the Labor–Management Advisory Committee to extend his concerns to the whole range of the '46 Employment Act" (206). See also Goldberg's remark in his memo to Wirtz that "the formal agenda sent to the members should be carefully worded so as not to . . . alarm the Council of Economic Advisors that we are taking over their function" (2).

101. James J. Reynolds Memoir, 9, and first Thomas J. Watson Jr. Memoir, 3–8, both in OHC, JFKL; USA–EBP, February 16, 1961, 34–39; Rowen, *The Free Enterprisers*, 61–70; Heath, *Kennedy and the Business Community*, 17–19; Schlesinger, *A Thousand Days*, 581–82; Sorensen, *Kennedy*, 275–76. In explaining to the USA Executive Board how the Advisory Committee on Labor–Management Policy would supplant the BAC, David McDonald complained that "this Commerce Department Advisory Committee . . . is made up of the big shots of American industry. . . . And this is sort of a closed club. It is almost a senate of American big business leaders and they advise the Secretary of Commerce. We have never had a labor advisory committee to the Secretary of Commerce, although the good Lord knows we have tried. We have never even had a labor advisory committee to the Secretary of Labor, although goodness knows we have tried" (USA–EBP, February 16, 1961, 35–36).

102. See "Kennedy Plans Labor Board in Bid to Bar Strife, Push 'Sound' Wage, Price Policy"; list of management members attached to Goldberg's "Memorandum to the Attorney-General," July 21, 1961, and Goldberg's letter, June 5, 1961, to Harold Gunmert, both in SLRF, roll 7, Labor Department Papers, JFKL. The third of these is the first of several letters Goldberg wrote in response to complaints that the committee's membership was not truly representative. Goldberg stated there that "although some of the members are drawn from labor and management, they do not represent any groups within labor and management." On Thomas Watson Jr.'s status in the BAC, see his first memoir in OHC, JFKL, 2. Watson attributed his election as vice-chairman solely to having backed Kennedy's successful candidacy. In Watson's words, "He [Kennedy] won, and among my business peers I went from a sort of questionable character to a man of high esteem very rapidly. I was invited to do a number of things which I thought were obviously connected with the fact that I had cast my vote and support toward a winner. And I was delighted at that, but at the same time somewhat disillusioned."

103. AJG; first Thomas J. Watson Jr. Memoir, OHC, JFKL, 5; USA–EBP, May 18, 1961, 162–63.

104. See "Kennedy Plans Labor Board in Bid to Bar Strife, Push 'Sound' Wage, Price Policy"; list of labor members attached to Goldberg's "Memorandum to the Attorney-General," July 21, 1961, SLRF, roll 7, Labor Department Papers, JFKL.

105. AJG.

106. See "Kennedy Plans Labor Board in Bid to Bar Strife, Push 'Sound' Wage, Price Policy"; list of "public" members attached to Goldberg's "Memorandum to the Attorney-General," July 21, 1961, SLRF, roll 7, Labor Department Papers, JFKL. My conclusions about the views of the various "public" members are based on Goldberg's 1958 speech, "Labor in a Free Society: A Trade Union Point of View," 7; USA–EBP, October 19, 1959, 1–2; "End of the Affair?" *Fortune*, July 1958, 222, 224; Stephen Ambrose, *Eisenhower: The President* (New York: Simon & Schuster, 1984), 158–59, 345, 423, 460, 528, 606; Stephen Ambrose, *Nixon: The Education of a Politician, 1913–62* (New York: Touchstone, 1987), 561–62, 563, 646, 660; Patrick Diggins, *The Proud Decades: America in War and Peace, 1941–1960* (New York: Norton, 1988), 134.

107. See PACLMP–CM, March 21, 1961; DKGD, March 25, 1961.

108. See PACLMP–CM, May 1, 1961, 1–5; USA–EBP, May 18, 1961, 161–65.

109. See PACLMP–CM, May 1, 1961, 2–7; Joseph Keenan Memoir, OHC, JFKL, 23–24; USA–EBP, May 18, 1961, 163–67. Watson had studied the issue of techno-logical change while at IBM and elaborated on his findings in a letter to Goldberg written one day later. See Goldberg's reply, March 28, 1961, SLRF, roll 4, Labor Department Papers, JFKL. See also Goldberg's letters to R. Ferris White and David Cunningham, May 16 and November 21, 1961, respectively, SLRF, rolls 6 and 12, Labor Department Papers, JFKL; "The Hard Realities of Retraining," *Fortune*, July 1961, 241–42, 246; "Retraining for Jobs," *Fortune*, April 1962, 219–20. The Swedish government's 1958 decision to spend heavily on retraining programs is noted in Gary Mucciaroni, "Political Learning and Economic Policy Innovation: The United States and Sweden in the Post–World War II Era," *Journal of Policy History* 1 (1989): 391, 394, 400–2. Organized labor's views during the early 1960s on automation, retraining, and the Swedish model are discussed in Rowen, *The Free Enterprisers*, 183–207. See also "Text of Speech by Andrew J. Biemiller Before IRRA December 1960," 4–6.

110. See PACLMP–CM, May 1, 1961, 8.

111. See PACLMP–CM, June 5, 1961, 1–7, 16–17; Rowen, *The Free Enterprisers*, 38.

112. PACLMP–CM, June 5, 1961, 8, also 7; Rowen, *The Free Enterprisers*, 43.

113. PACLMP–CM, June 5, 1961, 8.

114. Ibid., 17, also 16, 18.

115. PACLMP–CM, July 10, 1961, 1; letter from Arthur J. Goldberg to R. E. Da-vidson, July 3, 1961, and Goldberg's MFP, July 11, 1961, both in SLRF, roll 8, Labor Department Papers, JFKL. The committee's new framework was patterned after that used by the Committee for Economic Development (CED), a business group that in the 1940s had led the way in developing managerial support for Keynesian economic policies. See Goldberg's MFP; PACLMP–CM, November 28, 1961, 1–2; Goldberg's letter to Henry Ford II, January 26, 1962, SLRF, roll 11, Labor Depart-ment Papers, JFKL; Collins, *The Business Response to Keynes*, 180–81; Mucciaroni, "Political Learning and Economic Policy Innovation," 391–409.

116. PACLMP–CM, July 10, 1961, 2–3.

117. Ibid., 3, also 4.

118. Ibid., 4–5.

119. Ibid. Only a few months earlier Ford had shown a far more cooperative attitude (Goldberg's letter to him, April 20, 1961, SLRF, roll 5, Labor Department Papers, JFKL). Goldberg's reasons for opposing any move to bring unions under the antitrust laws are contained in his letter Clyde Hall, March 17, 1961, SLRF, roll 3, Labor Department Papers, JFKL.

120. PACLMP–CM, July 10, 1961, 6, also 4.

121. Ibid., 5, also 8–9, 12, 14–17. On the disagreements over how worker productivity should be calculated, see "Statistical Donnybrook," *Fortune*, January 1960, 184.

122. PACLMP–CM, July 10, 1961, 9, also 3–8, 10–15.

123. Ibid., 9–15. See also Goldberg's June 1, 1962, letter to Robert Kennedy, SLRF, roll 14, Labor Department Papers, JFKL.

124. PACLMP–CM, July 10, 1961, 15, also 10–14.

125. Ibid., 5–6, also 2–4, 6–15. Meany signaled his willingness to allow such intervention before the making of such settlements only when their negotiation raised the possibility of a so-called national emergency dispute (14).

126. Ibid., 15–18. For evidence of interest among labor economists in strengthening the government's ability to gather such data, see the letter from Harvard professor of economics Wassily Leontief to Kennedy. The letter, January 27, 1961, was routed through Goldberg and can be found in SLRF, roll 2, Labor Department Papers, JFKL.

127. See PACLMP–CM, July 10, 1961, 18; Goldberg's "Memorandum for Labor Relations Experts' Meeting," August 4, 1961, and Goldberg's letter to Meyer Bernstein, January 5, 1962, both in SLRF, rolls 9 and 13, Labor Department Papers, JFKL.

128. AJG; Goldberg's letter to Bertil Olsson, head of the Swedish Labor Market Board, April 18, 1961, and Goldberg's letter, June 13, 1961, to Everett Kassalow, IUD research director, thanking him for "your memorandum on Swedish economic policies and institutions." Both are in SLRF, roll 5, Labor Department Papers, JFKL.

129. DKGD, September 18, 1961. See also the undated entry in which Dorothy Goldberg recorded that "Drew Pearson's column says that Prime Minister Eslander [*sic*] of Sweden has a high regard for . . . Arthur . . . and hopes he will visit Sweden." See also Goldberg, *A Private View*, 78; Goldberg's letter to Clyde Summers, April 27, 1961, and his letter to Tage Erlander, August 21, 1961. Interest in Sweden was not confined to government officials. The president of the First National Bank of Chicago had recently visited there and sent a copy of his notes on the trip to Goldberg. See Goldberg's letter, September 6, 1961, to Gaylord Freeman Jr. thanking him for those observations. All three letters are in SLRF, rolls 5, 9, and 10, Labor Department Papers, JFKL.

130. See Goldberg's letter to J. Graham Parsons, July 13, 1962, SLRF, roll 18, Labor Department Papers, JFKL; DKGD, September 18–25, 1961; Shaplen, "Peacemaker," pt. 2, 52, 54; Goldberg, *A Private View*, 81–82.

131. Arthur J. Goldberg to Torsten Nilsson, October 26, 1961, SLRF, roll 11, Labor Department Papers, JFKL.

132. See Goldberg's letters to J. Graham Parsons, Sven T. Aberg, and J. Graham Parsons and his "Memorandum to George Weaver and Esther Peterson," December 5, October 16, and October 26, 1961, and January 18, 1962, respectively, SLRF, roll 11, Labor Department Papers, JFKL. New York senator Jacob Javits, who had pushed another version of the Advisory Committee on Labor–Management Policy, asked to be included in any sessions held with the Swedish experts (Goldberg's acceptance, October 10, 1961, also roll 11; Labor Department Papers).

133. See PACLMP–CM, October 16–17, 1961, 3–31; USA–EBP, October 5, 1961, 219–20.

134. See PACLMP–CM, October 16–17, 1961, 3–4, 7–10; USA–EBP, October 5, 1961, 219–20; McDonald, *Union Man*, 293. For Goldberg's rejection of the shorter-hours idea for reasons of military necessity and the need to discourage imports, see his letter to union official G. H. Cassler, March 20, 1962. See also his letter to business executive H. S. Harrison, in which Goldberg ruled out an increase in tariffs as a way of coping with less expensive foreign imports. In this letter, December 1, 1961, Goldberg wrote that the administration's goal was "to maintain our international competitive position within the framework of a liberal trade policy." Both letters are in SLRF, rolls 15 and 11, respectively, Labor Department Papers, JFKL.

135. PACLMP–CM, October 16–17, 1961, 6, also 4–5.

136. Ibid., 7, also 6.

137. See ibid., 5–6. Goldberg noted the seriousness of the committee's split over the passages dealing with the full-employment issue in a letter to Thomas Watson Jr. written shortly after the meeting (October 25, 1961, in SLRF, roll 11, Labor Department Papers, JFKL).

138. PACLMP–CM, October 16–17, 1961, 5, 9.

139. Ibid., 10–11, 15–16.

140. Ibid., 22.

141. See ibid., 22–31.

142. Ibid., 22–23. Goldberg did understand that the tendency of the collective bargaining process to erode managerial prerogatives made the task of defining them very difficult. See his letter to Senator Alexander Wiley, June 19, 1961, SLRF, roll 6, Labor Department Papers, JFKL.

143. PACLMP–CM, October 16–17, 1961, 24.

144. Ibid., 25.

145. Ibid., 25–28.

146. Ibid., 25–31.

147. PACLMP–CM, November 28, 1961, 1–2.

148. See ibid., 2–10; Goldberg's MTP, November 28, 1961, SLRF, roll 10, Labor Department Papers, JFKL.

149. W. Willard Wirtz to Arthur J. Goldberg, December 22, 1961, 2, in the Secretary of Labor's Office Files, folder marked "Personal Correspondence, 1961 & 1962, G," box 22, Wirtz Papers. On USA rank-and-file pressure for a shorter work-week and McDonald's unhappiness with the committee's failure to endorse it, see USA–EBP, January 10, 1962, 136–39, February 6, 1962, 121–27.

150. See PACLMP–CM, January 11–12, 1962, 1–9. Goldberg had noted as early as the preceding October the business-as-usual mentality shared by several committee members. See his letter to Thomas Watson Jr., October 25, 1961, in which Goldberg wrote of "the importance of trying to work more fully into the Committee's operation the sense — and the fact — of urgency which all of us here in Washington (and certainly you) feel so strongly" (SLRF, roll 11, Labor Department Papers, JFKL).

151. See PACLMP–CM, January 11–12, 1962, 3–8.

152. Ibid., 5, also 3–4.

153. See ibid., 5–6.

154. Ibid., 3.

155. See ibid., 7.

156. Ibid., 12, also 8–11. On Goldberg's view of the final automation report, see his MTP, January 15, 1962, SLRF, roll 11, Labor Department Papers, JFKL. See also

Arthur Goldberg, "The Role of Government," *Annals of the American Academy of Political and Social Science*, March 1962, 110–16. The entire issue is devoted to the topic of automation.

157. See PACLMP–CM, January 11–12, 1962, 12–15.

158. See ibid., 13. Syndicated columnist Victor Reisel had reported two days earlier that Goldberg had invited the Swedish representatives. See "Goldberg Warns Against Big Pay, Price Hikes," *Canton Repository*, January 10, 1962, 4. Reisel's report aroused alarm in the business community. For evidence of that concern and Goldberg's efforts to defuse it, see his letters to business executive J. E. Beardsley Jr. and Senate GOP leader Everett Dirksen, February 15 and 28, 1962, respectively, SLRF, roll 13, Labor Department Papers, JFKL.

159. See PACLMP–CM, January 11–12, 1962, 13–15.

160. See PACLMP–CM, January 16, 1961, 1, 5, 8–12, and February 6, 1962, 1; Goldberg's letter to Henry Ford II, January 26, 1962, SLRF, roll 11, Labor Department Papers, JFKL.

161. PACLMP–CM, February 6, 1962, 2, also 1, 3. A copy of the letter, dated that same day and signed by both Goldberg and Luther Hodges, is in SLRF, roll 11, Labor Department Papers, JFKL.

162. See PACLMP–CM, February 6, 1962, 3.

163. Ibid., 3–4.

164. Ibid., 4–5.

165. See Goldberg's MFP, December 12, 1961, and his letter to the editor of the *Washington Post*, December 13, 1961, SLRF, rolls 10 and 12, Labor Department Papers, JFKL; "Those Perplexing 'Guideposts,'" *Fortune*, September 1962, 219–20, 224; Goldberg, *A Private View*, 106–7; Shaplen, "Peacemaker," pt. 1, 54; "Goldberg Warns Against Big Pay, Price Hikes," *Canton Repository*, January 10, 1962, 4; James J. Reynolds Memoir, OHC, JFKL, 49; Boris Shiskin's memo to George Meany, June 6, 1961, AFL–CIO Papers, JFKL; "Administration Again Asks Unions, Firms to Use Restraint in Wage, Price Increases," *Wall Street Journal*, June 6, 1961; Goldberg's memo to Walter Heller, "Comments on the Annual Report of the Council of Economic Advisors," January 3, 1962, SLRF, roll 12, Labor Department Papers, JFKL, 2–3.

166. See copy of Goldberg's speech, reprinted in Daniel P. Moynihan, ed., *The Defenses of Freedom: The Public Papers of Arthur J. Goldberg* (New York: Random House, 1964), 181–88. See also Goldberg, *A Private View*, 106–7; Shaplen, "Peacemaker," pt. 1, 54.

167. Goldberg, *A Private View*, 108, also 106–7; Goldberg's MFP, March 6, 1962, SLRF, roll 11, Labor Department Papers, JFKL; Moynihan, *The Defenses of Freedom*, 187–88; Archie Robinson, *George Meany and His Times* (New York: Simon & Schuster, 1981), 223–24; "The National Interest in Bargaining," *Fortune*, April 1962, 94, 96; Shaplen, "Peacemaker," pt. 1, 54; McDonald, *Union Man*, 298; Rowen, *The Free Enterprisers*, 92, 187–88. Reuther, on the other hand, endorsed Goldberg's speech. See his letter to Goldberg, April 2, 1962, and the latter's response, April 10 1962, thanking the UAW chief for his support. Goldberg added pointedly that "I am particularly appreciative of your strong support of this viewpoint since, as we both know, there have been other voices in the labor movement not so perceptive and understanding as you have been." Copies of both letters are in folder 13, box 377, Reuther Papers.

168. Meany tended to defend his position in terms pleasing to managerial ears, stressing the dangers to business as well as to the unions of more statist solutions. Although that tack could often make him sound like a spokesman for the U.S. Cham-

ber of Commerce, Meany's motive in making such remarks was to protect the interests of American workers. Meany's views are discussed briefly in "The National Interest in Bargaining," *Fortune*, April 1962, 94, 96. For an example of Meany's way of addressing the issue of government coercion, see Robinson, *George Meany*, 223–24.

169. See DKGD, April 14, 1962; Goldberg, *A Private View*, 107–8; Shaplen, "Peacemaker," pt. 1, 54; Rowen, *The Free Enterprisers*, 92, 187–88.

170. See PACLMP–CM, March 6–7, 1962, 1–2; Goldberg's MFP, March 28, 1962, SLRF, roll 11, Labor Department Papers, JFKL.

171. PACLMP–CM, March 6–7, 1962, 2. For evidence of committee members' views of the Block and Burns's proposal, see also the discussion in the minutes for the August 7, 1962, meeting, 19–21. On Goldberg's view of the labor monopoly issue, see "Unions and the Anti-Trust Laws: Three Viewpoints," *Labor Law Journal* 7 (1956): 133–36; and his letter to Clyde Hall, March 17, 1961, SLRF, roll 3, Labor Department Papers, JFKL. On the roots of the antimonopoly impulse, see Bernard Bailyn, *Ideological Origins of the American Revolution* (Cambridge, Mass.: Harvard University Press, 1967), 94–159; Eric Foner, "Politics, Ideology, and the Origins of the American Civil War," in Eric Foner, *Politics and Ideology in the Age of the Civil War* (New York: Oxford University Press, 1980), 34–53; Alan Brinkley, *Voices of Protest: Huey Long, Father Coughlin and the Great Depression* (New York: Vintage Books, 1982), 143–68.

172. PACLMP–CM, March 6–7, 1962, 2.

173. Ibid., 5, also 4.

174. Ibid., 5.

175. Ibid., 7, also 6.

176. See ibid., 7; Goldberg's MFPs, March 6 and 28, 1962, SLRF, roll 11, Labor Department Papers, JFKL.

177. PACLMP–CM, April 3–4, 1962, 2, also 3–4.

178. Ibid., 3, also 2.

179. Ibid., 2–6.

180. Ibid., 4, also 3.

181. Ibid.

182. Ibid., 5–7.

183. Ibid., 7.

184. Ibid., 8, also 7.

185. Ibid., 8–9.

186. See ibid., 9–11. See also the discussion (3–4) of this issue in the minutes for the February 6, 1962, meeting; "Those Perplexing 'Guideposts,'" *Fortune*, September 1962, 219–20, 224; William Simkin Memoir, OHC, JFKL, 55–57.

187. See PACLMP–CM, April 3–4, 1962, 11–12.

188. AJG. On the strength of the Swedish "peak" organizations, the weakness of their American counterparts, and the implications of that key difference for the fate of social democratic policies in those two countries, see Mucciaroni, "Political Learning and Economic Policy Innovation," 391–418.

189. AJG. My conclusions about the motives of the business managers in opposing Goldberg's plan are necessarily somewhat tentative. The views expressed by the management members of the Advisory Committee on Labor–Management Policy do, however, point clearly in that direction.

190. On the 1961 auto industry contract talks, see Goldberg's MFP, August 29, 1961; his telegrams to Louis Seaton, vice-president of General Motors, and Walter Reuther, both dated September 6, 1961, his MTP, September 12, 1961, memo from Robert J. Myers to H. M. Douty, September 27, 1961, "The General Motors–UAW

Agreement—Revised," all in SLRF, rolls 8, 10, and 53, Labor Department Papers, JFKL; USA–EBP, February 16, 1961, 38–39; "How Hard Will Reuther Push?" *Fortune*, May 1961, 231–32, 234, 236; Heath, *Kennedy and the Business Community*, 68; Roger M. Blough, *The Washington Embrace of Business* (New York: Columbia University Press, 1975), 90–93.

Chapter 9. Limited Victory

1. DKGD, January 11, 1961. See also USA–EBP, March 15, 1960, 130–38, April 28, 1960, 97–101, August 9, 1960, 136–74; David J. McDonald, *Union Man* (New York: Dutton, 1969), 292; John Herling, *Right to Challenge: People and Power in the Steelworkers Union* (New York: Harper & Row, 1972), 96–97.

2. See USA–EBP, March 15, 1960, 130–34, April 28, 1960, 99, August 9, 1960, 163–65, 167–69, February 16, 1961, 9–81.

3. AJG; USA–EBP, March 15, 1960, 130–34, April 28, 1960, 99, August 9, 1960, 163–65, 167–69, February 16, 1961, 9–81.

4. AJG; USA–EBP, February 16, 1961, 9–66.

5. USA–EBP, February 16, 1961, 28, also 21–27, 29–66.

6. Ibid., 37–38, also 29–36, 39–64. Abel also grumbled about rumored government intervention in the auto industry negotiations. He said that he "was shocked to read [in the *Wall Street Journal*] that already plans are being made to say to the Auto Workers . . . prior to their beginning negotiations this year that the government will call the parties in and say 'Here is what your decision is going to be. Now, you can go through the preliminary motions and make it appear like you are going to have negotiations, but this will be it. This will be the wages and benefits to the employees. This will be the amount of [the price] increase, if any, that the . . . industry is entitled to.' Well, if we get ourselves into that kind of condition, then, of course, the labor movement is useless any further to the people, it is useless any further to the over-all good of society,—and I don't think any of us want that" (38–39).

7. Ibid., 58–59.

8. See ibid., 37–64.

9. Ibid., 32–33, also 24–32, 36–58, 60–66, 69–71; I. W. Abel, *Collective Bargaining– Labor Relations in Steel: Then and Now* (New York: Columbia University Press, 1976), 52–53; Richard W. Kalwa, "Collective Bargaining in Basic Steel, 1946–83" (Ph.D. diss., Cornell University, 1985), 39; Philip W. Nyden, *Steelworkers Rank-and-File: The Political Economy of a Reform Movement* (New York: Praeger, 1984), 48–49; Herling, *Right to Challenge*, 96–99.

10. See USA–EBP, February 16, 1961, 24–28, 33–70, May 18, 1961, 149–50.

11. See USA–EBP, February 16, 1961, 66–68.

12. See ibid., 68–71.

13. See ibid., 75–78.

14. Ibid., 78, also 77.

15. Ibid., 78.

16. Ibid., 79, also 78.

17. See ibid., 78–79.

18. Ibid., 73, also see 71–72, 74.

19. Ibid., 74, also see 75.

20. AJG; USA–EBP, February 16, 1961, 75–81; Arthur J. Goldberg letter to Alvin

F. Franz, June 22, 1961, SLRF, roll 7, Labor Department Papers, JFKL; Kalwa, "Collective Bargaining in Basic Steel," 5–7.

21. See USA–EBP, March 15, 1960, 134–38, April 28, 1960, 97–101; Kalwa, "Collective Bargaining in Basic Steel," 37.

22. See USA–EBP, March 15, 1960, 134–38, April 28, 1960, 97–101, August 9, 1960, 136–45; John A. Orr, "The Rise and Fall of Steel's Human Relations Committee," *Labor History* 14 (1973): 69–70; Kalwa, "Collective Bargaining in Basic Steel," 37.

23. USA–EBP, August 9, 1960, 145.

24. Ibid., 146, also 145, 147.

25. Ibid., 150, also 147–49; Orr, "The Rise and Fall of Steel's Human Relations Committee," 70; Kalwa, "Collective Bargaining in Basic Steel," 37.

26. See USA–EBP, August 9, 1960, 151–62, 164–67.

27. See USA–EBP, February 18, 1961, 210–11, May 18, 1961, 158–61; October 5, 1961, 220; Kalwa, "Collective Bargaining in Basic Steel," 86; Herling, *Right to Challenge*, 73–76; "Employment and Unemployment in the Steel Industry Since 1959," SLRF, roll 56, Labor Department Papers, JFKL.

28. USA–EBP, May 18, 1961, 197, also 196, 198–204.

29. Ibid., 199–201; Orr, "The Rise and Fall of Steel's Human Relations Committee," 69–70.

30. See USA–EBP, May 18, 1961, 200, also 199, 201.

31. Ibid., 202.

32. See ibid., 203, and October 5, 1961, 185–90, for Miller's discussion of the seniority problem.

33. See USA–EBP, May 18, 1961, 203, October 5, 1961, 185–90.

34. USA–EBP, May 18, 1961, 205, also 202–4.

35. Letter from Conrad Cooper to David J. McDonald, April 4, 1961, reprinted in USA–EBP, May 18, 1961, 207.

36. USA–EBP, October 5, 1961, 179.

37. Ibid., 182, also 179–81. See also Herling, *Right to Challenge*, 97.

38. See USA–EBP, October 5, 1961, 181–82.

39. See ibid., 181–96.

40. Ibid., 183–84, also 186.

41. See Goldberg's letter to Tom Patton, August 29, 1961, SLRF, roll 9, Labor Department Papers, JFKL; Hobart Rowen, *The Free Enterprisers: Kennedy, Johnson and the Business Establishment* (New York: Putnam, 1964), 90–92; George J. McManus, *The Inside Story of Steel Wages and Prices 1959–1967* (Philadelphia: Chilton, 1967), 28–31; Jim F. Heath, *John F. Kennedy and the Business Community* (Chicago: University of Chicago Press, 1964), 67–68; Roger M. Blough, *The Washington Embrace of Business* (New York: Columbia University Press, 1975), 76–77, 121–22, also 186.

42. AJG; Goldberg's letter to McDonald, February 12, 1962, SLRF, roll 13, Labor Department Papers, JFKL; McDonald, *Union Man*, 294–98; Theodore Sorensen, *Kennedy* (New York: Harper & Row, 1965), 443–46; Arthur M. Schlesinger Jr., *A Thousand Days: John F. Kennedy in the White House* (Boston: Houghton Mifflin, 1965), 583; Dorothy Goldberg, *A Private View of a Private Life* (New York: Charterhouse, 1975), 104–8.

43. AJG; Blough, *The Washington Embrace of Business*, 90–94; Heath, *Kennedy and the Business Community*, 88–89; McDonald, *Union Man*, 294–98; Sorensen, *Kennedy*, 443–46; Schlesinger, *A Thousand Days*, 583; Goldberg, *A Private View*, 104–8.

44. See William Simkin Memoir, OHC, JFKL, 55–57; Blough, *The Washington Embrace of Business*, 92–93; Kalwa, "Collective Bargaining in Basic Steel," ii–iii; McDonald, *Union Man*, 294–98; Goldberg, *A Private View*, 104–8; Rowen, *The Free Enterprisers*, 90–91; Herling, *Right to Challenge*, 96–100.

45. The steel industry's annual rate of after-tax profit on stockholders' equity had averaged 11.2 percent during the 1950– 57 period, and then dropped to 7.2 percent over the next four years (Kalwa, "Collective Bargaining in Basic Steel," 13). See also Blough, *The Washington Embrace of Business*, 38–40, 76–94; Roy Hoopes, *The Steel Crisis* (New York: John Day, 1963), 31–56, 111–36; McManus, *Inside Story of Steel Wages*, 86–89; McDonald, *Union Man*, 294–98; Goldberg, *A Private View*, 104–8; and Herling, *Right to Challenge*, 96–100.

46. See David McDonald's report to the USA leadership in USA–EBP, January 10, 1962, 136–54, for details of the events leading up to formal negotiations. See also Goldberg's MTP, dated January 15, 1962; his telegrams to the eleven major steel companies' chief executive officers and McDonald, February 5 and 6, 1962; memo from Herbert Klotz to Hyman Bookbinder, March 19, 1962, "Briefing for the President," all in SLRF, rolls 11, 13, and 73, Labor Department Papers, JFKL; Rowen, *The Free Enterprisers*, 92.

47. See USA–EBP, October 5, 1961, 181–85, 217–19; Hoopes, *The Steel Crisis*, 31–37, 87–88. On the link between price stability and the problems of foreign competition, Goldberg said privately less than a year later that "ten years ago . . . I [had] never even heard the term 'balance of payments.' Today, it has to be a consideration at every bargaining table" (Rowen, *The Free Enterprisers*, 91). After a decline following the end of the 1959 strike, the share of the U.S. market for steel claimed by imports began rising again during 1961. Even though the total remained small, the trend heightened the Kennedy administration's concern about keeping stable the price of American-made steel. On the growth in imported steel during the early 1960s, see Donald F. Barnett and Louis Schorsch, *Steel: Upheaval in a Basic Industry* (Cambridge, Mass.: Ballinger, 1983), 47–52, 60–69; Nyden, *Steelworkers Rank-and-File*, 44–45; Kalwa, "Collective Bargaining in Basic Steel," 8–10.

48. See USA–EBP, January 10, 1962, 141–42; February 5, 1962, 3–8; David J. McDonald Memoir, OHC, JFKL, 13–14; McDonald, *Union Man*, 294–97; Rowen, *The Free Enterprisers*, 92, 97, 99–102; Heath, *Kennedy and the Business Community*, 68; McManus, *Inside Story of Steel Wages*, 35–36; Blough, *The Washington Embrace of Business*, 38–39, 78–81.

49. See USA–EBP, February 5, 1962, 19, 52–53, 60, February 6, 1962, 171–72; first Thomas J. Watson Jr. Memoir, 12–14, OHC, JFKL; McDonald, *Union Man*, 303–4; McManus, *Inside Story of Steel Wages*, 35–36; Rowen, *The Free Enterprisers*, 92–93.

50. See USA–EBP, February 5, 1962, 8–9, 10–37, 55-62, 66–67, February 6, 1962, 83–121, 171–72; Goldberg's MTP, February 13, 1962, his MFP, February 20, 1962, his telegrams to the steel executives, February 5, 1962, and to McDonald, February 6, 1962, all in SLRF, rolls 11 and 13, Labor Department Papers, JFKL; McDonald, *Union Man*, 297–98; McManus, *Inside Story of Steel Wages*, 36–37; Herling, *Right to Challenge*, 96–99.

51. See USA–EBP, February 5, 1962, 8–9, 16–40, 55-62, 66–67, February 6, 1962, 170–71; Goldberg's MTP, February 13, 1962, SLRF, roll 11, Labor Department Papers, JFKL; Kalwa, "Collective Bargaining in Basic Steel," 37, 39; John P. Hoerr, *And the Wolf Finally Came: The Decline of the American Steel Industry* (Pittsburgh: University of Pittsburgh, 1988), 327; Nyden, *Steelworkers Rank-and-File*, 48–49; Herling, *Right to Challenge*, 96–99.

52. See USA–EBP, February 5, 1962, 8–9, 16–40, 55–62, 66–67; February 6, 1962, 170–71; Goldberg's MTP, February 13, 1962, SLRF, roll 11, Labor Department Papers, JFKL; Kalwa, "Collective Bargaining in Basic Steel," 37, 39; Nyden, *Steelworkers Rank-and-File*, 48–49; Herling, *Right to Challenge*, 96–99.

53. Memo from Robert J. Myers to the secretary [of labor], March 9, 1962, "Review of the Steel Situation"; also memo, "Employment and Unemployment in the Steel Industry Since 1959." The latter pointed out that even though the decline in steel industry employment had halted in January 1961 and that employment had grown by 75,000 through September of that year, employment in steel had been stagnant thereafter, in marked contrast to most other areas of the economy. The memo also noted that long-term unemployment was far higher in the primary metals sector than for the economy as a whole. Both memos are in SLRF, roll 56, Labor Department Papers, JFKL.

54. Memo, "Technological Developments, Investment and Research in the Steel Industry," 2, SLRF, roll 56, Labor Department Papers, JFKL. See also "Steel: It's a Brand-New Industry," *Fortune*, December 1960, 123–27, 249–50, 254, 256, 261–62, 264.

55. See memo from Robert J. Myers to the secretary [of labor], March 9, 1962, "Review of the Steel Situation." Myers had sent Goldberg a memo nine days earlier, "Indexes of Unit Labor Cost for Production Workers in the Iron and Steel Industry in Ten Countries, 1950–60." It concluded that the rate of increase in such costs in the United States was the highest of the ten. The memo clearly implied that the trend, which had been broken by the 1959 strike, must not be allowed to continue lest foreign competition grow steadily worse. Both memos are in SLRF, roll 56, Labor Department Papers, JFKL. See also McDonald, *Union Man*, 298–99.

56. See USA–EBP, October 5, 1961, 217–19, January 10, 1962, 136–42, 145–46, February 6, 1962, 121–27, March 31, 1962, 3–5; Goldberg's MTP, February 27, 1962, his MFPs March 6 and 13, 1962, and his MTP March 28, 1962, all in SLRF, roll 11; memo "Significance of 1962 Steel Settlement—Draft for Mr. Reynolds," April 6 1962, same collection, roll 56, all in the Labor Department Papers, JFKL; Kalwa, "Collective Bargaining in Basic Steel," 37–38, 113; William T. Hogan, *Economic History of the Iron and Steel Industry in the United States* (Lexington, Mass.: Lexington Books, 1971), vol. 4, 1641–43; McDonald, *Union Man*, 299–300; Rowen, *The Free Enterprisers*, 93–94, 97–98; McManus, *Inside Story of Steel Wages*, 37–42; Herling, *Right to Challenge*, 97–98; first Thomas J. Watson Jr. Memoir, OHC, JFKL, 12–14. Blough later claimed that he had continued hinting all along that U.S. Steel executives would order a general price increase in 1962 and that "if there was any suggestion of a 'social contract,' . . . in the case of steel it escaped me completely," but the evidence suggests otherwise (*The Washington Embrace of Business*, 78). See also 38–39, 76–94. See DKGD, April 14, 1962, in which Dorothy Goldberg recorded her husband's telling Robert Kennedy over the telephone that "we continuously said to them that the whole purpose is price stability. [And] . . . they didn't say anything [about a price increase]." See also McManus, *Inside Story of Steel Wages*, 49. Although most of these sources contend that the contract provided for a 2.5 percent increase in employment costs, the most recent and comprehensive study puts the figure at just 2.2 percent (Kalwa, "Collective Bargaining in Basic Steel," 113).

57. MFP, April 3, 1962, SLRF, roll 15, Labor Department Papers, JFKL. See also USA–EBP, March 31, 1962, 3–5; "Steel's Good Example," *The Economist*, March 31, 1962, 1253; McDonald, *Union Man*, 300–1; McManus, *Inside Story of Steel Wages*, 39–42; Heath, *Kennedy and the Business Community*, 68; Rowen, *The Free Enterprisers*, 94.

58. On the reopening clause, see memo, "Significance of 1962 Steel Settlement—Draft for Mr. Reynolds" (2), April 6, 1962, SLRF, roll 56, Labor Department Papers, JFKL. See also Joseph Block's comments in PACLMP–CM, August 7, 1962, 14; McManus, *Inside Story of Steel Wages*, 39–40; Hogan, *Economic History of the Iron and Steel Industry*, 1642.

59. Rowen, *The Free Enterprisers*, 95, also 94; Hoopes, *The Steel Crisis*, 16–20; Sorensen, *Kennedy*, 447–48; Blough, *The Washington Embrace of Business*, 81–84; Goldberg, *A Private View*, 108–9; McManus, *Inside Story of Steel Wages*, 44; Schlesinger, *A Thousand Days*, 583–84; Walter Heller's handwritten notes, 6:55 P.M., Tuesday, April 10, 1962, in Walter Heller Papers, JFKL.

60. On the details of this meeting, see Hoopes, *The Steel Crisis*, 20–22; Goldberg, *A Private View*, 108–9; Rowen, *The Free Enterprisers*, 95; Blough, *The Washington Embrace of Business*, 84; Schlesinger, *A Thousand Days*, 583–84; Sorensen, *Kennedy*, 448; first Thomas J. Watson Jr. Memoir, OHC, JFKL, 12–16; Walter Heller notes.

61. See Hoopes, *The Steel Crisis*, 22–24; Sorensen, *Kennedy*, 448–50; Schlesinger, *A Thousand Days*, 584–85; McManus, *Inside Story of Steel Wages*, 45–46; Rowen, *The Free Enterprisers*, 95–96; Walter Heller notes. For an indication of the strong feelings aroused by Blough's actions, see Heller's notes, where he recorded that in evidence at the meeting afterward were "much dismay & profanity . . . kicked in the nuts—s.o.b. [were] among the milder expressions [used]."

62. See Hoopes, *The Steel Crisis*, 26; Sorensen, *Kennedy*, 449; Walter Heller notes; McDonald, *Union Man*, 305; Rowen, *The Free Enterprisers*, 96; McManus, *Inside Story of Steel Wages*, 46; Heath, *Kennedy and the Business Community*, 52–53; Goldberg, *A Private View*, 113–15.

63. See Hoopes, *The Steel Crisis*, 24–25; Sorensen, *Kennedy*, 449; David J. McDonald Memoir, OHC, JFKL, 14–16; McDonald, *Union Man*, 301–3; Rowen, *The Free Enterprisers*, 95; McManus, *Inside Story of Steel Wages*, 46; Blough, *The Washington Embrace of Business*, 88–89; Walter Heller notes. See also DKGD, April 12, 1962, where Dorothy Goldberg recorded her husband as having said about Kennedy's actions, "I almost feel sorry for the industry. Wait till they see . . . all hell is going to break loose." See also April 14 1962.

64. See DKGD, April 12, 1962; Sorensen, *Kennedy*, 449–50; Hoopes, *The Steel Crisis*, 27–28; Walter Heller notes.

65. See DKGD, April 12, 1962; Goldberg, *A Private View*, 111. Shortly thereafter Kennedy had repeated the thought to members of his staff, saying this time, "My father always told me that steel men were sons-of-bitches, but I never realized till now how right he was" (Sorensen, *Kennedy*, 449; McManus, *Inside Story of Steel Wages*, 45–46). Upon learning of the remark, the press distorted it, reporting that Kennedy had referred to all businessmen in those terms. The change robbed the statement of both Kennedys' intended meaning: The remark reflected their understanding that the steel industry had for so long played a leading role in the business community that its managers tended to act in a very rigid and high-handed fashion. On steel managers' richly deserved reputation for arrogance even among their fellow business executives and Kennedy's views on that subject, see Chapter 7; DKGD, April 14, 1962; Hoopes, *The Steel Crisis*, 58; James J. Reynolds Memoir, OHC, JFKL, 54; Sorensen, *Kennedy*, 448–50; Schlesinger, *A Thousand Days*, 584; Arthur M. Schlesinger Jr., *Robert Kennedy and His Times* (Boston: Houghton Mifflin, 1978), 436.

66. Sorensen, *Kennedy*, 450. See also Schlesinger, *A Thousand Days*, 585; Rowen, *The Free Enterprisers*, 101–3; McManus, *Inside Story of Steel Wages*, 46–48, 54–56; Heath, *Kennedy and the Business Community*, 69; McDonald, *Union Man*, 304. Block's

greater willingness to cooperate with the administration's policy no doubt stemmed, at least in part, from Inland's greater degree of insulation from the problems facing the steel industry. Inland's particular advantages are described briefly in Kenneth Warren, *The American Steel Industry, 1850–1970: A Geographical Interpretation* (Pittsburgh: University of Pittsburgh Press, 1973), 313. See also Hoopes, *The Steel Crisis*, 69–70.

67. Rowen, *The Free Enterprisers*, 90. See also McManus, *Inside Story of Steel Wages*, 48.

68. Sorensen, *Kennedy*, 451. See also Rowen, *The Free Enterprisers*, 89; McManus, *Inside Story of Steel Wages*, 48.

69. AJG.

70. See DKGD, April 12 and 14, 1962; Sorensen, *Kennedy*, 452–57; Goldberg, *A Private View*, 110–11; Rowen, *The Free Enterprisers*, 89–90, 101–2; McManus, *Inside Story of Steel Wages*, 55–56; Heath, *Kennedy and the Business Community*, 69; Blough, *The Washington Embrace of Business*, 94–102; Schlesinger, *A Thousand Days*, 585–86.

71. DKGD, April 14, 1962, also April 12 and 13, 1962; first Thomas J. Watson Jr. Memoir, OHC, JFKL, 12–16; Hoopes, *The Steel Crisis*, 106–7, 139, 146–65; Rowen, *The Free Enterprisers*, 101–7; McManus, *Inside Story of Steel Wages*, 49–56; Sorensen, *Kennedy*, 452–58; Blough, *The Washington Embrace of Business*, 94–103; Schlesinger, *A Thousand Days*, 585–86. Robert Kennedy's decision to send two hundred FBI agents hunting for managerial wrongdoing, an act that generated enormous hostility in the business community, appears to have been far less important to persuading steel managers to back down than those other factors. For details of Robert Kennedy's activities, see second Thomas J. Watson Jr. Memoir, OHC, JFKL, 1–2; Schlesinger, *Robert Kennedy*, 433–39.

72. DKGD, April 13, 1962.

73. Blough, *The Washington Embrace of Business*, 103, also 102; Hoopes, *The Steel Crisis*, 164–65; McManus, *Inside Story of Steel Wages*, 56; Rowen, *The Free Enterprisers*, 105–6; Sorensen, *Kennedy*, 458; Schlesinger, *A Thousand Days*, 586.

74. See DKGD, April 14, 1962; Frederick Kappel Memoir, OHC, JFKL, 18–19; Hoopes, *The Steel Crisis*, 222–60; Schlesinger, *A Thousand Days*, 586–88; Rowen, *The Free Enterprisers*, 106–50; McManus, *Inside Story of Steel Wages*, 57–72; Heath, *Kennedy and the Business Community*, 16, 66–85; Schlesinger, *Robert Kennedy*, 435–39; Sorensen, *Kennedy*, 459–69; Blough, *The Washington Embrace of Business*, 107–11. Frederick Kappel, who at that time was chairman of the board of AT&T, later described the managerial reaction to the 1962 steel episode: "I think whether the steel thing was justifiable in its own details, I wouldn't know, but I think it was a glorious example of what every businessman figured sooner or later he was going to have to face up to in one way or another. . . . That is[,] that you have to bear down on other things than prices if you are going to contain inflation. Otherwise you squeeze profits out of the picture to the extent that you can't finance your growth. Then everything stops" (Kappel Memoir, 19).

75. Even an historian as sympathetic to Kennedy as Arthur Schlesinger Jr. later wrote: "His policy toward business [after the steel dispute] . . . was one of mild appeasement" (*Robert Kennedy*, 436). See also Goldberg's memo to Theodore Sorensen, July 31, 1962, SLRF, roll 18, Labor Department Papers, JFKL; McManus, *Inside Story of Steel Wages*, 81–99. On the stalemate at Kaiser and in the HRRC, see Goldberg's letter to Edgar Kaiser, July 5, 1962, SLRF, roll 18, Labor Department Papers, JFKL; USA– EBP, July 12, 1962, 180–94, September 11, 1962, 102–3. The union and Kaiser's management did eventually reach an agreement in January 1963, but it was unacceptable to managers at the other major steel firms. See Paul F. Clark, Peter

Gottlieb, and Donald Kennedy, eds., *Forging a Union of Steel: Philip Murray, SWOC and the United Steelworkers* (Ithaca, N.Y.: Cornell University Press, 1987), 142; McManus, *Inside Story of Steel Wages*, 86–89.

76. See first Thomas J. Watson Jr. Memoir, OHC, JFKL, 14–16; Hoopes, *The Steel Crisis*, 118–37; Barnett and Schorsch, *Steel*, 37–74; McManus, *Inside Story of Steel Wages*, 51–53, 62–65; Heath, *Kennedy and the Business Community*, 88–89.

77. "The Private Strategy of Bethlehem Steel," *Fortune*, April 1962, 105, also 106, 109, 112, 242, 244 246, 248, 253; Frederick Kappel Memoir, OHC, JFKL, 19.

78. On the trends toward diversification and the establishment of foreign subsidiaries during the 1960s, see Paul A. Tiffany, *The Decline of American Steel: How Management, Labor and the Government Went Wrong* (New York: Oxford University Press, 1988), 180–82. By 1968, the front cover of U.S. Steel's annual report contained a statement describing the company as "A Diversified Producer of Materials and Services," clearly marking a watershed in the firm's history (Hogan, *Economic History of the Iron and Steel Industry*, 1668, also 1665–69, 1704, 1737–38, 1783, 1787–91, 1814–17, 1839–40). The simultaneous emergence of smaller, highly automated minimills and the construction of steelmaking plants in areas of the United States where unions were weakest are noted in Warren, *The American Steel Industry*, 255–57, 277–82. At the same time, encouraged by rising prices after 1961, exports' share of American steel consumption rose steadily for the next seven years, from 4.6 percent to 16.4 percent (Kalwa, "Collective Bargaining in Basic Steel," 8–12). This in turn only encouraged the use of substitutes. Even steel managers' efforts to cope with that problem by developing lighter-weight steel products contributed to the industry's decline because they required less steel to fabricate, thereby aggravating the existing problem of excess plant capacity (Barnett and Schorsch, *Steel*, 38–47).

79. See PACLMP–CM, May 1, 1962, 1–2; Goldberg's letters to George Meany and Martha W. Griffiths, April 4 and May 9, 1962, respectively, Goldberg's MFPs March 28 and May 1, 1962, his MTP dated May 22, 1962, in SLRF, rolls 14, 15, 11, and 15, respectively, Labor Department Papers, JFKL; Rowen, *The Free Enterprisers*, 107, 124–29.

80. See PACLMP–CM, May 1, 1962, 3; Goldberg's MFP, April 30, 1962, SLRF, roll 15, Labor Department Papers, JFKL; William Simkin Memoir, OHC, JFKL, 62–63. What few changes in the Taft–Hartley Act that the report endorsed went nowhere. Kennedy and Goldberg declined to press for their enactment, out of a belief that the lack of a real consensus in favor of such amendments meant that such an effort would prove fruitless. See "President to Ask Labor Act Revision in '62 to Deal with Big Strikes, Goldberg Says," *Wall Street Journal*, February 1, 1962, 3; Goldberg's letter to Wayne Morse, June 22, 1962, Eugene Foley's memo to Hyman Bookbinder, July 27, 1962, SLRF, rolls 17 and 73, Labor Department Papers, JFKL; James J. Reynolds Memoir, 8, and Millard Cass Memoir, 19, both in OHC, JFKL; Rowen, *The Free Enterprisers*, 188; Heath, *Kennedy and the Business Community*, 63.

81. See PACLMP–CM, May 22, 1962, 3; Goldberg's letter to Luther Hodges, November 27, 1961; Eugene Foley's memo to Hyman Bookbinder, July 2, 1962. Press reports about the committee's failure began appearing that same spring. See Goldberg's MTP, April 10, 1962. See also Goldberg's letter, June 1, 1962, to Robert Kennedy, in which Goldberg conceded that the results of the Advisory Committee on Labor–Management Policy experiment "thus far have not been spectacular." These sources are in SLRF, rolls 12, 73, 15, and 17, respectively, Labor Department Papers, JFKL.

82. See PACLMP–CM, August 7, 1962, 1–18.

83. Ibid., 19–21; Eugene Foley's memo, "Briefing for the President," August 27, 1962, and his memo to Timothy Reardon, August 28, 1962, SLRF, roll 73, Labor Department Papers, JFKL.

84. PACLMP–CM, September 10, 1962, 5. An earlier proposal to endorse the call for regional meetings patterned after the national economic conference had drawn even more opposition (see PACLMP–CM, August 7, 1962, 21).

85. See PACLMP–CM, September 10, 1962, 5–6. Although a few such smaller committees did spring up, in retrospect what is most striking about the whole idea was how limited its reach proved to be. See Goldberg's letters to L. S. Hollinger, June 14, 1961, and Keith Prouty, July 5, 1961, SLRF, rolls 7 and 8, Labor Department Papers, JFKL.

86. See PACLMP–CM, October 2, 1962, 1–10, Goldberg's "Memorandum to George Weaver and Esther Peterson," January 18, 1962, Goldberg's letters to J. Graham Parsons, Dr. Bertil Kugelberg, and Torsten Nilsson, January 18, May 4, and September 5, 1962, respectively, in SLRF, rolls 11, 15, 17, and 19, Labor Department Papers, JFKL; Joseph Keenan Memoir, 23–24, and first Thomas J. Watson Jr. Memoir, 18, both in OHC, JFKL. After meeting with the Advisory Committee on Labor–Management Policy, the Swedes embarked on a thirty-day tour of the United States and Puerto Rico, during which they met with employer and union groups from around the country. See Goldberg's letter to Torsten Nilsson and his two letters to Martin Wagner, May 1 and August 15, 1962, SLRF, rolls 15 and 19, Labor Department Papers, JFKL.

87. See PACLMP–CM, October 2, 1962, 1–5. On the Swedish experience during the 1930s, see Chapter 2.

88. PACLMP–CM, October 2, 1962, 6.

89. Geijer observed that "every fourth person [in Sweden] is working for a foreign market" (PACLMP–CM, October 2, 1962, 6). See also Goldberg's letter to J. E. Beardsley Jr., in which he wrote, "Sweden's problems in world markets are also a reason why they have . . . more centralized control by labor and management groups and the government. To allow there the free forces that play here would in all probability bring disaster to their foreign trade activities upon which the Swedish economy rests. You must remember that about 45–50 percent of Sweden's total products are exported, compared with only 5 percent in the United States" (February 15, 1962, SLRF, roll 13, Labor Department Papers, JFKL).

90. PACLMP–CM, October 2, 1962, 7–8.

91. AJG. The inability of the AFL–CIO national apparatus to restrain all its affiliates' wage demands became readily apparent during the first half of 1962. Among the worst offenders were the building trades. See Goldberg's MTPs, January 23, May 22, and May 29, 1962, all in SLRF, rolls 11 and 15, Labor Department Papers, JFKL; first Thomas J. Watson Jr. Memoir, OHC, JFKL, 12. James J. Reynolds Memoir, 48–49, and William Simkin Memoir, 55–57, both in OHC, JFKL; "Those Perplexing 'Guideposts,'" *Fortune*, September 1962, 219–20, 224; Hobart Rowen, "Mr. Goldberg and the Labor Leaders," *The Reporter*, May 10, 1962, 34; Rowen, *The Free Enterprisers*, 197–98.

92. AJG.

93. In 1962, the percentage of the U.S. nonfarm workforce belonging to unions fell below 30 percent for the first time in two decades, a level never again reached to this day. See Michael Goldfield, *The Decline of Organized Labor in the United States* (Chicago: University of Chicago Press, 1987), 10–11; Taft–Hartley's and Landrum–Griffin's effect on union organizing is discussed on pp. 32–33, 85, 105–8, 154–59,

184–89. See also Goldberg's MFPs October 17 and December 12, 1961; his letter to Warren Magnuson, November 17, 1961; his MFPs April 3 and 10, 1962; Klotz's memo to Hyman Bookbinder, "Briefing for the President," April 24, 1962; Goldberg's MFP, May 1, May 8, May 22, May 29, June 5, June 12, June 26, July 17, July 24, August 7, August 14, August 21, and August 28, 1962; his letter to Kennedy, June 6, 1962; his letter to Wayne Morse, June 22, 1962. All these documents are in SLRF, rolls 10, 12, 15, 18, and 73, Labor Department Papers, JFKL. See also "The Changing Geography of American Industry" and "Factories on the Move," *Fortune*, July 1954, 35–36, 38, 40; "Pressures in the Print Shop," *Fortune*, July 1960, 212, 217; "The Greatest Unresolved Problem," *Fortune*, February 1962, 199–200; "The Personal Touch," *Time*, September 22, 1961, 21–25; "Labour's New Frontier," *The Economist*, April 14, 1962, 147–48; Richard B. Freeman and James L. Medoff, *What Do Unions Do?* (New York: Basic Books, 1984), 221–45; Mike Davis, *Prisoners of the American Dream* (London: Verso, 1986), 124–27.

94. AJG; memo from John L. Holcombe to Goldberg, "Regulations Under the LMRDA," January 26, 1961, Goldberg's letters to Archibald Cox, Robert Kennedy, George Meany, Lister Hill, George Harrison, and Richard Poff, February 14, March 8, August 8, August 14, 1961, and November 7, 1961, and June 15, 1962, respectively, all in SLRF, rolls 3, 4, 8, 9, 12, and 16, Labor Department Papers, JFKL; Joseph Keenan Memoir, 4–5, and James J. Reynolds Memoir, 19–29, 35–41, both in OHC, JFKL; "Making Landrum–Griffin Work," *Fortune*, December 1960, 220, 225–26; "Advise and Dissent," *Fortune*, February 1961, 193–94.

95. See USA–EBP, September 13, 1960, 255–57; Joseph Keenan Memoir, OHC, JFKL, 4–5; Davis, *Prisoners of the American Dream*, 126.

96. See USA–EBP, March 15, 1960, 7–29, April 28, 1960, 10–33, September 13, 1960, 255–57, September 15, 1960, 264–75, July 12, 1962, 196–97.

97. See USA–EBP, September 15, 1960, 264–75, May 18, 1961, 188, July 11, 1962, 12–107, July 12, 1962, 196–232, August 22, 1962, 655–61. See also Goldberg's letter to Robert Kennedy, March 8, 1961, which noted the complaint filed with the Labor Department by leading USA dissident Donald Rarick. Rarick had been assaulted at the 1960 Steelworkers convention, apparently for having spoken against the leadership's policies. See Rarick's telegram to James P. Mitchell, September 21, 1960, the reply from Undersecretary of Labor James O'Connell, and the attached memoranda in the folder marked "1960 – Landrum–Griffin Act – Investigation and Enforcement," box 115, Mitchell Papers; Herling, *Right to Challenge*, 70–71.

98. USA–EBP, July 12, 1962, 219, also 217–18; USA–EBP, September 11, 1962, 73–102. Goldberg's determination to enforce the law also infuriated Maritime Union leader Joe Curran and IUE president James Carey (James J. Reynolds Memoir, OHC, JFKL, 19–20).

99. USA–EBP, July 12, 1962, 219.

100. Ibid., 221, also 222.

101. AJG; Rowen, "Mr. Goldberg and the Labor Leaders," 33–34; Rowen, *The Free Enterprisers*, 183–207; Archie Robinson, *George Meany and His Times* (New York: Simon & Schuster, 1981), 251–75; John Barnard, *Walter Reuther and the Rise of the Auto Workers* (Boston: Little, Brown, 1983), 177–214.

102. See "Who's Raiding Whom?" *Fortune*, May 1957, 252, 256, 259; "Trouble at Headquarters" and "Again the Raiders," *Fortune*, March 1958, 218, 221; "Ethics or Carpenters?" *Fortune*, January 1959, 157–58; Alan K. McAdams, *Power and Politics in Labor Legislation* (New York: Columbia University Press, 1964), 65–68.

103. See "Ethics or Carpenters?" *Fortune*, January 1959, 157–58; "Solidarity Under the Palms," *Fortune*, April 1959, 200; "Flexible Ethics," *Fortune*, October 1959, 224, 227, 229; Robert Shaplen, "Peacemaker," *New Yorker*, pt. 1, April 7, 1962, 108.

104. See "Solidarity Under the Palms," *Fortune*, April 1959, 200; "Unsolidarity Forever," *Fortune*, November 1959, 273–74; USA–EBP, February 18, 1961, 149–51, July 12, 1962, 244–55, September 11, 1962, 73–80; Walter Reuther's letter to Goldberg, April 18, 1961, folder 12, box 377, Reuther Papers; Goldberg's telegram to George Meany, December 13, 1961, Goldberg's letter to Joseph Curran, July 11, 1962, and memo from Eugene Foley to Hyman Bookbinder, "Briefing for the President," November 8, 1962, all in SLRF, rolls 12, 17, and 73, Labor Department Papers, JFKL; "A Breakup of AFL–CIO over Job Rights Would Harm U.S.: Goldberg," *Wall Street Journal*, August ?, 1962, clipping in Steelworkers Papers.

105. AJG; "Bias in Unions," *Fortune*, June 1957, 144, 146; "Labor's 'Race Problem,'" *Fortune*, March 1959, 191–92, 194; William H. Harris, *The Harder We Run: Black Workers Since the Civil War* (New York: Oxford University Press, 1982), 140–42, 160–62.

106. USA–EBP, October 5, 1961, 144, also 143, 145–46; Harris, *The Harder We Run*, 140–42, 160–62.

107. See USA–EBP, October 5, 1961, 145–46; Norman Hill, "Blacks and the Unions: Progress Made, Problems Ahead," *Dissent* 36 (1989): 496; Robert J. Norrell, "Caste in Steel: Jim Crow Careers in Birmingham, Alabama," *Journal of American History* 73 (1986): 672–89; Edward Greer, *Big Steel: Black Politics and Corporate Power in Gary, Indiana* (New York: Monthly Review Press, 1979), 91–93, 100–2; William Kornblum, *Blue Collar Community* (Chicago: University of Chicago Press, 1974), 54–57, 125–26; Hoerr, *And the Wolf Finally Came*, 174–75; McDonald, *Union Man*, 199–201; Herling, *Right to Challenge*, 219–20.

108. See Norrell, "Caste in Steel," 669–94; Greer, *Big Steel*, 91–93, 100–2; Kornblum, *Blue Collar Community*, 54–57; Hoerr, *And the Wolf Finally Came*, 174–75; McDonald, *Union Man*, 51–52, 55, 142, 198–202.

109. See Norrell, "Caste in Steel," 674–94; Greer, *Big Steel*, 100–7; Kornblum, *Blue Collar Community*, 54–57, 125–26; Hoerr, *And the Wolf Finally Came*, 174–75; Herling, *Right to Challenge*, 219–20.

110. AJG; Norrell, "Caste in Steel," 673–94; Greer, *Big Steel*, 104–7; Hoerr, *And the Wolf Finally Came*, 174–75; McDonald, *Union Man*, 51–52, 55, 142, 198–202.

111. AJG. On the 1962 steel contract's antidiscrimination clause, see Goldberg's telegram congratulating McDonald on the change. A copy of the telegram, April 11, 1962, is in SLRF, roll 15, Labor Department Papers, JFKL. That same year, the UAW elected its first black vice-president (Harris, *The Harder We Run*, 139). On the larger changes slowly emerging from the USA and organized labor more generally on this issue, see 161–62; Norrell, "Caste in Steel," 689–94; Kornblum, *Blue Collar Community*, 54, 126–27; Greer, *Big Steel*, 100–4; Hill, "Blacks and the Unions," 496.

112. See USA–EBP, July 12, 1962, 241–55, August 22, 1962, 652–55; Robinson, *George Meany*, 122–40, 227–32.

113. USA–EBP, July 12, 1962, 244–45, also 241–43, 246–55.

114. Meany formally apologized to McDonald. For the details of their reconciliation, see USA–EBP, August 22, 1962, 652–55.

115. AJG. See DKGD, entry not dated, for Goldberg's views on the Bay of Pigs fiasco; Robert Shaplen, "Peacemaker," *New Yorker*, pt. 2, April 14, 1962, 50. Goldberg's address was reprinted in *Vital Speeches of the Day*, July 15, 1961, 595–97.

116. See Rowen, "Mr. Goldberg and the Labor Leaders," 33–34; Rowen, *The Free Enterprisers*, 186.

117. For Goldberg's views on the merger's ultimate results, see his Memoir, AFL–CIO MOHC, 20–21. On the merger's legacy, see also David McDonald's Memoir in that same collection, 6–8, 10–17; Jacob Weinstein's letter to Goldberg, January 14, 1962, Weinstein Papers. Growing sentiment in labor circles for Goldberg's departure from his cabinet post is noted in Rowen, "Mr. Goldberg and the Labor Leaders," 33–34; Rowen, *The Free Enterprisers*, 186.

118. See Schlesinger, *A Thousand Days*, 641; Schlesinger, *Robert Kennedy*, 404–8; Sorensen, *Kennedy*, 273.

119. AJG; Shaplen, "Peacemaker," pt. 2, 62; Goldberg, *A Private View*, 18–20; Schlesinger, *A Thousand Days*, 641; Schlesinger, *Robert Kennedy*, 404–8; Sorensen, *Kennedy*, 273.

120. See Schlesinger, *A Thousand Days*, 134, 641; Schlesinger, *Robert Kennedy*, 248, 407.

121. AJG; DKGD, December 26, 1960, August 28, 1962, September 1, 1962; Shaplen, "Peacemaker," pt. 2, 62; Goldberg, *A Private View*, 120–21, 131–34; Schlesinger, *A Thousand Days*, 641; Schlesinger, *Robert Kennedy*, 407; Sorensen, *Kennedy*, 273. Kennedy later wrote Dorothy Goldberg that in appointing her husband to the Court he, Kennedy, "gave away my right arm." The letter is reprinted in Goldberg, *A Private View*, 132.

122. See Goldberg's "Draft Letter from the President to Senator Clark," July 17, 1961; his letter to Adam Clayton Powell, July 20, 1961; his MTPs, November 7, 1961, 2, February 13 and March 6, 1962; his "Memorandum for the Honorable Theodore C. Sorensen," January 8, 1962; and memo from Lawrence O'Brien to Kennedy, February 5, 1962, 4, all in SLRF, rolls 7, 8, 10, and 11, Labor Department Papers, JFKL; Willard Wirtz's "Confidential Memorandum to the Secretary Re: The Economic Situation, July 1961," July 21, 1961, folder marked "Department of Labor Memos to Goldberg," box 24, Wirtz Papers. See also the Council of Economic Advisers Memoir, OHC, JFKL, 291, where Kermit Gordon recalled that Kennedy was disturbed that "considering where he started from in the unemployment situation, unless he was able to make real progress in lowering the unemployment rate and holding it down, he faced the prospect in the '64 campaign of meeting the charge that he had the highest unemployment rate of any president since the war." As late as June 20, 1962, George Meany told Kennedy in a memo: "We are afraid that the pickup from the recession will be aborted." See first page of press release for June 20, AFL–CIO Papers, JFKL. On the Eisenhower record on unemployment for 1958 to 1960 and the continuities during the following two years, see Chapter 6; Rowen, *The Free Enterprisers*, 253–60; Sorensen, *Kennedy*, 421.

123. "Comments on the Annual Report of the Council of Economic Advisors," 1, January 3, 1962, SLRF, roll 12, Labor Department Papers, JFKL. See also the accompanying cover letter from Goldberg to Walter Heller. For a detailed exposition of Heller's position, see Rowen, *The Free Enterprisers*, 255–61.

124. "Comments on the Annual Report of the Council of Economic Advisors," 1.

125. Arthur J. Goldberg to Walter W. Heller, January 15, 1962. See also "Comments on the Annual Report of the Council of Economic Advisors," 1–2, and Goldberg's letter to Walter Heller, January 10, 1962. All three are in SLRF, rolls 12 and 13, Labor Department Papers, JFKL.

126. See "Comments on the Annual Report of the Council of Economic Advisors," his letters to Walter Heller, January 10 and 15, 1962, and his letter to L. Fanninger Jr., November 21, 1961, all in SLRF, rolls 12 and 13, Labor Department Papers, JFKL; Rowen, *The Free Enterprisers*, 260–71.

127. See Hyman Bookbinder's memo to the cabinet secretary, April 4, 1962, "Items for Cabinet Meeting, April 5," SLRF, roll 73, Labor Department Papers, JFKL; Council of Economic Advisors Memoir, OHC, JFKL, 298, 340–41, 392–401; Rowen, *The Free Enterprisers*, 231–32; Robert M. Collins, *The Business Response to Keynes, 1929–1964* (New York: Columbia University Press, 1981), 177–84; Steven M. Gillon, *Politics and Vision: The ADA and American Liberalism, 1947–1985* (New York: Oxford University Press, 1987), 147; Heath, *Kennedy and the Business Community*, 114–17; Sorensen, *Kennedy*, 427–33; Schlesinger, *A Thousand Days*, 577–80, 595–99.

128. See Hyman Bookbinder's memo to the cabinet secretary, April 4, 1962, "Items for Cabinet Meeting, April 5," SLRF, roll 73, Labor Department Papers, JFKL; Council of Economic Advisors Memoir, 392–401, Robert Nathan Memoir, 24, and Frederick Kappel Memoir, 19–21, all in OHC, JFKL; pp. 2–4 of June 20, 1962, press release, AFL–CIO Papers, JFKL; Rowen, *The Free Enterprisers*, 231–52; Collins, *The Business Response to Keynes*, 171–95; Gillon, *Politics and Vision*, 147; Heath, *Kennedy and the Business Community*, 114–22; Sorensen, *Kennedy*, 427–33; Schlesinger, *A Thousand Days*, 577–80, 595–99.

129. The remark is quoted in Schlesinger, *A Thousand Days*, 579.

130. See Gilbert S. Gall, *The Politics of Right to Work: The Labor Federations as Special Interests, 1943–79* (Westport, Conn.: Greenwood Press, 1988), 129–225; Rowen, "Goldberg and the Labor Leaders," 34; Rowen, *The Free Enterprisers*, 186–87; Shaplen, "Peacemaker," pt. 2, 78, 80; McAdams, *Power and Politics*, 133; "Labour's New Frontier," *The Economist*, April 14, 1962, 147; memo, "To Walter from Irving," May 17, 1961, folder 8, box 392, Reuther Papers; "Closing the Labor Gap," *Fortune*, April 1961, 211–12, 217; Goldberg's letter to C. A. McNeill, May 25, 1961, SLRF, roll 6, Labor Department Papers, JFKL. Even in many of the states that passed so-called right-to-work legislation, this step was less than completely effective in outlawing union-security arrangements. In 1959 the USA pioneered a form of union security that soon became known as the *agency shop*. During the 1960s the NLRB and the courts quickly endorsed that innovation, thereby undercutting the union-shop bans ("The Agency Shop," *Fortune*, January 1961, 176, 178).

131. AJG. See also Frank McCulloch Memoir, OHC, JFKL, 1, 9–10, 15–16, 20–21; "A 'Strong-Minded' Chairman for NLRB," *Fortune*, April 1961, 212; "NLRB on the New Frontier," *Fortune*, July 1962, 255–56, 258; Lee Modjeska, "Labor and the Warren Court," *Industrial Relations Law Journal* 8 (1986): 479–546; Davis, *Prisoners of the American Dream*, 117–25; Joel Edward Rogers, "Divide and Conquer: The Legal Foundations of Postwar U.S. Labor Policy" (Ph.D. diss., Princeton University, 1984), 310–64.

132. See Goldberg's "Letter to All Department and Agency Heads," July 14, 1961, his letters to Adam Clayton Powell and Nora Friel, July 20 and August 24, 1961, respectively, his MTP November 28, 1961, his letters to Hugh Sandlin and President Kennedy, April 10 and 20, 1962, respectively, all in SLRF, rolls 8, 9, 10, and 15, Labor Department Papers, JFKL; "White-Collar Lag," *Fortune*, April 1955, 76, 79–80, 82; "A Little Wagner Act," *Fortune*, May 1955, 60, 62, 64; "Jerry Wurf's Causes," *Fortune*, May 1959, 222. On the other hand, labor's efforts to organize so-called white-collar workers in the private sector made little progress. See "No Sale," *Fortune*,

September 1956, 210, 212; "A New Social Revolution," *Fortune*, April 1958, 215–16, 218; "Organized Labor—The Dwindling Minority?" *Fortune*, November 1958, 242; "The Greatest Unresolved Problem," *Fortune*, February 1962, 199–200; USA–EBP, August 8, 1960, 87–89; "Policies for Industrial Peace," 2–4, an address given by James P. Mitchell to the National Association of Food Chains on October 22, 1962, copy in folder marked "1962 – Political," box 29, Wirtz Papers.

133. For an overview of the western European experience during this period, see Alain Touraine, "Management and the Working Class in Western Europe," *Daedalus* 93 (1964): 304–34; Robert O. Paxton, *Europe in the Twentieth Century* (New York: Harcourt Brace, 1985), 589–97, 599–603.

134. On Japan, see USA–EBP, August 8, 1960, 102–6, August 9, 1960, 174–77; Goldberg's letters to Ralph Yarborough, Robert Blum, Nobuo Noda, and Thurgood Marshall, June 22, July 17, October 9, and October 10, 1961, respectively; Goldberg's MTP, November 7, 1961, his letters to Eleanor G. Colt, Dean Rusk, Kenji Fukunage, and Dean Rusk, January 12, March 22, July 12, and August 10 1962, all in SLRF, rolls 7, 8, 10, 11, 13, 15, 18, and 19, Labor Department Papers, JFKL; Sheldon Garon, *The State and Labor in Postwar Japan* (Berkeley and Los Angeles: University of California, 1987), 242–48. Western European workers' rather different experience is discussed in Touraine, "Management and the Working Class in Western Europe," 304–34; Paxton, *Europe in the Twentieth Century*, 589–97, 599–603.

135. Japan's lower-wage "productivity campaign" of the 1950s and 1960s, in which organized labor participated, is noted in Garon, *The State and Labor in Postwar Japan*, 244.

136. See Goldberg's letter to President Kennedy, May 4, 1961, his "Memorandum for the Honorable Frederick Dutton," June 19, 1961, his draft "Memorandum from the President" and cover letter to Richard N. Goodwin, July 11, 1961, his letters to Dean Rusk, September 18 and November 22, 1961, his letters to George Meany, December 4, 1961, January 9, 1962, and February 28, 1962, his letters to J. Caleb Boggs, Dean Rusk, and Hubert Humphrey, December 5, 1961, March 2, 1961, and January 13, 1962, respectively, his MFP, January 17, 1962, his "Memorandum to the Honorable McGeorge Bundy," March 19, 1962, his letters to George Meany, February 16 and 19, 1962, his letters to Raymond Hackney and Serafino Romualdi, February 16 and August 15, 1962, all in SLRF, rolls 7–8, 10–13, 15, and 19, Labor Department Papers, JFKL. See also Goldberg's letter to Dean Rusk, February 4, 1961, Rusk's reply, March 8, 1961, Goldberg's letter to Chester Bowles, May 15, 1961, and Bowles's letters to Goldberg, September 14 and October 19, 1961, all in Bowles Papers.

137. See Goldberg's letter to President Kennedy, May 4, 1961, his "Memorandum for the Honorable Frederick Dutton," June 19, 1961, his draft "Memorandum from the President" and cover letter to Richard N. Goodwin, July 11, 1961; his memo, "Winning Foreign Worker Support for U.S. Foreign Policy," October 26, 1961, his letter to J. Caleb Boggs, December 5, 1961, and the attached memo entitled "Analysis of Letter from Jose M. Martin," all in SLRF, rolls 7, 10, 11, and 12, Labor Department Papers, JFKL; Andrew Biemiller's letter to members of Congress, August 22, 1961, folder 24, box 30, Legislative Reference Files, AFL–CIO Legislative Department Papers.

138. *Fortune*'s labor columnist Daniel Bell had apparently sensed the impending change even earlier. In mid-1958 he resigned his position to enter teaching. See his letter to Andrew P. Biemiller, June 23, 1958, folder 20, box 85, Staff Working Files, AFL–CIO Legislative Department Papers.

Chapter 10. Rupture

1. See Alpheus T. Mason, *The Supreme Court from Taft to Burger* (Baton Rouge: Louisiana State University Press, 1979), 1–128, 147–50; William E. Leuchtenburg, "The Origins of Franklin D. Roosevelt's 'Court-Packing' Plan," *Supreme Court Review* (1966): 347–400.

2. See Paul A. Freund, *On Understanding the Supreme Court* (Boston: Little, Brown, 1950); Paul A. Freund, *The Supreme Court of the United States: Its Business, Purposes and Performance* (Cleveland: World, 1961); Charles L. Black Jr., *Old and New Ways in Judicial Review* (Brunswick, Maine: Bowdoin College Press, 1958); Charles L. Black Jr., *The People and the Court: Judicial Review in a Democracy* (New York: Macmillan, 1960); Martin Shapiro, "Fathers and Sons: The Court, The Commentators, and the Search for Values," in Vincent Blasi ed., *The Burger Court: The Counter-Revolution That Wasn't* (New Haven, Conn.: Yale University Press, 1983), 218–38.

3. DKGD, September 1, 1962. See also Dorothy Goldberg's letter to her son, September 30, 1963, also in DKGD; Dorothy Goldberg, *A Private View of a Public Life* (New York: Charterhouse, 1975), 127–29, 164, 171–72; Bernard Schwartz, *Super Chief: Earl Warren and His Supreme Court—A Judicial Biography* (New York: New York University Press, 1983), 447–48; David M. O'Brien, *Storm Center: The Supreme Court in American Politics* (New York: Norton, 1986), 45; Henry J. Abraham, *Justices and Presidents: A Political History of the Supreme Court* (New York: Oxford University Press, 1974), 258; Freund, *The Supreme Court*; Black, *The People and the Court*.

4. On the importance of Frankfurter's replacement with Goldberg, see Eva Redfield Rubin, "The Judicial Apprenticeship of Arthur J. Goldberg, 1962–1965" (Ph.D. diss., Johns Hopkins University, 1967), iii–v, 250–58; Russell W. Galloway Jr., "The Third Period of the Warren Court: Liberal Dominance (1962–1969)," *Santa Clara Law Review* 20 (1980): 773–829; Goldberg, *A Private View*, 127–29; Schwartz, *Super Chief*, 1–492. Galloway concluded that the change in Court personnel from Frankfurter to Goldberg "was one of the most important in the history of the United States Supreme Court" (775).

5. See Schwartz, *Super Chief*, 445–48, 486–87; Rubin, "The Judicial Apprenticeship," vii–viii; Ira H. Carmen, "One Civil Libertarian Among Many: The Case of Mr. Justice Goldberg," *Michigan Law Review* 65 (1966): 310; Shapiro, "Fathers and Sons," 218–38; Felix Frankfurter Memoir, OHC, JFKL, 52–54; Arthur J. Goldberg, *Equal Justice Under Law: The Warren Era of the Supreme Court* (New York: Farrar, Straus & Giroux, 1971), 3–113; Mason, *The Supreme Court*, 6–7.

6. See Rubin, "The Judicial Apprenticeship," 59–61.

7. The Warren Court's labor decisions during Goldberg's tenure on it are discussed in Lee Modjeska, "Labor and the Warren Court," *Industrial Relations Law Journal* 8 (1986): 479–546; Rubin, "The Judicial Apprenticeship," 31–61.

8. See *Smith* v. *Evening News Association*, 371 U.S. 195 (1962); Modjeska, "Labor and the Warren Court," 543; Katherine Van Wezel Stone, "The Post-War Paradigm in American Labor Law," *Yale Law Journal* 90 (1981): 1535–38; Paul Weiler, "Promises to Keep: Securing Workers' Rights to Self-Organization Under the NLRA," *Harvard Law Review* 96 (1983): 1778–80; Douglas L. Leslie, *Labor Law* (St. Paul: West, 1979), 289, 313.

9. See Stone, "The Post-War Paradigm," 1535–38.

10. See *NLRB* v. *Reliance Fuel Oil Corporation*, 371 U.S. 224 (1963); Modjeska, "Labor and the Warren Court," 532–33; Archibald Cox, Derek Bok, and Robert

Gorman, *Cases and Materials on Labor Law*, 9th ed. (Mineola, N.Y.: Foundation Press, 1981), 89.

11. See *Brotherhood of Railway Clerks* v. *Allen*, 373 U.S. 113 (1963); Modjeska, "Labor and the Warren Court," 523–24; Cox, Bok, and Gorman, *Cases and Materials on Labor Law*, 1074; William E. Forbath, "The Shaping of the American Labor Movement," *Harvard Law Review* 102 (1989): 1111–256.

12. See *NLRB* v. *Erie Resistor Company*, 373 U.S. 221 (1963); Modjeska, "Labor and the Warren Court," 503–5; Leslie, *Labor Law*, 102–5; USA–EBP, May 14, 1963, 33–34.

13. See *Plumbers* v. *Borden*, 373 U.S. 690 (1963); *NLRB* v. *General Motors Corporation*, 373 U.S. 734 (1963); *Retail Clerks, Local 1625* v. *Schermerhorn*, 373 U.S. 746 (1963); Modjeska, "Labor and the Warren Court," 519–22, 536; Cox, Bok, and Gorman, *Cases and Materials on Labor Law*, 1078–79; Leslie, *Labor Law*, 336, 338–39. The emergence of agency-shop agreements is discussed briefly in Chapter 9, n. 130.

14. See, generally, Modjeska, "Labor and the Warren Court," 479–546.

15. See *Smith* v. *Evening News Association*, 371 U.S. 195 (1962) 201–5; *NLRB* v. *Reliance Fuel Oil Corporation*, 371 U.S. 224 (1963) 227; *Brotherhood of Railway Clerks* v. *Allen*, 373 U.S. 113 (1963) 124.

16. See *Brotherhood of Railway Clerks* v. *Allen*, 373 U.S. (1963), 129–31; *NLRB* v. *Erie Resistor Company*, 373 U.S. 221 (1963), 237.

17. See *Plumbers* v. *Borden*, 373 U.S. 690 (1963), 698–700.

18. See *Carey* v. *Westinghouse Electric Corporation*, 375 U.S. 261 (1964); Stone, "The Post-War Paradigm," 1532–33; Modjeska, "Labor and the Warren Court," 543; Leslie, *Labor Law*, 187, 188.

19. See *Humphrey* v. *Moore*, 375 U.S. 261 (1964); Modjeska, "Labor and the Warren Court," 531–32; Stone, "The Post-War Paradigm," 1541–42; Rubin, "The Judicial Apprenticeship," 37–39; Cox, Bok, and Gorman, *Cases and Materials on Labor Law*, 1037–38.

20. See *NLRB* v. *Exchange Parts, Inc.*, 375 U.S. 405 (1964); Modjeska, "Labor and the Warren Court," 489–90; Leslie, *Labor Law*, 107.

21. See *United Steelworkers of America* v. *NLRB*, 376 U.S. 492 (1964); Modjeska, "Labor and the Warren Court," 509–10; Leslie, *Labor Law*, 147–48.

22. See *John Wiley & Sons, Inc.* v. *Livingston*, 376 U.S. 543 (1964); Modjeska, "Labor and the Warren Court," 515–16.

23. See *NLRB* v. *Servette, Inc.*, 377 U.S. 46 (1964); Modjeska, "Labor and the Warren Court," 507–8; Cox, Bok, and Gorman, *Cases and Materials on Labor Law*, 749–50; Leslie, *Labor Law*, 152–53.

24. See *NLRB* v. *Fruit & Vegetable Packers & Warehousemen, Local 760 (Tree Fruits)*, 377 U.S. 58 (1964); Modjeska, "Labor and the Warren Court," 508–9; Leslie, *Labor Law*, 153–56.

25. See *Teamsters Local 20* v. *Morton*, 377 U.S. 252 (1964); Modjeska, "Labor and the Warren Court," 536–37; Leslie, *Labor Law*, 188–89; 330–31; Cox, Bok, and Gorman, *Cases and Materials on Labor Law*, 811.

26. See *Carey* v. *Westinghouse Electric Corporation*, 375 U.S. 261 (1964), 273–76.

27. See *Humphrey* v. *Moore*, 375 U.S. 335 (1964), 351–60. Harlan also contended that the Court should have set the case for reargument to determine whether federal labor laws preempted state courts from hearing such suits (360). See also Rubin, "The Judicial Apprenticeship," 39–42.

28. See *NLRB* v. *Fruit & Vegetable Packers, Local 760 (Tree Fruits)*, 377 U.S. 58 (1964), 76–94.

29. See *NLRB* v. *Burnup & Sims, Inc.*, 379 U.S. 21 (1964); Modjeska, "Labor and the Warren Court," 490; Leslie, *Labor Law*, 93.

30. See *NLRB* v. *Fibreboard Paper Products Corporation*, 379 U.S. 203 (1964); Modjeska, "Labor and the Warren Court," 496–99; Cox, Bok, and Gorman, *Cases and Materials on Labor Law*, 434–41; Leslie, *Labor Law*, 206–7; James B. Atleson, *Values and Assumptions in American Labor Law* (Amherst: University of Massachusetts Press, 1983), 124–26. The union involved in this case was the USA, which was appealing a federal appeals court's $300,000 verdict against it (USA–EBP, September 11, 1962, 72).

31. See *NLRB* v. *Fibreboard Paper Products Corporation*, 379 U.S. 203 (1964); Modjeska, "Labor and the Warren Court," 498–99; Leslie, *Labor Law*, 206–7; Atleson, *Values and Assumptions*, 124–26.

32. See Modjeska, "Labor and the Warren Court," 497–99; Cox, Bok, and Gorman, *Cases and Materials on Labor Law*, 434–41; Atleson, *Values and Assumptions*, 124–29; Leslie, *Labor Law*, 206–7.

33. The clear purpose behind the employer's action in the Fibreboard case is noted in Leslie, *Labor Law*, 206. See also USA–EBP, September 11, 1962, 69–72; Modjeska, "Labor and the Warren Court," 498, n. 124.

34. See *Textile Workers Union* v. *Darlington Manufacturing Company*, 380 U.S. 263 (1965); Modjeska, "Labor and the Warren Court," 491–92; Leslie, *Labor Law*, 111–14. The Court ordered the case remanded to the NLRB to determine whether the employer in the case had decided to close the plant in question for an antiunion reason. The board so found, and its conclusion was upheld by the U.S. Court of Appeals for the Fourth Circuit. See Leslie, *Labor Law*, 113; Cox, Bok, and Gorman, *Cases and Materials on Labor Law*, 247.

35. See *NLRB* v. *Brown*, 380 U.S. 278 (1965); Rubin, "The Judicial Apprenticeship," 46–47; Leslie, *Labor Law*, 117–19.

36. See *American Shipbuilding Company* v. *NLRB*, 380 U.S. 300 (1965); Rubin, "The Judicial Apprenticeship," 42–45, 47; Leslie, *Labor Law*, 119–23.

37. See *NLRB* v. *Brown*, 380 U.S. 278 (1965); *American Shipbuilding Company* v. *NLRB*, 380 U.S. 300 (1965); Rubin, "The Judicial Apprenticeship," 42–47; Leslie, *Labor Law*, 117–23.

38. See *United States* v. *Brown*, 381 U.S. 437 (1965); Cox, Bok, and Gorman, *Cases and Materials on Labor Law*, 1188–89; Schwartz, *Super Chief*, 562.

39. See *United States* v. *Brown*, 381 U.S. 437 (1965), 437–62; Cox, Bok, and Gorman, *Cases and Materials on Labor Law*, 1188–89; Schwartz, *Super Chief*, 562.

40. See Cox, Bok, and Gorman, *Cases and Materials on Labor Law*, 1188–89; Rubin, "The Judicial Apprenticeship," 60; Shapiro, *Super Chief*, 562. On Goldberg's long-standing opposition to the Taft–Hartley provision barring Communist Party members from serving as union officers or employees, see "Testimony of Arthur J. Goldberg, General Counsel, Congress of Industrial Organizations and United Steelworkers of America, Before the Senate Labor and Public Welfare Committee on S. 249 on February 3, 1949," copy in Goldberg Papers; Arthur J. Goldberg, *Labor United* (New York: McGraw-Hill, 1956), 183. For the earlier Supreme Court ruling upholding the Taft–Hartley ban, see *American Communications Association* v. *Douds*, 339 U.S. 382 (1950).

41. The central importance of the ban on radicals in winning managerial support for the postwar New Deal is noted in Chapters 3–5. On the other issues, see *United States* v. *Brown*, 381 U.S. 437 (1965).

42. See *United Mine Workers* v. *Pennington*, 381 U.S. 657 (1965); *Local 189,*

Amalgamated Meatcutters & Butcher Workmen v. *Jewel Tea Company*, 381 U.S. 676 (1965); Modjeska, "Labor and the Warren Court," 511–12; Rubin, "The Judicial Apprenticeship," 47–50, 56–59; Leslie, *Labor Law*, 249–51; 255–57.

43. See *United Mine Workers* v. *Pennington*, 381 U.S. 657 (1965); *Local 189, Amalgamated Meatcutters & Butcher Workmen* v. *Jewel Tea Company*, 381 U.S. 676 (1965); Modjeska, "Labor and the Warren Court," 511–12; Rubin, "The Judicial Apprenticeship," 47–50; Leslie, *Labor Law*, 249–62.

44. See *NLRB* v. *Burnup & Sims, Inc.*, 379 U.S. 21 (1964), 24–25.

45. See *NLRB* v. *Fibreboard Paper Products Corporation*, 379 U.S. 203 (1964), 217–26; Leslie, *Labor Law*, 207–8; Atleson, *Values and Assumptions*, 124–28; Stone, "The Post-War Paradigm," 1548.

46. See *NLRB* v. *Brown*, 380 U.S. 278 (1965); Rubin, "The Judicial Apprenticeship," 42–47; Leslie, *Labor Law*, 117–23.

47. See *American Shipbuilding Company* v. *NLRB*, 380 U.S. 300 (1965); Rubin, "The Judicial Apprenticeship," 42–45, 47; Leslie, *Labor Law*, 119–23.

48. See *United States* v. *Brown*, 381 U.S. 437 (1965), 462–78; Schwartz, *Super Chief*, 562.

49. See *United Mine Workers* v. *Pennington*, 381 U.S. 657 (1965), 659–72; Modjeska, "Labor and the Warren Court," 511–12; Rubin, "The Judicial Apprenticeship," 47–50, 55–59; Leslie, *Labor Law*, 249–53. Modjeska concluded that despite the White opinion's finding that labor was not entirely exempt from the Sherman Act when bargaining in an industrywide context, "through pragmatic awareness of the industry, table-pounding declarations of 'unilateral' goals, and a wink-and-nod, sophisticated negotiators remain essentially unhampered by the Court's token obeisance to antitrust law" ("Labor and the Warren Court," 512).

50. See *Local 189, Amalgamated Meatcutters & Butcher Workmen* v. *Jewel Tea Company*, 381 U.S. 676 (1965), 679–97; Modjeska, "Labor and the Warren Court," 511–12; Rubin, "The Judicial Apprenticeship," 55–59; Leslie, *Labor Law*, 255–60.

51. See *United Mine Workers* v. *Pennington*, 381 U.S. 657 (1965), 672–75; Rubin, "The Judicial Apprenticeship," 56–59; Leslie, *Labor Law*, 253.

52. See *Local 189, Amalgamated Meatcutters & Butcher Workmen* v. *Jewel Tea*, 381 U.S. 676 (1965), 735–38; Rubin, "The Judicial Apprenticeship," 56–59; Leslie, *Labor Law*, 261.

53. See 381 U.S. 676 (1965), 697–732; Rubin, "The Judicial Apprenticeship," 50–61, 257–58.

54. See Modjeska, "Labor and the Warren Court," 511–12; Rubin, "The Judicial Apprenticeship," 257–58; Alan Draper, *A Rope of Sand: The AFL–CIO Committee on Political Education, 1955–67* (New York: Praeger, 1989).

55. Modjeska concluded that "the reality is that the Court diverted the potential antiunion impact of the Taft–Hartley and Landrum–Griffin labor relations amendments. Destructive impact was both patent and incipient in the statutory language as written by Congress and as applied by the NLRB. Neutralization of such impact must surely be viewed as the Warren Court's most significant contribution to labor's cause" ("Labor and the Warren Court," 545). On the ways in which more conservative Court majorities have subsequently eroded those decisions, see also 546; Leslie, *Labor Law*; and Archibald Cox, Derek Curtis Bok, and Robert A. Gorman, *Cases and Materials on Labor Law*, 11th ed. (Westbury, N.Y.: Foundation Press, 1991).

56. See *Baker* v. *Carr*, 369 U.S. 186 (1962); *Gray* v. *Sanders*, 372 U.S. 368 (1963); *Wesberry* v. *Sanders*, 376 U.S. 1 (1964); *Reynolds* v. *Sims*, 377 U.S. 533 (1964); Schwartz, *Super Chief*, 410–27, 465–66, 501–8; Mason, *The Supreme Court*, 234–82;

Rubin, "The Judicial Apprenticeship," vii–viii; the discussion of those cases in Gerald Gunther, *Cases and Materials on Constitutional Law,* 10th ed. (Mineola, N.Y.: Foundation Press, 1980).

57. *Kennedy* v. *Mendoza-Martinez* and *Rusk* v. *Cort,* 372 U.S. 144 (1963).

58. *U.S.* v. *Seeger,* 380 U.S. 163 (1965).

59. *Henry* v. *Mississippi,* 379 U.S. 443 (1965); *Wong Sun* v. *U.S.,* 371 U.S. 471 (1963); *Townsend* v. *Sain,* 372 U.S. 293 (1963); *Jackson* v. *Denno,* 378 U.S. 368 (1964).

60. *Malloy* v. *Hogan,* 378 U.S. 1 (1964); *Pointer* v. *Texas,* 380 U.S. 400 (1965).

61. *Gideon* v. *Wainwright,* 372 U.S. 335 (1963); *Massiah* v. *U.S.,* 377 U.S. 201 (1964); *Escobedo* v. *Illinois,* 378 U.S. 478 (1964).

62. *U.S.* v. *Gainey,* 380 U.S. 63 (1965).

63. *Fay* v. *Noia,* 372 U.S. (1963).

64. *Sanders* v. *U.S.,* 373 U.S. 1 (1963).

65. *New York Times* v. *Sullivan,* 376 U.S. 254 (1964); *Garrison* v. *Louisiana,* 379 U.S. 64 (1964).

66. *Cox* v. *Louisiana,* 379 U.S. 536, 559 (1965).

67. *Freedman* v. *Maryland,* 380 U.S. 51 (1965).

68. *Griswold* v. *Connecticut,* 381 U.S. 479 (1965).

69. *American Committee for Protection of Foreign Born* v. *Subversive Activities Control Board,* 380 U.S. 503 (1965).

70. *Lamont* v. *Postmaster General,* 381 U.S. 301 (1965).

71. *Stanford* v. *Texas,* 379 U.S. 476 (1965). In fully one-third of those decisions, the Court divided five to four, with Goldberg consistently in the majority. For more information about the specifics of each case, see Schwartz, *Super Chief,* 449–50, 453–60, 470–75, 527–29, 531–41, 557–80; Peter Arenella, "Rethinking the Functions of Criminal Procedure: The Warren and Burger Courts' Competing Ideologies," *Georgetown Law Journal* 72 (1983): 185–248; Rubin, "The Judicial Apprenticeship," 150–248; the discussion of the relevant cases in Gunther, *Cases and Materials on Constitutional Law.*

72. *National Association for the Advanced of Colored People* v. *Button,* 371 U.S. 415 (1963).

73. *Peterson* v. *Greenville,* 373 U.S. 244 (1963); *Avent* v. *North Carolina,* 373 U.S. 244 (1963); *Gober* v. *Birmingham,* 373 U.S. 244 (1963); *Lombard* v. *Louisiana,* 373 U.S. 267 (1963); *Shuttlesworth* v. *Birmingham,* 373 U.S. 262 (1963); *Griffin* v. *Maryland,* 378 U.S. 130 (1964); *Bell* v. *Maryland,* 378 U.S. 226 (1964); *Barr* v. *Columbia,* 378 U.S. 153 (1964); *Bouie* v. *Columbia,* 378 U.S. 130 (1964); 378 U.S. 226 (1964); *Robinson* v. *Florida,* 378 U.S. 153 (1964); *Abernathy* v. *Alabama,* 380 U.S. 447 (1965); *Cameron* v. *Johnson,* 381 U.S. 741 (1965).

74. *Hamm* v. *Rock Hill,* 379 U.S. 306 (1964).

75. *Heart of Atlanta Motel* v. *United States,* 379 U.S. 241 (1964); *Katzenbach* v. *McClung,* 379 U.S. 294 (1964).

76. *McLaughlin* v. *Florida,* 379 U.S. 184 (1964).

77. *Harman* v. *Forssenius,* 380 U.S. 528 (1965).

78. For the details of each decision, see also Schwartz, *Super Chief,* 450–53, 479–86, 508–25, 529–30, 552–60; Rubin, "The Judicial Apprenticeship," 103–49; Gunther, *Cases and Materials on Constitutional Law.*

79. Both the scholarly and more popular literature on the Warren Court's rulings in the areas of reapportionment, crime, and civil rights is enormous. See the sources for the relevant cases in Gerald Gunther, *Cases and Materials on Constitutional Law,* 11th ed. (Mineola, N.Y.: Foundation Press, 1985). On the importance that Goldberg

510 Notes to pages 336–340

and other labor leaders attributed to organizing the southern workforce, see Chapters 3–5, 7, and 9.

80. See Bob Blauner, *Black Lives, White Lives* (Berkeley and Los Angeles: University of California Press, 1989), esp. 122–36. In explaining the opposition particularly in the white working class to the Court's actions and those of the federal government more generally, Blauner observed that "even though the position of white workers was insecure, their racial privilege modest, black militants targeted them along with more affluent whites as equally exploitive of racial minorities. Caught in the middle, many workers vented their anger and frustration at blacks, students, and antiwar activists" (122).

81. The deep-seated roots of popular hostility toward concentrated power are noted in Chapter 8. On the twentieth-century South in particular, see Alan Brinkley, *Voices of Protest: Huey Long, Father Coughlin and the Great Depression* (New York: Vintage Books, 1982), 143–68. The way in which this sentiment was manifested during the 1960s, much of it through George Wallace's presidential campaigns, is discussed in Dewey Grantham, *The Life & Death of the Solid South: A Political History* (Lexington: University of Kentucky Press, 1988), 149–76; Kevin Phillips, *The Emerging Republican Majority* (New Rochelle, N.Y.: Arlington House, 1969), 187–289; Marshall Frady, *Wallace* (New York: World, 1968), 137–246. See also George C. Wallace, *Stand up for America* (Garden City, N.Y.: Doubleday), 71–137; the entry on Wallace in Charles Reagan Wilson and William Ferris, eds., *Encyclopedia of Southern Culture* (Chapel Hill: University of North Carolina Press, 1989), 1199–1200.

82. For examples of the standpat critique, see the discussion of Eisenhower's views in Stephen Ambrose, *Eisenhower: The President* (New York: Simon & Schuster, 1984), 497–99, 528–29; those of Felix Frankfurter and John Harlan, in Schwartz, *Super Chief*, 410–555.

83. USA–EBP, February 15, 1963, 257. See also the discussion of unemployment in the early 1960s in Chapter 9; the data on USA membership in Chapter 5; USA–EBP, August 22, 1962, 661, March 19, 1963, 246; John Herling, *Right to Challenge: People and Power in the Steelworkers Union* (New York: Harper & Row, 1972), 74.

84. See USA–EBP, September 11, 1962, 14–15, 72–73, February 15, 1963, 204–8, 251–52, March 19, 1963, 188–211, 245–47, November 14, 1963, 45–46, September 12, 1962, 139–41; Herling, *Right to Challenge*, 75–77.

85. See USA–EBP, September 11, 1962, 69–72.

86. USA–EBP, March 19, 1963, 219–21. See also USA–EBP, May 14, 1963, 3–30, November 14, 1963, 44–45; Chapter 9.

87. See USA–EBP, July 12, 1962, 180–92, February 14, 1963, 89–102, May 14, 1963, 20–24; Richard W. Kalwa, "Collective Bargaining in Basic Steel, 1946–83" (Ph.D. diss., Cornell University, 1985), 38–39; John A. Orr, "The Rise and Fall of Steel's Human Relations Committee," *Labor History* 14 (1973): 69–79; Herling, *Right to Challenge*, 98–99; George J. McManus, *The Inside Story of Steel Wages and Prices 1959–1967* (Philadelphia: Chilton, 1967), 81–99. On the 1963 price increases in steel, see memo from Fred Raines to the Council of Economic Advisers (CEA), October 5, 1963, "Steel's Competitive Position Abroad and Price Stability at Home" and the "Excerpt from Transcript of Press Conference No. 62 of the President of the United States," October 9, 1963, both in Walter Heller Papers, JFKL.

88. USA–EBP, May 14, 1963, 21, also 20, 23–24.

89. See USA–EBP, May 14, 1963, 20–24; Herling, *Right to Challenge*, 96–100.

90. See "Steel and Union Reach Contract for 2-Year Peace," *New York Times*, June 21, 1963, and "Steel Labor Contract Extended 22 Months; Workers to Get Periodic

13-Week Vacations," *Wall Street Journal,* June 13, 1963, clippings in Heller Papers; also "Steel's Competitive Position Abroad and Price Stability at Home"; "Excerpt from the Transcript of Press Conference"; letter from Walter Heller to Otto Eckstein, May 7, 1964; table, "Steel–Auto Wage Comparison," May 26, 1964, all in Heller Papers; Orr, "The Rise and Fall of Steel's Human Relations Committee," 69–79; Kalwa, "Collective Bargaining in Basic Steel," 39; McManus, *Inside Story of Steel Wages,* 81–99; Herling, *Right to Challenge,* 96–102. Herling chronicles graphically the growing opposition to McDonald's policy but fails to spell out why the USA president refused to change course. The 1963 agreement between the USA and steel management provided for no general wage increase. The threat posed by imported steel during this period is discussed in Donald F. Barnett and Louis Schorsch, *Steel: Upheaval in a Basic Industry* (Cambridge, Mass.: Ballinger, 1983), 32, 47–51. Between 1961 and 1965, imports' share of the U.S. steel market, according to the most meaningful measure, roughly tripled. At the same time, American steel firms' profits, though still quite large and steadily rising, lagged behind the average for the manufacturing sector (48, 71–73). See also Kalwa, "Collective Bargaining in Basic Steel," 13; Roger M. Blough, *The Washington Embrace of Business* (New York: Columbia University Press, 1975), 110.

91. See Cyrus Ching Memoir, OHC, RBML–CU, 615; Kalwa, "Collective Bargaining in Basic Steel," 38–39; Orr, "The Rise and Fall of Steel's Human Relations Committee," 69–79; Herling, *Right to Challenge,* 98–100.

92. See USA–EBP, May 6, 1964, 65–85, November 10, 1964, 7–8, November 16, 1964, 113–17; Kalwa, "Collective Bargaining in Basic Steel," 37–39; Herling, *Right to Challenge,* 96–100; Orr, "The Rise and Fall of Steel's Human Relations Committee," 69–79; McManus, *Inside Story of Steel Wages,* 86–89; Paul F. Clark, Peter Gottlieb, and Donald Kennedy, eds., *Forging a Union of Steel: Philip Murray, SWOC and the United Steelworkers* (Ithaca, N.Y.: Cornell University Press, 1987), 142; John Hoerr, *And the Wolf Finally Came: The Decline of the American Steel Industry* (Pittsburgh: University of Pittsburgh Press, 1988), 327–29.

93. See USA–EBP, May 6–7, 1964, 97, 136–39, July 23, 1964, 51–54; David J. McDonald, *Union Man* (New York: Dutton, 1969), 311–13, 315; Norman Hill, "Blacks and the Unions: Progress Made, Problems Ahead," *Dissent* 36 (1989): 496; Robert J. Norrell, "Caste in Steel: Jim Crow Careers in Birmingham, Alabama," *Journal of American History* 73 (1986): 689–90; Philip Taft, *Organizing Dixie: Alabama Workers in the Industrial Era* (Westport, Conn.: Greenwood Press, 1981), 171–75.

94. USA–EBP, May 6, 1964, 63, also 11, 62; USA–EBP, January 23, 1964, 3–5, 9, 117–18; Frederick Kappel Memoir, OHC, JFKL, 19–21; letter from Edward Mason to Lyndon Johnson, June 10, 1964; memo from Stanley Ruttenberg to Walter Heller, "Possible Impact of the Auto Settlement," September 14, 1964; attached list of impending collective bargaining negotiations; clipping from *Wall Street Journal,* September 15, 1964, "Businessmen See Pact at Chrysler Creating an Inflationary Pressure"; Walter Heller's memo for the president, "One Poll That's Not So Good!" October 27, 1964, all in Heller Papers; also Theodore Sorensen, *Kennedy* (New York: Harper & Row, 1965), 427–33; Kalwa, "Collective Bargaining in Basic Steel," 39; Orr, "The Rise and Fall of Steel's Human Relations Committee," 71, 77–79; McManus, *Inside Story of Steel Wages,* 100–16. AT&T executive Frederick Kappel later observed that the Kennedy–Johnson tax measure ultimately "turned out to be a bill not too different from our [the Business Advisory Council's] views" (Kappel Memoir, 21).

95. USA–EBP, May 6, 1964, 91.

96. See USA–EBP, February 15, 1963, 204, July 24, 1964, 84–91, 105–7, September 2, 1964, 78–107, 113–29, September 15, 1964, 210–12, November 10, 1964, 3–21, November 19, 1964, 2–3, 112–34; Kalwa, "Collective Bargaining in Basic Steel," 39, 146–48; Orr, "The Rise and Fall of Steel's Human Relations Committee," 77–79; John A. Orr, "The Steelworker Election of 1965 – The Reasons for the Upset," *Labor Law Journal* 20 (1969): 100–5; Herling, *Right to Challenge*, 1–80; McDonald, *Union Man*, 307–9.

97. See cover letter, May 22, 1963, from Walter Heller to Arthur J. Goldberg and attached memos; memo from Heller to Goldberg, October 30, 1964, and the attached documents, all in Heller Papers; Herling, *Right to Challenge*, 86, 96, 117, 129; FSG.

98. See USA–EBP, August 21, 1962, 655–56, May 14, 1963, 34–35, July 24, 1964, 105–7, September 2, 1964, 113–17, September 15, 1964, 210–12, November 17, 1964, 113–39; I. W. Abel Memoir, OHC, LBJL, 4; Chapter 9; Orr, "The Steelworker Election of 1965," 100–12; McManus, *Inside Story of Steel Wages*, 117–82; Herling, *Right to Challenge*, 83–311; Orr, "The Rise and Fall of Steel's Human Relations Committee," 69–71, 77–82; McDonald, *Union Man*, 315–25. John Herling's book tells the story of the McDonald–Abel contest, although in a journalistic way that focuses on the surface issues rather than the underlying split over questions of political and economic policy. Soon after winning the election, Abel and his followers negotiated a new contract providing for substantial increases in pay and benefits, thereby spurring another round of steel price increases and encouraging further steel imports. See R. Conrad Cooper Memoir, 2–23, Roger M. Blough Memoir, 17–21, both in OHC, LBJL; Kalwa, "Collective Bargaining in Basic Steel," 39–41, 145–49; McManus, *Inside Story of Steel Wages*, 136–240; Herling, *Right to Challenge*, 301–5; Orr, "The Rise and Fall of Steel's Human Relations Committee," 80–82; Barnett and Schorsch, *Steel*, 48.

99. See Mike Davis, *Prisoners of the American Dream* (London: Verso, 1986), 126–27; John Barnard, *Walter Reuther and the Rise of the Auto Workers* (Boston: Little, Brown, 1983), 195–98; Herling, *Right to Challenge*, 330–37, 373.

100. AJG; Herling, *Right to Challenge*, 330–35. On the worsening inflation rate and the related problems, see Raymond Saulnier Memoir, OHC, DDEL, 51, 65; Luther Hodges's letter to Johnson and attached memo, December 4, 1964, folder 728, box 402, LBJ presidential papers, LBJL; Roger M. Blough Memoir, 12, and James J. Reynolds Memoir, 41–45, both in OHC, LBJL; James J. Reynolds Memoir, 48, and John Henning Memoir, 10–11, both in OHC, JFKL; Karen Orren, "Union Politics and Postwar Liberalism in the United States, 1946–1979," in Karen Orren and Stephen Skowronek, eds., *Studies in American Political Development* (New Haven, Conn.: Yale University Press, 1986), 235–37.

101. See Davis, *Prisoners of the American Dream*, 126–27.

102. See Chapters 6–9; Sorensen, *Kennedy*, 393–506; Arthur M. Schlesinger Jr., *A Thousand Days: John F. Kennedy in the White House* (Boston: Houghton Mifflin, 1965), 843–92; Arthur M. Schlesinger Jr. *Robert Kennedy and His Times* (Boston: Houghton Mifflin, 1978), 307–48; Carl Brauer, *John F. Kennedy and the Second Reconstruction* (New York: Columbia University Press, 1977), 230–320; Cynthia Harrison, *On Account of Sex: The Politics of Women's Issues, 1945–68* (Berkeley and Los Angeles: University of California Press, 1988), 89–165; Roger M. Blough Memoir, 3–4, Eugene B. Germany Memoir, 5–8, 38, and James J. Reynolds Memoir, 17–19, 41–45, all in OHC, LBJL; John Morton Blum, *The Progressive Presidents – Roosevelt, Wilson, Roosevelt, Johnson* (New York: Norton, 1980), 163–203; Joseph Keenan Memoir 23, and

John Henning Memoir 14, both in OHC, JFKL; notes from a White House dinner held on June 22, 1965, letter from Jack Stieber to Joseph Block, March 29, 1966, and Lyndon Johnson's letter to Block, April 21, 1966, all in folder marked "AC–77–1 Joseph Block," box 546, Joseph L. Block Papers, LBJL; Doris Kearns, *Lyndon Johnson and the American Dream* (New York: Harper & Row, 1976), 170–352. Business Advisory Council chairman Roger Blough later said of Johnson that "of all the Presidents that I've known since Hoover, he [Johnson] understood the business [community's] problems better than any of the other Presidents" (Blough Memoir, 3).

103. See Eric F. Goldman, *The Tragedy of Lyndon Johnson* (London: Macdonald, 1969), 35–56, 65–66, 378–417, 510; Kearns, *Lyndon Johnson*, 210–52; Blum, *The Progressive Presidents*, 167, 169, 175–76, 180–203; USA–EBP, February 14 and 15, 1963, 37–89, 251, 257–58, March 18 and 19, 1963, 4–110, 217–19; Joseph Krislov, "Organizing, Union Growth, and the Cycle, 1949–1966," *Labor History* 11 (1970): 212–22; Ray F. Marshall, *Labor in the South* (Cambridge, Mass.: Harvard University Press, 1967), 270–82, 297–343; Davis, *Prisoners of the American Dream*, 128–31; David C. Plotke, "The Democratic Political Order, 1932–1972" (Ph.D. diss., University of California at Berkeley, 1985), 827–29.

104. See Chapters 3–7 and 9; Blum, *The Progressive Presidents*, 181–203; Kearns, *Lyndon Johnson*, 251–352; George C. Herring, *America's Longest War: The United States and Vietnam, 1950–1975*, 2nd ed. (New York: Random House, 1986), 108–220.

105. See Chapters 2–7; John Bartlow Martin, "Election of 1964," in Arthur M. Schlesinger Jr. and Fred L. Israel, *History of American Presidential Elections*, vol. 4 (New York: McGraw-Hill, 1971), 3585–88.

106. See USA–EBP, July 11, 1962, 237–39, July 23, 1964, 49–65, September 2–3, 1964, 88–89, 128–29, 242–44; Martin, "Election of 1964," 3565–94; Arthur C. Wolfe, "Trends in Labor Union Voting Behavior, 1948–1968," *Industrial Relations* 9 (1969): 1–10; Draper, *A Rope of Sand*, 117–19; Sidney Blumenthal, *The Rise of the Counter-Establishment* (New York: Harper & Row, 1986); Maurice Isserman and Michael Kazin, "The Failure and Success of the New Radicalism," in Steve Fraser and Gary Gerstle, eds., *The Rise and Fall of the New Deal Order, 1930–80* (Princeton, N.J.: Princeton University Press, 1989), 212–42.

107. See Draper, *A Rope of Sand*, 99–144; James L. Sundquist, *Dynamics of the Party System* (Washington, D.C.: Brookings Institution, 1973), 218–44, 216–17, 370–73; Kent M. Beck, "What Was Liberalism in the 1950s?" *Political Science Quarterly* 102 (1987): 253–56; Plotke, "The Democratic Political Order," 697–98, 718, 765–76. For the most part, the neoliberal Democrats hailed from what James Sundquist described as a northern tier of states stretching from Maine to Oregon. David Plotke pointed to the growing amount of business contributions to the Democrats as a key indicator of the party's changing base of support. The level of such contributions rose sharply in 1964. In that year, one-third of all Democratic campaign funds came from business (Plotke, "The Democratic Political Order," 765–66, n. 33).

108. See George Meany Memoir 14–15, Joseph Beirne Memoir 23–24, both in OHC, LBJL; Gilbert S. Gall, *The Politics of Right to Work: The Labor Federations as Special Interests, 1943–79* (Westport, Conn.: Greenwood Press, 1988), 155–88; Plotke, "The Democratic Political Order," 783–84; Draper, *A Rope of Sand*, 119; Archie Robinson, *George Meany and His Times* (New York: Simon & Schuster, 1981), 244–47; David Brody, *Workers in Industrial America: Essays on the Twentieth Century Struggle* (New York: Oxford University Press, 1980), 233–34; Davis, *Prisoners of the American Dream*, 135. Union leader Joseph Keenan later contended unpersuasively that Johnson tried his utmost to secure repeal of 14(b) (Joseph Keenan Memoir, 16, in

OHC, LBJL). Far less flattering and more accurate assessments of Johnson's role can be found in the Meany and Beirne Memoirs and the works by Gilbert Gall and David Plotke. See also antiunion steel executive Eugene Germany's approving observation that after winning election to the Senate, Johnson thereafter never wavered on 14(b). The remark is in Germany's Memoir, 7–8, in OHC, LBJL. In marked contrast to Johnson's record, leaders of Canada's Liberal Party, which returned to power in 1963, pushed through a legislative program more protective of organized labor. As a result, the fraction of the Canadian workforce organized by unions – which trailed that in the United States from the mid-1930s through the mid-1950s before moving slightly ahead over the following decade – rose sharply during the next decade and a half, whereas the percentage of the U.S. workforce that was unionized dropped (Weiler, "Promises to Keep," 1804–27).

109. The important role of the unions in winning passage of civil rights legislation was noted by Norman Hill: "By the early 1960's organized labor was the staunchest institutional supporter of civil-rights legislation apart from the civil rights movement itself" ("Blacks and the Unions," 496). On the civil rights laws passed in the mid-1960s and their divisive results, see Blum, *The Progressive Presidents*, 167–69, 174–75; Robinson, *George Meany*, 233–43; Barnard, *Walter Reuther*, 185–87; Alan Draper, "Labor and the 1966 Elections," *Labor History* 30 (1989): 76–92; Draper, *A Rope of Sand*, 121–38; Jonathan Rieder, "The Rise of the 'Silent Majority,'" in Steve Fraser and Gary Gerstle, eds., *The Rise and Fall of the New Deal Order, 1930–80* (Princeton, N.J.: Princeton University Press, 1989), 243–68.

110. On labor's key role in winning Medicare's enactment, see Charles McKinney, "The Role of Organized Labor in the Quest for Compulsory Health Insurance, 1912–65" (Ph.D. diss., University of Wisconsin, 1969); Brody, *Workers in Industrial America*, 232; Draper, *A Rope of Sand*, 119. Passage of the two major education bills is discussed in Blum, *The Progressive Presidents*, 173–74; Goldman, *The Tragedy of Lyndon Johnson*, 306–8. Labor's strong support for retraining schemes from the late 1950s onward is detailed in Chapters 6 and 8.

111. On the War on Poverty and its consequences, see Draper, *A Rope of Sand*, 117–38; Ira Katznelson, "Was the Great Society a Lost Opportunity?" Rieder, "The Rise of the 'Silent Majority,'" and Thomas Byrne Edsall, "The Changing Shape of Power: A Realignment in Public Policy," all in Fraser and Gerstle, eds., *The Rise and Fall of the New Deal Order*, 185–211, 243–68, and 269–98, respectively.

112. On the 1966 off-year elections, in which the GOP gained forty-seven seats in the House and four in the Senate, see Draper, *A Rope of Sand*, 120–38; Draper, "Labor and the 1966 Elections," 76–92; Wolfe, "Trends in Labor Union Voting Behavior," 1–10. Among those labor supporters defeated was Illinois Senator Paul Douglas, who lost to neoliberal Republican Charles Percy. On the significance of this election in particular, see Draper, who observed, "The most bitter loss here [in the senatorial races], from labor's point of view, was the defeat of Senator Paul Douglas[,] who labor could always count on to defend it in the Senate's chambers" ("Labor and the 1966 Elections," 78). The significance of Pat Brown's election in 1958 is discussed in Chapters 6–7. On the rise of Ronald Reagan and the conservative movement for which he spoke, see William E. Leuchtenburg, *In the Shadow of FDR: From Harry Truman to Ronald Reagan*, rev. ed. (Ithaca, N.Y.: Cornell University Press, 1985), 209–35; Rieder, "The Rise of the 'Silent Majority,'" 243–68.

113. See John Bartlow Martin, *Adlai Stevenson and the World* (Garden City, N.Y.: Doubleday, 1977), 556–863; Sorensen, *Kennedy*, 236–737; Schlesinger, *A Thousand*

Days, 22–766; Schlesinger, *Robert Kennedy*, 452–746; John Kenneth Galbraith, *A Life in Our Times* (Boston: Houghton Mifflin, 1981), 456.

114. See Galbraith, *A Life in Our Times*, 455–57; Larry M. Roth, "Remembering 1965: Abe Fortas and the Supreme Court," *Mercer Law Review* 28 (1977): 961–76; Abraham, *Justices and Presidents*, 259–64; AJG.

115. See Goldberg, *A Private View*, 193; Roth, "Remembering 1965," 963–64. Johnson's own disingenuous account of how he first came to be interested in appointing Goldberg is in his memoir, *The Vantage Point: Perspectives of the Presidency, 1963–1969* (New York: Holt, Rinehart and Winston, 1971), 543–44. Johnson claimed that Goldberg had sought the job. See also Goldberg, *A Private View*, 193.

116. Arthur J. Goldberg Memoir, OHC, LBJL, 1–5; AJG; Goldberg, *A Private View*, 193–94; Roth, "Remembering 1965," 964; William O. Douglas, *The Court Years, 1939–1975: The Autobiography of William O. Douglas* (New York: Random House, 1980), 251. On Goldberg's restlessness while on the Court, see also his correspondence with Cass Canfield of Harper & Row, which indicates that during July 1964 Goldberg began to think about writing a book about the Court's work. See also John Fischer's memo of his two-hour conversation with Goldberg on March 17, 1965, during which Goldberg said that "he feels strongly that Supreme Court justices are now too cloistered, and that they ought to do considerably more to present their views on the philosophy of law and government to the public by way of speeches, books and articles without of course discussing subjects likely to come before the Court." The correspondence with Canfield and Fischer's memo to Jeanette Hopkins, March 23, 1965, are in Harper & Row Papers, RBML–CU.

117. AJG. See also Goldberg Memoir, OHC, LBJL, 3; Goldberg, *A Private View*, 194.

118. Goldberg Memoir, 1–3; AJG; Goldberg, *A Private View*, 194; Roth, "Remembering 1965," 963.

119. AJG; Abraham, *Justices and Presidents*, 259; Schwartz, *Super Chief*, 681–83, 720. Unbeknownst to Goldberg, Johnson, almost immediately after persuading him to leave the Court, apparently promised Fortas that when Warren retired he, Fortas, would be named chief justice. The pledge was intended to help persuade Fortas to accept the appointment to the seat Goldberg had vacated, which Fortas soon did (Schwartz, *Super Chief*, 584).

120. AJG. See also the Goldberg Memoir, OHC, LBJL, 1–2; Goldberg, *A Private View*, 195–97; Elizabeth Black, *Mr. Justice and Mrs. Black: The Memoirs of Hugo L. Black and Elizabeth Black* (New York: Random House, 1986), 118–19.

121. AJG.

122. See Jerry Holleman Memoir, OHC, LBJL, 46–48. On Johnson's role in the enactment of Landrum–Griffin and Goldberg's view of his conduct, see Chapters 6–7.

123. See Jerry Holleman Memoir 46–48. On Holleman's appointment as assistant secretary of labor, see Chapter 8.

124. Jerry Holleman Memoir, OHC, LBJL, 47, also 46.

125. Ibid., 46–47; Goldberg, *A Private View*, 88–93.

126. Jerry Holleman Memoir, 49, also 46–48.

127. Ibid., 49, 53. See also Goldberg, *A Private View*, 92–93. Holleman's version of this story leaves unclear whether the funds he collected ultimately made their way into Goldberg's own bank account or whether they went directly to the caterers, who then reduced the amounts of the bills sent to Goldberg, the remainder of which he paid with personal checks, the records of which he later produced for the press.

128. Jerry Holleman Memoir, 53, also 54.

129. Ibid., 53–54.

130. On the differences in Kennedy's and Johnson's outlook, see Chapters 6–9. See also Jerry Holleman's observation that Johnson was more "liberal" than Kennedy, except that "he [Johnson] was not as prolabor as John Kennedy" (Holleman Memoir, 32). When he resigned from the Court, in addition to giving up a lifetime appointment, Goldberg took a $10,000-a-year pay cut and lost the pension for his wife to which incumbent justices were entitled (Goldberg, *A Private View*, 197).

Chapter 11. A Time of Troubles

1. See John Bartlow Martin, *Adlai Stevenson and the World* (Garden City, N.Y.: Doubleday, 1977), 556–863; Theodore Sorenson, *Kennedy* (New York: Harper & Row, 1965), 236–737; Arthur M. Schlesinger Jr., *A Thousand Days: John F. Kennedy in the White House* (Boston: Houghton Mifflin, 1965), 22–766; Arthur M. Schlesinger Jr., *Robert Kennedy and His Times* (Boston: Houghton Mifflin, 1978), 452–746; John Kenneth Galbraith, *A Life in Our Times* (Boston: Houghton Mifflin, 1981), 456; Seymour Maxwell Finger, *American Ambassadors at the UN: People, Politics and Bureaucracy in Making Foreign Policy* (New York: Holmes & Meier, 1988), 109–94; Dorothy Goldberg, *A Private View of a Public Life* (New York: Charterhouse, 1975), 192–263.

2. Finger, *American Ambassadors at the UN*, 132–41, 170; John G. Stoessinger, *The United Nations and the Superpowers: China, Russia and America* (New York: Random House, 1973), 103–20.

3. Finger, *American Ambassadors at the UN*, 132–41; Stoessinger, *The United Nations and the Superpowers*, 115–20.

4. Donald Grant, "Goldberg at the U.N.," *The Progressive*, November 1965, 32; Finger, *American Ambassadors at the UN*, 170–71; Stoessinger, *The United Nations and the Superpowers*, 120–21; Goldberg, *A Private View*, 255–57.

5. Finger, *American Ambassadors at the UN*, 132–41, 170–72; Stoessinger, *The United Nations and the Superpowers*, 120–21. Finger observed that "the Article 19 controversy was really a conflict between those who wanted to maintain the United Nations as 'static conference machinery' (the USSR and Gaullist France) and those who wished to endow it with increasing strength and executive authority" (*American Ambassadors at the UN*, 141).

6. Goldberg Memoir, OHC, LBJL, 20; Grant, "Goldberg at the U.N.," 32–33; Finger, *American Ambassadors at the UN*, 172–77; Goldberg, *A Private View*, 202–3.

7. Finger, *American Ambassadors at the UN*, 177–78.

8. Goldberg Memoir, OHC, LBJL, 16–18, 21–31; Goldberg, *A Private View*, 255. On the authorship of UN Resolution 242, see Finger, *American Ambassadors at the UN*: "The resolution finally agreed upon unanimously in the Security Council was put forward by Lord Caradon, the British representative, but the draft was largely Goldberg's" (185, also 179–86).

9. "Cyprus Tension Reaches Climax; West Seeks Calm," *New York Times*, November 23, 1967; "Threat of a War over Cyprus Issue Appears to Ease" and "U.N. Standing by on Cyprus Crisis," *New York Times*, November 26, 1967; "War over Cyprus Averted by Pact," *New York Times*, December 1, 1967; Goldberg Memoir, OHC, LBJL, 9–10, 20; Arthur J. Goldberg Memoir, OHC, RBML–CU, 40–41;

Goldberg, *A Private View*, 250–51, 260; Finger, *American Ambassadors at the UN*, 186–89.

10. On Goldberg's negotiating technique while at the UN, see Goldberg Memoir, OHC, RBML–CU, 3–49.

11. George C. Herring, *America's Longest War: The United States and Vietnam, 1950–1975*, 2nd ed. (New York: Random House, 1986), 108–43; Stanley Karnow, *Vietnam: A History* (New York: Penguin Books, 1984), 395–426; Gabriel Kolko, *Anatomy of a War: Vietnam, the United States and the Modern Historical Experience* (New York: Pantheon, 1985), 163–67.

12. Goldberg Memoir, LBJL, 3, also 1–2, 5, 34–36; Goldberg, *A Private View*, 193–94, 260; AJG; George F. Kennan, *Memoirs: 1950–1963* (New York: Pantheon, 1972), 39–60; Ronald Steel, *Walter Lippmann and the American Century* (Boston: Little, Brown, 1980), 557–82; Karnow, *Vietnam*, 486–87.

13. Goldberg Memoir, OHC, LBJL, 3–5, 35–36; Goldberg, *A Private View*, 243–44.

14. AJG.

15. Escalation's consistency with the containment policy's logic is discussed in Herring, *America's Longest War*, 108–43. See also Karnow, *Vietnam*, 395–426; Kolko, *Anatomy of a War*, 163–75. For the way in which the support of liberals such as Goldberg for that policy contributed to the American military intervention in Vietnam, see Chapters 7, 9–10. The New Deal liberals who supported escalation deserved, of course, far more blame for its consequences. A leading example is Illinois Senator Paul Douglas. For an indication of how the issue divided New Deal liberals, see the highly revealing exchange of letters between Jacob Weinstein and Douglas, February 23 and March 7, 1966, in Weinstein Papers, CHS; Paul H. Douglas, *In the Fullness of Time* (New York: Harcourt Brace Jovanovich, 1971), 583–94.

16. Goldberg Memoir, OHC, LBJL, 4. See also Goldberg, *A Private View*, 195.

17. See Goldberg Memoir, OHC, LBJL; Goldberg, *A Private View*, 195; Herring, *America's Longest War*, 138–41; Karnow, *Vietnam*, 424–26.

18. AJG. Ball's willingness to cloak his own views in that way, essentially abandoning any real challenge to Johnson's policies, goes a long way toward explaining why he, unlike Goldberg, was able to maintain a good working relationship with Johnson and his hawkish advisers. See Henry F. Graff, *The Tuesday Cabinet: Deliberation and Decision on Peace and War Under Lyndon B. Johnson* (Englewood Cliffs, N.J.: Prentice-Hall, 1970). Graff recorded Dean Rusk's observation that "Ball had only played that [devil's advocate] role when he was 'assigned' it" (136). George Ball's more self-serving version of his role as "house dove" is contained in his memoirs, *The Past Has Another Pattern* (New York: Norton, 1982) 360–433.

19. See the memo from VM[?] to Johnson, dated May 24, 1966, comparing Johnson's frequency of contact with Goldberg during his first ten months as UN ambassador, as opposed to Stevenson during the preceding twenty months. Johnson communicated or met with Goldberg during that period at a rate almost four times greater than he had with Stevenson. The memo, which has no title, is in folder marked "Appointment File, May 24, 1966," President's Appointment File, [Diary Backup], box 35, LBJL. See also Ball, *The Past Has Another Pattern*, 428.

20. Herring, *America's Longest War*, 164–67; Karnow, *Vietnam*, 480–84; Goldberg, *A Private View*, 242–46; letter from Goldberg to Joseph Harold Crown, January 24, 1966, in Lawyers Committee on American Policy Towards Vietnam Collection, RBML–CU.

21. Goldberg Memoir, OHC, LBJL, 19. See also Goldberg, *A Private View*, 242–44; Herring, *America's Longest War*, 166–67; Karnow, *Vietnam*, 483–84.

22. AJG; Goldberg Memoir, OHC, LBJL, 19; Goldberg, *A Private View*, 242–44; Herring, *America's Longest War*, 166–67; Karnow, *Vietnam*, 483–84.

23. Letter from Arthur J. Goldberg to the president, May 13, 1966, folder marked "Appointment File, May 24, 1966," box 35, President's Appointment File [Diary Backup], LBJL, 1–2. On the growing U.S. military role in Vietnam during early 1966, see Herring, *America's Longest War*, 166–67; Karnow, *Vietnam*, 484–87. In *A Private View*, Dorothy Goldberg noted her husband's decision to write the letter but stated incorrectly that it was sent on December 4, 1965 (245). Goldberg did not take a copy of it with him when leaving the administration, which helps explain the error.

24. Arthur J. Goldberg to the president, May 13, 1966, 2.

25. Ibid., 3, also 2, 4; Herring, *America's Longest War*, 144–85.

26. Arthur J. Goldberg to the president, May 13, 1966, 3.

27. Ibid., 4.

28. Arthur J. Goldberg to the president, May 13, 1966, 4. Cabinet secretary Robert Kintner, to whom Johnson apparently showed the memo, also passed it along to his national security adviser Walt Rostow (who had replaced McGeorge Bundy earlier that year) with a cover sheet reading, "I thought you would like to see this." The cover sheet, May 17, 1966, in file marked "CO 312 3/11/66–6/2/66," box 80, President Ex CO 312 Collection, LBJL.

29. On seeing the letter in December 1989 for the first time in more than two decades, even Goldberg himself seemed surprised by its tameness (AJG). On the overwhelming support among Johnson's foreign policy advisers for escalation and the short list of covert dissenters, see Ball, *The Past Has Another Pattern*, 428–29. For Goldberg's claim that he favored de-escalation from the very beginning, see Goldberg Memoir, OHC, LBJL, 15: "Like any person trying to negotiate, [with] a stubborn employer or president, I had various fall back positions and so on. But basically, as my early memoranda show, I felt that we ought to get out."

30. Goldberg Memoir, OHC, LBJL, 36. See also Goldberg, *A Private View*, 245–46.

31. Goldberg, *A Private View*, 246. See also the Goldberg Memoir, OHC, LBJL, 36.

32. Goldberg, *A Private View*, 246.

33. Although no transcript of the exchange between Goldberg and Johnson exists, the candid snapshots taken during the meeting by a White House staff photographer testify to the explosive nature of their discussion. The photos show a conversation that moved from tense to furious disagreement. See White House Office Photo Collection, May 24, 1966, 11:37 A.M.–12:25 P.M., LBJL. The dual purpose of the meeting is evident from the memos contained in Johnson's personal file for it, which includes Goldberg's May 13 letter and a memo from Dean Rusk to Johnson about China's representation at the UN. Both Goldberg's letter and Rusk's memo, May 14, 1966, are in folder marked "Appointment File, May 24, 1966," box 35, President's Appointment File [Diary Backup], LBJL. The president's daily diary indicates that this session was the first direct communication between Johnson and Goldberg since Goldberg had sent his May 13 letter. That diary also details the meeting times and who was present when. See President's Daily Diary, May 13–24, 1966, LBJL. On Johnson's fury over Goldberg's assertion that he spoke for the liberal community, see Ball, *The Past Has Another Pattern*: "I was fully aware of the President's anger and resentment at that suggestion; Johnson spoke to me of it in scatological terms" (428).

34. Minutes, folder marked "17 June 1966, 6:05 P.M. NSC," Presidential Meeting Notes File, LBJL, 5.

35. Ibid.

36. Ibid.

37. Ibid.

38. Ibid., 6.

39. See ibid. and Minutes, folder marked "22 June 1966 NSC," both in Presidential Meeting Notes File, LBJL.

40. Minutes, "22 June 1966 NSC," 5.

41. Goldberg Memoir, OHC, LBJL 13, also 12, 15; Minutes, "22 June 1966 NSC"; AJG; Herring, *America's Longest War*, 146–47.

42. AJG. See also Goldberg Memoir, OHC, LBJL, 13.

43. Interview with Harry McPherson, November 19, 1990; HFG; Finger, *American Ambassadors at the UN*, 164.

44. AJG. See Ball, *The Past Has Another Pattern*, for the accusation that Goldberg undermined his own efforts at persuasion "by insisting to the President that he also had a constituency, thus implicitly threatening the President's own position, which was no way to treat a Texan" (428). Goldberg much later said that he did not really understand what Ball was talking about (Goldberg Memoir, OHC, LBJL, 10). See also Herring, *America's Longest War*, 170–77; Karnow, *Vietnam*, 479–91.

45. AJG; the President's Daily Diary, June 18–September 29, 1966, LBJL; Herring, *America's Longest War*, 184. Goldberg later claimed that before 1968, Johnson had never invited him to participate in the Wise Men sessions, but the President's Daily Diary entries for July 1965 through June 1966 indicate that Goldberg had attended a few such meetings before the breakdown in his relationship with Johnson. See Goldberg Memoir, OHC, 6–7, and President's Daily Diary, July 1965–June 1966, both in LBJL.

46. Dorothy Goldberg contended in her memoirs that her husband stayed on, first, out of a desire to continue giving Johnson an opposing view to the hawkish advice that others were providing and, second, so as to complete other UN assignments. This version of events seems incomplete at best. For her account, see *A Private View*, 245–46. Also see Ball, *The Past Has Another Pattern*, 424–33; HFG; AJG; Chapters 9–10.

47. See message from Bob Cox to John Macy, October 20, 1966, in folder marked "Arthur Goldberg," box 215, Macy Files, and President's Daily Diary, October 1, 1966–June 24, 1968, both in LBJL.

48. President's Daily Diary, October 1, 1966–June 24, 1968; HFG; AJG; minutes for NSC meetings held during this period, LBJL; Graff, *The Tuesday Cabinet*; "Memorandum for the President" from George Christian, December 7 and 8, 1967, in file marked "IT 47–26 1/12/67–8/21/68," box 14, Presidential Papers, Ex IT 47–23 Collection, LBJL.

49. Herring, *America's Longest War*, 186–92; Karnow, *Vietnam*, 523–52; Kolko, *Anatomy of a War*, 303–15, 327–37.

50. AJG; Herring, *America's Longest War*, 192–202; Karnow, *Vietnam*, 545–59; Herbert Schandler, *The Unmaking of a President: Lyndon Johnson and Vietnam* (Princeton, N.J.: Princeton University Press, 1977), 105–231, 237–38. Like many others, Goldberg appears to have initially misinterpreted the New Hampshire primary results, in which the Minnesota senator had come within three hundred votes of defeating Johnson out of fifty thousand cast. Although the news media tended to interpret the large McCarthy vote as an indication of the growing antiwar sentiment, many of those casting ballots for him had done so to protest Johnson's failure to

prosecute the war even more vigorously. What the New Hampshire result truly signaled, then, was erosion in popular support for Johnson's middle position, which was somewhere between all-out war and de-escalation. See Herring, *America's Longest War*, 202; Karnow, *Vietnam*, 558–9.

51. Memo in telegram form from Arthur J. Goldberg, Section 1, March 15, 1968, folder marked "National Security File: U.N. Vol. 9, box 69," box 2, DSDUF Vietnam Collection, LBJL, 1.

52. Ibid.

53. Ibid.

54. Ibid., 2.

55. Ibid.

56. Ibid., 2–3; Herring, *America's Longest War*, 180; Schandler, *The Unmaking of a President*, 130–31.

57. Goldberg memo, Section 2, March 15, 1968, 2, also 1. Goldberg noted that the bombing halt could help the United States obtain real Soviet assistance: "We would also be in a strong position, having followed Soviet and bloc advice on stopping the bombing, to urge that they use their supply leverage in support of a political settlement." Goldberg's three other suggestions were recommendations that the United States seek similar aid from other countries—mainly France, India, and the so-called nonaligned nations—from the pope, the UN secretary-general, and the UN Security Council (2).

58. Ibid., 2.

59. DKGD, March 21, 1968; AJG–DLS; Ball, *The Past Has Another Pattern*, 428–29; Herring, *America's Longest War*, 192–201; Karnow, *Vietnam*, 548–58. The telegram was sent in two parts, with the first received at the State Department at 7:36 P.M. and the second at 9:10 P.M., on March 15, 1968. Rusk evidently passed the memo to national security adviser Walt Rostow, who, before handing it to Johnson, scrawled the following note on the first page: "For the President[,] From Walt Rostow[,] Herewith Goldberg[.] Proposes we go for a bombing cessation and a negotiation promptly. Rostow: In my judgement the right time will be a few months from now—assuming Westy [General William Westmoreland, U.S. military commander in Vietnam] and the GVN [government of South Vietnam] weather the winter–spring offensive in tolerably good shape" (Goldberg memo, Section 1, March 15, 1968, 1).

60. Schlesinger, *Robert Kennedy*, 917, also 883–916; AJG; FSG; Chapters 6–7, and 9.

61. AJG; Schlesinger, *Robert Kennedy*, 917–30; Herring, *America's Longest War*, 202; Karnow, *Vietnam*, 559–60; Schandler, *The Unmaking of a President*, 224–25. Goldberg also seems to have avoided involvement in the 1968 Democratic primaries out of a desire to maintain the "nonpolitical" stance that he saw as befitting a former and possibly future Supreme Court justice (DKGD, 1 April 1, 1968).

62. Goldberg Memoir, OHC, LBJL, 6. See also Schandler, *The Unmaking of a President*, which quotes Rostow as saying that Johnson responded to the memo "vividly" and "negatively." Schandler also noted there that others reported that "in discussing the Goldberg proposal with his advisers in the White House on March 16, the president exploded in a rage, waved the memo in the air, and denounced it in colorful language" (239).

63. See Schandler, *The Unmaking of a President*, 237–40, 247–50; Herring, *America's Longest War*, 199–200; Karnow, *Vietnam*, 556, 559–61.

64. DKGD, March 21, 1968. See also the handwritten minutes of this meeting, in folder marked "20 March 1968 Meeting with Advisors on Vietnam," box 2, Presiden-

tial Meeting Notes File, LBJL; Schandler, *The Unmaking of a President*, 250–55; Herring, *America's Longest War*, 203–6; Karnow, *Vietnam*, 559–60.

65. Handwritten minutes; Schandler, *The Unmaking of a President*, 250–55; Herring, *America's Longest War*, 203–6; Karnow, *Vietnam*, 559–60.

66. Goldberg Memoir, OHC, LBJL, 7, 15–16, 32; Schandler, *The Unmaking of a President*, 254–55, 258–59; Herring, *America's Longest War*, 206; Karnow, *Vietnam*, 561.

67. Schandler, *The Unmaking of a President*, 259; Karnow, *Vietnam*, 561.

68. AJG; Schandler, *The Unmaking of a President*, 237–61; Herring, *America's Longest War*, 184; Karnow, *Vietnam*, 561–62.

69. Schandler, *The Unmaking of a President*, 260–61, also 259. Other sources for this key exchange include AJG; Goldberg Memoir, OHC, LBJL, 7–8; Goldberg, *A Private View*, 249–50; David Halberstam, *The Best and the Brightest* (New York: Random House, 1969), 653. The various accounts have Dupuy and Goldberg using somewhat different casualty figures, but in each case with the same absurd result: Based on U.S. military and CIA estimates, by March 26, the North Vietnamese and Viet Cong had no effective forces left in the field, even as the fighting continued. On the briefings more generally, see Karnow, *Vietnam*, 561–62.

70. Goldberg Memoir, OHC, LBJL, 8. On the basis of interviews with some of those present the session, Halberstam described the silence that followed Goldberg's ultimate question as "long and very devastating" (*The Best and the Brightest*, 653).

71. Schandler, *The Unmaking of a President*, 257–58, 261; Karnow, *Vietnam*, 562.

72. AJG; Goldberg Memoir, OHC, LBJL, 8–9, 15; Summary of Notes, in folder marked "26 March 1968 Meeting with Special Advisory Group," box 2, Presidential Meeting Notes File, LBJL, 1–2, 4–5; Schandler, *The Unmaking of a President*, 261–65; Herring, *America's Longest War*, 206; Karnow, *Vietnam*, 562. The meeting notes indicate that General Bradley favored continuing the existing policy, but the other accounts contradict that view.

73. Schandler, *The Unmaking of a President*, 264; Goldberg Memoir, OHC, LBJL, 8. See also DKGD, April 4, 1968.

74. DKGD, April 1, 1968; Schandler, *The Unmaking of a President*, 264–89; Herring, *America's Longest War*, 206–7; Karnow, *Vietnam*, 562–66.

75. Goldberg Memoir, OHC, LBJL, 2, 9; DKGD, April 1, 1968; Chapter 10; Schandler, *The Unmaking of a President*, 283–84; Herring, *America's Longest War*, 207; Karnow, *Vietnam*, 565; Clark Clifford, *Counsel to the President: A Memoir* (New York: Random House, 1991), 488–596.

76. Text of a letter from Arthur J. Goldberg to Lyndon Baines Johnson, April 23, 1968, 1–2, copy in DKGD. See also DKGD, March 21, 1968; "Goldberg's Final Slot: Law Career," *Chicago Daily News*, April 26, 1968; "Goldberg Exit: He Deserved Better," *Chicago Sun-Times*, April 28, 1968.

77. Goldberg Memoir, LBJL, 9–10; DKGD, April 28, 1968; "UN Ambassador Goldberg Quits; President Appoints George Ball" and "Goldberg's Final Slot," *Chicago Sun-Times*, April 26, 1968; Goldberg, *A Private View*, 247.

78. AJG; "U.N. Ambassador Goldberg Quits; President Appoints George Ball," *Chicago Sun-Times*, April 26, 1968; "Goldberg Quits as UN Delegate; Ball to Get Post" and "Goldberg Denies Discord on War," *New York Times*, April 26, 1968; "Chilly Tone Marked Exchanges Between Johnson and Goldberg," *New York Times*, April 29, 1968. Even though Goldberg specifically denied that his resignation stemmed from policy differences over Vietnam, press accounts noted Goldberg's role

as an in-house dissenter and rightly attributed his departure to this basic disagreement with Johnson.

79. DKGD, March 21, 1968; Bernard Schwartz, *Super Chief: Earl Warren and His Supreme Court—A Judicial Biography* (New York: New York University Press, 1983), 680– 82. On Warren's opinion of Nixon and his backers, see 336–38, 390, 399–400; Roger Morris, *Richard Milhous Nixon: The Rise of an American Politician* (New York: Henry Holt, 1990), 276–710.

80. The details of this meeting are recorded in DKGD, March 21, 1968.

81. AJG; Schwartz, *Super Chief*, 680–82, 720.

82. AJG; President's Daily Diary, June 24, 1968, LBJL; Ball, *The Past Has Another Pattern*, 436–38; Laura Kalman, *Abe Fortas: A Biography* (New Haven, Conn.: Yale University Press, 1990), 327–28. Goldberg and Thornberry had clashed nine years earlier, when the then Texas congressman had helped round up the crucial votes in his state's delegation for passage of the Landrum–Griffin act (see Chapter 7).

83. On the behavior of Johnson's other senior foreign policy advisers, see Graff, *The Tuesday Cabinet*; Halberstam, *The Best and the Brightest*; Schandler, *The Unmaking of a President*; Herring, *America's Longest War*, 108–220; Karnow, *Vietnam*, 312– 566; Kolko, *Anatomy of a War*, 111–326; Ball, *The Past Has Another Pattern*, 360–448; Clifford, *Counsel to the President*, 403–596; Kalman, *Abe Fortas*, 199–248, 293–358.

84. AJG; "Goldberg's Final Slot," *Chicago Daily News*, April 26, 1968.

85. Kalman, *Abe Fortas*, 319–58; Schwartz, *Super Chief*, 720–22; Clifford, *Counsel to the President*, 554–59. On the Warren Court innovations that aroused conservative opposition, see Schwartz, *Super Chief*, 289–722; Chapters 6–7, and 10.

86. Goldberg Memoir, OHC, LBJL, 33. Other sources for this event include AJG; President's Daily Diary, October 10, 1968, LBJL.

87. Goldberg Memoir, 33; President's Daily Diary, October 10–11, 1968; AJG. Johnson added insult to injury by releasing the news of his decision to the press before informing Goldberg (Kalman, *Abe Fortas*, 355–56).

88. AJG; David S. Broder, "Election of 1968," in Arthur M. Schlesinger Jr. and Fred L. Israel, eds., *History of American Presidential Elections*, vol. 4 (New York: McGraw-Hill, 1971), 3705–7, 3727–52. After the election, perhaps feeling pangs of remorse, Johnson gave some final thought to appointing Goldberg before concluding that it was too late. Instead, Johnson advised Nixon to appoint him, but the likelihood of that happening, as Goldberg himself later acknowledged, was nil. See "Memorandum for the President," from Barefoot Sanders to Johnson, December 9, 1968, in folder marked "Arthur J. Goldberg," box 164, Name File, White House Central File, and Goldberg Memoir, OHC, 33, both in LBJL.

89. Kalman, *Abe Fortas*, 330–57; Schwartz, *Super Chief*, 680–83, 720–22; Clifford, *Counsel to the President*, 554–59. Laura Kalman asserts that Goldberg would have fared better with Republicans than Fortas did because GOP Senator Robert Griffin, who led the opposition in his own party to the Fortas nomination, stated publicly that he could support Goldberg, but not Fortas, as Warren's successor. This remark cannot be taken at face value, however, given the substantial disagreements between Goldberg and the man who had cosponsored the Landrum–Griffin Act. Griffin almost surely made the comment out of a desire to appear fair, by listing the one liberal whom he could feel confident that Johnson would not choose. For Kalman's view, see *Abe Fortas*, 357.

90. "Memorandum for the President," from Barefoot Sanders to Johnson, December 9, 1968; Kalman, *Abe Fortas*, 327–58; Schwartz, *Super Chief*, 680–83, 720–22;

Clifford, *Counsel to the President*, 554–59. On the likelihood that conservative southern Democrats on the Senate Judiciary Committee would have opposed a Goldberg nomination, see "Memorandum," in which Johnson aide Barefoot Sanders reported to Johnson that "the 3 Southern Democrats on the Committee—Eastland, Ervin, and McClellan—would probably oppose [a Goldberg nomination]; I know of no reason why they would rush to support Goldberg after opposing Fortas."

91. Kalman, *Abe Fortas*, 319–58; Schwartz, *Super Chief*, 680–83, 720–22; Clifford, *Counsel to the President*, 554–59; Goldberg, *A Private View*, 197.

92. "Memorandum for the President," from Barefoot Sanders to Johnson, December 9, 1968; Kalman, *Abe Fortas*, 327–58; Schwartz, *Super Chief*, 680–83, 720–22; Clifford, *Counsel to the President*, 554–59; Broder, "Election of 1968," 3705–52; Chapter 10. Johnson's decision to nominate Fortas instead of Goldberg did, however, have one lasting consequence. By exposing Fortas to the Senate confirmation process in 1968, Johnson so weakened him as to prompt his resignation from the Court on May 14, 1969, thus giving Nixon the chance to name not one but two new justices in his first year as president. On the reasons for Fortas's resignation, see Kalman, *Abe Fortas*, 359–76.

93. Letter from Arthur J. Goldberg to Lyndon Baines Johnson, April 23, 1968, copy in DKGD, 1; "Goldberg Quits as UN Delegate; Ball to Get Post" and "Goldberg Denies Discord on War," *New York Times*, April 26, 1968; "Goldberg Asserts He Will Not Run for Office in '70," *New York Times*, December 10, 1969.

94. AJG; "Goldberg Asserts He Will Not Run for Office in '70" and "Rockefeller Backs Goodell for 1970," *New York Times*, December 10, 1969.

95. FSG; "Goldberg Asserts He Will Not Run for Office in '70," *New York Times*, December 10, 1970; Richard Reeves, "This Is the Battle of the Titans?" *New York Times Magazine*, November 1, 1970. On Rockefeller and his record as governor, see Robert H. Connery and Gerald Benjamin, *Rockefeller of New York: Executive Power in the Statehouse* (Ithaca, N.Y.: Cornell University Press, 1979); James E. Underwood and William J. Daniels, *Governor Rockefeller in New York: The Apex of Pragmatic Liberalism in the United States* (Westport, Conn.: Greenwood Press, 1982); Joseph E. Persico, *The Imperial Rockefeller: A Biography of Nelson A. Rockefeller* (New York: Simon & Schuster, 1982).

96. Reeves, "This Is the Battle of the Titans?"; Connery and Benjamin, *Rockefeller of New York*, 189–439; Underwood and Daniels, *Governor Rockefeller in New York*, 3–215; John Bartlow Martin, "Election of 1964," in Arthur M. Schlesinger Jr. and Fred L. Israel, eds., *History of American Presidential Elections*, vol. 4 (New York: McGraw-Hill, 1971), 3565–85.

97. Reeves, "This Is the Battle of the Titans?"; Connery and Benjamin, *Rockefeller of New York*, 40–76. In the 1966 gubernatorial race, Rockefeller won only 44.8 percent of all votes cast for the four major parties, enough to win reelection by a fairly narrow margin (Underwood and Daniels, *Governor Rockefeller in New York*, 65–70).

98. AJG; "Goldberg Asserts He Will Not Run for Office in '70," *New York Times*, December 10, 1969; "Goldberg to Seek the Governorship," *New York Times*, March 20, 1970; Reeves, "This Is the Battle of the Titans?" 23–24, 58, 65.

99. AJG; "Democratic Aspirants Are Cool to Goldberg's Entry in Race," *New York Times*, March 20, 1970; "Democrats Pick Goldberg but He 'Waives' Selection; Plans a Race by Petition," *New York Times*, April 2, 1970.

100. AJG; "Morgenthau Withdraws from Governor's Race," *New York Times*, May 13, 1970; "Goldberg and Patterson Win; Ottinger Tops 3 Senate Rivals; Powell and

Farbstein Beaten" and "Goldberg Edges Rival in Suburbs," *New York Times*, June 24, 1970; Reeves, "This Is the Battle of the Titans?" 23–25, 58.

101. Reeves, "This Is the Battle of the Titans?" 23–25, 58–59. On Goldberg's deficiencies as an orator, see Finger, *American Ambassadors at the U.N.*, 164.

102. Reeves, "This Is the Battle of the Titans?" 23, 65, 68, 69, 75–77; Connery and Benjamin, *Rockefeller of New York*, 40–59; Underwood and Daniels, *Governor Rockefeller in New York*, 40–71; Persico, *The Imperial Rockefeller*, 120–31. Rockefeller's eagerness to win the votes of these so-called neoconservatives proved so great that he even took to reminding supposedly receptive audiences that he had been Spiro Agnew's first choice for president two years earlier (Reeves, "This Is the Battle of the Titans?" 69).

103. Reeves, "This Is the Battle of the Titans?" 58; Underwood and Daniels, *Governor Rockefeller in New York*, 63–64; Persico, *The Imperial Rockefeller*, 122–24. On the traditional AFL position and the reasons for its revival during the 1960s, see Chapters 8–10.

104. AJG. The one Rockefeller campaign move that did surprise and deeply anger Goldberg was its decision to fund an unfriendly campaign "biography" of Goldberg, written by conservative author Victor Lasky. The book, a collection of distortions, half-truths, and outright lies of the sort for which Lasky was notorious, appeared that summer and proved to be a source of continuing embarrassment to Rockefeller and his more starry-eyed supporters. See Underwood and Daniels, *Governor Rockefeller in New York*, 59–60; Persico, *The Imperial Rockefeller*, 131, 252–53; Victor Lasky, *Arthur Goldberg: The Old and the New* (New Rochelle, N.Y.: Arlington House, 1970).

105. See "Goldberg Assails Costly Campaign," *New York Times*, May 13, 1970; "4-Term Governor" and "Goldberg Keeps Dignity in Defeat," *New York Times*, November 4, 1970; "Big Turnout Laid to Vice President," *New York Times*, November 5, 1970; Connery and Benjamin, *Rockefeller of New York*, 40–59; Underwood and Daniels, *Governor Rockefeller in New York*, 56–71; Persico, *The Imperial Rockefeller*, 124–28.

106. See Thomas Byrne Edsall, "The Changing Shape of Power: A Realignment of Public Policy," in Steve Fraser and Gary Gerstle, eds., *The Rise and Fall of the New Deal Order, 1930–80* (Princeton, N.J.: Princeton University Press, 1989), 269–93; Paul Starr, "The Deadly Marathon," *American Prospect* 10 (1992): 7–11.

107. Edsall, "The Changing Shape of Power," 269–93.

Chapter 12. Return to Private Life

1. AJG; *In Memoriam: Honorable Arthur J. Goldberg: Proceedings of the Bar and Officers of the Supreme Court of the United States* (Washington, D.C.: U.S. Supreme Court of the United States, 1990), 32–33.

2. AJG; *In Memoriam*, 32–33; "Notes on People," *New York Times*, July 27, 1978. Carter's national security adviser, Zbigniew Brzezinski, later wrote that Goldberg acquitted himself "admirably" at the Belgrade conference. See Zbigniew Brzezinski, *Power and Principle: Memoirs of the National Security Adviser, 1977–1981* (New York: Farrar, Straus & Giroux, 1983), 96.

3. AJG; "Dorothy K. Goldberg, 79, Is Dead; Artist, Writer and Rights Figure," *New York Times*, February 14, 1988; "Arthur J. Goldberg Dies at 81; Ex-Justice and Envoy to U.N.," *New York Times*, January 20, 1990.

Index

Abel, I. W., 112, 116, 127, 129, 133, 135, 164, 178, 181, 182, 197, 198, 213, 280, 281, 282, 286, 341, 342
Acheson, Dean, 368, 369
Adams, Avery, 205
Adams, Sherman, 116
Adenauer, Konrad, 149
Affirmative action. *See* Employment discrimination
AFL–CIO. *See* American Federation of Labor–Congress of Industrial Organizations
African-Americans. *See* Blacks
Agency shop
  court rulings on, 320
  emergence of, 503 n. 130
Amalgamated Clothing Workers Union (ACW), 9, 33, 51, 136
  and garment industry, 9–10, 402 n. 99
Amalgamated Labor Bank, 9, 25
America First Committee, 22, 23
American Civil Liberties Union (ACLU), 8
American Federation of Labor (AFL), 5
  98. *See also* American Federation of Labor–Congress of Industrial Organizations, merger of; Meany, George
  anti-statism of, 54–55, 57, 73, 147, 186–87
  influence upon AFL–CIO, 271–72, 304, 305–9, 342, 377–78, 379

and rift with CIO, 12–15, 33, 50, 70, 81, 103, 104–6
American Federation of Labor–Congress of Industrial Organizations (AFL–CIO)
  Ethical Practices Committee, 161–63, 165–67, 306
  Industrial Union Department (IUD), 122, 145, 163–64, 263, 308
  merger of, 117, 119, 120–25
  no-raiding agreement between, 110–11, 114–16
  political action efforts, 143–44, 180, 182–84, 226–28, 230–31, 309, 312–13, 344
  and racial segregation, 144–45, 230–31, 244–45, 306–8, 344–45
  tensions within, 124–25, 143–44, 145, 147, 161–67, 172–75, 188–90, 192–97, 216–17, 218–19, 223–24, 226–27, 233–34, 235, 258, 271–72, 304–9, 342, 377–78, 379
American Newspaper Guild (ANG), 11–12, 18
  Chicago strike of 1938–40, 12–18
Americans for Democratic Action (ADA), 76, 184
Anderson, Clinton, 71, 242
Anti-communism. *See also* Anti-radical hysteria
  liberals and, 10–11, 17, 19, 33, 39, 43,